www.wadsworth.com

wadsworth.com is the World Wide Web site for Wadsworth and is your direct source to dozens of online resources.

At *wadsworth.com* you can find out about supplements, demonstration software, and student resources. You can also send email to many of our authors and preview new publications and exciting new technologies.

wadsworth.com
Changing the way the world learns®

Invitation to Public Speaking

Cindy L. Griffin
Colorado State University

THOMSON
™
WADSWORTH

Australia • Canada • Mexico • Singapore • Spain
United Kingdom • United States

Publisher: Holly J. Allen
Editor: Annie Mitchell
Development Editor: Greer Lleuad
Assistant Editor: Amber Fawson
Marketing Manager: Kimberly Russell
Technology Project Manager: Jeanette Wiseman
Editorial Assistant: Breanna Gilbert
Marketing Assistant: Neena Chandra
Signing Representative: Jane Pohlenz Hetherington
Project Manager, Editorial Production: Cathy Linberg

Print/Media Buyer: Karen Hunt
Permissions Editor: Joohee Lee
Production Service: Thompson Steele, Inc.
Text Designer: Jeanne Calabrese Design
Photo Researcher: Sarah Evertson/Image Quest
Copy Editor: Thompson Steele, Inc.
Cover Designer: Preston Thomas
Cover Illustrator: Zita Asbaghi
Compositor: Thompson Steele, Inc.
Printer: Transcontinental Printing/Interglobe

Printed in Canada
5 6 7 06 05

Chapter-Opening Photos: p. 2 © Hulton-Deutsch Collection/CORBIS; **p. 22** © Charles Gupton/CORBIS Stock Market; **p. 48** © Joseph Nettis/Stock Boston; **p. 76** © Najlah Feanny/Stock Boston; **p. 100** © Jack Kurtz/The Image Works; **p. 124** © Journal-Courier/Joe Fasel Jr./The Image Works; **p. 154** 1998 © Syracuse Newspapers/John Berry/The Image Works; **p. 180** © James Nubile/The Image Works; **p. 202** © David Young Wolff/PhotoEdit; **p. 226** © Carol Cohen/CORBIS; **p. 248** © Robert Severi/Woodfin Camp & Associates; **p. 274** © Al Stephenson/Woodfin Camp & Associates; **p. 294** © Marilyn Humphries/The Image Works; **p. 320** © John Madere/CORBIS/Stock Market; **p. 350** © Syracuse Newspapers/The Image Works; **p. 372** © James Marshall/The Image Works; **p. 400** © Bettmann/CORBIS; **p. 424** © Shelley Gazin/CORBIS.

For more information about our products, contact us at:
Thomson Learning Academic Resource Center
1-800-423-0563
For permission to use material from this text, contact us by:
Phone: 1-800-730-2214   **Fax: 1-800-730-2215**
Web: http://www.thomsonrights.com

Library of Congress Control Number: 2003105657

Student Edition: ISBN 0-534-57924-8

Annotated Instructor's Edition: ISBN 0-534-57926-4

Wadsworth/Thomson Learning
10 Davis Drive
Belmont, CA 94002-3098
USA

Asia
Thomson Learning
5 Shenton Way #01-01
UIC Building
Singapore 068808

Australia
Nelson Thomson Learning
102 Dodds Street
South Melbourne, Victoria 3205
Australia

Canada
Nelson Thomson Learning
1120 Birchmount Road
Toronto, Ontario M1K 5G4
Canada

Europe/Middle East/Africa
Thomson Learning
High Holborn House
50/51 Bedford Row
London WC1R 4LR
United Kingdom

Brief Contents

Contents

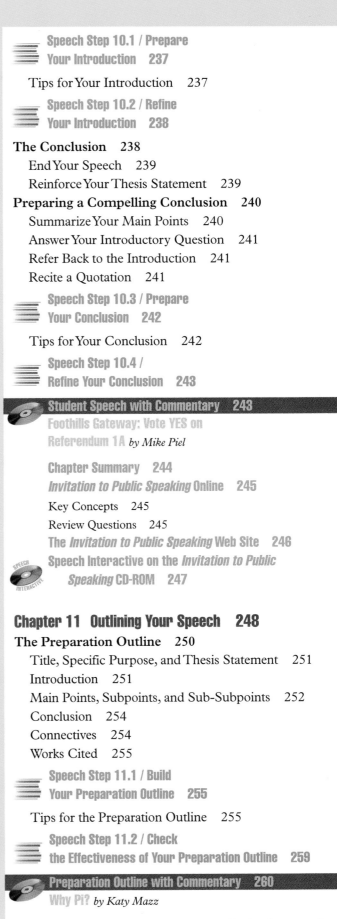

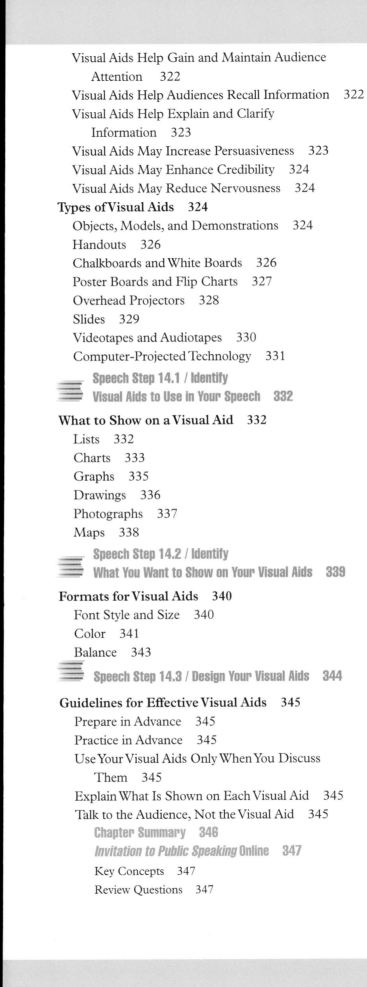

Preface

Our best public speaking courses focus their efforts and energies on teaching students the skills needed to speak effectively in public settings. To accomplish this goal, public speaking texts follow a familiar and practical framework that teaches students to give informative, persuasive, and special occasion speeches. Public speaking texts are designed to expose students to the wide array of steps and components involved in public speaking and to allow students to practice these various elements in the classroom.

Invitation to Public Speaking not only grounds itself in this successful approach, but expands it to focus on *public speaking as public dialogue*, encouraging students to see themselves as significant contributors to their larger communities. In this expanded context, public speaking reflects the many changes that have been taking place in our communities and our larger society, changes that call for public dialogue and an exploration of the many perspectives offered on a number of important topics (Ellinor & Gerard, 1998). When framed as a public dialogue, public speaking emphasizes the right to be heard and the responsibility to listen to others (Public Dialogue Consortium, 1998). Thus, *Invitation to Public Speaking* explores public speaking in relation to a modern definition of eloquence, where differences, civility, narratives, visual aids, and even self-disclosure play a larger role than they tend to in traditional rhetoric.

Invitation to Public Speaking encourages students to see public speaking as a meaningful and useful skill *beyond* the classroom setting by expanding the range of venues for public speaking. The text prompts students to speak not only in required classroom speaking situations, but also when they are asked to do so (for example, in the workplace) and when they decide to do so (perhaps as voices of their communities). Thus the text exposes them to the wide range of situations that causes us to assume the public platform and contribute to the public dialogue. It also allows instructors, if they desire, to incorporate a service-learning component into their course without preventing them from teaching public speaking using the familiar required speech format. Additionally, the text's pragmatic approach in combination with numerous dynamic, real-life examples allows working students to design speeches with their employment settings in mind.

Invitation to Public Speaking also frames the act of speaking in public to emphasize the ethical and audience-centered nature of public speaking.

Throughout the text, students are reminded that they speak to and for an audience, and they are encouraged to consider this audience at every step of the speech-making process. This audience-centered approach reminds students of the responsibilities associated with speaking publicly and the importance of advanced planning and preparation. It also eases some of the familiar speech anxiety students have, because it turns their attention toward speech preparation and effective communication with others and away from the performance aspect of public speaking.

Most existing texts focus primarily on informational and persuasive speaking, often also preparing students to give speeches that entertain or celebrate others. *Invitation to Public Speaking* includes this focus, but also introduces students to invitational speaking, a type of speaking that is becoming increasingly common. In invitational speaking, speakers enter into a dialogue with an audience in order to clarify positions, explore issues and ideas, or share beliefs and values. When we speak to invite, we want to set the stage for open dialogue and exploration of ideas and issues—we want to come to a fuller understanding of an issue, regardless of our different positions. This speech type is introduced early on in the text, when other speech types are defined and discussed, and is included in the discussion of the speech-making process throughout the text.

Finally, *Invitation to Public Speaking* emphasizes interconnections not only among each of the components of the speech-making process, but also between the speaker and the audience. In this way, the text helps students view public speaking as a layering of skills and issues rather than as a series of actions existing in isolation. Although the speaking process is presented systematically and in discrete steps, the end result is a smooth integration of material and speaking techniques. Additionally, the text's audience-centered approach and thorough integration of diversity help students better understand their audiences so they can establish credibility and communicate effectively.

Features of the Book

Coverage and Use of Technology

Invitation to Public Speaking was written with technology in mind. Thoughtful integration on nearly every page continually helps the student understand the links between the text and the technology. The text not only covers technology as it relates to speechmaking, but also incorporates the use of technology as a powerful learning tool. The Internet and online databases are discussed as tools for speech topic selection, research, and support, while presentation technology such as Microsoft® *PowerPoint*® is presented as a resource for creating professional visual aids. To guide students' use of technology in speech preparation, delivery, and analysis, the text integrates digital resources that will help students complete speech assignments and model their own public speaking performance.

Each chapter points students to numerous Web sites, video clips of student and professional speakers, InfoTrac College Edition exercises, and other online activities that can be accessed using the *Invitation to Public Speaking* CD-ROM and the *Invitation to Public Speaking* Web site. Each technology suggestion is represented in the text with an icon. Integrated throughout the chapter and summarized at the end of each chapter, these integrated icons direct students to use their CD-ROM and the text's companion Web site to complete speech preparation steps and enrich the concepts presented.

Focus on Skills

Invitation to Public Speaking prepares students to give speeches and enter the public dialogue via a solid, pragmatic, skills-based foundation in public speaking. Beginning with Chapter 2, "Entering the Public Dialogue with Confidence: Your First Speech," and continuing through Chapter 14, "Visual Aids," each chapter guides students through specific speech construction, delivery, or strategy steps. The text provides straightforward instruction in speechmaking that is based on my own classroom experience and knowledge of students' expectations for skill training.

Speech Step boxes frame and highlight critical instructions and prompt students to utilize Speech Builder Express™ to complete speech outlining assignments. Working through the Speech Step exercises exposes students to each component of the speechmaking process and gives them strategies for tackling the informative, invitational, persuasive, and special occasion speeches found in Chapters 15 through 19. Speech models included in the text are consistent with the principles presented.

Additionally, Review Questions conclude each chapter and give students the opportunity to further hone their skills. These questions range from straightforward true/false statements to activities that require more research and student involvement and reflection.

Speaking Venues and Service Learning

Invitation to Public Speaking covers a variety of speaking venues and provides ample opportunity to incorporate a service-learning component into the course. The text's flexible organization allows instructors who do not want to include service learning to easily maintain the traditional classroom-based speaking situation throughout the term.

Chapter 1, "Why Speak in Public?" offers students a comprehensive view of public speaking as public dialogue and discusses speaking when someone is asked to speak, decides to speak, or is required to speak. This allows students and instructors to step outside the speech classroom if they desire, and to take the public speaking skills taught and learned in the classroom into their communities. If they choose to stay with the traditional classroom speech format, the service learning information prompts students to select and deliver speeches that address larger social issues and dilemmas.

In addition, Invitation to Service Learning boxes appear in select chapters. Based on actual projects, these narratives reinforce for students the role and power of public speaking outside the classroom and in the public dialogue. The *Invitation to Public Speaking Instructor's Manual* and the *Invitation to Public Speaking Annotated Instructor's Edition* provide a definition of service learning and instruction for how to use service-learning projects as a source for speech topics, speech research, and possibly an environment for delivery.

Expansive Coverage of Speech Types

Some courses emphasize particular speech, but *Invitation to Public Speaking* was specifically developed to cover and support the entire array of public speaking types. The text's coverage of multiple speaking forms invites students to discuss audience centeredness and difference, as well as the ways that speakers can acknowledge, incorporate, and respond to difference with respect and integrity.

Beginning in Chapter 2, "Entering the Public Dialogue with Confidence: Your First Speech," the text presents a synopsis of five types of speaking: informative, invitational, persuasive, speaking on special occasions, and speaking in small groups. Each type of speech previewed in Chapter 2 is covered in depth in Chapters 15 through 20, and is given equal attention with regard to examples and tips in Chapters 3 through 14, furthering the text's goal of preparing readers for public speaking in a range of venues beyond the classroom.

Coverage of Social Diversity

Through reviewer-praised examples and discussion of key concepts, the text makes a comprehensive, yet subtle, integration of diversity. *Invitation to Public Speaking* offers meaningful coverage of diversity by exploring culture and speaking styles, culture and listening styles, speaking to diverse audiences, and language and culture.

Rather than isolate issues of diversity into separate chapters, *Invitation to Public Speaking* presents ideas and issues of diversity in examples, discussions, activities, and exercises throughout the text. In the process, the text provides sufficient information so that instructors do not need to do additional research in order to have meaningful conversations with their students. This "learn-as-you-go" approach benefits students and instructors as they add to their layers of knowledge about difference.

Coverage of Reasoning

The text emphasizes the important skill of reasoning in informative, invitational, and persuasive speaking situations. Chapter 8, "Reasoning," encourages students to recognize the validity of sound reasoning and evidence in any speaking context, while Chapter 18, "Persuasion and Reasoning," provides superior coverage of the critical importance of sound reasoning in persuasion.

Resources for Students

Invitation to Public Speaking features an outstanding array of supplements to assist in making this course as meaningful and effective as possible.

- **Invitation to Public Speaking CD-ROM** includes *Speech Interactive for Invitation to Public Speaking. Speech Interactive* includes video of 34 student and 21 professional speeches, which are included or referenced in the text. This multimedia tool helps students prepare for their own speech performances and provide effective feedback to their peers by evaluating and critiquing the introductory, informative, invitational, persuasive and special occasion speeches contained on the CD-ROM, using the questions provided. They can compare their evaluation with the author's and, if requested, submit their response electronically to their instructor.

- **Invitation to Public Speaking Web Site** will enhance student learning and build public speaking skills by including all of the Web Links, Interactive Activities, and InfoTrac College Edition Exercises referenced in the text and listed at the end of each chapter. In addition to student resources such as an interactive version of the Personal Report of Communication Apprehension

(PRCA) and the Research Inventory Worksheet, the Web site features *Speech Builder Express* Speech Outlining Program.

- **Speech Builder Express Speech Outlining Program** is a Web-based tool that coaches students through the speech organization and outlining process. By completing interactive sessions based on the in-text Speech Steps covering speech goal and specific purpose; organizational patterns; thesis statement, main points, supporting material, transitions, speech introduction, conclusion, and bibliography, students can create formal, speaking, and keyword outlines, formatted according to the principles presented in the text. Text and video models reinforce their interactive practice.

- **InfoTrac College Edition.** A fully searchable, online database provides students with access to complete articles from more than 4000 scholarly and popular periodicals, updated daily, and dating back over twenty years. This database allows students to complete their speech research using contemporary articles from all the major media. A four-month subscription to InfoTrac College Edition is included in the purchase price of this new text, and exercises for using InfoTrac are integrated into each chapter. Look for the InfoTrac College Edition logo to signal the InfoTrac College Edition feature.

- *InfoTrac College Edition Student Activities Workbook for Public Speaking,* by Nancy Goulden of Kansas State University, can be bundled with the text. The workbook features guidelines and an extensive selection of individual and group activities designed to help instructors and students get the most from InfoTrac College Edition.

- *Student Workbook for Invitation to Public Speaking* features extensive individual and group activities that support assignments suggested in the *Annotated Instructor's Edition* and the *Instructor's Manual.*

- *A Guide to the Basic Course for ESL Students,* by Esther Yook of Mary Washington College, is designed to assist the non-native speaker. Features FAQs, helpful URLs, and strategies for accent management and speech apprehension. Referenced throughout the *Annotation Instructor's Edition.*

- *Service Learning in Communication Studies: A Handbook* by Rick Isaacson, San Francisco State University; Bruce Dorries, Radford University; and Kevin Brown, Montana State University, is an invaluable resource for students in the basic course that integrates or is planning to integrate a service-learning component. Referenced throughout the *Annotated Instructor's Edition,* the handbook provides guidelines for connecting service learning work with classroom concepts and advice for working effectively with agencies and organizations. It also provides model forms and reports and a directory of online resources.

Resources for Instructors

Invitation to Public Speaking also features a full suite of resources for instructors. To evaluate any of these instructor or student resources, please contact your local Wadsworth representative for an examination copy, contact our Academic Resource Center at 800-423-0563, or visit us at http://communication.wadsworth.com.

- **Annotated Instructor's Edition (AIE)**, by Cindy L. Griffin of Colorado State University and Linda Scholz of Front Range Community College. The *Invitation to Public Speaking AIE* is a student copy of the text with marginal class-tested and reviewer-validated teaching tips and suggestions for integrating the extensive ancillary program. Fully cross-referenced with the *Instructor's Manual,* the test bank, the ESL and Service Learning handbooks, the *Multimedia Manager,* and the *Invitation to Public Speaking* CD-ROM, this tool is a must-have for the first-time instructor or graduate teaching assistant and a great refresher for the veteran professor.

- *Instructor's Manual,* by Cindy L. Griffin of Colorado State University and Linda Scholz of Front Range Community College. Cross-referenced with the *Annotated Instructor's Edition* and the student workbook, the *Instructor's Manual* provides a comprehensive teaching system. Included in the manual are suggested public speaking assignments and criteria for evaluation, chapter outlines, and in-class activities. All of the Weblinks, Interactive Activities, InfoTrac College Edition Exercises listed at the end of each chapter are included in detail in the Instructor's Manual in the case that online access is unavailable or inconvenient. The *Instructor's Manual* is available in print or electronically with a Word file of the test bank.

- **Transition Notes for *Invitation to Public Speaking,*** by Linda Scholz of Front Range Community College. This instructor's resource can help ease conversion of class notes and syllabi from select public speaking texts to Griffin's *Invitation to Public Speaking.* The 75-page manual features side-by-side comparison of the texts' table of contents. Annotated tables of contents help faculty see where the text overlap and where they differ.

- **Test Bank,** by Cindy L. Griffin of Colorado State University and Linda Scholz of Front Range Community College, features class-tested and reliability rated multiple choice, true-false, short answer, essay, and fill-in-the-blank test questions. Fully cross-referenced with the *Instructor's Manual.*

- **ExamView computerized testing.** Create, deliver, and customize tests and study guides (both print and online) in minutes with this easy-to-use assessment and tutorial system. ExamView offers both a Quick Test Wizard and Online Test Wizard that guide you step-by-step through the process of creating tests, while the unique "WYSIWYG" capability allows you to see the test you are creating on the screen exactly as it will print or display online. You can build tests of up to 250 questions using up to 12 question types. Using ExamView's complete word-processing capabilities, you can enter an unlimited number of new questions or add existing questions.

- **Overhead transparencies.** To facilitate lecture presentation in classrooms that are not wired for presentation software, overhead transparencies are available to demonstrate the resources such as models and key charts, diagrams, and forms used in speech preparation and delivery and included in the text.

- *Multimedia Manager for Invitation to Public Speaking: A Microsoft® PowerPoint® Presentation and Lecture Tool* is text-specific software designed to work with the PowerPoint presentation program and is available on a cross-platform CD-ROM. All the student speeches featured on the *Invitation to Public Speaking* CD-ROM and selected professional speeches are embedded into this outstanding presentation tool. If you have a computer and LCD display, you do not need a television and VCR to show the sample speeches in class.

- *The Teaching Assistant's Guide to the Basic Course,* by Katherine G. Hendrix of the University of Memphis. This guidebook is designed for the new communication teacher or for those who want to refresh their approach. Based on leading communication teacher training programs, the guide covers general teaching and course management topics, as well as specific strategies for communication instruction, such as providing effective feedback on performance, managing sensitive class discussions, and conducting mock interviews. This guide is available free to adopters of the text and as a saleable item to other interested parties.

- **CNN Videos** help stimulate class discussions. The series of CNN videos, with video segments keyed to material in the text, is available for qualifying adopters. Ask your Wadsworth/Thomson Learning representative for more information. *CNN Today: Public Speaking, Volume 1* includes Clinton's "apology" speech, a speech from the Dali Lama, and Queen Elizabeth II's address on the death of Princess Diana. *CNN Today: Public Speaking, Volume III* includes George W. Bush's acceptance speech and Al Gore's concession speech. *CNN Today: Public Speaking, Volume IV* includes President George W. Bush's Address to the Joint Session of Congress on September 20, 2001, Mary Fisher's "Whisper of Aids" and Nelson Mandela's Inaugural Address.

- **Wadsworth Video Library** is a resource of more than thirty videos, including seven volumes of "Student Speeches for Critique and Analysis." This series features sample narrative, self-introduction, informative, invitational, persuasive, and impromptu student speeches. Volume 7 includes all of the student speeches featured on the *Invitation to Public Speaking* CD-ROM.

- *WebTutor™ ToolBox for WebCT and Blackboard* is preloaded with content and available FREE via PIN code when packaged with this text. WebTutor ToolBox pairs all the content of this text's rich Book Companion Web Site with all the sophisticated course management functionality of a WebCT or Blackboard product. You can assign materials (including online quizzes) and have the results flow automatically to your gradebook. Contact your Thomson representative for more information or to package WebTutor ToolBox with this text.

- **MyCourse 2.0.** My Course is a free online course builder. Whether you want only the easy-to-use tools to build it or the content to furnish it, we offer you a simple solution for a custom course Web site that allows you to assign, track, and report on student progress; load your syllabus; and more.

Contact your Wadsworth/Thomson Learning representative for details or a demonstration of any of these teaching and learning resources. Available to qualified adopters. Please consult your local sales representative for details.

Acknowledgments

I believe writing and scholarship are both individual and collaborative efforts. Acknowledging the individuals who assisted me throughout the process of writing this book is one small way of recognizing that collaboration and thanking those who offered invaluable assistance and endless support. To Deirdre Anderson, former Executive Editor, and Greer Lleuad, Development Editor, I express my deepest and heartfelt appreciation. For their invitation to embark on this journey, their incredible vision and talent, their endless guidance, support, kindness, and laughter, I am honored and grateful. My writing process and life are richer because of the two of them. To Kim Russell, Marketing Manager; Jeanette Wiseman, Senior Technology Project Manager; Cathy Linberg, Senior Production Project Manager, Editorial Production; Mele Alusa, former Editorial Assistant; Photo Researcher Sarah Everston; Project Editor Andrea Fincke at Thompson Steele; and Becky Stovall, CNN Producer, I express my sincerest thanks. These amazing women shared their talents, time, and energy enhancing the book every step of the way. They also generously offered insight, wisdom, and expertise in response to my never-ending requests and questions.

To Linda Scholz, Lead Speech Instructor at Front Range Community College, and Jennifer Emerling Bone, former Lecturer at Colorado State University and Front Range Community College, and now Ph.D. student at University of Colorado, Boulder, friends in every way and collaborators on various aspects during various stages of this book, I am forever indebted. Their excellent ideas and insights, love and support, steady stream of laughter, smiles, and hugs, and willingness to test out the early versions of this book in their own classes are acts of courage and connection that never went unnoticed or unappreciated. The speeches of their students grace the chapters of this book, which reflects not only the talents of those students, but also the extraordinary skill Linda and Jennifer possess as teachers. I am lucky to have them in my life. My sincerest appreciation also goes to Tim Borchers at Minnesota State University Moorhead for his talent and expertise in integrating technology throughout each chapter of this book and for his assistance with the material in Chapter 20. His scholarship and perspective have greatly enhanced the pedagogy of this text and have paved the way for a truly meaningful and instructive Web site.

To Matt Petrunia and Anne Trump, Lecturers at Colorado State University, many, many thanks. Their hours and hours in the library, on the Internet, and in my office assisting me with research are invaluable. Working with the two of them gave me the confidence to complete this project on time and the assurance that the ideas in this book are supported by the very best of scholarship, both historical and contemporary. My colleagues at Colorado State University, Karrin Anderson, Eric Aoki, Carl Burgchardt, Greg Dickenson, Ann Gill, Brian Ott, Sue Pendell, Dennis Phillips, David Vancil, and David Vest shared their rich knowledge about teaching public speaking, material from their own libraries, and anecdotes from their own experiences, which energized and encouraged my work. The support they offered, the confidence they expressed, and their excellent scholarship reminded me to continue to strive for the richness that is possible in teaching and writing about public speaking. And along those lines, thanks very much to all the reviewers and class testers, listed on the inside front cover of this book, for their invaluable feedback and early support of this book.

Thanks also to Colorado State University Lecturers, graduate students, and special-appointment faculty Cara Buckley-Ott, Kathleen Creamer, Erin Cunningham, Ian Dawe, Brian DeVeney, Bill Herman, Jeffery Ho, Lori Irwin, Jill Lippman, Katheryn Maguire, Jeremy Mellott, Kirsten Pullen, Virginia Ramos, Allison Searle, Jamie Skerski, Derek Sweet, and Elizabeth Terry, who at various times (and sometimes without even realizing it) shared speech ideas, outlines, assignments, and stories that added to the depth and strength of this project. Many thanks also to their students, whose speeches are found in pages of this text. And finally, a sincere thank you to my public speaking students and to the students from other parts of the country whose voices enhance this text, for their creativity, flexibility, and talents.

Without a doubt, the strongest collaborative force in my life comes from my family. My husband, Mike Harte; my son, Joseph Griffin-Harte; my sisters, Tracy Zerr and Wendy Stewart; my brother John Griffin; my mother, Joan Christiansen; my father, John Griffin; and my dear friend Jana Webster keep strong and steady the flame that fuels my energy. Their unending love and support have enriched this project and reminded me daily that the public dialogue is enhanced by our willingness to listen to others and by our commitment to speak as clearly and honestly as possible. To them, I offer my love and thanks, and the acknowledgment that their care for me gives me great strength and peace.

Cindy L. Griffin is an Associate Professor of Speech Communication at Colorado State University. She received her B.S. from California State University, Northridge, her M.A. in Communication from the University of Oregon, and her Ph.D. from Indiana University. Cindy teaches Public Speaking, Women and Communication, Contemporary Rhetorical Theory, Feminist Rhetorical Theory, Rhetorical Criticism, and Rhetoric and Civility. A proponent of service learning, Cindy integrates service learning assignments into her coursework and has presented at regional and national conventions regarding service learning. In addition to her teaching and research, she has been the co-chair of Colorado State University's Commission on Ethnic Diversity and has served on the Diversity Advisory Committee as well as the University Mentoring Program. She currently co-facilitates the Women's Studies Project on Curriculum Transformation, is a member of the Graduate Committee, and is a member of the Bridges to the Future Service Integration Project. She and her husband, Mike Harte, have a son, Joseph, and live in Fort Collins, Colorado.

Timothy A. Borchers, technology contributor, is Associate Professor of Speech Communication at Minnesota State University Moorhead, where he has taught for seven years. He received his B.A. from the University of Nebraska–Lincoln and his M.A. and Ph.D. from Wayne State University in Detroit, Michigan. Timothy teaches classes in Persuasion, Argumentation, Rhetorical Theory and Criticism, and Public Speaking. He is the author of *Persuasion in the Media Ag*e and numerous articles, book chapters, and convention papers. Additionally, he coached collegiate forensics for ten years and served as editor of the National Forensic Journal, and he is currently active at MSUM in departmental and university governance. He and his wife, Susanne Williams, have one son, Oliver, and live in Moorhead, Minnesota. Timothy enjoys sports, cooking, home improvement projects, and watching movies.

T. M. Linda Scholz, author of the Annotated Instructor's Edition and co-author of the Instructor's Manual, has been an active, contributing member of the Fort Collins community for ten years. She received her B.A. and M.A. in Speech Communication and a master's certification in Women's Studies from Colorado State University. Linda has taught Public Speaking, Introduction to Intercultural Communication, Women's Studies, Oral Reading, and Interpersonal Communication. She is a passionate faculty member of Front Range Community College, Larimer Campus, and is committed to promoting diversity on campus among her colleagues and students, and among the Northern Colorado academic and business communities. Raised in Guatemala and California, Linda currently shares a home in Loveland, Colorado, with her lovingly patient partner and her two demanding cats.

Invitation to Public Speaking

Chapter One

Why Speak in Public?

In this chapter you will learn

About the power and influence of public speaking

About the influence of culture on speaking styles

What makes public speaking different from other kinds of communication

Why people speak publicly

I have come to tell you something about slavery—what I know of it, as I have felt it . . . . they cannot speak as I can from experience; they cannot refer you to a back covered with scars, as I can; for I have felt these wounds; I have suffered under the lash without the power of resisting. And yet my master has the reputation of being a pious man and a good Christian.

—Frederick Douglass, 1841, "I have Come to Tell You Something About Slavery," Lynn, Massachusetts[1]

The strength of America's response, please understand, flows from the principles upon which we stand. Americans are not a single ethnic group. Americans are not of one race or one religion. Americans emerge from all of your nations. We're defined as Americans by our beliefs, not by our ethnic origins, our race, or our religion.

—Rudolph W. Giuliani, 2001, Address to the United Nations after the September 11, 2001, terrorist attacks in New York and Washington, D.C.[2]

How many times you have been directly influenced or even changed by the words of someone else? Most of us, at some point in our lives, have listened carefully to another person speak publicly. Most of us, at least once, have left a public speech or lecture feeling different about the world, the issues that concern us, and even ourselves. None of us witnessed Frederick Douglass's 1841 speech against slavery. None of us heard Abraham Lincoln, almost twenty years later, explain, "If I could save the union without freeing any slaves, I would do it, and if I could do it by freeing all the slaves, I would do it, and if I could do it by freeing some and leaving others alone, I would also do that. What I do about the colored race I do to save the union."[3] Only some of us heard Rudy Giuliani speak. Yet all of us have been powerfully influenced by these speakers. Their speeches contribute to our understanding of very complicated and important events.

This book will facilitate your success as a beginning public speaker. It presents the practice of speaking in as many natural settings as possible and allows you to practice this skill in a classroom environment. The components of the public speaking process are broken down into discrete steps in the chapters that follow, and you will be asked to incorporate these into your speeches. Some of the techniques and steps presented in this text may seem contrived at first, but they will allow you to develop a strong base of knowledge regarding effective speech making. As you gain confidence, you will use this knowledge to branch out on your own, incorporating various aspects learned in this book into your own real-life speaking experiences.

Public speaking is a learned skill that gets more rewarding over time. Every speaker had to learn how to give effective speeches—even Frederick Douglass, Abraham Lincoln, Rudy Giuliani, and the many others you will read about in this text. The more you try out this new skill, the more quickly you will feel competent at giving speeches. After you finish your public speaking course, you will find that you give speeches at work and in your community. You will speak to give directions, share information, explain procedures, encourage or influence decisions, and more. The public dialogue you will read about in this text is lively and engaging. With care and practice, you will find that you too can influence the discussions that take place in the public dialogue in positive ways.

Even skilled speakers like New York Mayor Rudy Giuliani had to learn how to give effective speeches. The mayor is speaking here about the September 11, 2001, terrorist attacks on New York City, a serious issue that affected us all. Even if you didn't hear his speech, do you think you have been influenced by it? In what way?

AP/Wide World Photos

This chapter introduces you to the power and influence of public speaking, the differences between public speaking and other forms of communication, and the reasons why people choose to enter the public dialogue. It invites you to consider the opportunities you will have to speak publicly and to recognize the importance of learning the basic skills necessary to do so successfully and effectively. When we consider the power these actions have to shape lives, we begin to get a sense of the challenges, responsibilities, and thoughtfulness that goes into designing, delivering, and listening to effective public speeches. To learn more about the power of communication in shaping community, visit the Web site for the Public Dialogue Consortium at http://www.publicdialogue.org/working.index.html.

The Power and Influence of Public Speaking

When you speak publicly, you have the power to influence others. With every speech you give, you make choices about the kind of influence you will have. If you watch television, listen to the radio, or read newspapers and magazines, you are familiar with public arguments and debates. We see politicians solve problems by taking sides on issues and "doing battle" with their "opponents." Social dilemmas are presented as "wars," and groups position themselves on either side of the "dispute" offering "*the* solution" while harshly critiquing and negating the "other" side. We even watch, read about, or listen to people engage in hostile or threatening exchanges over differences in belief and action. The power to influence others through opposition and even anger seems quite common and almost normal.

But there are other ways to influence people when you give speeches. As you've watched and listened to combative exchanges, you may have heard critics of this approach call for more civility in public exchanges. The word *civility* comes from a root word meaning "to be a member of a household." In ancient Greece, *civility* referred to displays of temperance, justice, wisdom, and courage. Over time, the definition has changed only slightly, and in public speaking **civility** has come to mean care and concern for others, the thoughtful use of words and language, and the flexibility to see the many sides of an issue. To be civil is to listen to the ideas and reasons of others and to give "the world a chance to explain itself."[4] To be uncivil is to have little respect for others, to be unwilling to consider their

civility
Care and concern for others, the thoughtful use of words and language, and the flexibility to see the many sides of an issue.

ideas and reasons, and to be unwilling to take responsibility for the effect of one's words, language, and behaviors on others. To learn more about the meaning of civility, go to the University of Colorado Conflict Research Consortium's Web site at http://www.colorado.edu/conflict/civility.htm.

Deborah Tannen, author of *The Argument Culture: Moving from Debate to Dialogue,* offers one of the most compelling descriptions of many people's views about the incivility that characterizes much of our present-day public debates. Tannen describes "a pervasive warlike atmosphere that makes us approach public dialogue, and just about anything we need to accomplish, as if it were a fight." [5] She explains that in an argument culture, people tend to approach people and situations with a me-against-you frame of mind. They see each issue, event, or situation as if it were a contest, a fight, a battle over which side is correct. They begin with the idea that the best way to discuss any topic is through attack and by pitting one party against another. Although conflict and disagreement are a familiar part of most people's lives, the seemingly automatic nature of this response is what creates the argument culture so common today.

Tannen and others concerned with the argument culture recognize there are times when strong opposition and verbal attack are called for, and most of us can think of instances too. [6] But this form of communication isn't the only way people discuss issues, offer solutions, or resolve differences. We can view public speaking not only as engaging in a public argument, but also as participating in a public dialogue.

A dialogue is a civil exchange of ideas and opinions between two people or a small group of people. The **public dialogue** is the civil exchange of ideas and opinions among communities about topics that affect the public. To participate in the public dialogue is to offer perspectives, share facts, raise questions, and engage others publicly in stimulating discussions. [7] When we enter the public dialogue we become active citizens, participating in our nation's democratic process. We can also become participants in the global dialogue when we speak about issues that affect the entire world, such as the environment. Giving a speech is a natural way to enter the public dialogue, because when we give a speech we have a chance to

public dialogue
The civil exchange of ideas and opinions among communities about topics that affect the public.

Daryl Varrett is shown here speaking to reporters about support for hate crimes legislation—his uncle, James Byrd, Jr., was the victim of a hate crime in Jasper, Texas, in 1998. This topic can be a difficult one to talk about, and opinions vary about what constitutes hate crimes and how they should be punished. How difficult do you think it would be to respond civilly to an audience that doesn't seem open to your topic? What could you do to make this situation easier for you and your audience?

AP/Wide World Photos

clearly state our own perspectives. We also have a chance to open the door to hearing other people's perspectives. In this sense, giving a speech can be like participating in an unending conversation in which your own ideas are organized and in which others will participate. Kenneth Burke describes this conversation as follows:

> Imagine that you enter a parlor. You come late. When you arrive, others have long preceded you, and they are engaged in a lively discussion, a discussion too passionate for them to pause and tell you exactly what it is about. In fact, the discussion had already begun long before any of them got there, so that no one present is qualified to retrace for you all the steps that had gone before. You listen for a while, until you decide that you have caught the tenor of the argument; then you put in your oar. Someone answers; you answer them; another perspective is shared. The hour grows late, you must depart. And you do depart, with the discussion still vigorously in progress.[8]

Throughout this book you will be exposed to the power and influence of public speaking. As you study this process, you are asked to take a civil approach to your speaking. You are encouraged to give speeches that help clarify issues and stimulate thinking even as you inform, persuade, or invite others to consider a perspective. Although you may have strong views on issues, a civil approach to public speaking often is the most powerful way to present those views.

 Speech Step 1.1 / Choose an Approach to Public Speaking

Consider how you might approach giving a speech in this class. Would you prefer the combative approach Tannen describes or the dialogue approach? Why would you prefer the style you chose? Can you think of times when you might use the combative approach? Can you think of times when you might use the dialogue approach? What might be the effect of using these very different approaches in a speech?

Culture and Speaking Style

Culture has a powerful effect on communication. Whether it be the culture that comes from our nationality (the country we grew up in) or the culture that comes to us via our ethnic heritage (Italian American, for example), we can't ignore the effect of culture on communication. When we give or listen to speeches, we bring our cultural styles with us. Consider a few examples of ways that culture influences public speaking:

> The traditional West African storyteller, called the griot, weaves a story with song and dance, and enlivens a tale with all sorts of sound effects. He or she changes the pitch to suit the characters and the action and adds all kinds of popping, clicking, clapping sounds to dramatize the events of the story. The members of the audience respond like a chorus. They interpose comments at convenient intervals, add their own sound effects, and sing the song of the tale along with the griot.[9]

> To this day, poets are held in the highest esteem in Arab societies. The Arab poet performs important political and social functions. In battle, the poet's tongue is as effective as is the bravery of the Arab people. In peace, the poet might prove a menace to public order with fiery harangues. Poems can arouse a tribe to action in the same manner as the tirade of a demagogue in a modern political campaign. Poetry frequently functions in a political context to motivate action, and, as such, it is accorded as much weight as a scholarly dissertation.[10]

Ann Richards's speaking style is dominated by the use of inductive and experiential reasoning, folk wisdom, and concrete examples and stories as the basis for political values and judgments. A favorite line she uses is, "Tell it so my Mama in Waco can understand it." Her accessible style . . . encourages audience participation and reduces distance between the speaker and audience.[11]

These examples may come from cultures very different from your own or very familiar to you. What they suggest is that the ways we approach a public speech often reflect our different cultures, and sometimes even our maleness or femaleness.

Research on cultural styles of communication helps explain some of these differences. In general, many white males are comfortable with the direct, competitive style of interaction found in public presentations. Because historically this group of people has held more public offices and positions of power in the United States, it makes sense that their preferred style of communication has become the norm for public speaking. However, many other communication styles are also used. African American men, for example, tend to be more comfortable with a complex style of speaking. This style may be competitive, but it is more subtle, indirect or exaggerated, intense, poetic, rhythmic, and lyrical. Hispanic or Latino males usually reject the competitive style, favoring a more elegant, expressive, or intense narrative form of public communication. Similarly, Arab Americans tend to use an emotional and poetic style (poets often respond to and interpret political events in Middle Eastern countries) and rely on rhythm and the sounds of words to express their ideas.[12]

Other research suggests that in most Native American cultures, framing an issue as having only two sides is rare. In many Native American cultures, multiple perspectives are welcomed and competition is discouraged, while cooperation is privileged when discussing important matters. In addition, a more circular and flexible style of presentation is common, as well as the use of stories to explain ideas or teach beliefs. Humor or teasing are often used to make a point or teach a lesson. In many Native American, as well as some Asian and Asian American cultures, direct eye contact is a sign of disrespect, and publicly proving that someone else is wrong is a serious insult.[13]

The research on styles of speaking specific to women is slight. We do know that, in general, African American and Hispanic or Latina women may use a style of speech similar to the lyrical, rhythmic, or poetic style used by the males of their cultures, but it tends to be more collaborative than adversarial. White and Asian American women seem to share this sense of comfort with collaboration rather than attack, but do not often incorporate the poetic or lyrical forms of speaking used in many African American and Hispanic communities. In general, we also know that women from many different cultural backgrounds tend to incorporate a more personal tone, use as evidence more personal experiences and anecdotes as well as concrete examples, and establish connection and common ground with their audiences in their public speeches.[14]

In reading about these differences, you may have recognized your own culture's influence on your style of communication. These differences suggest there is more than one way to approach public speaking. Public speaking can occur when we argue with others or take sides on an issue. It can take place when we connect, collaborate, and share stories or humor with our audience. It also happens when speakers use various styles of language or delivery. To enter the public dialogue is to recognize the many different styles of speaking and to use those that fit you and the audience best. To explore ways to think about bridging cultural communication differences, go to http://www.ksu.edu/counseling/ispeak/people_to_people.htm and visit the Web site Intercultural Competence: Moving Beyond Appreciation and Celebration of Difference.

The elder is a well-respected storyteller in the Native American culture. Is story-telling a style of speaking familiar to you? What style, or combinations of styles, of speaking do you think you'd like to use in a speech?

© Eastcott/Momatiuk/The Image Works

What Is Public Speaking?

On any given day, we are bombarded with information: computers, televisions, radios, newspapers, magazines, movies, billboards, logos on cups and clothing and cars, even bosses, teachers, friends, and family fill our days with words, sounds, symbols, and conversation. We receive so much communication in a single day that researchers estimate 70 to 80 percent of most people's days are spent listening to others communicate. In fact, so much communication crosses our paths every day that we have come to call this era the information age.

How does public speaking fit into the information age? Consider the different sources of communication that contribute to the present information age and that we study in communication classrooms:

Intrapersonal communication: Communication with ourselves via the dialogue that goes on in our heads.

Interpersonal communication: Communication with other people that ranges from the highly personal to the highly impersonal. Interpersonal communication allows us to establish, maintain, and disengage from relationships with other people.

Group communication: Communication among members of a team or a collective about topics such as goals, strategies, and conflict.

Mass communication: Communication generated by media organizations that is designed to reach large audiences. This type of communication is transmitted via television, the Internet, radio, print media, and even the entertainment industry.

Public communication: Communication in which one person gives a speech to other people, most often in a public setting. This speech has predetermined goals and is about a topic that affects a larger community. In public speaking, one person, called the speaker, is responsible for selecting a topic and focus for the speech, organizing his or her ideas, and practicing his or her delivery. The speaker also is responsible for responding to audience questions and feedback.

intrapersonal communication
Communication with ourselves via the dialogue that goes on in our heads.

interpersonal communication
Communication with other people that ranges from the highly personal to the highly impersonal.

group communication
Communication among members of a team or a collective about topics such as goals, strategies, and conflict.

mass communication
Communication generated by media organizations that is designed to reach large audiences.

public communication
Communication in which one person gives a speech to other people, most often in a public setting.

How does the communication shown in the photo on the left differ from that shown in the photo on the right? How does the communication in both these photos differ from intrapersonal, small group, or mass communication?

Unlike casual conversations with friends and family, public speaking contains a structure and purpose that adds a level of responsibility not found in many everyday interactions. Unlike mass communication, the ability of the audience to respond directly sets it apart from many sources of information. And, unlike private conversations with one's self or with friends, public speaking is public. It is directed at groups of people and designed to be shared with those outside the immediate audience.

From these definitions, we can see that public speaking is unique because the responsibility for the organization, delivery, and flow of communication falls mostly on one person. However, if we think of public speaking as participating in the public dialogue, additional differences between public speaking and other forms of communication emerge.

Public Speaking Creates a Community

We often think of public speaking as an isolated, individual act. We imagine one person standing in front of a group of people presenting information to them. We forget that public speaking occurs because individuals belong to a community and are affected by one another. We speak publicly because we recognize this connection. When we share ideas and information and consider questions and possibilities with others, we recognize we are "members of a household." Even if we disagree with members of that household (our audience), we recognize we are connected to them. We create a community when we speak because we are talking about topics that affect us as well as each member of the audience.

At times we may forget we belong to a larger community and can participate in discussions that affect us all. Sometimes we feel isolated or think our interests and needs are not important to society. However, we are members of a larger social community, and we can and do add our voices to the public conversation. When we do, we recognize the need to stimulate the public dialogue, to answer the claims or statements of those who spoke before us, and to offer the larger community ideas for consideration and discussion. To think more about which issues in your community you can address as a public speaker and how you can go about it, complete Interactive Activity 1.1, "Convening Public Dialogue," online under Student Resources for Chapter 1 at the *Invitation to Public Speaking* Web site.

WEB SITE

Public Speaking Is Audience Centered

Public speaking also stands apart from other forms of communication because speakers recognize the central role of their audience. Speakers speak to audiences—without them we are not engaged in public speaking. Moreover, in public speaking the makeup of the audience directly influences the speaker's message. Consider the following scenarios:

> Su Lin's older brother recently had a near miss while riding his bike across town. Upset by the lack of awareness on the part of motorists, Su Lin wants to speak out at the next city council meeting to argue for motorist education programs.

> Gretchen's brother recently had a near miss while riding his bike across town. Upset by the lack of awareness on the part of motorists, Gretchen has decided to give a speech on motorist safety in her public speaking course.

> Arturo rides his bicycle to work every day and has persuaded many of his coworkers to do the same. He recently had a near miss with a distracted and rushed motorist and he wants to speak to his coworkers about what they can do to educate motorists about safe riding practices.

The audience in these three scenarios dictates the choices each speaker will make. Each of the three audiences, the city council, the public speaking class, and the other cyclists, have different positions, beliefs, values, and needs regarding motorist safety. City councils have financial limitations, time constraints, as well as voter preferences that Su Lin will need to consider. Gretchen's classmates probably struggle with issues of relevance of the topic to their lives (they may ride the bus) and busy schedules that make them want to drive quickly (getting from work to school and back in a limited time). At Arturo's workplace, the other cyclists probably worry about their own vulnerability too, whether riding to work is really worth the risk, and how to manage one more responsibility—motorist education.

What these three examples suggest is that public speaking is distinctly **audience centered,** or considerate of the positions, beliefs, values, and needs of an audience. To be audience centered is to keep your audience in your mind with every step of the public speaking process, including your research, organization, and presentation. You can learn how to analyze an audience and stay audience centered by completing Interactive Activity 1.2, "Thinking About Your Audience," online under Student Resources for Chapter 1 at the *Invitation to Public Speaking* Web site.

audience centered
Considerate of the positions, beliefs, values, and needs of an audience.

WEB SITE

Although conversations with friends are, in some sense, audience centered, consider the very different role of the audience (and even the speaker) in this scenario:

> Peter's older brother recently barely avoided an accident while riding his bike across town. Upset by the lack of awareness on the part of motorists, Peter vents his frustrations to his friends while they work out at the local gym.

Certainly Peter's friends are his audience, but he likely is more concerned with airing his feelings and anger and getting support from his friends than he is with framing his position in a particular way.

Public speaking also is audience centered because speakers "listen" to their audiences during speeches. They monitor the **feedback** given to them by audiences, the verbal and nonverbal signals an audience gives a speaker. Audience

feedback
Verbal and nonverbal signals an audience gives a speaker.

feedback often indicates they understand, are interested in, and receptive to the speaker's ideas. This feedback assists the speaker in many ways. It helps the speaker know when to slow down, explain something more carefully, or even tell the audience she or he will return to an issue in a question-and-answer session at the close of the speech. Audience feedback assists the speaker in creating a connection with the audience so they feel acknowledged, important, and able to participate if they wish.

We often think of public speaking as distinct because it is what a speaker does in front of an audience, when it actually is distinct because of the ways the speaker relates the ideas in the speech to the audience.

Public Speaking Encourages Dialogue

A final difference between public speaking and other kinds of communication is that public speaking sets the stage for the unending conversation Kenneth Burke described earlier in this chapter. The speaker is responsible for framing this conversation, or dialogue, and for laying the foundation for future discussions. Public speaking encourages dialogue because speakers want the people who hear the speech to be able to engage others, and perhaps even the speaker, in a conversation about the topic or issue after the speech is given. Public speaking encourages dialogue because the speaker is interested in discussing issues and in hearing more about them from the audience.

 To review the unique aspects of public speaking you've just read about, complete the InfoTrac® College Edition Exercise 1.1, "Defining Public Speaking," featured online under Student Resources for Chapter 1.

Speech Step 1.2 / Consider the Unique Aspects of Public Speaking

Choose a speech topic for a speech you might give in class. How would you speak about this topic in a way that differs from presenting it intrapersonally, interpersonally, in a group setting, or via mass media? How do you think a speech about this topic would begin to create community or contribute to the public dialogue? How would you make this speech audience centered?

A Public Speaking Model

Consider the following components to the public speaking process as it has been discussed thus far:

speaker
Person who stimulates public dialogue by delivering an oral message.

Speaker: A person who stimulates public dialogue by delivering an oral message. The speaker researches the topic of the speech, organizes the material that results from the research, presents the message, and manages discussion after or, in some cases, during a speech. Throughout this process, the speaker considers the needs and characteristics of the audience.

message
Information conveyed by the speaker to the audience.

Message: The information conveyed by the speaker to the audience. Messages can be verbal or nonverbal. For example, a speaker giving a speech about his interest in playing guitar would use words to describe his first guitar and use facial

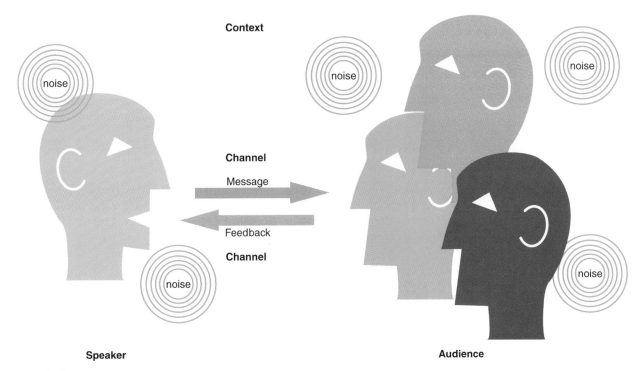

Figure 1.1

The Public Speaking Process Represented Visually

expressions, gestures, and tone of voice to convey his excitement about learning to play his first song. The goal of the speaker is to craft a message relevant to the audience. Most of our messages are intentional, but sometimes we send an unintentional message to our audience. An unintentional message can be an unplanned pause, a sigh, or a frown that conveys an idea or a feeling we had not planned to communicate. Messages connect people with ideas and are framed so they enhance or stimulate public discussion. When we speak, we convey messages by **encoding**, or translating ideas and feelings into words, sounds, and gestures. When we receive the message we **decode** it, or translate words, sounds, and gestures into ideas and feelings in an attempt to understand the message.

Audience: The complex and varied group of people the speaker addresses. Because of the audience-centered nature of public speaking, the speaker must consider the positions, beliefs, values, and needs of the audience throughout the design and delivery of a speech.

Channel: The means by which the message is conveyed. A message can be conveyed through spoken words, vocal tone and gestures, and visual aids. Additionally, messages can be conveyed through technological means such as a telephone, a microphone, or the Internet.

Noise: Anything that interferes with understanding the message being communicated. Noise may be external or internal. External noise, interference outside the speaker or audience, might be construction work going on outside the classroom window or a microphone that doesn't work in a large lecture hall. Internal noise, interference within the speaker or audience, might be a headache that affects one's concentration or cultural differences that make it hard to understand a message.

Feedback: The verbal and nonverbal signals the audience gives the speaker. Feedback from an audience indicates to the speaker the need to slow down, clarify, respond to questions, alter delivery, and the like.

encoding
Translating ideas and feelings into words, sounds, and gestures.

decoding
Translating words, sounds, and gestures into ideas and feelings in an attempt to understand the message.

audience
The complex and varied group of people the speaker addresses.

channel
Means by which the message is conveyed.

noise
Anything that interferes with understanding the message being communicated.

context
Environment or situation in which a speech occurs.

Context: The environment or situation in which a speech occurs. The context includes components such as the time of day and the place in which the speech is given, the expectations the audience has about the speech, and the traditions associated with a speech. For example, in a church setting a sermon could be given in the late morning, in a sunny church with hard wooden pews. The audience would expect the sermon to deliver an inspirational, moral message, and the sermon would follow a traditional organization based on a reading from the Bible.

Notice the interconnected nature of each of these components. Also note that the speaker is both a "speaker" as well as a "listener," attending to feedback from the audience. The audience also has a key role, listening to the message so they can contribute to the discussion that may occur when the speech is done. Look for the interconnection of these components as you complete the InfoTrac College Edition Exercise 1.2, "The Speaking Model," featured online under Student Resources for Chapter 1.

When Do We Speak in a Public Setting?

Public speaking occurs in certain contexts or circumstances. The context is the environment or situation in which a speech occurs. There are many different contexts for speaking (formal or informal settings, large audiences or small audiences, serious issues or lighthearted ones, and so on), and you will learn more about these as your read this text. However, certain contexts will prompt some people to speak, whereas others do not motivate us to give a speech at all. Understanding three of the most basic contexts helps us recognize when we might speak publicly.

In the following descriptions, notice that everyday people, not just famous or politically powerful ones, insert their voices into the public dialogue in order to share their knowledge, experiences, or perspectives. Each of these people began their speaking careers for different reasons, but each became well-known speakers without setting out to do so. Each person, in addition, decided to speak for different reasons, yet each has had a powerful impact on the lives of everyday people.

We Decide to Speak on Matters of Importance

We often find we are compelled to speak because an issue is of such importance that to let it go would do a disservice to ourselves and others around us. Consider the story of Lois Gibbs, who, prior to 1978, described herself as a "typical American woman" with a "typical American family" living in a "typical American town." When Gibbs learned that 20,000 tons of toxic chemicals were buried beneath her home and those of her neighbors in the Love Canal section of Niagara Falls, New York, she decided to speak out.

The issue and hazards of dioxin, the chemical poisoning her community and causing numerous illnesses, birth defects, and miscarriages in the families that lived there, was of such importance that Gibbs began giving speeches. Over a thirty-year period, Gibbs spoke about hazardous wastes and environmental activism to neighbors, friends, and home owners. She delivered speeches to city planners, legislators, and to other officials in her civic, state, and national governments. She even traveled internationally to speak out about hazardous waste disposal and was twice an invited guest on *The Phil Donahue Show,* a popular and influential television talk show that aired from 1970 to 1996.

Gibbs is a compelling and extraordinary example of the impact of someone who decided to speak out. Not only has she received international recognition as an environmental activist, but she is credited with bringing the issue of hazardous waste disposal to the attention of people nationally and internationally. Equally compelling, though, is how she describes her evolution as a speaker. When she first began to give speeches, Gibbs "was nervous." She repeatedly referred to herself as a "typical housewife," whose biggest decision before she decided to speak publicly was "what color wallpaper to use" in her kitchen. She describes her first speaking experiences as "intimidating" attempts to understand the "jibber jabber" of officials who did not want her nosing around. She "was so self-conscious that everything [she] said seemed to come out wrong"; she "got a little silly." Part of it was "nerves"; she "wanted a cigarette and a cold drink."[15]

After several years of speaking, Gibbs recognized her own evolution and perhaps some of the motivation and endurance required to accomplish what she did: "Fifty or sixty people came out [for a rally] . . . . I stood up and shouted: 'Do you want out?' and they shouted back, 'Yes!' . . . It was exhilarating to be in touch with the crowd that way. I had come a long way since that first time, when I was so scared."

Gibbs spoke in the context of deciding to speak out. In doing so, she exposed dangerous hazardous waste disposal practices and pressured officials to take responsibility for their actions and decisions. She encourages others to act on their motivations as well. Find "the courage to change the way the government works," she says, because, in "order for things to change, the truth has to be understood by a large group of people who then use this knowledge to fuel their efforts to win justice."[16] To learn more about Lois Gibbs and her reasons for speaking, go to http://www.goldmanprize.org/recipients/recipientProfile.cfm?recipientID=15n.

We Are Asked to Speak About Our Experiences and Expertise

People often speak publicly because they have important experiences or expertise to share. Ryan White, only a child when he began his public speaking career, is an example of someone who was asked to speak and share his experiences with others. White, a hemophiliac, received a blood transfusion at the age of 13 that changed his life: the blood-clotting agent Hemofil contained the AIDS virus, and he became infected. In 1985 White's school superintendent banned him from attending Western Middle School, near Kokomo, Indiana, White's hometown. Although the state health board recommended he be readmitted, and the family filed suit with the U.S. District Court in Indianapolis, the parents of Kokomo school children signed 117 claim forms threatening to file a civil suit if White was allowed in the classroom.

After two years of protests and school boycotts by parents and children, court orders and injunctions that kept White in and out of school, and continual health problems, White and his family moved to Cicero, Indiana, to escape the publicity in Kokomo. Shy about speaking out publicly and mistrustful of being in the spotlight, White was selective about the speaking engagements he agreed to. At the age of 16, he traveled to Omaha to speak to reporters, a religion class at Father Flanagan's Boys Town, and adults at the Joslyn Witherspoon Concert Hall:

> "Are you afraid of dying?" asks a student at Boys Town. "No," Ryan says. "If I were worried about dying, I'd die. I'm not afraid, I'm just not ready yet. I want to go to Indiana University." . . . "What was it like in Kokomo?" a girl asks . . . . "A lot of people would back away from me on the street," Ryan says. "They'd run from me. Maybe I would have been afraid of AIDS too, but I wouldn't have been mean about it." . . . Afterward, a reporter asks Ryan what was the worst thing about Kokomo. "I had no friends," Ryan says. "I was lonely. All I wanted was to go to school and fit in."

Reluctant to deliberately put himself in the spotlight, White explained, "It's embarrassing . . . . I'm helping people, I think, and I don't want people treated like me. But now I just want to be like everyone else."[17]

As a result of the speaking invitations White received and his willingness to share his experiences, the public education process about AIDS and HIV improved. In one of his last public appearances, in 1990, White appeared in Los Angeles with former president and first lady Ronald and Nancy Reagan. At this event, the Ryan White National Program for AIDS Education was established by Athletes and Entertainers for Kids.[18] Born in 1971, White died on April 8, 1990. He never made it to Indiana University, but because of the national exposure he received and his willingness to speak publicly about his experiences, White is described as "one of the nation's most persuasive advocates for AIDS patients' rights" and "a miracle of humanity."[19] Watch a video clip of a student speaker, Mike Piel, who was also able to make a connection with his audience and remain audience centered. You can find this clip under Speech Interactive on your *Invitation to Public Speaking* CD-ROM.

We Are Required to Speak in Class or at Work

Occasionally, people become public speakers out of necessity. Either our jobs require us to speak, we take a course that has public speaking as a component, or we discover we are in a situation where we have no choice but to speak out. Although these can be challenging moments, when people are required to speak they often discover they have the potential to make profound contributions to the public dialogue.

If you are required to speak in class, what topics would you like to speak about? How do you think you could use the experience of speaking in class to prepare yourself for the larger public discussion?

In the 1950s, Senator Joseph McCarthy campaigned ruthlessly against what he saw as a communist threat to the United States. McCarthy's efforts caught the attention of the country, and by 1953 this senator from Wisconsin had reached the height of his political power. He had the authority to subpoena individuals from all walks of life, to scrutinize their professional and personal activities, and to charge them with communist activities with little or no evidence of such affiliations. Even President Eisenhower and his leading aides and cabinet officers seemed anxious to please McCarthy, and McCarthy's senate colleagues knew and feared his influence.

However, in 1954 the national sentiment began to change, and people began to challenge McCarthy's power. McCarthy's ability to find communists and communist affiliations in every corner of society turned from being seen as potentially useful information to being viewed as absurd, unfounded, and slanderous accusations of innocent people.

McCarthy's reign came to a close in the Army-McCarthy hearings when he relentlessly charged a young law clerk who had served two weeks on the investigation team for the military special counsel with communist affiliations. Joseph Welch, the military special investigator, was required to speak in response to the accusations. Here is what he said to McCarthy during the hearings in 1954:

> Until this moment, Senator, I think I never really gauged your cruelty or your recklessness . . . . Little did I dream you could be so reckless and so cruel as to do an injury to that lad . . . . I fear he shall always bear a scar needlessly inflicted by you . . . . I like to think I am a gentleman, but your forgiveness will have to come from someone other than me . . . . Let us not assassinate this lad further, Senator. You have done enough. Have you no sense of decency, sir, at long last? Have you left no sense of decency?

At the close of his speech, the hearing room burst into applause and McCarthy, "flushed and stunned, sat in silence."[20] To hear a clip of Welch's speech, go to http://www.webcorp.com/mccarthy/mccarthypage.htm.

Unless we are in a classroom setting, or required to speak as part of our job, being required to speak out publicly is a rare occasion for most of us. However, even in a classroom, you can contribute positively to the public dialogue by selecting topics that are relevant and engaging. Similarly, required public speaking prepares you for situations in which you decide to or are asked to speak. It also allows you to practice for those times you find yourself entering Burke's room, listening to the conversation, and inserting your voice into the larger discussion.

To learn more about how you can continue your public speaking training after this class, go to the Toastmaster Web site at http://www.toastmasters.org. To examine several recent instances of speaking and determine why speakers engage the public, complete the InfoTrac College Edition Exercise 1.3, "Deciding to Speak," featured online under Student Resources for Chapter 1.

Speech Step 1.3 / Consider Why You Would Speak in Public

Outside of your public speaking classroom, when would you decide to speak publicly or agree to give a speech if you were asked? In this class, what topics will you choose to speak about? What do your answers to these questions indicate about your possible contributions to the public dialogue discussed in this chapter?

Sam

When I was asked to speak at my high school graduation, I was a little scared, but I knew it would be okay. I wrote my speech early and rehearsed it. I asked my family to sit down and listen to me practice over and over again. On graduation day, I thought I was going to be sick—I knew there was going to be a lot of people there, but there ended up being more than I expected. I was so scared! My family was sitting in the front row, which made me even more nervous. But every time I looked at my dad, he would make funny faces. I knew I was shaking, but thanks to the inventor of the podium, no one noticed. When I look back on that day, I am so glad that someone asked me to enter the public dialogue and give a speech. It was worth it!

Chapter Summary

When people give speeches, their words have the power to influence people and to shape actions and decisions. Whether we hear the actual speech or not, the ideas expressed in a speech enter and shape the public dialogue for years to come. The public dialogue is the open and honest discussion that occurs among groups of people about topics that affect those groups. It takes place when a speaker offers perspectives, shares facts, raises questions, and engages others in stimulating discussions. As we join that dialogue with our own speeches, we rely on and respond to these earlier speakers.

In this book, you will learn to enter this dialogue civilly, which is to display care, respect, thoughtfulness, and flexibility. And, although there may be great passion in your speeches, that passion is informed by the desire to contribute to the public dialogue in productive ways. As you enter the public dialogue, you will notice your speaking style is shaped by your culture as well as your gender. You also will be exposed to styles different from your own. This range of styles is essential to the health of the public dialogue, and understanding these differences assists you in responding civilly to others.

Although we live in the information age and are surrounded by communication every day, public speaking is unique from other forms of communication. It has a structure, purpose, and role for the speaker that are different from other forms of communication. Other forms of communication, such as intrapersonal, interpersonal, group, and mass communication, do not place as much responsibility on the speaker, nor do they have the same purpose (addressing issues that affect the larger community) or structure (one individual is responsible for the bulk of communication).

Public speaking also is unique from other kinds of communication because it creates community, is audience centered, and encourages dialogue in ways that other types of communication do not. The model of the public speaking process highlights the role of the speaker and explains the message, audience, and channel as well as the influence of noise and feedback. Understanding these components, as well as the differences between the various types of communication, will help you learn to give effective speeches.

We speak publicly either because we have decided to speak, we are asked to speak, or we are required to speak. These three reasons make up the foundation of any context for speaking—whether it be formal or casual, serious or lighthearted, or otherwise. You will probably encounter all three reasons for speaking in your lifetime. Recognize that public speaking is an essential part of communication. It has been used to help us understand, grapple with, and make decisions about our world and our lives. This book invites you learn to speak publicly so you can enter the rich and complex conversation that not only is unending, but makes up the public dialogue so important to our lives.

After reading this chapter, use your CD-ROM and the *Invitation to Public Speaking* Web site to review the following concepts, answer the review questions, and complete the suggested activities.

Key Concepts

civility (5)
public dialogue (6)
intrapersonal communication (9)
interpersonal communication (9)
group communication (9)

mass communication (9)
public communication (9)
audience centered (11)
feedback (11)
speaker (12)
message (12)

encoding (13)
decoding (13)
audience (13)
channel (13)
noise (13)
context (14)

Review Questions

1. Who are the most compelling speakers you have encountered? Why did they speak: did they decide, were they asked, or was it required? What issues did they discuss? How do these issues relate to the public dialogue discussed in this chapter? What made these speakers such strong presenters?

2. In this chapter, Deborah Tannen's notion of the argument culture is discussed. What is your perception of this culture? Have you been exposed to public communication as an argument? What were your reactions to this kind of interaction? If the people engaged in this interaction were to communicate civilly, what specific things would change?

3. Make a list of the issues you find interesting and have followed for some time. Who spoke publicly on those issues? If you don't know who gave speeches on these issues, spend time in the library and on the Internet finding these speeches. How do these speeches affect your own positions on these issues? How does this activity shape your perception of the unending conversation discussed in this chapter?

4. What cultural or gendered influences do you think will become (or already are) a part of your speaking style? Are these similar to those discussed in this chapter? If they are different, identify the differences and how they affect communication. Discuss this topic in your own public speaking class so that you and your classmates begin with a recognition of the differences you will encounter as you all give speeches.

5. Make a list of all the times you have presented information publicly. Include in your list occasions that range from formal to informal, carefully prepared in advance to impromptu, and presentations to a variety of audiences. Given this list, how much experience speaking publicly would you say you actually have had? Which situations were more comfortable for you than others? Why?

6. Write your own definition of public speaking. Now compare that definition to the one offered in this chapter. Compare it also to the model of public speaking. Now design your own model of the public speaking process, and label each of the components. How many of the components of the model described in this chapter (speaker, message, audience, channel, feedback, and noise) did you include? Be as creative and honest as you can with your model. What did you highlight or emphasize? Why?

7. When and why are you motivated to speak publicly? Would you decide to speak? Would you say yes if you were asked to speak? What if you were required to speak? Are there reasons you absolutely would or would not speak publicly? What are those reasons?

The *Invitation to Public Speaking* Web Site

The *Invitation to Public Speaking* Web site features the review questions about the Web sites suggested on pages 5, 6, 8, 15, and 17, the interactive activities suggested on page 11, and the InfoTrac College Edition exercises suggested on pages 12, 14, and 17. You can access this site via your CD-ROM or at http://www.wadsworth.com/product/griffin.

Web Links

1.1: Public Dialogue Consortium (5)
1.2: The Meaning of Civility (6)
1.3: Intercultural Competence (8)
1.4: Lois Gibbs (15)
1.5: Joseph Welch (17)
1.6: Toastmasters (17)

Interactive Activities

1.1: Convening Public Dialogue (11)
Purpose: To think about how you can help start a public dialogue in your community.

1.2: Thinking About Your Audience (11)
Purpose: To consider your classroom audience.

InfoTrac College Edition Exercises

1.1: Defining Public Speaking (12)
Purpose: To illustrate the differences between public speaking and other forms of communication

1.2: The Speaking Model (14)
Purpose: To apply the speaking model to a contemporary speech.

1.3: Deciding to Speak (17)
Purpose: To consider the various reasons for speaking.

Speech Interactive on the *Invitation to Public Speaking* CD-ROM

Use your *Invitation to Public Speaking* CD-ROM to access Speech Interactive and **Video Clip 1: Remaining Audience Centered: Mike Piel (16).** As you watch Mike speak, consider the language strategies he uses to communicate the importance of his topic to his audience. Click on "critique" to answer the following questions: What does Mike say to connect his topic to his audience? How does his language help him remain audience centered?

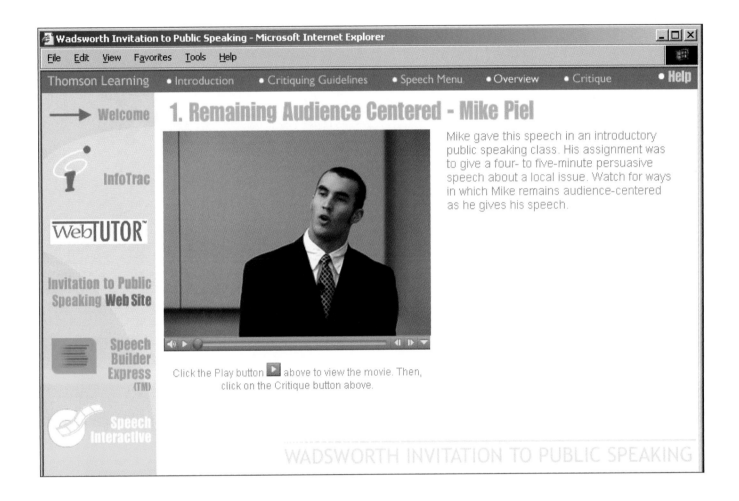

Chapter Two
Entering the Public Dialogue with Confidence: Your First Speech

In this chapter you will learn to

Identify the types of speeches most commonly given in the public dialogue

Explain the five basic steps of preparing a speech: invention, arrangement, style, memory, and delivery

Understand the most common reasons speakers are nervous about giving speeches

Apply six techniques for reducing some of the nervousness associated with giving speeches

Give your first speech

The yearning for dialogue among civilizations is not a novel aspiration. The quest for peace, justice, tolerance and respect for human rights and fundamental freedoms has been with us all at different stages in our lives and in the histories of our countries. However, something very important and new indeed emanates from the General Assembly resolution . . . which proclaims the year 2001 as the United Nations Year of Dialogue among civilizations. That important decision . . . was a collective realization . . . that we all are human beings and we all deserve . . . basic peace, security and sustainable development.

—Sam Nujoma, president of Namibia. Speech given at the United Nations Roundtable: Dialogue Among Civilizations, September 2000.

Your first speech is your entry into the public dialogue. It is your chance to begin to develop the skills you will need to enter this conversation effectively. In order to help you with this process, this chapter describes the basic components of giving your first speech. It begins with a description of the different types of speeches common to the public dialogue. Understanding these speech types will help you identify your own goals and reasons for speaking. You then will read an overview of the speaking process, which will help you prepare and deliver your first speech. Next is a summary of the ten steps to successful speaking. Last, you will explore why you may be nervous about public speaking and how to lessen that nervousness. By the end of this chapter you will be ready to give your first speech, which in a public speaking course is often a speech of self-introduction. A sample speech of self-introduction is featured under Speech Interactive on the *Invitation to Public Speaking* CD-ROM. You can find the full text of this speech at the end of this chapter, and you can find an outline of the speech at the *Invitation to Public Speaking* Web site.

Types of Public Speaking

Whether you have decided, been asked, or are required to participate in the public dialogue, you must first select the type of speech you will give. There are four different types of speeches: speaking to inform, invite, or persuade, and speaking on special occasions. Each type has its own distinctive goal and character. In this section you'll also read about speaking in small groups. Small group speaking isn't a type of speaking but rather a speech setting. However, it is introduced here because the goals of small group speaking are often similar to those of informative, invitational, persuasive, and special occasion speaking.

Informative Speeches

informative speech
A speech that communicates knowledge and understanding about a process, an event, a person or place, an object, or a concept.

When the goal of a speech is to pass along information others need but do not have, the speech is informative. An **informative speech** communicates knowledge and understanding about a process, an event, a person or place, an object, or a concept (Chapter 15). Informative speeches describe, explain, clarify, or demonstrate. They are given in a wide range of situations, from informal to formal, and can vary in length depending on the situation and the audience's need.

In an informative speech, your ethical responsibilities are to focus on accuracy and respect. Although you are providing the audience with new information, that information must be true, relevant, and clear. Not only must you present information honestly, but the audience also needs to understand what you are talking about. They also must understand why that information is important to them and how they can use that information to respond to or improve a situation or participate in the public dialogue.

Civil rights leader Jesse Jackson (left) and Rubin "Hurricane" Carter (right) speak to inmates at a California correctional facility. Carter was wrongly imprisoned nineteen years for a murder he didn't commit. Why do you think he's speaking to this particular audience? How does speaking about his experiences help his audience improve their situation or participate in the public dialogue?

AP/Wide World Photos

invitational speech
A speech that allows the speaker to enter into a dialogue with an audience in order to clarify positions, explore issues and ideas, or share beliefs and values.

Invitational Speeches

When you give an **invitational speech**, you enter into a dialogue with an audience in order to clarify positions, explore issues and ideas, or share beliefs and values (Chapter 16). When you speak invitationally, you set the stage for a interaction with your audience. Your goal is a reciprocal exchange of ideas and information, an exchange in which many sides of an issue are explored through audience participation. As a result, both you and the audience leave the interaction with a better understanding of the issues and why people hold the positions they do. Thus invitational speaking most closely resembles an actual dialogue. You begin that dialogue with your speech, set the stage for an exchange of ideas, and facilitate that exchange during or after the speech.

Invitational speeches are usually given in two contexts. In the first context, we give invitational speeches when there are many sides to an issue and we want to be sure we explore and understand them as fully as possible. In this context, an invitational speech helps us explore an issue thoroughly before we make decisions about what to do. In the second context, we give invitational speeches when an audience is polarized about an issue and we know we can't persuade them to change. In this context, an invitational speech allows us and our audiences to continue communicating with one another, even when we disagree profoundly. Rather than try to *change* other people, we speak invitationally to try to *understand* them. We try to see the world as they do and understand their views so that we can be more respectful of their positions and perspectives.

The primary ethical consideration in invitational speaking is your relationship to an audience. As an invitational speaker you want to share your own views, but at the same time you want to hear the views of others, especially if they are very different from your own. Because of this relationship, people who speak invitationally are ethically bound to create an environment in which all involved are able to articulate their differences, similarities, and perspectives without judgment or attempts to change. Their goal is to create an atmosphere in which people can listen to one another with respect and openness. To study an example of invitational speaking and learn how speakers can create the conditions to spark discussion about a topic, complete the InfoTrac College Edition Activity 2.1, "An Invitation to Speak," featured online under Student Resources for Chapter 2.

Persuasive Speeches

Speakers who engage in persuasive speaking want to change or reinforce the ways that other people think or behave. A **persuasive speech** is one whose message attempts to change or reinforce an audience's thoughts, feelings, or actions (Chapter 17). When we speak to persuade we act as advocates, encouraging or discouraging certain thoughts and actions. We urge our audience to accept our views or solutions, take a particular action, buy our products, or adopt our proposals. When we persuade others, we defend an idea, asking our audience to agree with us rather than someone else. Our goal is to change or reinforce our audience's attitudes (positive or negative feelings about something), beliefs (ideas about what is real or true), or values (ideas of what is good or worthy). Attitudes, beliefs, and values are discussed more fully in Chapter 5.

Because persuasive speakers act as advocates for what usually are very complicated issues, persuasive speeches have unique ethical dimensions. You must advocate your position without threatening, intimidating, or belittling the audience. You also must offer a fair presentation of the information, not distorting or omitting important details or facts. Finally, you must recognize the audience's right to decide for themselves about complex issues that are significant to the public dialogue.

Speaking on Special Occasions

Special occasions such as award ceremonies, banquets, weddings, and retirement parties often call for speeches. The type of speech you give at special occasions is very different from speeches to inform, invite, or persuade. Our goal with a special occasion speech is to mark an event as distinct and to help our audience reflect on the special nature of the gathering. With special occasion speeches we introduce (yourself, someone else, or an event), commemorate (another person for his or her accomplishments), or accept (an award or special recognition).

Introductory speeches. When you present information about yourself, another person, or an event to an audience, you are giving an **introductory speech** (Chapter 19). In an introductory speech, your goal is to give the audience a sense of the unique perspective of the person you are introducing or to welcome and make the audience familiar with an event. Introductory speeches often take place in formal settings (ceremonial events, job interviews, professional gatherings) and usually are quite short.

When you introduce yourself, you share with an audience what is interesting about you and relevant to the occasion. You describe your skills and talents, events in your life that have shaped who you are and what you value, and what makes you qualified or unique. When you introduce yourself, you want your audience to be glad they've had the opportunity to meet you and to want to get more acquainted with you when your speech is over. For tips on how to give a speech of self-introduction, complete Speech Step 2.1 later in this chapter.

When you introduce another person, you describe that person's contributions, qualifications, or talents. Like a speech of self-introduction, when you introduce another person, you want the audience to be interested in knowing that person better. When you introduce an event, you set the stage for a particular program or activity. You explain the importance of the event, what's to come, and how the audience can find the activities they want to participate in. Remember, when you give a speech of introduction, talk only about those things that will help the audience understand the qualities of the person or event they are about to experience. Remember, too, that at the heart of an introductory speech are a person's or event's reputation and credibility. As such, ethically you are bound to tell the truth and to create an environment of awareness, appreciation, respect, and understanding.

Using your *Invitation to Public Speaking* CD-ROM, watch the video clip of Tiffany under Speech Interactive. Consider the content of her speech as well as her delivery. To explore speeches of introduction even further, complete Interactive Activity 2.1, "Introducing the Future President," online under Student Resources for Chapter 2 at the *Invitation to Public Speaking* Web site.

WEB SITE

Commemorative speeches. When you give a **commemorative speech,** sometimes called a speech of tribute, you praise, honor, recognize, or pay tribute to a person, an event, an idea, or an institution (Chapter 19). Commemorative speeches often take place in formal settings such as retirement parties, weddings, anniversaries, birthdays, and memorial services. Although these speeches are often planned beforehand, speeches of commemoration can be spontaneous and unrehearsed. Your goal in a commemorative speech is to share what is unique and special about someone or something, and to express appreciation for special qualities and contributions.

commemorative speech
Speech that praises, honors, recognizes, or pays tribute to a person, an event, an idea, or an institution.

In creating commemorative environments, emphasize values and celebrate accomplishments and contributions that have positively affected others. When commemorating a person, you'll also want the person to feel a sense of pride at being recognized and praised. Your ethical responsibility as a speaker is to tell the truth about who or what you are commemorating. This means you want to share information that is appropriate, relevant, and helps an audience understand and appreciate the accomplishments and contributions of that person, event, or idea.

Using your *Invitation to Public Speaking* CD-ROM, watch the video clip of former Vice President Al Gore's commemorative speech under Speech Interactive. The vice-president gave this speech on April 25, 1999, at the memorial service for victims of the Columbine school shootings in Colorado. How well did he incorporate the principles of an effective commemorative speech?

Acceptance speeches. Speeches of acceptance are delivered when you receive an award or special recognition for your accomplishments. When you give an **acceptance speech,** your goal is to acknowledge your gratitude, appreciation, and pleasure at receiving an honor or a gift (Chapter 19). Acceptance speeches tend to be short and are usually humble and appreciative in tone. They are often given at formal gatherings, such as awards ceremonies or banquets, but they may also be given in more informal or casual situations, such as after a competition. When you give a speech of acceptance, your goal is to communicate your pleasure at receiving special recognition.

acceptance speech
A speech that acknowledges gratitude, appreciation, and pleasure at receiving an honor or a gift.

In acceptance speeches, the speaker is being recognized as an exceptional individual, as someone who stands apart from others and is worthy of recognition. When you give an acceptance speech, your ethical responsibilities are to express sincere appreciation for this recognition. You can do this by conveying your understanding of the meaning and importance of the award you are receiving. You also can do so by acknowledging those who have helped you reach your goals. Using your *Invitation to Public Speaking* CD-ROM, watch the video clip of Aboriginal Australian athlete Cathy Freeman's acceptance speech under Speech Interactive. How well did she incorporate the principles of an effective acceptance speech?

Speaking in Small Groups

If you take a moment to consider your workplaces, classrooms, families, and gatherings of friends, you will recognize yourself as a public speaker in small groups. In **small group speaking**, we give a presentation to a small collection of individuals or as part of a small group of people (Chapter 20). People generally give speeches in small groups in order to

Introduce oneself or a team	Raise questions
Establish the agenda for a meeting	Encourage an action or decision
Identify a problem	Help clarify an issue
Generate possible solutions	Draw others into the discussion
Assess the feasibility of those solutions	Resolve group conflict
Assign tasks	Build or increase group morale
Share information	Report on group findings or decisions

Because we speak in small groups for so many different reasons, there is often overlap between small group public speaking and the other types of speaking discussed in this text. When you speak in groups, you conduct meetings, give group presentations, participate in panel discussions, present at symposiums, and give team presentations. Your goals may include informing, inviting, or persuading, but you speak in a small group rather than by yourself in front of an audience. Additionally, when you speak in a small group, you must attend to group processes and dynamics, facilitate disagreements with maturity and respect, include all members of the group in the process, and accomplish the task you have been asked or assigned to complete. Your ethical responsibilities are tied to your leadership abilities and to the different roles you and the other group members take on.

To consider how effective you might be as a small group leader, go to http://www.albany.net?~sschuman/Definitions.htm and read the various definitions of a group facilitator. To learn techniques you can use to guide discussions in small groups, complete Interactive Activity 2.2, "Leading Small Group Discussions," online under Student Resources for Chapter 2 at the *Invitation to Public Speaking* Web site.

WEB SITE

When you enter the public dialogue, you speak to inform, invite, persuade, introduce, commemorate, or accept, or you speak as a member of a small group. As you learn to give the various types of speeches, you will discover that each requires a particular kind of environment or tone and is appropriate to a different kind of situation. As you practice many of these speeches in your public speaking course, you may find you are more comfortable with some than you are with others. However, note that each type of speaking has its place in the public dialogue, and learning to give any or even all of these types of speeches will help you be more successful in that dialogue once you complete your public speaking class. For more information about the differences between each type of speech, refer to Table 2.2 in the next section.

An Overview of the Speaking Process

The five basic steps most people take as they put together a speech come from scholarship on public speaking that began over two thousand years ago. These steps follow the five canons of rhetoric: invention, arrangement, style, memory, and delivery. A **canon** is an authoritative list, an accepted principle or rule, or an accepted standard of judgment. The five canons discussed here are the accepted list, principles, and standards of basic speech preparation.

Invention: Choosing Your Topic and Purpose and Gathering Your Materials

The **canon of invention** provides guidelines for generating effective content for your speech. It is the first step most people take when they put together a speech. There are five parts to the canon of invention: identifying your audience, selecting your topic, determining your purpose, deciding on your main points, and collecting materials to support your ideas.

canon of invention
Guidelines for generating effective content for a speech.

Audience. The first step in the invention process is to identify your audience (Chapter 5). Make every choice from the moment you are asked, decide, or are required to speak with the audience in mind. Your goal is to consider the kind of information your audience needs or wants and the best, most ethical way to present this information to them. You can do this by asking the following questions: Who is my audience? What are their interests, views, and experiences? How many of them are there? What do they know about me? Are they required to listen, or do they have a choice? The audience is your reason for speaking so you must consider them in each step of your speech preparation process.

Topic. Your next step in the invention process is to consider the topic, or the subject, of your speech. If you are asked or decide to speak, your topic either is given to you or you already know what you want to speak about. When you are required to speak, you often have to come up with a topic on your own. For required speeches that have no predetermined topic, Table 2.1 lists two simple techniques for selecting a topic (see also Chapter 4).

As you use these techniques, ask yourself why your audience might be interested in your topic, how they feel about your topic, and what their previous experience with that topic might be. Your goal is to stay audience centered, that is, to

Table 2.1

Two Techniques for Selecting a Speech Topic

Develop a topic based on your interests, hobbies, and skills	• Do you want to know more about something (a political issue, a craft or activity, an event in history, even a person, place, or thing)?
	• Are you actively involved in something (an art or skill, a club or group, a listserv or chat room)?
	• Are you good at some task or activity (music, dance, sports, working with animals)?
Develop a topic by brainstorming using free association, categories, or technology	• Sit with paper and pen or at a computer and look around the room. Pick one item and then list everything that comes to mind whether it is related or not.
	• Jot down category headings like "events," "natural phenomena," "concepts," "objects," "problems," or "processes," and brainstorm under these categories. Write down whatever comes to mind within each of these categories.
	• Log on to a search engine (Chapter 6) and review the list of subjects displayed on the home page.

Table 2.2

The Most Common General Purposes for Public Speaking

To inform	Share with an audience an area of expertise or body of knowledge.
To invite	Gain a fuller understanding of all perspectives by engaging in a dialogue with your audience in order to clarify positions, explore issues and ideas, or share beliefs or values.
To persuade	Advocate or encourage an audience to adopt a particular view, position, or plan.
To introduce	Acquaint an audience with someone, something, or some event.
To commemorate	Share with an audience praise, honor, tribute, or recognition for a person, event, or even an idea or institution.
To accept	Express gratitude, appreciation, and pleasure at being recognized, as well as accept an award or nomination.
To speak in or as a small group	Lead or facilitate a discussion with a small group of people (3–12), or speak collectively as a small group, in order to inform, invite, persuade, or all three.

keep your audience in mind with each choice you make during topic selection. Remember, you are speaking to them and you want them to be interested in and appreciate your subject.

Purpose. The third step under the canon of invention is to determine your purpose or reason for speaking (Chapter 4). Your purpose relates to the type of speech you will give. Table 2.2 lists the most common *general purposes* for public speaking, including those for speeches to introduce, commemorate, and accept, and for small-group speeches. When you select your general purpose you are deciding what, very generally, you would like to do in your speech. Note that the general purpose of a speech is expressed as an infinitive verb that parallels the type of speech you're giving (for example, the general purpose of a persuasive speech is *to persuade*). In your public speaking course, your general purpose is usually assigned by your instructor as part of your speech assignment.

Your next step is to identify your *specific purpose* and *thesis statement*. A specific purpose helps you refine your topic and purpose so you are more focused. A statement of a specific purpose includes exactly what you hope to accomplish with your audience in the time you have to speak. You usually include your specific purpose in your speech outline but don't state it in your speech. However, often you state your thesis statement as part of your speech introduction. The thesis statement is important because it allows you to state, in a single sentence, the content of your speech. The thesis statement, sometimes called the *central idea,* is the main proposition, assumption, or argument you want to express. It helps you identify your main points for your speech.

Here's how Missy expressed her specific purpose and thesis statement for a required speech, "The Mysterious World of Hiccups":

Topic:	Hiccups
General purpose:	To inform
Specific purpose:	To inform my audience of the "anatomy" of a hiccup, the most common causes of hiccups, and some of the ways to cure them.
Thesis statement:	Hiccups, or involuntary spasms of the diaphragm, are most often caused by food, beverages, and medicines, but can be cured easily with a few simple techniques.

Notice the use of "to inform" and "my audience" in the statement of specific purpose. Every specific purpose statement should include these two important phrases. The infinitive phrase "to inform" (or to accept, to persuade, and so on) reminds you of your general purpose. The phrase "my audience" reminds you that you are speaking to a specific group of individuals and should consider them in each step of the speech. Also notice that the specific purpose and the thesis statement are complete sentences. This ensures that you have a concise goal and a fully developed thesis or argument at the very start of your speech preparation process. If you follow these guidelines, your efforts will be directed toward a specific plan rather than a loosely formed one.

Main points. The fourth step in the invention process grows out of your specific purpose and thesis statement—identifying your main points (Chapter 9). Your main points are your most important claims, arguments, or concepts in the speech. They allow you to accomplish your specific purpose and to flesh out your thesis statement. Use your specific purpose and thesis statement to help you determine those main points. If you think of your thesis statement as the center of your speech, then your main points connect to and elaborate on this center. Using the specific purpose and thesis statement for her speech about hiccups, Missy decided on the following main ideas:

I. Hiccups are involuntary spasms of the diaphragm that cause the space between the vocal cords to close suddenly and make a peculiar sound.

II. Hiccups are most often caused by the foods we eat, the beverages we drink, and the medicines we ingest.

III. Mild cases of hiccups can be cured with a few simple techniques.

She identified these main points by asking herself what ideas support the thesis statement, what makes it true, and what fills out or adds detail to that thesis statement.

Gathering supporting materials. Your final step in the invention process is to gather supporting material for you speech (Chapter 6). When you need to find material to support your ideas, and almost all speakers do, focus your efforts in three places: the Internet, the library, and personal interviews. The Internet is a valuable source of materials, and many speakers incorporate facts from this source into their speeches. The Internet makes information from around the world accessible to users of computers, modems, and dial-up services, and it can provide you with the most current information on a topic. The library is the most comprehensive source of material you can use. Libraries house enormous amounts of information in a variety of formats and are designed to help users find that material easily. When you can't find the information you want in the library or on the Internet, or when you want specific, personalized information for your speech, you might conduct an interview. Personal interviews can provide you with the most direct or relevant stories, facts, and examples.

As you gather materials from any of these three sources, look for the following kinds of information so you can develop your ideas effectively (Chapter 7):

Examples:	Specific instances used to illustrate a concept, experience, issue, or problem. Examples help you clarify a point or argument, specify the nature of something, or make sure your audience understands your explanation.
Narratives:	Stories that recreate or foretell real or hypothetical events. Narratives develop, illustrate, clarify, or draw an audience into a

What are the advantages of using an animal as a visual aid? What are the disadvantages? How could a speaker reduce the likelihood of problems with Ginger, the two-toed sloth shown here, and make the most of this visual aid?

AP/Wide World Photos

claim you are making. They have characters, a sequence of events, and a setting or location. They can be very short, as in an anecdote, or longer, and they can be developed over the course of the speech, told all at once, or even be an entire speech.

Statistics: Numerical summaries of facts, figures, and research findings. Statistics numerically quantify, estimate, measure, and represent events, issues, positions, actions, beliefs, and the like.

Testimony: The opinions or observations of others. Testimony, often in the form of quotations, can come from an authority, an average person who has relevant experience with your topic, or from your own experiences.

Definitions: Statement of the exact meaning of a word or phrase. Definitions help clarify claims and ideas, especially when new terminology is being introduced or when a topic is controversial or emotional.

Audio/ visual aids: Materials or objects that display your ideas so the audience can see or hear your points (Chapter 14). These aids include handwritten and computer-generated images, displays, demonstrations, sound recordings, and the like. They are important because they clarify, reinforce, and maintain the audience's interest.

The invention process is the process of generating effective material for your speech. It involves focusing your attention on your audience, selecting and narrowing your topic, deciding on your main points, and gathering material to support your ideas. It is the first step speakers take in putting together a speech.

Arrangement: Organizing Your Ideas

canon of arrangement
Guidelines for ordering the ideas in a speech.

The second canon in the process of developing a speech is the **canon of arrangement,** or guidelines for ordering the ideas in a speech (Chapter 9). As you think about the structure your first speech might take, consider your audience, your thesis statement, and the ways you want to develop your main points. The three most basic components of almost every speech—an introduction, body, and conclusion—are the easiest place to start in a first speech, and they allow you to keep your audience, goal, and main ideas at the forefront of your thinking.

Introduction. However long or short, detailed or concise, introductions set the stage for a speech (Chapter 10). They open up the conversation, invite or demand attention, and acquaint the audience with your topic. Even though there are a few formulas you can use to develop your introductions, remember that not all speeches should begin in the same way. Some speeches need elaborate and dramatic introductions. Others are much better off beginning with something short and simple. One type of introduction is not better than another, but certain types of introductions do fit better for an audience, setting, speaking goal, or even your style.

An introduction should accomplish four objectives:

*   Introduce you and your topic to the audience.
*   Capture the audience's attention and get them interested in or curious about your topic.
*   Establish your credibility.
*   Preview the main ideas of the speech.

Missy followed these four principles to come up with the following introduction for her speech about hiccups:

> I'm here today to share information about one of life's great mysteries. No, I'm not referring to Stonehenge or the Great Pyramids, but to something everyone in this room has experienced: hiccups! Yes, I'm talking about the mysterious world of hiccups, which seem to be a universal occurrence. However, although this mystery is universal, hiccups appear to serve no physiologic function.

> I recently was blessed with an overwhelming occurrence of the hiccups, and this sparked my interest and curiosity in the subject. This "blessing" caused me to do some research and investigation, during which I discovered some interesting information about hiccups. I would like to share this information with you today. Specifically, my focus will be on three aspects of hiccups that I find especially informative. First, I'll explain the anatomy of a hiccup, or what a hiccup is and how it occurs. Second, I'll explain the three most common causes of hiccups, which are food, beverages, and medicine. Third, I'll share some simple techniques for curing those milder cases of hiccups.

In this short introduction, Missy follows each of the guidelines: she introduces her topic (the class already knew her fairly well, so she didn't need to introduce herself); she catches their interest by relating her topic to the mysteries of the world, her audience, and herself; she establishes her credibility by sharing that not only has she had an unusual experience with her topic, but she's done some research on it as well; and she previews her main points before she begins to elaborate on any one of them.

The body of the speech. The body of the speech is the longest part of a speech and contains the information you have gathered to develop your main ideas (Chapter 9). There are many ways to organize this material, and your thesis statement should help you narrow your numerous options. In public speaking courses, instructors often emphasize certain patterns over others to give students specific kinds of practice with organization. You also will notice that some speeches seem to fall naturally into one organizational pattern or another. The most common patterns are chronological, spatial, causal, problem-and-solution, and topical (Chapter 9). Other speeches are not so easy to arrange and may take more careful reflection and effort. Still, there are some basic rules you can follow to organize your main ideas and subpoints.

First, identify your main ideas and arrange them according to an appropriate organizational pattern. To help you do this, ask yourself which ideas necessarily go before others. Certain ideas must be developed before you can address others, and they must come first in your speech. If there is no necessary order, ask yourself what you think the audience will be most interested in, and place those ideas first. Or ask which ideas will draw the audience into the topic, and place those first.

Second, whatever organizational pattern you choose, you will want to be able to explain the logic of it—the reason it makes sense to present your ideas in the manner you have selected. You will also want to make sure your main ideas follow a systematic, logical, or natural progression that supports and develops your thesis statement.

Third, you will want to link your ideas together with words and phrases called *connectives*. Connectives (Chapter 9) help you transition from one point to another in order to introduce new points, preview or summarize ideas, and call attention to a particularly important idea.

Conclusion. The conclusion of a speech brings closure to your ideas, claims, arguments, and proposals, and, like introductions, conclusions can take many forms (Chapter 10). Although there is no one best way to conclude a speech, try to do two things as you bring closure to a presentation:

- Signal to the audience you are done.
- Summarize or restate your thesis statement.

Conclusions tend to be the shortest part of a speech, but they are very important. They remind the audience of the main ideas you developed in the body of your speech, and they can provide an audience with some final thoughts to reflect on. Let's take a look at the conclusion to Missy's speech:

> So, now you see that there is more to learn about the mysterious world of hiccups than you might have imagined. In this speech, I've shared some very enlightening information about what a hiccup is, the reasons why hiccups occur, and the process of curing them. Now, if someday you find *yourself* in the mysterious world of hiccups, you'll be well prepared to fight back with several of the remedies you've heard about today.

By stating, "In this speech, I've shared some very enlightening information," Missy signals to her audience that she is concluding her speech. She then summarizes her thesis statement and leaves her audience to ponder how they'll be able to use the information she's provided to cure their own bouts with hiccups.

Style: Considering Language and Figures of Speech

canon of style
Guidelines for using language effectively and appropriately.

The third canon to consider as you put together your first speech is the **canon of style,** or the guidelines for using language effectively and appropriately (Chapters 3 and 12). In this step of the speech process, you pay careful attention to the words and phrases you use in your speech.

In your first speech, consider your audience, your topic, and your goals. Certain kinds of language and images go better with certain kinds of audiences, topics, and speaking goals. At the most obvious level, you would not speak the same way to a group of children as you would to a group of adults. At more subtle

What kind of language would you use—or not use—in order to connect with this audience and give an effective speech?

levels, you likely will use different styles of speaking with supporters and opponents of a position, with those you want to have a dialogue rather than a debate with, and when you are commemorating or introducing people. Because of these differences, consider the following questions as you select the style of language you want to use:

- What kinds of vocabulary, imagery, and rhythms best match my audience, topic, and goals?
- Have I included vocabulary, imagery, and rhythms that draw my audience into my speech and help me express my ideas vividly?
- What kinds of vocabulary, imagery, and rhythms have the potential to offend, hurt, or alienate my listeners?
- What vocabulary needs to be defined, explained, or illustrated by examples?
- Am I speaking at a level appropriate to my audience?
- Have I omitted slang, euphemisms, or other unfamiliar or inappropriate words and phrases?

As you gather materials and organize your speech, keep your own ears and eyes open for language that enhances your material, for ways you can express your ideas appropriately, and for ways to rephrase potentially confusing, disturbing, or offensive terms and phrases. As you listen to others, and practice this skill yourself, you will find that language can be one of your most important tools for entering the public conversation and for creating the kind of speaking environment you want.

Memory: Practicing Your Speech

Two thousand years ago, the canon of memory referred to the actual memorization of a speech and the techniques for doing so. However, in your speech class, you'll be expected to give most of your assigned speeches in a conversational rather than a memorized style, or *extemporaneously*. Because of this change in

Illinois Lieutenant Governor Corinne Wood is pictured here rehearsing a speech in front of her family. Who would you practice your speech in front of? Why would you choose that person (or those people)?

AP/Wide World Photos

canon of memory
Guidelines for the time taken to rehearse a speech and the ways you prompt yourself to remember the speech as you give it.

preference of delivery styles, the **canon of memory** now refers to the time you take to rehearse your speech, and the ways you prompt yourself to remember the speech as you give it (Chapter 13). Like song writers who learn to play a song they have written by practicing it over and over again, speakers must learn the speeches they prepare. Additionally, if you are using technology, visual aids, or other materials, practicing your speech with them beforehand is a must.

Later in this text you'll learn several techniques for practicing a speech and prompting yourself as you give it. For your first speech, here is a brief summary of those techniques:

- Begin your practice sessions alone. At first, practice only segments of your speech. For example, try getting the introduction down, then the body, then the conclusion. You may even find it useful to break the body down by practicing each main point separately.

- Make notes on your speaking outline to help you remember your material and delivery techniques. If you plan to use any visual aids or technology, practice using it until you can manage it easily as you speak.

- Once you've practiced each segment of your speech individually, practice the speech as a whole. Try practicing in front of a mirror. Go back and rehearse the places where you seem to stumble or get lost. Make sure your visual aids and technology work as you planned.

- Before you give your speech, practice it three to six times from start to finish, depending on the level of spontaneity or polish you want in your speech.

Delivery: Giving Your Speech

canon of delivery
Guidelines for managing your voice, gestures, posture, facial expressions, and visual aids as you present your speech.

Your final step in your speech is delivery, actually presenting the speech to an audience. The **canon of delivery** provides guidelines for managing your voice, gestures, posture, facial expressions, and visual aids as you present your speech

(Chapter 13). As you give your first speech, use these suggestions to help you with delivery:

- Visualize a successful speech before you deliver it.
- Know your introduction well so you can begin your speech feeling confident.
- Use your notes as prompts and as a source of security.
- Make eye contact during the speech.
- Remember to breathe, gesture naturally, and pause as needed during your speech.

The five canons of rhetoric—invention, arrangement, style, memory, and delivery—are a part of every speech you decide, are asked, or are required to give. Using the canons as your road map, you will be prepared to enter most any public dialogue.

Ten Steps to Entering the Public Dialogue Successfully

Even the most eloquent, successful speeches take time and effort to create and deliver. As you read this textbook and practice giving speeches in your public speaking course, you will learn much more about how to give effective and interesting speeches. To get you started with your first speech, the speech types and the five canons of rhetoric can be summarized as ten steps for giving a successful first speech.

1. *Determine whether you decided, were asked, or are required to enter this dialogue.* How does context affect you, your speech, and your audience?

2. *Identify your audience and their characteristics.* Who are they? Why are they present? What is your relationship to them?

3. *Determine your topic, purpose, and thesis statement.* Are they relevant, appropriate, and manageable? Have you crafted them with your audience in mind? Begin thinking about ethical choices you may have to make in order to meet your audience's needs.

4. *Formulate your main points.* Do the main points reflect your thesis statement and purpose? Do they follow a systematic progression? Can you manage the material you'd need to present in the time you have for the speech?

5. *Gather your materials.* Have you used the Internet, library, and interviews? Have you gathered material for visual aids? Is your material relevant to your audience as well as to your topic and purpose? Have you done your research ethically and responsibly?

6. *Organize your ideas into an introduction, body, and conclusion.* Is there a logic to your organization? Do the introduction, body, and conclusion fit together to make a coherent whole? Remember to incorporate connectives, which help your audience keep track of your information.

7. *Select language that enhances your ideas.* Are you using language that is clear and appropriate to your subject, audience, and yourself? Have you rephrased confusing or potentially offensive language? Are you clear about the reasons why you might *not* rephrase certain language?

8. *Practice your speech.* Have you practiced the speech three to six times? Have you practiced with your visual aids? Have you used any strategies to help with nervousness?

9. *Deliver the speech.* Have you visualized a successful speech beforehand? Do your notes have prompts to help you remember to make eye contact with the audience, relax, gesture naturally, and breathe?

10. *Congratulate yourself on your successful first speech.* What did you do well? Where there any pleasant surprises? What successes and strengths will you carry over into your next speech?

Speech Step 2.1 / Design a Speech of Introduction or Self-Introduction

Using the ten steps for entering the public dialogue successfully, prepare a speech in which you introduce yourself, someone you know, or a person you admire. As you prepare this speech, consider whether the information you want to share is relevant, interesting, and carefully organized. If you are introducing yourself, take time to develop the details you want to share. If you are introducing someone else, be sure to gather enough information about the other person to give a developed speech. Be sure your delivery is extemporaneous (conversational), not memorized, and that you take time to practice your speech before you give it. Speech Builder Express can help you organize and outline your introductory speech. To access this online resource, click on "Speech Builder Express" on your CD-ROM for the username and password and to link to the Speech Builder Express site.

Overcoming Nervousness in Public Speaking

Many people, even the most experienced speakers, get nervous before they give a speech. One of the reasons we get anxious is that we care about our topic and our performance. We want to do well and are invested in giving a successful speech. Another reason we might be nervous before a speech is because we experience **communication apprehension,** "the level of fear or anxiety associated with either real or anticipated communication with another person or persons."[1]

Communication apprehension, or nervousness, can take two forms. People who are apprehensive about communicating with others in any situation are said to have **trait anxiety.** People who are apprehensive about communicating with others in a particular situation are said to have **state,** or **situational, anxiety.** Take a moment to consider whether you are trait anxious or state anxious in communication situations. Do you fear all kinds of interactions or only certain kinds? Most of us experience some level of state anxiety about some communication events, such as asking a boss for a raise, verbally evaluating another's performance, or introducing ourselves to a group of strangers.

In addition, most people experience some level of state anxiety about public speaking. This is called **public speaking anxiety** (**PSA**), the anxiety we feel when we learn we have to give a speech or take a public speaking course.[2] PSA can be alleviated with practice and by following the tips provided in this chapter. However, sometimes a few of us are extraordinarily nervous about giving speeches. If you think you are one of those people, see your instructor for special assistance with your fears.

Research on communication apprehension related to public speaking is complex, but it suggests that most people's state anxiety about public speaking exists for six reasons. Many people are state anxious because public speaking is

- *Novel:* We don't do it regularly and lack necessary skills as a result.

communication apprehension
The level of fear or anxiety associated with either real or anticipated communication with another person or persons.

trait anxiety
Apprehension about communicating with others in any situation.

state, or **situational, anxiety**
Apprehension about communicating with others in a particular situation.

public speaking anxiety (PSA)
The anxiety we feel when we learn we have to give a speech or take a public speaking course.

- *Done in formal settings:* Our behaviors when giving a speech are more prescribed and rigid.

- *Often done from a subordinate position:* An instructor or boss sets the rules for giving a speech, and the audience acts as a critic.

- *Conspicuous or obvious:* The speaker stands apart from the audience.

- *Done in front of an audience that is unfamiliar:* Most people are more comfortable talking with people they know. Also, we fear audiences won't be interested in what we have to say.

- *A unique situation in which the degree of attention paid to the speaker is quite noticeable:* Audience members either stare at us or ignore us, so we become unusually self-focused.[3]

Research also suggests that people are usually nervous only about specific aspects of public speaking. When people ranked what they fear while giving a speech, here's what they said:[4]

Trembling or shaking	80%
Mind going blank	74%
Doing or saying something embarrassing	64%
Being unable to continue talking	63%
Not making sense	59%
Sounding foolish	59%

When this list is combined with the six reasons for state anxiety, a pattern emerges. Because public speaking is novel, and because many people are less comfortable in highly structured and formal situations, they shake or tremble. Because it is an obvious act, people fear their minds will go blank, they will say something embarrassing, or they will be unable to continue to talk. Because it is done in front of an unfamiliar audience and speakers see themselves as being evaluated, they fear not making sense and sounding foolish.

There are several ways to ease most of the fears we have about giving speeches. The suggestions offered here should help you manage your nervousness and use it to your advantage.

Be Prepared by Doing Your Research

One way to reduce the nervousness that comes with giving a speech is to be as prepared as you can.[5] Careful preparation will help you feel more confident about what you will say (and what others will think) and ease fears about drawing a blank or not being able to answer a question. Here's an example of how one speaker eased his nervousness regarding these issues:

> Ahmad knew his promotion depended on this next sales presentation. He had given a weak presentation at a job fair last month, and he knew his boss had been disappointed. He'd been asked questions he couldn't answer, and he hadn't know statistics and figures he should have known. As he'd watched his boss frown and lean back in her chair, he'd become even more nervous. This month, he would do everything he could to be prepared for whatever issue or question came up—and to avoid that unnerving stare his boss so easily cast at her staff.

> Ahmad set about to do a more thorough job of identifying, gathering, organizing, and remembering material. As a result, when he spoke, he was confident about his material and was able to answer the questions his audience asked.

Speakers who research their topics thoroughly before they speak feel confident. They tend to be much more relaxed and effective during their presentations.

Practice Your Speech

Many people are nervous about giving speeches because they haven't given many before and they don't like the formal setting. If you fall into this category, practicing your speech many times before you give it can help. Here is an example of how this can be done.

> Randy was terrified to give his first speech. His instructor suggested a solution he reluctantly agreed to try out. Feeling a little silly, Randy began by practicing his speech in his head. Then, when no one else was home, he began to present his speech out loud and alone in his room. He then stood in front of a mirror and delivered his speech to his own reflection. After several horrifying attempts, he began to feel more comfortable.
>
> Soon after, he began to trust his speaking ability enough to deliver his speech to his older sister, whom he trusted to be kind and constructive. First, he asked her to look interested, even if she wasn't. After doing this a few times, he asked her to give him honest nonverbal feedback. Then he asked her to share her suggestions and comments verbally. Finally, he practiced once more in the clothing he planned to wear and delivered his speech in his kitchen, which he arranged so it resembled, as closely as possible, his classroom.

When speakers practice their speech before they give it, they become more familiar with the process of speaking and the formality of the situation. As they gain comfort by practicing it alone, they can then move to the more obvious rehearsals (with an audience). They also have time to make changes in their presentation and to smooth out the rough spots before they actually give the speech. This practice is part of a process known as **systematic desensitization**, a technique for reducing anxiety that involves teaching your body to feel calm and relaxed rather than fearful during your speeches. This technique can help you give successful speeches and build your confidence, thus breaking the cycle of fear associated with public speaking. Talk to your instructor if you'd like to learn more about this technique.[6]

systematic desensitization
A technique for reducing anxiety that involves teaching your body to feel calm and relaxed rather than fearful during your speeches.

Sarah

In the past I have had no problem with public speaking, even in front of large groups of people. But when I stood up in front of our speech class to do my informative speech, I was shaking. I had to speak last, so I had to sit through all of my classmates' speeches while my stomach turned and turned. I was well prepared for my speech, so I didn't understand why I was so nervous. It was finally my turn. I stood up, took a few deep breaths, and I was on my way. I felt hot, as though my face was gleaming red. I tried my hardest to keep talking at a steady pace, breathing, and not fidgeting. Before I knew it, I was halfway done and beginning to relax. When it was all over I felt so much better and told myself that next time I wouldn't let myself get so nervous. The class said they couldn't see my nervousness anyway.

Have Realistic Expectations About Your Delivery

Sometimes people fear public speaking because they have unrealistic expectations about delivery. They expect their speeches to sound like professional performances rather than speeches, and they worry about their hands shaking or their voices faltering.[7] If this is one of your fears, adjust your expectations to a more realistic level. Here's how this fear affected one student.

> Brita, a perfectionist, expected to excel at whatever she did. When she took a public speaking course, she thought she should deliver flawless speeches from the start. As she listened to her classmates give their first speeches, she thought of the first speaker:

"I don't want to stumble like he did"; of the second speaker: "I must never lose my place"; of the third speaker: "Oh, no, her neck is turning red! How will I control that?"; of the fourth speaker: "I see he's not making continuous eye contact with his audience. I have to remember to do that"; and so on, until she had very unrealistic expectations for her first speech. However, when all the speakers had finished, and the instructor and students shared their comments, she adjusted her expectations. They all agreed that, for the most part, the deliveries were quite good for first speeches. Brita began to realize that her ideas of a so-called perfect delivery were unrealistic and unnecessary.

Remember, speakers pause, cough, rely on their notes for prompts, occasionally say "um," and even exhibit physical signs of nervousness, such as blushing or sweating. As we give more speeches, these "flaws" either go away, become less noticeable, or we learn to manage them effectively. Even Lois Gibbs, in Chapter 1, gave speeches she felt were full of "mistakes." Nonetheless, her speeches made a difference early on in her career. Here are a few realistic expectations for beginning speakers:

- Take a calming breath before you begin your speech.

- Remember your introduction.

- Strike a balance between using your notes and making eye contact with your audience.

- Make eye contact with more than one person.

- Gesture naturally rather than holding on to the podium.

- Deliver your conclusion the way you practiced it at home.

Practice Visualization and Affirmations

Sometimes when we imagine giving a speech, we see the worst case scenario. We see ourselves trembling, forgetting what we planned to say, dropping our notes, tripping on the way to the podium, and so on. Although a speech rarely goes this badly, these negative images stay in our minds. They increase our anxiety and often set up what is called a self-fulfilling prophecy: if you see yourself doing poorly in your mind before your speech, you set yourself up to do so in the speech. There are two solutions to this negative dynamic: visualization and affirmations.

Visualization. **Visualization** is a process in which you construct an image of yourself in your mind's eye giving a successful speech. Research on the benefits of visualization before giving a speech suggests that one session of visualization (about fifteen minutes) has a significant positive effect on communication apprehension.[8] The techniques of visualization are used by a wide range of people—athletes, performers, executives—and can range from elaborate processes to quite simple ones. For public speakers, the most effective process works as follows:

Find a quiet comfortable place where you can sit in a relaxed position for approximately fifteen minutes. Close your eyes and breathe slowly and deeply through your nose, feeling relaxation flow through your body. In great detail, visualize the morning of the day you are to give your speech.

You get up filled with confidence and energy and you choose the perfect clothing for your speech. You drive, walk, or ride to campus filled with this same positive, confident energy. As you enter the classroom, you see yourself relaxed, interacting with your classmates, full of confidence because you have thoroughly prepared for your speech. Your classmates are friendly and cordial in their greetings and conversations with you. You are *absolutely* sure of your material and your ability to present that material in the way you would like.

Next, visualize yourself beginning your speech. You see yourself approaching the place in your classroom from which you will speak. You are sure of yourself,

visualization
Process in which you construct an image of yourself in your mind's eye giving a successful speech.

Athletes commonly use visualization techniques to help them reduce their nervousness. What images do you use, or would you use, when you visualize yourself giving a successful speech?

cognitive restructuring
A process that helps reduce anxiety by replacing negative thoughts with positive ones, called affirmations.

affirmations
Positive, motivating statements that replace negative self-talk.

eager to begin, positive in your abilities as a speaker. You know you are organized and ready to use all your visual aids with ease. Now you see yourself presenting your speech. Your introduction is wonderful. Your transitions are smooth and interesting. Your main points are articulated brilliantly. Your evidence is presented elegantly. Your organization is perfect. Take as much time as you can in visualizing this part of your process. Be as specific and positive as you can.

Visualize the end of the speech: it could not have gone better. You are relaxed and confident, the audience is eager to ask questions, and you respond with the same talent as you gave your speech. As you return to your seat, you are filled with energy and appreciation for the job well done. You are ready for the next events of your day, and you accomplish them with success and confidence.

Now take a deep breath and return to the present. Breathe in, hold it, and release it. Do this several times as you return to the present. Take as much time as you need to make this transition.[9]

Research on visualization for public speakers suggests that the more detail we are able to give to our visualizations (what shoes we wear, exactly how we feel as we see ourselves, imagining the specifics of our speech), the more effective the technique is in reducing apprehension. Visualization has a significant effect on reducing the nervousness we feel because it systematically replaces negative images with positive ones. For more tips and information about visualization, go to Dr. Steve Ginley's Web site http://www.morton.cc.il.us/morton%20web%20courses /spe101/visualization.htm.

Affirmations. Negative self-talk often is a reflection of the harsh judge many people carry within. When we tell ourselves, "I'm no good at this," "I know I'll embarrass myself," or "Other people are far more talented than I," we engage in negative self-talk. We judge ourselves as inferior or less competent than others. Although it is natural to evaluate our own performances critically (it's how we motivate ourselves to improve), negative self-talk in public speaking situations can be quite unhelpful. When our internal voices tell us we can't succeed, our communication apprehension only increases.[10]

To counter the negative self-talk that might be going on in your head before a speech, try the following technique. For every negative assessment you hear yourself give, replace it with an honest assessment, reframed to be positive. This technique, sometimes called **cognitive restructuring**, is a process that helps reduce anxiety by replacing negative thoughts with positive ones, called affirmations.[11] **Affirmations** are positive, motivating statements that replace negative self-talk. They are very helpful in turning our immobilizing self-doubts into realistic assessments and options. Consider the following examples:

NEGATIVE	POSITIVE
I'll never find an interesting topic.	I am as able as anyone to find an interesting topic. I am an interesting person. I have creative ideas.
I don't know how to organize this material.	I can find a way to make this make sense. I have a good sense of organization. I can get help if I need it.
I know I'll get up there and make a fool of myself.	I am capable of giving a wonderful speech. I know lots of strategies to do so.
I'll forget what I want to say.	I'll remember what I want to say, and I'll have notes to help me.

I'm too scared to look at my audience.	I'll make eye contact with at least five people in the audience.
I'm scared to death!	I care about my performance and will do very well.
I'll be the worst in the class!	I'll give my speech well and am looking forward to a fine presentation. We are all learning how to do this.

Positive affirmations reframe negative energy and evaluations and shed light on your anxieties. To say you're terrified is immobilizing—to say you care about your performance gives you room to continue to develop your speech. It also is a more accurate description of what is going on inside. Affirmations assist you in minimizing the impact of the internal judge and, along with visualization, can reduce some of the anxieties we have about being judged.

Find Points of Connection with Your Audience

Sometimes our nervousness comes from our view of the audience (Chapter 5). When we give a speech, we sometimes see the audience as a group of strangers and think of ourselves as distant from them. In the public dialogue, though, the audience really is a part of our own community. So one way to reduce some of the nervousness connected to our view of the audience is to find points of connection between ourselves and the audience.

As you prepare your speech, identify ways you are similar to your audience. The similarities may be as general as living in the same town or working for the same company or as specific as sharing the same views on issues. Whatever the level of comparison, finding out about your audience reminds you that we all share many aspects of our daily lives. This helps you see that, despite differences, we do share similar views and experiences.

To further explore some of the ways you can make connections with your audience and feel less nervous about speaking, complete Interactive Activity 2.3, "Connecting with the Audience," online under Student Resources for Chapter 2 at the *Invitation to Public Speaking* Web site.

WEB SITE

Be a Good Member of an Audience Yourself

Some of our nervousness about audiences also comes from the fact that we don't always behave in the most supportive ways when *we* are members of an audience. When you are listening to a speech, do you make eye contact with the speaker? Do you sit with an attentive and alert posture, showing interest in the presentation? Do you take notes about the speaker's presentation? Do you ask relevant questions of the speaker when the speech is over or offer constructive comments if you have the opportunity to evaluate his or her performance? Speakers who fail to behave as engaged and interested audiences often fear the very same response to their speeches.

One way to overcome this fear of disrespectful audiences is to behave as an audience member as you would want others to behave when you speak. Doing so helps establish rapport (if you are kind to a speaker, she or he likely will respond similarly to you). It also helps you learn about not only the speaker's topic, but how to put together and deliver an effective speech. Behaving as an audience member in the ways you would like *your* audiences to behave can help you feel less nervous while speaking publicly.

Student Speech with Commentary
Self-Introduction *by Tiffany Brisco*

Specific purpose: To introduce myself to my classmates in my public speaking course.
Thesis statement: I am an 18-year-old Southern California native whose public speaking experience over the years has prepared me well for this class and will help me fulfill my career goal of being a lawyer.

Commentary

Tiffany begins with a series of questions to catch her audience's attention.
She reveals the subject of her speech in her introduction.

Offering only a brief overview of her childhood, Tiffany describes her early years speaking in front of people. Thus she sets the stage for her next point, her more recent speaking experience.

Beginning with a quick transition, she provides several examples of her speaking experiences as a teen and an adult. She then uses these examples to help her develop her thesis: her experiences have prepared her for a career as a lawyer.

Tiffany signals the end of her speech with language that lets the audience know she is wrapping up.

She concludes by stating her goals for the future, reminding her audience of the link between public speaking and becoming a lawyer.

If you have been assigned an introductory speech, such as a speech of self-introduction, a speech to introduce a classmate, or a narrative speech, you can use the following speech as a model. Using your Invitation to Public Speaking *CD-ROM, watch the video clip of Tiffany Brisco's speech of self-introduction. Tiffany gave this speech in an introductory public speaking class. The assignment was to give a one- to two-minute speech, and students were asked to share a bit of information about themselves so the class could get to know one another. Students were also asked to share any background they had in speech and why they were taking a public speaking course, besides the fact that it was required.*

Introduction

Where to start with something so intricate? Should I start at the beginning or begin at the end and trace back? What is this intricate object that I'm going to talk to you about today, you ask? Well, my subject is, of course, myself, Tiffany Nicole Brisco, born some eighteen years ago in Southern California.

Body

I grew up an only child in a single-parent household. My mother always drove me to do my best, and at an early age I won first place in a speech contest for the reading of the poem "Little Chocolate Child." Since then, I have been in several drama classes and a few plays, and have even done extra parts in movies and TV shows.

Since then, because I was very involved in school projects, I found myself on a few occasions giving speeches when running for student council offices. I was also honored enough to be able to do a speech at my graduation. Oddly enough, all this experience came before I had even had my first speech class, which came in my senior year in high school. It was a great class and taught me many skills, and prepared me for this speech course in which I am currently enrolled. Because of my prior speaking experience, I feel very comfortable and confident when giving my speeches in this class. I decided to take this speech course at CSU because speaking skills can always come in handy, especially with the career goal of becoming a lawyer—I need to learn how to become a successful public speaker.

Conclusion

So, in a nutshell, that's me. Tiffany Nicole Brisco, an 18-year-old Southern California native who aspires to become a successful lawyer and, in turn, a successful public speaker.

The solutions offered in this section may help you reduce some of the speech anxiety so common to beginning public speakers. Preparing, practicing, being realistic, visualizing and affirming, finding connections, and modeling appropriate audience behavior are options that even experienced public speakers use. As your confidence increases, modify some of these techniques to fit your needs and the special circumstances of your speaking activities. Learning to relax while giving speeches enhances our ability to contribute to the public dialogue and encourages us to participate in this important and necessary activity.

Speech Step 2.2 / Reduce
Any Anxiety You Feel About Giving a Speech

Make a list of what makes you feel nervous about public speaking. Now sort this list into categories that reflect your view of yourself, your audience, the process of designing your presentation, and giving your speech. Identify which aspect or aspects of the public speaking process are most fearful for you. Work on easing your fears by using some of the techniques for overcoming nervousness discussed in this chapter.

Chapter Summary

Whether your first speech informs, invites, persuades, introduces, commemorates, accepts, or is to a small group or as part of a small group, each kind of speaking creates a particular environment, relies on a certain structure, and creates unique relationships between the speaker and the audience.

As you give your first speech, and then practice many of the types of speaking throughout your public speaking course, remember the five canons of the speaking process: invention, arrangement, style, memory, and delivery. These canons provide the guidelines that will help determine your speaking purpose and topic, gather materials for your speech, organize your ideas, practice your speech, and present your speech to an audience.

Many people are nervous about speaking in public, especially for the first time. To help you reduce any nervousness you might experience, try some of the following techniques. Research your speech topic thoroughly so you feel confident about the material and are prepared to answer questions. Practice your speech to work out any problems with the speech before you give it and to feel comfortable giving it in front of an audience. Have realistic expectations about your delivery so you don't feel you have to give a perfect presentation. Visualize yourself giving a successful speech, and replace any negative self-talk with positive affirmations. Find points of connection with your audience so you view them as part of your community rather than strangers who want to judge you. And, finally, model good behavior when you are an audience member so you establish rapport with the people who may be a member of your audience.

Remember, the public dialogue is a place for the lively exchange of ideas. With some forethought and practice, you can add to this dynamic and stimulating exchange.

Invitation to Public Speaking Online

After reading this chapter, use your CD-ROM and the *Invitation to Public Speaking* Web site to review the follow-

ing concepts, answer the review questions, and complete the suggested activities.

Key Concepts

informative speech (24)
invitational speech (25)
persuasive speech (26)
introductory speech (26)
commemorative speech (27)
acceptance speech (27)
small group speaking (28)

canon (28)
canon of invention (29)
canon of arrangement (32)
canon of style (34)
canon of memory (36)
canon of delivery (36)
communication
   apprehension (38)

trait anxiety (38)
state, or situational, anxiety (38)
public speaking anxiety
   (PSA) (38)
systematic desensitization (40)
visualization (41)
cognitive restructuring (42)
affirmations (42)

Review Questions

1. Pretend you are giving a speech introducing the events of your day to a visiting friend. What does this person need to know to come along with you? To occupy themselves while you are busy? To get food, shelter, or rest? To respond to being lost, should that happen? Now deliver that speech to someone (a classmate, for example), and see what remaining questions they have that you did not think to include in your speech.

2. Identify the differences between speeches to inform, invite, and persuade. What do you enjoy or appreciate about each of these speeches? Why? Under what conditions would you choose each of these types of speaking?

3. Observe the communication patterns in the next group in which you participate. What kinds of communication take place? Does anyone dominate the conversation? Does anyone not participate? What roles do people assume? Is the communication ethical, as described in this chapter? How is conflict handled? What suggestions do you have to make the group speaking more successful?

4. Set aside fifteen minutes of alone time the day before your first speech. Take time to visualize that speech as the process is described in this chapter. Go through each step carefully and with detail. Do not rush or overlook any aspect of the speech process. After you give your speech, compare having visualized the speech and your level of nervousness to a situation in which you were nervous but did not visualize. Was the visualization helpful in reducing your nervousness? Why or why not?

5. Either alone or with a friend, list or discuss the negative self-talk you use to describe your ability to give speeches. Identify the specific negative phrases you use, and turn them into positive affirmations. Be realistic in reframing your negative self-talk into positive self-talk, using the examples in this chapter as a guide.

6. As you listen to other students give their speeches, see if you can find similarities and differences between them and you. This will help you find points of connection with your audience, one of the techniques for reducing your nervousness before a speech. It also will help you stay audience-centered, which is covered in Chapter 1 and in this chapter as well.

The *Invitation to Public Speaking* Web Site

The *Invitation to Public Speaking* Web site features review questions about the Web sites suggested on pages 28 and 42, the interactive activities suggested on pages 27, 28, and 43, and the InfoTrac College Edition exercise suggested on page 25. You can access this site via your CD-ROM or

at http://www.wadsworth.com/product/griffin. To access Speech Builder Express in order to complete Speech Step 2.1 on page 38, you will need the username and password included under "Speech Builder Express" on your CD-ROM.

Web Links

2.1: Types of Leaders (28)
2.2: Visualization Tips (42)

Interactive Activities

2.1: Introducing the Future President (27)
Purpose: To study a famous speech of introduction

2.2: Leading Small Group Discussions (28)
Purpose: To identify effective group leadership techniques

2.3: Connecting with the Audience (43)
Purpose: To consider ways in which speakers connect with audiences

InfoTrac College Edition Exercise

2.1: An Invitation to Speak (25)
Purpose: To understand the conditions necessary for invitational speaking

Speech Interactive on the *Invitation to Public Speaking* CD-ROM

The following video clips of speeches referenced in this chapter are included under Speech Interactive on your *Invitation to Public Speaking* CD-ROM. After you have watched the clips, click on "Critique" to answer the questions for analysis.

Video Clip 1: Former Vice-President Al Gore's Commemoration of Columbine Shooting Victims (27). What are the values Gore celebrates in this speech at the memorial service for victims of the Columbine school shootings in Colorado? How does he say the victims lived by those values? What special language does he use in the speech? How does Gore use emotion to bring the Columbine community together?

Video Clip 2: Cathy Freeman's Acceptance of the 2001 ESPY Awards' Arthur Ashe Courage and Humanitar- ian Award (27). Cathy Freeman's acceptance speech at the 2001 ESPY Awards was recognized as highly effective. To what degree does Freeman display humility in accepting the Arthur Ashe Courage and Humanitarian Award? Does she acknowledge others? How does she acknowledge the significance of the award? What kind of language did she use?

Video Clip 3: Self-Introduction: Tiffany Brisco (44). As you watch Tiffany Brisco's speech of self-introduction, consider whether she provides relevant and appropriate information about herself. Is the information appropriate to the speaking situation? What supporting details does she offer? Do these details give the audience the kind of information they would like to hear? How is the speech organized? How effective was Tiffany's language and delivery? What are the strengths and weaknesses of this speech of introduction?

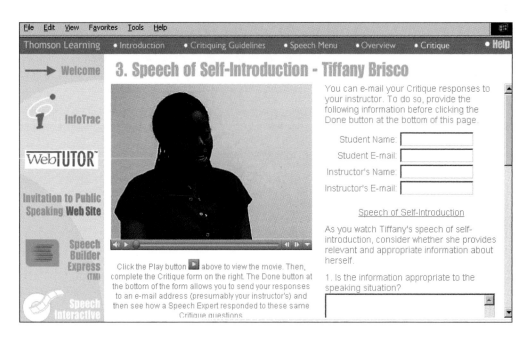

Chapter Three
Effective Listening

In this chapter you will learn to

Explain why listening to others is important

Identify the reasons why we sometimes fail to listen to others

Implement strategies for becoming a more effective listener

Implement strategies for becoming a more critical listener

Implement strategies for becoming a more ethical listener

Describe how your roles as a speaker and as a listener are related

Most of us, despite our best intentions, tend to spend our conversational time waiting for the first opportunity to offer our own comments or opinions. And when things heat up, the pace of our conversation resembles a gunfight on Main Street: "You're wrong!" "That's crazy!" The points go to the one who can draw the fastest or who can hold his ground the longest. As one person I know recently joked, "People do not listen, they reload."

—William Isaacs, *Dialogue and the Art of Thinking Together,* 1999[1]

Throughout your public speaking course, you will spend far more time listening to others than giving your own speeches. Over the course of one public speaking class, you may speak for a total of only 20 to 30 minutes, but in a class of thirty students, you'll *listen* to speeches for about 10 to 14 hours! Similarly, in the workplace or as a member of a community group, you may occasionally speak for long periods, but most of your presentations will last only from 10 to 30 minutes. Most likely, you'll spend much more of your time listening to others.

Even though most of us do more listening than speaking, the statistics on the amount of information we *retain* from listening to speeches are surprising. After a 10-minute oral presentation, the average person understands and retains only 50 percent of the information presented. Forty-eight hours after the presentation, those same listeners retain only 25 percent of the information.[2] To read more interesting facts about listening, go to the International Listening Association Web page at http://www.listen.org/pages/factoids.html.

Can you recall the last speech you heard? How much of its content do you remember? Now think of the last presentation you gave. How much of that information did you want your audience to remember? Is it inevitable that listeners lose so much information? As speakers, we definitely want our audiences to retain more than one-quarter of the information we worked so hard to present. And as listeners, most of us want to make the time we spend listening more profitable. Listening research indicates that we can improve our overall listening ability if we understand why listening to others is important, why people fail to listen well, what speakers do to complicate listening, and what specific listening skills we can cultivate. To assess your listening skills at this point in your public speaking **WEB SITE** course, complete Interactive Activity 3.1, "Assessing Your Listening," online under Student Resources for Chapter 3 at the *Invitation to Public Speaking* Web site.

Why Listen to Others?

confirming
Recognizing, acknowledging, and expressing value for another person.

hearing
Vibration of sound waves on our eardrums and the impulses then sent to the brain.

Listening to others is perhaps one of the most powerful ways in which we communicate as members of a community. When we listen to others, we confirm their humanity, presence, and worth. When we listen and **confirm,** we recognize, acknowledge, and express value for another person. So central is the act of listening that the philosopher Martin Buber claimed in the 1920s, "A society may be termed human in the measure to which its members confirm one another."[3] Note that listening is different from hearing. **Hearing** refers to the vibration of sound

One of former President Bill Clinton's strengths as a speaker was his ability to confirm others. In what ways does Clinton appear to be confirming his audience here?

AP/Wide World Photos

waves on our eardrums and the impulses that are then sent to the brain. When you listen to someone, you do more than simply receive sound waves—you contribute to a healthy society. To learn more about Buber's thoughts on the importance of listening, go to the Martin Buber Web site at http://www.buber.de/en/.

To confirm others by listening to them is not necessarily to agree with them or even to be persuaded by them. **Listening** is simply the process of giving thoughtful attention to another person's words and understanding what you hear. When you listen to others, you do not have to agree with them but you do have to give them your full attention. By listening to another's words, you recognize those words as expressions of that person's experiences, values, and beliefs.

If we are to participate in the public dialogue of our communities and make a space for others to do so also, we must listen. If we are to be effective public speakers and audiences, we must also understand why we sometimes fail to listen.

listening
The process of giving thoughtful attention to another person's words and understanding what you hear.

Why We Sometimes Fail to Listen

Why do we immediately shut down our willingness to listen to some messages but allow others to open us up to new ideas and ways of thinking? Why do we willingly confirm some people but refuse to even consider confirming others? Similarly, why are we sometimes surprisingly good at understanding some speakers, but no matter how hard we try, we are unable to follow the ideas of others? Listening researcher Paul Nichols explains that we sometimes fail to listen because "the simple art of listening isn't always so simple." Rather, it is often work. The "sustained attention of careful listening—that may take heroic and unselfish restraint. To listen well we must forget ourselves" and give our focused attention to another.[4]

As listeners, we fail to focus our attention for four reasons: listener interference, differing listening styles, speaker interference, and an inability to get beyond

interference
Anything that stops or hinders a listener from receiving a message.

differences. **Interference** is anything that stops or hinders a listener from receiving a message. Interference can be external to the listener (auditory or visual distractions) or internal (distracting thoughts or feelings). As you read this section, see if you recognize some of your own weaknesses as a listener or a speaker.

Listener Interference

Even though we occasionally hear a speaker that very few people understand, most of our listening problems stem from our own poor listening habits. Consider the following list of bad habits that many listeners fall into. Can you identify times you've done some of the following?

- Think you're not interest in the subject before the speech really gets going.
- Assume you know what the speaker is going to say before it's even said.
- Get so focused on the details that you miss the bigger point.
- Adopt a passive physical stance—slouching, reclining, making no eye contact.
- Adopt a defensive physical stance—turning away, crossing arms, making hostile eye contact.
- Pay attention to distractions—or create them yourself.
- Be so preoccupied with the messenger that you miss the message.
- Tune out difficult information.
- Tune out information you don't agree with or argue with the speaker's message in your own mind.
- Prepare your response while the speaker is speaking.
- Daydream or pretend you are listening when you really aren't.

At one time or another, most of us have fallen into many of these habits. We may think we've heard all there is to hear on a subject, so we begin daydreaming or simply pretend to listen. We become so enamored or so frustrated with a speaker that we forget to listen to the content of a speech. We find the material too challenging or difficult to understand, so we give up listening, begin talking to the person next to us, or even open the newspaper and begin to read. We even "reload," as this chapter's opening quote suggests, getting ourselves ready for the fight on "Main Street." Although we might want to blame the speaker for these lapses in listening, we really are responsible for our failure to listen when we practice these habits. At the end of this section, we will learn how to replace these bad habits with more productive ones. The International Listening Association describes additional listening habits that cause listener interference. You can find their list of "Irritating Listening Habits" at http://www.listen.org/pages/irritating_listening_habits.html.

Differences in Listening Styles

Some people listen better when certain senses are stimulated. The phrases "let me try that," "explain it to me," and "show me" are clues to how a person listens best. Consider the following examples:

> To her surprise, Rosa loved her geography course. As her professor lectured, she was able to touch and examine samples of the rocks and minerals discussed. On field trips, she always stood or walked at the front of the group, exploring the soils and formations with her hands. When she went back over her notes, she could see the particular hillside, rock, or mineral in her mind and remember its content and formation process. Even though she hadn't really wanted to take this required course, Rosa did very well in it.

Mileah was an excellent student of languages. In her experience, nothing stuck with her more than listening to the sounds of a particular language over and over. Sure, she read the books to help her, but she learned most quickly when she heard the language spoken out loud by her instructor, on the tapes in the language labs, and on the films shown in the course. Not surprisingly, in all of her classes she discovered that no matter the subject, she learned more from the lecture or discussion than from her reading.

Stuart took an art history seminar at the local college and realized he had a knack for understanding the art of any given period. Although the instructor's lectures were interesting, Stuart didn't *really* understand what the instructor was talking about until he saw the actual slides. Even though he might see over a hundred slides of art in one lecture, he always left class with a clear understanding of the period and the artists' work, because he could see what the professor was talking about.

If you recognized yourself in any of these scenarios, you know that people "listen" in different ways. In the first scenario, Rosa is an **experiential listener.** She understands best when she can touch, explore, and participate in what is being described. Rosa is the kind of person who often says "let me try that" in order to learn something. In the second example, Mileah is the "explain it to me" person. She's an **auditory listener** because she needs to hear verbal explanations and descriptions to learn well. In the final example, Stuart is a **visual listener,** characterized by his "show me" response. Stuart is the kind of person who has to see something to understand it and how it works.[5]

We sometimes fail to listen when we do not receive a message in the way that best matches our preferred listening style. Although we cannot control this variable, we can minimize its impact. Later in this chapter we'll explore ways to adjust to information presented in a style not well suited to our listening preferences, and we'll learn ways in which speakers can try to satisfy different listening styles. To read about ideas related to this discussion of listening styles, go to the "Learning Styles Explained" Web site at http://www.ldpride.net/learningstyles.MI.htm#Learning%20Styles%20Explained.

Speaker Interference Caused by Information

Although as speakers we might want to blame all listening troubles on our audience, we can affect our audience's ability to listen in very direct ways. We want to create speeches that are "listenable." A **listenable speech** is considerate and delivered in an oral style.[6] That is, a listenable speech uses words meant to be heard (oral style) rather than words meant to be read (written style). **Considerate speeches** ease the audience's burden of processing information. One of the ways we can construct considerate speeches is by reducing interference caused by information.

Listeners generally stop listening, or become very frustrated, when we present information that is too complicated, challenging, or basic. When we share ideas that are too complicated, audiences can have difficulty following our line of reasoning. When our ideas seriously challenge an audience's belief systems, the audience can get caught up in the differences in values and lose sight of the point we are trying to make. When we present stories or arguments that are too basic, our audiences may simply become bored and stop listening.

In the following example, the information is both too complicated and too challenging for some audiences. The speaker's dilemma, presented in an excerpt from Amy Tan's *The Kitchen God's Wife,* illustrates that although Winnie, the storyteller, decided to share her complicated and challenging history with her immediate audience, she chose not to even attempt to explain it to others:

experiential listener
Listener who needs to touch, explore, and participate in what is being described.

auditory listener
Listener who needs to hear verbal explanations and descriptions to learn well.

visual listener
Listener who needs to see something to understand it and how it works.

listenable speech
Speech that is considerate and delivered in an oral style.

considerate speech
Speech that eases the audience's burden of processing information.

For nearly forty years, I have told people Helen is my sister-in-law. But she is not. I have told people she is the wife of my brother, Kun, the one who was killed during the war. This is not the truth. But I did not say this to deceive anyone. The truth was too complicated to tell. No one would understand even if I could explain it all. In truth, he was only my half brother—related not even by blood, just by marriage. And he did not die in the war. He died before the war, his head chopped off in Changsha for selling three bolts of cloth to the revolutionaries, bragging that he cheated them by charging them a ridiculously high price, laughing that the cloth was of poor quality. But how could I ever reveal this?—that a member of my family meant to cheat his customers . . . . When I came to this new country, I thought I could finally forget about this half brother Kun.

But then Helen wanted to come from Formosa. I had to let her come. She told me I had a debt from many years before, now I had to pay her back. So I told the U.S. immigration officials in 1953 that Helen was my sister, born to one of my father's other five wives. And once she was here, I couldn't tell our church friends that my father had five wives. How could I say that? I was the wife of a minister. [7]

Winnie is an excellent example of a speaker who has information that is too complicated for some audiences (the immigration officials, for example) and too challenging for others (members of her church, who grew up in a culture very different from hers). She also gives us an example of a speaker who struggles with a common ethical dilemma: how to bridge cultural differences while staying as close to the truth as possible. Winnie decides to communicate only the background and cultural information her audience needs in order to understand her story. She made this decision because she did not want to overwhelm or overly challenge her listeners by sharing the entire story. Do you think she made the best choice? What would you do in her situation to make the information listenable?

Other information is difficult to listen to because it is too basic. Consider the following example: Katherine, a graduating senior, was the student speaker at her recent college graduation. Recognizing that graduation is a time of huge transition and uncertainty, but also of excitement, she decided to read passages from one of her favorite books, Dr. Seuss's *Oh, The Places You'll Go!* After her opening remarks to the audience and the other graduates, she began to read:

> Congratulations! Today is your day. You're off to Great Places! You're off and away! You have brains in your head. You have feet in your shoes. You can steer yourself any direction you choose. You're on your own. And you know what you know. And YOU are the guy who'll decide where to go.

If she had stopped here and continued in her own words, her speech may have been a success—most people love the messages in Dr. Seuss stories, so he is an excellent author to cite in a speech. However, Katherine continued to read lengthy passages from the book. After a while, people stopped listening to her speech because the language was too basic. Her audience began to shift and shuffle, to lose interest, and to strike up small side conversations while she was speaking. Although it can be interesting and meaningful for adults, *Oh, The Places You'll Go!* is written for children. Thus Katherine's speech on change and the excitement of the unknown used language that was too basic for college graduates and their families.

Speaker Interference Caused by Language

Another way we can give listenable, considerate speeches is by reducing interference caused by language. Most communication students view language as a tool, as something we use to describe our thoughts and experiences to others. Some would say that objects exist in the world around us and that people use language to describe those objects as they truly are. However, most now believe the way we know something is through the words we use to describe it.[8] For example, even though a dog may sit directly in front of a group of people, one person may describe the dog as a large, clumsy, furry, lovable animal; another as an unpredictable, aggressive, frightening nuisance; and another as a hairy, smelly extra mouth to feed and clean up after. Language, it seems, can be a tool we use to shape and describe the things around us. You'll learn more about how to use language as an effective speaking tool in Chapter 12. Here you'll explore how to use language as a tool to encourage better listening.

Listening can fail simply because the speaker's language is unclear. The language may be too formal or technical, too casual, too noninclusive, or too cluttered.

Formal or technical language. Most of us have heard the following phrases or sayings many times in our lives. Can you recognize them?

1. Scintillate, scintillate, asteroid minific.

2. Members of an avian species of identical plumage congregate.

3. Surveillance should precede saltation.

4. Pulchritude possesses a solely cutaneous profundity.

5. It is fruitless to become lachrymose over precipitately departed lacteal fluid.

6. Freedom from encrustations of grime is contiguous to rectitude.

7. Eschew the implement of correction and vitiate the scion.

8. It is fruitless to attempt to indoctrinate a superannuated canine with innovative maneuvers.

9. The temperature of aqueous content of an unremittingly ogled saucepan does not reach 212 degrees F.

10. All articles that coruscate with resplendence are not truly aurifeous.[9]

You may not recognize these common sayings because they are expressed in very formal and technical language. In some situations, this style of language may be quite appropriate, but most audiences stop listening when the speaker's language is more formal or technical than they can understand. These ten very formal sentences simply say:

1. Twinkle, twinkle, little star.

2. Birds of a feather flock together.

3. Look before you leap.

4. Beauty is only skin deep.

5. Don't cry over spilled milk.

6. Cleanliness is next to godliness.

7. Spare the rod and spoil the child.

8. You can't teach an old dog new tricks.

9. A watched pot never boils.

10. All that glitters is not gold.

Firefighters use jargon to communicate efficiently with one another. How might these firefighters describe the scene here to someone who isn't a firefighter? What jargon do you use in your profession that you might need to explain to an audience?

© George Hall/Woodfin Camp & Associates

Richard

I experienced a case of a speaker's language causing interference during a speech about computer programming. The speaker was talking about how to develop a game on the computer, and he was using terminology that I just didn't understand. It was probably a good speech, but I couldn't figure out what he was talking about. This was frustrating for me because he had caught my attention in the beginning and he had good visual aids, but once he got into the body of the speech, he lost me. About halfway through the speech, I just gave up trying to figure him out, and to this day I still have no clue how to develop a computer game. This experience gave me insight into how I should give my speeches. Now I concentrate on using familiar words, words my audience will understand.

jargon
Technical language used by a special group or for a special activity.

A specific type of language that is too technical is **jargon**, technical language used by a special group or for a special activity. You've probably used jargon if you play sports (a *bogey* is a type of score in golf) or are a member of a specialized group (in the military a *bogey* is an unidentified, possibly hostile, aircraft). You also may have used jargon in your job to identify processes or objects specific to your occupation (truck mechanics know a *bogie* is a type of wheel assembly used in some automotive trucks).

Jargon can be confusing because your audience may not know what a particular word means. What do you think the following sentence means?

We staged at the farmhouse about a mile away and after five days were demobed.

If you're a wildland firefighter, you might recognize this sentence as meaning "We camped [staged] at the farmhouse about a mile from the fire, and after five days of fighting fire there, we either went home or were sent to another fire [demobed]." As you can see from this example, jargon is often too technical for most audiences. A firefighter using this jargon in a speech to his colleagues would be easily understood. But if he used this language in a speech to high school students interested in pursuing a career in fire fighting, he'd probably get a lot of confused looks. As a speaker, use jargon only if it will help your audience better understand your message.

Casual language. Language also can be difficult to listen to if it is too casual. We often fall into our familiar, everyday language patterns, which can be too informal for our audience. **Slang** is an informal nonstandard vocabulary, usually made up of arbitrarily changed words. A **colloquialism** is a local or regional informal dialect or expression. A **euphemism** substitutes an agreeable or inoffensive expression for one that may offend or suggest something unpleasant. When our language is too casual, audiences might not be able to follow the main ideas of the speech, or they become confused or uncomfortable. Either way, they stop listening to our message. Consider these examples:

Slang	Dogg, this track is off the hook!
	(Buddy, this song is great! I love it.)
	Let me drop some science.
	(I'll explain the facts to you; also, to "drop" or release a CD.)[10]
Colloquialism	He done flew off his chair at the news.
	(He was so surprised by the news that it seemed as though he'd fall out of his chair.)
Euphemism	I'm going to go powder my nose. (I have to use the bathroom.)
	Due to changing market forces, the company will be downsizing. (Because the company is not making enough profit, employees will be laid off.)

In some settings, such as at a party with your friends, casual language is easily understood. However, in public speaking settings, translate casual slang, colloquialisms, and euphemisms into expressions an audience is more likely to understand. Some casual language may even be offensive to some members of an audience, causing them to stop listening or focus on the speaker's language rather than the speaker's ideas. Remember, as a speaker you want your audience to be able to listen to you without working too hard. When your audience is confused or offended by your language, they won't hear the message you want to send.

Language that is noninclusive. Listening can break down when you use words that seem to refer to only certain groups of people, or *noninclusive language*. A common example of noninclusive language is language that seems to describe only men, not men and women both. **Gender-inclusive language** recognizes that both women and men are active participants in the world. Using gender-inclusive language is one of the simplest ways you can improve listening, yet some people criticize and resist it. They argue that the pronoun *he* includes both women and men, and using *man* to describe all people is perfectly acceptable. For others, worrying about "gender stuff" is an issue that was resolved years ago. Yet research indicates that when we use noninclusive nouns and pronouns, listeners visualize men far more often then they do women or men and women together.

slang
Informal nonstandard vocabulary, usually made up of arbitrarily changed words.

colloquialism
Local or regional informal dialect or expression.

euphemism
A word or phrase that substitutes an agreeable or inoffensive expression for one that may offend or suggest something unpleasant.

gender-inclusive language
Language recognizing that both women and men are active participants in the world.

If you doubt the narrowness of language that is not gender inclusive, consider the research. In 1973, children were asked to select photographs for textbooks titled "Urban Man" and "Man in Politics" or "Urban Life" and "Political Behavior." The children nearly always chose pictures of men when the titles included the male nouns. When the titles were not specifically male oriented, the children chose more pictures that contained both women and men. Fifteen years later, in 1988, researchers asked first grade students to write a story about an average student. When the researchers used the word "he" to describe the assignment, only 12 percent of the students wrote a story about a female. When they used "he or she," 42 percent of the students wrote stories about females. [11]

In 1995, to determine whether gender bias was still an issue, researchers asked college students to fill in the blanks to sentences such as, "Before a judge can give a final ruling, _____," and "Before a doctor can make a final diagnosis, _____." What pronouns did the students choose to finish the sentences? Even though women today participate in almost all aspects of public and professional life, students chose predominantly masculine pronouns to finish the sentences. [12]

Using gender-biased language prevents listeners from hearing the main arguments and ideas of a speech. Whether we mean it to or not, noninclusive language tends to reflect a noninclusive attitude. By using the "universal he," we give the impression that we do not recognize women as competent, professional individuals or we are unaware of the research indicating that using only male pronouns serves to exclude women. Either way, listeners spend energy focusing on our use of language rather than paying attention to our arguments.

Additionally, gender-biased language can be quite ambiguous and thus confusing. When we say, "If a person wants to be treated as an adult, he must earn the respect worthy of such treatment," is the "person" a man (only), a woman (only), or a human being of either sex? [13] How is the listener to know for sure? What if Jane wants to be treated as an adult? Can she earn the respect worthy of such treatment? How would a listener know? It is easier to include Jane in the argument—and reduce the work for the listener—by saying, "If people want to be treated as adults, they must earn the respect worthy of such treatment." Regardless of your own stance on the position of women in the world relative to men, avoiding noninclusive terms can help clarify ambiguous arguments or claims. It also helps listeners understand the intended message. To learn more about gender-neutral language, go to http://www.stetson.edu/departments/history/nongenderlang.html and read Carolyn Jacobson's "Some Notes on Gender-Neutral Language."

Another example of noninclusive language is language that does not acknowledge cultural diversity. **Culturally inclusive language** is language that respectfully recognizes the differences among the many cultures in our society. Although it may seem obvious that we need to consider diversity when we speak to diverse audiences, at times our language does not reflect our attention to diversity.

A common example of language that is not culturally inclusive is **spotlighting**, the practice of highlighting a person's race or ethnicity (or sex, sexual orientation, physical disability, and the like) during a speech. Speakers who spotlight describe a lawyer as a Hispanic lawyer, a doctor as an Asian American doctor, and a friend as an African American friend. Spotlighting is most common among members of the dominant culture in a society, and it marks differences as being unusual. Consider the following examples:

The jury includes five men and two African American women.

The panel includes three professionals and a disabled lawyer.

culturally inclusive language
Language that respectfully recognizes the differences among the many cultures in our society.

spotlighting
Practice of highlighting a person's race or ethnicity (or sex, sexual orientation, physical disability, and the like) during a speech.

The meeting is going to be chaired by a Hispanic professor and a university administrator.

He's a talented gay artist.[14]

None of these sentences refers specifically to whiteness, heterosexuality, or physical ability, because these are all characteristics of the dominant culture in the United States. Thus they are considered normal. Spotlighting identifies people thought to belong to a special, and hence an unusual, category. As a result of spotlighting, differences get marked as abnormal, slightly strange, or surprising. A speaker using culturally inclusive language would describe the people in these examples as five white men and two African American women (or as seven people), four professionals (a lawyer is professionally employed), two employees of the university (or a Hispanic professor and a white administrator), and a talented artist.

Also make sure your speech topics, source citations, and examples represent a range of cultural perspectives. Additionally, when you cite statistics, consider how culture and ethnicity have affected them. Speakers often fail to cite authorities and information from cultures other than their own. For example, we often hear that women earn approximately 76 cents to every dollar a man earns, but which women? Culturally inclusive language reveals that white women earn approximately 80 cents to every dollar a white man earns, African American women earn approximately 63 cents, and Hispanic women earn approximately 56 cents to every dollar a white man makes. Noninclusive language erases this important disparity. Culturally inclusive language recognizes these important differences.[15]

Using culturally and gender-inclusive language communicates to an audience that you are aware of the diversity in our society and of the influence of culture. Your speech becomes more listenable because audiences gain a more holistic view of an issue. Your goal as a speaker is to connect with your audience and to share your ideas with them, so make listening as easy as possible. Using language that includes *all* members of your audience assists you in doing just that.

Verbal clutter. Sometimes audiences have a difficult time listening to a speaker because of **verbal clutter**, extra words that pad sentences and claims but don't add meaning. Even though listeners can mentally process far more words than speakers can speak per minute (the average speaker speaks at a rate of 125 to 175 words per minute, but trained listeners can process 350 to 450 words per minute), verbal clutter impedes listening because listeners must process words that are unnecessary, redundant, and don't help develop an idea.[16]

verbal clutter
Extra words that pad sentences and claims but don't add meaning.

Examples of verbal clutter are such common words and phrases as "you know," "it's like," "I'm like," "um," "and all," "and stuff," "stuff like that," and "then I go." These small additions to a speech, although commonly used in casual conversation, distract listeners and add no useful meaning.

Similarly, descriptions loaded with adjectives and adverbs act as verbal clutter. Hard to spot sometimes, we often use this type of verbal clutter when we try to create vivid descriptions. Which of these sentences would you prefer to process during a speech?

Cluttered: Good, effective public speakers use carefully selected and chosen words, sentences, and phrases, correctly and accurately.

Uncluttered: Skilled speakers present their ideas clearly.

Cluttered: If nothing else, he was first and foremost, above all, a man of considerable honor and principled integrity.

Uncluttered: Above all, he was a man of integrity.

The uncluttered sentences are much easier on the ears. They hold our attention and focus our listening efforts. Without the clutter, audiences have a far easier time listening for our main points and ideas.

But how much clutter do you really want to eliminate? Notice the differences in the level of clutter in the next three examples:

Cluttered: At some point during the day, every single day of her life, no matter the weather or the distractions, she would make the long, steep trek 3 miles one way to the distant, far-off waterfall.

Less cluttered: At some point during the day, every day of her life, she made the 3-mile trek to the waterfall.

Uncluttered: Every day she hiked 3 miles to the waterfall.

Notice that some of what might be called "clutter" in one speech adds richness and detail to another, setting a particular tone or mood. Go back and reread the cluttered example. If we simply took out the words "the distant, far-off," we might have a nice description for a commemorative speech or a speech of introduction. But in a persuasive or informative speech, the focus might be on the daily hike to a waterfall, not on the characteristics of the woman. Thus the less cluttered or uncluttered versions might make the point far more effectively.

Ask yourself two questions when you want to eliminate verbal clutter. First, do the words you use help develop your argument or make more work for the listener? You might use this question to decide on language for the speech about the woman who hiked to a waterfall. Second, how many words in your speech are redundant? Consider the examples about the "man of integrity." If you look up "integrity" in the thesaurus, you will find "honor" listed as a synonym: both words mean the same thing in this context. Additionally, the phrases "first and foremost," "above all," and "if nothing else" mean the same thing. To say "considerable" in the cluttered example detracts from the direct power of the simple claim "man of integrity." And to be "principled" is to adhere to certain standards, or to

WEB SITE have integrity, so "principled" isn't necessary either. To learn more about how to eliminate verbal clutter, complete Interactive Activity 3.2, "Eliminating Verbal Clutter," online under Student Resources for Chapter 3 at the *Invitation to Public Speaking* Web site.

We often use language without thinking and sometimes present information that is inappropriate or too complicated, challenging, or basic. However, by paying careful attention to our words and to the ideas we want to express, we can create speeches that are listenable and considerate, speeches that audiences will want to listen to. To further explore information and language factors that may interfere with a speaker's message, complete the InfoTrac College Edition Exercise 3.1, "Interfering with the Message," online under Student Resources for Chapter 3.

Speaker Interference Caused by Differences

Differences between a speaker and an audience can also cause problems with listening. Although we are all similar in many ways, none of us exactly matches our audience in appearance, mannerisms, values, or background. When we are faced with differences, we sometimes see them in terms of a hierarchy (such as seeing a person of a certain age or sex as more trustworthy or credible than another person). When we see differences in this way, we become preoccupied with questions of right and wrong and have trouble focusing on what a speaker is saying. Here are some of the ways speakers and audiences are different and the ways those differences can prevent effective listening:

Speech style: Accents, tonal and rhythmic qualities, stuttering, nonnative speakers of a language, and gendered speech differences affect listening. We sometimes see these differences as strange, funny, or inappropriate and have trouble paying attention to the message.

Background and occupation: Differences in race, ethnicity, nationality, regional upbringing, religion, education, occupation, and economic status can affect listening. When we see these differences as right or wrong, we forget to be open to the value of other experiences and influences and often stop listening.

Appearance: Styles of dress, height, weight, hair, body adornment, and even a speaker's posture affect listening. Audiences sometimes have difficulty listening because they are so focused on the speaker's appearance that they can't focus on the message.

Values: When a speaker holds values that are different from members of the audience, listening sometimes is difficult. When listeners are so convinced that certain values are "worthy" and "good" and others are "wrong" and "bad," they rarely listen in order to understand why that position makes sense to the speaker. Instead, they listen as though they were in a gunfight, reading their responses as challenges.

How do we minimize our differences, or explain and account for them, so audiences and speakers can more easily confirm one another? We can go a long way toward that goal by defining *difference* as meaning simply *different*, as not the same but still worth listening to. Thus we can open up the possibility for listening that confirms others rather than listening that means we must agree with everything they say.

Although listeners are responsible for interference caused by differences, as speakers we also contribute to this listening problem. Here are a few ways we can minimize the impact of differences:

© Neal Preston/CORBIS

- Acknowledge and explain differences in speech styles or appearance. Act as an interpreter for the audience, explaining what those differences mean.

- Explain your background and how it affects your position or presentation of information. In this way you become a source of information regarding your differences not just someone unusual or unfamiliar.

As a member of an audience, what about this speaker might cause interference for you as a listener? What could you do to reduce this interference? What could the speaker do?

- Invite others to consider your values without attempting to persuade. Assume an invitational stance that attempts to confirm the audience as well as offer your own perspective. (See Chapter 16 for more about invitational speaking.)

Using your *Invitation to Public Speaking* CD-ROM, watch the video clip of Barbara Bush's commencement speech at Wellesley College under Speech Interactive. How does she bridge differences with her audience?

Even though differences can seem like permanent obstacles to listening, both audiences and speakers must recognize that difference is the foundation of a healthy public dialogue. Once we invite dialogue, rather than monologue, we encourage the exchange of ideas, information, perspectives, and even creative solutions to many of the dilemmas we face. Both audiences and speakers are responsible for creating this healthy dialogue, and a public speaking course is an excellent place to practice listening and speaking in ways that confirm and respect differences.

Speech Step 3.1 / Help Your Audience Listen to Your Speech

Consider the many reasons why your audience might fail to listen to your next speech. How many of these reasons can you eliminate before you actually give the speech? How many can you eliminate or address during your speech? Identify the specific steps you will take to help your audience listen to, and retain, your message.

How to Listen Effectively

Even though the act of listening poses many challenges, we as listeners can improve our skills and increase the amount of information we retain. In the process, we will also become better speakers. In fact, the listening strategies you'll read about in this and the next two sections involve listening for many of the components you will incorporate later into your own speeches.

One of the most important obstacles to overcome as a listener is your own interference, or the bad habits discussed earlier in this chapter. However, if you learn to listen effectively, these bad habits are relatively easy to minimize. An **effective listener** overcomes listener interference in order to better understand a speaker's message. To minimize your own bad listening habits and reduce interference, try the following.

effective listener
Overcomes listener interference in order to better understand a speaker's message.

Listen for the Speaker's Purpose

Try to determine the speaker's goal. Is the speaker attempting to introduce, inform, invite, persuade, or commemorate? Can you determine who or what is being introduced, and why? What information are you about to receive, and why is it important? What are you being invited to consider? What are you being persuaded to do, think, or feel?

Listen for the Main Ideas

As the speech unfolds, identify each of the speaker's main points or arguments. Are there two, three, or more main points or arguments? Is each point clearly articulated, and do you see why it is a main point?

Listen for the Links Between the Ideas

How does the speaker connect each main point or idea? Listen to see if you can follow the development of the ideas. Can you find the relationship between and among the claims made and their connection to the speaker's goal? Listen for previews before main ideas, transitions, connectives from one idea to the next, and summaries at the ends of main ideas.

Listen for Supporting Evidence and Sources

What kind of evidence does the speaker use to support ideas? Identify the specific kinds of evidence used by speakers, such as narratives, personal disclosure, statistics, comparisons, and expert testimony (Chapter 7). Does the speaker use enough evidence, and does it actually help the speaker make the argument?

Listen for Consistency of Delivery and Content

Compare the speaker's style of delivery to the actual content of the speech. Are the two consistent? For example, if the topic is serious, does the delivery match that seriousness? How does the speaker use delivery to enhance the content or build a particular kind of environment? Using your *Invitation to Public Speaking* CD-ROM, watch the video clip of President George W. Bush's address regarding the U.S. response to terrorism under Speech Interactive. Pay attention to his purpose for making the speech, his main ideas, the links between his ideas, his evidence, and the consistency between his delivery and content.

Write Down New Words and Ideas

Keep paper beside you as you listen, and jot down any unfamiliar words, phrases, or ideas. Keeping notes will help you listen for information that explains these words, phrases, and ideas and keep you focused on the content of the speech.

Write Down Questions

As you listen to the speech, questions will probably come to your mind. Write them down as they occur, and ask the speaker about them at the end of the speech or find the answers on your own. Keeping notes about your own questions will keep you focused on finding the answers as the speech progresses.

Offer Nonverbal Feedback

Rather than sitting passively or falling prey to distractions, listen by sitting in an upright (but relaxed) posture, and engage the speaker by making eye contact (if it is culturally appropriate). Use culturally appropriate nonverbal cues such as smiles of encouragement and head nods that signal understanding and attention. Taking notes is another nonverbal way of showing the speaker you are listening and keeping your attention focused.

Listen for the Conclusion

Many speeches have a distinct conclusion (see Chapter 10). Listen to the speaker to see if you can discover the moment the conclusion begins. Does the speaker summarize the main points, tell a story to wrap up the speech, ask the audience to participate in some action, or do something else to bring the presentation to a close? Consider whether the content and delivery of the conclusion match the purpose of the speech.

Which members of this audience are not listening effectively? What nonverbal cues tell you that one person is paying less attention than another? Do you recognize your listening habits in any of the members of this audience?

© Bob Daemmrich/Stock Boston

Take Stock at the End of the Speech

At the close of the speech, review in your own mind the goal, main points, evidence, and conclusion of the speech. Is there consistency among each of these? Review your notes and determine what questions you might want to ask the speaker, or find answers on your own.

Make Adjustments for Listening Styles

Although speakers should consider accommodating the three listening styles discussed in this chapter into their speeches, sometimes they do not and, occasionally, they cannot. As a member of the audience, making adjustments for preferred listening styles can be hard to do, but if the speaker fails to present information in a style you are comfortable with, you are not at a complete loss. In fact, most of us learn to listen to information presented in all three styles. Try the following techniques if you are having trouble paying attention to a speaker.

Experiential listeners may find it hardest to adapt to speakers who fail to accommodate tactile styles of listening. However, speakers often neglect this style because hands-on processes during speeches can be unwieldy and time consuming. If you are a tactile listener, try to listen carefully to the content of a speech so that afterward you can find a tangible example of what the speaker is discussing, or after the speech is over, ask the speaker to show you what she or he meant. Although these are not complete solutions, they may help you stay focused when you are beginning to lose concentration and falling prey to distractions.

As an auditory listener, you usually are at an advantage because speakers have to explain verbally what they mean. In fact, speakers usually rely more on verbal explanations than on presenting information that can be touched and examined or seen visually. However, you may get lost in visual aids, especially if they aren't explained well or when speakers hand out objects without much description. When this happens, take notes during the presentation so you can ask for a verbal explanation during the question-and-answer session or after the speech is over.

If you are a visual learner, you can adapt by creating mental images of what the speaker is saying, drawing a diagram in your notes, and writing down key words, especially those that bring concrete images to mind. Seeing the speech's information in your head or on paper should help you listen more effectively. After the speech, you can ask the speaker if your images or notes match the intended message.

To learn more about adapting your listening style to a speaker's approach, complete Interactive Activity 3.3, "Adapting to Your Listening Style," online under Student Resources for Chapter 3 at the *Invitation to Public Speaking* Web site. To apply what you have just learned about becoming a better listener, complete InfoTrac College Edition Exercise 3.2, "Sharpening Your Listening Skills," featured at the end of this chapter and online under Student Resources for Chapter 3. Additionally, you can find the Effective Listening Checklist online under Student Resources for Chapter 3. You can use this checklist to guide your listening behaviors next time you listen to a speech.

WEB SITE

Speech Step 3.2 / Assess Your Effectiveness as a Listener

Assess your effectiveness as a listener by completing the online Effective Listening Checklist. As you listen to the next round of speeches in your class, use the checklist to guide your listening behaviors. When you use the checklist, how much more information do you recall from the speech? After the speech, how much more involved do you get in the question-and-answer or class critique session?

How to Listen Critically

When we listen to speeches, we want to listen not only effectively but also critically. When you listen to a speech critically, you mentally check it for accuracy, comparing what the speaker says with what you personally know and what your own research tells you. You also listen to assess the strengths and weaknesses of the reasoning and supporting materials presented in a speech. Note that listening critically is different from listening to judge or find fault with a message. Rather, **critical listeners** listen for the accuracy of a speech's content and the implications of a speaker's message. Critical listeners benefit by remaining open to new ideas, but they also listen carefully to how speakers develop those ideas into arguments. Additionally, they consider the impact of a speaker's ideas and how they may affect immediate audiences as well as larger communities.

critical listener
Listener who listens for the accuracy of a speech's content and the implications of a speaker's message.

To help you listen to speeches critically, ask yourself the questions shown in Table 3.1, then follow the suggested guidelines. Asking these types of who, what, and how questions will help you assess a speaker's claims and arguments before you make decisions about their value or strength.

Table 3.1

Guidelines for Critical Listening

QUESTION	GUIDELINE
• How fully has the speaker developed an idea? Is something left out, exaggerated, or understated? Does the speaker use sound reasoning? Are claims based on fact or opinion? (Chapters 8 and 18)	• Speakers must develop all major arguments fully rather than present them without explanation and development. Speakers should not exaggerate arguments or understate their importance. Major ideas should be supported by evidence in the form of examples, statistics, testimony, and the like.
• What sources does the speaker rely on? Are they credible? How are they related to the speaker's topic? Will the sources benefit if facts are presented in a certain way? For example, is the tobacco industry arguing that smoking isn't harmful? (Chapter 7)	• Speakers must support major and supporting claims with credible sources that are as unbiased as possible. Speakers must cite sources for all new information. Sources should be cited carefully and with enough detail so the audience knows why the source is acceptable.
• Are the claims the speaker makes realistic? What are the implications of those claims? Who is affected by them? In what way? Has the speaker acknowledged these effects, or are they left unstated? Are there other aspects of the issue the speaker should address?	• Speakers must make realistic and logical claims and acknowledge different perspectives. Claims of a solution or a cause-and-effect relationship must clearly show that the solution will work and the relationship exists. When speakers take a position, they must not present their position as absolute or the only one possible.
• How does this speech fit with what I know to be true? What is new to me? Can I accept this new information? Why or why not?	• Some speakers will make claims that go against your personal experience. If this happens, see if you can discover why. Sometimes the answer lies in cultural differences or in a speaker's research of an issue. Try to be open to different views of the world while at the same time assessing the speaker's evidence and reasoning objectively. Before you reject a speaker's claims out of hand, engage the speaker in a civil discussion to find out why your perspective differs.
• What is at stake for the speaker? How invested is the speaker in the topic and the arguments being made? How will the speaker be affected if the audience disagrees?	• All speakers are invested in some way in their topics and arguments. However, some arguments benefit a speaker more than anyone else. Identify the speaker's motives so you can better understand why she or he is making particular claims.

When we listen critically, we allow for dialogue because we avoid making quick decisions about good and bad, right and wrong. Listening critically encourages us to ask questions about ideas so we are better able to respond to claims and explore issues with others.

 Speech Step 3.3 / Practice Listening Critically

Listen critically to the next speech you hear, asking yourself the questions listed in Table 3.1. When you listen critically, do you find you better understand the speaker's position and retain more information than when you don't listen critically? Are you able to engage the speaker in the question-and-answer session more meaningfully? Now listen critically to your own speech before you give it in class. Ask yourself the first two questions listed in Table 3.1. Are you satisfied with the arguments you make and the sources you cite? How do you think your audience will respond to the last three questions?

How to Listen Ethically

Listening effectively encourages audiences to pay attention to the process of listening in order to reduce interference. Listening critically encourages listeners to listen for the accuracy of the reasoning in a speech. Listening ethically encourages audiences to pay attention to the ethical implications of a message. *Ethics* refer to the study of moral standards and how those standards affect our conduct. When we speak of ethics, we are talking about the moral principles we use to guide our behaviors and decisions. An **ethical listener,** then, considers the moral impact of a speaker's message on one's self and one's community. Ethical listeners attend to the standards and principles advocated by a speaker. In order to listen ethically, listeners must suspend judgment, assess the information they hear, and, at times, respond to the speaker's message.

ethical listener
Listener who considers the moral impact of a speaker's message on one's self and one's community.

Suspend Judgment

Ethical listeners suspend judgment when they are willing to enter an "opinion holding pattern" for the duration of a speech. They are willing to listen to a speaker's message, without assigning "right" and "wrong" to it, in order to gather as much information as they can. Ethical listeners consciously avoid reacting immediately to a statement they disagree with. This allows them to hear the complete message and not jump to conclusions before the speaker is finished. And when they hear the complete message, they can contribute to the public dialogue in more informed ways.

Consider an example. Two students are listening to a speaker on their campus argue for free speech and the right of hate groups to say or print anything they want. Early on in the presentation the speaker says, "It's our constitutional right to express ourselves; this country was founded on that principle. Two hundred plus years later, I argue we are guaranteed the right to say anything we want to anyone."

> *Listener who rushes to judgment:* "That's ridiculous, how can he say that? People don't have the right to say anything they want whenever and wherever they want. That's harassment, and we don't have the right to do that to anyone!"

By rushing to judgment, this listener may stop listening altogether or may focus on a response to the speaker rather than listening to more of what the speaker has to say. By doing so, she may miss the speaker's later claim that our right to express ourselves also guarantees that we can freely criticize hate speech, a freedom not all societies enjoy.

Now consider the speaker who listens ethically, suspending judgment in order to listen to the full message:

> *Listener who suspends judgment:* "Wow, that sounds extreme to me, but maybe he's got a reason for making that claim. Let me see if I can understand why he makes such a strong statement."

Even though this student disagrees with the speaker, he's willing to put aside his disagreement until he's heard all the speaker has to say. Thus he'll have an easier time following the speaker's ideas, confirming them, and responding intelligently to the speaker's claims. Suspending judgment does not mean that we as listeners sit by passively and let speakers say whatever they wish without scrutiny. You can still question and disagree with a speaker's message. Suspending judgment is simply a tool to help you listen more effectively and hear a speaker's entire message.

WEB SITE For more information about suspending judgment as you listen, complete Interactive Activity 3.4, "Using Dialogic Listening," online under Student Resources for Chapter 3 at the *Invitation to Public Speaking* Web site.

Assess Information and Respond to the Speaker's Ideas

Ethical listening also requires that listeners assess a message (listen critically) first and then respond to the speaker's ideas. Listeners can respond during the speech or in a conversation with the speaker and other audience members after the speech is given. When ethical listeners respond to a speaker's ideas, they participate in a constructive dialogue with a speaker. Even if they do not agree with a speaker's position, ethical listeners join the public dialogue so they can better understand a position, explore differences, and share their own views. In their attempts to understand, ethical listeners recognize, acknowledge, and show value for others, even if their positions are vastly different from the speaker's.

WEB SITE To practice assessing and responding to a speech, use the Speech Evaluation Checklist shown in Figure 3.1 (and under Student Resources for Chapter 3 at the *Invitation to Public Speaking* Web site). This checklist will help you focus your attention as you listen to a speech and identify areas you'd like to explore with a speaker when the speech is over. Remember, public speaking can be viewed as an extended conversation, and ethical listening helps you participate in this conversation.

Speakers as Listeners

Although this chapter has focused extensively on how we as members of an audience can improve our listening skills, speakers are also listeners. In front of an audience, speakers do more than produce a steady stream of words. They listen to their audiences during the presentation by monitoring their expressions, posture, feedback, and level of attention. Speakers use this information to adapt to audience needs throughout the speech by slowing down or speeding up, taking more time to explain, omitting information, or adding extra examples to clarify. In Chapter 5, you'll learn more about your broader relationship to your audience. Here you'll focus on how you can listen effectively to your audience.

When you give a speech, remember that audience members bring with them many bad listening habits. What follows are some examples of problematic audiences and ways you can counter their bad habits to help them listen better.

Tiffany Brisco

Audiences Who Are Uninterested

Sometimes audience members appear uninterested in your speech from the start or seem to assume they already know what you will say. Address this behavior by making your introduction and first main points compelling, innovative, and attentive to your audience's particular biases. Genet began his speech by saying, "You say you already know. You say, 'There's nothing new here!' You might even be thinking, 'This will never happen to me' and, maybe—just maybe—you're right. But what if you're wrong? What if you're *probably* wrong? Are you willing to be the two out of three who didn't listen?" After this introduction, he had the full attention of the class and was able to maintain their attention throughout his speech on alcohol and drug addiction. Using your *Invitation to Public Speaking* CD-ROM, watch the video clip of Tiffany under Speech Interactive. What does she say in her introduction to make it easy for her audience to listen to her speech?

Figure 3.1
Speech Evaluation Checklist

Speaker _____ **Topic** _____

Introduction

_____   Is the purpose of the speech clear? What is the purpose? _____

_____

_____   Does the speaker establish credibility?

_____   Are the topic and purpose relevant to the audience?

_____   Does the speaker preview the speech?

Body

_____   Are the main points clearly identified? What are the main points? _____

_____

_____   Are the main points fully supported? Why or why not?

_____   Are the sources credible? Why or why not?

_____   Is the reasoning sound? Why or why not?

_____   Are other perspectives addressed?

_____   Is the speech listenable? Why or why not? (Consider language, organization, and interference.)

At what points do I suspend judgment in order to listen ethically and effectively? _____

_____

_____

Conclusion

_____   Does the speaker signal the end of the speech?

_____   Does the speaker summarize the main points?

Discussion

What questions would I like to ask the speaker? _____

What information would I like clarified? _____

What would I like the speaker to talk more about? _____

What would I like the speaker to think more about? _____

What information do I have that I want to share with the speaker? _____

_____

_____

These hecklers disrupted a recent speech given by President George W. Bush in praise of local volunteering efforts. How could he have adapted to these audience members during his speech to help them listen to his message more effectively?

AP/Wide World Photos

Audiences Who Are Distracted or Disruptive

Some audience members may slouch, fail to make eye contact, daydream, and make or attend to distractions. To counter this behavior, ask questions of the entire audience or of particular members. Ask them to complete an activity related to your topic, such as making a list or jotting down what they already know about your topic. Bring particularly disruptive people into your speech verbally or by bringing them to the front of the audience for a legitimate reason (for example, to give a demonstration or to record discussion ideas on a white board). Here's how Seth handled this situation:

> Noticing that several of his audience members were reading the newspaper during his speech, Seth paused mid-sentence to catch his audience's attention and said, "You know, I bet that whatever's in that paper isn't as current or relevant to our lives as my next point. Because, at this moment in time, our government is spending billions of dollars to cover up . . . ," and he continued on with his topic. At that point, he had the full, and respectful, attention of the audience.

Note that you want to be careful about singling out audience members. Make sure the speaking environment is such that you won't embarrass those people or make the rest of the audience feel uncomfortable. Approaching this type of situation with good-natured humor can go a long way toward making your audience feel that you value them.

Audiences Who Are Distracted by the Speaker

If your audience is staring at your unusual style of clothing or is straining to understand because of differences is speech styles, take a moment to explain what the distraction means to you and why it's there. Angelique, a student with a strong accent, shared with her audience that she was from the Dominican Republic. She explained that her husband kept trying to correct her accent but she told him, "It's my accent and I like it." Sharing this story in the introduction of her speech helped reduce the focus on her accent and enabled her audience to listen to her message instead.

Audiences Who Are Confused

You can use a number of strategies to help audiences who appear to be confused by the information in your speech. Slow down, explain with more detail, reduce your number of main points, alter your language, or use all three listening styles to share your message. Even if you had not planned to use visual aids, use an overhead projector or board, or ask someone from the audience to demonstrate your ideas. Marilyn saw her audience looking confused, so she proceeded to outline her main points on the board and jot down key words and phrases. The audience applauded her efforts and acknowledged that her speech was much easier to follow with a visual map.

Audiences Who Plan Their Responses Rather Than Listen

Sometimes particular audience members appear to be planning their responses to you during your speech. Acknowledge their eagerness to participate, and recognize it as a positive sign of interest. Make a space for conversation at the close of the speech. Acknowledging someone's interest can bring a listener into your speech and create an environment in which everyone feels they can express themselves. Hallie watched a member of her audience react with dismay to one of her claims and then fidget and sit on the edge of his seat. She acknowledged his desire to respond by saying, "I see I've struck a chord with some of you. If you'll hang on to your questions and hear me out, I'd love to hear your reactions at the end of the speech." Her resister relaxed a bit and was able to put his opposition aside enough to listen to her full arguments and reasons. The conversation at the end of the speech was lively and dynamic, and both Hallie and the audience member benefited from it.

Although in Chapter 5 you will discover other excellent ways to help your audience listen to you, you cannot do so unless you listen to your audience yourself. When you as a speaker listen to your audience, you make your message more listenable and memorable, and you make it easier for your audience to give you the attention and respect you deserve. You can find the Speaker's Listening **WEB SITE** Checklist online under Student Resources for Chapter 3. Use this checklist to help you listen to your audience before and during your next speech.

Chapter Summary

We listen to others so we can confirm their ideas and enter the public dialogue in ways that are intelligent and rewarding. Although listening is one of the most important communicative acts, we sometimes fail to listen because of listener interference or differences in listening styles. Our failure to listen well is also caused by speaker interference due to information, language, or other differences in style, background, appearance, and values. However, there are many ways to improve our listening.

To listen effectively, listen for the speaker's purpose, main ideas, and the links made between ideas. Listen for supporting evidence. Listen for consistency between the speech's content and the speaker's delivery style. Write down new words, ideas, and questions you have for the speaker. Provide the speaker with positive nonverbal feedback. Listen for the conclusion of the speech, and review the material you have just heard. Finally, adapt your listening during a speech so the information matches your preferred listening style.

When we listen critically, we assess the strengths and weaknesses of a speaker's reasoning and evidence and remain open to new ideas and information. When we listen ethically, we listen for the moral implications of a message. Ethical listeners practice two listening behaviors: (1) suspending judgment and (2) assessing and responding to the speaker's ideas.

Even though we usually think of our audience as the listeners in a speech, speakers are also listeners. When you give a speech, listen to your audience for signs of disinterest, hostility, or opposition. Also listen to make sure your style and mannerisms aren't confusing or distracting. Finally, listen for signs that your audience is confused. Each of these signals helps you adapt your message so your speech is a listenable one.

By using the information provided in this chapter, you can improve your listening skills both as a speaker and as a member of an audience. Many of the suggestions offered in this chapter are discussed in detail in later chapters. This reflects the fact that listening plays a central role in the public dialogue, and our task as speakers is to listen carefully to others as well as ourselves.

When you listen to your audience as you speak, you can help them become better listeners and understand your message more fully. Which of the listening strategies discussed in this chapter do you think you'd feel comfortable using in your next speech?

Invitation to Public Speaking Online

After reading this chapter, use your CD-ROM and the *Invitation to Public Speaking* Web site to review the follow-ing concepts, answer the review questions, and complete the suggested activities.

Key Concepts

confirming (50)
hearing (50)
listening (51)
interference (52)
experiential listener (53)
auditory listener (53)

visual listener (53)
listenable speech (53)
considerate speech (53)
jargon (56)
slang (57)
colloquialism (57)
euphemism (57)

gender-inclusive language (57)
culturally inclusive language (58)
spotlighting (58)
verbal clutter (59)
effective listener (62)
critical listener (65)
ethical listener (67)

Review Questions

1. Identify the times you have listened to confirm others. Were you able to recognize, acknowledge, and express value for another individual? How did you do this—verbally or nonverbally? Now identify the times you listened with "guns loaded." What are the differences between the two types of listening? Do you have a preference for one over the other? Why?

2. Monitor your listening for a day, and write down five ways your listening failed. How might you change these bad listening habits?

3. Attend a speech given by someone very different from you. Pay attention to how you manage the listening interference that comes from differences. Can you listen nonjudgmentally? Can you accommodate different speech styles, mannerisms, dress, and backgrounds? How are you able to listen even though differences may be present?

4. What listening styles best agree with you? Are you an experiential listener, an auditory listener, or a visual listener? If you can, compare your style with those of your classmates. Discuss with your classmates how you might adapt to the various styles of listening in your speeches.

5. A considerate speech eases an audience's burden of processing information by reducing interference. For your next speech assignment, make a list of three ways you can reduce interference caused by information and three ways you can reduce interference caused by language. Refer to this list as you prepare your speech.

6. What kinds of jargon do you use in your everyday interactions at school, at work, or at home? Make a list of some of the jargon you use, and define each word or phrase on your list. Now think about your next speech topic and your audience. What would be the benefits or the drawbacks of using some of this jargon in your speech?

7. Watch two speeches on the videotape that accompanies this text. Assess the speakers you listen to. Which of the interferences do they tend to produce? Do they seem conscious of their interference based on information or language? How would you work to minimize these interferences? How could they have worked to minimize the interference?

8. Make a list of the ways to listen effectively described in this chapter. Bring this list to the next speech day in your class. Using this list, practice the strategies for effective listening. Compare your experiences listening in this way to other days you have listened to speeches. What differences do you notice?

9. Watch one of the speeches on the *Invitation to Public Speaking* CD-ROM or on the videotape that accompanies this text. As you watch the speech, assess the effectiveness of your listening by completing the Effective Listening Checklist. How effectively did you listen? In what areas could you improve? How would you have interacted with the speaker if the speech was live?

10. Review the definition of ethical listening. What is the role of ethical listening in the public dialogue? Do you believe it is your responsibility to listen ethically? Do you think you can suspend judgment and listen to assess and respond to the information? Explain your answers.

11. Describe a time when you did not listen to your audience. What was the impact of this failure? How might you have remedied this situation?

12. Keep a listening journal for a week. For each day, record at least three of your listening behaviors, three successes, and three failures. How much time do you spend listening effectively, critically, and ethically? What are the advantages of each type of listening?

The *Invitation to Public Speaking* Web Site

The *Invitation to Public Speaking* Web site features the review questions about the Web sites suggested on pages 50–53 and 58, the interactive activities suggested on pages 50, 60, 65, and 68, and the InfoTrac College Edition exercises suggested on pages 60 and 65. You can access this site via your CD-ROM or at http://www.wadsworth.com/product/griffin.

Web Links

Interactive Activities

3.1: Assessing Your Listening (50)
Purpose: To assess your listening skills at this point in your public speaking course.

3.2: Eliminating Verbal Clutter (60)
Purpose: To practice eliminating excess words in a speech.

3.3: Adapting to Your Listening Style (65)
Purpose: To learn how to maximize your learning and listening styles.

3.4: Using Dialogic Listening (68)
Purpose: To learn how to use dialogic listening.

InfoTrac College Edition Exercises

3.1: Interfering with the Message (60)
Purpose: To learn how speakers can make it difficult to listen.

3.2: Sharpening Your Listening Skills (65)
Purpose: To think critically about information that speakers present.

Speech Interactive on the *Invitation to Public Speaking* CD-ROM

The following video clips of speeches referenced in this chapter are included under Speech Interactive on your *Invitation to Public Speaking* CD-ROM. After you have watched the clips, click on "Critique" to answer the questions for analysis.

Video Clip 1: Barbara Bush's Speech at Wellesley College (61). In her speech, how did Barbara Bush deal with the differences between her and her audience? How did she acknowledge differences in speech styles or appearances? How did she invite others to consider their values? How did she assume an invitational stance?

Video Clip 2: President Bush's Address to the Nation on October 7, 2001 (63). As you watch President Bush's speech, consider his speech's purpose and main points. How did he connect or relate main points? What evidence did he provide to support his main points? Also consider his delivery. Did it suit the content of his speech?

Video Clip 3: Encouraging Effective Listening: Tiffany Brisco (68). As you watch Tiffany's speech, consider how well she helps her audience listen to her speech. In what ways is her introduction compelling, dynamic, and innovative? How do you think it encouraged her audience to continue listening to her?

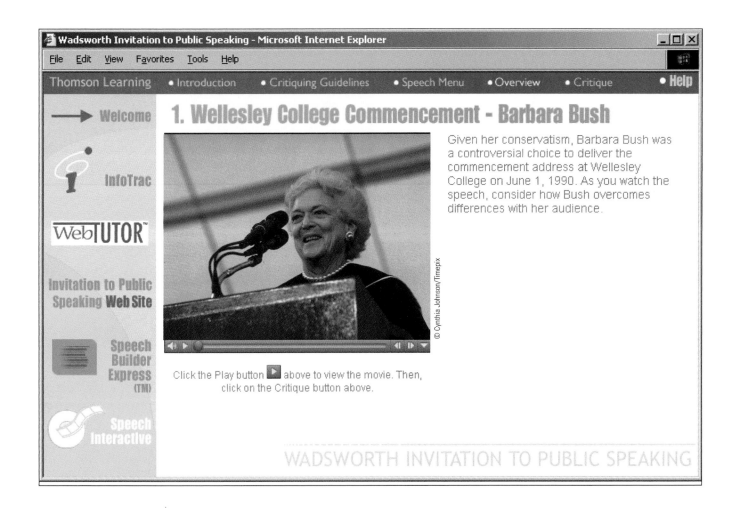

Chapter Four

Developing Your Speech Topic and Purpose

In this chapter you will learn to

Identify how context influences your speaking goals

Choose a speech topic whether you decide to speak, are asked to speak, or are required to speak

Develop clear statements of purpose for your speech

Develop the thesis statement of your speech

I am one of the most indecisive people in the world. I cannot pick out a candy bar in less than five minutes. If you can't decide on a candy bar, then imagine how hard it is to choose a speech topic. It's not that I don't have a lot of ideas. It is just that I either want to do them all and can't decide, or that I don't want to choose something that's not going to turn out well. In the end I usually decide on a topic that interests me. I figure that if it interests me then I can show true interest to the audience and captivate them that way.

—Candice Andrews, public speaking student, Colorado State University, Fall 2001

Angela has worked at her job for almost nine months. During this time, she has noticed that her company could improve its customer base if staff members paid greater attention to the quality of service they provide during customer contact. After watching one of her peers lose a third potential client in a week, she decides to talk to her boss about possible solutions to this increasingly common problem. Although she is nervous about approaching her boss, she meets with him to discuss her ideas. After a lengthy discussion, Angela and her boss decide she should put together a presentation so she can share her ideas with her coworkers at an upcoming meeting. Later, Angela wonders how she got herself into this presentation. Regardless, she figures she better start planning what she wants to say and why because her presentation is as important to her as it is to the company.

Julio is a member of the speaker's bureau for Rocks to the Top, a community-based organization that promotes rock climbing as a form of exercise, team building, self-esteem, and environmental awareness. Julio's coordinator calls him one afternoon to ask if he would speak to a group of newly hired employees at a local computer firm. The firm is interested in Rocks to the Top programs and possible training sessions for their new employees. Julio knows he is an effective speaker when he is in front of teens or local community members, but he has never presented to members of the corporate world. Before he accepts or declines the offer, he asks for some time to consider the kinds of adjustments he would need to make in his current presentation in order to meet the needs of this new audience.

Oscar put off taking public speaking until his last semester of college. For the first assignment, the professor assigns the students an informative speech on a topic they feel deeply interested in, committed to, or passionate about. Terrified, Oscar is certain he has no interests or passions and that his only commitment is to get out of the assignment somehow. "My roommate took this class," Oscar says to himself. "I'll ask him how he got out of it!" Instead, his roommate helps him brainstorm possible topics. Oscar realizes he is interested in black-and-white photography, passionate about ethical hunting and fishing, and committed to the practice of martial arts. "You could narrow any one of these into a great speech," his roommate says. "Let's think about why you'd want to talk to your class about any of these topics."

Do successful public speakers know intuitively or naturally what to say and how to say it? Your own experience probably tells you that successful public speaking is usually the result of careful planning and forethought rather than any so-called intuitive or natural speaking ability. No doubt, we can and do find ourselves in front of audiences without much advance notice. But as the examples here suggest, we are more likely to find ourselves speaking when we've had time to prepare.

Although advance preparation means work, careful planning before you speak helps you decide your speaking purpose or what you want to accomplish with your speech. It also helps you determine the best way to frame your topic so you fulfill your speaking purpose. In this chapter, we explore how you can choose speech topics and then narrow them and your purpose to accommodate three speaking contexts: when you decide to speak, when you have been asked to speak, and when you are required to speak.

How Context Influences Our Speaking Goals

In Chapter 1, you read about Lois Gibbs, who decided to speak; Ryan White, who was asked to speak; and Joseph Welch, who was required to speak. Similarly, the three scenarios at the opening of this chapter reflect the three reasons we speak publicly: Angela decided to speak, Julio was asked, and Oscar was required. Identifying the context in which you speak publicly will help you understand the connection between why we speak publicly and what we speak about.

Deciding to Speak

The most common reason to speak is that we find an issue so important or our experience so relevant, we decide to speak about it. This is also perhaps the most powerful reason people become public speakers. Before the advent of television and radio, people used a variety of platforms to share their opinions and ideas. They spoke out in churches and town halls, at street corners, in town squares or centers, and on soapboxes—wooden platforms made of soapboxes that people stood on to give a speech. So important was the power of public speech in shaping opinions and influencing actions that until the 1850s, legislation in the United States prevented certain people, such as women, from speaking publicly.

Today, people often view mass media as the voice of the public, forgetting we can and do insert our own voices into public discussions. Although most of us do not have free and easy access to the airwaves—or carry soapboxes around with us!—we do decide to speak on many occasions. In educational settings, we give class presentations and participate in student government. In social gatherings, we offer toasts and congratulations to others, or we debate current issues. In business and professional meetings, we discuss ideas and create plans. And in community forums, we speak about the environment, population growth, education, and the like. To see, for example, what the California Parent-Teacher Association (PTA) says about speaking in public about educational issues, go to http://www.capta.org/HotTips/communication.html.

When people decide to speak, as Lois Gibbs and Angela did, they generally speak about issues central to their lives and well-being. To decide to speak publicly is to decide you can offer an audience important knowledge or a valuable perspective.

Being Asked to Speak

To be asked to speak is probably the most flattering context for a public speaker. When we are asked to speak, we are asked to share a part of ourselves with others. Like Ryan White or Julio, we can share our knowledge, skills, experiences, and perspectives with others. When we are asked to speak, we are recognized as experts, or at least as someone who has information others want.

Ryan White (shown here on the left) was asked to speak publicly many times about his experiences with HIV and AIDS. For what reasons do you think you might be asked to speak? Although you may not have experienced health issues as grave as Ryan's, can you think of other experiences or expertise you have that you might be asked to speak about? If you weren't asked, would you decide or choose to speak about them in a required setting, such as your speech class?

AP/Wide World Photos

It can be exciting to think about sharing our experiences and knowledge with other people. As you move through life, you might find you are asked to speak in educational settings, at service clubs, or at formal or professional gatherings. For example, Marjorie Brody is a professional speaker who conducts workshops on how to succeed in business. Go to her Web site at http://www.marjoriebrody.com/, and consider her background and the unique experiences she brings to speaking situations. Like Brody, if you are asked to speak publicly, it is because people want to hear your views and ideas. But remember that although you may be considered an expert, you'll be a more successful speaker if you follow the principles of speech preparation discussed in this book. Expertise in a particular subject area does not always guarantee you are an expert at giving speeches.

Being Required to Speak

Being required to speak can be a regular part of our lives. For example, you're now taking a public speaking course, just like Oscar. You may have a job in marketing or as a tour guide. Occasionally, you may have to fulfill a civic or legal obligation, such as Joseph Welch did when he was asked to speak before a Senate hearing. Even though this last speaking venue might seem intimidating, recall how Welch's speech helped bring about enormous change.

When you are required to speak, you often must follow strict guidelines. For example, in a professional setting your boss may provide you with a topic, a specified amount of time, and a speaking goal and then ask you to give a presentation at a meeting. In a typical public speaking assignment, you may be asked to give an informative speech that is three minutes long, cites two sources, and includes a visual aid. Although we may not like required public speaking, learning to give speeches in a public speaking course can be invaluable. If you view a classroom speaking requirement as an opportunity to prepare for other speaking contexts, you can make the most of the time you spend in class. In a public speaking course, you are given structure and guidance that can help you improve your presentational skills and participate in the public dialogue.

These three contexts—deciding, being asked, and being required to speak—are the reasons why people enter the public dialogue. Understanding how you become a public speaker is the first step in preparing a successful presentation. Once you recognize why you are speaking, you can turn your attention to selecting and narrowing your speech topic and deciding on your purpose for speaking.

Choosing Your Speech Topic

Your **speech topic** is the subject of your speech. Selecting a topic for a speech can be a very creative and energizing part of putting a speech together. With a little systematic thought and inventive organization, speakers often come up with a wide range of interesting speech topics. By now you've probably discovered in your public speaking course that you need to choose a topic of interest to both you and your audience. The steps described in this section will help you find interesting and relevant speech topics for your required speeches. When you decide or are asked to speak, your topic is usually predetermined. Your task in these contexts is to make sure you understand your topic fully. You can do this by asking yourself several questions, which are discussed at the end of this section.

speech topic
Subject of your speech.

The Classroom Setting

Before you can select an appropriate and interesting topic for your assigned speech, you must consider the requirements of your assignment. Assigned speeches usually have several constraints because they are given in a classroom setting.

- *Preselected purpose.* An instructor usually tells you to give a particular type of speech such as a speech to inform or persuade. You do not have the freedom to select your speech purpose, and you must select a topic compatible with the purpose.

- *Time limits.* Class size determines speech length—your instructor wants to make sure everyone in the class has time to give their speeches. Classroom speeches often last only a few minutes, and you may be penalized for going over time. You must select and narrow your topic to satisfy the assignment's time limits.

- *Highly structured assignment.* You're usually asked to incorporate several specific speech components. You may be required to cite a specific number of outside sources, use visual aids, incorporate a specific style of language, or use a particular organizational pattern. The structure of an assigned speech often influences topic selection.

- *Instructor as an audience.* You give your classroom speeches to an instructor who is already a skilled public speaker. You must select a stimulating topic that your instructor, who has listened to many other speeches, will appreciate.

- *Class members as an audience.* Your classmates may become the best audience for you as a beginning public speaker—they're also learning the ropes of public speaking, and they'll appreciate your hard efforts. But they can also be a challenge because they may be interested in topics your instructor doesn't want to hear about. Additionally, they're also searching for interesting topics, so try to avoid commonly used topics.

So how do you select a manageable, interesting, and dynamic topic for your required speeches? The process takes a bit of planning and effort, but you will discover that you have a wealth of usable ideas once you organize your thoughts about who you are, what you know, and what issues and events capture your own attention.

Choosing Your Topic When You Are Required to Speak

One of the most basic ways to select a topic for a required speech is to make a list of your interests and give a speech about one of them. In this section you'll discover that with some care and time, you can build on this basic process to come up with unique and exciting slants on topics that at first may seem uninteresting.

Kate

For me, topic selection has always been random. My mind wanders, and then I roam around the library or the Internet to find what I might like to research and if I can find adequate information. I like to use many different references, such as articles, books, TV programs, and the Internet to guide my quest in finding an appropriate topic. I usually sway toward topics that interest me and will, I hope, interest others.

In a public speaking classroom, the first step to selecting a topic is to outline the requirements of the speech assignment. Write down your speech requirements at the top of your computer screen page or a piece of paper. Your assignment might look like this:

Informative purpose; 4 minutes long; 3–4 sources; 1 statistic; 1 of the following: metaphor, analogy, narrative, or alliteration; inclusive language.

The second step is to match your interests or expertise to these requirements.

Suppose you were asked to give a speech about nineteenth-century Dutch painter Vincent van Gogh. Some possible topics could be the importance of his art, the life of painters during the period in which he worked, a visit to the van Gogh museum in Amsterdam, or links between genius and insanity. What other topics can you think of that relate to van Gogh?

Matching your interests to a speaking assignment. Before you can match your interests to a particular assignment, you must determine what they are. Divide your interests into the following categories: what you like to do, what you like to talk about, and what you would like to know more about.

Most people can identify many activities they like to participate in. Make a list of them, including those that seem serious as well as playful or silly. Try to be as detailed as possible. Krista, a 23-year-old college senior, likes to do the following:

Swim, run, cycle	Spend time with her friends
Play soccer, volleyball, tennis, and Frisbee golf	Coach children in sports during the summer
Ski, roller-blade, and hike	Get good grades
Watch television and movies	Stay up late
Work with computers	Eat pizza, hamburgers, anything barbecued, and some vegetables

With a little adjustment and creativity, any of these interests could be turned into an interesting informative topic. Krista could inform her audience about any of the following:

the top ten medal-earning swimmers in the world

the history of marathon running

how to play Frisbee golf

who invented roller blades

the longest running television sitcom

the first chat room on the Web

gender differences in friendship styles

the role of laughter in reducing stress

the relationship between grades and annual income

medical research on optimal sleeping patterns

the origins of pizza

These are just a few of the many informative topics that Krista could speak about, all relevant to her instructor, her classmates, and the public dialogue.

Another good way to find speech topics is to take inventory of what you like to talk about. To do this, ask yourself the following questions:

- When do you find yourself participating in discussions?

- When do you feel like you have a lot to say about an issue but don't?

- What topics do you raise in conversations?

- What topics do you repeatedly return to or seek more information about?

For example, Keenan loves to talk about basketball. He could turn this very broad topic into a dynamic speech by going beyond the obvious. What does he love about the sport? Is it the players' skill, the strategy of the game, the politics of athletics, or the behaviors of sports fans? He could fashion a speech out of any of these topics:

He could trace the evolution of basketball as a sport.

He could discuss the advantages and disadvantages of starting children in the sport at a young age.

He could discuss the money behind the game.

He could discuss the balance between athletic talent and game strategy.

He could outline the role of sports fans in supporting individual teams.

With some creativity and effort, Keenan could turn his love of basketball into an informative, invitational, or persuasive speech.

Issues, events, people, and ideas you are curious about also often make excellent speech topics. You could give a speech that informs others of a particular event, or you could persuade them to participate in that event. If you are intrigued by a famous person, you could give a commemorative or informative speech about that person's life and accomplishments. If you are curious about a place, an idea, an object, or an animal, you could explore it with others in an informative or invitational speech. If you've always wanted to participate in an activity, but aren't sure why or how, give a persuasive, informative, or invitational speech about it. To do your own research about any of these topic ideas, you might use the Internet search engine Altavista. Go to http://www.altavista.com/sites/help to learn how. Or try Google at http://www.google.com/help. Speeches that grow out of a speaker's curiosity often capture the attention, interest, and curiosity of an audience as well.

Matching your expertise to a speech assignment. *Expertise* can be an intimidating label, but whether we realize it or not, almost everyone is an expert in some area of life. Some people are experts in obvious ways, such as playing a musical instrument, painting, or computer programming. Other people are experts in less obvious ways. They may have an unfailing sense of direction, know the right gift to buy for any occasion, or tell jokes that make people laugh. Dynamic speech topics can come from your own skills and talents. Consider the following examples:

- Rachael has a great sense of direction. She decides to give an informative speech on traveling and the five most important things to do to avoid getting lost.

- Tomás is an excellent cook. He decides to give an informative speech on the differences between traditional Bolivian and Spanish foods.

- April is fluent in American Sign Language. She decides to give a speech persuading her audience to learn a second language.

- Wilson comes from a family of artists. He decides to give a speech inviting his audience to consider the importance of supporting the arts.

These are interesting speech topics about activities or skills that may seem mundane to the person who has them. You can identify areas in which you may be considered an expert by asking yourself the following questions:

- What comes naturally to me?

- What runs in my family?

- Do I often get compliments when I do a particular thing?

- Do others repeatedly ask me to take the lead, take care of some situation, or solve a problem for them?

- Have I ever had special training or lessons?

- Have I spent years studying, practicing, or doing something?

- Do I have degrees, certifications, licenses, or other markers of my accomplishments?

If you answered yes to any of these questions, you may be an expert in some area that would make an interesting topic for a required speech. Although not all of our experiences make us experts, you might find you have expertise because of an event you've witnessed or an environment you've been in. Consider these possibilities:

- Did you live or grow up in another country?

- Did you play sports in high school or college?

- Is there something about your family that is unique or unusual?

- Have you had unexpected or momentous experiences in your life?

- Have you been exposed to other cultures, religions, and philosophies?

Situations like these can generate short speeches that satisfy the requirements of an assignment, capture the attention of your instructor and classmates, and relate directly to the public dialogue. A few final tips: As you translate your experiences into speech topics, be certain you can talk about them easily without getting upset or revealing more than you are comfortable with. And note that although you might know a lot about a topic, you should still research it to discover aspects you might be unaware of. You can use search engines like AskJeeves to help you locate information. Find out about AskJeeves at http://www.askjeeves.com/docs/about /whatIsAskJeeves.html.

Brainstorming

Brainstorming is the process of generating ideas randomly and uncritically, without attention to logic, connections, or relevance. This process requires you to free-associate rather than plan, and it is often used as a problem-solving strategy in business settings. Brainstorming can be an effective tool for coming up with speech topics in required speaking situations, and you can use this technique by yourself, in groups, or in pairs. Here are some tips for successful brainstorming:

brainstorming
Process of generating ideas randomly and uncritically, without attention to logic, connections, or relevance.

- Let your thoughts go where they will. Don't censor yourself or others. Allow all ideas, even those that seem trivial or odd.

- Write your ideas down quickly. Don't worry about spelling or punctuation, and abbreviate whenever you can.

- Keep your list handy over the course of several days, and add to it as new thoughts come to you.

There are several ways to approach brainstorming: by free association, by clustering, by categories, and by technology.

Brainstorming by free association. Brainstorming can be as unstructured as sitting at your desk with a pencil and paper, or at your computer with a blank screen, and recording all ideas that come to your mind. Although it might take a moment for the first idea to come to mind, more will come in rapid succession after that.

Brainstorming on a computer is especially effective because many people can type faster than they can write in longhand. When you record your ideas quickly, your thoughts will also flow quickly. If you use a computer, consider starting by free-associating with the computer screen turned off. Sometimes the blank screen allows you to free-associate without the pressure of filling up a blank page. At other times, seeing your ideas on the screen stimulates your thinking and spurs additional ideas.[1] After only a minute, a typical free association list might look like this:

hands, keyboard, letters, movement, running, wind, kites, children, play, laughter, skinned knees, Band-Aids, nurses, hospitals, sterile, feral cats, tiger, cougars, wilderness, encroachment, farming, ranching, cows, cowboys, rodeos, circus, clowns, entertainment, containment, buckets, garage, car, war, peace, hostility, conflict, harm, warm, cold, snow skiing, skis, lifts, chairs, dining rooms, meals, holidays, families, celebration, gifts

A free association list can go on and on until you run out of ideas. When you're trying to come up with a speech topic, try to spend at least several minutes brainstorming by free association to generate as many ideas as possible. Once you've compiled your list, explore it to determine if one of your ideas might be an appropriate speech topic. The free association list here could generate the following interesting speech topics:

the inventor of the Band-Aid

what to do when you encounter a feral cat

different kinds of clowns

how different countries celebrate holidays or the starts of new seasons

WEB SITE To practice brainstorming a speech topic by free association, complete Interactive Activity 4.1, "Basic Brainstorming," online under Student Resources for Chapter 4 at the *Invitation to Public Speaking* Web site. If brainstorming by free association doesn't generate the kinds of topics you think might make an interesting speech, other techniques might help.

Brainstorming by clustering. Clustering is a visual way to brainstorm. Write down an idea in the center of a piece of paper, and then draw four or five lines extending from it. At the ends of these lines, write down other ideas that relate to your first idea. Then, extend lines from these new ideas to even more ideas. Let's take a look at Jeret's clustering diagram. He began scuba diving at a very young age, so he used this as his general idea and developed the cluster of ideas shown in Figure 4.1.

Figure 4.1

Cluster Diagram

The figure shows that from scuba diving, his general idea, Jeret was able to branch out to many additional ideas. Brainstorming by clustering is a good way to generate speech topics because it gives some structure to the brainstorming process without limiting your possibilities too much.

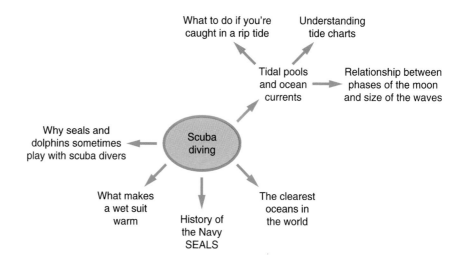

Brainstorming by categories. Most speeches given in public speaking classrooms are about concepts, events, natural phenomena, objects, people, places, plans and policies, problems, and processes. As you've probably noticed, these topics represent different categories. Brainstorming by categories is an excellent way to generate a speech topic, and it provides more structure than free association or clustering. To brainstorm by categories, list the following nine categories on your computer screen or a piece of paper. Then list five or six different words under each heading that fit into the indicated categories. Two students working together came up with this list:

Concepts	Events	Natural phenomena
world peace	Valentine's Day	aurora borealis
white supremacy	September 11, 2001	avalanches
interstellar travel	Chinese New Year	snow
communism	*quinceanera*	whirlpools
theme dining	World AIDS Day	drought
co-housing	Super Bowl	lightning

Objects	People	Places
guns	Bill Clinton	Mexico
kayaks	John Elway	Hawaii
backpacks	Ellen DeGeneres	Alaska
espresso machines	Snoop Doggy Dog	Italy
coral reefs	Condoleeza Rice	Japan
laptop computers	Bill Gates	Australia

Plans and policies	Problems	Processes
a balanced U.S. budget	national budget	making wine
socialized medicine	world hunger	puberty
decreased crime	substance abuse	making bread
eliminating unemployment	sexism	negotiating
quality public education	racism	developing film

If none of the words you write down immediately strikes you as a good speech topic, select one or two and use free association or clustering to narrow your scope, generate new ideas, or frame the topic in a way that is interesting and fits the requirements of your assignment.

Similarly, if none of your brainstormed topics catches your interest, link several of them together. Can you find a connection among Hawaii, Alaska, and Mexico? What about these locations and kayaks or whirlpools? How about laptops, espresso machines, and theme dining? Linking any of these topics together, randomly or with purpose, gives you additional opportunities to develop interesting speech topics. You might also try a method of brainstorming that assigns numerical values to topics. Learn more about this method by completing Interactive Activity 4.2, "Brainstorming for Topics," online under Student Resources for Chapter 4 at the *Invitation to Public Speaking* Web site.

WEB SITE

Brainstorming by technology. You can use technology in a number of ways to find a suitable speech topic. If you have access to the Internet, you can discover possible topics by browsing a search engine's subject indexes. Yahoo!, Lycos, and AskJeeves are popular search engines that many people are familiar with. By accessing this resource, you can explore an array of topics, click on a general subject, and link to more and more specific Web sites until you find a topic that interests you and fits the requirements of your speech assignment.

Libraries also provide many online indexes for journals, newspapers, magazines, and the like. Browse through the *Reader's Guide to Periodical Literature*, InfoTrac College Edition, *The New York Times Index,* or subject-specific indexes about medicine, physics, science, or women's studies. (In Chapter 6 you'll explore how to use these types of resources more fully.)

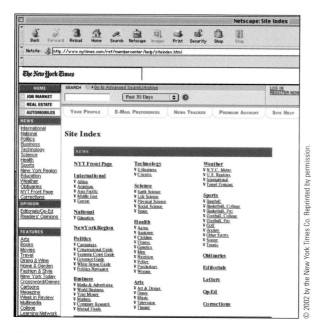

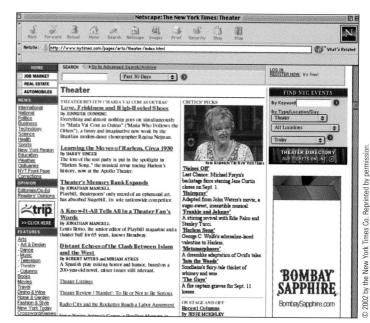

To use technology to brainstorm for a speech topic on American theater, you could click on the key word "theater" in the *New York Times Index* (left). You could then explore the articles generated by your search (right).

WEB SITE

Brainstorming with technology helps stimulate your thinking about very contemporary topics. Do your own brainstorming with technology by completing Interactive Activity 4.3, "Brainstorming with Technology," online under Student Resources for Chapter 4 at the *Invitation to Public Speaking* Web site.

Narrowing Your Topic When You Are Asked to or Decide to Speak

When we decide to speak, we are generally responding to an issue we are interested in or concerned about. When we are asked to speak, we are usually given a topic that a specific audience wants to hear about. Even though your speech topics in these contexts are predetermined, when you decide or are asked to speak you want to be sure you clearly understand what your topic is and what's expected of you as a speaker. Sometimes we decide to speak about issues that are complex or controversial, and when we are asked to speak, the requests aren't always very clear. When you decide or are asked to speak, take a moment to ask yourself, or the person who's asked you to speak, the following questions:

- What *exactly* is the topic of my speech? If I have decided to speak, what *specific* topic do I want to talk about? If I have been asked to speak, what *specific* topic does my audience want to hear about?

- Can I discuss this topic in the time allowed, or do I need to narrow or broaden my scope? Is there some aspect of this topic that I might be better able to cover in the time allowed?

- Who is my audience? What is my relationship to them? If I've decided to speak, am I qualified to speak about this topic? Will my audience see me as qualified? If not, could I change my topic or strengthen my qualifications in some way? If I've been asked to speak, why am I qualified to speak about this topic?

These questions will help you focus and narrow your topic so it is appropriate for your speaking situation. They'll also help you better understand why you want to speak or why you've been asked to speak, and what you're most qualified and prepared to speak about.

Whether you take inventory of your interests and skills, use brainstorming techniques, decide what you are motivated to speak about, or are given a topic to speak about, recognize that you are capable of generating any number of speech topics. With a little bit of creativity and organization, you can come up with speech topics that are interesting and relevant to the public dialogue.

Speech Step 4.1 / Generate a List of Possible Speech Topics

Make a list of what you like to do or want to know more about. Make this list as detailed as you can, including what you find yourself discussing with friends or what people say you're good at. Now brainstorm additional topics, using one of the techniques you read about in this chapter. Next, organize the topics you've listed by categories to help you see connections between your topics and possibly generate more. Choose ten possible speech topics for your next speech. Set them aside for now.

Articulating Your Purpose

We learned in Chapter 2 about several types of speaking and context: speaking to inform, invite, persuade and speaking on special occasions and in small groups. For each of these speaking types, the speaker has a different goal: to inform, invite, and persuade, or to introduce, commemorate, and accept. These are the goals we focus on in this chapter. Note that as a speaker in or as part of a small group, your speaking goal generally falls into one of these six categories. As such, we'll save the discussion of small group speaking's unique components until Chapter 20.

Speaking goals can be explained in terms of general purposes and specific purposes. The **general purpose** of a speech is its broad goal: to inform, invite, or persuade or to introduce, commemorate, and accept. The **specific purpose** of a speech is a focused statement that identifies exactly what a speaker wants to accomplish with a speech. Let's take a look at how you use each of these purposes to organize your thoughts about your speeches.

general purpose
A speech's broad goal: to inform, invite, persuade, introduce, commemorate, or accept.

specific purpose
Focused statement that identifies exactly what a speaker wants to accomplish with a speech.

General Speaking Purposes

Suppose your instructor asks you to speak about organic farming. You could speak about many aspects of this topic. Without knowing your purpose for your speech, it can be difficult to know where to begin. Do you describe organic farming, what it is, and who practices it (informative)? Do you ask your audience to consider the impact of organic farming on the environment and the average family's grocery bills (invitational)? Do you attempt to convince your classmates that organic farming is the most efficient type of farming (persuasive)? Do you commemorate organic farming or something about it (commemorative)? Your first step toward answering these questions is to determine your overall goal for your speech, or your general purpose:

To inform: describe, clarify, explain, define

To invite: explore, interact, exchange

To persuade: change, shape, influence, motivate

To introduce:	acquaint, present, familiarize
To commemorate:	praise, honor, pay tribute
To accept:	receive an award, express gratitude

Notice that each of these overall goals is quite different from the others. For example, the goal of acquainting is quite different from the goal of praising, which is quite different from the goal of clarifying. So, by determining your general purpose, you begin to find a focus for your speech. To consider how speaking context helps determine a speaker's general purpose, complete InfoTrac College Edition Exercise 4.1, "Speaking Publicly," featured online under Student Resources for Chapter 4.

Specific Speaking Purposes

Once you determine your general purpose, you must then determine what exactly you want to communicate to your audience, or your specific purpose. Specific speaking purposes help you narrow the focus of your speech. Similar to road maps, statements of your specific speaking purposes show you your destination and keep you from making wrong turns or missing important exits. A specific purpose states exactly what you want to accomplish in the speech. To understand the importance of a speech's specific purpose, consider again the example of Angela that opens this chapter.

Angela has decided that her general speaking purpose is to persuade. She knows she wants to convince her coworkers to change. But how exactly does she want them to change? What does she want to persuade them to do or think? If she doesn't figure this out, she will find herself going in circles as she prepares her speech—she'll research supporting material she doesn't need, and she'll get frustrated as she loses sight of what she wants to accomplish with her speech.

Angela needs to develop a specific-purpose statement, but how does she do this? First, she must identify her **behavioral objectives,** the actions she wants her audience to take at the end of her speech. After some thought, she decides that she wants her coworkers to behave differently with potential customers. She writes on a piece of paper, "I want my coworkers to respond differently with potential customers." This speech purpose is still fairly broad, but it is more focused than her general purpose, to persuade her coworkers to change.

Angela's next step is to narrow the focus of her behavioral objective even further. She must define what she means by "respond differently." She knows that her coworkers need to be more courteous, take more time answering the customer's questions, and describe the company's products more carefully. She thinks she has a pretty good system in place when she interacts with potential clients. After some thought, Angela realizes that more specifically than wanting her coworkers to respond differently, she wants them to adopt her style of working with new contacts.

So, while Angela generally wants to persuade her audience to act differently with customers, she specifically wants to persuade them to adopt her customer service program. Thus her specific-purpose statement is "I want to persuade my coworkers to adopt my customer service program." She now has a very focused idea of what she wants to communicate to her audience. She'll find it much easier to prepare a speech with a specific purpose than she would have if she'd stopped at her general purpose of wanting her audience to change.

Table 4.1 shows more examples of general and specific purposes, this time for the speech topics Julio and Oscar were considering at the opening of this chapter, as well as for the topic of organic gardening. Notice the differences between the general purposes and the specific purposes. From the six general purposes, you

behavioral objectives
The actions a speaker wants the audience to take at the end of a speech.

Table 4.1

General and Specific Speaking Purposes

GENERAL PURPOSE	SPECIFIC PURPOSE
To inform	I want to inform my audience of the programs offered by Rocks to the Top.
	I want to inform my audience of the process of planting, harvesting, and preparing organic produce.
To invite	I want to invite my audience to consider the merits of the three martial arts experts who have interviewed for our school.
	I want to invite my audience to consider the implications of turning part of our community park into organic gardening space.
To persuade	I want to persuade my audience to adopt my customer service program.
	I want to persuade my audience to buy organic produce.
To introduce	I want to introduce my audience to Maria Rodale, the editor of *Organic Gardening*.
	I want to introduce my audience to the schedule for the day's Rocks to the Top training session.
To commemorate	I want to commemorate for my audience my grandparents and the values they taught me during my summers on their organic farm.
	I want to commemorate for my audience Wong Fei Hung, one of the first well-known masters of the martial arts.
To accept	I want to accept the award from my employer for the most innovative training program successfully implemented this year.
	I want to accept the City Council's "Outstanding Community Project" award for my efforts at establishing organic community gardens in my neighborhood.

could generate specific purposes for at least twelve very different speeches. Using your *Invitation to Public Speaking* CD-ROM, watch President George W. Bush speaking to the nation after the September 11, 2001, terrorist attacks on the United States. How did the nation's expectations of him the night he gave his speech influence his purpose for speaking?

When you state your specific speaking purpose, state it clearly, remain audience centered, and use a complete sentence. Consider the following tips:

State your specific speaking purpose clearly. Begin your specific-purpose statements with the infinitive phrases *to inform, to invite, to persuade, to introduce, to commemorate,* or *to accept.* These phrases clearly indicate what your general purpose is and what you hope to accomplish with your speech. Compare the following correct and incorrect statements of purpose:

Correct	Incorrect
I will introduce Master Cho and three of his most noteworthy accomplishments to my audience.	Master Cho is talented.
I will inform my audience of the history of martial arts in the United States.	I'm going to talk about martial arts.
I will persuade my audience that practicing martial arts is an excellent form of exercise.	The martial arts are good for you.

Notice that the incorrect statements are vague, unfocused, and don't indicate the overall goal of the speech. For example, the statement "I'm going to talk about martial arts" won't help the speaker focus on a particular aspect of martial arts and prepare a manageable speech. Nor will it give an audience a sense of what direction the speech will take. In contrast, each of the correct statements provides you with a focused, solid framework from which to prepare your speech, and each lets audiences know what they can expect to hear in your speech.

Keep your audience in the forefront of your mind. Remember, you are speaking to and for a particular audience, and you research and organize your speech with this fact in mind. Your specific purpose should clearly reflect the presence of your audience. To this end, be sure your specific-purpose statement includes the words *my audience,* or a more specific synonym. Compare the following correct and incorrect statements of purpose:

Correct	Incorrect
I want to inform my audience of the process of planting, harvesting, and preparing organic produce.	The methods of growing organic produce.
I want to invite my coworkers to consider altering our current training program.	Shall we alter our training methods?
I want to persuade my audience of the importance of growing and eating organic fruit.	We should grow and eat organic fruit.
I want to commemorate for my audience Johnny Appleseed as he appears in different cultures.	Johnny Appleseed is a myth that exists in many cultures.
I want to accept and express my gratitude to the City Council and my neighbors for the "Outstanding Community Project" award.	Thank you for this "Outstanding Community Project" award.

Notice how the correct examples encourage you to reflect on the makeup of your audience in ways that the incorrect examples do not. The words "my audience," "the City Council and my neighbors," and "my coworkers" encourage the speaker to focus not on some unspecified entity, but on a specific group of people with particular traits and characteristics.

Use definitive, complete sentences. Always use definitive, complete sentences to express your specific speaking purposes. When you use a definitive statement, you assert your purpose directly and concretely. Similarly, when you use complete sentences, you articulate a purpose that is well thought out and audience centered. Compare the following correct and incorrect statements of purpose:

Correct	Incorrect
I will inform my audience of one very popular form of marital arts, karate.	Karate
I want to invite my coworkers to consider supporting local community organic gardens.	Supporting community gardening
I want to persuade my audience to work with Rocks to the Top.	Aren't they the best?

Although it may seem that the incorrect statements leave greater room for a speaker's creativity, they are too vague to be of much help when you prepare your speech. "Karate" functions better as a speech topic than as a statement of purpose. Similarly, the phrase "supporting community gardens" doesn't indicate the speaker's speech goal at all. And the question "Aren't they the best?" suggests the speaker thinks Rocks to the Top is a good organization but doesn't indicate that he wants to persuade an audience to share his views. Complete, definitive statements provide speakers with specific details from which to build a speech.

As you begin to organize your materials about your speech, write your general and specific statements of purpose at the top of all your research notes. Like any good road map, clear statements of purpose help you select and navigate the path toward putting the final touches on your presentation. For practice in thinking about specific-purpose statements, complete InfoTrac College Edition Exercise 4.2, "Creating the Specific-Purpose Statement," online under Student Resources for Chapter 4.

Library research is useful because it helps you determine your topic and then narrow it down so you can write your specific statement of purpose. What types of library materials might you search for that would help you narrow your topic?

Speech Step 4.2 / Write a General-Purpose Statement and a Specific-Purpose Statement

Using the list of topics you selected in Speech Step 4.1, write a general-purpose statement and a specific-purpose statement for each of the ten topics. For each of your speech assignments, you can complete this step and all of the subsequent Speech Steps in this text, using Speech Builder Express, your online speech organization and outlining tool accessible via your *Invitation to Public Speaking* CD-ROM. Speech Builder Express uses interactive activities, a tutor feature, and video clips to coach you from speech topic to presentation outline. Once you log in, you can create and save up to four speech outlines and, if requested, email them to your instructor.

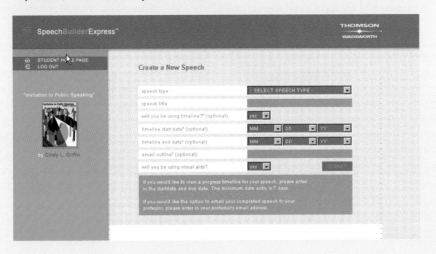

Stating Your Thesis

thesis statement
Statement that summarizes in a single declarative sentence the main proposition, assumption, or argument you want to express in your speech.

So far in this chapter you've explored how context affects your speaking goals, how to select a speech topic, and what your general and specific purposes are. Now you are ready to take the final step to complete this initial part of the speech preparation process. Every successful speech has a *thesis statement*, sometimes called a *central idea*. A **thesis statement** is a statement that summarizes in a single declarative sentence the main ideas, assumptions, or arguments you want to express in your speech. It adds focus to your specific purpose because in a thesis statement you state, in a single sentence, the exact content of your speech.

Note that the thesis statement is closely related to the specific purpose. Recall that the specific-purpose statement indicates what you want your audience to understand or do as a result of your speech. The thesis statement helps you accomplish this goal by allowing you to state in a single sentence the specific ideas you will cover in the speech. The thesis statement helps you identify the main ideas of your speech, which will become your main points for the speech (Chapter 9).

Let's look again at some specific-purpose statements from this chapter to see how they relate to thesis statements (see also Table 4.2):

Specific purpose: I want to inform my audience of the different belts in the martial arts.

With this statement, Oscar claims it is useful to understand the different belt levels in the martial arts. To focus his speech on a manageable aspect of this topic, he must determine exactly what he wants the audience to know about the martial arts belt system. He considers what he is asked most often about this topic. Thus his thesis statement looks like this:

Thesis statement: In the three most common schools of martial arts in the United States—judo, karate, and tae kwon do—the black belt is the most esteemed belt level among the slightly differing belt systems.

With his thesis statement, Oscar considers how much common knowledge there is about the marital arts as well as what people are most curious about. Additionally, his thesis statement summarizes and previews two main points:

I. Judo, karate, and tae kwon do are the most common schools of martial arts in the United States.

II. Each school has a slightly different belt system, but the black belt is the most esteemed belt level in all the schools.

Consider a second example:

Specific purpose: I want to invite my audience to consider working with Rocks to the Top.

With this specific-purpose statement, Julio claims that Rocks to the Top is a worthwhile organization. However, he doesn't want to persuade his audience to work with his agency because he wants them to be sure it's the best program for them. The thesis statement for this invitational speech is as follows:

Thesis statement: Agencies that work with Rocks to the Top improve employee attendance, productivity, and creativity, and a frank discussion about our services could help my audience decide whether Rocks to the Top is the right program for them.

Table 4.2

General and Specific Purpose and Thesis Statement

INFORMATIVE SPEECH

General purpose:	To inform
Specific purpose:	To inform my audience of the three most important things to do to avoid getting lost while traveling
Thesis statement:	The three simple things travelers can do to avoid getting lost are to carry maps, plan out the route before-hand, and ask directions from knowledgeable sources.
General purpose:	To inform
Specific purpose:	To inform my audience about where to seek shelter during a tornado
Thesis statement:	When a tornado strikes, seek shelter in a storm cellar, a fortified storm closet, or your bathtub.

INVITATIONAL SPEECH

General purpose:	To invite
Specific purpose:	To invite my audience to consider supporting the arts in our community
Thesis statement:	The arts have played a very important role in my life, enhance the quality of life in any community, and may be something my audience wants to support.
General purpose:	To invite
Specific purpose:	To invite my audience to explore the pros and cons of retaining the death penalty in the United States
Thesis statement:	I'd like to describe the benefits and drawbacks of retaining the death penalty in the United States, then explore with my audience whether this punishment is still appropriate for serious crimes.

PERSUASIVE SPEECH

General purpose:	To persuade
Specific purpose:	To persuade my audience to spay or neuter their pets
Thesis statement:	Spaying or neutering pets is easy and affordable, and helps prevent having to put down thousands of unwanted kittens and puppies each year.
General purpose:	To persuade
Specific purpose:	To persuade my audience to learn a second language
Thesis statement:	When we learn a second language, not only do we learn to appreciate the culture of the people who speak that language, we also increase our understanding of our own culture.

This thesis statement summarizes and previews three main points, two that address content and one that opens the floor to discussion:

I. Rocks to the Top has helped decrease employee illness and burnout and increase employee creativity.

II. Rocks to the Top provides a range of services, including hands-on activities as well as those that require personal reflection rather than activity.

III. Given this overview, a discussion could help my audience decide if Rocks to the Top is appropriate for them.

Now consider a third example:

Specific purpose: I want to persuade my audience to eat organic fruit.

This statement makes the claim that organic fruit is good for you. To persuade your audience to eat it (what you want to accomplish), you must refine this statement to explain *why* eating organic fruit is good for you (what you will say to accomplish your goal). In explaining why, your thesis statement begins to take shape:

Thesis statement: Because organic fruit does not contain the dangerous chemicals found in nonorganic fruit, it is far healthier for people to eat and better for the environment.

This thesis statement indicates that the speech will consist of four main points:

I. Organic fruits do not contain dangerous chemicals.

II. Organic fruits are grown in ways that make them healthier to eat than nonorganic fruits.

III. Organic fruits are grown in ways that are safe for the environment.

WEB SITE To help you distinguish between effective and ineffective thesis statements, complete Interactive Activity 4.4, "Identifying Thesis Statements," online under Student Resources for Chapter 4 at the *Invitation to Public Speaking* Web site. The clarity and focus you get when you develop your thesis statement and main points guides your research efforts and supporting materials, your reasoning, and your organizational patterns (Chapters 6, 7, 8, and 9). Use your thesis statement in combination with your general and specific statements of purpose and to help you identify your main points. You can then move to the next steps of putting your speech together.

Speech Step 4.3 / Write a Thesis Statement

Choose five of the topics you wrote purpose statements for in Speech Step 4.2. Write a thesis statement for each. Is your thesis statement a single declarative sentence? Does it state the main ideas, assumptions, or arguments you want to express? Does it include the ideas you want to cover in your speech?

Review this list and select the speech you're most interested in. Why do you like this one more than the others? Does it best fit the assignment your instructor has given you, your audience, or your own personal preferences? Access Speech Builder Express for help in writing thesis statements and to watch a video clip of a speech introduction that includes an effective thesis statement. You can also watch video clips of two student speakers, Rebecca Ewing and Jesse Rosser, delivering thesis statements under Speech Interactive on the *Invitation to Public Speaking* CD-ROM.

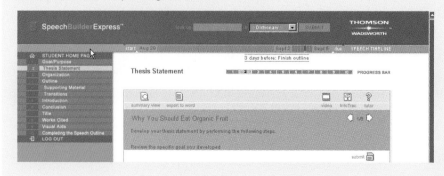

Chapter Summary

Understanding the context in which you speak will help you prepare effective speeches. When you decide to speak, you do so because an issue is so important that you feel drawn to speak out about it. When you are asked to speak, you do so because you have been asked to share information with others. When you are required to speak, you do so because you are obligated to give a speech. Although you may be required to speak in your public speaking class, you will find that in the future you will more often decide or be asked to give speeches.

When you choose a speech topic, consider the purpose of your speech, your time constraints, and your audience. If you are giving a speech in a classroom setting, also consider the specifics of your assignment. You can choose a speech topic randomly or by using a more systematic approach. Take stock of your interests by making a list of what you like to talk about or of what people say you're good at. Narrow the focus of your speech by matching your interests and expertise to your speech assignment. Or generate a list of possible speech topics by brainstorming. You can brainstorm by free association, by clustering, by categories, or by using technology.

Once you've identified possible topics for your speech, determine your general purpose for your speech: to inform, to invite, to persuade, to introduce, to commemorate, or to accept. Your next step is to identify your specific purpose by stating exactly what you want to accomplish with your speech. Write specific-purpose statements so your speaking purpose is clear, you're keeping the audience in the forefront of your mind, and you're using definitive and complete sentences. Finally, refine your speech topic further by writing your thesis statement, a single declarative sentence that summarizes the main points of your speech. Thesis statements indicate what you want to say in your speech in order to accomplish your speaking goal. They also preview the content of your speech for your audience.

How do successful speakers seem to know naturally what to say and how to say it? Much of what we label "natural talent" is really the result of advanced planning, careful organization, and a willingness to use the resources available. Although speech preparation does take time, the guidelines provided in this chapter will help you begin to put together a speech that meets the needs of your speaking context and your audience.

Invitation to Public Speaking Online

After reading this chapter, use your CD-ROM and the *Invitation to Public Speaking* Web site to review the following concepts, answer the review questions, and complete the suggested activities.

Key Concepts

speech topic (81)

brainstorming (85)

general purpose (89)

specific purpose (89)

behavioral objectives (90)

thesis statement (94)

Review Questions

1. List the occasions when you have decided, been asked, or been required to speak publicly. What did you like about each speaking occasion? What do you wish you could have changed? If you've never decided to speak publicly, or haven't been asked, when do you think you would be?

2. Use the strategies suggested in this chapter to make a list of four different speech topics you might like to speak about. How do you think the classroom setting

would affect what you would say about these topics? What would you do to make these topics suitable for a classroom setting?

3. Rewrite the following incorrect specific-purpose statements so they are correct:

   To give 10 percent of your annual income to charity

   Geraldine Ferraro, Elizabeth Dole, and Hillary Rodham Clinton

   The Nobel Peace Prize

   Terrorism

   Isn't the level of water pollution in our local river too high?

4. Make a list of speech topics you might decide to speak about. For each topic, identify why you've decided to speak and who your audience would be. How might your reasons for speaking and your audience affect what you say about your topics? Write a general-purpose and a specific-purpose statement for at least one of these topics. Is this a speech you might give in your speech course? Why or why not?

5. Make a list of speech topics you might be asked to speak about. For each topic, identify why someone might ask you to speak and who your audience would be. Now write a general and a specific statement of purpose for at least one of these topics. Is this a speech you might give in your speech course? Why or why not?

6. Practice writing a general and a specific statement of purpose for a speech on each of the following topics:

   teen violence   mandatory military service

   women in athletics   bilingual education

   Now write a thesis statement for each of these possible speeches and identify the main points for each. Could you choose one of these possible speeches for your next speech? Why or why not?

The *Invitation to Public Speaking* Web Site

The *Invitation to Public Speaking* Web site features the review questions about the Web sites suggested on pages 79–80 and 84–85, the interactive activities suggested on pages 86, 87, 88, and 96, and the InfoTrac College Edition exercises suggested on pages 90 and 93. You can access this site via your CD-ROM or at http://www.wadsworth.com/product/griffin. To access Speech Builder Express in order to complete Speech Steps 4.2 and 4.3, you will need the username and password included under "Speech Builder Express" on your CD-ROM.

Web Links

4.1: California PTA Communicating Tips (79)
4.2: Marjorie Brody (80)
4.3: Altavista and Google Help (84)
4.4: AskJeeves.com (85)

Interactive Activities

4.1: Basic Brainstorming (86)
Purpose: To explore basic brainstorming techniques.

4.2: Brainstorming for Topics (87)
Purpose: To explore a point-value system of brainstorming for topics.

4.3: Brainstorming with Technology (88)
Purpose: To explore brainstorming with technology.

4.4: Identifying Thesis Statements (96)
Purpose: To identify and evaluate thesis statements.

 ## InfoTrac College Edition Exercises

4.1: Speaking Publicly (90)
Purpose: To understand the constraints and restrictions of various speaking contexts.

4.2: Creating the Specific-Purpose Statement (93)
Purpose: To assess a speaker's specific purpose.

Speech Interactive on the *Invitation to Public Speaking* CD-ROM

The following video clips of speeches referenced in this chapter are included under Speech Interactive on your *Invitation to Public Speaking* CD-ROM. After you have watched the clip, click on "Critique" to answer the questions for analysis.

Video Clip 1: President Bush's Speech on September 11, 2001 (91). Did President Bush decide to speak after the attacks on New York City and Washington, D.C., on September 11, 2001? Was he asked to speak? Was he required to speak? What were the expectations of his audience on this occasion? To what degree do you think Bush fulfilled those expectations?

Video Clips 2 and 3: Student Speeches: Effective Thesis Statements (96). Watch the introduction of Rebecca Ewing's persuasive speech on graduated licensing and listen for her thesis statement. Does her thesis statement state in a declarative sentence the main proposition, assumption, or argument she wants to express in her speech? Now watch the introduction of Jesse Rosser's persuasive speech on preventing school violence and listen for his thesis statement. Does his thesis statement state the specific ideas he will cover in his speech?

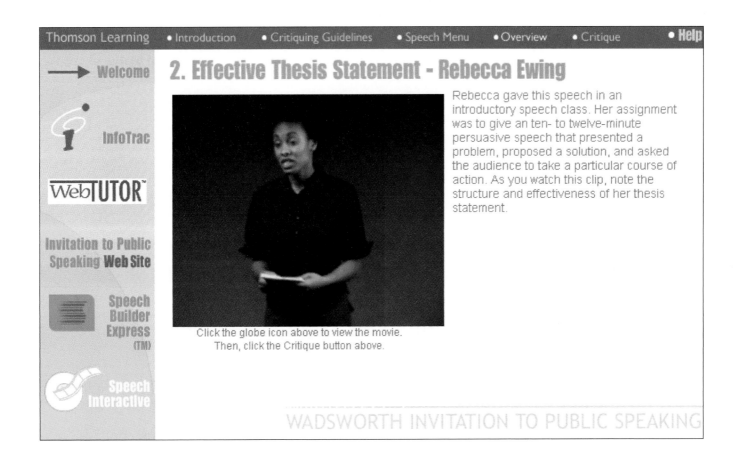

Chapter Five

Your Audience and Speaking Environment

In this chapter you will learn to

Define what an audience is

Conduct a demographic audience analysis

Adapt to an audience that is both a diverse group of people and a unique community

Identify the influence of a speaking environment on an audience

Identify strategies for adapting to audience expectations for a speech

It is "the hearer that determines the speech's end and object," Aristotle said. In tackling the problems of the community, the speaker's art is in deciding, in choosing theme and thought, structure and style. All elements dictated by purpose, yes, but also as influenced by the audience and occasion.

—Harold Barrett, *Rhetoric and Civility: Human Development, Narcissism, and the Good Audience,* 1991[1]

dialogue
An interaction, connection, and exchange of ideas and opinions with others.

audience centered
Acknowledging your audience by considering and listening to the unique, diverse, and common perspectives of its members before, during, and after your speech.

When you give a speech, you add your voice to the public dialogue. By definition, a dialogue involves more than one person, more than just a speaker presenting a message to some unknown, unseen entity. To engage in a **dialogue** is to interact, connect, and exchange ideas and opinions with others. When you engage in the *public* dialogue, you recognize that the speaker and the audience are equally important, that both have opinions, feelings, and beliefs. To be a successful public speaker, you must acknowledge these realities and listen carefully to your audience before, during, and after your speech.

One of the most effective ways you can listen to your audience is by adopting an audience-centered perspective. To be **audience centered** is to acknowledge your audience by considering and listening to the unique, diverse, and common perspectives of its members before, during, and after your speech. Although you want to consider what your audience thinks, feels, and believes, being audience centered does not mean you can manipulate your audience or that you must compromise your message. In other words, you don't want to say only what your audience agrees with or wants to hear. Rather, being audience centered means you understand the positions and perspectives of your audience so you can craft a listenable message. To help you begin to think about being audience centered, visit http://www.ncte.org/traci/tens/013.html and consider how you might relate to your audience more effectively.

In Chapter 3, you learned how to listen to your audience during a speech in order to better respond to their needs. In this chapter you will build on those skills and learn how to best understand your audiences by exploring what an audience is, why there are different types of audiences, how speaking environments affect audiences, and how you can apply what you learn about your audience and speaking environment to help others listen to your speech.

What Is an Audience?

We often use the term *audience* without much thought. We prepare our speeches with our "audience in mind," we want to "persuade our audience" of something, and we "sit in the audience" as we listen. But what does the term *audience* really mean? Who and what makes up an audience, and how should speakers think about this very important group of people? Tracing the evolution of the word *audience* helps us understand the diverse nature of audiences and gain insight into how we can best communicate with them.

The word *audience* comes from the Latin root *audire,* which means "to hear." The English word *audience* was coined in the fourteenth century, and at that time it referred to a formal hearing in front of a court official, magistrate, or sovereign. People were granted "an audience" by someone in a position of authority, meaning they were given the privilege of having their concerns heard and, they hoped, of receiving some sort of assistance.

People did not gather together to form "an audience" as we commonly think of the term until the eighteenth century. By that time, European and North American societies had changed a great deal. Trade routes had opened up, cities had grown and become centers of commerce and information exchange, and groups of people had started to meet and discuss publicly their common issues of interest. By the 1700s, the term *audience* came to mean "the hearing of one that speaks, or the Assembly of Hearers."[2]

In the nineteenth and twentieth centuries, with the advent of mass media and technologies such as offset printing, the telegraph, television, and computers, the definition of an audience changed again. Because technology allows us to be an audience member and never leave our homes or computer screens, an "audience" has become simply "people who listen."

For the purpose of this public speaking text, **audience** is defined as a group of people who gather to listen. Although this definition is simple, we recognize that audiences are far more complex than the definition suggests. Modern audiences are composed of a diverse group of people exposed to endless messages from the media, their workplaces, their families and friends, and many other sources. Despite all these demands on the listening time of a highly diverse group of people, you can learn a number of skills to help you address an audience effectively. Let's start by exploring both the individual and collective nature of audiences.

audience
Group of people who gather to listen.

Considering an Audience as a Group of Diverse People

Have you ever noticed that for each similarity you find you have with someone, you also find a difference? Perhaps you and a friend love action films, popcorn, and state-of-the-art theaters. Yet one of you loves a bargain matinee, to sit up close, and to pour on the butter, whereas the other is happiest settling in at the back of the theater for the late night show with no butter at all. You are similar, yet you are different.

People are unique for a variety of reasons that relate to some combination of culture, upbringing, experiences, personality, and even genetics.[3] Like you and your movie-going friend, no two people are alike, and it is this uniqueness that sets us apart and makes us interesting. But groups of people are often also similar to one another in many ways. As public speakers, how can we give a speech that takes into consideration an audience's conflicting differences and similarities? First, try to consider how your audiences view the world by analyzing their master statuses and their standpoints.

Master Statuses

Groups of people share common experiences, perspectives, and attitudes because they occupy certain master statuses. **Master statuses** are significant positions occupied by a person within society that affect that person's identity in almost all social situations.[4] A person's master statuses might include race or ethnicity, sex, physical ability, sexual orientation, age, economic standing, religion or spirituality, and educational level. They could include positions in society like being a parent, child, or sibling, or being employed or unemployed, and so on, if those positions affect someone's identity in almost every social situation.

master statuses
Significant positions occupied by a person within society that affect that person's identity in almost all social situations.

Master statuses are an important part of our identity that affect us in almost all social situations. What master statuses might be affecting the ability of this audience to listen to the speaker? What master statuses might be affecting the speaker's ability to connect with the audience?

© Wolfgang Kaehler/CORBIS

Miranda

I have many master statuses. I am a daughter dedicated to her family and her family values. I am forever a student, always craving new knowledge. I am a first-generation student, boldly going where no one else in my family has gone before—college. I am a Mexican American living life for my ancestors. Last, but not least, I am curious, always searching for new adventures in life. All of this makes up who I am and affects every decision I make each day, from what clothes I choose to wear to the books I choose to read. It also affects what topics I choose to speak about and how effectively I listen to other speakers.

A status is a *master* status when it profoundly influences a person's identity and the way in which he or she is perceived by others. Whether we intend to or not, we often respond to other people based on one or more master statuses. For example, teenagers with rumpled and baggy clothes are often treated differently in a grocery store than are neatly dressed women in their 30s who have children. Whether or not our assumptions about these people are correct (teenagers will cause problems, mothers are responsible and will manage their children), we categorize and respond to people based on the positions they hold in society.

Master statuses affect our view of the world because certain master statuses are seen as more valuable than others. For example, whether we are comfortable acknowledging such differences or not, our culture tends to rank whiteness, heterosexuality, and masculinity higher than being a person of color, gay or lesbian, and female. Because the first three statuses are considered more valuable, they are rewarded more (higher salaries, more acceptance and protections, more personal freedoms) than the last three (lower salaries, less acceptance and fewer protections, and greater threats to physical safety).[5]

Standpoints, Attitudes, Beliefs, and Values

standpoint
Perspective from which a person views and evaluates society.

The impact of unequal treatment because of master statuses can affect an individual's **standpoint**, the perspective from which a person views and evaluates society. Members of your audiences will have different standpoints, or views of society. This is because they will have different master statuses and thus different experiences. For example, teenagers often see life as unfairly biased against them, and the mother often sees the world as expecting her and her children to behave perfectly in all situations.

Note that although master statuses can have a powerful influence on a person's view of the world, master statuses do not *determine* a person's standpoint. For example, not all women believe they need to have children to fully experience womanhood, just as not all men believe their masculinity is weakened if they are not the primary breadwinners for their families. Additionally, we all occupy numerous master statuses throughout our lives, and each influences us in different ways. For example, although we maintain our ethnicity throughout our lives, we move from young to old, child to parent, unemployed to employed, and so on.

Our standpoints influence our attitudes, beliefs, and values. An **attitude** is a general positive or negative feeling a person has about something. Attitudes reflect our likes and dislikes, our approval or disapproval of events, people, or ideas.[6] A **belief** is a person's idea of what is real or true or not. Beliefs are more conceptual than attitudes and reflect what we think we know about the world. A **value** is a person's idea of what is good, worthy, or important. Our values reflect what we think is an ideal world or state of being. Values help us determine whether we think a person, idea, or thing is acceptable in our worldview.[7]

Conversations, debates, and arguments held as part of the public dialogue are heavily influenced by the different attitudes, beliefs, and values that result from our different standpoints and master statuses. Additionally, attitudes, beliefs, and values are influenced by our cultural backgrounds. All cultures have unique ways of explaining and organizing the world. As a speaker, you must make a point to recognize these different worldviews and guard against ethnocentrism. **Ethnocentrism** is the belief that our own cultural perspectives, norms, and ways of organizing society are superior to others. When we hold ethnocentric views, we see other cultures as odd, wrong, or deficient because they do not do things the way we do. Speakers who let ethnocentric views come through in their speeches run the risk of alienating audiences who do not hold similar views. To consider how President George W. Bush addressed ethnocentrism in a speech he made about terrorism, complete Interactive Activity 5.1, "Avoiding Ethnocentrism," online under Student Resources for Chapter 5 at the *Invitation to Public Speaking* Web site.

To be audience centered, speakers must consider the significant influence of master statuses, standpoints, attitudes, beliefs, values, and culture on audiences. When speakers take these things into consideration, they increase their chances of giving effective speeches. Professional speaker Lenny Laskowski offers a handy mnemonic device to help you consider the importance of adapting to your audience. (A mnemonic device is a rhyme, phrase, or other verbal device that makes information easier to remember.) Check out his Web site at http://www.ljlseminars.com/audience.htm. To think about adapting a message to five different audience types, go to the Web site Five Audience Types at http://www.engr.washington.edu/~tc231/audience_analysis/5audiences.html.

Demographic Audience Analysis

How does recognizing your audience's master statuses and standpoints help you become a better speaker? By using master statuses as guideposts for crafting your speech, you can try to anticipate the potential impact your speech topic, language, and so on, might have on your audience. Are members of your audience first-year high school students or married graduate students? Are they of a

attitude
General positive or negative feeling a person has about something.

belief
A person's idea of what is real or true or not.

value
A person's idea of what is good, worthy, or important.

ethnocentrism
Belief that our own cultural perspectives, norms, and ways of organizing society are superior to others.

WEB SITE

certain ethnicity? What types of jobs do they hold? Are they grandparents? What are their educational backgrounds? How might each of these master statuses influence the standpoints of your audience members? Once you've answered these types of questions, you can consider the attitudes, beliefs, and values of your audience more completely. This will help you adapt the message of your speech to your audience.

A common way to determine the master statuses of an audience is to conduct a demographic audience analysis. A **demographic audience analysis** is an analysis that identifies the particular population traits of an audience. Demographic characteristics include age, country of birth or origin, ethnicity and race, physical ability or disability, position in a family (parent, child), religious orientation, and sex (male or female). You can gather demographic information by interviewing your audience personally, through a survey, or by researching the Internet. Using the Internet is best when you want to find information about a large general group of people, such as the citizens of a town, county, or region. For example, you can find demographics for cities and regions at About.com's Geography site at http://geography.about.com (start at the Subject list on the left of the page). Or you can explore a variety of demographic statistics about the United States by going to the Web site of the U.S. Census at http://www.census.gov. However, to gather targeted information about your specific audience, you must interview your audience directly or conduct a survey.

You can conduct a demographic analysis before your speech by asking your audience to fill out a survey that asks about demographic information and attitudes, beliefs, and values. Surveys ask two primary types of questions: open ended and close ended. **Open-ended questions** are questions that allow respondents to answer in an unrestricted way. An example of an open-ended question is "What are your reactions to the president's policy on terrorism?" People asked this question are free to respond with any answer they like. A **closed-ended question** requires respondents to choose an answer from two or more alternatives. Examples of closed-ended questions are "Do you support the president's policy on terrorism?" (requires a yes or no answer) and "On a scale of 1 to 5, with 5 indicating the highest support, how do you rate the president's policy on terrorism?" (requires one rating out of five possible alternatives).

You can find a sample survey online under Student Resources for Chapter 5 at the *Invitation to Public Speaking* Web site. When you construct your survey, follow these guidelines:

- Keep your survey short (one or two pages).
- Keep your questions short and focused on one idea at a time.
- Use clear and simple language.
- Keep your own biases out of the survey.
- Provide room for respondents to write their comments.

Your goal in analyzing your audience is to give an audience-centered speech. Remember that although master statuses can be powerfully influential, people can experience them in very different ways. Speakers must understand that we are all unique, that we experience life differently, and that we grow and change over time. When conducting a demographic analysis and considering master statuses, it can sometimes be easy to forget individual differences and resort to stereotyping. A **stereotype** is a broad generalization about an entire group based on limited knowledge or exposure to only certain members of that group. Stereotyping is harmful because we make assumptions based on incomplete information. It may seem comforting to be able to predict certain behaviors based on a stereotype, but we can usually find many exceptions to any stereotype. Remember, audiences are

---

demographic audience analysis
Analysis that identifies the particular population traits of an audience.

open-ended question
Question that allows the respondent to answer in an unrestricted way.

close-ended question
Question that requires the respondent to choose an answer from two or more alternatives.

stereotype
Broad generalization about an entire group based on limited knowledge or exposure to only certain members of that group.

WEB SITE

Surveys are an excellent way to gather information about your audience's attitudes, beliefs, and values. What kind of information would you want to gather about your audience? Would you use open-ended or closed-ended questions to obtain this information?

© Michael Newman/PhotoEdit

a collection of people with unique experiences and personalities, and you cannot lump them into one universal category.

You can explore a wide range of audience analysis tools by completing Interactive Activity 5.2, "Learning About Your Audience," online under Student Resources for Chapter 5 at the *Invitation to Public Speaking* Web site. A specific type of audience analysis tool is a psychographic analysis. To explore one type of psychographic analysis, a VALS survey, and create and administer a similar survey for your audience, complete Interactive Activity 5.3, "Using Psychographic Analysis," online under Student Resources for Chapter 5 at the *Invitation to Public Speaking* Web site.

WEB SITE

WEB SITE

Speech Step 5.1 / Conduct a Demographic Audience Analysis

To learn about the group of people who make up your audience, use the sample survey on the *Invitation to Public Speaking* Web site to conduct a demographic audience analysis before your next speech. Using the information you gather, identify your audience's master statuses, standpoints, attitudes, beliefs, and values. As you prepare your speech, be sure to remain flexible about the influences of master statuses on your audience, and avoid stereotyping.

Considering an Audience as a Community

Although audiences begin with individuals who bring various standpoints to a presentation, they rapidly become a community of people joined together in some way, if only temporarily. Understanding how an audience comes together as a temporary community helps speakers stay audience centered.

Angelina Grimke is an example of a speaker who managed to stay audience centered despite speaking in a hostile environment.

Voluntary Audiences

Just as speakers decide something is significant enough to speak out about, people come together as audiences because they find something significant enough to listen to. These audiences are voluntary: they have chosen to be present. An example of a voluntary audience is the Million Man March in Washington, D.C., in 1994, which brought African American men from across the country together to discuss issues of family, race, and masculinity. Public celebrations and commemorations, such as Super Bowl victories or the return of a famous person to a hometown, also bring audiences together voluntarily. And tragedies, like the Oklahoma bombings or the Columbine school shootings, often draw people together.

The need to listen unites people with various master statuses and standpoints. This means that most audiences are quite diverse. As a result, they may agree or disagree with a speaker or with one another. Consider the true story of Angelina Grimke and the choices she made when speaking to a voluntary, but very diverse, audience. Speaking in Philadelphia in 1838, Angelina Grimke faced an audience of several thousand people. Although some were supportive of her cause, abolition and the right of women to speak in public, others were quite hostile. Even before she began to speak, an angry mob gathered outside the speaking hall and began to push at the bolted doors, shout insults, and throw rocks at the side of the building.

When she stood to speak, some of her audience began to howl. But Grimke had considered her audience well in advance, and she knew that many would disagree with both her message and her presence on the stage. (At the time it was illegal for women to speak in public to audiences of both women and men.) Months earlier she had worked out a speaking strategy she thought might encourage audiences to get past their resistance to her. In this earlier speech, Grimke adopted a biblical persona as she spoke, comparing herself to the biblical heroine Esther. Esther had dared to speak to the king of Persia and plead for the lives of her fellow slaves, and Grimke likened her situation to Esther's. The strategy worked and although the audience was hostile at first, they calmed down enough to listen to her speak.

In her speech in Philadelphia, Grimke changed her strategy slightly, adopting a masculine persona, some say that of the prophet Isaiah. In this more assertive tone, she challenged the violence taking place outside the building, saying, "Those voices without tell us that the spirit of slavery is *here*." She demanded her audience think: "What is a mob? . . . What if the mob should now burst in upon us, break up our meeting and commit violence upon our persons—would this be anything compared with what the slaves endure?" [8]

Grimke's strategy worked, and her audience quieted enough for her to speak. The heckling from inside the hall stopped soon after she began to speak, and not a person in the audience left her speech, even though they too were in danger from the mob outside. Considered one of the most important speakers of the abolition and women's rights movements, Angelina Grimke is an excellent example of an audience-centered speaker, even in the most difficult of situations.

Although it is tempting to think that voluntary audiences are easier for speakers to address, the example of Angelina Grimke suggests this is not always so. However, voluntary audiences usually have an active interest in your topic. This fact certainly works to your advantage as a speaker, and staying audience centered will only help you deliver your message effectively, no matter what your speaking situation. For practice in identifying whether a speaker is audience centered or not, complete InfoTrac College Edition Exercise 5.1, "Being Audience Centered," online under Student Resources for Chapter 5 at the *Invitation to Public Speaking* Web site.

When speakers face involuntary audiences, they face a number of challenges. What might this speaker do to minimize these challenges and stay audience centered?

Involuntary Audiences

Just as speakers are sometimes required to give a speech, people sometimes form an audience because they must. These audiences are involuntary: they might prefer to not be present. Examples of involuntary audiences are students in required public speaking courses and employees in mandatory business meetings. Some involuntary audiences have little or no interest in your topic. As such, they may display open hostility toward you and your topic or a disconcerting lack of attention and involvement. For example, in your public speaking class, some of your classmates would rather not hear about certain topics because of their own strong beliefs, yet they are forced to sit and listen. Others seem to only stare blankly at you. Still others ignore you and work on other projects while you are speaking. Unfortunately, you may encounter the same behaviors in your professional and social worlds—some audiences attend a speech only because their job requires it or because of family or social obligations. However, with a little forethought and effort, most involuntary audiences can be brought into the public dialogue.

For the speaker facing an involuntary audience, being audience centered may mean the difference between an ineffective and a successful speech. Before you give your speech, talk with the person who asked you to speak. Discover why your audience is required to attend. Or at the beginning of your speech, ask your audience members why they've been asked to listen to you. Then address those issues in your speech. For example, if you are presenting to an audience that is part of a mandatory training program, ask about the rationale for the training, the goals of the training, and what your audience hopes to gain by the training. Knowing this information will help you design and present a message that is relevant and useful.

Similarly, if an audience opposes your topic, learn why so you can confirm and be confirmed by an involuntary audience. Before you speak, ask your audience to write down their concerns and pass them to you, or gather this information several days earlier. The feedback you receive will help you thoughtfully address an audience's concerns, frustrations, or resistance. This audience-centered approach opens up dialogue rather than forcing ideas on people. You let your audience know you are working to understand them as you ask them to do the same for you.

Think back to the times you have been forced to listen to a presentation. What caused you not to want to be there? What caused you to shut down and remain unreceptive? Was it the topic, the setting, the speaker, or simply because you felt you had little choice about being present? The answers to these questions can help you adjust your message, design a presentation that is relevant and interesting, and demonstrate understanding for your audience.

Finally, if you are speaking to an involuntary audience, try a little **empathy** by trying to see and understand the world as another person does. What would motivate you to listen to a topic you disagreed with or a presentation you were required to listen to? If you adopt this empathic, audience-centered approach, your involuntary audience may be delightfully surprised by your presentation and welcome you as a speaker.

 To consider the type of a particular audience and the degree to which the speaker was able to adjust the message for the audience, complete InfoTrac College Edition Exercise 5.2, "Identifying Audiences," online under Student Resources for Chapter 5 at the *Invitation to Public Speaking* Web site.

So far you've discovered you must consider both the individual and collective nature of audiences, you've explored why audiences come together at all, and you've learned how you can engage an involuntary audience. Audience-centered speakers keep all these factors in mind as they prepare and present their speeches. In the next section, you'll learn techniques to help you manage your speaking environment effectively.

empathy
Trying to see and understand the world as another person does.

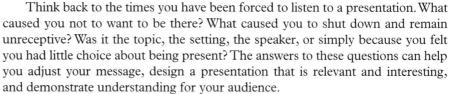

Speech Step 5.2 / Determine Whether Your Audience Is Voluntary or Involuntary

Consider the audience of your next speech. Are they a voluntary audience, present because they are interested in your topic and want to hear what you have to say? Or are they involuntary, present because they have to be? If they are a voluntary audience, adapt to your audience by identifying the various perspectives they have about your topic. If they are an involuntary audience, discover why and adapt your speech to better suit their needs. What are some ways in which you can communicate your empathy for them?

Considering Your Speaking Environment

Before audience-centered speakers give a speech, they must discover as much as they can about their *speaking environment* or where and when they will speak, so they can manage their speaking situation with relative ease. Effective speakers must consider such situational factors as the size of the audience and the physical arrangement of the speaking site, the availability of technology, what time of day they'll be speaking, where their speech falls in a series of presentations, and the length of time they have to speak.

Size and Physical Arrangement

The size of an audience and the physical arrangement of a speaking situation may seem like small matters, but they can have a powerful effect on a speaking environment. You can enhance your ability to connect with your audience if you consider these matters carefully before your speech and adapt to them during your speech. Consider the following example:

> I found [him] alone in an empty basketball locker room moments before he was to speak before a crowd of six thousand at Arizona State University, calmly sipping tea. "Your Holiness, if you're ready . . ."
>
> He briskly rose, and without hesitation he left the room, emerging into the thick backstage throng of local reporters, photographers, security personnel, and students—the seekers, the curious, and the skeptical. He walked through the crowd smiling broadly and greeting people as he passed by. Finally passing through a curtain, he walked on stage, bowed, folded his hands, and smiled. He was greeted with thunderous applause. At his request, the house lights were not dimmed so he could clearly see his audience, and for several moments he simply stood there, quietly surveying the audience with an unmistakable expression of warmth and good will. For those who had never seen the Dalai Lama before, his maroon and saffron monk's robes may have created a somewhat exotic impression, yet his remarkable ability to establish rapport with his audience was quickly revealed as he sat down and began his talk.
>
> "I think that this is the first time I am meeting most of you. But to me, whether it is an old friend or new friend, there's not much difference anyway, because I always believe we are the same; we are all human beings. . . ."[9]

It might seem that a large audience, a group of journalists and security guards, and a wide stage would mean distance and disruption for a speaker, but not necessarily. Despite these potentially difficult physical settings, the Dalai Lama stayed audience centered by engaging with his audience personally. He asked that the house lights be left on, and he took the time to make eye contact with his audience, acknowledging a connection to each audience member. He took advantage of his setting rather than letting it control him. But how does a speaker do this?

To establish rapport with our audiences, we must consider the dynamics of audience size and physical arrangement before we speak, and we must adjust to any changes immediately before or during our speech. To stay audience centered with respect to size and place, ask yourself the following questions:

- How many people will be present?
- Will they stand or be seated? Where will they stand or sit?
- From where will I be speaking?
- Does this arrangement help or hinder the speaking environment I wish to create?
- What adjustments will I want to make before the presentation begins?
- What will I do if I cannot make these adjustments?
- What kinds of adjustments might I make during a presentation if I want to alter the environment?

You probably won't be able to change the size of most audiences, but you should be able to work with the physical setting to create the kind of speaking environment you want. Consider whether you want to stand or sit, where you want your audience to sit (for example, in rows, in a circle, on chairs, on the floor), and how these decisions will affect your ability to connect with your audience. Ideally, you would make arrangements to establish your speaking environment ahead of time, as well as plans to make adjustments during your speech as needed. Remember, your speaking goal is to connect with your audience before, during, and after the speech. To learn more about how physical location affects a speech, go to The Advanced Public Speaking Institute Web site at http://www.public-speaking.org/public-speaking-roomsetup-article.htm.

Technology

To public speakers, technology provides the various tools speakers use to help them deliver their message. Technology can be as elaborate as a computer and LCD panel or as simple as a pen and a flip chart. Technologies that speakers typically use are microphones; podiums for notes; tables or easels for displays, visual aids, or handouts; chalk, chalkboards, and erasers; ink markers, white boards and erasers; markers, pens, and flip charts; tacks, pins, or tape; overhead projectors, laptop computers, and LCD projectors; slide projectors, screens, and extension cords; and VCRs, cassette players, or CD players. When you're thinking of using technology for your speech, stay audience centered by asking yourself the following questions:

- Have I asked what types of technology will be available for me to use?
- Do I have time to prepare the materials I need to use that technology?
- Do I have the time to practice using the technology? Have I worked out any glitches?
- Am I prepared to speak if the technology fails?
- Am I sure that my decision to use or not use technology helps me create the kind of environment I want?
- Does the technology help me communicate my messages clearly? Does it enhance my speech or detract from it?

Note that audience-centered speakers use technology to do more than simply enhance or project their message. They also make a commitment to their audience to use that technology competently. Consider the importance of this commitment in the following example:

> Landon was a wonderful photographer and wanted to enhance his speech by showing slides of his photos. He knew there would be a slide projector in the room in which he was scheduled to speak, so he selected his slides carefully and had his carousel ready the day before the speech. The next morning, just before he was to be introduced to

Strong speakers take stock of their environment before they begin to speak. What questions might you ask yourself to prepare to speak in this environment? If you're planning to use technology, what will you to do make sure your speech is successful even if your technology fails?

© Zephyr Picture/Index Stock

his audience, he tried to put his carousel on the projector and discovered it didn't fit—his projector and the one made available for him to use during his speech were not compatible! Undaunted, he quickly moved the slides into the available carousel. But he wasn't familiar with the projector's remote control, and several times during his speech he sent slides backward rather than forward. As a result, his presentation didn't flow the way he'd wanted it to, and he'd had to spend time studying the remote rather than connecting with his audience.

In this scenario, Landon had to spend time and energy working out technology problems rather than connecting with his audience. He did what he could to recover, but after his speech he felt he hadn't really created the kind of environment he had wanted. He'd wanted people to get excited by his material, but he felt they had simply been patient with him instead.

In Chapter 14, you will learn more about visual aids that rely on technology. Remember, although technology is a tool that can help you give a more effective speech, it has its drawbacks. If your speech *relies* on technology to be effective but the technology you need is not available when you arrive to speak, your presentation will be negatively affected. That's why you need to take the time also to consider how to present your speech without technology. Putting this time into your speech before you give it will help you stay audience centered by keeping your attention focused on *delivering your message* to your audience in a way that they appreciate.

Temporal Factors

Audience-centered speakers also consider issues of time, sometimes called *chronemics,* when they think about connecting with their audiences. Three important time considerations are the time of day you'll be speaking, where your speech falls in a series of presentations (will you speak first, last, or somewhere in the middle?), and how much time you'll have to speak.

Time of day. The time of day a speech is scheduled is significant. Take a moment to consider your moods throughout a day. Is your energy different in the morning than it is in the evening? How about before or after a meal? Just as *our* levels of energy are affected by the time of the day, so too is the mood of an audience.

In the mornings, audiences tend to be fresher, but they may also be anxious about the responsibilities they have that day. In the evening, audiences may be weary, tired from all the work they've done. Around lunchtime, they are hungry and preoccupied with getting some food, or they have just eaten and may be drowsy as their bodies work to digest food rather than your message.

Let's consider Julio from Chapter 4 and how he adjusts his message about Rocks to the Top for his audience.

In the morning, Julio begins by encouraging his audience to refill their cups of coffee and tea as he speaks. He then acknowledges the demands on their time by speaking for 15 minutes, asking them to participate in an activity for 20 minutes, then breaking for 15 minutes so they can check voice mail and email. When they reconvene, they follow up on the activity for about an hour.

After lunch, Julio also engages his audience verbally because he knows their energy will be a bit lower than it was in the morning. When he speaks for longer than half an hour or so, he incorporates a break so audiences can check messages. If he speaks before lunch, Julio clearly defines his speaking schedule so his audience knows when they can expect to eat.

In the evening, Julio acknowledges that it's the end of a working day that was probably very busy for most of the audience. Rather than beginning by explaining the program, he immediately engages them verbally by asking them a few questions about a typical workday that they can answer by raising their hands. This strategy keeps them connected to him in a more direct way—he knows they are probably tired, and he wants them to stay actively involved in the speech rather than sitting back passively.

Julio stays audience centered, regardless of the time of day, by acknowledging the audience's needs at specific times of the day and by organizing his presentations accordingly.

Speaking order. To be audience centered, you must also consider speaking order, or the place you occupy in a series of speakers. If you are the first speaker, you get the audience when they are fresh, listening more actively, and usually more willing to process your message. You also get to set the stage for later speakers, make the first impression, and direct the audience's energy without interference by previous speakers. Additionally, you get to connect with an audience before anyone else does, especially because audiences sometimes ask more questions of first speakers.

If you are the last speaker, or near the end of a series, your audience may be tired and weary of processing the information presented by previous speakers. They will have had their attention pulled in lots of different directions, and they may be more inclined to tune out a speaker or leave than to sit and listen to another speech. As such, start by acknowledging previous speakers and the information they presented. Then try to use your speech to reenergize the audience and redirect their focus as needed. At the end of your speech, the audience may have asked previous speakers most of their questions, so don't be disappointed if they have none for you. Or be prepared to share the stage with previous presenters who will also be answering the audience's questions.

If you are in the middle, you have the advantage of a warmed-up audience that isn't yet anxious to leave, but such an audience is also able to compare the information in your speech to the information given in previous speeches. Thus engage an audience by making connections to previous speakers. As needed, recast or reshape the audience's mood or tone so they're able to hear your message more effectively. At the end of your speech, keep in mind that the audience may ask questions that attempt to pull together information from prior speeches or to rectify discrepancies in claims. If you can help audiences synthesize the information from your and previous speaker's speeches, you stand a better chance of sticking in their memories—people tend to remember beginnings and endings rather than what comes in the middle.

Audiences react to speakers differently depending on speaking order. By being prepared for the expectations audiences have of speakers at various times in a series, and by making simple adjustments to your content and delivery as a result, you will be more of an audience-centered speaker.

Length of speech. Students of public speaking often groan when an instructor sets a specific time limit to a speech and refuses to accept an infraction of that limit without penalty to the student. Why the strict time limits? What is the big deal? Time limitations, although invisible to the audience, are an important structural component of a speech.

When speakers go over the time constraints, they do several undesirable things. If they are speaking in a series, they communicate to their audience that their presentations are more important than those of the speakers following them. Or they communicate a sense of arrogance, suggesting the audience would rather hear their words than those of the speakers coming later. If they are the only speaker, they communicate that they don't understand or care about the many demands on an audience's time—generally, audiences want to hear and process a speaker's message, then move on to other commitments. Speakers who go over time limits also suggest they are unorganized and cannot prioritize and organize their material to fit into a predetermined time. Thus they communicate an air of incompetence. But most importantly, speakers who do not prepare a speech that fits within time limits risk not being able to give their entire speech, which means their audience won't receive their entire message.

The responsibility for staying within time constraints falls on the speaker. When you agree to speak, find out how much time you will have for your presentation, then stay within that time frame. If your audience wants more of your information, they can ask you to continue, elaborate, or engage you later in a question-and-answer session. (Question-and-answer sessions are discussed at the end of this chapter.) If you do not know what your time limitations are and there are other speakers who want to speak, do some quick mental math: divide the total time for the event by the number of speakers, allowing time for questions and discussion. Remember, audience-centered speakers manage their time efficiently and responsibly, creating an environment in which audiences feel respected and appreciated. For more information about time limits, see Chapters 10 and 13.

 Speech Step 5.3 / Consider Your Speaking Environment

For your next speech, think about the size of your audience, the physical arrangement of the room, and the technology you want to use. What elements of your speaking environment will help you stay audience centered? What problems might come up during your speech? How could you solve them? Now consider the time of day in which you give your speech, your speaking order, and the length of your speech. How will you work with these temporal factors to stay audience centered?

Adapting to Audience Expectations

What expectations do you bring with you when you go to a ball game? When a friend invites you to dinner? When you attend a dance performance? When you watch a favorite television program or listen to a new CD? When we attend events or engage in familiar activities, we have certain expectations about how they will progress. For example, when we attend a ball game, we expect bleachers, announcers, players, referees, rules, a scoring system, and an end to the game. We expect the game to progress in a certain way, and we know when it doesn't progress properly.

When audiences attend public speaking events, they also bring expectations with them. They expect public speaking events to follow a certain structure, and they base their interpretation of a speaker's message on those expectations. Audiences have expectations about the form of a speech, the credibility of the speaker, and how the speaker interacts with the audience in discussions. Audience-centered speakers must address these expectations, because audiences use them to help decide whether or not a speaker "did a good job."

Expectations About the Form of a Speech

Communication scholar and theorist Kenneth Burke defines *form* as "the creation of an appetite" in the minds of an audience and the "adequate satisfying of that appetite." He suggests that a speech has form when one part of it leads an audience to "anticipate another part, to be gratified by the sequence."[10] In other words, audiences expect a speech to follow a certain progression of events and those events to progress as they'd anticipated. For audiences with a Western cultural background, audiences expect speeches to take the following form:

- The speaker will do most of the speaking or facilitating and share information the audience does not already have.

- The audience will listen during the speech and ask most of their questions at the end of the speech.

- Certain types of speaking will follow certain sequences: at the opening of an event, speeches of introduction are given; at public lectures, speeches of information, invitation, or persuasion are likely; at a celebration, speeches of commemoration or acceptance are given; and at business meetings, speeches take the form of presenting ideas, facilitating discussions, or gathering information.

To stay audience centered, do your best to recognize which form your audience will expect for your speech. Then try to follow that form or explain your reasons for altering it. If you don't, your audience's expectations will be violated, and they may react negatively to your speech. For example, if you are asked to commemorate a colleague, be sure to prepare a speech that praises that person and highlights her contributions. Even if you don't feel your colleague has contributed as much as the company thinks she has, try to focus on the positive aspects of your interactions with her so your speech is appropriate for the occasion. Don't take the opportunity to give a persuasive speech that tries to convince the audience your colleague isn't at all praiseworthy. By violating the form of a commemorative speech, you'll only frustrate your audience's expectations and make them feel uncomfortable. In our next example, the speaker doesn't follow the form he knows his audience expects, but he explains why he doesn't and so gives a successful speech.

Jeff Ho had been invited to speak to a class on communication and culture about representations of race in the media. As an Asian American who had studied the subject fairly extensively and was a dynamic and engaging speaker, Jeff had often been asked to give similar presentations. As a result, he was quite familiar with his material and with his audiences' expectations about how he should present it. Students expected him to lecture and present facts and research so they could take notes. But he really wanted to connect with his audience and create a dialogue, so he decided to violate his audience's expectations.

When he began his presentation, he told the students that he knew they expected him to lecture and they were prepared to sit back and maintain a certain distance. He said, "I'm going to make it really hard for you to stay distant, because I can't be distant from the issue of race and the media—and neither can you. You see, how the media present us as individuals, as people engaged with one another, affects us too powerfully to pretend we can understand by simply listening to someone lecture for fifty minutes. So, I am going to tell you some of my stories, experiences, and perspectives, and I'm asking that you tell me some of yours during this time we have together."

Jeff's presentation was a huge success. His audience understood why he'd violated their expectations of form because he'd explained why. In fact, he'd set up new expectations—the exchange of stories and experiences. He created a new appetite, which he satisfied during his time with them.

Audience-centered speakers understand that audiences have certain expectations of form for certain types of speeches. They recognize that when they choose to alter these forms, they must help their audience understand why. Remember, staying audience centered isn't saying only what the audience wants to hear—it is creating an appetite in them to hear what you have to say. To assess the degree to which a Memorial Day speaker met his audience expectations, complete InfoTrac College Edition Exercise 5.3, "Expectations of a Memorial," online under Student Resources for Chapter 5 at the *Invitation to Public Speaking* Web site.

Expectations About the Speaker

Audiences also bring expectations with them about you, the speaker. When audiences take the time to listen to a speech, they want the speaker to be competent (qualified) and credible (believable). You'll explore competency and credibility in more detail in Chapters 8, 10, and 18, but here you'll learn how audiences use master statuses to assess whether or not a speaker is qualified and believable.

As you learned earlier in this chapter, master statuses are the positions people hold in society that affect their identities in almost all social situations. Whether we like it or not, once an audience identifies a speaker's master statuses, they usually form expectations about that speaker based on what they believe about particular master statuses. For example, Dennis is a 55-year-old white attorney. A Georgia native, he travels to law schools across the country to meet with prospective new hires for his law firm. At every presentation, he is asked about racism and sexism in the South. He is also often challenged, both overtly and subtly, about whether he is able to recognize forms of discrimination that could be present in his firm. As a white male from the South, audiences often don't expect Dennis to be able to speak credibly about issues of race and gender.

To understand what an audience might expect of you as a speaker, take a moment to identify your own master statuses. Are you a woman or a man? What is your age and physical state? What is your race and ethnicity? Do you have an accent or unusual style of speech? Will you acknowledge your marital status, parental status, or sexuality in your speech? What is your educational level? Are you often labeled or marked by society in a particular way? Your answers to questions like these will help you adjust to your audience's expectations of you as you begin a presentation.

Consider how Carolyn Calloway Thomas, a professor in the Department of Communication and Culture at Indiana University, has addressed the issue of audience expectations of her as a speaker. She once asked a group of students, "What do you notice about me?" They listed a number of items—her height, dress, style of presentation, occupation, and so on. "Yes, yes," she said, "those all are significant. Go on." Finally, one student said, "You are a black woman." "Yes," she responded, "and although that affects almost every aspect of my life, as well as almost every aspect of how you respond to me, if you can't get past the fact that I am black, if that's all you see about me, we've got a communication problem. You'll get stuck there. I am a black woman, yet I also am a very complex human being."

Professor Calloway Thomas offers speakers a useful strategy for working with audience assumptions about master statuses: simply acknowledge them. Master statuses do affect us, but help your audience move beyond them, because they are not the totality of who we are. Speakers can use many nonthreatening phrases to help audiences move beyond their assumptions. They include phrases such as "I'm often asked that question," "Audiences generally assume," "As a woman (or other master status), people expect me to," and "Now, you might be wondering why someone like me is speaking on this topic today." Phrases that can help audiences shift their focus from unfamiliar styles or mannerisms include "Let me explain the symbolism behind the clothing I'm wearing today," "I'll be using an interpreter today and, as fascinating as they are to watch, I'd love it if you look at me as I speak and ask your questions directly to me," and "Even though I've lived in the United States for ten years now, the English language still stumps me at times. I hear it occasionally stumps some of you native speakers as well, so maybe we can help each other out with some of what we don't understand."

These kinds of phrases acknowledge, directly and kindly, that an audience's assumptions may prevent them from hearing a speaker's message. They also acknowledge differences in a positive way and encourage audiences to better understand those differences—as an audience-centered speaker, you certainly want to understand the positions of your audience, but you also want your audience to understand *your* positions. To help audiences understand you, encourage them to move beyond simply defining you by your master statuses by asking them to recognize you as a unique individual. To assess the degree to which Joe Lieberman, the first Jewish person to be nominated as a major party vice-presidential candidate, acknowledged audience expectations about him, complete Interactive Activity 5.4, "Acknowledging Expectations of the Speaker," online under Student Resources for Chapter 5 at the *Invitation to Public Speaking* Web site. You can also watch Senator Lieberman accept the nomination for the 2000 Democratic candidate for vice-president under Speech Interactive on your CD-ROM.

WEB SITE

SPEECH
INTERACTIVE

Expectations About Speaker-Audience Discussions

An important part of the public dialogue is responding to an audience when they ask questions or want to discuss the ideas you present. Speakers are often expected to make time for question-and-answer sessions at the end of a speech or to manage brainstorming sessions and discussions. This sort of audience interaction can be challenging because when you share the floor with others, you lose some of the control you had when you were presenting—you cannot always predict what will happen or what the audience will ask or say.

Despite the unpredictability of discussions and question-and-answer sessions, you can use several strategies to stay audience centered and manage this flow of information effectively. First, consider why people ask questions. They usually ask because they want to clarify points you raised, get more information about a position you advocate, satisfy their curiosity about an issue or an idea, identify or establish connections between ideas, or support or challenge you or the ideas you presented.[11] In addition to asking questions, audience members participate in discussions for many of the same reasons that they ask questions. They also may want to share specific information with the group, restate information in a way that may be easier to understand, or even dominate the conversation.

Identifying which of these reasons motivates someone to participate in a speaking event can help you enormously. If an audience asks you for more information or to clarify a point, try to recognize that they are interested in your topic, not commenting on your ability to present information clearly. If an audience attempts to make connections between what they previously believed and the new information you've presented, help them make those connections rather than get frustrated that they just don't "get it." Similarly, when audience members try to organize their thoughts about a complicated topic, work with them rather than against them, and perhaps incorporate their ideas into your plan for the discussion.

Audiences often ask questions because they want to know more about a speaker's viewpoint. What kinds of questions do you think you might get in your next speech? How might you respond to them?

Recognizing what motivates an audience to attack or challenge a speaker is a particularly valuable tool. Addressing attacks or challenges from an audience during a question-and-answer session is often a speaker's greatest fear. When an audience attacks or challenges you, it is usually because they doubt the validity of your information or your credibility as a speaker. When you recognize why audiences do these things, you are more likely to respond appropriately rather than feel intimidated or engage in unproductive sparring. Consider the following example:

Ramón is a small young-looking man with a graduate degree in communication. Fluent in both Spanish and English, he works as an interpreter for a health care collective that serves migrant workers in his community. The collective consists of physicians, physician's assistants, nurses, and interpreters. Ramón is the only minority at the collective and the only one who has had extensive conversations with the migrant workers the collective serves.

At a recent meeting Ramón attended, he gave a presentation addressing some of the problems people on his staff were having managing cases. Ramón offered a solution based on his experiences with the workers. He was immediately challenged by one of the physicians, who questioned his suggestions and labeled them "impractical." He told Ramón that there were factors at work he couldn't possibly recognize, then quickly moved the discussion in another direction. Although Ramón had the knowledge, education, and experience to make useful suggestions, he was challenged by someone with more "credibility" than he.

Ramón's challenge to his credibility was the result of his master statuses. As a small, young-looking minority, Ramón occupied a less authoritative position than the other people at the meeting, who were all older looking, white, and seen as having more credible credentials. Although Ramón's facts were correct, his audience could not see past his status, and so, however unconsciously, they labeled him as less knowledgeable than they. Ramón understood why his coworker challenged him and responded by saying, "You know, I often get overlooked as a source of ideas because of my age, and I realize that being a minority can sometimes throw people off. But I've lived in this community all my life and am quite familiar with the migrant and farming culture. I've also spoken with many of our clients outside the context of the clinic, and they've told me what they think would help them. I still think there might be ways to translate their suggestions into a feasible plan." Once Ramón explained how his experience and communication skills lent his ideas credibility, the rest of the group were able to move beyond their assumptions and work with his ideas and suggestions.

Despite their unpredictable nature, speeches that allow time for questions or incorporate discussion can be particularly rewarding for both audiences and speakers. In these speeches, speakers communicate to audiences that they're interested in the speaker's thoughts, beliefs, and concerns. They also communicate that they want to interact with the audience to provide more information if necessary or perhaps learn something new themselves. They are engaging in a healthy public dialogue by making a space for conversation, confirmation, and the exchange of perspectives. For more information about question-and-answer sessions, see Chapter 13. Additionally, you can find additional suggestions for how to manage question-and-answer sessions online under Student Resources for Chapter 5 at the *Invitation to Public Speaking* Web site.

WEB SITE

Using your *Invitation to Public Speaking* CD-ROM, watch the video clip of the question-and-answer session of the final 2000 presidential debate under Speech Interactive. Consider how well the candidates addressed the questions the audience asked. Also watch the video clip of President George W. Bush's news conference of October 11, 2001, under Speech Interactive. How clearly did he communicate his points to his audience?

Chapter Summary

An audience is a collection of people who have gathered to listen to a speaker's message. Although the definition of the term *audience* has changed over time, the need to stay audience centered in a speech has not. In order to stay audience centered, consider the various master statuses, standpoints, attitudes, values, and beliefs of your audience members. You can gather this information by conducting a demographic analysis, a survey that will give you specific information about the particular population traits of your audience.

As you consider your audience, also recognize that audiences form a community. Sometimes, this community is a voluntary one interested in your topic and what you have to say. At other times, your audience is involuntary, required to listen to you. With either group, a successful speaker stays audience centered, acknowledging why people are present as well as their master statuses and standpoints.

An audience-centered speaker also pays careful attention to the speaking environment. This environment includes the size and physical arrangement of the speaking situation, the available technology, and temporal factors such as the time of day and the speaking order. You will be able to give a more effective speech in almost any environment if you assess the environment beforehand and adapt to it during your speech. Audience-centered speakers also adapt to audience expectations. These expectations focus on the form of the speech (for example, commemorative versus persuasive), how qualified and believable the speaker is, and the speaker's ability to lead discussions.

In short, audience-centered speakers understand their own positions about a topic, those of their audience, and how they might present their own perspectives without violating another's worldview. They recognize the expectations audiences have of them and take time to manage those expectations as best they can.

After reading this chapter, use your CD-ROM and the *Invitation to Public Speaking* Web site to review the follow-ing concepts, answer the review questions, and complete the suggested activities.

Key Concepts

dialogue (102)
audience-centered (102)
audience (103)
master status (103)
standpoint (104)

attitude (105)
belief (105)
value (105)
ethnocentrism (105)
demographic audience
    analysis (106)

open-ended question
    (106)
close-ended question
    (106)
stereotype (106)
empathy (110)

Review Questions

1. Identify the following statements as true or false:

    _____ A dialogue is simply taking turns in a conversation.

    _____ When preparing my speech, I need to think more about what I want to say than the background and experiences of my audience.

    _____ All cultures and subcultures have the same basic idea of how the world works.

    _____ Audiences will interpret my message in just the way I want them to.

    _____ To be audience centered, I must say only what the audience wants to hear.

    _____ Temporal and situational factors have little effect on my speech.

    _____ When I open up my speech for questions or discussion, I lose all control of the flow of communication.

    Each of these statements is false. Can you explain why?

2. Consider the times that as an audience member you held a very different standpoint from the other audience members. Consider the times you held a very similar standpoint to other audience members. How did these situations affect your experience? Did the speaker address these differences or similarities? What was the effect of the speaker's actions?

3. Discuss with your classmates the differences between voluntary and involuntary audiences. In your public speaking class, you will speak to involuntary audiences. What strategies will you use as a speaker to communicate an audience-centered perspective to your audience?

4. Imagine you are giving a speech to introduce your audience to rock climbing and to encourage them to take up the sport. Describe how your speech might change for each of the following audiences:

    • Thirty sixth graders, voluntarily present
    • Thirty corporate executives, asked to attend by their bosses
    • Seven pregnant women and their partners, voluntarily present
    • Fifteen people over the age of 60, voluntarily present
    • Twelve lower income teenagers who are part of an environmental education program and quite frightened by the prospect of rock climbing
    • Your boss at the sporting goods store (you want her to invest more money in supplies for rock climbers)

    With your classmates, discuss the changes you would make in your approach, content, and presentation.

5. Consider the room in which your public speaking class is held. Describe the physical setting, options for the placement of speakers, time constraints, and other temporal factors. How is your audience limited or enhanced by these environmental factors? How are *you* limited or enhanced? Identify specific strategies you can use to enhance this environment so your audience is more open to your message and better understands it.

6. Do discussions and question-and-answer sessions make you feel nervous? If so, what are your biggest fears regarding these speech elements? Using this chapter as your guide, identify three ways you might ease some of your fears.

The *Invitation to Public Speaking* Web Site

The *Invitation to Public Speaking* Web site features the review questions about the Web sites suggested on pages 102, 105–106 and 111, the interactive activities suggested on pages 105, 107, and 118, and the InfoTrac College Edition exercises suggested on pages 108, 110, and 117.

You can access this site via your CD-ROM or at http://www.wadsworth.com/product/griffin. To access Speech Builder Express, you will need the username and password included under "Speech Builder Express" on your CD-ROM.

Web Links

5.1: Being Audienced Centered (102)
5.2: Audience Analysis (105)
5.3: Five Audience Types (105)
5.4: Demographics for Cities and Regions (106)
5.5: U.S. Census (106)
5.6: Advanced Public Speaking Institute (111)

Interactive Activities

5.1: Avoiding Ethnocentrism (105)
Purpose: To understand how speakers can guard against being ethnocentric.

5.2: Learning About Your Audience (107)
Purpose: To learn about creating and interpreting surveys for audiences.

5.3: Using Psychographic Analysis (107)
Purpose: To learn how psychographic analysis can improve audience centeredness.

5.4: Acknowledging Expectations of the Speaker (118)
Purpose: To understand how speakers can acknowledge the expectations that audiences have of them.

InfoTrac College Edition Exercises

5.1: **Being Audience Centered** (108)
Purpose: To learn how speakers communicate to diverse audiences.

5.2: **Identifying Audiences** (110)
Purpose: To isolate characteristics of an audience and assess how well speakers adapt to these audiences.

5.3: **Expectations of a Memorial** (117)
Purpose: To understand how speakers adapt to their audience's expectations about form.

Speech Interactive on the *Invitation to Public Speaking* CD-ROM

The following video clips of speeches referenced in this chapter are included under Speech Interactive on your *Invitation to Public Speaking* CD-ROM. After you have watched the clips, click on "Critique" to answer the questions for analysis.

Video Clip 1: Senator Joseph Lieberman Accepting Nomination as Democratic Candidate for Vice-President (118). How did Senator Lieberman acknowledge audience expectations about him as the first Jewish person to be nominated as a major party vice-presidential candidate? What kinds of phrases did he use in his acceptance speech?

Video Clip 2: Answering Questions in a Presidential Debate (120). Al Gore and George W. Bush fielded ques-

tions from the audience in the final debate of the 2000 presidential campaign. How well does each answer the questions asked? Do they respond to the questions? Do the questions pose any unique challenges to the candidates? Does the questioner challenge information or credibility? Are the questions complicated or uncomfortable?

Video Clip 3: President Bush's Press Conference on October 11, 2001 (120). How clearly does President Bush communicate with his audience during his press conference on October 11, 2001? What are some possible interpretations of what he says? What is the danger of misinterpreting Bush's remarks in this situation?

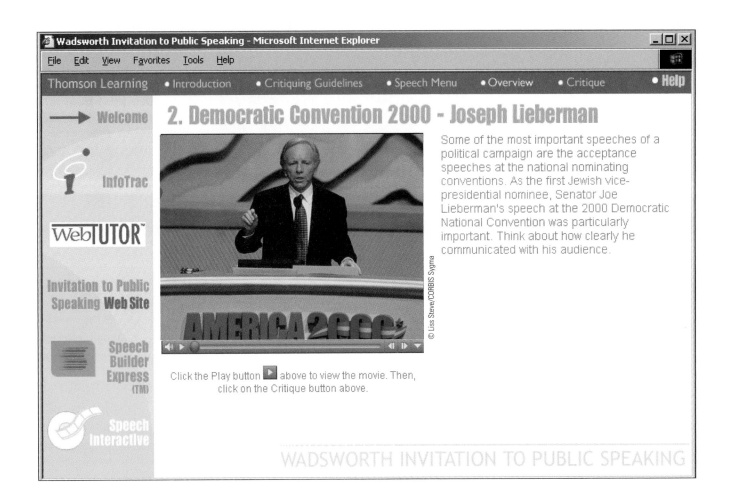

Chapter Six

Gathering Supporting Materials

In this chapter you will learn to

Determine the types of supporting materials you need to gather for your speech

Search for information on the Internet, in the library, and through personal interviews

Evaluate the information you find

Apply several tips that will help you with your research efforts

Knowledge is of two kinds. We know a subject ourselves, or we know where we can find information about it.

—Samuel Johnson, eighteenth-century essayist, from James Boswell's *The Life Of Samuel Johnson, LL.D.*, 1791

One of our primary responsibilities as public speakers is to provide audiences with accurate information so public conversations can be well informed. In addition to giving our opinions on the topics we speak about, we must also provide facts, examples, and evidence. We can find this type of information, called *supporting material,* by considering our own experiences and knowledge, searching the Internet, researching at the library, or interviewing people who are related to our speech topic in some way.

Conducting all this research may seem intimidating at first, but if you organize your research efforts, your search for materials can fill notebooks and folders with an impressive range of supporting materials that keep you excited about your projects and your audiences interested in your speeches.

This chapter will help you collect the materials you need to enter the public dialogue. You will learn how to organize your efforts into three categories: determining what types of information you need to gather; identifying where you might find that information; and assessing the strengths and weaknesses of the information you find. If you are organized and systematic in your search efforts, you will spend your research time productively, reduce your frustration, and increase your chances of finding excellent materials to support your ideas.

Determine What Types of Information You Need

Before you begin your research in earnest, take some time to organize your thoughts about what types of supporting material you already have and what types you still need. Start by asking yourself the following sorts of questions (note that in Chapter 7 we'll discuss examples, stories, statistics, testimony, and definitions in detail):

- What examples and stories do I have?
- What statistics will my audience want to know?
- What kinds of testimony will they want to hear?
- What terms and phrases can I define clearly on my own?
- Is the information I already have accurate, relevant, and credible?
- How will I evaluate the accuracy, relevance, and credibility of the information I find?
- What ideas or points can I develop or support from my own experiences?

research inventory
List of the types of information you have for your speech and the types you want to find.

WEB SITE

As you consider these questions, you can construct a **research inventory,** a list of the types of information you have and the types you want to find. (A Research Inventory Worksheet is shown in Figure 6.5 on page 149 and is available online as a download under Student Resources at the *Invitation to Public Speaking* Web site.) A research inventory helps you take stock of what you have and what you will need. It helps you focus your research efforts and identify areas that need special attention. It is your first step toward making the time you spend gathering materials productive.

Consider the sample research inventory in Figure 6.1. This inventory was developed by Lin, who gave a speech on road rage to her public speaking class. The thirty minutes she spent identifying what information she had and what she needed

Figure 6.1

Sample Research Inventory

Speech topic:	Strategies for managing road rage
General purpose:	To inform
Specific purpose:	I want to inform my audience of some strategies for managing road rage.
Thesis statement:	In the past decade, as incidents of road rage have increased dramatically, several strategies have been developed to manage road rage caused by the stress of driving.
My audience is:	My public speaking classmates

I currently have:

Examples and stories:

A poem about road rage (from Henna Man: Poems)

Statistics:

A dissertation about the characteristics of people with high/low driving anger (from Linda Filetti), includes statistics about who typically exhibits road rage

Testimony:

Definitions:

This information is relevant, accurate, and credible because:

The poem illustrates one person's experience with road rage (put in the intro to catch audience's attention)

The dissertation was heavily researched by a Ph.D. student who has done extensive study on the problems and effects of road rage.

My audience will want to hear:

Examples of the following:

Specific incidents of road rage

Statistics for the following:

Statistics to back up the claim that road rage incidents have increased dramatically over past 10 years

Statistics to back up the strategies I suggest (do they really work?)

Testimony about the following:

The experiences of people who've exhibited road rage

The experiences of people who have used the strategies to overcome it

Definitions of the following:

What road rage is (esp. as opposed to normal driving frustrations)

Deep breathing (stress reduction technique)

The kinds of sources they will find trustworthy are:

Government documents about road rage

People who've experienced road rage and learned to manage it

Experts on driving, or experts on stress management

I need to find the following information:

A few more examples of road rage incidents

More statistics, especially about how the strategies work for people

Testimony (from at least two people)

A more concise definition of deep breathing than the one I have now

Sources for this information:

Library database (published studies of how road rage has increased over the past 10 years)

InfoTrac (articles about road rage and how to deal with it)

Government Web sites (statistics)

Web sites about driving information and techniques (strategies)

Possibly interview a driving instructor or psychologist who specializes in stress management (ask Linda Filetti who she knows)

information overload
When we take in more information than we can process but realize there still is more information we are expected to know.

to gather saved her hours of time on the Internet, in the library, and in interviews. In addition to saving you time, preparing a research inventory before you start gathering support materials helps you avoid experiencing what futurist Alvin Toffler calls *information overload*. In his now famous book *Future Shock*,[1] Toffler explained that **information overload** happens when we take in more information than we can process but realize there still is more information we are expected to know. Educators believe information overload will continue to increase, so much so that by the year 2020 the "available body of information [will] double every 73 days!"[2]

Toffler offers a useful strategy for managing information overload: classify information so it fits into manageable units. This is what you do with your research inventory—you organize the information for your speech into two classifications, what you have and what you need. The next step is to determine *where* you'll find the information you need.

Notice that the last item on the Research Inventory Worksheet is "Sources for this information." Once you know what types of information you want, you can classify that information even further by identifying where you are most likely to find it. In the next few sections you will explore four common sources of information: your own experiences and knowledge, the Internet, libraries, and personal interviews. Understanding how best to access information from these sources and what you will most likely gather from each will help you evaluate each source's strengths and weaknesses. Equipped with this understanding, you'll focus your research time and energy on sources that are most likely to give you what you need To read an article that offers helpful advice, see Jim Owen's "Coping with Information Overload" at http://www.careerbuilder.com/wl_work_9905_overload.html.

Speech Step 6.1 / Prepare Your Research Inventory

Identify the topic for your next speech. Use the Research Inventory Worksheet to brainstorm the research you might do. Consider the advantages and disadvantages of your sources for the material you might find. Remember to consider your speech goals, your audience, and the need to vary your sources of information.

Use Your Personal Knowledge and Experience

After reading Chapter 4 you probably recognized that you have personal, firsthand knowledge about a number of subjects that would make excellent speeches. After you've selected your topic, use this personal experience as a source of research. Before you begin other research, take a moment to consider what knowledge you already have about your topic. This knowledge can come from your own experiences and training, your family background, hobbies, job, or profession, or even things you have read or observed.

For example, the information in Cindy's speech on folding the American flag (Chapter 15) relies on her personal experience in the military and with folding the flag during ceremonial events. Similarly, Carol's source of research for her speech on fat discrimination (Chapter 18) was her own personal experiences. If you're interested in a topic but don't have personal experience with it, you can gain personal experience as part of your research. For example, suppose you wanted to give a speech about a particular agency in your community. You could visit that agency and shadow someone for a day to get the personal experience you need.

Search for Materials on the Internet

Whether you've ever logged on or not, the Internet is currently the most popular research tool for college students in the United States. The **Internet** links computer networks around the world via telephone lines, cables, and communication satellites, allowing users to access information from millions of sources. Most people access information on the Internet by using the **World Wide Web**, a system that allows users to easily navigate the millions of sites on the Internet. For public speaking students, the Internet offers access to dialogues and research around the globe and can link you to the most current opinions and findings. You can find data for local, regional, national, and international events and issues, and sometimes the most current interpretations of that data. When you use the Internet, you have at your disposal a truly staggering range of ideas. You may have free Internet access through your college or univeristy. If you don't, check out another source of free Internet access, NetZero, at http://www.netzero.com.

Note that the Internet is not without its weaknesses. Because it is easy to access and open to anyone, information from all sorts of sources is posted on the Internet that may not be accurate. Many sites include old or incomplete information or information based on personal opinions and biases. Additionally, identifying a credible Internet site can be difficult because many are well designed and look like professional postings even if they're not.

The Internet can be a fast and exciting way to collect material for your speech, but use it as only one of several approaches you take to building a strong presentation. Although you may already have experience with Internet research, a quick overview of how to access it will help you consider ways to evaluate the strengths and weaknesses of the information you find there.

Internet Basics

A **browser** is a software program that allows you to search for, find, and display information on your computer screen. Netscape Navigator and Microsoft Internet Explorer are two common browsers, and most publicly accessible computers have these, or similar, browsers installed on them. From your browser, you can access Web sites and Web pages with the help of URLs and links. A **Web site** is a location on the World Wide Web that links to related **Web pages**, individual screens that represent specific parts of a Web site. A **URL**, or **uniform resource locator**, is the address of a specific Web site or page. URLs function like phone numbers or mailing addresses, taking you to specific sources of information. An example of a URL is http://www.itworks.be/, the address of a site devoted to giving Internet users information about the Internet itself. Another is http://www.newslink.org, the address of NewsLink, a site that can link you to newspapers, magazines, and broadcasts from around the world. **Links** are icons or highlighted words and phrases that take you from site to site or from one part of a site to another. Navigating sites with links is much like skipping to a chapter in a book or changing television channels.

If you find a site you think you might want to return to, you can use your browser's **bookmark** feature to save its URL for quick and easy access later. Clicking on a bookmark, also called a *favorite*, allows you to return directly to a site without typing in its URL or linking to it through other sites. If you are not using a computer of your own and can't use the bookmark feature, copy the URL carefully and note the reason you found this site useful. You also may be able to print out the relevant information to take with you or even download (copy) it to a personal disk to use later.

Internet
An electronic communications network that links computer networks around the world via telephone lines, cables, and communication satellites.

World Wide Web
System that allows users to easily navigate the millions of sites on the Internet.

browser
Software program that allows you to search for, find, and display information on your computer screen.

Web site
Location on the World Wide Web.

Web page
Individual screens that represent specific parts of a Web site.

URL (uniform resource locator)
Address of a specific Web site or page.

links
Icons or highlighted words and phrases that take you from site to site or from one part of a site to another.

bookmark
A menu entry or icon that allows you to return directly to a site without typing in its URL or linking to it through other sites (also called a *favorite*).

If you know exactly where you want to go on the Internet, these basics may be all you need to know. But when you're gathering materials for a speech, you may not always know which specific site to access. Simply linking from site to site can lead to endless searching in all the wrong places. When you do not know the URL of the site you want to find, search engines can be enormously helpful.

Search Engines

search engines
Sites that index Web pages and, based on subjects you provide, search them to locate relevant sites.

Boolean operators
Words you can use to create specific phrases that broaden or narrow your search on the Internet.

Search engines are sites that index Web pages and, based on subjects you provide, search them to locate relevant sites. See Figure 6.2 for a list of the most common search engines and their URLs. Using a search engine is like looking for phone numbers in the yellow pages of a phone book. Suppose Lin wanted to interview driving instructors for her road rage speech but didn't know any personally. She could go to the yellow pages, look up "driving instruction," and find a list of instructors she might contact. If she couldn't find any instructors in her local phone book, she could use a phone book from another community. Her "search engines" are the phone books, and these sources link her to a number of possibilities she might pursue. On the Internet, she could access one of the search engines listed in Figure 6.2, search for "road rage and driving instructors," and the search engine would list a number of sites she could explore.

Note that Lin used a Boolean operator in her search. **Boolean operators** are words you can use to create specific phrases that broaden or narrow your search. Three of the most commonly used are *and, or,* and *not.* In her search for links on road rage, Lin used the Boolean operator *and,* so she got a listing of links to sites about both driving instructors and road rage. If she had used *or* she would have called up links that related to either driving instructors or road rage. If she'd searched on "driving instructors *not* road rage," she would have gotten only links to sites about driving instructors that did not refer to road rage at all. Using Boolean operators helps you tailor your searches to find as much or as little information as you need.

Be aware that at the rate information becomes available today, no single search engine can find every available Web site that pertains to your topic. In fact,

Figure 6.2
Search Engines

Yahoo	http://www.yahoo.com
Alta Vista	http://www.altavista.digital.com
Open Text	http://www.opentext.com
Lycos	http://www.lycos.com
InfoSeek	http://www2.infoseek.com
Excite NetSearch	http://www.excite.com
Highway 61	http://www.highway61.com
Savvy Search	http://guaraldi.cs.colostate.edu:2000
All-in-One Search Page	http://www.albany.net.alinone
All The Web	http://www.alltheweb.com
Metacrawler	http://www.metacrawler.com
Dogpile	http://www.dogpile.com
HotBot	http://www.hotbot.com
Google	http://www.google.com

it's estimated that most search engines can search on only about one-third of the available sites on the Web.[3] So, just as you would not limit your research efforts to one book or magazine, use more than one search engine to research your topic.

Evaluating Internet Information

The Internet can be an excellent source of information, but remember you must use this tool properly in order to get the best results. Knowing how to evaluate the quality of information you find on the Internet will save you time and frustration and ensure that you develop your speech ideas completely and responsibly.

Many Web sites are maintained and regularly updated by reputable people, companies, and institutions, but just as many others are not. Web sites are regularly abandoned, and thus never updated, by owners who lose funding or simply lose interest. As a result, Web sites range dramatically in accuracy, complexity, and usefulness. Given the fluid nature of the Internet, how do you know whether or not a source found there is one you can use in your speech? As you would with any other source of information, evaluate your data according to the following criteria:

Is the information reliable? Check the domain in the URL. Is it .com (a commercial enterprise that might be trying to sell you something), .org (a nonprofit organization, more interested in services and issues than in commerce), .edu (an educational institution), or .gov (a government agency)? What bias might the owners of this site have about your topic? Do they make any disclaimers about the information they post on the site? What makes this information reliable or not?

Is the information authoritative? URLs that include a tilde (~) often indicate that a single individual is responsible for the information on a Web site. Can you find the person's credentials posted on the site? Can you contact the person and ask for credentials? Can you find the person's credentials in any print sources, such as a Who's Who reference? Regardless of whether the material was authored by a single person, an organization, an institution, or a company, is the author an expert on the subject of the site?

How current is the information? Many Web pages include a date that tells you when it was posted or last updated. If you don't see such a date, you may be able to find it in your browser's View or Document menu. If you still can't find a date, check to see if you've found an abandoned, or ghost, site by checking out the directory at http://www.disobey.com/ghostsites/. If you determine that the Web site is current, is the time frame relevant to your subject or arguments? You may find great information, but if it doesn't relate to the time frame of your speech, it's not relevant.

How complete is the information? Much of the text posted on the Internet consists of excerpts from printed material, and what is left out may be of more use than what is included. For example, a site may contain one paragraph from a newspaper article, but that paragraph may not reflect the overall message of the article. If you want to use an excerpted portion of a printed work, be sure to track down the complete work. A site is also incomplete if it presents only one side of an issue. Be sure to consider as many positions on your topic as possible. To guarantee the completeness of your supporting materials, search for your topic on several search engines and in print documents.

Assess the information you see on these home pages. Does the information look current and complete? How reliable do you think each of these sites is?

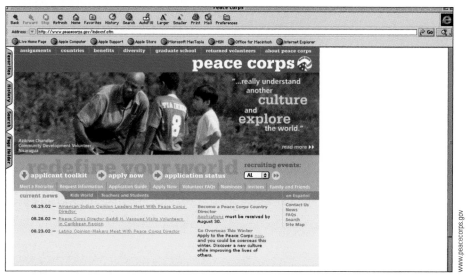

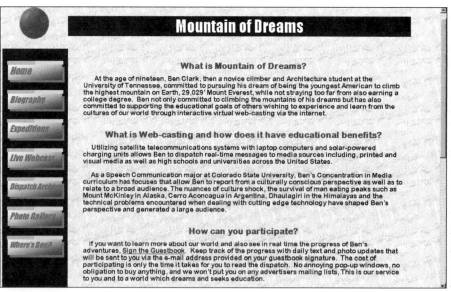

Is the information relevant? Does the information fit your needs? Is it what you were looking for? Does it help develop your main ideas and points or does it take you in a different direction? Many facts and stories are on the Web—be sure you use those that do more than tell a great story. They must also help you develop your thesis (Chapters 8 and 18).

Is the information consistent? Is the information you find consistent with information you find on other sites, from printed sources, or from interviews? Can you find other sources to support the statements, claims, and facts provided by a Web site? If the information is inconsistent with other sources, it may reflect new findings about a topic, but it also may reflect an unfounded or unsubstantiated claim. Be wary of outrageous or controversial claims that can't be checked for accuracy or aren't grounded in reasonable arguments or sources.[4]

If you keep these six criteria in mind as you research your speech topic on the Internet, you'll be more likely to use supporting materials that are credible. Recall from Chapter 5 that you increase your chances for giving a successful speech by remaining audience centered, and audiences expect information that is reliable, authoritative, current, complete, relevant, and consistent. The Internet is certainly a source of much credible material, but it should be only one of many tools you use to gather materials for your speech. For a checklist that will help you evaluate Internet resources, look online under Student Resources for Chapter 6 at the *Invitation to Public Speaking* Web site.   WEB SITE

Research Materials at the Library

The library probably is your most comprehensive tool for gathering materials. Not only can you access the Internet from most libraries, but you also have access to librarians, databases, indexes, journals, magazines, newspapers, books, documents, and many other useful resources. These materials cover an extensive range of topics and time frames. And, although libraries might not always seem as up to date as the Internet, they are still far more reliable because all the materials in a library are routinely evaluated and systematically organized.

But libraries also have their weaknesses. Libraries are only open on a set schedule, and you sometimes have to maneuver what may seem like a confusing coding system and a maze of shelves. One library may not have the exact source you want, so you have to look for other sources or go to another library to get the material. Until you get to know them, libraries can seem quite foreign. In fact, library research can seem so difficult that Ernest Boyer suggested in a report for the Carnegie Foundation that about "one out of every four undergraduates spends no time in the library during a normal week."[5]

However, once you understand the strengths and weaknesses of a library, you can easily combine Internet research with library research and gather a wide range of useful and credible materials for your speeches.

Orientations

If you are new to library research or are unfamiliar with the library you will be using, schedule a tour of the library before you begin your research. Getting a library orientation may sound silly or boring, but it can save you countless hours wandering around a place you don't understand. Additionally, libraries often differ slightly from one another in how they are organized or what materials they offer, so an orientation can help you get used to a new library. Most orientations take about an hour, and they can give you the confidence you need to begin your research on the right foot.

Librarians

Librarians are one of your most useful resources in the library. Surprisingly, though, many students ask a librarian for assistance only as a last resort and then are frustrated because the librarian knows exactly where to find the information they've just spent hours looking for. If you find yourself spending more than half an hour searching for materials you can't find, ask for assistance. Consider what a librarian is trained to know: how materials are catalogued or stored, what materials are on databases, how to search through databases, how to refine subject and word searches, where materials are located in the library, and how to request materials from other libraries. These skills can be invaluable to someone who is looking for supporting materials for a speech. When you do seek out a librarian in the course of your research, consider the following tips:

- If you haven't used the library before, schedule an orientation. A basic knowledge of the library will help both you and the librarian helping you enormously.

- Fill out your research inventory before you begin your search and bring it with you to the library. Refer to it as you work with the librarian.

- Ask specific questions. For example, rather than asking, "Where can I find information on road rage?" ask where you might find statistics for the number of accidents caused by road rage, or testimony by driving instructors about road rage, or examples of the most common forms of road rage.

- Share the specifics of your assignment with the librarian: "It's only a four-minute speech," "My instructor wants three sources from this year and two from within the last ten years," "My audience is a potential source of funding for my proposal," "I want a really dramatic story for my introduction," and so on. Information like this will give the librarian the same focus you've got for your speech and will help you avoid information overload.

- Treat the librarian with respect. Librarians are highly trained people whose specialty is finding information. They are eager to help but only if you recognize their talents and worth.

To access librarians through the Internet, go to http://www.ipl.org/ref, the Web site of the Internet Public Library. Librarians affiliated with this site will answer questions you have about specific topics via email. Remember, librarians won't do the work for you, but they can make the work you do much more efficient and fruitful.

Melissa

For my persuasive speech, I chose to speak against prosecuting pregnant women who use drugs during their pregnancy. Because I am not an expert on this topic, I needed to enhance my credibility by finding reliable information. I asked the college librarian to help me conduct a search. She helped me locate information on a full-text database. I used mostly journal articles for my sources because I was able to locate information to support my argument. I felt more confident with my speech by using information from the American Medical Association and the American Psychiatric Association. Once I found solid information, I was ready to write my speech.

Print and Online Catalogs

Print and online catalogs are the first sources most students turn to in their search for supporting materials. If you are new to library research, catalogs can be the most user-friendly place to start. Catalogs allow you to search by title, author, or subject for books, journals, magazines, and many other print and electronic materials.

Most catalogs are computerized now, but you may find some libraries that still use print card catalogs that you search through by hand. Card catalogs organize sources by subject matter or by the title or author of a work. Each card features basic information about a particular source, such as when it was published, who published it, and whether it contains illustrations, photographs, or maps. Each card also indicates that source's call number, an alphabetical or numerical code that indicates exactly where that material is stored in the library. To learn more about call numbers and how they can help make your research more efficient, check out the Web site Understanding Call Numbers at http://www.hcc.hawaii.edu/education/hcc/library/callno.html.

Online catalogs display the same information that print catalogs do, but they often also provide a bit more detail, such as whether the material is checked out or not and how to obtain it if it is checked out. Online catalogs are particularly helpful because they allow you to perform keyword and subject searches. For example, if you don't know the full title of the source you want, you can search with a word that is included in the title. The computer will bring up a listing of all titles that include that word. You then can scan the list to find the specific source you want. Subject searches allow you to find all the sources that include information about a particular topic. For example, suppose Lin wanted to know if any recent books or magazine articles have been written about road rage. She doesn't have a specific author or title, so she searches on the subject of *driving*. This search would probably produce way too many sources to look through. She could then search on a more specific term, *road rage*. The results of this search would probably be much more manageable. Note that she also could have used Boolean operators to narrow or broaden her searches as necessary.

Once you have used a library's catalog to explore all the possible sources of information about your speech topic, you can then move to more specific information, such as databases, government documents, and reference works.

Databases and Indexes

Databases are collections of information stored electronically so they are easy to find and retrieve. Before computers were commonly used, researchers had to search manually through pages and pages of written text. They now use computer terminals to easily access the same materials. Databases are wonderful to use for several reasons. Computer searches take only minutes, so you can save valuable research time. Searches are more efficient because you can search using keywords and subjects in a way you can't do with printed materials. You can access materials from many other libraries besides your own. Sources are very current because records can be entered into a computerized database immediately and updated regularly. And databases conveniently allow you to copy information easily and search from computers inside and outside the library.

But databases also have their drawbacks. The so-called logic of databases is sometimes hard to understand, so searches can yield *false hits*, or citations unrelated to your topic. For example, a search for articles on "road rage" may yield articles on road construction and anger management techniques. Additionally,

database
Collections of information stored electronically so they are easy to find and retrieve.

bibliographic database
A database that indexes publishing data for books, periodical articles, government reports, statistics, patents, research reports, conference proceedings, and dissertations.

full-text database
A database that indexes the complete text of newspapers, periodicals, encyclopedias, research reports, court cases, books, and the like.

abstract
Summary of the text contained in an article or publication.

index
Alphabetical listing of the topics discussed in a specific publication, along with the corresponding year, volume, and page numbers.

many electronic databases (except catalogs) do not include material that is more than five to ten years old. So, if you are looking for historical trends, you will need to research other sources of information.

You will find two kinds of databases in libraries. **Bibliographic databases** index publishing data for books, periodical articles, government reports, statistics, patents, research reports, conference proceedings, and dissertations. **Full-text databases** index the complete text of newspapers, periodicals, encyclopedias, research reports, court cases, books, and the like. Bibliographic databases help you find a specific source of information, such as the title of a particular journal article, and a full-text database provides the entire text of that item. A new copy of this book features access to InfoTrac College Edition, a full-text database that you will find useful for your speech research. Note that because full-text databases store so much text, they are more likely to yield false hits. To avoid being overwhelmed by false hits, take a few minutes to complete InfoTrac College Edition Exercise 6.1, "Using InfoTrac College Edition," online under Student Resources for Chapter 6 at the *Invitation to Public Speaking* Web site.

Some databases provide abstracts of documents. An **abstract** is a summary of the text contained in an article or publication. An abstract can be very useful because it tells you whether or not a document includes the information you need, which can save you from searching for text you can't use. Most abstracts are about a paragraph long, but some can be lengthy. However long the abstract is, you need to track down the full text if you want to cite it in your speech—abstracts help you find relevant sources, but they are not the sources themselves.

When you want to search through materials that are published regularly, such as magazines, newspapers, yearbooks, scholarly journals, and proceedings from conferences, an index can be very helpful. An **index** is an alphabetical listing of the topics discussed in a specific publication, along with the corresponding year, volume, and page numbers. Many indexes are computerized, but some libraries still rely on the print versions. You can find indexes from almost every academic discipline and area of interest, such as agriculture, art, economics, ethnic studies, language, political science, speech communication, and women's studies. See

InfoTrac College Edition features millions of up-to-date full-text articles from hundreds of journals and magazines. You can access InfoTrac College Edition online at the *Invitation to Public Speaking* Web site by using the password that accompanied a new copy of this text.

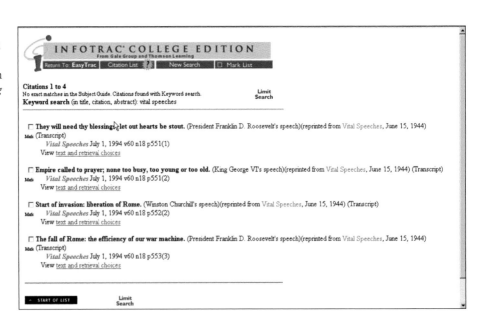

Figure 6.3

Indexes

InfoTrac/SearchBank	Citations, abstracts and full-text articles from more than 1,000 magazines, journals, and newspapers
LEXIS/NEXIS	Full-text database for legal, business, and current issues. Includes U.S. Supreme Court and lower court cases
CARL UnCover	Indexes scholarly journals and delivers documents. A fee is charged for document delivery
Readers Guide to Periodical Literature	Indexes 240 popular and general interest magazines, including *The New Yorker, Newsweek,* and *Time*
DataTimes	On-line newspaper database, including *Washington Post, Dallas Morning News,* and *San Francisco Chronicle*
Christian Science Monitor	Indexes the *Christian Science Monitor International Daily Newspaper*
New York Times Index	Indexes the *New York Times* newspaper
NewsBank	Microfiche collection covering current events from newspapers in over 100 cities
The Times Index (London)	Index to the daily *Times,* the *Sunday Times,* the *Times Literary Supplement,* the *Times Educational Supplement,* and the *Times Higher Education Supplement*
Wall Street Journal Index	Emphasizes financial news from the *Journal.* Includes Barron's Index, a subject and corporate index to *Barron's Business and Financial Weekly*
Washington Post Newspaper	Index of the newspaper from the nation's capital

Figure 6.3 for a list of commonly used indexes. Keep a few tips in mind when you search indexes for materials:

- Subject and keyword searches are crucial to finding what you want in an index, so be as specific and concise as you can.

- Indexes vary in how they classify topics, so a particular search term might not yield useful results from all indexes.

- You can usually find *something* on your topic in almost any index, so be sure you are searching indexes relevant to your topic.

Government Documents

Government documents can help you make a well-informed contribution to the public conversation. They contain all kinds of useful information:

- Statistics on population, personal income, education, crime, health, and the like
- Information about social issues such as employment, hunger, teen pregnancy, and the environment
- Issues discussed in Congress, such as gun control, seat belts, and education
- Information about historical events, such as wars or elections

- Information on local issues, such as funding for public education or charter schools, land disputes, water rights, and so on

- Research sponsored by the government

- Maps, charts, and posters that you can download or photocopy to make excellent visual aids for your speeches (Chapter 14)

You can find government documents in print, on CD-ROM, and sometimes on database indexes. Most government information now is available on the Internet, thanks to a 1996 mandate by Congress to cease publishing government information in microfiche and paper formats.[6] To find this information on the Internet, go to http:///www.infoctr.edu/fwl or search for "Federal Web Locator" on any search engine. The Federal Web Locator site is organized into six sections: legislative branch, judicial branch, executive branch, independent agencies, quasi-official agencies, and nongovernmental federally related sites. Each of these sections provides numerous links that can take you quickly and easily to all sorts of useful information. For access to the congressional record, go to http://www.access.gpo.gov/sudocs/aces/aces003.html. For statistical sources by subject, go to http://lcweb.loc.gov/global/legislative/congrec.html. For full-text statutes and legislation, try http://www.prairienet.org/~scruffy/f.htm. To access county and city government Web sites, try http://local.yahoo.com/local/.

Reference Works

What is the definition of the word *metamorphosis*? When and where was Oprah Winfrey born? Who was the first person to fly around the world? What was the worst storm in recorded history? When you are looking for simple facts and answers to general questions, consult the reference works in the reference section of your library. Reference works contain useful facts and information and can provide you with quick answers, thus saving you hours of time searching the Internet or digging through indexes and abstracts. If you are unsure of exactly which reference work to consult, ask you librarian for guidance. These are some of the more commonly used references and examples of each:

- *Almanacs:* Collections of facts on various subjects, such as the depth of Lake Michigan (*The World Almanac and Book of Facts*). For information about an online almanac, complete Interactive Activity 6.1, "Using an Almanac," online under Student Resources for Chapter 6 at the *Invitation to Public Speaking* Web site.

WEB SITE

- *Atlases:* Books of maps and geographical information (*The Times Atlas of World History, Goode's World Atlas*). For information about an online atlas, complete Interactive Activity 6.2, "Using an Atlas," online under Student Resources for Chapter 6 at the *Invitation to Public Speaking* Web site.

WEB SITE

- *Biographical dictionaries:* Information about famous and important people (*Dictionary of American Biography, Who's Who*). For information about an online biographical dictionary, complete Interactive Activity 6.3, "Using a Biographical Dictionary," online under Student Resources for Chapter 6 at the *Invitation to Public Speaking* Web site.

WEB SITE

- *Dictionaries:* Compilations of words and their definitions, correct spellings and pronunciations, origins, and synonyms and antonyms (*Oxford English Dictionary; Collins German-English, English-German Dictionary*).

- *Encyclopedias:* Overviews or surveys of a wide range of topics, such as butterflies, chemical warfare, or Toronto (*Encyclopedia Britannica, World Book*

Encyclopedia). Explore Britannica.com by completing Interactive Activity 6.4, "Using an Encyclopedia," online under Student Resources for Chapter 6 at the *Invitation to Public Speaking* Web site.

WEB SITE

- *Gazetteers or guidebooks:* Dictionaries or descriptions of geographical places. Guidebooks contain maps; gazetteers do not (*Chambers World Gazetteer: An A–Z of Geographical Information, Baedeker Guidebooks, Fodor's Travel Guides*).

- *Handbooks:* Summaries or survey of a single broad subject, such as meetings (*Robert's Rules of Order*).

- *Manuals:* Works that explain how to do something or how an organization operates (*United States Government Manual*).

- *Quotation dictionaries:* Compilations of historical and contemporary quotations (*The Oxford Dictionary of Quotations*).

- *Reviews:* Analyses and comments on the work of another, often authors of books, movies, plays, or other performances; artists; or people who make significant public arguments or claims (*Book Review Digest, Index to Scientific Reviews*).

- *Yearbooks:* Summaries of trends and events of the previous year. Can be limited to one subject or to one geographical area (*Information Please Almanac, Atlas and Yearbook; Americana Annual: An Encyclopedia of Events; Statistical Abstract of the United States*).[7]

Reference works can be helpful for a number of reasons that aren't always immediately obvious. They are quick to use and can give you a jump start on your research efforts. They can give you an overview of a topic and get you started on gathering supporting materials. Reference sources can help you cross-check information you find on the Internet or in another source. They can help you track

Reference materials are a rich source of interesting material for your speech. Use your research inventory to help you plan your trip to the library and keep track of the information you find there.

Table 6.1

Internet versus Library Research

USE THE INTERNET WHEN YOU	USE THE LIBRARY WHEN YOU
Can access a computer	May want assistance with your search
Want the most current ideas	Want comprehensive materials
Want to explore less established sources	Want established sources
Want shortened versions of print documents	Want the full text of a document
Know your specific subject or URL	Want to review databases
Can verify the accuracy and credibility of the information found	Can evaluate the appropriateness and relevance of the information found

down someone's credentials or give you the specific details of a person's life. Reference works tend to be timely or to give you the information you need for a specific time frame. And they can give you ideas for other places to look for the materials you need.

Evaluating Library Resources

Although the information in libraries is generally more reliable than materials on the Internet, you still must evaluate library sources and use them with care. Not all the sources you find will be credible or appropriate for your particular speech and audience. Evaluate library sources by using the same strategies you use to assess Internet sources: check that the source is reliable, authoritative, current, complete, relevant, and consistent. For detailed information about evaluating library sources, **WEB SITE** look online under Student Resources for Chapter 6 at the *Invitation to Public* *Speaking* Web site. Apply your skill at evaluating library resources by completing InfoTrac College Edition Exercise 6.2, "Evaluating Library Information," online under Student Resources for Chapter 6 at the *Invitation to Public Speaking* Web site. For a summary of when to use Internet or library research, see Table 6.1.

Speech Step 6.2 / Research and Evaluate Internet and Library Sources

Begin to research on the Internet and at the library for the materials you will use to support your speech. As you research, consider the strengths and weaknesses of both sources given your topic, speech goals, and audience. Follow the guidelines in this chapter to evaluate the strength of the information you find. Discard any information that does not seem reliable, authoritative, current, complete, relevant, or consistent.

Conduct Research Interviews

The Internet and the library are both sources of information that will provide you with relevant and interesting material for your speeches. But both lack one thing: the dynamic exchange of information you can get from talking to another person about your speech topic. To help you add this component to your speech, you can gather supporting materials by interviewing others.

Using the words of other people in a speech can provide a sense of immediacy, bring abstract concepts and arguments to life, and make seemingly distant issues hit home. As such, including the results of an interview in your speech can be a powerful way to present your ideas. An **interview** is a planned interaction with another person that is organized around inquiry and response, with one person asking questions while the other person answers them.[8] As this definition indicates, interviews require planning, and productive interviews involve more than simply asking a few questions. You must first decide who you'll interview, then schedule the interview, decide on what questions to ask, conduct the interview in a professional and ethical manner, then follow up with a letter of thanks.

interview
Planned interaction with another person that is organized around inquiry and response, with one person asking questions while the other person answers them.

Determine Who to Interview

Your first step in conducting interviews is to determine who you want to interview. There are several criteria you can use to identify the best interview subjects for your speech. Who are the experts on my speech topic? Who has personal experience with the topic? Who will my audience find interesting and credible? Who has time to speak with me? Who do I have the time to contact?

As you gather other supporting materials from the Internet and the library, also keep your eyes open for people in your area who might be excellent sources of information. If you have time, you also might consider contacting people who live outside your area via email or the telephone. Choose interview subjects who have credentials and experiences relevant to your topic and so can speak intelligently

Reporters often use interviews to gather information to be sure their stories are accurate and interesting. If you're planning to conduct an interview for your next speech, who might you interview? How could the information this person provides make your speech more interesting and relevant?

about it. A good interview subject might be a well-known expert or scholar, a head of an agency or company, someone on staff or in a support position, or a member of a community group, club, or organization.

Schedule the Interview

Although there are exceptions, most people are flattered to be asked for an interview and will agree if you present yourself and your request respectfully. To ensure that a potential source sees you as credible and professional, take a moment to consider why you want the interview and why this person is an appropriate interview subject, what specific types of information you want to gather, roughly what questions you'll ask, and approximately how much time you want to spend with this person. When people are asked for an interview, they want to know the answers to all of these questions. Before you contact someone to request the interview, rehearse what you'll say a few times (like you would a speech) so you sound organized and professional. In your request, include the following:

- Identify who you are, providing your full name, where you're from (school, place of business), the public speaking course you're in, and your instructor's name.

- Specify the requirements of your assignment, such as its purpose, length, and topic.

- Describe why you've chosen to contact the person (for example, she's an expert in the field, he's the head of an agency).

- Request the interview, letting the person know how much time it will take and what kinds of questions you'll ask. Include two or three of your most important or engaging questions.

Note that by describing the types of questions you'll ask, your interview subjects can determine whether they can answer them and if they need to prepare before you arrive. And by letting them know how long you need for the interview, they can schedule time for you. Additionally, longer interviews often mean they're expected to give more detailed answers than they would in a shorter interview. For a sample interview request, look online under Student Resources for Chapter 6 at **WEB SITE** the *Invitation to Public Speaking* Web site.

Prepare for the Interview

Preparing for interviews often takes longer than conducting them, but the payoffs of being well prepared outweigh the extra time you spend. The two components of preparing for interviews are designing your questions and deciding how you will record your interview.

Designing interview questions. Take time with your interview questions because they are your guide for an interview. Showing up with a plan to "just see how it develops" may be a good strategy for meeting a new friend, but it usually does not get you what you need in an interview. Even seasoned interviewers plan their questions carefully before they begin an interview, and most of them also research their interview subjects extensively.[9]

As you design your questions, think about what you want to know by the time you leave an interview. The goal of your questions should be to obtain information that you couldn't find through your Internet and library research. For example, in her speech on road rage, Lin couldn't find information about the personality profiles of people prone to road rage. When she interviewed the driving instructor, she asked him about his experiences with students who fell into road rage. Thus she was able to get the information she needed.

Three kinds of questions are commonly used in interviews: open-ended questions, closed-ended questions, and probes (open-ended and closed-ended questions are also discussed in Chapter 5). Open-ended questions invite a wide range of possible responses. They can be as broad as "How did you become a driving instructor?" and "What are your thoughts on this most recent form of legislation?" Open-ended questions are useful for several reasons. They are usually nonthreatening and so prompt interviewees to do most of the talking. They do not restrict the form or content of an answer, and they allow interviewees to offer information voluntarily. Finally, they encourage interviewees to pull together ideas, knowledge, and experiences in interesting ways.

A closed-ended question invites a brief, focused answer and allows the interviewer to keep tighter control of the direction of the conversation. A closed-ended question might be "How long have you been a driving instructor?" or "Do many of your students display road rage?" Closed-ended questions are useful because they can be answered easily and quickly, encourage interviewees to give you specific information, and result in shorter answers for you to process.

Most research on interviewing suggests that using a combination of open-ended and closed-ended questions yields the best results in an interview. Open-ended questions give you more stories and details than closed-ended questions, but when you just need facts, there's nothing like a closed-ended question to prompt the specific answer you need.[10]

Another type of interview question is a **probe**, a question that fills out or follows up an answer to a previous question. Probes function in many ways. Some probes are nonverbal, such as head nods or questioning eyes that indicate interest and a request to continue. Other probes take the form of minimal responses, slight vocalizations such as "Oh?" "Really?" "Um-hmm," and "Is that so?" Some probes are more direct. They ask for clarification, as in "Let me see if I've got this right. Did you say that . . . ?" or "Could you explain what those figures mean for our community?" Or they ask for elaboration, as in "Why do you say you're angry about this new legislation?" or "When that first driver went crazy with you in the car, what was your reaction?" Probes are excellent interview tools because they allow you to take an initial question further than you'd planned and to get a more comprehensive answer.

probe
Question that fills out or follows up an answer to a previous question.

Recording the interview. As you prepare for an interview, consider whether you want to tape-record your conversation or record it on paper. Both methods have advantages and disadvantages. On tape you have a record of your exact conversation, but you have to transcribe the whole thing to find the exact quotes you want, which can be time consuming. A tape recorder can also sometimes make an interviewee nervous and less prone to share stories and ideas. However, with a tape recorder you are free to relax a bit during the interview and make more extensive eye contact because you aren't busy writing things down.

When you record your interview on paper, you have the advantage of being able to make notes about nonverbal aspects of the interview that may help you when you repeat a quote in your speech, and when it is over, you already have a written transcript of your conversation. However, because you are trying to record all that is said, it can be harder to relax and simply engage in a conversation with your interviewee.

Whatever your choice, be prepared and come to the interview with a tape recorder and tapes or plenty of paper and a working pen. Check your equipment before the interview, and set up the recorder before you begin asking questions. Whether you plan to take notes on paper or record on tape, ask your interviewee if you have permission to record your conversation.

Conduct the Interview

The guidelines for conducting interviews are essentially grounded in the rules of common courtesy, so are not difficult to follow. Show up on time for your interviews, and begin and end them promptly. This communicates respect for your interviewees and their schedules. Begin interviews by introducing yourself to your interviewee. Request permission to record the interview and set up your equipment as needed. Then restate your purpose for the interview and a little bit about your assignment. Begin with questions that will put the interviewee at ease, and then follow those with your most important questions. As the interview progresses, remember that although you are having a conversation with your interviewee, you need to listen more than you talk—you are there to get the other person's perspectives and ideas, and you can't do this if you dominate the conversation.

At the end of your interviews, ask your interviewees if they would like to add any additional information. You may get a piece of information or a story you did not think to ask directly for but that fits into your speech perfectly. Finally, thank your interviewees verbally for their time, and be sure you have recorded names, professional titles, and addresses correctly so you can cite them accurately and send letters of thanks. For additional information about conducting an interview, see the Prepared Question Interview Web site at http://www.tpub.com/journalist/57.htm.

Follow Up the Interview

Review your notes or transcribe your tapes as soon after the interview as you can, filling in details that are fresh in your mind and extending abbreviations you might have used in recording words on paper. Make notes of ideas that came to you as you listened to your interviewees, such as places in your speech that a particular quote or story might go or ways you might use some of the interview information in your opening and closing comments. And remember, always send formal letters of thanks to your interviewees, communicating your appreciation for their time and willingness to share information with you. You might even share with them some of the interview material you've decided to include in your speech.

Act Professionally and Dress Appropriately

Being professional does not necessarily mean acting formally or dressing in your finest clothes. Being professional means you take your job seriously, you are reliable, and you treat others with respect. In interviews, being professional means you are prepared, you dress according to the environment and situation, and you are ethical. In the last few sections we explored how you can prepare for interviews. In this section we discuss appropriate dress, and in the next section we discuss the principles of ethical interviewing.

The rule of thumb in dressing for a job interview is to dress at, or at one level nicer than, the level you would ordinarily dress for that job. The same rule holds true for interviews you conduct for speech research. If you would wear jeans and a T-shirt to work where you are conducting your interview, then wear clean jeans and a shirt or slacks and slightly dressy shirt. If you would wear a suit to work where you're conducting the interview, then wear business clothing. Although this guideline might sound silly, communication research confirms that appearance matters and our professionalism does get communicated by what we wear. When you wear appropriate clothing to your interviews, your interviewees will feel you are taking yourself and the interview seriously.

Ethical Interviews

Being an ethical public speaker is especially important when you conduct interviews, because your interview subjects are entrusting you with their words—and hence their reputations. Ethical interviewing means preparing for interviews, asking appropriate questions, using quotes and information honestly, including only what was said and staying true to the intention of the speaker, and giving credit to interviewees for the words and ideas you include in your speech.

At times it may be tempting to alter a statement, embellish a story, or change a number or example just slightly to fit your needs. However, if the public dialogue is to function in any meaningful way, we must present material that is accurate and true. Information is inaccurate even if it's been changed *only slightly,* and people cannot make rational and reasonable choices if they have incorrect information.

Of course, ethics also apply to interviewees. If an interviewee provides information that seems inconsistent with what your other research supports, take the time to double-check your own research and the credentials of your interview subject, and ask your interviewee for documentation or sources that support unusual claims. If an interviewee provides information that is highly personal or would compromise the integrity or reputation of others, do not use that information in your speech. And, of course, if an individual shares something with you "off the record," that information should stay out of your speech and out of your conversations with others.

Using your *Invitation to Public Speaking* CD-ROM, watch the video clip of Katie Couric interviewing two aid workers detained in Afghanistan in 2001. Assess the ethics of the interview.

Preparing for, conducting, and following up an interview can be a detailed, time-consuming process. However, all your hard work will result in a conversation with someone who may give you the information you need to make your speech come alive. The supporting materials you gather from interviews also supplement and confirm the materials you find in your Internet and library research. Now that you've explored what type of supporting material you need for your speeches and how to go about obtaining it, let's look at some ways to make your research efforts a little easier.

Research Tips

Researching your speech topic can take time, but if done in an organized and systematic way, it can provide you with the supporting materials you need for a successful presentation. To make the research process manageable, remember to give yourself plenty of time, and consider the following tips for doing research.

Begin by Filling Out Your Research Inventory

Take the time to fill out your research inventory so you can figure out what you have and what you need. Use the last section in the inventory, "Sources for this information," to help you remember where you might search for material. Update your inventory as you begin finding information and discovering other sources.

Take Notes and Make Copies

Keep careful, complete notes and records of sources to ensure you've got accurate information. If you find later you've got an incomplete record of a source, your careful documentation will help you locate that item again, saving you much time and frustration. For Internet and library sources, include in your notes the *full name* of the author, book or magazine, article or document, publisher, and place of publication; the exact URL of a Web site or page; the publication or posting date; and the page numbers where you found your information. For interviews, include in your notes the full name of the interviewee, his or her title, and place of business; and the date of the interview. All of your notes should include the exact, complete phrases or words you are citing or quoting.

In addition to taking notes, photocopy and print out pages of the more extensive material you want to cite, paraphrase, or quote. Be sure to check spelling, titles, dates, and sources twice for accuracy. When you record a URL, make sure it is absolutely accurate. Any mistake, even a missing period or a misspelling, may lead to an incorrect site or a dead end. Check each note for completeness by asking yourself, "If someone else wanted to go to this exact source, could they do so by looking at my bibliography or typing in this URL?" and, "If I want to cite this in my speech, do I have all the information I need?" Watch how Carol Godart cites her source material orally in her persuasive speech on fat discrimination, by accessing the video clips for Chapter 6 under Speech Interactive on your CD-ROM.

Avoid Plagiarism

plagiarism
Presenting another person's words and ideas as your own.

patchwork plagiarism
Constructing a complete speech that you present as your own from portions of several different sources.

global plagiarism
Stealing an entire speech from a single source and presenting it as your own.

incremental plagiarism
Presenting select portions from a single speech as your own.

Plagiarism is presenting another person's words and ideas as your own. That is, plagiarism is stealing someone else's work and taking credit for it. Plagiarism is a serious issue in public speaking because it's dishonest and detrimental to a healthy public dialogue. There are three types of plagiarism. **Patchwork plagiarism** is constructing a complete speech that you present as your own from portions of several different sources. **Global plagiarism** is stealing an entire speech from a single source and presenting it as your own. **Incremental plagiarism** is presenting select portions from a single speech as your own.

All three forms of plagiarism are extremely unethical. However, they are easy to avoid. As you do your research, avoid unintentional plagiarism by taking careful notes, documenting the source of each idea. Remember to cite these sources in your speech, even if you are paraphrasing an idea or borrowing only one phrase. And consider the consequences of plagiarizing: loss of credibility, failing the assignment or course, and perhaps even expulsion from your school. Finally, the most obvious way to avoid plagiarism is to do your own work and to give credit to others for their ideas and words.

Set Up a Filing System

As you gather information, it is tempting to put it all in one folder and wait to organize it when you sit down to draft your speech. This may save you time in the beginning of your search, but it will add time toward the end. It is much more efficient to organize your information as you go. Not only does filing as you go help you be sure you've found the information you set out to find, but it helps you keep track of what you've already found.

Begin by organizing your materials according to your research inventory. Set up separate files for examples and stories, statistics, testimony, and definitions (Chapter 7) or color-code your materials by type of evidence with a highlighter or other system. Make notations on your notes and copies, identifying the type of evidence, the date, the point the material makes, and where you might use it in your speech (for example, "good for introduction"). As you gather more material, also organize your materials by main points and subpoints (Chapters 4 and 9). To get started on a filing system for your research, complete InfoTrac College Edition Exercise 6.3, "Filing Your Research," online under Student Resources for Chapter 6 at the *Invitation to Public Speaking* Web site.

Gather More Material Than You Think You'll Need

We often underestimate the amount of material we need to support our ideas. Or we think we've found the perfect example, only to discover that when we put the speech together, we can't use it after all. For these reasons, gather more information than you think you'll need. Collect several possibilities for your introduction and conclusion, not just one. If your instructor asks for three sources from one time frame, gather six and use the best three. If you need one great example of what a statistic really means, ask your interviewee for a few, and choose the one that best illustrates your point.

When you have finished organizing your speech, you should have supporting material left over. The extra time you spent gathering these materials will not go to waste, because they will help you in your question-and-answer session, especially if an audience member asks you to elaborate on a point you made. Extra supporting materials will also give you confidence as you present your speech—you will know that you're speaking with plenty of support at your fingertips.

Begin Your Bibliography with Your First Source

A bibliography is a record of each of the sources you use in your speech, and exactness is the key to a good bibliography. There are many different styles for bibliographies. Be sure to check with your instructor, or your employer if a work presentation requires a bibliography, for which style to follow. You can see samples of bibliographic entries by buying a style manual or checking one out from the library or by looking online under Student Resources for Chapter 6 at the *Invitation to Public Speaking* Web site.

WEB SITE

Start your bibliography the moment you collect your first source. Choose the style you want to use with the first entry, and stick to it as you construct your bibliography. By doing so, you will have the citations you need before you log off the Internet or leave the library or interview. And when you've finished your research, you will have a **preliminary bibliography,** a list of all the potential sources you'll use as you prepare your speech. (See Figure 6.4 for a sample of a preliminary bibliography.) As you organize your speech, you'll decide which information to include or not include and remove entries you don't need. When you finish putting your speech together, you will find your bibliography is complete—and you didn't have to rush to finish it just before your speech.

preliminary bibliography
List of all the potential sources you'll use as you prepare your speech.

Thank Others for Their Assistance

We rarely work in isolation, and many people will help you gather materials for your speeches. Remember to thank each of these people, formally or informally, depending on their efforts and contributions. If you interviewed someone, thank them in writing. If you received assistance from a librarian, a teaching assistant, or your instructor, thank them verbally and, as appropriate, mention to their supervisor how helpful they were. If people from the community share a valuable

Figure 6.4

Sample Preliminary Bibliography

Preliminary Bibliography
U.S. Department of Transportation. <u>Aggressive Driving: Help Get the Word Out.</u> Washington, D.C.: National Highway Traffic Safety Administration, 1998.
Browne, Timothy. Conahan's Driving School, Inc. Personal interview. Denver, CO. 23 February 2002,
Filetti, Linda Baker. "Characteristics of Individuals with High and Low Driving Anger." Ph.D. diss., Colorado State University, 2000.
Gilbert, Derrick I.M. "Road Rage." <u>Henna Man: Poems.</u> New York: Riverhead Books, 2000.
James, Leon. "Traffic Psychologist Confesses to Road Rage." <u>Driver Alert: Electronic Magazine</u> 1, no. 1 (November 1997). Accessed 4 June 2002. http://www.aloha.net/~dyc/driveralert/behavior.html.

resource, be sure to thank them for their help. Your success at gathering materials depends just as much on the generosity of people who assist you as your willingness to spend time on research. Acknowledge their contributions, and you will almost certainly receive their help again if you ever need it.

For additional research tips, check out Sandra Whitman's Web page, Research Tips, at http://servercc.oakton.edu/~wittman/find/research.htm.

Speech Step 6.3 / Prepare Your Preliminary Bibliography

With the supporting materials you've collected for your speech so far, prepare your preliminary bibliography. Use a style of your choosing or a style your instructor asks you to use. Remember to record the materials you find on the Internet, at the library, and through interviews. Speech Builder Express can help you prepare your preliminary bibliography with whatever citation style you choose or are assigned.

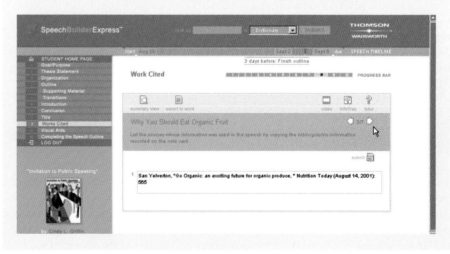

Figure 6.5

Research Inventory Worksheet

Speech topic: _____

General purpose: _____

Specific purpose: _____

Thesis statement: _____

My audience is: _____

I currently have:

    Examples and stories:

    Statistics:

    Testimony:

    Definitions:

    This information is relevant, accurate, and credible because:

My audience will want to hear:

    Examples of the following:

    Statistics for the following:

    Testimony about the following:

    Definitions of the following:

The kinds of sources they will find trustworthy are:

I need to find the following information:

Sources for this information:

Chapter Summary

When you take time to take stock of your personal knowledge and experience, use the Internet, use the library, and conduct quality interviews, you can gather the range of materials you need to enter the public dialogue with integrity. By using search engines, librarians, catalogs, databases and indexes, government documents, reference works, and professional interviewing practices, you can collect a strong base of supporting materials for your speeches. When you learn to evaluate the strengths and weaknesses of your sources by assessing their reliability, authoritativeness, currency, completeness, relevancy, and consistency, you then can present ethical arguments and proposals to your audiences.

Doing research may seem like a lot of work, or it may seem easier to gather information from a computer or a book rather than a face-to-face interview. However, with a bit of planning, you can make the process easier and very productive. Start your research by filling out your research inventory. As you gather materials, take notes and make copies to avoid plagiarism and to help you prepare your bibliography. Set up a filing system early to keep careful track of your materials, and gather more than you think you'll need. Finally, thank the people who helped you gather your materials for their assistance.

Without a doubt, gathering materials takes time. But the time you spend can be rewarding if you are systematic and careful in your approach. The public dialogue depends on a wide range of information and perspectives. Gathering materials so you can present and respond to this range ensures that the conversation continues, evolves, and stays lively and healthy.

Don't be afraid to ask librarians for help. Their job is to help you, and you'll find that they'll usually be able to point you toward just the information you want.

After reading this chapter, use your CD-ROM and the *Invitation to Public Speaking* Web site to review the following concepts, answer the review questions, and complete the suggested activities.

Key Concepts

research inventory (126)
information overload (128)
Internet (129)
World Wide Web (129)
browser (129)
Web site (129)
Web page (129)

URL (uniform resource locator) (129)
links (129)
bookmark (129)
search engines (130)
Boolean operators (130)
database (135)
bibliographic database (136)
full-text database (136)

abstract (136)
index (136)
interview (141)
probe (143)
plagiarism (146)
patchwork plagiarism (146)
global plagiarism (146)
incremental plagiarism (146)
preliminary bibliography (147)

Review Questions

1. Fernando is planning to do research for his speech on the impact of AIDS in the Hispanic community. His audience is a group of students, parents, and teachers from a high school located in his community who have become interested in the issue and want to raise awareness and money. What kind of research do you suggest he include? What might be the strengths and weaknesses of this research?

2. If you are doing service learning in your public speaking course, take time to consider your speech topic and the supporting materials you will need. If you are gathering information for an agency, set up time to talk with someone there to help you identify what kind of material you should gather. If you are presenting your speech about the agency, what information sources will you use? Will you use the Internet, the library, personal interviews, or all three?

3. Log on to http://www.prairienet.org/~scruffy/f.htm and browse through the site. Can you find "scruffy's" credentials? If you can't find this person's credentials, how else might you evaluate the strength or weaknesses of this site? Will you rely on it as a site to give you reliable and accurate information? Why or why not?

4. Use the evaluation criteria described in this chapter to evaluate the strengths and weaknesses of the informa-

tion you have gathered for your next speech. Is it reliable, authoritative, current, complete, relevant, and consistent? Based on your assessment, identify information you might discard, and consider whether you need to continue to do more research for your speech.

5. Draft a list of questions you would like to ask a personal contact for your next speech. Keep in mind your speech goals, time limitations, and your audience. Now organize that list so the most important questions are first and the least important ones are last. Next consider how you will begin your interview. Will you start with your most important questions or some warm-up questions? With what questions will you close the interview?

6. Bring the material you've gathered for your next speech to class. In groups of two or three, help one another organize this material. What suggestions can you make to help keep track of information and remember what has been gathered?

7. Using the same material you used in question 6, discuss in groups of two or three what research you might cite directly in your speeches and what material you might use as background material. Consider your speech goals, your audience, and the ethics of public speaking in your discussion.

The *Invitation to Public Speaking* Web Site

The *Invitation to Public Speaking* Web site features the review questions about the Web sites suggested on pages 128, 129, 135, 144, and 148, the interactive activities suggested on pages 138–139 and the InfoTrac College Edition exercises suggested on pages 136, 140, and 147.

You can access this site via your CD-ROM or at http://www.wadsworth.com/product/griffin. To access Speech Builder Express in order to complete Speech Step 6.3, you will need the username and password included under "Speech Builder Express" on your CD-ROM.

Web Links

Interactive Activities

6.1: Using an Almanac (138)
Purpose: To find evidence in an almanac.

6.2: Using an Atlas (138)
Purpose: To find evidence using an atlas.

6.3: Using a Biographical Dictionary (138)
Purpose: To find evidence using a biographical dictionary.

6.4: Using an Encyclopedia (139)
Purpose: To find evidence using an encyclopedia.

InfoTrac College Edition Exercises

6.1: Using InfoTrac College Edition (136)
Purpose: To learn how to conduct simple and advanced searches of InfoTrac College Edition.

6.2: Evaluating Library Information (140)
Purpose: To apply the evaluation criteria for library materials.

6.3: Filing Your Research (147)
Purpose: To create a filing system for your speech research.

Speech Interactive on the *Invitation to Public Speaking* CD-ROM

The following video clips of speeches referenced in this chapter are included under Speech Interactive on your *Invitation to Public Speaking* CD-ROM. After you have watched the clips, click on "Critique" to answer the questions for analysis.

Video Clip 1: Using a Variety of Sources: Carol Godart (146). Watch how Carol Godart cites her source material in her persuasive speech on fat discrimination. How many different sources does Carol cite in her speech? What are

the sources she uses to convince her audience that fat discrimination is a serious problem? Does she include all necessary information with each citation?

Video Clip 2: Katie Couric Interview on *Dateline*, November 27, 2001 (145). Watch Katie Couric's interview with two aid workers who were detained in Afghanistan in 2001 and later released. What kind of questions does Couric ask? Why did she use these type of questions? Was the interview ethical?

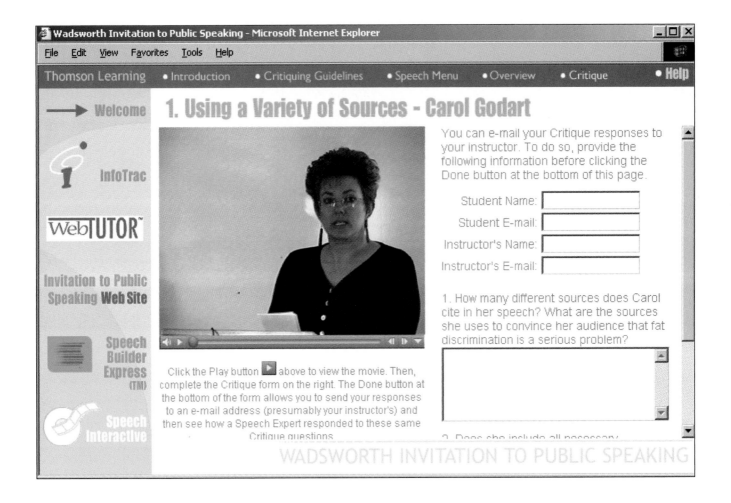

Developing and Supporting Your Ideas

In this chapter you will learn to

Explain the importance of supporting materials in
a speech

Identify and provide examples of the five main
types of supporting material

Apply tips for using each of the five types of
supporting materials effectively

The public dialogue is kindled by claims. The word claim *comes from the Latin* clamare, *which means "to call or cry out." There is something social about a claim: someone calls out to someone else. When one person asserts something, there is the expectation that another person can hear the call and understand the claim.*

—Adapted from James Crosswhite, *The Rhetoric of Reason: Writing and the Attractions of Argument*, 1996 [1]

claim
Assertion that must be proved.

evidence
The materials that speakers use to support their ideas.

When we enter the public dialogue, we take part in a social interaction—one person makes a claim about a topic to an audience, "calling out" to them. In public speaking, a **claim** is defined as an assertion that must be proved. When we make claims, we explore and exchange ideas, we respond to one another, and we clarify, refine, and revise our positions. When we communicate our claims effectively, the public dialogue is stimulated and enhanced.

To communicate effectively we must understand how to support our claims or prove our assertions. We prove our assertions by using **evidence,** the materials speakers use to support their ideas. Evidence is the supporting material that allows you to explain a process with confidence, share a perspective in a way that encourages a positive audience response, identify a problem and pose a solution, motivate an audience to action, or acknowledge someone's accomplishments. Evidence comes from the information you gather in your research on the Internet, at the library, and in interviews. Your evidence is your proof, and strong evidence helps you build your credibility. In Chapter 8, you'll read about how you can enhance your personal credibility. In this chapter you'll learn how to assess the credibility, or believability, of your evidence. Credible evidence is the foundation of the common language in the public sphere.

The five most common types of supporting material are examples, narratives, statistics, testimony, and definitions. You are probably familiar with these types of evidence, but you may not be sure when to use them or how to evaluate their strengths and weaknesses. When to use and how to evaluate supporting material is the focus of this chapter. Let's start with examples as evidence.

Oprah Winfrey is a credible source of information for millions of people in the United States. Yet some people question her credibility because of her enormous popularity, asserting that she holds too much influence over what people think. What makes a person credible in your eyes?

AP/Wide World Photos

Examples

Examples are specific instances used to illustrate a concept, experience, issue, or problem. Examples can be brief, only a word or a sentence or two, or they can be detailed and developed quite fully. Examples can also be real or hypothetical. A **real example** is an instance that actually took place. A **hypothetical example** is an instance that did not take place but could have. Generally, real examples are more credible and convey a sense of immediacy. Consider the following real examples from student speeches:

> In her speech on binge drinking, Eileen used a powerful example of a binge drinker by describing her friend who "consumed 12 to 15 beers, 5 nights a week, and stopped each evening only because she ran out of beer, time, or money."

> In his speech on the dangers of exotic pets, Kyle used an example provided by the head of his city's Pest Control and Wildlife Department: "According to the Department's head, one man had a gaboon viper, a cobra, a black-tailed rattlesnake, a copperhead, three large boas, and a full-grown alligator who acted as a 'guard dog.'" Kyle explained to his audience that these pets were hazardous because the owner was "bitten by his gaboon viper and died from the bite. The remaining so-called pets? They went to the Humane Society to be adopted by other people or to be euthanized."

> As examples of the negative side effects of anabolic steroids, Jon cited "cosmetic changes, infertility, heart disease, stroke, prostate problems, and liver toxicity." In addition, he mentioned "disfigurement, specifically jutting foreheads, prominent cheek-bones, and elongated jaws."

These students used examples to help them clarify exactly what they meant when they used the terms *binge drinker, hazardous pets,* and *negative side effects.*

Occasionally you can clarify a point with a hypothetical example. A hypothetical example usually begins with words like *imagine, suppose,* or *let's say that.* For example, when Clara addressed a group of teenagers in an after-school program on proper eating, she could have simply said, "Skipping breakfast isn't good for you." Instead, to be a more effective speaker, she supported her claim with a hypothetical example:

> Suppose you skipped breakfast this morning. Let's see what that would do to your energy level by about 9 or 10 o'clock—that's during second period, right? If you haven't eaten by then, you'll probably feel bored or restless, and maybe sad or unmotivated. You might also feel angry or irritable, kind of grouchy and crabby. And maybe you'll feel a little lightheaded or dizzy if you stand up fast. You might have a headache. You'll definitely have trouble concentrating on your school work because your blood sugar is low or because all you can think about is how hungry you are. Sound familiar to any of you?

Clara's hypothetical example, although not a real example about a real person, was grounded in her research and helped her audience understand more clearly why skipping meals isn't good for them.

Several criteria can help you decide when using an example would be most effective. Consider the following guidelines, all of which help you answer in advance any questions your audience may have about your topic.

Use Examples to Clarify Concepts

Identify the concepts in your speech that your audience might consider complex or unfamiliar, and then use an example to help you frame those concepts in terms your audience will understand. In other words, try to anticipate what parts of your speech might prompt your audience to ask, "What do you mean by that?" Examples

example
Specific instance used to illustrate a concept, experience, issue, or problem.

real example
Instance that actually took place.

hypothetical example
Instance that did not take place but could have.

Canadian figure skaters Jamie Sale and David Pelletier received a silver, rather than a gold, medal at the 2002 Winter Olympics as a result of biased judging. They were later co-awarded a gold medal. If you were giving a speech about biased judging in the Olympics, you could use this pair of skaters as an example of how biased judging can affect the outcome of an event. Can you think of other examples you could use in a speech about this topic?

frame abstract concepts and experiences in terms of concrete actions, events, people, and things. Thus an example can make an abstract or complex point clearer.

In Clara's case, she anticipated her audience's question "what does she mean by 'isn't good' for me?" Her detailed example about the physical and mental impacts of skipping breakfast clarified what she meant by "isn't good." For another instance of an example used to clarify a concept, use your *Invitation to Public Speaking* CD-ROM to watch a video clip of former Texas governor Ann Richards under Speech Interactive. Richards uses an example of former U.S. representative Barbara Jordan's resolve and fortitude to give her audience a better sense of Jordan and her character.

Use Examples to Reinforce Points

What parts of your speech might prompt the audience to say, "I don't see that it matters"? Examples help an audience see your points in terms of the common human experience. As such, examples help audiences recognize the relevance and importance of your points in their own lives. Kyle used an example of how unpredictable exotic pets can be, reinforcing his point that owning exotic pets is a dangerous hobby. By describing what happened to an owner of such pets, and then what happened to the animals after the owner died, Kyle encouraged his audience to see themselves in the owner's shoes.

Use Examples to Bring Concepts to Life or to Elicit Emotions

When someone says, "I'm not affected by that issue," an example helps bring a concept to life by providing specific images an audience can picture in their minds. When they're able to create a mental picture, one that is filtered through their own thoughts and experiences, they can better understand how an issue affects them or someone they know. Jon's illustration of the various negative side effects from steroids drew his audience into a topic that seemed remote to many of them. Most of his audience knew the use of steroids was "bad," but with his example they could imagine jutting foreheads, strokes, and heart disease in some of their favorite athletes. Jon's example made the use of steroids seem more real and personal to them. Similarly, Kyle's example of the exotic pets being euthanized brought out the emotions in his audience. No longer were the exotic pets curiosities; they became real animals who died through no fault of their own.

Use Examples to Build Your Case or Make Credible Generalizations

When someone says, "It's not as common or prevalent as you say," using a number of examples helps them see that it is. A series of examples can help you build a case or help you make a plausible generalization. For example, if you can cite numerous examples of the prevalence of binge drinkers in college dorms, you can make a stronger claim for binge drinking as a significant problem.

Tips for Using Examples Effectively

Not all examples are equal. Some don't illustrate your point well and others won't resonate with your audience. To evaluate an example for its strengths and weaknesses, consider the following questions.[2]

Is the example relevant? Does it refer to the point you are making or to something else? In her speech about binge drinking, if Eileen offers an example of treatment programs for older adults as her "success story solution," but her target population is teens and individuals in their 20s, her example isn't relevant. It's a great example of a solution, but not the solution to her specific problem.

Is the hypothetical example ethical? Use hypothetical examples carefully because audiences don't like to be misled or lied to. When you offer a hypothetical example, make sure it represents events or information grounded in fact. Your hypothetical example should be plausible; it really could be true or have happened. You also should tell your audience it is hypothetical. Don't try to trick them into believing a made-up example, however plausible, is real when it isn't.

Are there enough examples to support your claim? Is one enough, or do you need several? If you can't find more than one example to support your point, perhaps your claim actually is unfounded. If you want to suggest something is common, but you can't find examples of it, it may not be as common as you thought. One example suggests an isolated incident and not a trend, so avoid generalizing from a single example. When you are making a case for the existence of something, like the problem of binge drinking in the dorms, you'll need quite a few examples. However, if you are illustrating what you mean by binge drinking, one example should suffice.

Have you accounted for the counterexamples? Counterexamples are those examples that contradict your claims—they make what you say false or at least weaken your assertions. If Jon found that some athletes who used anabolic steroids experienced no negative side effects, he would have to explain why this is so. If he can't explain these counterexamples, he has to change his claim to "some athletes experience some negative side effects when they take anabolic steroids"—he can't claim that anabolic steroids affect all athletes negatively because he has examples of athletes who aren't affected negatively.

Is the example appropriate for my audience? Some examples are too graphic, emotional, detailed, or personal for an audience. Use caution with examples that contain violent details, the manipulation of emotions, overly technical material, or the use of explicit personal details. For example, when Judy Sheperd speaks about the murder of her son Matthew, she describes his body wrapped in bandages with tubes coming out from everywhere. She shares that his ear had been reattached by surgeons and continued to bleed as she and her family stayed with him in his final days of life. However, she does not offer more graphic details of his physical condition, recognizing they would prevent her audience from listening to her message if they remained caught in the violence of his death. She draws them in emotionally but does not provide overly graphic details.

 Using examples is an excellent way to support your claims and develop or clarify your information. Examples are important parts of speeches, and, when used appropriately, they can help you make your points clear and compelling. To think more about the effectiveness and ethics of using examples in your speeches, complete InfoTrac College Edition Exercise 7.1, "Tax Cut Beneficiaries" online under Student Resources for Chapter 7.

Narratives

A **narrative** is a story that re-creates or foretells real or hypothetical events. Narratives often are highly symbolic, which explains part of the attraction of people to stories, and they help us explain, interpret, and understand events in our lives or the lives of others.[3] Speakers can use **brief narratives**, sometimes called *vignettes,* which take only a short time to tell and illustrate a specific point, or **extended narratives,** which take longer to tell and can be integrated into your speech more fully. Whatever the length of a story, it should organize the events you describe in your speech, flesh out characters, and tell of actions, settings, and plots.

Narratives capture experiences, appeal to various senses, and call out to our emotions, intellects, and imaginations. They transport us to other places and show us other ways of seeing and living. However long or short a narrative, speakers entering the public dialogue use them to remind, predict, explain, and connect ideas and experiences. They use narratives to draw in emotions and to teach lessons or share vivid experiences or incidents.

Because stories are so appealing to audiences, and because they can make a point in dramatic or compelling ways, look for stories as you gather your material and consider using them in your speeches. A carefully selected and well-told story can add a personal touch, make a point, or move an audience in significant ways. There are several criteria to use when you are thinking about incorporating a narrative into your speech.

Use Narratives to Personalize a Point

Former U.S. president Ronald Reagan was an expert at using stories to make his point in personal ways. An advocate of private action rather than government assistance, he told the story of Jose Salcido, whose wife had died of cancer.

[Her death left Jose] both father and mother of thirteen children. In an accident only the Lord can explain, one day the brakes on his truck didn't hold and he was crushed against a brick wall as he walked in front of the vehicle. The children who had lost their mother now had lost their father. But even they were not orphaned.

Reagan told of family, neighbors, members of their church parish, even strangers, who stepped in to help the children. He finished his story by reading a letter from one of the people who assisted the children: "This is for the children of Jose Salcido. It is for them to know there are always others who care; that despite personal tragedy, the world is not always the dark place it seems to be." In this one story, Reagan drew his audience personally into his argument. As they listened to his story, they actually could see themselves assisting the children.[4]

One of Ronald Reagan's strengths as a speaker was his ability to personalize his speeches with narratives. For example, he personalized a speech about replacing government assistance with personal action by telling the story of a community that came to the aid of an orphaned family of thirteen children. What stories might you use to personalize your ideas and draw your audience into your speech?

© Larry Downing/Woodfin Camp & Associates

Use Narratives to Challenge an Audience to Think in New Ways

A narrative can challenge an audience to think differently or to understand the world in new ways. Curtis began his speech on the various kinds of racism in the following way: "Let me tell you the story of Ishmael."

> Ishmael was sitting at a restaurant in town, minding his own business, eating dinner with some of his friends. At another table nearby, he and his friends heard snickering and laughter, but ignored it because they didn't think it related to them. Pretty soon, the laughter got louder and two guys from that table began to address Ishmael and his friends. At first they thought it was going to be a friendly exchange but soon realized they were the butt of the jokes being told—racist jokes, about the shape of Ishmael's eyes and the color of his skin. The so-called jokes soon turned to taunts and verbal abuse, with the girlfriends joining in. Not sure what to do, Ishmael and his friends were saved, so to speak, by the owner of the restaurant, who asked Ishmael and his friends to leave.

Curtis paused here to let the story sink in. He began again: "You think I might be making this up? It happened to my best friend a couple of years ago while he was a student at this very university."

As we tell a story, we share our perspectives with an audience in personal, yet organized, ways. As we listen to a story, we may find a commonality we hadn't recognized before. Or we may gain a new or deeper understanding of an issue, as did the audience in the example just cited, who believed racism no longer exists.

Use Narratives to Draw an Audience in Emotionally

Facts, statistics, and examples are important, but they can lack the personalized, emotional component of a story. Use a story when you want to draw your audience into the speech emotionally. Erin used this brief story, found in a newspaper as she gathered materials for her speech: "The latest issue of *U.S. News and World Report* told it this way, 'There I sat, driving behind the car when I saw the tire disintegrate. The vehicle flipped over and over—no one knows how many times—and two teenagers on a family vacation to Disneyland died on Interstate 5.'" Erin could have offered statistics to make her point ("Firestone tires are linked to 101 deaths in the United States and 46 in Venezuela"), but, instead, she drew her audience in emotionally with a brief story of the implications of defective tires.

Use Narratives to Unite the Speaker and the Audience

Stories often describe common, profound, or dramatic experiences, and you can share stories to create unity between you and your audience. When you share a story about an experience that is just like everyone else's experience, you establish common ground with your audience. When you relate a powerful moment in your life, you reveal a personal aspect of yourself that allows your audience to identify with you more fully. When you tell dramatic or exciting stories, you can connect with your audience by sharing a way of thinking about the world that may be new to them. Because of their content and the personalized way they are told, stories often create a sense of togetherness for speakers and their audiences. Using your *Invitation to Public Speaking* CD-ROM, watch the video clip of U.S. secretary of state Colin Powell under Speech Interactive. To create unity between him and his audience, Powell tells a story about his parents' experiences as immigrants to the United States.

Tips for Using Narratives Effectively

In speeches, narratives are more than just stories that entertain: they convey something specific to an audience. Use the following questions to determine whether the narrative you want to use in your speech actually does more than simply "tell a good story."

Does your narrative make a specific point? When you tell a story in a speech, you must tell it for a specific reason to make a specific point. The purpose of the story might be to reaffirm values, challenge perspectives, remind your audience of important events and beliefs, or teach ways of being and thinking. Examine the narrative you want to tell in your speech to be sure it has a clear point. Remember, many great stories are available, but not every story makes your point well. Reagan told the story of the orphaned children in such a way that his point could not be missed—without assistance from everyday people, rather than from the government, the children would have suffered more than they already had.

Is the length appropriate? Speeches often have time limits, and stories, especially extended ones, take time to tell. Brief stories often fit better into speeches, like Erin's story about the car accident, but don't discard an extended story immediately. A brief story allows you to make your point quickly. An extended story can draw the audience in more fully and with more detail. To use an extended story in a speech, open with a part of the story, add pieces of it as you develop your speech, and then conclude with the remainder of the story. This use of an extended story can keep the audience listening in order to "hear how the story ends" throughout the speech.

Is the language vivid and the delivery appropriate to the story? The language you use in a story must do more than just tell the story. It should bring your message to life. This doesn't mean you must use flowery or complicated language. Rather, think about the language you choose in a story and the images and messages that language conveys and creates. Notice how the tire "disintegrated" in Erin's example from *U.S. News and World Report* and the "world isn't always a dark place" in Reagan's speech. The language you select makes a difference in the kind of image you can create. Similarly, the manner in which you tell the story is significant. Practice telling your story several times until you get your pauses, emphasis, gestures, and expressions the way you want them. When telling a story, the delivery often is as important as the content.

Is the story appropriate for my audience? You can apply the same criteria you use to determine the appropriateness of examples to narratives. Is your story too graphic, too personal, or simply inappropriate for a particular audience? As you do for examples, make sure the stories you tell ring true for your audience. For certain cultures, ethnic or otherwise, some stories simply don't tell a familiar tale or recount a common experience. If you suspect certain parts of your story will be too culturally unfamiliar for your audience, make sure you explain those parts. Or choose a different story altogether if you anticipate that too much of the story won't ring true.

Similarly, stories often reference other stories or rely on parts of other stories to be complete. This process is called **intertextuality**, and it is very common in television programs—for example, one show refers to another or relies on part of a narrative from another show to make its point. Because so many of our stories come from television, intertextuality in everyday communication is becoming very common. Make sure your audience has the references necessary to follow these types of intertextual narratives.

intertextuality
Process in which stories reference other stories or rely on parts of other stories to be complete.

A carefully selected and well-told story can add a personal touch, make a point, or move an audience in ways that are worth considering. To help you harness the power of narratives for your speeches, complete InfoTrac College Edition Exercise 7.2, "Narratives of Personal Success," online under Student Resources for Chapter 7.

Statistics

Statistics are numerical summaries of facts, figures, and research findings. They help audiences understand amounts (100 individuals participated), proportions (that's almost half of the people in this organization), and percentages (fully 50 percent said they'd participate again). Numbers summarize and help audiences make sense of large chunks of information (eight glasses of water a day, every day of the year, is the equivalent of almost three thousand glasses of water a year), and they help people see where something is in relation to other things (he's the third fastest runner in the world).

statistics
Numerical summaries of facts, figures, and research findings.

Numbers and statistics may seem less glamorous than a story or a clever example, but relevant, surprising, or little known statistics can grab an audience's attention. Statistics can help your audience understand the magnitude or impact of an event or issue, help you synthesize large amounts of data, or help you point out exceptions to trends or generalizations. Statistics help you make and refine your claims, and they can highlight certain aspects of your topic that other types of evidence cannot. According to Cynthia Crossen, author of *Tainted Truth: The*

Manipulation of Fact in America, 82 percent of people surveyed said statistics increase a story's credibility.[5] One of the best sources of statistics is the *Statistical Abstract of the United States,* located at http://www.census.gov/prod/www/statistical-abstract-us.html. This resource includes statistics related to crime, population, health, and many other topics. (You can also find a print version of this document in many libraries.)

Types of Statistics

Common statistics include totals and amounts, costs, scales and ranges, ratios, rates, dates and times, measurements, and percentages. Other, more technical, statistics are the *mean, median,* and *mode.* The mean, median, and mode can cause confusion because they are numbers that *summarize* other sets of numbers. When you use them correctly, they can be an important source of evidence, but why, how, and when to use them isn't always clear. The descriptions that follow will help you determine the type of statistics you need in your speech.

The **mean** tells you the average of a group of numbers. Find it by adding all the numbers in your data set and then dividing by the total number of items. Use the mean when you want to describe averages, patterns, tendencies, generalizations, and trends, especially for large groups of data. For example, the mean is what you need if you want to find the average weight of a group of teenagers, like Clara did in her speech to the after-school youth in our earlier example. To find her mean, Clara added together the weight of each of the teens in her audience (they weighed 115, 121, 126, 132, 154, 159, 163, 167, and 170) and then divided that number by the total number of teens she had weighed (9). This gave her the mean, 145 pounds, the average weight in her audience. She then used that average, or mean, to compare her audience's average to the average weight of teenagers fifty years ago, then to teen athletes and nonathletes. She and her audience then entered into a discussion about average weights for teenagers in general.

Finding the mean isn't useful when your data sets include extreme values, or what are called *outliers.*[6] A group of students speaking to county commissioners about affordable housing illustrates why this is so. The students presented information about the average cost of housing in their area. Most of the houses rented for $900 to $1,100 a month, but one particular home rented for $2,250 a month. In this case, the students couldn't have used the mean because the outlier in this set of data ($2,250) would have distorted the average. The students would then have presented a distorted picture of the housing costs in their area. To provide a more accurate statistic, the students would have had to use the mode or the median (described next), or leave out the $2,250 rental and explain why.

The **median** is the middle number in a series or set of numbers arranged in a ranked order. A median tells you where the midpoint is in your set of data. It shows you that one-half of your observations will be smaller and one-half larger than that midpoint. Use the median when you want to identify the midpoint and make claims about its significance or about the items that fall above or below it. For example, the median weight of Clara's teens is 154. This means that half the teens weighed more than 154 and half weighed less. Both Clara and her audience now have more information than simply the average weight of teens (145 pounds) and, for example, can begin to explain weight in relation to body type or height (those below the median ranged in height from 4'11" to 5'8" and those above the median ranged from 5'6" to 6'1").

The students speaking about affordable housing used the median to explain that one-half of the homes they assessed rented for less than $950 a month and one-half rented for more than that. They then explained that once the housing that

mean
Average of a group of numbers.

median
Middle number in a series or set of numbers arranged in a ranked order.

Class of admission

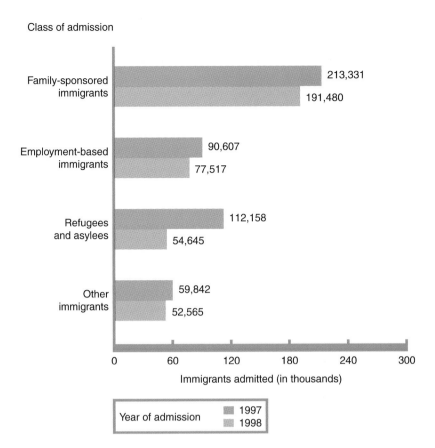

Figure 7.1

Visual Representation of Statistics

Visual representations of statistics help an audience understand complex or abstract information. This graph shows the number of immigrants admitted to the United States in 1997 and 1998 by class of admission.

Source: U.S. Census Bureau, Statistical Abstract of the United States, 2000.

rented for less than the median had been rented, families looking for rentals in their area had to be able to pay more than $950 a month. They discussed the monthly income necessary to support such housing costs. Using the median in this way helped them make a case for building Habitat for Humanity homes in a particular neighborhood so more families could afford to live there.

The disadvantage of using the median is that significant numbers below and above the midpoint might not be discussed. For example, is it significant for a teen to weigh 39 pounds lighter than the median weight, as the lightest person does, or 16 pounds heavier than the median, as the heaviest does?) Similarly, if the students failed to explain that below the median rent of $950, houses rented for only as low as $875, their audience could get the sense that some housing was much more affordable than that. And if they didn't note that above the median homes rented for as high as $1,300, their audience might not understand that about half of the housing in the area was too expensive for most families. Thus their audience could get the impression that families easily could afford to live in a certain neighborhood, when actually they could not.

The **mode** is the number that occurs most often in a set of numbers. Use the mode when you want to illustrate the most frequent or typical item in your data set in order to establish the occurrence, availability, demand, or need for something. For example, if Clara found that of the 9 in her group, 7 ate five times a day and the 2 others ate four times a day, then the modal rate of food consumption is five times a day—that's the most common number of meals her audience eats in a day. She then could talk about metabolism during growth spurts and the need for many teens to eat more than three times a day as they are growing. Similarly, if the

mode
Number that occurs most often in a set of numbers.

students showed that the most common monthly income for people looking for rental homes was $1,200, they could use the mode to show that most of the homes for rent in their area were priced too high for these people. Thus they could argue that Habitat for Humanity homes were crucial.

Numbers help you make claims and establish the importance of your ideas. To learn more about mean, median, mode, and other statistics, go to The Statistics Homepage at http://www.statsoftinc.com/textbook/stathome.html. This resource provides detailed information about all sorts of statistics. You can download the entire textbook featured on the site to your computer. Because audiences give numbers so much credibility, consider the following guidelines when you want to use statistics.

Use Statistics to Synthesize Large Amounts of Information

Numbers allow you to present large amounts of data in a very precise way. They make it possible for you to talk in terms of hundreds, thousands, or more, rather than every single instance. For example, in a speech on the process of newspaper production, Josh explained that in his hometown of approximately 1 million people, 31,000 copies of the paper were printed each weekday, and 37,000 copies were printed on Sunday. And, he explained, "if you took one average-sized newspaper and cut it into the size of a paperback book, you have a book about 350 pages thick." Use statistics when you want your audience to appreciate the numerical force behind something or when you want them to understand the size or quantity of an event.

Use Statistics When the Numbers Tell a Powerful Story

In a speech on cradle-to-grave marketing, Jess could have told the story of a child heavily influenced by television advertising. Instead, he chose to use statistics:

> The average 12-year-old spends four hours a day watching television—the equivalent of two months of nonstop TV watching per year. The result is what marketers call the "nag factor," children badgering their parents to buy products, culminating in 188 billion children-influenced dollars spent on products in 1997. So powerful is the nag factor, that advertisers spend $2 billion annually on advertising directed specifically at children.

The story Jess told with these numbers, two months total television watching that resulted in parents spending an enormous amount of money and increased focus on this market by advertisers, is far more powerful than the story of one child begging a parent to buy products on a shopping trip.

Using your *Invitation to Public Speaking* CD-ROM, watch the video clip of gun control advocate Sarah Brady under Speech Interactive. In her speech to the 1996 Democratic National Convention, she makes her argument for gun control more compelling by informing her audience that every two hours, a child is killed by a gun.

Use Statistics When Numerical Evidence Strengthens a Claim

Statistics can strengthen a claim, especially one made in an example or a story, because they quantify or measure the impact of an event. They also allow you to make the same claim in a new way. After Tasha used verbal and visual examples to describe the damage done by the *Exxon Valdez* oil spill, she used statistics to strengthen her claim that the spill caused an enormous amount of damage: "You can see why this spill is known as the worst oil spill in history. The oil from the *Exxon Valdez* spread over a total of 10,000 square miles in Alaska. It covered 1,500 miles of shoreline and traveled as far as 600 miles from the original spill." Tasha's description and examples affected the audience on one level, her visual aids impacted them on another, and her dramatic statistics reinforced her claims about the impact of the spill.

Tips for Using Statistics Effectively

There are many ways to misuse statistics or to cause considerable confusion with them. Recall from our housing example that the mean rent misrepresented the affordability of housing in a particular neighborhood. Similarly, if Clara suggests that the modal number of meals for teens is five per day, we can easily overlook the thousands of teens who go without food each day or even those who have eating disorders. Because statistics can be manipulated, some guidelines will help you use them responsibly and accurately.

Evaluate your statistics carefully. In Chapter 6, you learned some guidelines for evaluating your supporting materials. You can use the same guidelines to assess the strength of a statistic. Be certain the source is credible, the data are not old, and the statistic represents what you claim it does. It is easy to manipulate a statistic to say what you want. For example, when only 10 percent of those surveyed say they would try a product again, but only fifteen people were sampled, you don't have a very strong statistic. Similarly, be wary when a source that is overly invested in a particular outcome provides a statistic. See if you can find other sources that agree with that statistic, or present statistics from various perspectives in order to make your claim more accurately.

Use statistics sparingly. Audiences will remember most of the stories you tell, but they will have a harder time remembering the numbers. In fact, the more numbers you use, the fewer your audience is likely to remember. How difficult do you think it would be to remember the numbers in the following example?

> Based on these 1992 figures, we can say of the 1,393 males between the ages of 18 and 21 with incomes above $24,000 a year and less than two years of training who attended this event more than three times but less than five, 743 drove their own vehicles, 259 rode with friends, 128 took the bus, and 11 walked. This leaves 252 unaccounted for. Now, let's look at the 2002 data. These figures change slightly.

Although this is a hypothetical example, it illustrates how beginning speakers sometimes tend to use too many numbers and use them randomly. The result is more information than audience members can remember, presented without a systematic structure to help them. To minimize this problem, try the following:

- Display statistics visually on an overhead, in a PowerPoint slide, in a handout, or on a board or flip chart. Displaying statistics visually reinforces your verbal presentation by helping your audience keep track of the statistics.
- Round your numbers up or down wherever possible. Notice how Tasha rounded her numbers about the *Exxon Valdez* oil spill to whole numbers. She spoke of 10,000 and 1,500, and 600 rather than 10,143 and 1,485 and 621. When you want to emphasize general size rather than the exact amount, round your numbers.

- When you must present a lot of numbers to make a point, find ways to group them together so your audience can digest them more easily. Although your audience will still have to keep track of quite a few numbers, "chunking" them makes them easier to follow: "Our 1992 survey included approximately 1,400 young men, aged 18 to 21, with incomes of over $24,000 annually. We found, roughly, 750 drivers, 250 passengers, 130 bus riders, and 10 walkers. We can't account for about 250 attendees, and previous attendance didn't seem to influence transportation choices." In this example, certain kinds of data are grouped together (demographic, mode of transportation, and insignificant data) so the audience can remember numbers that are related to one another.

- Translate your statistics for the audience. How big is 1,500 miles of shoreline? Show them it's the distance between two familiar points, say New York City to the southern tip of Florida. What does it mean to say one in ten? Represent that number by asking one in ten of your audience members to stand up. How large is a protected wilderness area of 10,000 acres? Ten thousand acres is equal to just over 7,500 football fields, including the end zones.[7]

- Of all the data your research will turn up, select only the statistics that will help you make your case. In the example at the beginning of this section, the statistic "attended this event more than three times but less than five" isn't essential to the speaker's argument, so she doesn't need to mention it in her speech. Instead, she could save it for the question-and-answer session at the end of her speech in case an audience member asked about it. Similarly, when you display statistics visually, direct your audience to the most significant data that will help you make your point or generate interest in your topic.

Statistics can be a very beneficial tool to use in a persuasive speech. To practice finding and using statistics that help you persuade an audience, complete **WEB SITE** Interactive Activity 7.1, "Persuasive Statistics," online under Student Resources for Chapter 7 at the *Invitation to Public Speaking* Web site.

Ronda

I would totally recommend that public speaking students use a lot of evidence in their speeches. Examples, testimony, and statistics are all very helpful tools to use in a speech. I think one of the best places to include evidence is in the introduction. Doing this catches the attention of the audience and gives them a better understanding of your topic. Adding evidence into the body section adds support to the claims you make. I think tying evidence from the introduction into the conclusion is a great way to wrap up the speech. I suggest using statistics when you are really trying to get your point across, because some statistics can really open the audience's eyes and make them more aware of a situation. I also like testimony because it gives the audience an idea of what something is like from a person who has experienced it or has studied it firsthand.

Testimony

testimony
Opinions or observations of others.

When speakers use the opinions or observations of others, they are using **testimony** as a source of evidence. Testimony is sometimes called "quoting others" or "citing the words of others." We usually think of testimony as coming from an authority, a person who has expertise, training, experience, or personal knowledge about a subject. This is often true, but testimony can also come from laypeople, average individuals who have relevant experience with your topic. Speakers sometimes also provide their own testimony, their own words and experiences and sources of evidence.

Testimony often takes the form of a **direct quotation**, an exact word-for-word presentation of another's testimony. At other times speakers **paraphrase** the words, or provide a summary of another's testimony in the speaker's own words. Direct quotations often are seen as more credible than paraphrasing, but sometimes a person's words or stories are too long, too complex, or simply contain inappropriate language for a particular audience, making paraphrasing more listenable.

Generally, use someone else's testimony when his or her words make your point more clearly, powerfully, or eloquently than your own. When you use the testimony of someone considered an authority in a particular field, you are using **expert testimony.** When you use the testimony of someone who has firsthand knowledge of a topic, you are using **peer testimony**, sometimes called *lay testimony.* You also can use your own testimony to convey your point. This type of testimony is called **personal testimony.** With each type of testimony, always give credit to the person you are quoting or paraphrasing, including his or her name and credentials. (See Chapter 9 for more about citing your sources in your speech.) Let's look at some more specific guidelines for using testimony in speech.

direct quotation
Exact word-for-word presentation of another's testimony.

paraphrase
Summary of another's testimony in the speaker's own words.

expert testimony
Testimony of someone considered an authority in a particular field.

peer testimony
Testimony of someone who has firsthand knowledge of a topic, sometimes called *lay testimony.*

personal testimony
Your own testimony that you use to convey your point.

Use Testimony When You Need the Voice of an Expert

Sometimes an audience may be interested in our descriptions of an issue or event, but we might not have enough credibility to make our assertions sufficiently believable. Expert testimony can give our ideas or claims an extra boost. Phrases like "According to the surgeon general" add the voice of authority to a speech. Darian enhanced his credibility by using expert testimony in his speech on the shortage of qualified schoolteachers:

> "We have good people coming in," said Sandra Feldman, president of the American Federation of Teachers, "but we lose almost 50 percent of them in the first five years." Why? The reason is money, according to Ms. Feldman: "If someone lasts four or five years, they see that they can teach, but they can't support themselves or their families."[8]

Incorporating the testimony of recognized experts lends an air of credibility to your own testimony and helps you build a stronger case.

Use Testimony to Illustrate Differences or Agreements

Speakers often use testimony when they want to illustrate the range of opinions about a topic. Testimony from several different sources gives an audience a sense of the diversity—or lack of diversity—of opinions circulating in the public dialogue. If you can cite a variety of expert opinions on your subject, you illustrate the complexity of an issue. Or, if all the experts agree and offer a unified voice, you illustrate the strength of a particular opinion. Consider statements like these: "In my review of the minutes for the planning commission meetings from January to September of this year, I found only one person on the nine-member city planning commission who disagreed. Let me share what Joel Phillips, the dissenting voice, said, and then tell what the other eight individuals had to say" or "There seems to be incredible diversity on this issue. Of the five professors I interviewed, none offered the same solution to the problem I posed. Here are some of their suggestions." When used in these ways, testimony sheds light on agreements or disagreements over issues that affect your audience.

Shawn Fanning created Napster, a software program that allows music fans to find and share music files from the Internet. Do you think he would be able to give credible testimony about copyright issues in the music industry? About artists getting compensation for their work? About alternative ways to distribute music to the public?

© AFP/CORBIS

Use Your Own Testimony When Your Experience Says It Best

Although the words of an expert can lend credibility to a speech, sometimes your own experiences make a stronger impression. In a speech on the peer pressure that contributes to the prevalence of eating disorders in young women, Rachael used her own testimony: "You know," she said to her audience, "no one has ever come up to me and said, 'Wow, Rachael, you look great! Have you gained ten?' It's always the opposite, isn't it? 'Have you *lost* ten?'" She could have used the testimony of a doctor or a psychologist, but her personal testimony about her own experiences with peer pressure strengthened her point about the peer pressure many young women encounter.

Paraphrase Testimony to Improve Listenability

The exact words of an expert may not always be appropriate for an audience, because they may be too complex or too vulgar. However, you can still use that person's words if you paraphrase, summarizing statements rather than repeating them exactly. For example, when Joel Phillips, the dissenting commissioner, explained, "residential zoning factors historically have an inverse effect on the growth this sector of the community feasibly can accommodate," Shatanna paraphrased his words by saying, "Mr. Phillips, the dissenting commission member, explained that, historically, zoning ordinances have a negative effect on the growth of our community." Her paraphrasing allowed her to use the commissioner's testimony without confusing her audience.

Similarly, try paraphrasing when your source uses profanity or vulgar language that may not be appropriate for a particular audience. But note that if your source feels strongly enough about an issue to use profanity, or if the use of profanity is an important part of that person's personality, your paraphrase should reflect this. Tell your audience that your source feels strongly enough about an idea to express it with swearing or that the person uses profanity liberally. Remember, paraphrasing is a summary of what was said, not a recasting of someone's feelings or beliefs. Also note that although profanity may not *always* be inappropriate in a speech, you should still think carefully about your reasons for including it and your audience's possible reactions to hearing it.

Tips for Using Testimony Effectively

Testimony enhances a claim or adds to a position much like a second opinion would. It brings in outside voices, adds other perspectives, and illustrates what others are thinking and saying about your issue. But to function as a common language, testimony must meet certain criteria.

Is the source of your testimony credible?
To be credible, testimony must come from people who know something about your subject, have been trained in the particular area you're speaking about, and whose reputations are respectable. When you select testimony, ask yourself if the people you are quoting are believable. Do they have the proper credentials or experiences, and will your audience see them as people worth listening to?

Advertisements often provide excellent examples of the misuse of testimony. Advertisers often use the testimony of celebrities to promote products, yet these celebrities may know very little about the actual product. In your speeches, make sure your testimony comes from someone who actually knows about your subject, not just from someone everyone might like or find interesting. When using testimony from yourself or a nonexpert, make certain your audience will see you or the layperson as credible. Testimony such as "my neighbor said" will not help your case, unless your neighbor has some legitimate connection to the issue you are speaking about.

Is the testimony biased?
Sometimes we tell others they are biased, that they have personal preferences or feelings about an issue. In the public dialogue, the term *bias* has a more specific meaning. **Bias** is an unreasoned distortion of judgment or prejudice about a topic, and a biased source will have an unreasoned personal stake in the outcome of an issue.[9] In contrast, an **objective** source is someone who does not have a personal stake in an issue and can provide a fair and undistorted view about a topic. Although objective sources certainly have preferences and feelings, they are not so strongly influenced by their own stake in an issue that they distort information.

bias
Unreasoned distortion of judgment or prejudice about a topic.

objective
Having a fair and undistorted view on a question or issue.

Obviously, no one can be completely objective. In fact, sometimes we *want* to use the testimony of someone who has a personal stake in an issue, because that person understands the issue as an insider. But we often need testimony from sources who are not personally invested in an issue and do not stand to gain from a particular outcome. For example, when a representative of the tobacco industry argues for the safety of smoking cigarettes, you have a biased source. The representative has a personal stake in the matter and will not be seen as even slightly objective by most audiences. Yet he could be an excellent source of testimony on issues of tobacco production or marketing.

To determine whether a source is biased or objective, ask yourself the following questions:

- What is this person's connection to the issue? How does that connection affect her or his perspective? Does he or she have a personal stake in the issue?

- Are this person's ideas about this topic so firmly rooted that she or he would be unable to speak credibly on another aspect of the topic?
- Are this person's words informed and reasoned? Is he or she making claims based on adequate exposure to the issue?

 Answering these questions can help you determine how to use the testimony you have and how to introduce it to your audience so they see it as credible. To practice evaluating sources for bias and credibility, complete InfoTrac College Edition Exercise 7.3, "Who Do You Believe?" online under Student Resources for Chapter 7.

Have you paraphrased accurately? When you summarize another person's testimony or change some of the language so it is more suitable to your audience, do so carefully. As you summarize, make sure you've retained essential material and haven't changed the testimony's tone or meaning. For example, one of the commissioners Shatanna interviewed said, "It's very complicated. Let me outline some of the issues for you." He then described seven distinct issues. Shatanna's paraphrasing reflected this complexity. In her speech, she said, "Commissioner Fields presented seven different issues. The issue that most directly affects my topic today is the first one he mentioned, the conflict between what residents and retailers want." Note that it is unethical to change the intended meaning of testimony or to place it in a context that your source did not intend. Although it can be tempting to use a great quote in a way your source did not mean, it is also deceptive.

Is the testimony connected to your point? In the public dialogue, we use testimony to strengthen a speech, not simply to share perspectives and experiences. This is important to consider when you use anyone's testimony but especially when you use your own. When you use personal testimony, make sure it enhances your speech and that you're not using it simply because you want to tell your story. If you think testimony about your own experience—or the testimony of another person—fits into your speech perfectly, connect it to the larger issue you are speaking about.[10] Rachael's testimony about the pressure to be thin followed this guideline. She used her experiences not to draw attention only to herself, but to call attention to a common experience for many young women. Rachel didn't just tell her own story. She told the story of numerous other women as well.

Definitions

As forms of evidence, definitions are essential to public speaking. Without them, the common language shared by speaker and audience breaks down quickly. A **definition** is a statement of the exact meaning of a word or phrase. Definitions can make the most technical, or the simplest, of terms clear and meaningful for your audiences. Provide a definition of a word in a speech when its meaning may be ambiguous and confuse an audience.

Every word has both a denotative and a connotative definition. The **denotative definition** is the objective definition you would find in a dictionary, the meaning of a word on which most everyone can agree. (To find the meanings of various words, consult Dictionary.com at http://www.dictionary.com/. This Web site also features a thesaurus you can use to locate words that have similar meanings.) In contrast, a **connotative definition** is the subjective meaning of a word or a phrase based on personal experiences and beliefs.

definition
Statement of the exact meaning of a word or phrase.

denotative definition
The objective definition of a word or a phrase you would find in a dictionary.

connotative definition
The subjective meaning of a word or phrase based on personal experiences and beliefs.

Be aware that providing the dictionary definition of a word may not always be enough to get your point across. Definitions come from personal experiences as well as from the dictionary. An example illustrates how powerful a connotative definition can be. Abolitionist Sojourner Truth, born a slave in New York in approximately 1797 and freed in 1827, focused one of her most famous speeches on the definition of the word *woman*. In "Ain't I a Woman?" she repeatedly questioned the definition of this word, asking her audience to decide whether or not she actually was "a woman":

> That man over there says that women need to be helped into carriages, and lifted over ditches, and to have the best place everywhere. Nobody ever helps me into carriages, or over mud-puddles, or gives me any best place. And, ain't I a woman? Look at me, look at my arm. I have plowed and planted and gathered into barns, and no man could head me—and ain't I a woman? I could work as much and eat as much as a man (when I could get it) and bear the lash as well—and ain't I a woman? I have borne thirteen children and seen them most all sold off into slavery, and when I cried out with a mother's grief, none but Jesus heard. And ain't I a woman?[11]

As this example illustrates, connotative definitions can move an audience in a way that denotative definitions sometimes can't. However, because connotative definitions are based on emotions and personal experiences, they can cloud an issue or confuse an audience. As such, be sure to identify the connotative definitions you use in your speech and take into account the varying connotations one word may have. Truth did this when she questioned the audience's connotative definitions of *woman*.

Although some speeches are built around a definition, as in Truth's example, others incorporate definitions in order to clarify words for audiences. The guidelines for using definitions in your speeches are as follows.

Use Definitions to Clarify and Create Understanding

Use a definition when you can hear your audience say to themselves, "I don't know what that word means" or "I've never heard the word used that way before." For technical terms, a denotative definition often suffices. For familiar words used in new ways, connotative definitions are a must. For example, in a speech to students at Moscow University, Ronald Reagan defined the word *freedom* as the recognition that no single authority has a monopoly on truth. At the time, democracy was new to the Soviet Union, so Reagan's definition helped his audience see more clearly what he believed are the benefits of a democracy.

Use Definitions to Clarify an Emotionally or Politically Charged Word

Many words in our language have become emotionally and politically charged. Words like *race, sexism, disability, discrimination, equality, liberal,* and *conservative* have become hotbeds of dispute. When you use words like these, provide a definition. Explain how you are using the word so you can minimize some of the emotions and politics associated with it. Otherwise, your audience may not be able to listen to you. For example, Jackson Katz, a speaker who travels around the country speaking about issues of feminism and masculinity, defines what he means by feminism early on in his presentations. In doing so, he relates feminism to equality, social justice, and freedom. He explains that feminism is "as American as apple pie," diffusing much of the anxiety people feel when they hear the word *feminism*. Katz works extensively with Marines in the U.S. Marine

Corps as well as with college students and educators. By defining his words, he ensures his audiences are able to listen to his ideas rather than worry he is advocating the anti-male stance commonly associated with feminism in the popular press.[12]

Use Definitions to Illustrate What Something Is *Not*

Definitions also explain to an audience what something isn't. In a student speech on the hostile environment created by sexual harassment, Hillary defined *hostile environment* and *harassment* first by what they are, then by what they aren't:

> According to the *Webb Report: A Newsletter on Sexual Harassment*, behavior is sexual harassment if it (1) is sexual in nature, (2) is unwelcome by the person it is directed at, and (3) is sufficiently severe or pervasive that it alters the conditions of that person's employment and creates an abusive working environment. This means it's not sexual harassment nor is it seen as creating a hostile environment if the behavior: (1) isn't sexual in nature, (2) is welcomed by the person it's directed at, and (3) doesn't negatively affect that individual's working environment and create an abusive climate. The behavior may be offensive, unproductive, or even harmful, but if it doesn't meet all three criteria, then it's not considered sexual harassment.

Hillary defined what sexual harassment is by illustrating for her audience what it isn't.

Use Definitions to Trace the History of a Word

etymology
The history of a word.

The history of a word, called its **etymology,** allows you to trace the original meaning of a word and to chart the changes it has undergone. The etymology of two words are traced in this text: *audience* in Chapter 5 and *claim* here in Chapter 7. Tracing the history of these two words offers insights into their origins and the ways those origins affect our understanding and use of those words today. In speeches, tracing the history of a word can help you build an argument for a position or tell a more comprehensive story about an issue. Many dictionaries provide the etymology of words, but *The Oxford English Dictionary* is a particularly good source for tracing a word's origins. Another good resource is Word Origins at http://www.wordorigins.org/home.htm. This Web site features a long list of words and their original meanings. This site is useful when you want to know why words we use today have the meanings they do.

Tips for Using Definitions Effectively

Using definitions seems fairly straightforward and simple, and it usually is. But, as with all forms of evidence, you must consider credibility, clarity, and accuracy. When you define a word, keep the following guidelines in mind.

Is the source of the definition credible? Where does your definition come from? Consider whether the dictionary you are using is credible. Some dictionaries are far more extensive than others, and if you want a recent definition, make sure you have the latest edition. Similarly, some dictionaries offer a more comprehensive history of a word. If you are tracing the etymology of a word, consult

You can find definitions in many sources other than the dictionary. Try researching encyclopedias, textbooks, and books about specific topics—such as music, law, or engineering. These types of books can also be excellent sources of definitions.

these. Finally, if you are using a particular person's definition of a word, make sure that person is a credible and qualified source.

Have you avoided proper meaning superstition? *Proper meaning superstition* is a term that was coined by I. A. Richards and C. K. Ogden in the late 1920s. Proper meaning superstition is the belief that everyone attaches the same meaning to a word, and that you are using that meaning. With proper meaning superstition, speakers use words believing their audiences will have exactly the same referent. If you decide not to define a term, check to be sure you haven't fallen prey to proper meaning superstition.[13] To find out how easy it can be to fall into using proper meaning superstition, complete Interactive Activity 7.2, "Avoiding Proper Meaning Superstition," online under Student Resources for Chapter 7 at the *Invitation to Public Speaking* Web site.

WEB SITE

Have you actually defined the term? Avoid using a term to define itself. This happens when we say, "by *younger* I mean people who aren't very old—they're still young." With this definition, the audience still won't know what you mean by "young"—is it 5 years of age, 20 years, or something else? Also avoid using unfamiliar words in a definition. This happens when we say something like "By *septifragal*, I mean to say dehiscing by breaking away from the dissepiments." This may be clear to scientists but not to very many other people. Finally, avoid circular definitions, such as "By *masculine*, I'm referring to those traits not feminine, and by *feminine*, I mean those not masculine." With this definition, the audience still won't know what is meant by either "masculine" or "feminine."

Review the supporting materials you have gathered for your next speech. Do you have enough evidence to support your main ideas? Separate your examples, narratives, statistics, testimony, and definitions. Do you have enough of each type of supporting material to support your ideas? Now use the tips in this chapter to evaluate your evidence. Will your audience see your evidence as credible? Do you think they will accept the claims you make in your speech?

Chapter Summary

Each type of supporting material has strengths and weaknesses, and each is important to the common language of public speaking. As you research and assemble your materials, you'll find you want to use a variety of evidence types to build and strengthen your claims, develop your ideas, and appeal to your audiences. When you use examples, you use specific instances to illustrate a concept, experience, issue, or problem. Your examples can be real or hypothetical, and they should help clarify or reinforce a claim or bring an idea to life or build your case for a position.

When you use narratives, you are sharing a story that recreates or foretells real or hypothetical events. Narratives can be brief or extended, and they help you personalize your claims, challenge your audience to think in new ways, draw out emotions, or bring the speaker and audience closer together.

Statistics are the use of numbers to summarize facts, figures, and research findings. The three types of statistics most commonly used in speeches are the mean (or average), the median (or middle point), or the mode (the most frequent). Use statistics to synthesize large amounts of information, help you tell a powerful story, or strengthen your claims.

Testimony involves using the opinions or observations of others to support your claims. Testimony can be peer, expert, or personal and is used when you need an expert's voice and to illustrate differences or similarities regarding an idea. Use your own testimony (personal testimony) when your voice illustrates your point best, and remember to paraphrase complex testimony to improve listenability.

Definitions are statements of the exact meaning of a word or phrase. Definitions can be denotative (commonly agreed on) or connotative (based on personal experiences or beliefs) and will help you make your claims in several ways. Definitions can be used to clarify or create understanding for your audience or to explain an emotionally or politically charged term. They also can be used to explain what something is *not* or to trace the history of a term.

As the opening quote for this chapter suggests, when speakers enter the public dialogue, they make claims—they call out to someone about an important issue. Because audiences respond to this call, either in their heads or via questions and dialogue with a speaker, speakers must present evidence that an audience is able to hear and understand. To make sure this happens, use evidence that is credible, relevant, appropriate, and organized. Take time to arrange your materials carefully and systematically, keeping your audience in mind throughout this process. When you take time with this step of speech preparation, you communicate to your audiences that you want to engage them in meaningful ways, and you want to contribute productively to the never-ending conversations that occur in the public dialogue.

After reading this chapter, use your CD-ROM and the *Invitation to Public Speaking* Web site to review the follow- ing concepts, answer the review questions, and complete the suggested activities.

Key Concepts

claim (156)
evidence (156)
example (157)
real example (157)
hypothetical example (157)
narrative (160)
brief narrative (160)
extended narrative (160)

intertextuality (163)
statistics (163)
mean (164)
median (164)
mode (165)
testimony (168)
direct quotation (169)
paraphrase (169)
expert testimony (169)

peer testimony (169)
personal testimony
    (169)
bias (171)
objective (171)
definition (172)
denotative definition (172)
connotative definition (172)
etymology (174)

Review Questions

1. Bring your research to class for your next speech. In groups, organize your research by example, narrative, statistic, testimony, and definition. Do you have an imbalance in the kinds of research you have gathered, or is your evidence fairly well balanced?

2. Consider the examples or narratives you have gathered for your speech. Are they real or hypothetical, brief or extended? Out loud, practice delivering one of your examples or narratives. Do you feel comfortable with your delivery? Why or why not? Practice delivering this material until it sounds natural and conversational.

3. Bring the statistics you have found in your research to class. In groups, discuss how you might work with these statistics to present them clearly, ethically, and smoothly to your audience. Identify your means, medians, and modes. Discuss what each of these types of evidence actually tell or illustrate for your audience, including a discussion of how to avoid misrepresenting an issue with your statistics.

4. Josiah and Keisha are working together on developing a community presentation for the local food bank. They have most of their materials—statistics, exam- ples, and narratives—and have developed a great slide presentation to accompany their presentation. They still need testimony, though, and are considering where to go, who they might speak to, and the ethics of gathering testimony from certain individuals. From whom do you suggest they gather testimony, and what might they want to consider as they speak with indi- viduals and then present this testimony?

5. In what instances might you be an expert and be able to offer your own testimony in a speech? What makes you an expert in this situation and not in others? How could you establish your credibility as an "expert" if you were to use this testimony?

6. Choose one article from a recent edition of your local or campus newspaper. Identify the various types of evidence used, whether you think it is effective or not, and the strengths and weaknesses of this evidence.

The *Invitation to Public Speaking* Web Site

The *Invitation to Public Speaking* Web site features the review questions about the Web sites suggested on pages 164, 166, 172, and 174, the interactive activities suggested on pages 168 and 175, and the InfoTrac College Edition exercises suggested on pages 160, 163, and 172. You can access this site via your CD-ROM or at http://www.wadsworth.com/product/griffin. To access Speech Builder Express, you will need the username and password included under "Speech Builder Express" on your CD-ROM.

Web Links

7.1: *Statistical Abstract of the United States* (164)
7.2: The Statistics Homepage (166)
7.3: Online Dictionary (172)
7.4: Word Origins (174)

Interactive Activities

7.1: Persuasive Statistics (168)
Purpose: To learn how statistics can be used to support persuasive arguments.

7.2: Avoiding Proper Meaning Superstition (175)
Purpose: To explore how some terms have multiple meanings and shape our conceptions of our ideas.

InfoTrac College Edition Exercises

7.1: Tax Cut Beneficiaries (160)
Purpose: To better understanding the power and limitations of examples used to support claims and clarify ideas.

7.2: Narratives of Personal Success (163)
Purpose: To help you harness the power of narratives for your speeches.

7.3: Who Do You Believe? (172)
Purpose: To practice evaluating sources for bias and credibility.

Speech Interactive on the *Invitation to Public Speaking* CD-ROM

The following video clips of speeches referenced in this chapter are included under Speech Interactive on your *Invitation to Public Speaking* CD-ROM. After you have watched the clips, click on "Critique" to answer the questions for analysis.

Video Clip 1: Ann Richards's Eulogy for Barbara Jordan (158). In her eulogy for former U.S. representative Barbara Jordan, former Texas governor Ann Richards describes how Jordan sought government help to remove a gate that a neighbor had built across the public access road to her house. Richards used the example to give her audience a better sense of Jordan and her character. Are there other examples Richards uses in the speech? Do the examples help to create a mental image of Jordan? What examples might be an effective form of support in a eulogy?

Video Clip 2: Colin Powell's Address to the 1996 Republican National Convention (162). Early in his political career, Secretary of State Colin Powell held relatively liberal views, and many members of the Republican Party did not embrace him immediately. In his speech at the 1996 Republican National Convention, Powell bridged the distance between him and his party by telling a narrative about his parents, who immigrated to the United States to work hard and enjoy justice and freedom. Briefly summarize Powell's narrative. how persuasive is his story? What other forms of support does he use? Are the other forms of support more or less persuasive than his use of narrative?

Video Clip 3: Sarah Brady's Address to the 1996 Democratic National Convention (166). In her speech to the 1996 Democratic National Convention, Brady explains that each year 40,000 Americans are killed and 100,000 wounded by guns. She makes her argument for gun control more compelling by informing her audience that every two hours, a child is killed by a gun. Evaluate Brady's use of statistics. Does she provide their source? Does she use appropriate statistics? Which form of support do you think would be most effective for Brady?

NOBODY'S BORN A BIGOT.

National Conference Of Christians And Jews
Learning To Live Together: The Unfinished Task.

GANNETT OUTDOOR

Chapter Eight

Reasoning

In this chapter you will learn to

Identify Aristotle's three modes of proof

Describe the five patterns of reasoning used to construct sound arguments

Test the strength of your claims with Toulmin's model of reasoning

Apply tips for reasoning ethically

If we are to conclude that something is "true," that some past deed was "good," or that some proposed course of action is "right," it is not enough for us to know that we, ourselves, are psychologically disposed to approve of the deed, or that the proposed course of action seems right . . . : we must have sound reasons for thinking that something is true.

—Stephen Toulmin, *The Place of Reason in Ethics*, 1950[1]

logos
The word Aristotle used to refer to the logical arrangement of evidence in a speech.

WEB SITE

ethos
The word Aristotle used to refer to the speaker's credibility.

pathos
The word Aristotle used to refer to emotional appeals made by a speaker.

inferences
The mental leaps we make when we agree that a speaker's evidence supports his or her claims.

argument
Set of statements that allows you to develop your evidence in order to establish the validity of your claim.

Whether your speaking goal is to inform, invite, or persuade, one of the most important aspects of entering the public dialogue is sound reasoning. Sound reasoning ensures that your issues and perspectives are developed and discussed fairly and ethically. It ensures that your claims make sense to you and your audience, and that you prove your points. Speakers accomplish sound reasoning when they use what Greek philosopher Aristotle labeled *logos*, *ethos*, and *pathos*. **Logos** refers to the logical arrangement of evidence in a speech. **Ethos** refers to the speaker's credibility, and **pathos** refers to the emotional appeals made by a speaker.[2] For practice in distinguishing among these three forms of proof, complete Interactive Activity 8.1, "Aristotle's Forms of Proof," online under Student Resources for Chapter 8 at the *Invitation to Public Speaking* Web site.

Recall that we enter the public dialogue because we feel strongly about an issue and want to share our knowledge and views with others. We share our knowledge and views most effectively when we reason with our audience. When you reason, you use logos, ethos, and pathos to justify the connections between your evidence and your claims. In other words, you arrange your evidence logically, establish and build your credibility, and appeal to emotion in order to show that your evidence supports your idea, position, or perspective. Reasoning helps an audience make **inferences**, which are the mental leaps we make when we agree that a speaker's evidence supports his or her claims.

When you reason logically, you offer evidence that you think most people in your audience would accept as legitimate, valid, and appropriate.[3] As you learned in Chapter 7, evidence is the material you use to support your ideas, or the examples, narratives, statistics, testimony, and definitions you've gathered through research and interviews. This evidence helps you develop what is often called an argument. Although the term *argument* may bring to mind an angry dispute, in the public dialogue an **argument** is a set of statements that allows you to develop your evidence in order to establish the validity of your claim.[4]

Each time you develop a main point or link ideas together logically in a speech, you use evidence and reasoning to develop a sound argument for your perspective. Just as you use organizational patterns to arrange your main points in a speech, you use patterns of reasoning to help you organize your evidence and claims.

Patterns of Reasoning

Although scholars have developed more than twenty-five different patterns of reasoning, we limit the discussion here to five of the most useful for beginning public speakers: reasoning by induction, deduction, cause, analogy, and sign.[5] These pat-

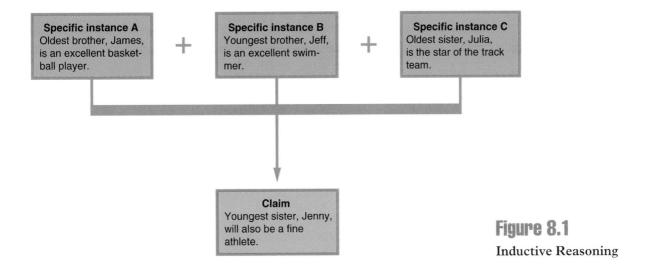

Figure 8.1
Inductive Reasoning

terns can help you develop logical arguments in all types of speeches. You probably are familiar with most of these patterns because almost everyone uses them every day. What makes them unique in public speaking is that speakers think about them consciously as they arrange their evidence and develop the logic of their main and subpoints.

Induction, or Reasoning from Specific Instances

James is an excellent basketball player.

His brother Jeff is an excellent swimmer.

Their sister Julia is the star of the track team.

Jenny, the youngest of the family, will be a fine athlete too.

Throughout our lives we often observe regularities, patterns of behavior, or trends. We can point to these repeating patterns to make a claim about something we expect to happen or be true. When we do so, we reason inductively. **Inductive reasoning** is a process of reasoning that uses specific instances, or examples, to make a claim about a general conclusion (see Figure 8.1).[6]

Inductive reasoning, sometimes also called *argument by example,* is best used when you can identify patterns in evidence that indicate something is expected to happen again or should hold true based on previous experience.[7] For example, in the scenario at the beginning of this section, the claim that Jenny, the youngest in a family of athletes, is likely to be a talented athlete is based on the trend her siblings have established.

Let's look at how inductive reasoning can be used in a speech. In her invitational speech on becoming a vegetarian, Karyl used inductive reasoning to describe her switch from eating meat. She gave examples from four slaughterhouses to illustrate the treatment of the animals and the reasons she chose to stop eating meat. This series of examples allowed Karyl to reason as follows:

Animals in the six slaughterhouses I researched experience harsh conditions and unnecessary cruelty *(her series of specific examples)*. Animals in slaughterhouses throughout the United States are treated inhumanely *(her generalization based on her examples),* and I decided not to support this treatment by not eating them *(her personal decision based on her inductive reasoning).*

inductive reasoning
Process of reasoning that uses specific instances, or examples, to make a claim about a general conclusion.

When you reason from specific instances, you can state your claim (general observation) first and then offer your supporting instances, or you can present the instances first and then make your claim. In the following example, Ruby stated her claim first and then provided specific instances:

> The amount of privacy we are allowed to keep is under siege everyday *(claim)*. Beverly Dennis, an Ohio grandmother, completed a questionnaire in order to get free product samples. Instead, she got a sexually graphic and threatening letter from a convict in Texas who was assigned the task of entering product data into computers for the company *(specific instance)*. Similarly, the dean of the Harvard Divinity School was forced to resign after downloading pornography to his home computer. He asked a Harvard technician to install more memory to his computer at home and, in the process of transferring files, the technician discovered, and reported, the pornography *(specific instance)*.

Ruby used inductive reasoning again later in her speech. In the following example, she withheld her claim until after she had described her specific instances. Also notice how she used statistics to reinforce the pattern in her specific instances:

> Like many of you, I thought my own life was safe because I do not download pornography or request free product samples. But as I continued to do research for my speech, I learned that my medical records, phone calls, and faxes to my doctor aren't as private as I thought. Nor are my emails at work. Medical records are passed along to numerous individuals and recorded or filed electronically—accessible to any determined employee or computer hacker *(specific instance)*. And phone calls and faxes can be monitored or picked up by anyone from the office staff to the other doctors *(specific instance)*.

> And, according to this year's report by the American Management Association, nearly three-quarters of U.S. companies say they are monitoring employees electronically. In fact, according to *The Unwanted Gaze,* some companies even use computer software that monitors and records every keystroke an employee makes. Using this software, called Spector, an employee at a Nissan dealership was fired after her employer opened one of her emails, a sexually explicit note to her boyfriend *(specific instance)*. Can you imagine your boss reading your emails to your boyfriend? Our privacy has gone public in ways we are only beginning to imagine *(claim)*.

Expressed as a formula, an inductive argument looks like this:

Specific instance A	or	Claim you want to establish
Specific instance B		Specific instance A
Specific instance C		Specific instance B
Specific instance D		Specific instance C
Claim based on the specific instances		Specific instance D

Guidelines for inductive reasoning. There are three guidelines for reasoning from specific instances:

- Make sure you have enough examples to make your claim.
- Make sure your generalizations are accurate.
- Support your inductive arguments with statistics or testimony.

Let's take a closer look at each of these guidelines. First, be sure you have enough examples to make your claim. For example, if only one person in Jenny's family is a fine athlete, you cannot claim she likely will be—you do not have enough specific instances to back that claim. Similarly, if only one or two slaughterhouses treat animals inhumanely, you cannot claim that most of them do.

In other words, avoid *anomalies*. Anomalies are exceptions to a rule, unique instances that do not represent the norm. When speakers rely on anomalies or use too few examples to make a claim, they may be guilty of making **hasty generalizations**, or of reaching a conclusion without enough evidence to support it. (For another explanation of hasty generalizations, go to http://gncurtis.home.texas.net/. When you get to the site, scroll down the left-hand navigation bar until you reach the letter *H* and "hasty generalization.") To support your claim, find more than three instances before you make any inferences about larger patterns. However, your audience probably needs no more than four specific instances, even if you have identified far more than that.

Second, make sure your generalizations are accurate. Although it can be tempting to make a claim about only a few instances, be careful not to overgeneralize. For example, if warmer winters are the trend for your region over the past decade, you can predict a warmer winter next year. But you probably can't extend that prediction to other parts of the country unless you have specific examples to support your claim. Don't be too hasty in extending examples from one area or group to another unless your data support that claim.

Third, support your inductive arguments with statistics or testimony. Although you cannot produce an endless list of examples without boring your audience, you can develop your case by supplementing your examples with statistics or testimony. For example, if you want to explain that organic farms produce competitively priced and tasty crops, offer examples of two or three farms that do so. Then strengthen your inductive process with statistics showing that organic farmers county-, state-, or nationwide are successfully competing with nonorganic farms. You also could support your examples with testimony from the head of the Department of Agriculture, validating the profitability of organic farming. Statistics and testimony help your audience better understand the validity of the larger trend you are describing.

To gain experience evaluating inductive arguments critically, complete Interactive Activity 8.2, "Assessing Inductive Reasoning," under Student Resources for Chapter 8 at the *Invitation to Public Speaking* Web site.   **WEB SITE**

hasty generalization
Error in reasoning in which a speaker reaches a conclusion without enough evidence to support it.

Deduction, or Reasoning from General Principle

Grade inflation negatively affects all college students.

Jody is a college student.

Jody is affected negatively by grade inflation.

When speakers reason from general principles to specific instances (the opposite of inductive reasoning), they reason deductively. **Deductive reasoning** is a process of reasoning that uses a familiar and commonly accepted claim to establish the truth of a very specific claim (see Figure 8.2). A common example of this form of reasoning is "All people are mortal. Socrates is a person. Therefore, Socrates is a mortal." The first statement, "All people are mortal," is called the **major premise,** or the general principle, and states a

Even Aristotle was unclear about how many examples to use for inductive reasoning. In one of the oldest surviving treatises on rhetoric, he stated, "If you put your examples first you must give a large number of them; if you put them last, a single one is sufficient; even a single witness will serve if he is a good one."[8]

© Bettmann/CORBIS

deductive reasoning
Process of reasoning that uses a familiar and commonly accepted claim to establish the truth of a very specific claim.

major premise
Claim in an argument that states a familiar, commonly accepted belief. Also called the *general principle.*

Figure 8.2

Deductive Reasoning

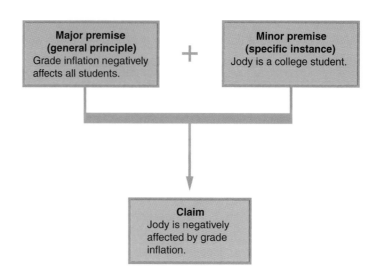

familiar, commonly accepted belief. The combination of the major premise with the second statement, called the **minor premise**, or the specific instance, establishes the truth of the third statement, called the **conclusion**. Taken apart, the example looks as follows:

minor premise
Claim in an argument that states a specific instance linked to the major premise.

conclusion
Logical outcome of an argument that results from the combination of the major and minor premises.

Major premise, or general principle; almost everyone accepts this claim.	All people are mortal.
Minor premise, or specific instance; the specific example linked to the major premise.	Socrates is a person.
Conclusion; the combination of the major and minor premises.	Socrates is mortal.

In the example about Jody and grade inflation, the major premise is that grade inflation negatively affects all students. A speaker could use this general principle to build a specific case about Jody. Here's how this line of reasoning looks:

Major premise, or general principle	Grade inflation negatively affects all college students.
Minor premise, or specific instance	Jody is a college student.
Conclusion	Jody is negatively affected by grade inflation.

Let's look at how Damon used deductive reasoning in his persuasive speech. He built his case for more proactive intervention for teenage boys in his community around the general principle that the rate of male teen suicide is especially high in the United States. He quickly established his major premise in his first main point:

> Since the 1950s, the rate of suicide for white teenage males has tripled and is nearly twice the rate for all other white Americans. For African American males, in only the last twelve years, the suicide rate for teens has risen a staggering 165 percent! In addition, even though more girls attempt suicide, four times more boys than girls actually succeed in killing themselves.

Damon then used deductive reasoning to conclude that the national suicide rate is affecting his own community. His line of reasoning in his first main point is as follows:

Major premise	The rate of male teen suicide is alarmingly high.
Minor premise	Our own community has experienced three such suicides in the last two months.
Conclusion	The unacceptably high rate of teen suicide among males is finding its way into our own community.

Although the topic of suicide is an emotionally difficult one, Damon's audience accepted his first main point because of his strong deductive reasoning. They then listened eagerly to his next points as he described the signs of teens considering suicide and the ways to respond appropriately to troubled teenage boys.

Expressed as a formula, a deductive argument looks as follows:

Major premise, or general principle

Minor premise, or specific instance of the general principle

Conclusion based on the combination of the major and minor premises

Guidelines for deductive reasoning. Reasoning from general principles to specific instances is an effective way to build a case for your claims. When your general principle is firmly established or commonly accepted, your reasoning should unfold quite smoothly. For example, general principles that are clearly established and commonly accepted are that asbestos causes lung cancer, driving drunk is dangerous to yourself and others, and elected officials should act with integrity.

This protestor's sign illustrates a general principle that is not accepted by everyone. Do you accept this principle? If not, what additional evidence would you need to accept it as valid?

Sometimes audiences won't accept your general principle. When they don't, you will need to strengthen it with additional evidence or reasoning. This process is called *establishing the validity of the major premise*. For example, if you assert that raising cattle for beef consumption is cruel and unethical, juvenile crime is out of control, or pornography is a violation of women's rights, your audience is more likely to need proof. If your audience does not accept your major premise, they are less likely to accept your conclusion. You will need to use careful reasoning to develop your case.

We often enter the public dialogue precisely *because* we want to establish the truth of a general principle. Let's see how one very famous speaker, Susan B. Anthony, worked from a controversial general principle. Anthony spoke in favor of women's right to vote in the 1870s. She built her reasoning for women's right to vote on the premise that the U.S. Constitution guarantees all citizens the right to vote. Her full line of reasoning looked as follows:

Major premise	The U.S. Constitution guarantees every citizen the right to vote.
Minor premise	Women are U.S. citizens.
Conclusion	The U.S. Constitution guarantees women the right to vote.

Although this deductive argument makes sense to us today, Anthony's major and minor premises were open to dispute more than 130 years ago. People did not agree that the Constitution guaranteed all citizens the right to vote, nor did they agree about who was a citizen. Anthony and many other suffragists spent much of their speeches trying to convince their audiences of their major and minor premises. Despite their passionate efforts, women did not get the right to vote in the United States until 1920.[9] Using your *Invitation to Public Speaking* CD-ROM, watch the video clip of Lisa's speech under Speech Interactive. Consider how she uses deduction, paying particular attention to how she establishes the major premise of her argument.

Causal Reasoning

If I don't study, then I'll do poorly on my exam.

If I use recreational drugs, then I'll eventually turn to more addictive ones.

If I study self-defense, then I'll be less likely to be hurt if someone attacks me.

causal reasoning
Process of reasoning that supports a claim by establishing a cause-and-effect relationship.

Causal reasoning is a process of reasoning that supports a claim by establishing a cause-and-effect relationship. Causal reasoning identifies an "if-then" relationship that suggests "if" one factor is present, "then" another is sure to follow.[10] The statements at the beginning of this section are examples of causal relationships. Each of them establishes a cause-and-effect relationship: lack of preparation (the cause) results in poor grades (the effect); use of recreational drugs (the cause) leads to the use of addictive ones (the effect); and learning self-defense (the cause) lessens the risk of harm in the event of an attack (the effect).

Speakers often use causal reasoning to develop their ideas with great success. In the following example, Kameron uses causal reasoning to develop his argument that Zebra mussels, native to the Caspian Sea in Europe but not to the waters of the United States, are seriously damaging the aquatic environment:

> Zebra mussels cause damage to every aspect of any aquatic ecosystem they encounter. They destroy the natural balance of the ecosystem by filtering the food from water at an insane rate of one liter of water each day. Not much you think? Well, these mollusks can live in colonies of up to 70,000 mussels. That's 70,000 liters of water cleared of all food each day. This means the Zebra mussels consume all the food usually eaten by animals lower in the food chain. The result is catastrophic repercussions on down the line. For example, a body of water whose food is filtered away cannot support any kind of life. The larger fish then have nothing to eat, resulting in fewer fish for anglers.

Kameron's causal reasoning allows him to argue compellingly that Zebra mussels (the cause) lead to aquatic devastation (the effect).

Guidelines for causal reasoning.
Causal reasoning is an effective form of reasoning because it allows you to link two events together. But because causal relationships are sometimes difficult to prove, select your causal evidence carefully. Consider the following three guidelines:

- Avoid false causes.
- Avoid assuming an event has only one cause.
- Cite supporting evidence to strengthen your cause-and-effect relationships.

Let's take a closer look at each of these guidelines. First, avoid false causes.[11] A **false cause** is an error in reasoning in which a speaker assumes that one event caused another simply because the first event happened before the second. It can be easy to assume a false cause. You pick up your "lucky" pen from your desk, and five minutes later you get a creative brainstorm for the project you are working on.

false cause
Error in reasoning in which a speaker assumes that one event caused another simply because the first event happened before the second.

Did the lucky pen cause the creative brainstorm? Perhaps, but it's hard to tell. Similarly, your nephew watches two hours of violent cartoon programming in the morning. When he sits down to lunch, he points his hot dog at his sister and makes shooting noises. Did the violence in the cartoons cause the behavior? Perhaps his behavior was prompted by the game he played with neighbors the day before or the joke his father told while making similar gestures. Again, the connection is not certain.

Although it is tempting to assume direct causes when one event happens shortly after another, the two events may not be directly related. When one event happens *immediately* after another, there may be a link, but you would have to investigate further to be sure. If you make a causal claim in a speech, you must be certain one event did in fact cause the other. Using your *Invitation to Public Speaking* CD-ROM, watch the video clip of Brent under Speech Interactive. Consider how he makes a causal claim. Is the stated cause-and-effect relationship accurate or inaccurate?

Brent Erb

Second, avoid assuming that an event has only one cause. Events often have many causes, especially those that become topics in the public dialogue. For example, it is unrealistic to try to pin the cause of teen suicide on one factor. It is far more appropriate to address the multiple factors that contribute to teen suicide: the home and school environment, social pressures, individual personality traits, the teen's support system and friendships. Similarly, it is inaccurate to suggest that watching violent television is the sole cause of violence in children. Many other factors contribute to violent behaviors, and a speaker's reasoning must address all these causes.

Third, strengthen your cause-and-effect relationships by citing strong supporting evidence. For example, in his informative speech about Zebra mussels, Kameron identified a very strong connection between the overpopulation of Zebra mussels and the damage done to boats, buoys, docks, and anchors. He was able to support his connection by providing testimony from local fishers who had seen buoys sink from the weight of too many mussels! However, in a persuasive speech about the relationship between power lines and cancer in people who live close to them, Christina could make only a very weak connection: her father, who died of cancer, had lived near power lines for years. However, the scientific evidence she provided to establish a strong link between cancer and proximity to power lines was sketchy and inconclusive. Thus, no matter how hard she tried, her audience would not accept her claim that power lines caused her father's cancer.

Consider the effectiveness of causal reasoning by completing InfoTracCollege Edition Exercise 8.1, "Determining Causation," featured online under Student Resources for Chapter 8.

Analogical Reasoning

It's like paying for your groceries and then leaving them at the store! If students want to pay tuition and then not show up for class or do the work, I guess that's their right.

Reversing this decision would be like slamming on the brakes at 90 miles an hour. I can't support those kinds of casualties. If we are going to make any changes now, we've got to apply the brakes gradually so no one gets hurt.

When we compare two similar things and suggest that what is true for the first will be true for the second, we are reasoning analogically. **Analogical reasoning** is

analogical reasoning
Process of reasoning suggesting that because two conditions or events resemble each other in ways that are certain, they will resemble each other in other ways that are less certain.

reasoning suggesting that because two conditions or events resemble each other in ways that are certain, they will resemble each other in other ways that are less certain. When we suggest that paying tuition but not doing class work is like buying groceries but leaving them behind, we are saying that students often pay for what they don't use. If we tell our coworkers or employees that a change now is like slamming on the brakes, we are comparing the hazards of sudden stops on the freeway to sudden changes in the workplace. In both cases, we are reasoning by analogy.

We also reason analogically when we compare differences in two similar conditions or events and draw inferences about what should be true for both but isn't. Consider how Stephanie used analogical reasoning to inform her audience about the differences in the way crimes against minorities are treated as compared to those against whites:

> I was living in Oak Harbor, Washington, when JonBenet Ramsey was killed. . . . Like everyone else, I was appalled and followed the coverage of her death for three months. Then, in my town of Oak Harbor, a 7-year-old girl named Deborah Palmer disappeared while walking to school one morning. . . . Her lifeless body was found washed up on a local beach, 6 miles from her house. Do you know who Deborah Palmer was? Well, JonBenet's murder ran as a cover story in almost every national newspaper and magazine. Her little face looked back at me for over a year every time I went into a grocery store. Deborah's story ran in the *Seattle Times,* the *Skaggit Valley Herald,* and the *Whidbey Island News* for a total of nine articles. In a very short period of time, Deborah's story disappeared completely.
>
> Why the difference when the crimes were so similar and neither murderer was ever found? JonBenet was a crowned beauty queen with blond hair and blue eyes. Deborah was the child of an African American father and a Filipino mother.

The analogy Stephanie used to draw her audience into her compelling speech is that JonBenet Ramsey and Deborah Palmer had much in common. They were little girls who died brutally and tragically within three months of one another. Police have yet to find either murderer. If one child received extensive news coverage, shouldn't the other one have too?

Although Stephanie held the audience's attention as she developed her analogy, analogies also can be short and straightforward. For example, when speaking to her audience about the importance of more than direct care, physician Deborah Prothrow-Stith used this simple and effective analogy: "We were just stitching them up and sending them back out on the streets, back to the domestic equivalent of a war zone."[12]

Speakers from many professions use analogies because they appeal to audiences—an analogy begins with what is familiar and is usually easy to understand. To read a discussion about analogical reasoning in politics and science, go to the Analogical Reasoning Web page at http://www.psych.mcgill.ca/perpg/fac/dunbar/analogy.html.

Guidelines for analogical reasoning. To increase the effectiveness of analogical reasoning, be sure what you are comparing is truly alike. When you compare two conditions or events that don't share characteristics, your analogy is invalid and will seem illogical to your audience. Most of us have heard invalid analogies and thought to ourselves, "That's like comparing apples to oranges." For example, it is invalid to suggest that proposed nonsmoking ordinances will succeed in Kentucky, Tennessee, and North Carolina because they succeeded in California, Oregon, and Washington. This analogy is invalid because people in southern states that grow tobacco and in western states whose economies do not depend on tobacco have different attitudes about smoking. If you make an analogy between two conditions or events, they must be similar in many respects for the analogy to be valid.

Reasoning by Sign

> The small bomb-like icon on your computer screen tells you that your program has frozen and you have problems.
>
> The silence from upper management is a sign that they're about to make changes.
>
> The bubbles around the perimeter of the boat indicate that divers are about to surface.

A **sign** is something that represents something else. It is one of the most common forms of reasoning we use in our daily lives: dark clouds are a sign of a storm rolling in; a decrease in the number of applications for a certain academic program is a sign of declining interest; the bailiff's command "all rise" is a sign that the judge is about to enter the courtroom. [13] Signs have an important function in the reasoning process because they prompt us to infer what is *likely* to be. They help speakers establish relationships and draw conclusions for their audiences based on those relationships. **Reasoning by sign** is reasoning that assumes something exists or will happen based on something else that exists or has happened.

Signs, like causal relationships, can have strong or weak relationships. Reasoning by sign is strengthened when you can point to the repetition of one example to build a case. For example, *every* time the bomb on the computer screen appears, the computer is frozen. But note that few signs are infallible, and most are open to question (sometimes those dark clouds don't bring rain).

sign
Something that represents something else.

reasoning by sign
Process of reasoning that assumes something exists or will happen based on something else that exists or has happened.

Guidelines for reasoning by sign. Because signs are fallible, consider three guidelines for using them:

- Think about whether an alternative explanation is more credible.

- Make sure a sign is not just an isolated instance.

- If you can find instances in which a sign does not indicate a particular event, you do not have a solid argument.

Let's take a closer look at each of these guidelines. First, is an alternative explanation more credible? In a speech on the standards for licensing teachers, Seogwan suggested that the low test scores in the nation's public schools were a sign of poorly trained teachers. He reasoned that low scores represented, or signaled, poor teaching. However, when his audience questioned him, they raised a number of equally credible explanations. Could the lower scores be a sign of outdated or biased tests? Of overcrowded classrooms? Of the need to restructure our classrooms? Of poor testing skills? Each of these explanations is as likely as the one Seogwan offered, and much evidence supports each of them. As a result, his audience thought Seogwan's reasoning was flawed. To avoid this pitfall, be sure that when you claim one thing is a sign of another, an alternative explanation isn't equally valid or better.

Second, when you reason by sign, make sure the sign is not just an isolated instance. Speaking in favor of pornography, Mark argued that all of his friends, women included, had no problems with pornography. This, he claimed, was a sign that most people accept pornography now. He ignored the nationwide debate over pornography and the thousands of people who campaign against it. He mistakenly assumed that one instance (his friends' support of pornography) represented a larger pattern.

Third, when you reason by sign, you are suggesting the sign almost always indicates a particular event. If you can find instances in which the sign does not indicate that event, you do not have a solid argument. Arguing against feminism, Tammi claimed, "My problem with feminism is that it's against men. Feminists want to reverse the power structure and take away the rights of men. When I hear the word *feminist,* I know it's a sign for angry, power-hungry women." However, her audience named many feminists (the sign) who were not anti-male or power hungry (what Tammi claims feminism represents). Her sign did not meet the test of reliability—her audience had many examples of the sign without the presence of what she argued it stood for.

 Good examples of reasoning by sign can be found in the field of medicine—one of the primary purposes of medical research is to identify the signs of certain diseases. To explore reasoning by sign in the medical community, complete InfoTrac College Edition Exercise 8.2, "Finding Symptoms and Cures," online under Student Resources for Chapter 8.

 ### Speech Step 8.1 / Test the Reasoning of Your Arguments

Examine the first main argument in your speech and determine which pattern of reasoning you've used to develop this argument (inductive, deductive, causal, analogical, and by sign). Test your reasoning, using the guidelines discussed in this chapter. If you are satisfied that your reasoning is sound for this argument, repeat this process for the other arguments in the speech. If you are dissatisfied, take the time to strengthen your reasoning process, then move on to your other arguments.

Scott

As a listener, it is important to identify reasoning throughout a speech because the speaker could be telling you things that are extremely biased or flat out not true. Being able to identify sound reasoning in the speech is critical so you don't just absorb what the speaker says and believe everything is true. You must search for the logic and reason (conclusion) behind what the speaker is saying and see if it makes sense.

A Map of Reasoning

By now, you are familiar with the various types of evidence introduced in Chapter 7 (examples, narratives, statistics, testimony, and definitions). You can use the patterns of reasoning you've explored in this chapter to assemble your evidence into a logical argument. One way to help you assemble your ideas logically and build your case, or construct your argument, is to develop a map of your reasoning process. A solid argument should follow this map of reasoning, which is adapted from Stephen Toulmin's model of a sound argument (see Figure 8.3).[14]

Claim	*What do you think or want to propose?*
Grounds	*Why do you think this or want to propose it?*
Warrant	*How do you know your grounds support your claim?*
Backing	*How do you know the warrant supports the grounds?*

This model of a sound argument helps you both as a speaker and as an audience member. As a speaker, you can use these questions to double-check the logic of your assertions—you can make a map of your own reasoning. As a listener, you can use the map to assess the reasons speakers give in support of their own claims.

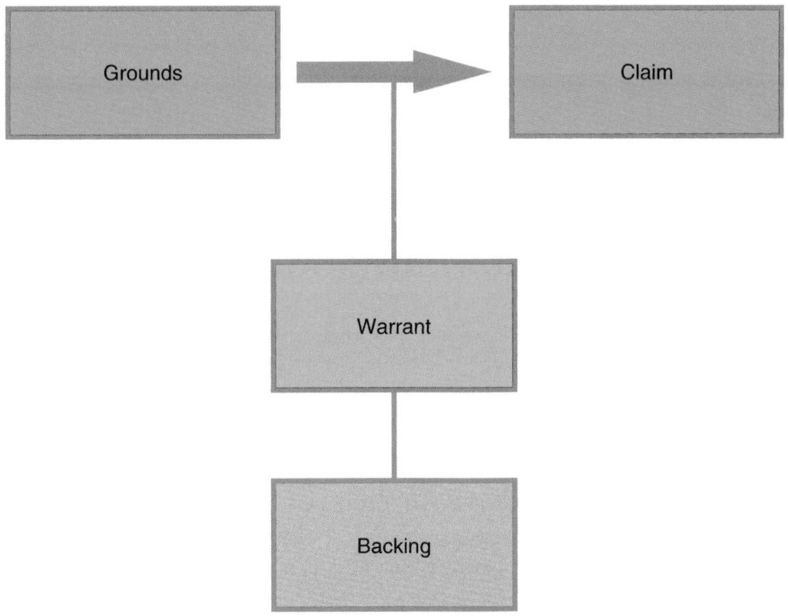

Figure 8.3

Toulmin's Model of Reasoning

To explore more information and illustrations of the Toulmin model, go to http://commfaculty.fullerton.edu/rgass/toulmin2.htm.

Let's look at a map of Damon's reasoning in his persuasive speech on teen suicide to see how this works in an acutal argument:

Claim   *What do you think or want to propose?*

The high rate of teen suicide for males is now a part of our community.

Grounds   *Why do you think this or want to propose it?*

Three boys have committed suicide in our own community in the past two months.

Warrant   *How do you know your grounds support your claim?*

Three suicides in two months meet the standard of a high rate of suicide.

Backing   *How do you know the warrant supports the grounds?*

Research indicates that three suicides in two months is an above average rate.

This map—a bit like a child's continually questioning "why?"—helps speakers and audiences track a line of reasoning and find any flaws or loopholes. The reasoning in Damon's speech is solid, and the map helps us see this. He has acceptable grounds, warrant, and backing for his claim.

This map also can be used to test your reasoning in other types of speeches. In Stephanie's informative speech, she explained that crimes against minorities are treated differently than those against whites (claim). She described the coverage of the murder of Deborah, a child with African American and Filipino heritage (grounds). Stephanie then described the coverage of JonBenet's murder (warrant), linking that coverage to JonBenet's whiteness as well as her status as a beauty queen (backing).

Now let's use the model to uncover flaws in Christina's causal arguments about power lines and cancer. Notice that after the warrant, her backing breaks down:

Claim   *What do you think or want to propose?*

     Living near power lines increases the risk of cancer.

Grounds   *Why do you think this or want to propose it?*

     My father died of cancer and we lived near a power line.

Warrant   *How do you know your grounds support your claim?*

     The reason my father had cancer was because of the power line.

Backing   *How do you know the warrant supports the grounds?*

     Scientific research has yet to confirm the connection between cancer and power lines.

Her causal reasoning fell prey to several problems: circular reasoning, overgeneralizing, and claiming only one cause. Using Toulmin's model, we see that Christina used a circular form of reasoning (you'll learn more about circular reasoning in Chapter 18):

Grounds   My father died because of the power line.

Warrant   The power lines caused my father's death.

Additionally, her backing discredits her argument—she produced no scientific evidence to support her claim. Her research turned up only speculation and inclusive evidence (her backing) rather than the definitive connection she needed. Mapping her grounds, warrant, and backing clearly illustrate the weakness of her argument.

How could Christina have improved her argument? If she had reasoned inductively, offering several examples of people who lived near power lines and died of cancer, her warrant would have been acceptable. She also could have offered statistics to support her claim, showing her audience the numerical correlation between power lines and cancer.

We can see a second example of flawed reasoning in Mark's speech about pornography. In this case, Mark did not gather enough research to support his claims, nor did he reason carefully. This became apparent when he tried to diagram his proposal using the map of reasoning:

Claim   *What do you think or want to propose?*

     Most people accept pornography as okay.

Grounds   *Why do you think this or want to propose it?*

     I like pornography and so do my friends.

Warrant   *How do you know your grounds support your claim?*

     Even my girlfriends don't think it's bad.

Backing   *How do you know the warrant supports the grounds?*

     If girls don't think it's bad, then it isn't.

Mapped out in this way, the speaker and the audience could see the weaknesses in his reasoning. First, his grounds (we like it) do not support his claim (it's okay). Liking something and establishing that thing as okay are two different things. Second, his warrant and backing are based not only on too few examples (his girlfriends) but also on a questionable sign (if some girls don't think pornography is bad, does that mean all girls don't?). Moreover, they do not even address his claim that "most people accept pornography as okay." He has provided no evidence that "most people" accept pornography or explained what he means by "okay." To explore more examples of how communicators use the Toulmin model, go to http://intra.som.umass.edu/buscomm/argument.html, a Web page created for business writers.

When you reason, trace each step of your argument with Toulmin's model. Mapping your arguments before you deliver your speech helps you find the flaws and fix them. As a member of an audience, when you find you are having trouble following a line of reasoning, ask the four questions of Toulmin's model: What is the speaker claiming or proposing? Why does the speaker think or want to propose this? What grounds support the speaker's claim? What backing supports the grounds? These questions should help you spot invalid claims and poorly developed arguments. To practice using Toulmin's model to assess a speech, complete InfoTrac College Edition Exercise 8.3, "Applying Toulmin's Model," online under Student Resources for Chapter 8.

Speech Step 8.2 / Apply Toulmin's Model of Reasoning to Your Arguments

Apply Toulmin's model of reasoning to each of your arguments in Speech Step 8.1. Identify your claims, grounds, warrant, and backing. Verify the logic of those four parts of your argument, and make any adjustments to your reasoning process now.

Tips for Reasoning Ethically

Evidence, reasoning, logic, and arguments are powerful tools in the public dialogue. With them, we can share information, express our perspective and invite dialogue, make a case for a certain position or debate an issue, and even celebrate someone's accomplishments. However, we can also manipulate, confuse, and misrepresent events, issues, and people. As such, we must consider the ethics of reasoning carefully. Speaking ethically requires our commitment to giving speeches that are accurate and well reasoned. The following tips will help you reason ethically in your speeches: build credibility, use accurate evidence, and verify the structure of your reasoning.

Build Your Credibility

When you develop your reasoning with your audience in mind, you develop your relationship with them. Not only do you design your reasoning so your audience can listen to you without feeling confused or criticized, but you design your reasoning to build your credibility. **Credibility** is the audience's perception of a speaker's competence and character. **Competence** is the audience's view of a speaker's intelligence, expertise, and knowledge of a subject. Competence is developed through reasoning, organization, and delivery. **Character** is the audience's view of a speaker's sincerity, trustworthiness, and concern for the well-being of the audience. Character is displayed through a speaker's honesty and regard for the audience.[15]

Through ethical reasoning, as discussed throughout this chapter, you communicate to an audience that you are competent and you care about them. You

credibility
Audience's perception of a speaker's competence and character.

competence
Audience's view of a speaker's intelligence, expertise, and knowledge of a subject.

character
Audience's view of a speaker's sincerity, trustworthiness, and concern for the well-being of the audience.

convey to the audience that you have thought about the best way to express your ideas and you want others to understand them. In short, a careful reasoning process communicates an audience-centered stance that enhances your credibility. This credibility is a critical component of the ethical reasoning process. (For more about credibility, especially in regard to persuasive speaking, see Chapter 18.)

Speech Step 8.3 / Build
Your Credibility with Sound Reasoning

Evaluate how you are building your credibility through your reasoning processes. Is your reasoning sound enough to communicate your competence and character to your audience? How does your reasoning help you stay audience centered throughout your speech? If you cannot identify the specific ways your reasoning builds your credibility, take time now to clarify how you convey you've thought about your ideas and how your audience can best understand them.

Use Accurate Evidence

Because speakers are adding to the ongoing discussion of issues that affect us all, they want to use accurate evidence. Recall from Chapter 7 that it is just as easy to find examples, statistics, and testimony from unreliable sources as it is to find them from credible ones. It also is possible to misrepresent or alter any statistic, example, narrative, or testimony you do find. However, a healthy public dialogue depends on legitimate evidence in order to build sound reasoning.

As a speaker, you are ethically obligated to use accurate evidence in all of your patterns of reasoning. Although you may be able to present a fully developed inductive argument based on fabricated examples or a compelling analogy that is false, you would be deceiving your audience. For example, when George W. Bush reasoned that drilling for oil in the Arctic National Wildlife Refuge would not affect that ecosystem negatively, the American public was skeptical. They had credible evidence that it would do just the opposite. Similarly, when Bush reasoned that the oil drilled from that area would contribute significantly to our oil supply, his evidence was challenged as inaccurate. Ethical speakers want to be certain of the accuracy of their arguments at every step of the process. Using your *Invitation to Public Speaking* CD-ROM, watch the video clip of the first Bush-Gore 2000 presidential debate included under Speech Interactive. Consider how each candidate used evidence to support his reasoning.

Verify the Structure of Your Reasoning

Applying Toulmin's model of reasoning to your arguments is the final way you can ensure the ethical nature of your reasoning. (In fact, Toulmin developed this framework to assist average people in discovering weaknesses in their reasoning processes.) By using this model as you develop your speech, you can check the warrants, grounds, and backing for your claims and ensure their accuracy. Note that it is unethical to assert a claim is true if you do not have evidence to support that claim (recall Mark's speech about pornography). Similarly, it is unethical to make unfounded arguments that could alarm audiences (recall Christina's speech about power lines and cancer). When you identify weaknesses and potentially disturbing claims before presenting them to your audiences, you are acting ethically.

When presidential candidates participate in a debate, they must make sure the evidence they present is accurate, particularly about issues of national interest. Otherwise, voters will doubt their credibility. How might you verify the accuracy of evidence in your speech? What are the implications for the public dialogue as a result of the misuse of evidence?

AP/Wide World Photos

Chapter Summary

The process of reasoning is basic to any kind of speech. Whether we inform, invite, or persuade, we offer reasons to our audiences, and we want those reasons to be sound. When we reason, we use logos, ethos, and pathos to offer explanations and justifications for our ideas and positions. The logic of our reasons depends on our evidence—the examples, narratives, statistics, and definitions we gather during our research process. This logic helps our audience make inferences and see the connections between our evidence and claims. Our goal is to develop an argument that our audience can contemplate and agree with or dispute.

Beginning speakers use five common patterns of reasoning:

- Inductive reasoning, or reasoning from specific instances, relies on a series of examples to develop a claim we expect to be true. When you reason inductively, have enough examples to support your claim, make sure your generalizations are accurate, and use statistics and testimony to support your arguments.

- Deductive reasoning, or reasoning from general principle, begins with a commonly accepted major premise. In combination with a specific instance, or minor premise, it then establishes the truth of a specific claim, or conclusion. If your general principle is one the audience will not accept immediately, you will need to establish its validity.

- Causal reasoning establishes an "if-then" relationship, suggesting that if one event happens (a cause), then another is sure to follow (effect). When you use causal reasoning, be careful not to claim a causal relationship if it can't be proven or to assume mistakenly there is only one cause for an event. In addition, try to identify the strength or weakness of the relationship you are establishing.

- Analogical reasoning suggests that when two objects are similar in known ways, they will be similar in other ways. However, be sure the two things you are comparing truly are alike.

- Reasoning by sign establishes the truth or probability of an event or an object based on a symbol of it. A sign represents something else and, when the sign is present, speakers reason that the other thing will be too. When you reason by sign, be sure there isn't a more credible explanation for your claim, that the sign is not an isolated instance, and that the sign is always present when what it represents is.

Using Toulmin's model of reasoning, speakers can verify the strength of their arguments. Listeners, too, can use this model to assess the strength of a speaker's reasoning. The model sets out four questions:

1. The claim: What do you think or want to propose?

2. The grounds: Why do you think this or want to propose it?

3. The warrant: How do you know your grounds support your claim?

4. And the backing: How do you know the warrant supports the grounds?

Like all other aspects of public speaking, reasoning has an ethical component. To be ethical during the reasoning process is to stay audience centered and to establish strong credibility through sound reasoning. Ethical speakers use their evidence accurately and do not make claims their evidence does not support. They take time during the speech writing and research process to verify the structure of their reasoning so they will not confuse or alienate their audience.

As you enter the public dialogue, you will discover that you rely on reasoning—your own and that of other speakers—to communicate and to exchange ideas and views. Although each component of the speaking process has its place, sound reasoning is one of the most powerful aspects of a healthy public dialogue.

Sound and ethical reasoning will help you not only in your speech class, but also in your other classes and in the workplace. Can you think of times when understanding reasoning methods and knowing how to verify your reasoning could have helped you solve a problem or make a point in these contexts?

© Courtesy of Beloit College. Photo by Chuck Savage. Property of Wadsworth./Thomson Learning.

Invitation to Public Speaking Online

After reading this chapter, use your CD-ROM and the *Invitation to Public Speaking* Web site to review the follow- ing concepts, answer the review questions, and complete the suggested activities.

Key Concepts

logos (182)
ethos (182)
pathos (182)
inferences (182)
argument (182)
inductive reasoning (183)

hasty generalization (185)
deductive reasoning (185)
major premise (185)
minor premise (186)
conclusion (186)
causal reasoning (188)

false cause (188)
analogical reasoning (189)
sign (191)
reasoning by sign (191)
credibility (195)
competence (195)
character (195)

Review Questions

1. Bring a copy of the morning paper to class with you. In groups, identify as many different types of reason- ing as you can find in the text, photographs, or adver- tisements. Label each item you find either *inductive, deductive, causal, analogical,* or *sign,* and evaluate the strength of each item's reasoning according to the guidelines discussed in this chapter.

2. Do you think Ruby offered enough examples to make her inductive claim valid in her speech on privacy rights? Why do you think what you do? How many examples do you think a speaker can reasonably pres- ent in a five-minute speech with three main points?

3. Map the reasoning you find in a newspaper editorial or a letter to the editor according to Toulmin's model of an argument. Does the writer make solid argu- ments, or can you find weaknesses in his or her war- rant, grounds, backing, or all three? Based on what you've read in this chapter, can you see ways in which to strengthen the writer's claims?

4. In this chapter, Mark claims that to like something makes that thing okay. What is the distinction between liking something and something being okay that is important to Mark's reasoning?

5. This chapter suggests that a speaker's credibility is an important part of the ethical process of using reason- ing. Do you agree? Why or why not? Can you identify speakers you have heard or read about who do not have much credibility and you would deem unethical? Compare those speakers lacking in credibility to a speaker you find credible. Whose arguments do you find more ethical?

The *Invitation to Public Speaking* Web Site

The *Invitation to Public Speaking* Web site features the review questions about the Web sites suggested on pages 185, 190, 193 and 195, the interactive activities suggested on pages 182 and 185, and the InfoTrac College Edition exercises suggested on pages 189, 192, and 195. You can access this site via your CD-ROM or at http://www.wadsworth.com/product/griffin.

Web Links

8.1: Hasty Generalization (185)
8.2: Analogical Reasoning (190)
8.3: Toulmin Model (193)
8.4: Toulmin Model and Business (195)

Interactive Activities

8.1: Aristotle's Forms of Proof (182)
Purpose: To learn how to distinguish among ethos, pathos, and logos.

8.2: Assessing Inductive Reasoning (185)
Purpose: To evaluate inductive arguments critically.

 ## InfoTrac College Edition Exercises

8.1: **Determining Causation** (189)
Purpose: To learn to evaluate causal reasoning.

8.2: **Finding Symptoms and Cures** (192)
Purpose: To explore how medical researchers identify relationships between signs and diseases.

8.3: **Applying Toulmin's Model** (195)
Purpose: To learn to spot invalid claims and poorly developed arguments.

Speech Interactive on the *Invitation to Public Speaking* CD-ROM

The following video clips of speeches referenced in this chapter are included under Speech Interactive on your *Invitation to Public Speaking* CD-ROM. After you have watched the clips, click on "Critique" to answer the questions for analysis.

Video Clip 1: Deduction: Lisa Alagna (188). As you watch Lisa use deductive reasoning, consider the tests of deduction discussed in this chapter. How does Lisa establish the validity of her major premise? Do you accept her premise? Why or why not?

Video Clip 2: Causal Reasoning: Brent Erb (189). Watch the video clip of Brent. Consider how he makes a causal claim. Is the causal relationship he states accurate or inaccurate?

Video Clip 3: Bush-Gore Presidential Debate (196). As you watch the video clip of the Bush-Gore debate about drilling for oil in the Arctic wilderness, consider how each candidate uses evidence. How does each question the other's use of evidence? What external sources do they use?

Chapter Nine
Organizing Your Speech

In this chapter you will learn to

Identify your main points for your speech

Determine the appropriate number of main points for your speech

Organize your main points according to five different patterns

Apply tips for preparing your main points effectively

Use four different kinds of connectives in your speech

Cite sources properly in your speech

Speak properly, and in as few words as you can, but always plainly; for the end of speech is not ostentation, but to be understood.

—William Penn, founder of Pennsylvania, c. 1695

Once you've gathered the information for your speech, you may be wondering how to organize it into a coherent presentation. There are several ways you can organize your ideas into interesting points. In this chapter, you will learn how important organization is in creating a clear and effective speech, how to structure your main points, and how to apply different patterns of organization.[1] You also will learn ways to move from one idea to the next, as well as techniques for citing sources in your speeches. Once you master the fundamental steps of organization and source citation, you can branch out to more elaborate techniques. For now, use these basic frameworks to help you build speeches that are clear, interesting, and easy to follow.

Organize for Clarity

Recall from Chapter 1 that one of the differences between public speaking and everyday conversation is that public speaking is more systematic or organized than a casual conversation. Public speakers usually take considerable time to organize their thoughts and ideas before they enter the public dialogue. They organize their ideas so their message is easy to follow and their supporting materials fall into place in a way that is logical to their audiences. Like many other aspects of your speeches, organization is another important audience-centered responsibility.

Let's look at an example that illustrates the importance of a well-organized speech. See if you can make sense of the following outline of ideas:

Take one of the corners and bring it to the center.

The history of this process is an intriguing one.

My mother had the flag given to her family when her brother died in the Vietnam War.

The stars on the edge of the flag are highly symbolic.

It should never touch the ground.

She describes the ceremony as quite beautiful and symbolic.

You need two people to fold a flag correctly.

There is a correct way to fold a flag.

The flag should always be displayed behind the speaker's left shoulder.

Can you follow this speaker's organizational logic? Although you begin to realize that the speech is about flags by the second subpoint, are you clear about the speaker's thesis? Is her speech informative, invitational, persuasive, or for a special occasion? Can you tell whether she was asked, required, or whether she decided to speak? It is hard to figure out what this speech is about from the outline just presented.

Now consider this speech organized in a way that is more linear, not to mention more appealing, to an audience:

Specific purpose: To inform my audience about the rules and regulation for handling the U.S. flag.

Cindy Gardner demonstrates the process of folding a flag.

Thesis statement:	The flag, a symbol of much that is great about this nation, should be hung, handled, and folded in a specific manner.
Main points:	I. Each part of the flag has a specific meaning or purpose dedicated to symbolizing patriotic ideas.
	II. Because of the symbolism of each of these parts, the flag should be hung in a specific manner.
	III. Flag etiquette, more than just stories told from generation to generation, tells us how to handle a flag properly.
	IV. Flags also should be folded in a specific way, with each fold representing important qualities of our country.

Notice how this outline gives you a much clearer sense of what Cindy will cover and how her ideas relate to one another. **Organization**, the systematic arrangement of ideas into a coherent whole, makes speeches listenable. It makes your ideas and arguments clear and easy to follow. Using your *Invitation to Public Speaking* CD-ROM, watch the video clip of Cindy giving the speech about flag folding under Speech Interactive. Notice how she organizes her ideas. To appreciate the importance of organization, complete InfoTrac College Edition Exercise 9.1, "Assessing Clarity," online under Student Resources for Chapter 9.

organization
Systematic arrangement of ideas into a coherent whole.

Main Points

One of the first steps in organizing a speech is to identify your main points. **Main points** are the most important, comprehensive ideas you address in your speech. They give your speech focus and help you decide which information to include and which to leave out. They are your overarching themes or subjects. To read more about the importance of main points, go to speech consultant Jan D'Arcy's Web site at http://www.cfug-md.org/SpeakerTips/775.html and read "Three Main Points in Your Speech."

main points
The most important ideas you address in your speech.

Identify Your Main Points

You can identify the main points of your speech in two ways. First, take stock of your speech assignment, your list of ideas, and your research (to help you, use your research inventory discussed in Chapter 7). You will know you have a main point when you realize that if you do not develop a particular idea, your speech topic will seem incomplete, nonsensical, or will not accomplish your goal for the speech.

Second, if you have already written your thesis statement, you should be able to find your main points within it. Notice in the example about folding a flag that Cindy's thesis statement defines her main points: (1) the symbolism in the U.S. flag and how a flag should be (2) hung, (3) handled, and (4) folded. Without a thesis statement (as in the first version of Cindy's outline), a speaker's ideas are simply a random collection of points. Consider how the thesis statement helps Robert define his main points in the following example:

Specific purpose:	To inform my audience of the history of theatrical lighting.
Thesis statement:	The history of theatrical lighting can be divided into three periods: before electricity, the discovery of electricity and the invention of light bulbs, and the invention of lighting instruments for the stage.

Main points:	I. Before electricity, actors and directors depended on the sun, oil lamps and torches, and chandeliers to light their stages.
	II. With the invention of electricity came the invention of the light bulb, a tremendous boon to lighting stages.
	III. New instruments, called the ellipsoidal, the fresnel, and the intelabeam, allowed lighting technicians to create more effects with theatrical lighting.

Notice that we can find the three main points in the thesis statement: the three periods in the history of theatrical lighting.

Your thesis statement may not always be as specific as Robert's, especially if you are giving a process, or how-to, speech. Nonetheless, even with the broad thesis statement in the next speech, Candice used it to develop her main points:

Specific purpose:	To inform my audience of the process of making a scrapbook.
Thesis statement:	There are four steps to making a quality scrapbook.
Main points:	I. Collect the materials you want to put into the book.
	II. Decide on the order of your materials.
	III. Arrange the materials in the book.
	IV. Cover or bind the book.

Notice how the four steps Candice mentioned in her thesis statement became the four steps she discussed in her speech. Also note that although making a scrapbook may seem like a fairly simple speech topic, Candice gave this speech as a part of a service learning project in her speech course (see the Invitation to Service Learning box below).

Invitation to Service Learning / Candice

Photo courtesy of Jennifer Emerling Bone

When I first found out that we had to volunteer as part of the course requirement, I felt a bit apprehensive. Then I discovered that one of the agencies I could volunteer for was a facility that housed juvenile delinquents. This intrigued me. I myself had a difficult childhood. My parents divorced when I was young. A few years later my father was in a severe motorcycle accident that left him permanently disabled. To make the situation even worse, my brother was diagnosed with cancer when he was only 16 years old. It took me a little while to find the positives in life and to realize that some people had it worse than I did. The decision to focus on the positives is what led me to making scrapbooks.

I started to collect happy memories in photographs and display them in a scrapbook. Once I had found my passion and creative outlet, I wanted to share it with others. That is what led me to Turning Point, a facility where I could help troubled teens.

The girls I worked with were challenged teenagers who were trying to turn their lives around, and I wanted to help. I soon discovered that the girls I worked with wanted to learn something new. I began by going to Turning Point on a Saturday morning and staying for ten hours. I spent the day snapping pictures of the girls having fun and playing. Next, I returned to give an interactive speech on how to make a scrapbook.

I brought along the photos I had taken and gave each girl several photos to include on her own scrapbook page. The girls had a great time designing their own page and learning how to focus their energy on something positive.

The public speaking class made me take my creative talents and my public speaking skills and combine them into one. Whether you give a speech because you are asked or because you are required, I believe you can have a profound effect on someone in the audience. A big part of giving a successful speech is in the voice and the choice of words you use. What you get out of a service learning project is what you put into it. And for me, it was touching someone's life through words and creativity.

Your thesis statement and your research should guide your selection of main points for other types of speeches as well. In an invitational speech on the problem of elder abuse, Peter developed the following main points:

Specific purpose: To invite my audience to consider two possible solutions to the problem of elder abuse.

Thesis statement: The problem of elder abuse is quite widespread, but may be solved by more thorough background checks of employees in care facilities and increased funding for training and salaries.

Main points:
I. More thorough background checks of employees in care facilities may help solve the widespread problem of elder abuse.
II. Increased funding for training and salaries may also help solve this problem.

In his speech, Peter used his thesis statement to identify the two primary solutions to elder abuse, and he used his research to develop those possibilities. To practice locating main points in your research, complete InfoTrac College Edition Exercise 9.2, "Identifying Main Points," online under Student Resources for Chapter 9.

Use an Appropriate Number of Main Points

Knowing how many main points to include can be difficult because we often gather more information than we need and our subjects can be complex. Additionally, classroom speeches often have other requirements, such as incorporating visual aids, citing a specific number of sources, and engaging in a question-and-answer-discussion with the audience. So how do you determine how many main points to include?

In any kind of speech, your time limit is your most important guideline for determining the number of main points. For even a two- to three-minute speech of introduction, you might start out with a long list of main points, as May did:

Specific purpose: To introduce myself to my audience.

Thesis statement: I have lived an interesting life thus far and have goals for the future.

Main points:
I. I was born in the air over China so I have dual citizenship.
II. I've lived in many different cities, states, and countries.
III. I love to do anything that pertains to water.
IV. I'll graduate next June and travel with friends for the summer.
V. After that, I'll join the navy.
VI. From there, I hope to become an aquatic research scientist for a university.

Although each of these points is interesting, there are far too many to cover—even if May had ten minutes. Also notice that her thesis statement is quite vague and does not help her focus her ideas.

When you have a long list of ideas for any kind of speech, recognize that you'll have to reduce your scope. Most classroom speeches are limited to two to four main points, depending on the length of your speech and your speaking goals. You can reduce your scope by returning to your thesis statement and tightening it up (as May needs to do) or by focusing on only the main points that develop your thesis statement best. Here's a solution for May's speech:

Specific purpose: To introduce myself to my audience.

Thesis statement: The first twenty-two years of my life have been nomadic ones, and this lifestyle is likely to continue for some time.

Main points:

     I. Even as I was being born—in an airplane over China—it seems I've been destined to travel.

     II. My love of water will take me into the navy and continue to nurture this nomadic spirit of mine.

By narrowing her scope and by organizing the six ideas into two main themes, May can present a far more coherent and interesting speech. Her audience will be able to follow two main points easily, rather than keep track of six points. And by focusing and reducing the number of points, May presents a more memorable image of herself.

    Remember, you want your ideas to be developed fully, and trying to incorporate too many into one speech will only create problems. If you suspect you have too many main points, review your thesis statement and then consider your time limits. Ask yourself if you can reasonably cover the amount of material you have planned in the time you are allowed (tips for managing the length of your main points are offered at the end of this section). If you have too much information, rewrite your thesis statement so it is narrower in scope. Then make the necessary adjustments in your main points. For practice identifying main points in a speech, **WEB SITE** complete Interactive Activity 9.1, "Choosing Main Points," online under Student Resources for Chapter 9.

Speech Step 9.1 / Identify and Narrow Down Your Main Points

Review the thesis statement for your next speech. How many main points have you prepared to develop your thesis statement? Do you think you can reasonably cover the material you need to in the time you have? If not, rewrite your thesis statement and main points so you cover a more practical amount of material. You can complete this Speech Step online using Speech Builder Express. Access your Speech Builder Express account using the username and password included on your *Invitation to Public Speaking* CD-ROM.

Order Your Main Points

Once you've determined the number of main points for your speech, you will want to determine the order in which you discuss them. Although there are numerous organizational patterns, the five covered here are the basic ones. As you become more skilled at speaking, you can adjust these patterns or add patterns that are more complex to your inventory. For now, use these basic patterns—chronological, spatial, causal, problem-and-solution, and topical—to help you improve your organizational skills.

Chronological pattern. Speeches that trace a sequence of events or ideas follow a **chronological pattern** of organization. If the ideas in your topic extend over a period of time or follow a sequence of first, second, third, you may want to use this pattern to organize your speech. In the next example, Serafina used a chronological organizational pattern to highlight the stages of a theory:

chronological pattern
Pattern of organization that traces a sequence of events or ideas.

Specific purpose:	To inform my audience of George Kinder's theory of money maturity.
Thesis statement:	The concept of money maturity relates to a person's relationship to money during childhood, adulthood, and on into the future.
Main points:	I. Kinder's first stage of money maturity focuses on the relationship to money a person acquires during childhood.
	II. The second state of money maturity addresses the relationship to money a person has as an adult.
	III. The third stage of money maturity occurs when we set healthy goals for our financial security in the future.

In the next example, Demetrius uses a chronological pattern to demonstrate and explain a process:

Specific purpose:	To inform my audience of how to make a safe ascent during a scuba dive of less than forty feet.
Thesis statement:	Safe ascents during scuba diving can be divided into three basic steps.
Main points:	I. The first step in making a safe ascent is the preparation step: signal your buddy and check the time.
	II. The second step is the "get ready" step: raise your right hand over your head and hold your buoyancy control device (BCD) with your left hand.
	III. The third step of the safe ascent is the actual ascent: slowly rotate upward, breath normally, and release air from your BCD as you go.

Using your *Invitation to Public Speaking* CD-ROM, watch the video clip of Jeff Malcolm's speech introduction. Jeff uses the chronological pattern to organize his speech. Consider the effectiveness of this pattern for his speech.

Spatial pattern. When ideas are arranged in terms of location or direction, they follow a **spatial pattern** of organization. For example, arranging ideas from left to right, top to bottom, or inside to outside helps your audience visualize the

spatial pattern
Pattern of organization in which ideas are arranged in terms of location or direction.

relationship between ideas or the structure of something. Spatial relationships can be abstract, as in the next example about eating according to the food pyramid. At other times, they indicate the location of real things or places, as in the second example about five Italian villages.

Specific purpose:	To inform my audience of some of the creative ways to eat according to the food pyramid.
Thesis statement:	The food pyramid can be used creatively to eat interesting and healthy foods.
Main points:	I. At the foundation of the food pyramid are the grain and vegetable servings that you can combine to make dishes from around the world, such as couscous salad with tomatoes and basil.
	II. You can complement this foundation with the middle level of the pyramid—the dairy, fruit, and protein servings—by making dishes such as curried chicken with apricots.
	III. The top of the pyramid includes the stuff we really like to eat, the fats and sweets that can be made into such delicacies as candied almonds.

In the second example, the spatial pattern is used to describe geographical locations:

Specific purpose:	To invite my audience to visit the Cinque Terre, five villages along the Mediterranean coast of Italy that are only accessible by boat or by footpath.
Thesis statement:	The Cinque Terre contains five villages set into a steep hillside that visitors to the Mediterranean coast of Italy may find enchanting.

The city and surrounding area of Winnipeg, Canada, could be discussed using a spatial pattern of organization. What main points could you write for this image that would follow this pattern? Could you also discuss this image using another pattern?

© Eastcott-Momatiuk//The Image Works

Main points:
    I. The farthest village, called Monterosso, is a popular attraction because of the huge statues carved into the rocks overlooking its beaches.

    II. The next two villages, Vernazza and Corniglia, display remarkable vineyards, homes, and a central promenade and piazza.

    III. A hike to the top of the fourth village, Manarola, gives you a stunning view of the ocean and all five of the villages.

    IV. Riomaggiore, the village of love, completes the Cinque Terre, or five villages, with its captivating display of homes and shops tucked into the final ravine of this remarkable Italian hillside.

Causal pattern. Speeches that describe a cause-and-effect relationship between ideas follow a **causal pattern** of organization. When you use this organizational pattern, you will have two main points, one discussing the cause and the other describing its effects. You can present either the cause first or the effect first, depending on your topic and your speaking goal. In the next example, Jeremy uses a causal pattern to organize the ideas presented in his informative speech on sibling rivalry.

causal pattern
Pattern of organization that describes a cause-and-effect relationship between ideas.

Specific purpose:
    To inform my audience of the causes and most serious effects of sibling rivalry.

Thesis statement:
    Sibling rivalry is caused by competition for attention and can become quite severe if not handled properly.

Main points:
    I. Sibling rivalry is caused by competition for positive attention from parents.

    II. If ignored, sibling rivalry can turn to hatred between siblings.

If the effects have already happened, you might choose to present the effects first, followed by the cause. In this next example, Chaundra discusses the effects of worker burnout first, and then she attempts to persuade the audience of one of its possible causes.

Specific purpose:
    To persuade my audience that the rapid pace of today's workplace is leading to an unusually high level of burnout.

Thesis statement:
    Today's workers are experiencing high levels of burnout, which is caused by increased demands on their time and energy.

Main points:
    I. Today's workers display levels of burnout that are higher than ever.

    II. Today's working environments contribute to burnout through a constant demand for more output in shorter amounts of time.

A causal organizational pattern is useful when your topic describes an event or situation and its consequences. It also is helpful when you want to describe an event that might happen and what its effect might be.

Problem-and-solution pattern. Speeches that identify a specific problem and offer a possible solution follow a **problem-and-solution pattern** of organization. This pattern is common in persuasive speeches because we can describe a

problem-and-solution pattern
Pattern of organization that identifies a specific problem and offers a possible solution.

problem and follow with a call to action. The problem-and-solution pattern has two main points: the description of the problem followed by a description of the solution. Solutions can be general or specific. In the following example, Molly's solution was a general recommendation:

Specific purpose: To persuade my audience that beef by-products have invaded our lives and that awareness is the first step to becoming an educated consumer.

Thesis statement: Becoming aware of the presence of beef by-products in such common items as deodorants, photographic film, marshmallows, gum, and candles is the first step in making educated consumer choices.

Main points:
I. Without our knowledge, beef by-products are included in many of the products we put on and in our bodies, as well as in and around our houses.
II. The solution to this invasion is to become aware of the presence of these beef by-products so we can make informed choices about what we buy and use.

In the next example, Brandon called for a very specific solution:

Specific purpose: To persuade my audience to vote in favor of bond measure 343 in November.

Thesis statement: Money going to support before- and after-school meal programs is at an all-time low, and this measure will ensure the improvement of these services to students in our public schools.

Main points:
I. There currently is not enough money available to provide adequate before- and after-school meal programs to students in our public schools.
II. Passing bond measure 343 will provide this necessary money at a cost of only $2.75 per taxpayer per year.

In Chapter 18, you'll learn more about the various types of solutions that speakers can suggest to their audiences.

Topical pattern. One of the most common patterns of organization is a topical pattern. Speakers often use this pattern when topics don't fit well into any of the other patterns we've discussed. A **topical pattern** of organization allows you to divide your topic into subtopics, each of which addresses a different aspect of the whole topic. When you use a topical pattern, you can organize your ideas by following a progression of ideas that suits your own style, by using the principle of *primacy* (putting your most important idea first) or *recency* (putting what you most want your audience to remember last), or by arranging them in many other ways. In the following example, Justin arranged his ideas topically to address the two major types of phobias:

Specific purpose: To inform my audience of the two major types of phobias.

Thesis statement: Although there are many specific phobias, these "irrational fears and dislikes" can be categorized in two ways.

Main points:
I. A social phobia is a fear of appearing stupid or being shamed in a social situation.
II. A specific phobia is a fear of specific objects or situations, like spiders, closed spaces, and so on.

topical pattern
Pattern of organization that allows the speaker to divide a topic into subtopics, each of which addresses a different aspect of the whole topic.

In the next example, Brooke discusses chili peppers, using three different short stories that take her from less personal facts to more personal ones:

Specific purpose: To inform my audience of the legends behind the chili pepper.

Thesis statement: The chili pepper's story can be told via global, national, and personal stories.

Main points:
    I. The first tale is a global story involving the eye-watering, nose-running heat from the hottest chili pepper around: the habanero.
    II. The second tale is a national story, the tale of Tabasco—both a sauce and a pepper.
    III. The final tale is my own story about growing up on and helping at my grandfather's produce farm, where chilies played a central role.

In the following example, Alex uses a topical pattern to persuade her audience that women in "glory sports" are just as talented as the men.

Specific purpose: To persuade my audience that very talented women engage in what are commonly called glory sports.

Thesis statement: Many women participate in glory sports, and even though most of us know very little about them, they are as talented as the men.

Main points:
    I. Layne Beachley is a professional surfer living in Sydney, Australia, who has held the world champion surfing title for three consecutive years.
    II. Cara Beth Burnside resides in Southern California and is a legendary skateboarder.
    III. Tara Dakides, also from California, is "the most progressive and influential female ever to strap on a snowboard," doing tricks "most guy pros haven't even done yet."

Topical patterns help you organize a speech that doesn't fit into a chronological, spatial, causal, or problem-solution organizational pattern. If you try to rearrange the three examples in this section into one of these other organizational patterns, you'll find that your ideas won't fit well. For practice in identifying appropriate organizational patterns, complete Interactive Activity 9.2, **WEB SITE** "Organizing Main Points," online under Student Resources for Chapter 9 at the *Invitation to Public Speaking* Web site. You can also complete Speech Step 9.2 to select an organizational pattern for your main points.

Speech Step 9.2 / Select an Organizational Pattern for Your Main Points

Revisit the main points you developed in Speech Step 9.1. Can you organize them according to a chronological, spatial, causal, problem-and-solution, or topical organizational pattern? Which pattern will help you best convey your ideas? Select the most appropriate pattern for your next speech.

Speech Builder Express will help you further outline your speech once you designate the organizational pattern your speech will follow.

Tips for Preparing Main Points

There are three keys to developing your main points. First, separate each main point—don't combine two points into one. Second, word your points as consistently as you can. Finally, balance your coverage by spending about the same amount of time discussing each main point.

Separate your main points. In order to be as clear as possible, each main point should be a separate idea. Once you've identified your likely main points, double-check them to be sure you have not combined two ideas into one main point. We may be tempted to combine two ideas in order to cover as much information as we can. But notice what happened when Aaron combined two ideas into a single point:

Ineffective main points

I. Electronic music is produced from a variety of machines that make noise electronically

II. Electronic music has become more popular in recent years and is performed by many well-known artists.

More effective main points

I. Electronic music is produced from a variety of machines that make noise electronically.

II. Electronic music has become popular in recent years.

III. Electronic music is performed by many well-known artists.

Although both columns cover the same ground, the points in the right-hand column are clearer because they each address only one idea. By separating the two points, Aaron can avoid confusing or overwhelming his audience.

By preparing your main points carefully, you'll be able to give an effective speech that your audience will find easy to follow. Consider your next speech. How will you order and present your main points so they have the greatest impact?

Word your main points consistently. Try to word your main points as consistently as possible. A parallel structure is easier to organize and remember. In the next example, Michael presented an informative speech on the reasons for stop signs. Notice how the parallel main points in the right-hand column are clearer and more memorable than those in the left-hand column:

Ineffective main points

I. Drivers need to know who has the right of way, and a stop sign tells us that.

II. Stop signs slow down drivers who are traveling at unsafe speeds.

III. Sometimes pedestrians need protection from vehicles, and stop signs give them that protection.

More effective main points

I. Stop signs assign the right of way to vehicles using an intersection.

II. Stop signs reduce the problem of speeding in certain areas.

III. Stop signs protect pedestrians in busy intersections or near schools.

With a simple reworking of phrasing, Michael made his main points parallel— stop signs assign, stop signs reduce, stop signs protect. Although this kind of parallel structure is not always possible, your ideas will be clearer and more memorable when you can use it. For useful suggestions for rewording your main points so they are parallel, go to http://webster.commnet.edu/grammar/parallelism.htm.

Balance your main points. Remember that your main points are your most important ideas. As such, give each point about the same amount of time during your speech. If you are spending very little time developing a point, consider whether it really is as important as you thought. If you are spending a lot of time on one point, perhaps you should divide it into two points. In preparing a speech on the art of batik, Martha discovered the following imbalance:

Specific purpose: To inform my audience about batik, a beautiful and diverse art form that has been practiced for centuries.

Thesis statement: The art of batik has an intriguing history as well as methods of production and designs that reflect the skill and politics of the artisan.

Main points:
I. The history of batik (65 percent of the speech)
II. The production of batik (15 percent of the speech)
III. The designs of batik (15 percent of the speech)
IV. Where to purchase batik (5 percent of the speech)

Martha realized she had spent so much time on her first point that she didn't have time to cover her remaining points. Although the history of batik is important, it wasn't the only information she wanted to share with her audience. She also wanted to show them the production process and some of the designs she loved. After some consideration, Martha reduced the scope of her speech by dropping her fourth point (which wasn't really a part of her thesis statement), and she condensed the details of her first point. She reworked her speech as follows, saving 20 percent of her time for her introduction and conclusion (see Chapter 10):

Specific purpose:	To inform my audience about batik, a beautiful and diverse art form that has been practiced for centuries.
Thesis statement:	The art of batik has an intriguing history as well as methods of production and designs that reflect the skill and politics of the artisan.
Main points:	I. The history of batik (30 percent)
	II. The production of batik (25 percent)
	III. The designs of batik (25 percent)

In a typical speech, a reasonable distribution of time for your main points would look like this:

Two-point speech	Three-point speech	Four-point speech
40 percent	27 percent	20 percent
40 percent	27 percent	20 percent
	27 percent	20 percent
		20 percent

However, if some points are more complex than others, you could vary your coverage to achieve a similarly balanced breakdown:

30 percent	20 percent	15 percent
50 percent	30 percent	25 percent
	30 percent	25 percent
		15 percent

Your goal is not necessarily to spend exactly the same amount of time on each point, but to offer a balanced presentation of your ideas.

Speech Step 9.3 / Refine the Wording and Balance of Your Main Points

Make sure your main points are distinct points and you haven't combined two separate points. If you have combined two points, separate them now. Now consider the phrasing of your main points. Is the wording of your points parallel? If not, make them parallel now. Finally, consider how balanced your main points are. If they are not comfortably balanced, adjust the balance now.

Connectives

Your main points are the heart of your speech. Once you have them down on paper and supported with your research, you must find ways to connect them to enhance the audience's understanding. The words and phrases we use to link ideas in a speech are called **connectives.** They show audiences the relationship between ideas.

Before you read the descriptions of the four types of connectives, consider some of the common connectives that speakers use unconsciously: "all right," "next," "now," "um," "and," "so," "so then," and "ah." These words are often called *fillers*—they take up airspace but tell the audience very little about the relationship between ideas. Fillers can be annoying, especially after the same one is

connective
A word or a phrase used to link ideas in a speech.

repeated again and again in a speech. The following section offers four useful alternatives to these fillers. Transitions, internal previews, internal summaries, and signposts add meaning and help your audience remember your ideas.

Transitions

Transitions are phrases that indicate you are finished with one point and are moving on to a new one. At their most effective, transitions state the idea that you are finishing as well as the one you're moving on to. In the following examples, the transitions are underlined:

> <u>Now that you understand</u> how our childhood memories influence our relationship to money, <u>let's explore</u> the relationship we have to money as adults.

> <u>Once you've</u> signaled your buddy and checked the time, <u>you're ready to move</u> to the second state of ascent, the "get ready" stage.

> <u>As you can see</u>, the second level of the food pyramid complements the first. <u>This takes me to</u> what many people think is the best part of the pyramid, the top level with the fats and sweets.

> <u>The evidence clearly shows</u> the level of burnout many workers are experiencing. <u>I'd now like to share</u> some of the causes of this burnout.

You can consciously insert transitions—such as "let's turn to," "now that you understand," "in addition to," and "that brings me to my next point." But many will come naturally as you close one point and begin a new one. Use transitions to guide your audience from point to point as you deliver your speech. To judge the effectiveness of transitions used by two speakers, complete InfoTrac College Edition Exercise 9.3, "Using Transitions," featured online under Student Resources for Chapter 9.

Internal Previews

An **internal preview** is a statement in the body of your speech that details what you plan to discuss next. Internal previews focus on what comes next in the speech rather than linking two points, as transitions do. Internal previews are very similar to the preview you offer in the introduction of a speech (covered in Chapter 10), except you use them to introduce a new point rather than the entire speech. In the next example, Martha introduces her second point, batik production, with an internal preview:

> In discussing the production of batik, I'll explain the four steps: the preparation of the cloth, the mixing of the dyes, the application of the dye, and the setting of the image in the cloth.

After hearing this preview, the audience is ready for four steps and begins to appreciate the intricacies of the batik process. Internal previews are often combined with transitions, as in this next example:

> <u>As you can see</u>, (*transition*) with the invention of the light bulb came exciting and safer possibilities for theatrical lighting. And the now familiar light bulb <u>takes me to my third point,</u> (*internal preview*) the invention of three instruments that revolutionized lighting in the theater: the ellipsoidal, the fresnel, and the intelabeam from Robert's speech.

Not every main point requires an internal preview, but the unfamiliar terminology in Robert's third point lends itself to a preview. Introducing new concepts or terminology before offering the details enhances your audience's understanding of your topic.

transition
A phrase that indicates a speaker is finished with one point and moving on to a new one.

internal preview
A statement in the body of a speech that details what the speaker plans to discuss next.

Internal Summaries

internal summary
A statement in the body of a speech that summarizes a point a speaker has already discussed.

An **internal summary** is the opposite of an internal preview. It is a statement in the body of your speech that summarizes a point you've already discussed. If you've just finished an important or complicated point, add an internal summary to remind your audience of its highlights. In Jeremy's speech on sibling rivalry, he could use an internal summary at the end of the first point:

> To summarize, the causes of sibling rivalry—birth order, sex, parental attitudes, and individual personality traits—can cause children to compete for their parents' affection and attention.

In Molly's speech about beef by-products, an internal summary helps the audience remember how common beef by-products are:

> I hope I've clarified for you the numerous places by-products are found. Outside our bodies, these by-products show up in emery boards and plasterboard; glue, bandages, and film; candles, cellophane, shaving cream, and even deodorant. Inside our bodies, we ingest these by-products when we eat marshmallows, mints, margarine, food coloring, gum, and sausage casings.

Internal summaries help audiences remember chunks of information and important ideas. Like internal previews, internal summaries can be combined with transitions so you can move efficiently into your next point. Here's an example from Brandon's speech:

> In short, (*internal summary*) the lack of funding for before- and after-school meal programs leads to poor academic performance, increased absences, and behavioral problems. But let's see (*transition*) what this bond issue will do to remedy many of these problems.

Internal summaries are excellent tools to use when you want your audience to remember key points before you move on to a new idea. When combined with transitions, internal summaries can help audiences move smoothly from one idea to the next.

Signposts

signpost
A simple word or statement that lets an audience know where a speaker is in a speech or that indicates an important idea.

A **signpost** is a simple word or statement that lets an audience know where you are in your speech or that indicates an important idea. Signposts help your audience keep track of where you are in a list or in the series of main points. Signposts can be numbers ("first," "second," "third"), phrases ("the most important thing to remember is," "you'll want to make note of this"), or questions you ask and then answer ("so, how do we solve this dilemma?"). Notice how Brooke used signposts to mark each of her three main points in her speech about chili peppers:

> I. The first tale is a global story . . .
>
> II. The second tale is a national story . . .
>
> III. The final tale is my own story . . .

In Alex's speech on women in glory sports, she asked questions to introduce each of her main points. For her first main point she asked,

> How many of you know who Layne Beachley is?

For her second she asked,

> So, you didn't know Layne Beachley. How about Cara Beth Burnside? Can anyone tell me her accomplishments?

And for her third she asked,

> Okay, I'll give you one more try. Who knows Tara Dakides's contributions to the world of glory sports?

Although you don't want to overuse these kinds of questions, they can be effective in getting an audience involved in your speech. Audience members will try to answer the questions in their own heads before you do.

The final use of signposts is to mark the most important ideas in your speech. When you hear any of the following phrases, or when you use one in a speech yourself, it's a signpost asking the audience to pay close attention:

> The most important thing to remember is . . .

> If you hear nothing else from today's speech, hear this . . .

> Let me repeat that last figure for you . . .

> This next point is crucial to understanding my arguments . . .

But note that you should use this kind of signpost only once in a speech. If you use it more often, the audience quickly loses confidence that what you are about to say is really "the most important thing."

You can use connectives singly or in combination with other connectives. Their purpose is to help you move smoothly from idea to idea and to help your audience follow your presentation. These tools add clarity to a speech and can make it flow. You can find a list of connectives that you can use as transitions and signposts at http://owl.english.purdue.edu/handouts/general/gl_transition.html.

Speech Step 9.4 / Prepare the Connectives for Your Speech

Identify the places between your main points where a connective would add clarity or help you move from one idea to the next. Incorporate at least one transition, one internal summary or preview, and, as appropriate, one or more signposts into your next speech. Speech Builder Express includes a section on transitions and will help you incorporate them into your speech outline. Using the username and password included on your *Invitation to Public Speaking* CD-ROM, you can access Speech Builder Express.

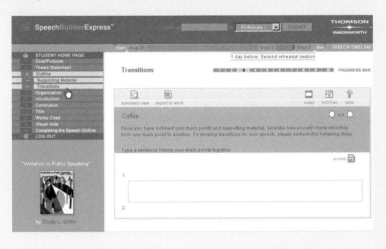

Citing Sources in Speeches

As you organize your ideas and develop your main points, you will want to cite some of the research you have gathered for your speech. There are three reasons to cite sources: they add credibility to your ideas, they add to your own credibility, and giving credit to your sources is ethical.

Citing Sources Adds Credibility to Your Ideas

When you cite the work or ideas of other people, particularly those viewed as experts, you communicate that your ideas have the backing of others. When you cite sources, you communicate that you have taken the time to find out what others think about your topic. You illustrate that your ideas are not yours alone—others support your views and think they are worthy. Additionally, when you want to bolster the credibility of a claim, cite the source so your audience recognizes the authority from which it came.

Citing Sources Enhances Your Own Credibility

When you cite sources in a speech, you indicate that you have done research. Citing sources communicates that you are interested in adding to your own knowledge base. It is a sign you value public dialogue over a personal monologue. Rather than presenting yourself as all knowing, citing sources communicates that you recognize others have something to offer the public dialogue and you are open to their perspectives.

Keeping your research well organized from the start helps you cite sources appropriately when you give your speech. How will the sources you cite in your next speech reflect your participation in the public dialogue?

© Michael Newman/PhotoEdit

Citing Sources Is Ethical

When you cite sources, you also communicate a sense of ethics because you give credit to others for their work. Our ideas about issues and beliefs about controversies rarely come from our own thoughts and experiences; they are almost always influenced by what others say and do. Especially in public speaking, we build our ideas from the ideas of others. Citing sources means that you do not claim their work as your own. Citing sources in speeches indicates that you recognize the influence of other people and you are not stealing their ideas. To read a discussion about the ethics of citing sources, go to Duke University's plagiarism Web page at http://www.lib.duke.edu/libguide/plagiarism.htm.

Rules for Citing Sources

Although your instructor may have specific rules for the number and format of sources you are to cite in a speech, there are also three general guidelines for citing sources during your speech. These guidelines rely on ethical principles as well as an audience-centered approach. The first one deals with when to give credit to others for their work. The second focuses on how to give that information. The third is a reminder to deliver all information accurately.

Give credit to others. When you rely on the specific ideas or words of others, give them credit during your speech. The guideline works like this: the more specifically you rely on someone else's ideas or words, the more responsible you are for citing them. If you use someone's study, quote or paraphrase someone, or share information from a magazine, book, newspaper, or other news source, you need to cite your source in your speech. You can use phrases like the following:

Last week's *New York Times* tells us that . . .

According to the 2000 Census, . . .

The director of the Center for Applied Studies in Appropriate Technology responded to my question in this way . . .

The *Farmer's Almanac* reports that this will be the wettest year this area has experienced since 1938.

Jane Kneller, professor of philosophy at this university, writes, . . .

Note that even though much of what we say comes from our research and the work of others, we do not need to provide a citation for every claim we make. Some claims are based on common knowledge. For example, the statement "Eating a balanced diet is good for your health" is common knowledge. But the statement "The foundation of a balanced diet is six to eleven servings a day of bread, cereal, rice, or pasta" requires a source citation such as "according to the U.S. Department of Agriculture's food pyramid."

Give specific information about your source. For your audience to see your claims as credible, they need to know the specific sources. General phrases such as "research shows," "evidence suggests," and "someone once said"—rarely substantiate a claim. If your audience is listening with care, they'll want to know your sources. They'll be asking "what research?" "whose evidence?" and "who said?" They'll want specifics in order to accept your research as credible. When you cite a source, include the following information:

Tiffany Brisco

*   The name of the person or the publication

*   The credentials of that person or publication

*   The date of the study, statistic, or piece of evidence

These three pieces of information generally are enough to show your audience that your source is valid and your statistics are reliable and relevant to your topic. You can usually omit details such as page numbers and place of publication from your actual speech, but you will want to include them in your list of works cited. Using your *Invitation to Public Speaking* CD-ROM, watch the video clips of Tiffany and Damien. Assess the degree to which they accurately cite sources and provide information about them.

Deliver all information accurately. When you cite a source, you must do so accurately. This means giving the name and title of the person correctly, pronouncing any unfamiliar words smoothly, and delivering all statistics and quotations accurately. Citing sources can seem awkward if you trip over the words. Mispronouncing names and titles, stumbling over dates and quotes, and leaving out important parts of a claim reduce your credibility. It can even alter the facts you are sharing with your audience. So, before you give your speech, check to be sure you have all the information recorded correctly, and rehearse it until it flows smoothly.

For more advice about citing sources efficiently and effectively, complete Interactive Activity 9.3, "Citing Sources," online under Student Resources for WEB SITE Chapter 9 at the *Invitation to Public Speaking* Web site.

Chapter Summary

Organization is the systematic arrangement of ideas into a coherent whole. It makes a speech listenable and is an audience-centered activity. It communicates to your audience that you care enough about them and your topic to be clear and easy to follow. To achieve this clarity, you must identify the main points of your speech. Main points are the most important ideas in a speech, and they can be developed from your research or your thesis statement.

The time limit of your speech is the most important guideline for determining the number of your main points. If you have too many points to cover in the time you have, return to your thesis statement and narrow the scope of your presentation. Covering too many points or trying to include too much detail only confuses your audience and reduces your chances of giving an effective speech.

Main points can be organized in five basic ways. With a chronological pattern, you organize your main points to trace a sequence of events or ideas. With a spatial pattern, you organize your ideas in terms of location or direction. With a causal pattern, you trace a cause-and-effect relationship—either the cause followed by the effect or vice versa. With a problem-and-solution pattern, you present a problem first, followed by a possible solution. Finally, with a topical pattern, you divide your main points into subpoints in order to address different aspects of your topic. The topical pattern is one of the most common for all types of speeches.

There are three tips for preparing your main points. First, be sure each main point covers only one aspect of your topic. Second, word your main points as consistently as possible. Third, balance the time you give to each main point. If you find you are spending too much time on any one point, consider revising your main points so you can spend about an equal amount of time covering each one.

To show the relationships between your main points, use connectives: transitions, internal previews, internal summaries, and signposts. Transitions indicate you are finished with one point and moving on to a new one. An internal preview introduces the key components of a new point; an internal summary recaps a point just covered. Signposts are words or phrases that mark important information or let the audience know where you are in your speech.

It is important to cite the sources you use in your speech. Citing sources adds credibility to your ideas because it communicates to your audience that you are not alone in thinking the way you do. Citing sources also adds credibility to you personally. When you cite your sources, you communicate to your audience that you have taken the time to learn what others think about your topic and you recognize you are part of a public dialogue. Finally, citing sources is ethical because it gives credit to others for their work.

When citing sources, remember the following tips. First, cite the sources you rely on specifically or quote directly. Second, provide enough specific information about your source so your audience knows the source is valid, reliable, and relevant. Third, cite sources accurately by recording all your research carefully and practicing your delivery.

You make a positive contribution to the public dialogue when you take the time to organize your ideas carefully and to report your research accurately. These tasks are just a few of the many steps speakers take to ensure that their ideas are sound and their audiences are able to follow their voice as it contributes to the public dialogue.

After reading this chapter, use your CD-ROM and the *Invitation to Public Speaking* Web site to review the follow- ing concepts, answer the review questions, and complete the suggested activities.

Key Concepts

organization (205)
main points (205)
chronological pattern (209)
spatial pattern (209)

causal pattern (211)
problem-and-solution pattern (211)
topical pattern (212)
connective (216)

transition (217)
internal preview (217)
internal summary (218)
signpost (218)

Review Questions

1. Write a specific purpose, thesis statement, main points, and subpoints for a speech on a topic of your choice. Now mix up those main points and subpoints, and try to deliver a sketch of the speech to your classmates. Can they follow your organization? Why or why not?

2. Choose one of the following topics: M&M's® candy, Valentine's Day, or "finals week." Using each of the five patterns of organization discussed in this chapter, write a specific purpose, thesis statement, and main points for a speech about the topic you chose. What is the emphasis in each speech, depending on its organizational pattern?

3. In class, write down a possible speech topic on a three- by-five card or a strip of paper. Pass your topic to your instructor. Your instructor will select several topics, ask you to get into groups of five, and distribute a topic to each group. With your group, write the specific purpose, thesis statement, and main points for a speech. Also write connectives for the speech, including each of the four types of connectives discussed in this chapter. Now deliver the sketch of your group's speech to the class (be sure to use your connectives).

4. Bring three or four of the sources you will use in your next speech to class. In small groups, practice delivering the citation of those sources with each other. Focus on those sources with especially long titles, with names that are difficult to pronounce, or that are just confusing. Work with one another to find the most comfortable way to cite these sources in your next speech.

The *Invitation to Public Speaking* Web Site

The *Invitation to Public Speaking* Web site features the review questions about the Web sites suggested on pages 205, 215, 219, and 220, the interactive activities suggested on pages 208, 213, and 221, and the InfoTrac College Edition exercises suggested on pages 205, 207, and 217.

You can access this site via your CD-ROM or at http://www.wadsworth.com/product/griffin. To access Speech Builder Express in order to complete Speech Steps 9.1, 9.2, and 9.4, you will need the username and password included under "Speech Builder Express" on your CD-ROM.

Web Links

9.1: Jan D'Arcy's Speaker's Tips (205)
9.2: Parallel Form (215)
9.3: Transition Words and Phrases (219)
9.4: Plagiarism: Its Nature and Consequences (220)

Interactive Activities

9.1: Choosing Main Points (208)
Purpose: To identify the main points used in a presidential address to Congress.

9.2: Organizing Main Points (213)
Purpose: To understand the methods of organizing main points.

9.3: Citing Sources (221)
Purpose: To learn how to avoid inaccurate source citations.

InfoTrac College Edition Exercises

9.1: Assessing Clarity (205)
Purpose: To appreciate the importance of organization.

9.2: Identifying Main Points (207)
Purpose: To learn how to locate main points in research.

9.3: Using Transitions (217)
Purpose: To identify and appreciate a communicator's use of transitions.

Speech Interactive on the *Invitation to Public Speaking* CD-ROM

The following video clips of speeches referenced in this chapter are included under Speech Interactive on your *Invitation to Public Speaking* CD-ROM. After you have watched the clips, click on "Critique" to answer the questions for analysis.

Video Clip 1: Organization of Main Points: Cindy Gardner (205). Watch Cindy's speech about the proper way to fold a flag. What are her main points? What are her subpoints? What organizational pattern does she use? How effective is this pattern for her particular topic?

Video Clip 2: Chronological Organization: Jeff Malcolm (209). Watch how Jeff uses a chronological pattern of organization in his speech. What are his main points? Is it easy to follow his organization? What are the advantages of using this pattern? What are the disadvantages?

Video Clip 3: Oral Citation of Source: Damien Beasley (221). Watch how Damien orally cites his source material in the short clip from his speech of entertainment at a forensics tournament. What information does he provide about his source?

Video Clip 4: Citing Sources: Tiffany Brisco (221). As you watch the video clip of Tiffany giving her speech, consider how she handles her sources. Does she cite sources in this clip? How effectively does she provide information about the sources she used?

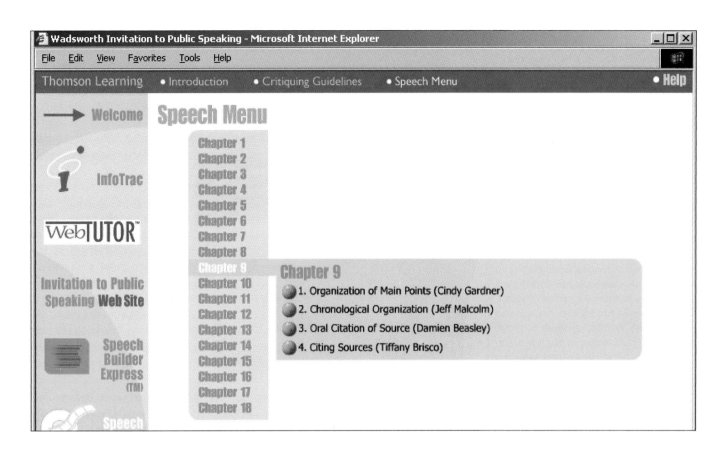

Chapter Ten

Introductions
and Conclusions

In this chapter you will learn to

Describe the four functions of an effective introduction

Prepare a compelling introduction

Describe the two functions of an effective conclusion

Prepare a compelling conclusion

Identify at least four tips each for preparing an introduction and a conclusion

What does it take to have passion and desire, to be determined and dedicated to fulfill your dreams of being a fighter pilot during World War II? I begin with this question because these are the qualities of the noble and respectable Tuskegee Airmen.

—Javad Fields, Colorado State University student, 2001

Both common sense and research tell us that a speech with an introduction, even a short one, makes an audience more willing to listen, think more highly of the speaker, and understand the speech better.[1] A conclusion adds additional components to your speech. Conclusions reinforce thesis statements, remind listeners of what you've just covered, and frame your ideas and arguments in just the way you want. Because the introduction and the conclusion are important parts of a speech, in this chapter you will learn the basic techniques for developing each. As you read the following discussions, keep in mind that your introduction and conclusion frame the way you enter and exit the public dialogue.

The Introduction

Your introduction is your first contact with your audience. In the opening words of your speech you set the stage for what's to come, connect your audience to your topic, and establish your purpose for speaking. Introductions are like first impressions—they are important and lasting. Because of this, they draw on all of your audience analysis skills (Chapter 5). In order to develop an introduction that allows you to connect with your audience in the way you want, consider the four functions of any introduction:

- Catch the audience's attention
- Reveal the topic to the audience
- Establish credibility with the audience
- Preview the speech for the audience

Notice that each objective is highly audience centered. Thus your introduction, like the body of your speech, is designed with the audience in mind. In each of the four components of the introduction, you consider the audience's perspectives, the reason the audience is there, as well as your own goals. Let's take a closer look at each of these components and then at some techniques for implementing them with effective introductions.

Catch the Audience's Attention

One of the most important tasks you have as a speaker is to capture the attention of your audience. You want them to listen to you, to be intrigued, curious, and eager to hear more. When you catch the audience's attention, you not only pique their curiosity about your topic, you also show them how the topic relates to them. Keep in mind that however you get your audience interested in your topic, you must be ethical. This means you must be honest, respectful, and consistent with the principles of an open and healthy public dialogue.

Establish your credibility early on in your introduction so your audience understands why you're qualified to speak on your topic. But be careful to represent your expertise accurately and ethically. Audiences don't like to be misled.

Reveal the Topic of Your Speech

In your introduction, you also want to let the audience know the subject of your speech. Although guessing games can be fun, your audiences want to know what you will be discussing. Keeping them in suspense for a moment or two is fine, but your introduction should reveal your topic before you begin your first main point.

Establish Your Credibility

As you've learned, to be credible is to inspire trust in your audience and to communicate to them that you have considerable knowledge of your topic. If your audience regards you as credible and competent, they will believe they have good reason to listen to your ideas. Establishing credibility contains an ethical dimension. Audiences do not like to be lied to or misled. If you distort your credibility on a subject, your audience is less likely to believe you or to be influenced by your speech.

Preview Your Speech

The fourth component of an introduction is to preview the main points of the speech. When you **preview** your speech, you share with your audience a brief overview of each of the main points in your speech. Previews are necessary in any introduction because they get your audience ready to hear your speech; they set

preview
Brief overview in the introduction of a speech of each of the main points in the speech.

the stage for the body of the speech. Previews also help your audience organize their thoughts about what's to come, and they communicate to your audience that you are organized and competent.

Preparing a Compelling Introduction

There are several creative ways in which you can gain your audience's attention, reveal your topic, establish your credibility, and preview your speech. Let's look at some techniques that will help you prepare compelling, memorable introductions.

Ask a Question

rhetorical question
Question a speaker asks that an audience isn't supposed to answer out loud but rather in their own minds.

A question can arouse your audience's curiosity and capture their attention as they try to figure out the answer. A question can also reveal the topic of your speech—the answer usually is your topic. Sometimes speakers use a **rhetorical question,** a question that the audience isn't supposed to answer out loud but rather in their own minds. At other times, they solicit answers directly from the audience.

In the next two examples, Nathan and Brooke ask rhetorical questions—they supply the answers to their own questions.

> Do you think you could walk from New York to just beyond Chicago? How about from Georgia to Maine? If you're up for such a hike, take the route from Georgia to Maine—that will put you on the Appalachian National Scenic Trail, a trail that stretches over 2,000 miles and traverses fourteen states. This trail is also the topic of my speech today.

> Chilly? No, it's not cold. Chili? No, it doesn't come in a can of beans. Chile? No, I'm not speaking of a country in South America, either. Today I'm speaking about the "chili," yes, and the chili pepper. That fiery vegetable, which, according to the Chile Today Web site, has conquered people's taste buds and cuisines around the world for over ten thousand years.

To read a discussion of a specific type of rhetorical question, go to http://humanities.byu.edu/rhetoric/Figures/rhetorical%20questions.htm. In the next example, Cassie solicits answers from the audience before revealing the topic.

> You've heard of the game "Strange but True"? Play with me for a minute. I'll read the headline, and you tell me if it's true or not. Ready? Okay.
>
> > "Surfer Sues Surfer for Theft of Wave." True or false?
>
> > "Deaf Bank Robber Wins Suit: Courts Say Alarm Exploited His Disability." True or false?
>
> > "College Student Falls Out Fourth-Story Window During Mooning Prank: Sues University for Negligence." True or false?
>
> Each of these lawsuits is real, and these "crazy lawsuits" are the subject of my speech today.

Beginning a speech with a question, rhetorical or not, engages your audience from the moment you begin to speak. It communicates to the audience that you'd like them to be actively involved in listening to you and prevents them from simply sitting back passively. If you open your speech with a question, be sure it relates directly to your topic, and remember to pause after each question so the audience has time to answer it, either aloud or in their heads.

Tell a Story

A second way to capture your audience's attention and reveal your topic is to tell a story. Stories draw an audience into your speech by offering characters and dramas they can relate to. Stories also personalize topics that might seem remote or disconnected to some members of an audience. Notice how Brandi uses language creatively to draw her audience into her story.

> It seemed like such a harmless thing to do. What could be wrong with putting out a little food to help the foxes and deer make it through a hard winter? Besides, seeing wildlife in your backyard is one of the many benefits to living in Colorado. Or so thought a family who set out dog food, hamburger, and grains for foxes and deer near their home in the wooded foothills just outside Denver. But guess who also came to dinner? Tasty treats left in the family's backyard lured hungry mountain lions into the neighborhood. Not only did the wild cats like the hamburger, but they also had their eyes on one of their favorite prey, the deer.

Brandi Lafferty

> It didn't take long for the real trouble to start. Residents' cats and dogs began disappearing from their yards. Fear and anger set in, and people began calling officials to do something about the mountain lions. What started as a well-meaning effort for deer and foxes ended in the death of one of Colorado's favorite wild animals. The mountain lion was killed in a trap set out to make the neighborhood safe again.

> Hi, my name is Brandi Lafferty and today I'd like to describe some of the negative consequences associated with feeding big game wildlife and encourage you to help keep our wildlife wild.

Using your *Invitation to Public Speaking* CD-ROM, watch the video clip of Brandi's introduction under Speech Interactive.

If you use a story in your opening, be sure it relates directly to your topic and clearly connects to the body of your speech. Sometimes it is tempting to tell a great story just because it is great. Avoid this pitfall, and use only stories that help you introduce your topic.

Most people enjoy a good story, so telling one is a particularly effective way to catch an audience's attention. What are some interesting stories from your life that you could tell in the introduction to a speech? Would one of these stories relate to the topic of your next speech?

Recite a Quotation or a Poem

You also can catch your audience's interest and reveal your topic through a quotation or poem. Quotations bring someone else's words into your speech and lend it the credibility of someone more famous or knowledgeable than you are. They also can teach lessons or illustrate perspectives that are relevant to your speech. Quotes can be quite simple or fairly complex. In a speech on adoption, Chad began with a simple quote:

> Dennis Rainey, author of the book *One Home at a Time,* states, "I have a wife and six children, two of which are adopted—but I can't remember which ones."

Speaking about the terrorist attacks on New York City and the Pentagon in September 2001, Mike began with a more complex quote:

> Mohandas K. Gandhi said, "When I despair, I remember that all through history the way of truth and love has always won. There have been murderers and tyrants, and for a time they can seem invincible. But in the end they always fail. Think of it: always."

In the next example, Jessica uses a poem to begin her speech. She uses this poem to set the tone of her speech and reveal her topic:

May your thoughts be as glad as the shamrocks,

May your heart be as light as the song.

May each day bring you bright happy hours,

That stay with you all year long.

For each petal on the shamrock,

This brings a wish your way—

Good health, good luck, and happiness

For today and everyday.

When some hear this Irish blessing, they think of a three-leaf clover. Others think of Ireland or St. Patrick. My family has its roots in Ireland, and we always think of all three. The shamrock has a long history of meaning for the Irish, and it represents the magical number 3. To fully understand the importance of the shamrock, though, you need to know how it became the symbol of Ireland. You must also understand how St. Patrick used it, and how it is represented every year by Saint Patrick's Day. Even if you're not Irish, a little bit of information about the shamrock will help you enjoy your next March 17 celebration, or understand those who make such a big deal of it.

Notice, too, how Jessica establishes her credibility early on in the introduction by referring to her family's roots in Ireland. She also connects her topic to her audience in the final sentences of the introduction.

When you use a quote or poem, be sure it relates directly to your topic or illustrates the importance of your subject. Like stories, there are a lot of great quotes and poems, but you want to use one that sums up your topic and grabs your audience's attention. Also remember to cite the source of the quote or poem and to deliver it so the audience knows it is a quote or poem rather than your own words (for tips on delivery, see Chapter 13). To explore places on the Internet **WEB SITE** where you can find quotations for your introduction, complete Interactive Activity 10.1, "Starting with a Quotation," online under Student Resources for Chapter 10 at the *Invitation to Public Speaking* Web site.

Give a Demonstration

When you demonstrate some aspect of your topic, you capture your audience's interest and make them want to see or hear more. In the following example, Megan began by singing. After she had captured her audience's attention, she revealed the topic of her speech, the author of her song. In the second paragraph, she previewed her speech so her audience knew exactly what she was going to cover.

(Begin by singing "Amazing Grace.")

Comfort is what I feel when I hear this song. No matter if I am at a funeral service or singing it in a choir, this song overwhelms me with a sense of peace. I know it has the same effect on others as well. But who was the man behind this song? And isn't it, as some say, a bit overdone? Dr. Ralph F. Wilson states that he used to think "Amazing Grace" was just that, overdone. Wilson says, "'saved a wretch like me,' come on, really now. But the author really was a wretch, a moral pariah." Wilson is the author of *The Story of John Newton,* and John Newton is the author of America's most popular hymn, "Amazing Grace."

But what happened to John Newton that made him a "moral pariah"? What happened in this man's life that it was only the "grace of God" that could save him? Well, today I'm going to share with you just how a "wretch" like John Newton wrote such a well-known hymn. I'll begin by telling you a little bit about his early life. Then, I'll tell you how he came to write "Amazing Grace." Finally, I'll conclude by discussing this hymn's legacy.

Although not everyone has the talent to stand up and sing for their audiences, many speeches can be opened with some type of demonstration. Speeches about activities, sports, arts and crafts—about how to do anything—are good possibilities for demonstrations.

When you use a demonstration to introduce your speech, make sure you can complete it in only a few minutes or even seconds. Recall from Chapter 9 that introductions and conclusions are a relatively small part of the speech. In fact, as you will see later in this chapter, your introduction and conclusion should be no more than 20 percent of your speech. Time your demonstration to make sure you'll have enough time for the rest of your speech. If your demonstration seems too long, think about using it in the body of your speech instead. In either case, practice your demonstration before the speech. A poorly delivered demonstration can make a negative first impression on the audience.

Make an Intriguing or Startling Statement

Making an intriguing or startling statement is an excellent way to draw your audience in with the unknown or the curious. Let's look at a few examples of this technique:

> *Ohayoo gozaimasu.* You probably don't know what I just said. I just gave you the greeting for "good morning" in Japanese, the ninth most spoken language in the world. Having studied Japanese for over three years now, I would like to share a little bit about this intriguing language with you today. I know you're probably wondering, "Why should I care about the Japanese language when I live in the United States?" Well, according to the *Encyclopedia Britannica,* there are currently over 125 million speakers of Japanese worldwide. In today's world, that means you're more than likely to meet a Japanese speaker at least once in your life. Wouldn't it be a good idea to know at least something about his or her language?
>
> Today, I'll share some of what I know about the Japanese language with you. I'll first talk about Japanese body language, which is both similar to and different from American body language. Then, I'll discuss spoken Japanese, which requires a lot of practice to learn. Finally, I'll tell you a little about the written language, which contains over fifty thousand characters and three alphabets.

In this example, Kelly illustrates all four criteria for a strong introduction. He catches the audience's interest in the first few lines, establishes his credibility in the third sentence, and relates the topic to his audience in his final lines of the first paragraph. In the second paragraph, Kelly previews his speech.

As you read this next example, see if you can identify all four of the criteria for a strong introduction. Notice how Katy takes a little extra time in her introduction to relate the topic to her audience and to establish her credibility:

> 3.14159265358979323846264433832795. Most of you know the name of the number I just recited. It's a number found in rainbows, pupils of eyes, sound waves, ripples in the water, and DNA—a ratio that both nature and music understand but that the human mind cannot quite comprehend. This number has sparked curiosity in many minds over the past four thousand years. I'm talking about pi—not the dessert, but the circle ratio.
>
> Now, a class of speech majors is probably wondering if they can survive a six-minute speech about math. My own interest came about when I was challenged to memorize more digits than a friend of mine could. As a result of that challenge, I have researched

U2 singer Bono is known for giving speeches with particularly memorable introductions, often making intriguing statements to great effect. Think about the last speech you watched or listened to. How well was the introduction presented? Was it interesting, or startling, or funny? Did it draw you into the speech?

this topic, finding information not only technical and historical, but also fanatical. Today, I plan to inform you of what pi is, the history of pi, and how pi has created an obsession in people's lives.

Janelle also used this technique to open her persuasive speech on women donating their ova, called oocyte donation, to women who aren't able to bear children:

> I haven't finished college yet, but I can make $10,000 to $50,000 in only three months. By selling my body? Well, almost. As a young, white, attractive female, I can make this money by selling my eggs to couples who want to have children but can't.

She then went on to describe the process of oocyte donation and to encourage her audience not to participate in this quick way to make money.

When you choose to introduce your speech with a startling statement, use caution. You want to startle rather than offend your audience. Beginning speakers sometimes fall into the trap of thinking that an offensive statement is appropriate because it will, indeed, startle. If you are thinking about using a statement that may be too graphic, inappropriate, or horrifying, find a more acceptable alternative. Your startling statement should invite the audience to listen, not shut down communication. The Web site Uselessfacts.net contains many interesting, unusual, and startling facts. Go to http://www.uselessfacts.net to find a fact that would be appropriate to include in your introduction.

State the Importance of the Topic

Sometimes speakers choose to begin their speeches with clear statements of the significance or magnitude of a topic. When you state the importance of the topic, you tell the audience why they should listen. Recall Justin's speech about phobias from Chapter 9. He introduced his speech by stating the importance of understanding phobias:

> More than 19 million Americans between the ages of 18 and 54 suffer from some sort of phobia every year. That's one in ten people, or at least two of us in this room today. That means if you don't have a phobia yourself, you probably know someone who does. I don't just mean a fear of scary stories, or public speaking, or a fear of the dark, either. I mean an intense and persistent fear that significantly affects a person's actions and decisions.

Tina also used this technique to introduce a speech on a topic that seemed fairly ordinary but was actually quite interesting to her audience:

> Okay. Everyone look down at your feet. How many of you have shoes on? Just as I thought. Each of us has a pair of shoes or sandals on our feet. But how many know where those shoes come from? And let's be honest. How many women in the audience have shoes with heels of an inch or more? Um-hmm, don't answer. And for the men, do you steer the women in your lives toward the heels in the shoe stores? Maybe even some of you men own a pair of heels? Well, when I look in my closet, I see one pair of sneakers, two pairs of boots, and a dozen high-heeled shoes. But do I know where these shoes come from or how heels were invented? No. At least not until I did some research into my shoe fetish.

> Today, I'd like to share the story of shoes with you. I'd like to discuss the origination of shoes, the changes they've gone through, the invention of high heels (which originally were made for men, by the way), and the troubles those heels have caused.

In these two examples, Justin and Tina state the importance of the topic in two different ways. In the first example, Justin tells his audience that his topic is important because significant numbers of people are affected by phobias. In the second example, Tina states the importance of her topic by reminding her audience that wearing shoes is something most everyone does.

A third way to state the importance of a topic is to show that although a practice or phenomenon is uncommon, it has a significant impact. Will did this in his speech about germ-line engineering and cloning:

> Imagine a world filled with humans who are genetically perfect, with no flaws or birth defects—humans who are superior to what we know today. Now imagine there's no shortage of body parts for transplants or to repair what we now call "irreparable" injuries, because an exact replica of each person is available—strictly for donation. Although these two notions seem farfetched, we may be coming closer to this imaginary world than we realize.

> The two processes I asked you to imagine are called germ-line engineering and cloning, the topic of my speech. I know most of you are familiar with these ideas from science fiction novels, movies, and television, but in the next few decades, you may be able to visit your local geneticist to create a designer baby or maybe even have yourself cloned. I realize there are serious moral and ethical concerns about genetic engineering. However, I'd like to invite you to consider that the benefits of these two forms of engineering far outweigh the disadvantages. Today, I'll describe the two processes for you, germ-line engineering and cloning, and then share the advantages of these processes. I'll then discuss two ways that those of us in this room are likely to be affected by these forms of genetic engineering, and then open the floor for discussion.

To learn more about how speakers establish the importance of their speech topic, complete InfoTrac College Edition Exercise 10.1, "Establishing Significance," online under Student Resources for Chapter 10.

Share Your Expertise

Although you know your qualifications for speaking on a subject, your audience may not. Establishing credibility does not mean boasting and bragging. Instead, it means you share your expertise with your audience. Recall how Jessica, Kelly, Katy, and Tina stated their credibility in their introductions:

Shamrocks. My family has its roots in Ireland.

Japanese Language. Having studied Japanese for over three years now, I would like to share a little bit about this intriguing language with you today.

Why Pi? As a result of that challenge, I have researched this topic, finding information not only technical and historical, but also fanatical.

History of Shoes. Well, when I look in my closet, I see one pair of sneakers, two pairs of boots, and a dozen high-heeled shoes. But do I know where these shoes come from or how heels were invented? No. At least not until I did some research into my shoe fetish.

Establishing your credibility often is a subtle process. In these examples, the speakers revealed their expertise by illustrating their qualifications to speak about their topics. They referred to family, study, research, and personal experience to communicate their competence to speak about their topics. Use these same techniques to establish your credibility in your speeches. And remember, your credibility also comes through your research (Chapter 6), the development of your ideas (Chapter 7), your reasoning (Chapters 8 and 18), your organization (Chapter 9), and your delivery (Chapter 13). To see how professional speakers talk about their credibility as they begin a dialogue with an audience, complete InfoTrac College Edition Exercise 10.2, "Establishing Credibility," online under Student Resources for Chapter 10.

State What's to Come

Previewing your speech is a necessary component of your introduction. When you preview your speech, you give your audience an overview of your main points. This is important because, as you learned in Chapter 3, even the best listeners need help following and remembering a speaker's ideas throughout a speech. When your audience hears a preview, they will anticipate your main points, be prepared to listen to them, and not be surprised or confused.

The best previews are brief—they set the audience up for what's to come but do not go into too much detail. Here's how Nathan, Brooke, and Cassie previewed their speeches:

Appalachian Trail. First, I'll give you a brief history of the trail's formation. Then, I'll share some facts with you about the trail itself and how it's maintained. Finally, I'll tell you the stories from some of those who have hiked the trail.

The Chili Pepper. The chili pepper legends I wish to share with you are the result of a variety of stories. First are the stories found across the globe. Second are the national stories originating in our own country. Third is a personal story about my grandfather, the person who introduced me to the chili pepper's legacy.

Crazy Lawsuits. In my research I found many crazy cases that actually have gone to court, and today I'll discuss some of the craziest. I'll begin with some basic legal terms that come up in these cases so you can follow them more easily. Then I'll share with you some of my favorite cases and give you a sample of the kinds of things that tie up our court system. Finally, I'll persuade you that we should help those who are organizing to control these lawsuits and stop the abuses of our legal system.

In each of these examples, the speakers used variations of "first, then, finally," to identify the order of main points. Although this language might seem unimaginative, spoken language is quite different from written language (Chapter 12). Audiences need extra tools to help them absorb and remember a speaker's ideas. (This is also why connectives are so helpful to audiences, as you learned in Chapter 9.) Explicit language like that used in the previews here increases the likelihood that your audience will understand your ideas, follow them throughout the speech, and remember them when the speech is over. Using your *Invitation to Public Speaking* CD-ROM, watch the video clip of Mike's preview under Speech Interactive. Does Mike clearly state what's to come during his speech?

Mike Piel

 ## Speech Step 10.1 / Prepare Your Introduction

For your next speech, choose one technique each for catching your audience's attention, revealing your topic, establishing your credibility, and previewing the speech. Begin preparing an introduction that incorporates the techniques you've chosen. Then put aside your introduction and continue reading. You can complete this Speech Step using Speech Builder Express. Once you complete the questions included on the program and type in your introduction, Speech Builder Express will save your entry as part of your overall outline until you are ready to complete the next Speech Step. Use Speech Builder Express to complete this Speech Step and add your conclusion to your draft outline.

Tips for Your Introduction

Look for introductory materials as you do your research. As you do your research, look for stories, quotations, startling facts or statements, and other material to use in your introduction. If you collect material you might use in your introduction, you will save yourself time when you write it. You also will have several options to choose from, so you can select the one that suits your audience and your goals best.

Prepare the wording after you prepare the body of the speech. If you wait until you have all your supporting materials and the exact wording of your main points, it will be easier to phrase your introduction so it matches the tone and language of your speech. Although you may be tempted to write the introduction first, save this step until the end. If you wait to write your introduction, you won't have to go back and change it to match the ideas in the body of your speech.

Prepare and practice the full introduction in detail. Do not leave your introduction to chance. Introductions are the first moment of connection you have with your audience, so prepare the introduction completely before you give your speech. If you are opening with a story, practice telling the full story until you can tell it with ease and flair. If you are opening with a quote, memorize it. If you plan to begin with a demonstration, rehearse it until you have it perfected. However you begin, practice that opening over and over so you are confident and can deliver it smoothly.

Because introductions set the stage for what's to come, you want this part of the speech to go as flawlessly as possible. You also want to deliver this part of the speech with a minimum of notes and a maximum of eye contact. So, practice your full introduction again and again until you can deliver it smoothly and confidently. A well-delivered introduction will not only enhance your credibility, but will also increase your confidence as you move into the body of your speech.

Be brief. Remember, introductions tell just a little of what's to come; they set the stage for the body of the speech. Introductions should be brief, only 10 to 15 percent of the speech. If they are longer, they become tedious. They also cut into the time you need for your main points. If your planned introduction is longer than 10 to 15 percent of your speech, you probably have included too much detail. Revisit it and see if you can shorten it. Your goal is not to give your speech in the introduction, but to get the audience ready to hear your speech.

Be creative. Creativity is one of the best ways of capturing an audience's attention and revealing your topic. "Creative" doesn't necessarily mean "elaborate and artistic" (although it can be that). In speeches, creativity often comes through simple measures. Creativity depends on imagination and new ideas and perspectives. Trying out several of the techniques in this chapter will help you prepare a creative and effective introduction. For additional tips on creating your introduction, go to http://www.odwyerpr.com/archived_stories_2001/june/0620prof_dev.htm.

 Speech Step 10.2 / Refine Your Introduction

Review the introduction you wrote in Speech Step 10.1. Is it worked out in full detail? Is it brief? Is it creative? If you answered no to any of these questions, revisit your introduction and strengthen it as needed.

The Conclusion

Your conclusion is your final contact with your audience. Just as the introduction is the first impression, the conclusion is the last impression the audience has of you, and this impression will last long after the speech is over. Because final impressions are lasting, take time to prepare your conclusion so your speech ends with as much care as it began. Then practice that conclusion so you can deliver it in just the way you want. When you deliver your conclusion, you have two primary goals:

- Bring your speech to an end.
- Reinforce your thesis statement.

End Your Speech

When you end a speech, you are signaling to the audience that your presentation is over. Rather than ending abruptly or just trailing off, you want to communicate clearly that the speech is wrapping up and then is over. This signal comes through your words as well as your style of delivery. The more audience centered you are, the more effective your conclusion will be.

Speakers can signal the end of their speech by altering the tone and rate of their delivery. Like the close of a conversation, the conclusion of a speech exhibits a shift in style.[2] Think back to when you wanted to close off a conversation or when someone abruptly ended one and caught you unprepared. What were the signals you gave or those you needed to hear from the other person?

Generally, closure in conversations is signaled by a pause, a change in the rate of speaking, and even a different tone of voice. In speeches we use these same nonverbal cues. When you've concluded your final main point, use these shifts in delivery to signal to your audience that you are about to wrap up. Using your *Invitation to Public Speaking* CD-ROM, watch the videotape of the conclusion to Dr. Martin Luther King Jr.'s "I Have a Dream" speech. Notice how he changes his voice as he nears the end of the speech.

Another very effective way to signal the end of your speech is with a concluding transition. These are simple words and phrases such as "in closing," "in summary," "in conclusion," "let me close by saying," and "my purpose today has been." (For additional concluding transitions, go to http://www.bgsu.edu/departments/writing-lab/transition_words.html and read the entries for "conclusion" and "summation.") Although these transitions seem obvious, they can be especially useful as you make your way from the body of your speech to your conclusion. These transitions also will help you incorporate the techniques discussed in the next section.

Reinforce Your Thesis Statement

The second function of your conclusion is to reinforce the thesis statement of your speech. Recall from Chapter 4 that your thesis statement is a statement that summarizes, in a single declarative sentence, the main ideas, assumptions, or arguments you want to express in your speech. When you restate or rephrase your thesis statement in your conclusion, you remind your audience of the core idea behind your descriptions and assertions. Notice how this reinforcement can be very succinct, as in Chad's speech on adoption, or more elaborate, as Katy's on pi:

> In my family, I have two parents, an older sister and two younger brothers. One of them is adopted, but in my heart I could not tell you which one.

> In conclusion, no one knows why pi has caused such a craze, or why several books, movies, and fanatical Web pages have been produced on this subject. What inspired the Chudnovsky brothers to devote their lives to the search for pi? What inspired me to write a speech on a silly number? The answer lies in the mystery. Exploring pi is an adventure, which is why people do it. I want you to remember pi not only as the circle ratio, not only as the biggest influence on math over the course of history, but as a number that has an influence on everything we do.

Restating your thesis statement reinforces the heart of your arguments and encourages your audience to remember your words. Using your *Invitation to Public Speaking* CD-ROM, watch the video clip of Mike's conclusion under Speech Interactive.

Preparing a Compelling Conclusion

There are several techniques for signaling the end of a speech and reinforcing your thesis statement. You likely will combine several of these techniques in order to deliver a comprehensive conclusion. As you develop your conclusion, remember to continually ask yourself, "What final ideas do I want to leave my audience with?"

Summarize Your Main Points

summary
Concise restatement of the main points at the end of a speech.

An effective tool for ending your speech and restating your thesis statement is a summary of your main points. A **summary** is a concise restatement of your main points at the end of your speech. You can use it to review your ideas and remind your audience about what's important in your speech. Several of the speakers featured in this chapter used this technique in their conclusions:

> In the past few minutes, I have shared with you some of the crazy things people go to court over. I've defined the terms *tort, civil suit,* and *frivolous lawsuit*. I've shared some representative examples of crazy lawsuits and encouraged you to get involved in reducing the time these suits take up in our court system. I'd like to leave you with the following quote . . . .

> As you've seen in these last few minutes, ideas that have been presented to us as fiction may soon be reality. Germ-line engineering and cloning may soon be processes that are used in our every day life. Both techniques raise ethical questions and concerns, especially as we consider the advantages and disadvantages of each. I have shared some of my own thoughts about these issues in this presentation; I'd now like to open it up for questions and discussion.

When you summarize your main points, remember to do three things. First, offer only a summary—don't restate too much of your speech. The audience has already heard the details, and you are only trying to reinforce the key ideas and help them remember what you've said. Second, don't introduce new ideas into the summary. If you didn't bring an idea up in the body of the speech, don't raise it in the conclusion. New ideas in a conclusion will only confuse your audience. Finally, try to use the same kind of language in your summary that you used in the body of your speech. Familiar phrasing will help your audience recall your main ideas rather than forcing them to figure out what the new wording means.

Todd

Conclusions are one of the more interesting aspects of a speech. These are your last words to really make an impact about the content in your speech. They can be funny, soothing, emotional, or sometimes downright wacky. Whatever type of conclusion it is, make it powerful. Leave the speech with an impression that the topic took a great amount of work and did not just waste people's time. It should enhance and stimulate the audience so their brains expand just a touch, embracing them with the new information on the topic. I am very interested in personable conclusions such as a poem, words of advice, or a strong statement. However you decide to shape your conclusion, make sure you review the main points in your speech in a manner that magnifies the relationship between you, your topic, and the audience.

Answer Your Introductory Question

If your speech begins with questions, answer them in the conclusion of your speech. This technique reminds the audience of what they've learned or of the importance of understanding more about a particular issue. Nathan, who began with questions about hiking the Appalachian Trail, returned to those questions in his conclusion:

> So, now do you think you could walk from New York to Chicago, or from Georgia to Maine? Well, even if you're not up for the hike, many others have been. As a result of the efforts to maintain the Appalachian Trail, individuals have hiked the 2,200-mile-long footpath to raise funds, overcome disabilities, and seek out spiritual insights. The next time someone asks you if you want to "take a hike," perhaps you'll say, "why not?"

Refer Back to the Introduction

Occasionally, a speaker opens with a word, phrase, or idea and then returns to it in the conclusion. Like answering introductory questions, this technique brings the speech full circle and provides a sense of completeness. It usually is combined with other techniques for conclusions, such as summarizing the main points. Recall Kelly's speech about the Japanese language. After he summarized his ideas, Kelly returned to his opening as he concluded his speech:

> Thank you for listening, or, as they say in Japan, *doomo arigatoo gozaimashita.*

Reggie, who opened his speech with a story of a boy's battles with health, finished the story in his conclusion. After restating his thesis he said,

> And that boy I told you about in the opening of my speech? Well, I'm that boy, I'm now 19, doing fine, and in fact, I haven't set foot in a hospital for over four years now.

Recite a Quotation

When you conclude with a quotation, you rely on someone else's words to reinforce your thesis statement. A concluding quotation should come from someone you cited in your speech or from someone famous the audience will recognize. In the following examples, both Cassie and Tina return to sources they had cited in their speeches:

> I'd like to conclude with a quote from Jon Opelt, from the CALA: "We support the rights of injured parties to use the legal system responsibly in seeking fair compensation. However, some lawsuits are just darn right absurd."

> As we've heard today, shoes have gone through great changes over time. What started with animal skins and then lace, transformed itself into the 24-inch heels worn by both men and women, and on to the modern look we know today. But as Dr. Rene Cailet says, "Shoes should protect the foot and not disturb it. Having sore feet is not normal. As in any body part, pain is a signal that something is wrong."

To help see how speakers use these techniques, complete InfoTrac College Edition Exercise 10.3, "Concluding Remarks," online under Student Resources for Chapter 10.

Speech Step 10.3 / Prepare Your Conclusion

Using the techniques described in this chapter, write a conclusion for the introduction you have prepared. Begin by incorporating a transition from the body of your speech to the conclusion. Then summarize your main points, answer your introductory question, refer back to your introduction, or recite a quotation. Make sure your conclusion is consistent with your introduction and the tone you want to set for the ending of your speech. Put your conclusion aside and continue reading. Use Speech Builder Express to complete this Speech Step and add your conclusion to your draft outline.

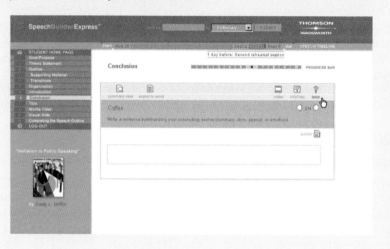

Tips for Your Conclusion

Look for concluding materials. As you research your speech, look for materials you can use in your conclusion. You may find just the right summary or technique if you keep in mind the kind of conclusion you want to create. If you find more quotations than you can use in the body of your speech, see if you can use one in your conclusion instead. Or, if a story is too long to tell in the introduction, think about saving part of it for the conclusion. As you research and develop your speech, you will come across interesting and effective materials for your conclusion. Save them, and then draw from these options to create an ending your audience will appreciate.

Be creative. Keep in mind that your conclusion is your last contact with your audience. Your creativity will keep them interested until the very end and will help them remember your ideas and arguments. As in the introduction, creativity in a conclusion does not need to be dramatic or elaborate. A creative conclusion, like Nathan's or Reggie's, can emerge from a clear summary and a reference back to the introduction. It may happen as you share a quote or finish a story begun in the introduction. Thinking creatively does not mean you become an expert entertainer. It does mean you think about the members of your audience, your speech goals, and the tone of your speech, then devise ways to make your final words innovative and imaginative.

Be brief. Conclusions are the shortest part of a speech. Because they summarize and end the speech, they should only be 5 to 10 percent of the total speech. Remember, conclusions don't introduce new information; they bring closure to the ideas already presented. If you find your conclusion is running too long, you may be finishing a main point you did not cover completely in the body or providing too much detail in your summary. Go back and reduce the scope of your conclusion if it's too long. Remember, the purposes of the conclusion are to bring the speech to an end and to reinforce the thesis statement. To assess the brevity of Laura Bush's conclusion in a recent radio address, complete Interactive Activity 10.2, "Focusing the Conclusion," online under Student Resources for Chapter 10 **WEB SITE** at the *Invitation to Public Speaking* Web site.

Don't leave the conclusion to chance. Take time to prepare the conclusion carefully before you deliver the speech. Work out all the details and practice delivering your conclusion until you have it just the way you want. Your last contact with your audience should be one that enhances your credibility. Make sure you know what you want to say and rehearse your closing words carefully so you can make eye contact with the audience and end your speech with confidence and assurance.

Speech Step 10.4 / Refine Your Conclusion

Review the conclusion you wrote in Speech Step 10.3. Have you followed the guidelines suggested in this section? If not, revisit your conclusion and strengthen it as needed.

Student Speech with Commentary

Foothills Gateway: Vote YES on Referendum 1A *by Mike Piel*

Specific purpose: To persuade my audience to vote yes on Referendum 1A.

Thesis statement: Voting yes on Referendum 1A is a good idea because it will save Foothills Gateway, a community organization that serves people with mental disabilities, at little cost to the taxpayer.

As you craft the introduction and conclusion of your next speech, you can use the following speech as a model. Using your Invitation to Public Speaking *CD-ROM, watch the video clip of Mike Piel's speech. As part of a service learning assignment, Mike gave this speech in an introductory public speaking class. The assignment was to give a four- to five-minute persuasive speech about a local issue. Analyze Mike's conclusion by answering the question included under Video Clip 4 at the end of the chapter.*

Commentary

Introduction

How many of you are planning on having children? How many of you are planning on having a child with a mental disability? None? Unfortunately, this is a reality that so many people in this world have to face day to day. In fact, one out of every four people in Larimer County alone is in some way

(continued on following page)

Mike begins with two rhetorical questions and a compelling statistic that captures the audience's attention and relates his topic to his audience.

Mike reveals his topic and states his goal. He establishes his credibility by explicitly stating this goal and by stating he will address the impact of this vote on taxpayers.

Mike finishes his introduction by previewing his speech. Notice how he clearly states his three main points and adapts his last point to his audience.

Mike signals the end of his speech with the phrase "in the last few minutes" and by restating his three main points.

Mike makes a direct appeal to his audience, reinforcing his thesis and reminding his audience of his purpose for speaking—to persuade them to vote yes on the referendum. Notice how he makes a direct, yet simple, appeal to their emotions, ending his speech on a strong note of human interest and compassion.

affected by someone with a mental disability. Luckily for these people, a community organization called Foothills Gateway is here to make their lives a little easier. Unfortunately, this great organization is in danger of losing its funding. The only way to prevent this from happening is to vote yes on referendum 1A in the upcoming election. To make you more aware of the situation, I'm going to take the next few minutes to inform you of several things. I will let you know what it is exactly that Foothills Gateway does, why passing this referendum is such a good idea, and lastly, how it's going to affect you, the taxpayer.

Conclusion

Now, over the last few minutes I have tried to inform you about what Foothills Gateway does, why this referendum is a good idea, and a little bit about how it's going to affect you, the taxpayer. I'll try to appeal to your good sense, your good nature as human beings—don't turn your back on people who are less fortunate than you, because if you don't take care of them, nobody else will. So please vote yes when you go to the ballot. Thank you.

Chapter Summary

An introduction is your first contact with your audience. Introductions have four objectives: to catch your audience's attention and interest, to reveal your topic, to establish your credibility, and to preview your speech. In order to accomplish these four goals, use a variety of techniques, such as asking a question, telling a story, reciting a quotation or poem, or giving a demonstration. You can also begin a speech with an intriguing or startling statement or by stating the importance of the topic.

Several tips are useful to remember when you create your introduction. First, look for introductory materials as you do your research. Second, prepare the exact wording of the introduction after you've prepared the body of the speech. Third, make the introduction brief, no more than 10 to 15 percent of the speech. Fourth, be creative as you develop the introduction. Finally, work out the full introduction and practice it carefully before you give the speech.

A conclusion is the final words in your speech. It has two goals: to signal the end of your speech and to reinforce your thesis statement. Conclusions are your last impression, so develop them with care. Several techniques can help you with conclusions. You can communicate to the audience that you are bringing the speech to an end by pausing and shifting the rate and tone of your delivery and by using transitions. Other effective techniques are summarizing your main points, providing the ending to a story you began in the introduction, answering a question you raised in the introduction, referring back to a comment you made in the introduction of the speech, and summing up your speech with a quotation.

Several tips will help you with your conclusion. As with the introduction, look for concluding materials during your research. Remember, too, to use creativity in the conclusion and to be brief. Conclusions should be no more than 5 to 10 percent of your speech. Finally, don't leave your conclusion to chance. Develop it carefully and practice it until you can deliver it with confidence.

Introductions and conclusions are very audience centered. In order to connect positively with your audience in the opening moments of your speech, consider who they are and what kinds of appeals will be appropriate and interesting to them. Similarly, to leave your audience with certain feelings and perspectives, consider how they feel about your topic. Like all aspects of the public dialogue, your introduction and conclusion can either contribute to or detract from healthy conversation and exchange. If you take time to prepare your introduction and conclusion, you will be more likely to participate in this dialogue successfully.

Invitation to Public Speaking Online

After reading this chapter, use your CD-ROM and the *Invitation to Public Speaking* Web site to review the following concepts, answer the review questions, and complete the suggested activities.

Key Concepts

preview (229)   rhetorical question (230)   summary (240)

Review Questions

1. Along with each of your classmates, write a potential speech topic and purpose on a slip of paper and hand it to your instructor. Your instructor will redistribute your topics to the class, making sure you do not receive your original topic. Now design an introduction to the topic your instructor has given you. Your introduction should (1) catch the attention and interest of your audience, (2) state your topic, (3) establish your credibility, and (4) preview your speech.

2. Consider the audience, topic, speaking goals, and main points of your next speech. How many of the techniques for introducing a speech can you develop? Write out several possibilities and select one. Practice delivering your introduction to your class or to a small group of students in your class.

3. Name the eight different techniques for catching the attention of the audience and revealing the topic of a speech. Identify the strengths of each technique.

4. Why should speakers establish their credibility and preview the main points of a speech? Are these components of an introduction important?

5. Suppose you have been asked to give a speech on the history of bubble gum. How would you establish your credibility on this topic? How creative do you think you could be in introducing this topic? Give examples of how you would establish credibility and your creativity.

6. Using the introduction you developed in question 2, write a conclusion for your speech, incorporating the techniques you've learned in this chapter. Practice your conclusion and deliver it to your class or a small group of students in your class.

7. Name the four different techniques for concluding a speech. Identify the strengths and weaknesses of each one.

8. Write a conclusion for the following speech:

Specific purpose — To persuade my audience to summarize their main points and reinforce their thesis statement in a conclusion to a speech.

Thesis statement — Summarizing main points and reinforcing the thesis statement of a speech are excellent audi-ence-centered techniques for concluding a presentation.

Main points

   I. Summarizing your main points reminds your audi-ence of the material you've covered in a speech.

  II. Reinforcing the thesis state-ment reminds your audience of your main ideas, assump-tions, or arguments.

The *Invitation to Public Speaking* Web Site

The *Invitation to Public Speaking* Web site features the review questions about the Web sites suggested on pages 230, 234, 238, and 239, the interactive activities suggested on pages 232 and 243, and the InfoTrac College Edition exercises suggested on pages 236 and 241. You can access this site via your CD-ROM or at http://www.wadsworth.com/product/griffin. To access Speech Builder Express in order to complete Speech Steps 10.1 and 10.3, you will need the username and password included under "Speech Builder Express" on your CD-ROM.

Web Links

10.1: Rhetorical Questions (230)
10.2: Uselessfacts.net (234)
10.3: The Speech Introduction (238)
10.4: Concluding Transitions (239)

Interactive Activities

10.1: Starting with a Quotation (232)
Purpose: To identify quotations that could be used in the introduction to a speech.

10.2: Focusing the Conclusion (243)
Purpose: To understand the importance of a brief conclusion.

InfoTrac College Edition Exercises

10.1: Establishing Significance (236)
Purpose: To understand how speakers establish the impor-tance of their speech.

10.2: Establishing Credibility (236)
Purpose: To explore how speakers establish credibility in their introductions.

10.3: Concluding Remarks (241)
Purpose: To understand how speakers conclude their speeches.

Speech Interactive on the *Invitation to Public Speaking* CD-ROM

The following video clips of speeches, referenced in this chapter, are included under Speech Interactive on your *Invitation to Public Speaking* CD-ROM. After you have watched the clips, click on "Critique" to answer the questions for analysis.

Video Clip 1: Speech Introduction: Brandi Lafferty (231). As you watch Brandi's story about feeding wildlife, notice at what point you realize the topic of the speech. At what point do you realize Brandi's position on this topic? Does her story motivate you to listen to the rest of her speech? Why or why not?

Video Clip 2: Speech Preview: Mike Piel (237). Watch Mike's preview of his speech. Based on his preview, do you think his speech will be easy to follow? What are the topics he will cover? Are there times when a speaker may not want to use a preview?

Video Clip 3: Dr. Martin Luther King Jr.'s "I Have a Dream" Speech (239). As you listen to the concluding remarks of Dr. King's "I Have a Dream" speech, listen to how we uses his voice to signal the end of the speech. How is King's energy different in these concluding sentences? What impact do you think this energy had on his audience?

Video Clip 4: Speech Conclusion: Mike Piel (242). Watch Mike Piel's conclusion and listen to how he recaps his main points and ends with a strong, decisive statement. Is his final statement something the audience will remember?

Outlining Your Speech

In this chapter you will learn to

Prepare a preparation outline

Prepare a speaking outline

Prepare note cards to use as prompts during a speech

Why bother outlining? It's a question millions of students have asked and ... we need to ponder the answers we offer them. ... Will it teach them logic? Save them time? Make the structure of their arguments and ideas visible?

Outlining is an activity that engages our reasoning powers and reorganizes our material into a visual structure. ... Over time, the outline takes on a lively meaning of its own, representing the author's earlier thoughts, without the distracting details of the full draft.

—Adapted from Jonathan Price's *Outlining Goes Electronic,* 1999[1]

Outlines have been with us from the early days of public speaking and are the subject of approximately seventy-five composition, rhetoric, and technical writing textbooks written in the past fifty years. Classical and Renaissance rhetoricians (teachers of public speaking) advocated the outline as a template, or pattern, to help prepare for court, church, and diplomatic presentations. In 1828 the rhetorician Richard Whately encouraged the use of an outline as a "brief visual preview" of a document. By 1933 the *Oxford English Dictionary* defined the term *outline* as "a description, giving a general idea of the whole, but leaving details to be filled in."[2]

An outline is as essential to your speech today as it was to speeches given hundreds of years ago. An outline is a short visual version of your speech that helps you organize your ideas in two important ways. First, when you outline your ideas, you create a *synopsis* of your speech, or a skeletal summary. With this synopsis in front of you, you can examine your arguments in a new light and can tell if they will make sense to your audience. When you write out an outline, you can follow the arrangement of your points and discover whether you've developed them logically. Outlines help you take what's in your head and put it on paper. You then can see if your ideas really are organized in the way you want.

Second, an outline helps you discover any weak or missing ideas and arguments. When you review your outline, you see how your ideas are mapped out. If you've skipped a point or failed to develop an idea completely, an outline will help you discover this before you give your speech. Even though you might think you can map out your ideas if you simply write up a complete draft of your entire speech, don't fall prey to this temptation. Compare any of the full texts of speeches in this book with the outlines. Which gives you a better sense of balance, of how arguments are developed, and of any missing points or ideas? An outline is a much better map of the logic of your presentation. In addition, a good outline can help reduce your anxiety about speaking. Read about how at the Scared Speechless Web site, http://www.back2college.com/publicspeaking.htm.

As you prepare your speech, make two different outlines. Develop the first, called a *preparation outline,* when you finish your research and begin identifying your main and supporting ideas. From your preparation outline, develop a second outline, called a *speaking outline.* This is a condensed version of your preparation outline, and you use it to practice and deliver your speech. Both outlines are important parts of your speech process.

The Preparation Outline

preparation outline
Detailed outline a speaker builds when preparing a speech that includes the title, specific purpose, thesis statement, introduction, main points and subpoints, connectives, conclusion, and source citations of the speech.

As its name suggests, the **preparation outline** helps you prepare your speech. Note that the preparation outline *is not* the full text of your speech. Instead, it is a detailed outline you build as you prepare your speech that includes the title, specific purpose, thesis statement, introduction, main points and subpoints, connectives, conclusion, and source citations of your speech. It contains enough detail to be certain your speech is organized and complete, but it does not include every word you will say. Note that it's never too early to begin creating a preparation outline for your speech. For information on getting started, go to the Web site Preparing and Using Outlines at http://webster.commnet.edu/mla/outlines.htm. Or complete Interactive Activity 11.1, "Outlining the Introduction," online under Student Resources for Chapter 11 at the *Invitation to Public Speaking* Web site.

WEB SITE

Title, Specific Purpose, and Thesis Statement

Because a preparation outline helps you focus your ideas and organize your materials, write out your specific purpose and thesis statement at the top of the outline (Chapter 4). Also give your speech a title that arouses your audience's curiosity and makes them want to listen to what you have to say. The title of a speech usually comes from its specific purpose and thesis statement, which both indicate the theme of your speech. A good title also reflects the tone of your speech. Let's take a look at how Brooke and Katy titled their speeches from Chapter 10.

Title:	The World's Fire
Specific purpose:	To inform my audience about the history and legends of the chili pepper.
Thesis statement:	The history of the chili pepper includes global, national, and personal stories.
Title:	Why Pi?
Specific purpose:	To inform my audience about the number pi.
Thesis statement:	Pi, a fascinating number with an unusual history, has become an obsession for some people.

Both speakers chose simple, yet appropriate, titles for their speeches. Each title is interesting so it draws an audience in, and each gives a hint of what the speech is about. (Katy's complete preparation outline for her speech, "Why Pi?", is featured at the end of this section.) To develop a title for your next speech, complete Interactive Activity 11.2, "Creating a Title," online under Student Resources for Chapter 11 at the *Invitation to Public Speaking* Web site.

WEB SITE

Introduction

Recall from Chapter 10 that your introduction should do four things: catch your audience's attention, reveal your speech topic, establish your credibility, and preview your main points. Identify these four steps in your preparation outline. This will help you be sure you have included each of them in your introduction. Here's how Nathan, Brooke, and Cassie outlined their introductions.

Nathan:

I. How far do you think you can walk? *(catch attention)*

    A. A hike from Georgia to Maine will put you on the Appalachian National Scenic Trail. *(reveal topic)*

    B. I've hiked this trail twice in my life, the most recent time being last summer. *(establish credibility)*

II. Today I'd like to share with you a brief history of this trail, some facts about the trail and how it's maintained, and stories from some people who've hiked the trail. *(preview main points)*

Brooke:

I. The words *chilly, chili,* and *Chile* refer to cold weather, spicy beans, and a country in South America. *(catch attention)*

    A. Today I'm speaking about the chili pepper. *(reveal topic)*

    B. The Chile Today Web site says the chili pepper has conquered taste buds and cuisines for ten thousand years.

    C. To me, the chili pepper is a legend, story, and tale. *(establish credibility)*

II. The chili pepper legends I'll discuss come from a variety of stories. *(preview main points)*

    A. Some stories are found across the globe.

    B. Others are the national stories originating in our own country.

    C. My final story is a personal one about my grandfather, the person who introduced me to the chili pepper's legacy. *(also establishes credibility)*

Cassie:

I. Play the game "Strange But True" with me for a minute. *(catch attention)*

    A. Each of these lawsuits is real, and these "crazy lawsuits" are the subject of my speech. *(reveal topic)*

    B. In my research I found many crazy cases that actually have gone to court. *(establish credibility)*

II. Today I'll discuss some of the craziest by defining basic legal terms, sharing some of my favorite cases, and persuading you that we should help control these lawsuits. *(preview main points)*

In these examples, the speakers summarized their introductions in outline form. These outlines do not include the full text of the speeches, but rather a synopsis of the main ideas. By using this format, the speakers could see they included the four components of a strong introduction. Using your *Invitation to Public Speaking* CD-ROM, watch the introduction to Katy's speech on the number pi. Compare what she says with what she wrote in her preparation outline at the end of this section. In her speech, does she clearly include all the components of the introduction she outlined?

Katy Mazz

Main Points, Subpoints, and Sub-Subpoints

As you learned in Chapter 9, the most important ideas in your speech are your main points. Your main points make up the body of your speech. When you want to elaborate on your main points, you use subpoints and sub-subpoints. A **subpoint** develops an aspect of a main point. A **sub-subpoint** goes deeper to develop an aspect of a subpoint. You can think of main points, subpoints, and sub-subpoints as moving from the whole to the parts, or from the general to the specific. Consider the following examples:

I. There is a difference between animal welfare and animal rights.

    A. Animal welfare is based on the philosophy that humans have a right to care for and use animals.

    B. Animal rights are based on the philosophy that animals have a right to a free and healthy existence and humans should not interfere with this.

subpoints
A point in a speech that develops an aspect of a main point.

sub-subpoints
A point in a speech that develops an aspect of a subpoint.

Notice that the idea in the main point (I) is broader than the ideas in the two sub-points (A and B). The subpoints develop specific aspects of the main point.

Consider a second example with sub-subpoints, this time from Kameron's speech in Chapter 8 about zebra mussels:

I. Zebra mussels cause damage to every aspect of any aquatic ecosystem they encounter.

    A. They destroy the natural balance of the ecosystem.

        1. They consume all the food available to those lower on the food chain.

        2. Larger fish no longer have smaller fish to feed on.

    B. They form large colonies that attach themselves to any solid object, making it difficult for commercial enterprises.

        1. They congregate on buoys and markers, causing them to sink.

        2. They clog intake ports by attaching themselves to anything solid.

Again, notice that the main point (I) is developed and supported by the two sub-points (A and B). Additionally, the subpoints are developed and supported by the sub-subpoints (points 1 and 2 under points A and B). In addition, notice that the points are organized according to the principle of **coordination**, or arranging your points into successive levels, with the points on a specific level having equal importance.

The importance of organizing ideas logically is apparent when Kameron's example is rearranged:

I. They congregate on buoys and markers, causing them to sink.

    A. They destroy the natural balance of the ecosystem.

        1. They form large colonies that attach themselves to any solid object.

        2. Zebra mussels cause damage to every aspect of any aquatic ecosystem they encounter.

    B. They consume all the food available to those lower on the food chain.

        1. They clog intake ports by attaching themselves to anything solid.

        2. Larger fish no longer have smaller fish to feed on.

Mixed up in this way, Kameron's interesting points become confusing. Remember, a main point is the broadest, most comprehensive idea; a subpoint supports and develops the main idea; and a sub-subpoint supports and develops the subpoint.

coordination
The process of arranging points into successive levels, with the points on a specific level having the same weight or value.

Ashley

My initial thought when creating a preparation outline was, "Why do we have to go through all this trouble?" I thought it was a big waste of time, and I would end up with the same outcome if I just wrote out my speech. But after I started my outline, I realized it does help organize your thoughts and supporting ideas. All the pieces of my speech puzzle started to come together. To make my preparation outline into a speaker's outline, I wrote down the most important pieces of information in each main point and then marked when I wanted to use my visual aid. Here's a tip: Don't wait until the last minute. I am very glad I learned how to write an outline like this. I think it really helped me, and I will use it from now on.

Conclusion

In Chapter 10 you learned that the conclusion has two goals: to signal the end of the speech and to reinforce your thesis statement. Thus you want to outline your conclusion to make sure it meets these goals. Like your introduction, the outline of the conclusion isn't a word-for-word transcript. Rather, it's a summary of what you'll say. Let's take a look at how Nathan and Will outlined the conclusions to their speeches in Chapter 10.

Nathan:
I. So, now do you think you could walk from New York to Chicago, or from Georgia to Maine? *(bring speech to an end)*

II. Even if you're not up for the hike, many people have hiked the 2,200-mile-long footpath to raise funds, overcome disabilities, and seek out spiritual insights. *(reinforce thesis statement)*

Will:
I. As you've seen in these last few minutes, ideas that were once regarded as fiction may soon be reality. *(bring speech to an end)*

II. Although there are ethical questions and concerns, germ-line engineering and cloning may soon be processes that are used every day. *(reinforce thesis statement)*

WEB SITE For help in outlining your conclusion, complete Interactive Activity 11.3, "Outlining the Conclusion," online under Student Resources for Chapter 11 at the *Invitation to Public Speaking* Web site. .

Connectives

Recall that connectives are words and phrases that link your main ideas, summarize your arguments, and help you transition from one point to the next (Chapter 9). Because most connectives are only about as long as a sentence, simply write them out rather than outline them. Here's how some of our speakers used connectives in their preparation outlines. In her speech on crazy lawsuits, Cassie previewed her main points in her introduction, and then she wrote the connective to her first main point:

Connective: Let's begin by looking at some definitions.

She then outlined her first main point:

I. Three terms come up in most of these cases.

    A. The first term is *tort.*

    B. The second term is *civil suit.*

    C. The third term is *frivolous lawsuit.*

Similarly, Kelly used a transition in his speech on the Japanese language to get him from his first main point to his second:

Connective: Now that I've introduced you to some Japanese body language, I would like to discuss a little bit about spoken Japanese.

And in his speech on germ-line engineering, Will incorporated an internal summary into his preparation outline:

Connective:	As you've just heard, germ-line engineering combines the age-old idea of manipulating DNA strands through selective breeding of animals and the newer research that is unpacking the human DNA code. But this isn't the only radical idea around today.

Will then moved on to cloning, his next main point.

Include connectives between the major sections of your preparation outline introduction, body, and conclusion, and between main points to help you track your transitions from one idea to the next. If you write out your connectives, you can easily see if you've overused a phrase (for example, "now let's" again and again), and you can see which points you might clarify with internal previews, summaries, or both. Identify your speech's connectives by completing Interactive Activity 11.4, "Adding Connectives," online under Student Resources for Chapter 11 at the *Invitation to Public Speaking* Web site.   **WEB SITE**

Works Cited

The final component of your preparation outline is a list of the works you have cited in your speech. Follow the guidelines for citing sources in Chapter 9 or those required by your instructor. Your instructor might require an established format for citing sources, such as that of the Modern Language Association (MLA) or the American Psychological Association (APA). For guidelines for these citation styles, see http://www.cox-internet.com/ruskhslib/cited.htm or http://www.library.uq.edu.au/training/citation/apa.html. Or look under Student Resources for Chapter 6 at the *Invitation to Public Speaking* Web site.   **WEB SITE**

Unless your instructor indicates otherwise, include only the sources you actually cited orally in your speech. By listing your sources, you'll see how many you relied on to build your arguments and establish your credibility. If you discover you have cited only one or two sources and you think you need more, you can go back and rework sections of your speech to include additional citations. Remember, citing the work of others enhances your ideas and increases your credibility. Using sources in your speech keeps your audience from discrediting your ideas as too personalized or uninformed.

 Speech Step 11.1 / Build Your Preparation Outline

Using the template provided by your instructor or the sample at the end of this section as a guide, build a preparation outline for your next speech. Start by creating a title and indicating your specific purpose and thesis statement. Then outline your introduction your main points, subpoints, and sub-subpoints, and your conclusion. Add connectives that will help you transition from one idea to the next. Finally, add a section of the works you intend to cite in your speech, following the format provided by your instructor or this book. Speech Builder Express can be used to create your preparation outline online. Using your desktop word processing software, you can save your outline online or email it to your instructor.

Tips for the Preparation Outline

Use complete sentences. As you develop your preparation outline, always write your ideas out in complete sentences. The difference between a full-sentence outline and a key-word outline is obvious when the two are compared:

Incorrect: Key-word outline

I. The Tuskegee Airmen

   A. Four squadrons

   B. The elite 332nd

   C. Their names

II. Obstacles

   A. The first

   B. No officers

   C. Recognition

Correct: Full-sentence outline

I. The Tuskegee Airmen were an elite group of African American fighter pilots who fought during the Second World War.

   A. The first five men graduated from four different squadrons at the Tuskegee training center in Alabama.

   B. The Tuskegee Airmen were considered one of the Allies' strongest weapons.

   C. Because of their talents, the Tuskegee Airmen were given nicknames in both German and English.

II. Although history books now recognize these men as heroes, they had to overcome many obstacles in order to be allowed to fly.

   A. At first they were not allowed to form a squadron because "no colored squadrons" were needed.

   B. They then were told no such unit was allowed because there were "no commissioned Negro officers" in the Air Force.

   C. Although they never lost a bomber they escorted, it wasn't until 1948 that the first African American pilot received his gold wings.

Although you do get a sense of Javad's topic and ideas in the key-word example, a full-sentence outline is far more useful as a tool to help you prepare and track the components of your speech. A key-word outline gives you very little sense of how fully developed your ideas are and whether you have thought them through completely. In contrast, a full-sentence outline clearly shows how well your speech is organized, what the contents of each point are, where there are inconsistencies, and where you might need to add more information.

Label the introduction, body, conclusion, and connectives. In addition to labeling the title, specific purpose, and thesis statement in your preparation outline, also label the introduction, body, conclusion, and connectives. Notice that the labels for the introduction, body, and conclusion are centered in the sample outline at the end of this section. These labels mark each component of your speech and encourage you to consider each one separately. They also help you see how much time you are devoting to each section. For example, you can tell whether your introduction is overly long or if your conclusion is too abrupt.

Use a consistent pattern of symbols and indentation. Outlines are based on the principles of **subordination**, or ranking ideas in order from the most to the least important. The most common way to indicate subordination in an outline is to use a traditional pattern of symbols and indentations. Symbols are the letters and numbers you use to label your main points, subpoints, and sub-subpoints. Main points are labeled with capital Roman numerals (I, II, III, IV, V, and so on). Subpoints are labeled with capital letters (A, B, C, D, and so on). Sub-subpoints are labeled with Arabic numbers (1, 2, 3, and so on). Indentations help you visually indicate the subordination of ideas. Your main ideas are set farthest left, and each level of subideas is indented progressively farther to the right (on your computer, use tab spaces). A traditional outline format looks like this:

I. Main point

    A. Subpoint

        1. Sub-subpoint

        2. Sub-subpoint

        3. Sub-subpoint

    B. Subpoint

II. Main point

    A. Subpoint

    B. Subpoint

        1. Sub-subpoint

        2. Sub-subpoint

In a complex outline, you may need sub-sub-subpoints and even sub-sub-sub-subpoints. Label sub-sub-subpoints with lowercase letters (a, b, c, d, and so on), and label sub-sub-sub-subpoints with lowercase Roman numerals (i, ii, iii, iv, v, and so on).

I. Main point

    A. Subpoint

    B. Subpoint

        1. Sub-subpoint

           a. Sub-sub-subpoint

              i. Sub-sub-sub-subpoint

              ii. Sub-sub-sub-subpoint

           b. Sub-sub-subpoint

        2. Sub-subpoint

When you indent, be sure you indent *all* the text that corresponds with the point, not just the first line of text. Doing so will help you see the ranking of each point clearly.

Incorrect

II. Although history books now recognize these men as heroes, they had to overcome many obstacles in order to be allowed to fly.

    A. At first they were not allowed to form a squadron because "no colored squadrons" were needed.

subordination
The process of ranking ideas in order from the most to the least important.

Correct

II. Although history books now recognize these men as heroes, they had to overcome many obstacles in order to be allowed to fly.

    A. At first they were not allowed to form a squadron because "no colored squadrons" were needed.

Divide points into at least two subpoints. When you support your broader ideas with more specific ideas, you divide your points. For example, in Javad's speech about the Tuskegee Airmen, he discussed the three obstacles the men overcame in his second point. He divided this main point about overcoming obstacles into three subpoints: (1) the belief that there was no need for a "colored" squadron, (2) the fact that there were no commissioned Negro officers in the Air Force, and (3) that fact that they were not formally recognized as pilots until 1948.

Common sense tells us that when we divide a point, we must divide it into at least two parts—you can't divide something into only one part. But what if a point doesn't seem to divide naturally into two or more parts? For example, when Cassie began working on her speech about frivolous lawsuits, she intended to define only one legal term, not three. As such, she wound up with only one subpoint for her main point about definitions. To solve this dilemma, she could have folded the definition into another point. For example, she could have defined the term *tort* while describing her first crazy lawsuit. Instead, she decided to expand her original point about important definitions and ended up with three subpoints.

Be careful when you fold one point into another. Make sure you discuss only one idea in each point so that your audience can follow your discussion and reasoning easily. For example, in Chapter 16, Shelley speaks about threatened and endangered species, dividing the two ideas "threatened" and "endangered" into separate points rather than collapsing them into one. In doing so, she is able to help her audience understand the differences between the two categories.

Check for balance. When you label and indent your main points, subpoints, and sub-subpoints, your preparation outline will show whether your ideas are complete and balanced. As you discovered in Chapter 9, a speaker's goal is to offer a fairly equal presentation of each main point. If your presentation outline shows that one or two points get far more discussion than the others, you need to reconsider your speech goals and how you have tried to accomplish them. Does your speech organization really reflect what you've identified in your thesis statement as the main points in your speech? Suppose your preparation outline showed the following structure:

I. Main point

II. Main point

    A. Subpoint

    B. Subpoint

        1. Sub-subpoint

        2. Sub-subpoint

        3. Sub-subpoint

    C. Subpoint

    D. Subpoint

E. Subpoint

    1. Sub-subpoint

    2. Sub-subpoint

    3. Sub-subpoint

    4. Sub-subpoint

    5. Sub-subpoint

III. Main point

    A. Subpoint

    B. Subpoint

Note that the second main point is developed in far more detail than the first or third main points. Additionally, subpoints B and E are more fully developed than the others are. The outline shows an imbalance that needs to be corrected. Either the speech can be refocused to make the second main point the thesis statement, or some material can be eliminated from the second main point and some material added to the other two main points. To help you identify the balance of your points in your outline, complete Interactive Activity 11.5, "Outlining Main Points and Subpoints," online under Student Resources for Chapter 11 at the *Invitation to Public Speaking* Web site.

WEB SITE

Keep an audience-centered focus. When you build your preparation outline, try to think of how your audience might answer the following questions:

- Is any part of the speech too complex or too simple?

- Are the main points clear?

- Are they sufficiently developed and meaningful?

- Are the introduction and conclusion clear, and what tone do they set?

- Are there connectives, and do they clearly relate the points and show the flow of ideas?

- Do the works cited adequately support the ideas and arguments?

Your preparation outline can help you answer each of these questions so you can connect with your audience and contribute to the public dialogue. Using your *Invitation to Public Speaking* CD-ROM, watch a video clip of Hillary Rodham Clinton's September 9, 1995, address to the United Nations Fourth World Conference on Women under Speech Interactive. As you watch the speech, create a preparation outline that she could have used.

Speech Step 11.2 / Check the Effectiveness of Your Preparation Outline

Review your preparation outline and translate any incomplete sentences or key words into full sentences. Make sure you've labeled the introduction, body, and conclusion of your speech. Also make sure you've used the proper symbols to indicate your main points, subpoints, and sub-subpoints and your points are indented properly. Correct any imbalances you discover in your points. Finally, make sure your outline has an audience-centered focus. If you've been completing your outline using Speech Builder Express, click on "Completing the Speech Outline" to view your preparation outline.

Preparation Outline with Commentary

Why Pi? *by Katy Mazz*

Specific purpose: To inform my audience about the number pi.

Thesis statement: Pi, a fascinating number with an unusual history, has become an obsession for some people.

Commentary

Katy indicates her specific purpose and thesis statement at the beginning of her preparation outline. This helps her stay audience centered, focused on her topic, and reminded of her speech goals.

Katy labels her introduction to help her keep her place as she gives her speech. The outline of her introduction is very detailed to help her account for and identify the four components of a strong introduction.

Katy catches her audience's attention by reciting pi to several decimal places and by getting them curious about its presence in their lives.

In subpoint E, she reveals the topic of her speech.

Katy adapts her topic to her audience by indicating she knows her audience quite well—she recognizes they are all speech majors. She establishes her credibility by indicating she has researched her topic and is personally interested in it.

In the last point of her introduction, Katy previews the three main points of her speech.

By marking the body of her speech with a heading, she can clearly see where she must shift from her introduction to her first main point.

Notice that she uses complete sentences for each point.

She divides her first main point into two subpoints. In the first one,

Are you ready to build your preparation outline? Use the following outline as a model. You can watch a video clip of the speech Katy Mazz gave based on this outline by using your Invitation to Public Speaking *CD-ROM. Katy gave this speech in an introductory public speaking class. The assignment was to give a four- to six-minute informative speech about any topic. Students were asked to create a preparation outline, to cite at least four sources, and to speak from a speaking outline or note cards. In addition, they were asked to end on a strong note. (You can read Katy's speaking outline later in this chapter.)*

Introduction

I. 3.14159265358979323846264433832795. (*catch attention*)

   A. Most of you know the name of the number I just recited.

   B. It is found in rainbows, pupils of eyes, sound waves, ripples in the water, and DNA.

   C. It is a ratio that nature and music understand but that the mind cannot comprehend.

   D. This number has sparked curiosity over the past 4000 years.

   E. I am talking about pi—not the dessert, but the circle ratio. (*reveals topic*)

II. I will try to present pi as the fascinating topic I think it is to a class of speech majors who wonder if they can survive a speech about math.

   A. I have researched this topic, finding information not only technical and historical, but also fanatical. (*establish credibility*)

   B. My own interest came about when I was challenged to memorize more digits than a friend of mine.

III. I plan to inform you of what pi is, the history of pi, and how pi has created obsessions in people's lives. (*preview main points*)

Body

I. Even if you don't know what it represents, pi is a number that almost everyone is familiar with.

   A. When you divide the circumference of a circle by its diameter, the result will always equal pi.

      1. No matter the size of the circle, this division results in what is called the circle ratio.

      2. Although we refer to pi as 3.14 or 22/7, it is actually an irrational number, meaning that it cannot be represented as a fraction.

3. The number pi is never-ending—or is it?

4. For ages, mathematicians have puzzled, and have been almost ashamed, that it is so difficult to find another value as simple as the circle ratio.

B. Pi is more than just the circle ratio.

1. According to David Blatner, who wrote "The Joy of Pi", this value can be found in all fields of math and science, architecture, the arts, and even in the Bible.

2. The world record for calculating pi to the greatest number of decimal places is 206 billion decimal places, calculated by Dr. Kanada at the University of Tokyo.

Transition: Although 206 billion digits have been calculated thus far, there was a time in antiquity when there was uncertainty of the second decimal place.

II. Woven among pi's infinite digits is a rich history, ranging from the great thinkers of ancient cultures to the supercomputers of the twentieth century.

A. Four thousand years ago, there was no decimal system, compass, paper, or pencil, yet people still found ways to calculate pi.

1. The Egyptians used a stake, a rope, and the sand to approximate pi as a little greater than 3.

2. The Greeks, Babylonians, Israelites, Chinese, and Mesopotamians also studied the circle ratio, yet none of them were certain of the third decimal place.

B. Whether pi is an infinite number remained a mystery until the sixteenth century.

1. Petr Beckmann, a former professor of engineering at Colorado University, likes to call this period the age of the digit hunters, with each generation popping out more digits than the next.

2. Keep in mind that at this point the electronic calculator had not yet been invented.

3. Famous mathematicians of the time continued to break records for calculating pi.

C. In the twentieth century, the invention of the computer allowed mathematicians to calculate pi to 16,000 digits, confirming that pi is infinite and totally random.

Transition: What is the fascination with pi that has caused people to be both fascinated and obsessed?

(continued on next page)

she explains what pi is and what makes it unusual. Notice how she uses a rhetorical question in her third sub-subpoint, to spark her audience's interest.

In her second subpoint, Katy continues to explain what pi is. Again, she presents intriguing information to help her audience appreciate pi's popularity and intrigue.

In this transition, Katy briefly restates her last point and introduces her second point, the history of pi, with her reference to antiquity. She sets the transition off so she can find it easily and see she is moving on to her second main point.

Katy divides her second main point into three subpoints that help her develop her discussion of pi's rich history. She develops her argument chronologically, from ancient history to the present era. Notice her use of subordination and that she indents each new point properly.

Katy shares interesting historical facts about math that appeal to her audience of speech majors.

Note her interesting language: "the age of the digit hunters" and "each generation popping out more digits." In this point, she uses her research creatively and stays audience centered.

Katy brings her audience up to the present era with her third subpoint.

By asking another rhetorical question, she previews her third main point.

In her final point, Katy explains the obsession some people have with the number pi. In her three subpoints, she discusses a different aspect of this obsession.

In subpoint A, Katy tells a story of the Chudnovsky brothers and the lengths to which they went to study pi.

Katy uses Goto as an example of someone obsessed with memorizing pi, then shares some memorization methods that are easier. Notice that subpoint B is slightly more developed than subpoints A or C, but that her three subpoints still are fairly evenly balanced.

Her third subpoint wraps up her discussion of the obsession with pi, using a lighthearted story of a tradition she learned on the Ridiculously Enhanced Pi Page Web site.

Katy includes a transition in her summary by returning to one of her questions from earlier in her speech. Also note that she marks her conclusion as a distinct part of her outline.

Katy begins her conclusion by answering her question about why pi has caused such a craze. She then summarizes her main points.

III. Blatner states, "People have calculated, memorized, philosophized, and expounded on" pi more than on any number in history.

   A.   The Chudnovsky brothers, Gregory and David, were both mathematicians from Russia who moved to New York to entertain their obsession with pi.

      1. In their own apartment, they built a supercomputer from scrap materials.

      2. With this computer they were able to calculate more digits and to study its use in various formulas.

   B.   Other people try to memorize pi.

      1. Some do it for sport or to be silly, but others are more serious.

      2. Blatner states that in 1995, Hiroyuko Goto spent over nine hours reciting 42,000 digits of pi from memory, far exceeding the world record.

         a. This was a rare case, but there are methods of memorization for the average memory.

         b. Some people remember pi through poems, clever mnemonics, and songs.

         c. Some simply memorize the digits in groups of fours, which is the method I've found easiest.

   C.   So many people are obsessed with pi that the number is celebrated on Pi Day every March 14, or 3/14.

      1. The Web site Ridiculously Enhanced Pi Page suggests that you gather with friends at 1:59 p.m. to celebrate.

      2. At this time, eat pie and share personal stories about pi.

Summary and transition: So ends my analysis of people's obsessions, but my earlier question was not fully answered.

Conclusion

I. No one knows for sure why pi has caused such a craze, why several books, movies, and Web pages have been devoted to this subject. (*brings speech to an end*)

   A.   What inspired the Chudnovsky brothers to devote their lives to the search for pi?

   B.   What inspired me to write a speech on a silly number?

C. The answer lies in the mystery of pi: People explore pi because it is an adventure to do so.

II. Remember that pi is not only the circle ratio, not only the biggest influence on math over history, but also a number that has a great affect on people and an influence on everything we do. (*reinforce thesis and summarize main points*)

III. William Schaaf, in "The Nature and History of Pi", concludes that "probably no symbol in mathematics has evoked as much mystery, romanticism, misconception and human interest as the number pi."

Works Cited

Beckmann, Petr. *A History of Pi*. New York: St. Martin's Press, 1971.

Blatner, David. *The Joy of Pi*. New York: Walker and Company, 1997.

Blatner, David. "Pi Facts and Figures." *The Joy of Pi*. Accessed 20 September 2000. http://joyofpi.com/.

Schaaf, William. "The Nature and History of Pi." *The Joy of Pi*. Accessed 20 September 2000. http://www.joyofpi.com/schaaf.htm.

Witcombe, Chris. "Notes on Pi". *Earth Mysteries*. Sweet Briar College. Accessed 23 September 2000. http://witcombe.sbc.edu/earthmysteries/EMPi.html.

Ridiculously Enhanced Pi Page. Posted 1998. *The Exploratorium. Accessed* 23 September 2000. http://www.exploratorium.edu/pi/pi98/

Notice that the outline of her conclusion includes a lot of detail. This helps her (1) make sure she has incorporated the two aspects of a strong conclusion, and (2) see that her conclusion is shorter than her introduction and will take only a few moments to deliver.

Katy ends her speech with a quotation, leaving her audience with a strong sense of the mystique of the number pi.

Katy includes a bibliography of the specific research she references in her speech. Note that her sources range from 1971 to 2000, indicating that she did both historical and current research. She also relies on both Internet and print sources, illustrating that she searched in several places for material rather than relying on only one kind of source.

The Speaking Outline

Your speaking outline is a brief version of your preparation outline. You use it when you deliver your speech. The **speaking outline**, sometimes called *speaking notes*, is a condensed form of your preparation outline, used to help you remember your ideas as you speak. Remember that you will almost never memorize a speech or read it from a manuscript. Most often you will choose the exact words of your speech as you are giving it. As such, you need a speaking outline to help you remember specific information that you plan to include in your speech. For example, your speaking outline might include the full text of quotations, statistics, names, and other material you want to remember exactly. It also includes delivery prompts, such as "make eye contact," "slow down," and "breathe."

The most effective speakers make frequent eye contact with their audience and speak directly to them. Their speaking outlines encourage them to do this. Because they do not have the full text written out in front of them, they are not tempted to read to the audience. Instead, they rely on the ideas, words, and phrases in their speaking outline to remind them of what they want to say.

speaking outline
Condensed form of a preparation outline, used to help a speaker remember his or her ideas when speaking.

Although you may feel you will give a better speech if much of it is written out fully on your speaking outline, experienced speakers have found this simply isn't so. The most dynamic speakers are those whose speaking outlines only prompt their memories and enable them to engage their audiences directly.

Speaking outlines are very personalized documents. As you gain experience speaking, you will discover what you need to include to be an effective speaker and what you can leave out. For now, use the following tips to help you build your speaking outline.

Tips for the Speaking Outline

Use key words and phrases. When you write your speaking outline, use key words and phrases rather than full sentences. As you prepare this outline, think carefully about what words and phrases will help you remember your full ideas.

In the example here, notice how Graham reduced his full sentences to key words, working from the larger idea to its most essential component:

Preparation outline

    I. Many people are not aware of what a voucher system is.

        A. Voucher programs take taxpayers' money and give it to families.

            1. Families then use money to send children to the school of their choice.

            2. The school of choice could be either a public or private school.

        B. In theory, money that normally goes to public schools now is distributed to a range of schools.

        C. The program is touted as a new solution to the old problem of inadequate public education.

Speaking outline

    I. The voucher system

        A. Taxpayers' money to families

        B. Money normally goes to public schools

        C. New solution to old problem

The key words capture the essence of Graham's ideas and help him remember the full thought when he looks down at his notes. The key words call to mind the full argument or explanation. They keep him talking and prevent him from reading his speech.

Use an outline format. As you look down at your speaking outline during a speech, you have to be able to find your place easily. For this reason, follow the traditional outline format for your speaking outline, and indent your subpoints and sub-subpoints. You can find your place far more quickly in an outline than in a written manuscript. If you are nervous and lose your place during a speech, you can easily find it and reduce your nervousness considerably.

In the example here, note the difference between a list that is left justified and a traditionally formatted outline. It's much easier to find a point in the indented outline.

Incorrect: Left-justified format

I. Most Americans unfamiliar with *El Día de Los Muertos.*

A. A holiday that honors deceased family members

B. Carlos Miller and the combination of ancient with Catholic rituals

C. "The loving dialogue between death and life"

II. Incense, skeletons, and family altar

A. Smell of incense heavy in the air

1. Copal incense sold weeks in advance

2. Elizabeth Carmichael and Chloe Sayer say incense "sanctifies the ceremony, just as it has done for many centuries"

B. Skeletons

1. Reminds us that death is the great equalizer

2. Editorial cartoons

3. Skulls are everywhere, particularly the *calaveras.*

Correct: Outline format

I. Most Americans unfamiliar with *El Día de Los Muertos*

   A. A holiday that honors deceased family members

   B. Carlos Miller and the combination of ancient with Catholic rituals

   C. "The loving dialogue between death and life"

II. Incense, skeletons, and family altar

   A. Smell of incense heavy in the air

      1. Copal incense sold weeks in advance

      2. Elizabeth Carmichael and Chloe Sayer say incense "sanctifies the ceremony, just as it has done for many centuries"

   B. Skeletons

      1. Reminds us that death is the great equalizer

      2. Editorial cartoons

      3. Skulls are everywhere, particularly the *calaveras*

Which speaking outline would you rather work from? Almost every speaker prefers the second version because the indentations make it easier to keep track of your place and to remember which is a main point and which is a subpoint.

Write clearly and legibly. Many speakers type their speaking outline on a computer because the print is more legible than their handwriting. They also use a plain, easy-to-read font, often in a larger size than normal. (Similarly, speakers who write their outline by hand print larger than they normally do.) Notice the difference between these two font sizes:

Reminds us that death is the great equalizer.

Reminds us that death is the great equalizer.

Although in most writing we wouldn't use the larger font size, in a speaking outline the bigger letters make our speech much easier to deliver, especially if we're nervous.

You need your speaking outline to remember specific information you plan to use in your speech. Many speakers add delivery cues to their outlines to help them remember to pause, make eye contact, or use a visual aid. What delivery cues do you think you would use in your next speech?

© Michael Dwyer/Stock Boston

Add cues for delivery. Add this final component of your speaking outline after you've written it up and have practiced your speech a few times. As you practice, notice where you tend to stumble, where you are too tied to the outline and forget to make eye contact, and where you move too quickly or slowly. Also notice where you have trouble with pronunciation or remembering what you want to say. Add cues to help you through these rough spots.

Cues are words and phrases like "slow down," "pause," "look up," "show visual aid," and "make eye contact." Also include cues for pronunciation of any words that are hard for you to say, especially names. And add a word or two to help you remember a complete idea or a part of a story or example you tend to forget. If you've typed your outline on a computer, handwrite your cues. If you've handwritten your speaking outline, use a different color for your cues.

Your cues will help you give your speech in the way you want and will remind you to stay connected to your audience. Be sure to keep the cues brief, so they don't distract you from your audience and your speech. Cues are especially valuable when you are up in front of an audience trying to remember several things at the same time. Practice developing a speaking outline by completing InfoTrac College Edition Exercise 11.1, "Creating a Speaking Outline," online under Student Resources for Chapter 11.

 Speech Step 11.3 / Build Your Speaking Outline

Using the template provided by your instructor or the sample at the end of this section as a guide, build a speaking outline for your next speech. Translate the complete sentences of your preparation outline into key words and phrases that will help you remember your key ideas as you give your speech.

Are you ready to build your speaking outline? You can use the following outline as a model. Katy based her speaking outline on her preparation outline, and she modified it in places to account for problems she encountered with her delivery as she practiced her speech.

(Breathe)
(Make eye contact)

Introduction

I. 3.14159265358979323846264338332795.
   (Pause)

   A. Most of you know the name of this number.

   B. In rainbows, pupils of eyes, sound waves, ripples in the water, and DNA.

   C. Nature and music understand, but the human mind cannot quite comprehend.

   D. 4000 years of curiosity.
      (Pause)
      (Make eye contact)

   E. I am talking about pi, the circle ratio.

II. Speech majors may wonder if they can survive a speech about math.

   A. My research turned up technical, historical, and fanatical information.

   B. What sparked my own interest.

III. Today I'll share with you what pi is, the history of pi, and how pi has created obsessions in people's lives.

Body

I. Pi is a symbol that most everyone is familiar with.

   A. The circumference of a circle divided by its diameter.
      (Slow)

      1. This number is also called the circle ratio.

      2. We refer to pi as 3.14 or 22/7, but it is an irrational number.

      3. Pi's mysticism is due to the fact it's never ending—or is it?

      4. Mathematicians have long puzzled about values as simple as the ratio of a circle.

   B. Pi is more than the circle ratio.

      1. According to David Blatner, who wrote The Joy of Pi, this value can be found in all fields of math and science, architecture, the arts, and even the Bible.

(continued on next page)

Commentary

At the top of her speaking outline, Katy makes notes to herself to breathe and make eye contact with her audience. She knows she'll be nervous, so she uses these notes to remind her to take a breath and look for friendly faces. She also makes a note to pause after she recites the digits of pi and before she goes on with her introduction.

Note that her introduction is an abbreviated version of her introduction in her preparation outline. She gives herself just enough cues to help her remember the four steps of her introduction.

To help her with her delivery, Katy reminds herself to pause and make eye contact here before stating the topic of her speech.

She previews her speech in point III, stating her three main points.

Katy titles the body of her speech to remind her that she is moving to the main points of her speech. This is also a visual cue to help her find her place after she makes eye contact with her audience.

She writes "slow" as she begins her first point to remind her to not rush through this information, which is new for many of her audience members.

Again, Katy gives herself enough text to remember her ideas, but not so much that she can fall prey to reading her speech to her audience.

(continued from previous page)

2. The world record for the most calculated pi to the greatest number of digits is **206 billion decimal places,** calculated by <u>Dr. Kanada at the University of Tokyo.</u>

(Pause)

Although 206 billion digits have been calculated thus far, there was a time in antiquity when there was uncertainty of the second decimal place.

II. Pi has a rich history.

A. Four thousand years ago, people could calculate pi, even without today's resources.

1. The Egyptians approximated pi as a little greater than 3.

2. The Greeks, Babylonians, Israelites, Chinese and Mesopotamians were not certain of the third decimal place.

B. The infinity of pi remained a mystery until the sixteenth century.

1. <u>Petr Beckmann,</u> a former professor of engineering at <u>Colorado University,</u> calls this period **"the age of the digit hunters, with each generation popping out more digits than the next."**

2. Keep in mind there was still no electronic calculator.

3. Famous mathematicians continued to break records.

C. In the twentieth century, the invention of the computer allowed mathematicians to calculate pi to **16,000 digits.**

What is the fascination with pi that has caused people to be both fascinated and obsessed?

(Pause)

III. As <u>Blatner</u> states, **"People have calculated, memorized, philosophized, and expounded on"** pi more than on any number in history.

A. The Chudnovsky (**Chud-nov-sky**) brothers, Gregory and David.

1. In their apartment, built a supercomputer from scrap.

2. Calculated more digits and studied the use of pi in various formulas.

B. Many other people try to memorize pi.

1. Some for sport or to be silly; others are more serious.

2. <u>Blatner</u> states that **in 1995, Hiroyuko (He-roy-uko) Goto spent over nine hours reciting 42,000 digits of pi from memory, far exceeding the world record.**

(Make eye contact)

a. This was a rare case.

b. Some people remember pi through poems, mnemonics, and songs.

c. Some memorize the digits in groups of fours.

Katy underlines the names of her sources and sets the numbers she wants to remember in bold so she'll deliver them correctly.

She makes a note to pause before her transition so she can shift her pace a little to signal she is moving to a new point. She also writes out her full transition to remind her to deliver it—she's concerned that her nervousness will cause her to skip it and jump into her second main point.

As she did in her first main point, she underlines the source and sets in bold the facts she wants to remember. Notice that she sets entire quotes in bold so she can find them easily and deliver them correctly.

Again, she writes out her transition, this time including a signal to pause after the transition before she begins her final main point.

In point III, Katy adds the phonetic spelling (spelled as they should sound) of two names so she will be sure to pronounce them correctly.

Her note to make eye contact signals her to look directly at her audience after she delivers the startling statistics of nine hours and 42,000 digits. This will help her to emphasize her point that this feat is rare but that people really are obsessed with pi.

C. The number is celebrated on Pi Day every March 14, or 3/14.

    1. The Ridiculously Enhanced Pi Page suggests gathering at 1:59 p.m.

    2. Eat pie and share stories about pi.

So ends my analysis of people's obsessions, but my earlier question was not fully answered.

Conclusion

(Slow down!)

(Make eye contact)

I. No one knows why pi has caused such a craze.

    A. What inspired the Chudnovsky brothers?

    B. What inspired me?

    C. The answer lies in the mystery and adventure.

II. The biggest influence on math over history and influences everything we do.

III. <u>William Schaaf,</u> in "The Nature and History of Pi," concludes that **"probably no symbol in mathematics has evoked as much mystery, romanticism, misconception and human interest as the number pi."**

* Adapted with permission from Katy Mazz.

When she practiced her speech, Katy noticed she tended to rush through her conclusion. So she added notes to slow down and make eye contact so she would take time to wrap up her speech.

Katy ends her speech with a quote, so she underlines the source's name and sets the quote in bold so she won't stumble when she delivers the final words of the speech.

Note Cards

Some speakers prefer note cards instead of a speaking outline. Note cards (3 x 5 or 4 x 6) are smaller and less obvious than full sheets of paper. Note cards also are sturdier and less likely to shake if a speaker's hands tremble. And they give us something to hold on to, sometimes making us feel a little more secure as we speak. If you feel more comfortable with note cards, follow these guidelines:

- Use key words and phrases and place no more than five or six lines on each card. As with speaking outlines, do not write the full text of the speech on the cards. Audiences inwardly groan when they see a tall stack of cards on the podium and expect a lengthy speech.

- Write clearly and legibly. You can glue typed portions of pages or even type directly on the card. If you handwrite your notes, use large, clear printing that is easy to read.

- Use only one side of the card. This prevents the audience from trying to read the back of a card. It also reduces the likelihood that cards will get out of order as you give your speech.

- Number each card so you can easily reorder them if they do get mixed up.

- Put cues for delivery on your cards so you can see them (use separate cards or different colors for these cues).

- When you deliver the speech, the cards should have a low profile. Try not to gesture with them, play with them, or tap them on the podium. You want the audience to pay attention to you, not the note cards.

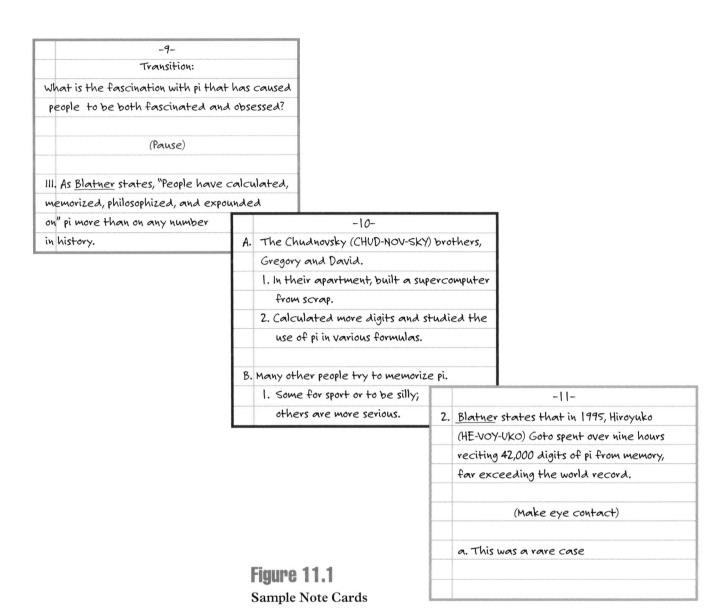

-9-

Transition:

What is the fascination with pi that has caused people to be both fascinated and obsessed?

(Pause)

III. As <u>Blatner</u> states, "People have calculated, memorized, philosophized, and expounded on" pi more than on any number in history.

-10-

A. The Chudnovsky (CHUD-NOV-SKY) brothers, Gregory and David.
   1. In their apartment, built a supercomputer from scrap.
   2. Calculated more digits and studied the use of pi in various formulas.

B. Many other people try to memorize pi.
   1. Some for sport or to be silly; others are more serious.

-11-

   2. <u>Blatner</u> states that in 1995, Hiroyuko (HE-VOY-UKO) Goto spent over nine hours reciting 42,000 digits of pi from memory, far exceeding the world record.

   (Make eye contact)

   a. This was a rare case

Figure 11.1
Sample Note Cards

Speech Step 11.4 / Check the Effectiveness of Your Speaking Outline

Make sure your ideas are outlined and easy to follow visually. Also make sure your computer-written text or handwriting is easy to read from a distance. If it isn't, adjust your printing, fonts, or type sizes so they are clear and legible. Finally, save a copy of your outline on your computer or make a few photocopies of it. If you are using Speech Builder Express, you can save up to four speech outlines for the semester.

Now practice your speech several times. As you practice, add your delivery cues. If you find your outline is too messy after several rounds of practice and adjustments, print out a new one and add only those cues that you find most helpful (or mark up one of your photocopies). Remember, your speaking outline should be legible—too many notes and changes will make it hard to read.

Chapter Summary

Outlines, shortened versions of a speech, are essential to the speaking process because they help you organize your ideas. They are a synopsis of your speech, displaying your main points, subpoints, and sub-subpoints. Students of public speaking use two kinds of outlines: the preparation outline and the speaking outline.

The preparation outline is the outline you use to prepare a speech. It contains your main points, subpoints, and sub-subpoints, written out in complete sentences. The preparation outline also includes the title of your speech, the specific purpose, and the thesis statement. It outlines your introduction and conclusion, labels each part of your speech clearly, and includes your connectives as well as a list of the research sources you plan to cite in the speech.

When you prepare the preparation outline, follow several guidelines that will help you with the clarity, organization, and delivery of your ideas. First, use complete sentences and not key words. Second, label the introduction, body, and conclusion clearly on the outline. Third, use a consistent pattern of symbolization and indentation on the preparation outline. Fourth, check for balance and make sure the information you want to present is weighted equally. Finally, as with every step of the speech process, review your preparation outline to see if you've kept an audience-centered focus in the speech.

The second type of outline you will prepare for a speech is the speaking outline. You use this document when you deliver your speech. Speaking outlines contain key words and phrases rather than full sentences, ensuring that you will deliver your speech in a conversational manner. There are three guidelines to follow when you develop your speaking outline. First, use key words and phrases as well as an outline format. Second, be sure the speaking outline is clear and legible. Finally, add cues for delivery after you have practiced with the outline several times.

Some speakers prefer note cards to speaking outlines. Note cards are smaller and sturdier than a full sheet of paper. If you prefer to speak from note cards, remember several things. Use key words and phrases rather than the full text. Write clearly and legibly and use only one side of the card. Number the cards and include cues for delivery on the cards. Finally, keep a low profile with the cards so the audience will pay attention to you and not your note cards.

Outlines are an essential step in the speech making process. They are excellent tools for organizing your ideas and improving your delivery. Take time to develop both the preparation outline and the speaking outline so you are confident and ready to contribute to the public dialogue in meaningful and audience-centered ways.

Taking the time to carefully outline your speech and prepare a speaking outline or notes will ensure you give a speech that is well researched, solidly constructed, and audience centered.

Invitation to Public Speaking Online

After reading this chapter, use your CD-ROM and the *Invitation to Public Speaking* Web site to review the following concepts, answer the review questions, and complete the suggested activities.

Key Concepts

preparation outline (250)
subpoints (252)

sub-subpoints (252)
coordination (253)

subordination (257)
speaking outline (263)

Review Questions

1. Imagine you're going to give a speech describing your day from breakfast through dinner. Prepare a preparation outline for this speech. Make sure your outline includes the title of your speech, your specific purpose and thesis statement, an introduction, four main points with at least two subpoints per main point, connectives, and a conclusion.

2. Identify and discuss the tips for writing a preparation outline. What benefits are gained from following these suggestions?

3. Using the preparation outline from question 1, construct a speaking outline for your speech on your day. Add delivery cues as needed. Discuss the differences between your preparation outline and your speaking outline. What are the strengths and weaknesses of each?

4. Identify and discuss the tips for writing a speaking outline. What benefits are gained from following these suggestions?

The *Invitation to Public Speaking* Web Site

The *Invitation to Public Speaking* Web site features the review questions about the Web sites suggested on pages 250, 251, and 255, the interactive activities suggested on pages 251, 254, 255, and 259 and the InfoTrac College Edition exercise suggested on page 266. You can access this site via your CD-ROM or at http://www.wadsworth.com/product/griffin. To access Speech Builder Express in order to complete Speech Step 11.2, you will need the username and password included under "Speech Builder Express" on your CD-ROM.

Web Links

11.1: Scared Speechless (250)
11.2: Preparing and Using Outlines (251)
11.3: MLA Works Cited and APA References Pages (255)

11.4: Adding Connectives (255)
Purpose: To add connectives to an outline.

11.5: Outlining Main Points and Subpoints (259)
Purpose: To outline the main points and subpoints of your speech.

Interactive Activities

11.1: Outlining the Introduction (251)
Purpose: To create an outline of an introduction.

11.2: Creating a Title (251)
Purpose: To create a title for your speech.

11.3: Outlining the Conclusion (254)
Purpose: To create an outline of the conclusion.

 InfoTrac College Edition Exercise

11.1: Creating a Speaking Outline (266)
Purpose: To learn how to write a speaking outline.

Speech Interactive on the *Invitation to Public Speaking* CD-ROM

The following video clips of speeches, referenced in this chapter, are included under Speech Interactive on your *Invitation to Public Speaking* CD-ROM. After you have watched the clips, click on "Critique" to answer the questions for analysis.

Video Clip 1: Introduction: Katy Mazz (252). Watch Katy's introduction. Compare what she says with what she wrote in her preparation outline. In her speech, does she clearly include all the components of the introduction she outlined?

Video Clip 2: Hillary Rodham Clinton's "Women's Rights Are Human Rights" (259). Watch the Hillary Rodham Clinton's address to the United Nations Fourth Conference on Women on September 9, 1995. Create a preparation outline of the speech. When you are finished, evaluate the degree to which the speech had a distinct introduction, body, and conclusion. Were the main points balanced? How was the speech audience centered? How does an outline help you make these judgments?

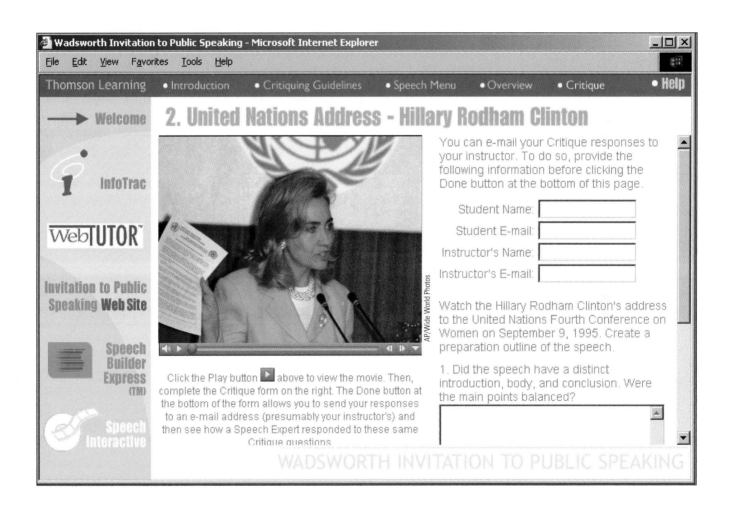

Chapter Twelve

Language

In this chapter you will learn to

Use clear and accurate language in your speeches

Use language that is culturally inclusive and gender inclusive

Explain the differences between spoken and written language

Describe at least two ways to use language to create memorable images

Describe at least five ways to use language to create a pleasing rhythm

We often take for granted the ability to use language to communicate experience. I have never visited Barrow, Alaska. However, my husband and two of his brothers have lived there. From their stories, from pictures, and from the things I have read, I know what the Arctic Ocean looks like when frozen. I know that a man's beard becomes covered with frost and icicles when he walks to the store in December. . . . I know that "Joe-the-water-boy" used to deliver desalinated ocean water in a truck with a broken window, wearing only a T-shirt and pants, and somehow he did not freeze. . . . These, along with most of the things I claim to know, I know not as a result of direct experience but because of language, of symbols.

—Ann Gill, *Rhetoric and Human Understanding*, 1994[1]

language
System of verbal or gestural symbols a community uses to communicate with one another.

Central to the speech making process is **language,** the system of verbal or gestural symbols a community uses to communicate with one another, to which the opening quote of this chapter refers. However, we often take language for granted, failing to realize how much we know because of language rather than direct experience. Communication scholars agree that language, the systematic code of a group of people, is central to establishing and maintaining societies. Scholars who study this process are sometimes called *symbolic interactionists.* To read about the theory of symbolic interaction and how language influences our experiences, go to http://www.acsu.buffalo.edu/~reymers/id-1.html.

In the public dialogue, language allows us to share our thoughts, question the ideas of others, and invite our audiences to consider our positions. In Chapter 3, we discussed language as it relates to listening. In this chapter, we explore language as it relates to speaking. Specifically, we discuss the ambiguity of language, culture and language, gender and language, the importance of accurate use of language, the importance of language to public speaking, and several of the linguistic devices public speakers use to create memorable images.

Language Is Ambiguous

If a speaker never utters a word but instead communicates through mime and gesture, how well do you think you would understand the speech? What if a speaker and an audience do not share a common language? Could you grasp the intricacies of the message? Obviously, understanding others when we do not share a common language is difficult. But if we share a common language with our audience, shouldn't communication be easier? Isn't it enough to use the same labels for things to communicate a message? How much attention do we need to give to the language in our speeches if we speak the same language as our audience? Consider the semantic triangle of meaning, created in 1923 by C. K. Ogden and I. A. Richards,[2] as shown in Figure 12.1:

On the left corner of the triangle is the **symbol,** the word or phrase spoken by the speaker. For example, when a speaker says "freedom," as did Martin Luther King Jr. in his "I Have a Dream" speech, or "AIDS" as did Mary Fisher in her speech to the Republican National Convention, those words are the symbols. On

symbol
Word or phrase spoken by a speaker.

Figure 12.1
Semantic Triangle of Meaning

the right corner of the triangle is the **referent,** the object, concept, or event the symbol represents. The referent is the actual experience of freedom or the disease known as AIDS. You might also think of this as the denotative definition of a word or event, as discussed in Chapter 7. This is the socially agreed upon definition of a word or the actual object or event named by the speaker.

At the top of the triangle is the **thought,** or **reference.** This is the memory and past experiences audience members have with an object, concept, or event. When a speaker offers a word or phrase, audience members recall their own experiences with that word or phrase. These are our connotative definitions (Chapter 7), our personalized, subjective interpretations of words, objects, or events. So the symbols "freedom" and "AIDS" call to mind a variety of connotative experiences and memories for the members of an audience. Given our diverse master statuses and standpoints (Chapter 5), as well as our unique personal experiences, we all have different memories and past experiences with freedom and AIDS.

The semantic triangle of meaning shows us that even though all the audience members might understand the symbol and even have a similar referent for it, they do not have the same thoughts, or references, for the symbol. This difference is what makes language ambiguous. The experience of freedom or AIDS (or any referent) differs among people and groups, depending on their culture, geographical location, and master status. For some, freedom is a given. For others, freedom is something that has been fought for over the centuries. Similarly, AIDS means different things to different people depending on their sexual orientation, religion, and personal experiences with the disease.

When speakers forget that words do not mean the same thing for everyone, they unintentionally create ambiguity for their audiences. When they forget that people may share symbols, but not experiences with those symbols, they run the risk of confusing or alienating their audiences. One way to clear up some of this ambiguity is to use words that are more concrete. A **concrete word** is a word that refers to a tangible object—a person, place, or thing. For example, rather than talking about politicians, speak about specific politicians: name them or their political parties so your audience knows exactly which politicians you are referring to. This will help you avoid **abstract words,** words that refer to ideas or concepts but not to specific objects.

As you think about whether the words you will use in your speech are concrete or abstract, diagram them on Ogden and Richards's semantic triangle of meaning. Ask yourself whether the words you use are as clear as you think they are. If they aren't, take time in your speech to define them for your audience. Review the discussion of definitions in Chapter 7 to familiarize yourself with some of the ways speakers can define words for their audiences to eliminate the ambiguity created by connotations. To read more about I. A. Richards, co-creator of the semantic triangle of meaning, and his contributions to our study of language and meaning, go to http://www.eng.as.fvsu.edu/richard.htm.

referent
Object, concept, or event a symbol represents.

thought, or reference
Memory and past experiences that audience members have with an object, concept, or event.

concrete word
Word that refers to a tangible object—a person, place, or thing.

abstract word
Word that refers to ideas or concepts but not to specific objects.

Language with multiple meanings is an integral part of rap music. Rap artist Missy "Misdemeanor" Elliot is particularly well known for challenging the meaning of certain words in some of her songs. You probably won't be rapping in your speech, but what words would you use that have multiple meanings? Why would you use them and how could you clarify them?

AP/Wide World Photos

idiom
Fixed, distinctive expression whose meaning is not indicated by its individual words.

WEB SITE

Language and Culture

In its most basic sense, language is an organized and learned symbol system. It is used to represent human experiences and to transmit messages. Language allows us to describe, label, and share events with others and to understand each other's perspectives and experiences. However, people in different cultures have different life experiences. As a result, different cultures name and define the world differently.

For example, in American Sign Language, which is a visual rather than spoken language, signs often are subtly altered to reflect the visual aspects of objects and events. The concepts "modest home" and "mansion" begin with the same basic sign for "home" but differ in their execution. In contrast, in spoken English, words are only occasionally modified to emphasize some aspect of appearance (for example, "huuuge house"). Usually, to emphasize some visual aspect, we add more words to the description or choose a different word.

Subcultures, or groups within a larger culture that share its language, may also use the language differently. For example, the language of rap music, which has roots in the African American tradition of "signifying," has clear differences from standard English. Signifying is governed by its own rules of grammar, semantics, and syntax. It allows people to make statements that have double, and often even multiple, meanings that are not understood by people outside the subculture.[3] The topics of rap music, the words it uses, and the ways those words are put together and delivered reflect these multiple meanings, as well as the experiences and perspectives of members of this subculture.

The culturally bound nature of language requires us to be aware of obvious, as well as subtle, differences. As speakers, either we can adapt our language choices to the culture of the people we are addressing, or, if we do not know their culture well enough to do so, we can acknowledge the differences as we speak. If we can identify which of our words our audience might not understand because of cultural or regional differences, then we can offer clarification for those words and promote understanding rather than confusion.

Idioms are especially difficult for people of other cultures to understand. An **idiom** is a fixed, distinctive expression whose meaning is not indicated by its individual words. "I was in stitches" and "they kept me in the dark" are examples of English idioms. In American Sign Language, "the train is gone" is an idiom that means you missed the joke or the heart of the matter. We often use idioms without realizing it: "I don't get it," "it's way over my head," and "go figure" are three common examples. Idioms can be especially difficult for nonnative speakers. To be fully understood, we must "unpack the meanings" (another idiom) of potentially confusing phrases and words. To learn more about some of the idioms English speakers use, complete Interactive Activity 12.1, "Exploring Idioms," online under Student Resources for Chapter 12 at the *Invitation to Public Speaking* Web site.

Table 12.1

Appropriate Labels for People of Different Cultures

Ethnicity	African American or black
	Asian American, or identify the country of heritage: Chinese American, Japanese American, Korean American. (Note that "Oriental" refers to an art object, like a rug, and not a person.)
	Hispanic, Latina or Latino, or identify the country of heritage: Cuban American, Mexican American
	Native American or American Indian, or identify the specific nation: Sioux, Navajo, Hopi. (Note that just "Indian" more often refers to people who come from India.)
	White, European American
Physical ability	A person with [name of disability]
	A person living with [name of disability]
	A person who has [name of disability]
Age	Boy or girl (a person 18 years old or younger)
	Young woman or young man (junior high or high school age)
	Man or woman (a person 19 years old or older)
	Older person (rather than *elderly*)
Sexual orientation	Bisexual man or woman
	Gay man or lesbian
	Straight or heterosexual man or woman
	Transgendered person
	Transvestite

Cultural differences can interfere with communication in other ways too. If we do not know how a cultural group prefers to identify itself, we may accidentally offend some members of our audience. Table 12.1 will help familiarize you with some of the preferred labels for different cultural groups. Because these labels change as society changes, try to stay current with the ways different groups label themselves. Two good sources of guidelines for these labels are Random House at http://www.randomhouse.com/words/language/avoid_guide.html and the American Heritage Book of English Usage at http://www.bartleby.com/64/6.html.

Although the use of appropriate labels sometimes is called "politically correct speech," appropriate labels really are about respecting others. Groups name themselves because they wish to emphasize aspects of their lives that are important to them. Speakers who are audience centered are aware of how cultures and subcultures name themselves and the characteristics or histories they are honoring. We show respect for our audience when we use appropriate labels.

Language and Gender

In Chapter 3, you learned that it's important to use gender-neutral language so your speeches address both women and men. To help you do this, consider the guidelines in Table 12.2 for translating some common gender-biased language into gender-inclusive language. These guidelines are from the American Psychological Association. They can be found in print in the *Publication Manual of the American Psychological Association* or online at http://www.library.uq.edu.au/training/citation/apa.html.

Table 12.2

Guidelines for Gender-Inclusive Language

PROBLEMATIC	PREFERRED
Man, mankind	People, humanity, human beings, humankind, human species
Man a project	Staff a project, hire personnel, employ staff
Manpower	Work force, personnel, workers, human resources, staff
Man's search for knowledge	The search for knowledge
Chairman	Chair, chairperson, moderator, discussion leader, facilitator
Foreman, mailman	Supervisor or superintendent, postal worker or mail carrier
Salesmanship	Selling ability
Sportsmanship	Teamwork, cooperation, conduct, respect for others, graciousness
He, his, him (universal "he" as a pronoun for a noun that refers to both women and men)	They (used with plural nouns), she or he, his or her, him or her
Dear Sir:	Dear Sir or Madam, To whom it may concern, Dear members of the _____ Committee (name the specific group)
Mr. and Mrs. John Smith	John and Jane Smith
Doctors and their wives	Doctors and their partners or significant others
Woman doctor, lady lawyer, woman driver	Doctor or physician; lawyer or attorney; driver

Increasingly, speakers are using gender-inclusive words and phrases in their speaking. In his speech to the American people after the terrorist attack on the World Trade Center in 2001, President George W. Bush referred to the "business men and women, mothers and fathers . . . " who lost their lives in the attack, acknowledging the professional as well as the personal roles of the women and men who died. Using gender-neutral and gender-inclusive language reflects your awareness of both men and women as valued and active participants in the world. To test your skills at translating gender-biased language into gender-neutral language, complete Interactive Activity 12.2, "Choosing Gender-Neutral Language," online under Student Resources for Chapter 12 at the *Invitation to Public Speaking* Web site.

WEB SITE

Language and Accuracy

Consider the following lists of words:

persecution	prosecution
simple	simplistic
patriarchal	patriarchic
good	well

What are the differences between the words in each column? If someone is *persecuted*, is that the same as being *prosecuted*? If you look in the dictionary, you'll see that to be persecuted is to be subjected to cruel or unfair treatment, whereas to be prosecuted is to be tried in a court of law for a criminal offense. The words mean different things, yet they often are confused. Similarly, many speakers like to add "-istic" to the end of words because they think it makes a concept sound more complex. Yet *simple* means easy, straightforward, or effortless, and *simplistic* means ignoring complexities. Although you should be able to find *patriarchal* in the dictionary, can you find *patriarchic*? It's not a word in the English language, although speakers sometimes use it, confusing it with *patriarchal*. How about *good* and *well*? Do you know the difference between the two? Does your favorite music group play good or do they play well? (They should play well and sound good.)

Knowing the correct definitions and usage of words is important because accurate language affects not only your meaning but also your credibility. For a list of several words that speakers typically have difficulty with, go to the Oxford Dictionary Web site at http://www.askoxford.com/betterwriting/classicerrors/confused/.

Here are three tips to improve the accuracy of your language. First, check the definitions of the words you are using. When a word is central to the meaning of a sentence or a claim, look it up in the dictionary (in print or online) to be sure you have the correct word. To look up words online, go to Merriam-Webster Online at http://www.m-w.com/. This site features a dictionary, a thesaurus, and a variety of other features to help you use words correctly. Looking up words can save you considerable embarrassment. In a commemorative speech, a student described her sister, saying, "She's incredible: she's kind, generous, and always thinks of others; she's notorious for this in my hometown." Although her sister was remarkable, "notorious" means well known for undesirable features, not desirable ones.

Second, if your use of language is not as strong as you'd like, work with someone who has strong language skills as you develop and practice your speech. Most colleges and universities have writing and tutoring labs, with people ready to help students with clarity and grammar. (Ask your instructor about resources available

Keeping a dictionary or a thesaurus near you when you read is an excellent way to increase your vocabulary and learn the correct meanings of words. Think about three words you've heard today whose meanings you were unsure of. Look them up in the dictionary.

on your campus if you aren't familiar with them.) If you take time to seek out this kind of help, you will find that not only will your speeches be clearer and your credibility enhanced, but your writing will improve as well.

Third, study the language. American civil rights leader Malcolm X copied the dictionary word by word to improve his language skills, but there are other ways to improve yours. Read more books, magazines, and newspapers; take courses that focus on language skills; and practice with language and vocabulary workbooks from the library, bookstores, and teaching supply stores. You can even study a foreign language, which will teach you about your own language in the process. Studying the language systematically not only will increase your vocabulary but also help you develop your arguments and ideas more clearly. You can also improve your skills by completing InfoTrac College Edition Exercise 12.1, "Learning New Words," online under Student Resources for Chapter 12.

Speech Step 12.1 / Evaluate the Inclusiveness and Accuracy of the Language in Your Speech

Using the preparation outline of your next speech (Chapter 11), identify the words and phrases you will use to communicate your ideas. Diagram the key-words of your main points on the semantic triangle of meaning. Do you think any of the words you plan to use may have referents other than those you intend? How will you define these words? Do you think any of the language you plan to use in your main points may confuse audience members of a different culture? How will you clarify that language? How gender inclusive is the language you plan to use? Finally, check the dictionary to be sure your language is accurate.

Language and Public Speaking

Because of the complexities of language, we may be tempted to write out our speeches beforehand to get every word right. And then we may be tempted to read the speech to our audience to avoid the ambiguities and errors discussed in this chapter. However, when we speak, we want to use language meant to be spoken, not read. Writing out a speech is appropriate only when speaking from a manuscript (see Chapter 13). Even though every speaker makes a mistake now and again, with care and attention to language, you can learn to address your audience with clarity and vividness most of the time.

oral style
Speaking style that reflects the spoken rather than the written word.

The most effective speakers use what is called an **oral style,** a style that reflects the spoken rather than the written word. They "talk" their speeches rather than read them. The differences between the spoken word and the written word are significant: spoken language is more interactive, more casual, and more repetitive than written language.[4]

Spoken Language Is More Interactive

When we write to someone, we produce a steady stream of words. However, when we speak to others, we interact with them: we make adjustments as we speak, monitor their interest and understanding, and we ask or respond to questions. When we speak publicly, our language reflects the shifts, pauses, and adjustments we make for our audience. We carry on a conversation with our audience in ways that we do not when we write to someone.

Former Texas governor Ann Richards is well known for her homespun oral style. (Use your *Invitation to Public Speaking* CD-ROM to watch a video clip of Ann Richards under Speech Interactive, Chapter 7.) Think about the language you plan to use in your next speech. What steps will you take to use an oral rather than written style?

AP/Wide World Photos

Our nonverbal communication also reflects this interactive mode. Our expressions and gestures reinforce our words, giving spoken language a different tone than written language. Written prose doesn't lend itself to this spontaneous nonverbal interaction. Speakers who read written-out speeches usually sound like they're delivering something the audience should be reading rather than listening to.

Spoken Language Is More Casual

Written language tends to be more formal than spoken language, although there are exceptions. If you open most any book or magazine and try to talk the text, you will notice that the words sound a little formal. Written and spoken languages differ in formality because writing tends to be more rule governed than speaking. When we speak, we use more contractions (for example, "can't" instead of "cannot") and colloquialisms ("No way!" instead of "That simply isn't possible"). We also run our words together when we speak (we read, "I'm going to ask" but say, "I'm gonna ask"). A speaker who delivers a speech in a written style sounds more distant and formal than one who talks to the audience. Using your *Invitation to Public Speaking* CD-ROM, watch the video clip of Brandi under Speech Interactive. Note the casual style of speaking she uses.

Brandi Lafferty

Spoken Language Is More Repetitive

In oral cultures, the narrative (story) form is the primary way to pass along information. Because information is not stored in writing, repetition is necessary to help audiences in oral cultures remember the stories. Because public speaking audiences also need help remembering what they hear, public speakers use more repetition than writers do.

Public speakers intentionally repeat main ideas and arguments. They summarize their main points and restate important arguments in order to help their audiences remember them. Recall from Chapters 9 and 10 that in your speeches you present an overview of your ideas (introduction), state those ideas (body), and then summarize them (conclusion). You also use repetitive tools like transitions, internal summaries, and internal previews to help audiences remember your ideas. This repetitive quality, so necessary to public speaking, is found less often in many forms of written communication. The need for repetition reinforces the importance of speaking rather than reading to audiences and sets spoken language apart from written in this third way.

We can encourage an exchange of ideas in the public dialogue through our style of language, as well as through the images we create. For practice identifying the differences between written and oral language, complete InfoTrac College Edition Exercise 12.2, "Comparing Written and Spoken Language," online under Student Resources for Chapter 12.

Language, Imagery, and Rhythm

Because much of what we know comes to us through language rather than direct experience, we want to pay careful attention to the images we create with our words. As you put together the final touches of your speeches, listen to your words and phrases. Do they inspire you? Do they create a picture in your mind of what you are describing? Are they pleasing to your ear? Do they make you want to hear more? If your language draws you into your speech, then it likely will draw in your audience. By carefully choosing the words you use in your speech, you can use language to create rich images and sensations.

In this section you will read about a number of verbal techniques you can use to draw your listeners into your ideas. These tools can be divided into two general categories: language that creates memorable imagery and language that creates a pleasing rhythm.

Speakers often use language to create powerful visual images for their audiences. Describe this 1959 Chevrolet Corvette using simile, metaphor, and personification. For example, how would you describe what it felt like to drive this car on a scenic highway? What words would you use to describe, say, excitement or apprehension about driving such an expensive car?

simile
Figure of speech that makes an explicit comparison of two things, using the words *like* or *as*.

Language That Creates Memorable Imagery

Our language can call to mind engaging sights, smells, tastes, and sounds. With language, we can bring an idea to life and make abstractions seem concrete. Figures of speech, such as similes, metaphors, and personification, can create powerful images for our audiences. Powerful images are often what make our speeches appealing, interesting, and memorable. In the following discussion, notice how these devices blend with the words around them. They call up the images without calling attention to themselves.

Simile. When we use **similes**, we are making an explicit comparison of two things that uses the words *like* or *as*. Although the two things we are comparing are different, they are similar in a way that we want to highlight in order to make a specific point. Consider the following examples of similes from speeches given by Patrick and Haley:

> Although he stands only five feet ten to my six feet two, *my father seems like a giant* to me, and probably always will. But he's a gentle giant, for the most part, and I look up to him and appreciate many of the lessons he taught me.

> From the time you first begin to consume it, the sugar in your body scratches the lining of the arteries leading to your heart. *The process is like sandpaper on wood,* and it never reverses itself.

Through similes, Patrick emphasized his respect for his father, and Haley dramatized the hazards of consuming sugar. Patrick could simply have said he respected his father, and Haley's statement that sugar scratches the lining of the heart was enough to make her point. However, by using similes, their audiences could "see" Patrick's respect for his father and Haley's description of the damage sugar does to arteries.

Amy

The use of language devices in a speech can send a more powerful message to your audience than simply stating the facts. Language devices create images and inspire audiences. One problem I came across when writing my speech is that different people can get different connotations from an image. For example, I used the simile "her spirit ran like the stream." I meant for this image to show her strength, but someone else might have taken it to mean flexibility, as in following the current of the stream. But when used carefully, language devices are great for illustrating your meanings within the speech. These language devices also can carry over into your English classes, especially when it comes to creative writing. Once you get a handle on them, language devices can definitely help your audience relate to you.

Metaphor. Aristotle described a command of metaphors as "the greatest thing by far." A **metaphor** is a comparison between two things that describes one thing as being something else. The word *metaphor* comes from a Greek term meaning "transference."[5] When we use metaphors, we are transferring the qualities of one thing to another, illustrating their similarities.

Although many metaphors create associations that are obvious (for example, "the war on drugs"), some are more subtle, such as Guatemalan human rights advocate Rigoberta Menchú's "we are not myths of the past, ruins in the jungle, or zoos."[6] In the "war on drugs," the comparison is explicit—the government is responding to drug trafficking in a warlike manner. In contrast, Menchú's comparison of the Mayan people to myths, ruins, and zoos is more subtle. Menchú is arguing for the rights of the Mayan people today by comparing them to what they are not. In both examples, the metaphors make the comparisons memorable. Two student speakers, Silas and Brooke, used metaphors quite successfully in the following ways:

> Melanoma is one of the most common cancers in Americans between the ages of 25 and 29. If it is caught early and removed, a person lives a normal life. Well, maybe it's normal. According to Matthew Brady, now 19, after summers on his boogie board and at the age of only 14, "they *cut a steak out of my back.*"

> As I ate, my mouth got hotter and hotter . . . and hotter. I took a sip of water. It kept right on heating up. The source of this *fire in my mouth*? The fairly well-known habanero chili.

metaphor
A figure of speech that makes a comparison between two things by describing one thing as being something else.

George W. Bush's 2001 inaugural address contained many metaphors (like most inaugural addresses). He described America's "faith in freedom and democracy" with the following metaphors:

> Through much of the last century, America's faith in freedom and democracy was *a rock in a raging sea*. Now it is *a seed upon the wind, taking root* in many nations.

President Bush also used several similes and metaphors in his address to Congress on September 20, 2001. To assess the effectiveness of his language choices in this speech, complete Interactive Activity 12.3, "Using Similes and Metaphors," online under Student Resources for Chapter 12 at the *Invitation to Public Speaking* Web site.

WEB SITE

mixed metaphor
Metaphor that makes illogical comparisons between two or more things.

Like similes, metaphors bring ideas to life with rich associations and comparisons. However, they can go astray sometimes in awkward ways. A **mixed metaphor** is a metaphor that makes illogical comparisons between two or more things. When speakers mix their metaphors, they begin with one metaphor and then switch to another midstream. The confusion, if not humor, that results from mixed metaphors is apparent in the following examples[7]:

> It appears as though the *Achilles' heel* of the Eagles' defense is about to *rear its ugly head*.

> I wanted all my ducks in a row, so if we did get into a posture, we could pretty much *slam-dunk this thing and put it to bed*.

In the first example, the speaker asks the audience to associate the metaphor of an Achilles' heel (a weak point) with the rearing of an ugly head. However, heels cannot raise their heads. In the second example, the speaker associates a slam dunk (a shot in basketball) with putting something to bed (finishing a task). Combined with the metaphor of ducks in a row (everything in order) and a posture (a bluff), the audience has trouble deciding which image to focus on. In short, mixed metaphors bring together too many or contradictory associations and are difficult to visualize.

personification
A figure of speech that attributes human characteristics to animals, objects, or concepts.

Personification. When we use **personification**, we attribute human characteristics to animals, objects, or concepts. Assigning sight, speech, hearing, thought, emotion, action, or sensation to objects (such as trees, rocks, buildings) or to concepts (such as love, bravery, sadness) is personification. "Confusion spoke," "the trees listen," and "the voice of democracy" are examples of personification. In the following examples, notice how easy it is to accept the traits assigned to things we don't typically see as having these human qualities:

> My *bones are tired*. Not tired of struggling, but tired of oppression. ("Queen Mother Moore," civil rights leader)[8]

With personification, the ideas expressed here come to life. Bones, which can break or weaken, can't become tired, although the image of deep fatigue stays with the audience long after the words are said.

In a speech about losing his job, Carl used personification to describe the letter he received and his reaction to it:

> Those *words just sat there staring* at me. *They wouldn't leave* and *they wouldn't explain themselves*. "You're fired," *they said*. And *they refused* to tell me anything else.

The image Carl created conveys the shock of being fired without explanation or recourse. Personification, in sum, can call up vivid images and sensations for your audience.

Look again at the language you plan to use in your speech. Does it follow an oral or a written style? (Hint: If you have written out your speech word for word, it probably follows a written rather than an oral style.) Adjust your language so it reflects the oral style necessary for effective public speaking. Now select one of your main points. What similes or metaphors could you use to describe some aspect of that point? Is there some element of that main point you could personify? Select two of your ideas and incorporate them into your speech.

Language That Creates a Pleasing Rhythm

We can strengthen the images we create with our words by focusing on the way the words sound when put together. When we think of rhythm, we may think of poetry, music, or children's stories, not speeches. However, some of the most effective public speakers in history are the ones who presented strong ideas rhythmically. Consider Jesse Jackson, John F. Kennedy, and Barbara Jordan. These speakers are all known for their powerful ideas and their rhythmic speeches. In speeches, **rhythm** is the arrangement of words into patterns so the sounds of the words together enhance the meaning of a phrase. Parallelism, repetition, alliteration, and antithesis are four ways to emphasize your ideas with rhythm.

Parallelism. When we arrange related words so they are balanced or related sentences so they have identical structures, we are using **parallelism**. The notion that "*beauty is* as *beauty does*" is an example of a simple but effective use of parallelism. A more complex example was expressed by former Massachusetts congressman Joe Moakley: "*It is never* a crime to speak up for the poor, the helpless, or the ill; *it is never* a crime to tell the truth; *it is never* a crime to demand justice; *it is never* a crime to teach people their rights; *it is never* a crime to struggle for a just peace. *It is never* a crime. *It is always* a duty." Because of its rhythm and symmetry, parallelism helps an audience remember a statement. Here are other examples of parallelism:

> The denial of human rights *anywhere* is a threat to human rights *everywhere*. Injustice *anywhere* is a threat to justice *everywhere*. (Jesse Jackson, civil rights leader)

> *Rich and poor, intelligent and ignorant, wise and foolish, virtuous and vicious, man and woman*—it is ever the same, each soul must depend wholly on itself. (Elizabeth Cady Stanton, nineteenth-century suffragist)

Repetition. When we use **repetition** in a speech, we repeat keywords or phrases at the beginnings or endings of sentences or clauses. President Franklin D. Roosevelt's "I see one-third of the nation ill-housed, ill-clad, and ill-nourished" is an example of repetition. The repetition of the word ill creates a rhythm that helped his audience remember his claims. Representative Barbara Jordan used repetition in her 1976 keynote address to the Democratic National Convention:

> *We are a people* in a quandary about the present. *We are a people* in search of our future. *We are a people* in search of a national community.

In the next example, educator Marva N. Collins used both repetition and rhyme to create a memorable message for the young people in her audience:

Advertisers often use personification to sell products. What language would you use to personify a box of sugary cereal for kids? Can you think of an opportunity when you might use personification in your own speech?

rhythm
Arrangement of words into patterns so the sounds of the words together enhance the meaning of a phrase.

parallelism
Arrangement of related words so they are balanced or of related sentences so they have identical structures.

repetition
Repetition of keywords or phrases at the beginnings or endings of sentences or clauses to create rhythm.

Thousands will tell you that it cannot be done, *thousands will tell you* that you will fail. But only you, child, will know how far you can sail. So say to yourself, "I shall not fail."

Repetition is one of the easier verbal techniques for beginning speakers to use. Consider these examples from student speeches:

Let me talk about my experiences as a first-year teacher. I'll tell you now, I loved it, but *I was not prepared.* For the endless energy of the students? *I was not prepared.* The demands on my time outside the classroom? *Not prepared.* Angry parents? *Not prepared.* Learning disabilities? *Not prepared.* Language differences? Personal tragedies? Trusting faces staring up at me? You got it: *I was not prepared.*

As students, we need to respond. *As students, we need* to care. *As students, we need* to step forward and share our positions.

Because repetition reinforces messages rhythmically, they stay with us long after the speech is over.

alliteration
Repetition of a particular sound in a sentence or a phrase.

mnemonic device
Rhyme, phrase, or other verbal device that makes information easier to remember.

Alliteration. **Alliteration** is the repetition of a particular sound in a sentence or a phrase. We can use alliteration to emphasize an idea, to create a humorous tone, or as a mnemonic device (a **mnemonic device** is a rhyme, phrase, or other verbal device that makes information easier to remember).[9] Alliteration is not just for children's rhyming games (such as Peter Piper and his pickled peppers). Consider these common phrases: the Wild West, feast or famine, the ballot or the bullet, compassionate conservatism, strong and silent, and the Million Man March. These phrases have become familiar, in part because of their alliteration. When used sparingly, alliteration can give a rhythm to your words that audiences find engaging and easy to remember. Consider these examples of alliteration and the ways the repetition of sounds makes it easier to remember the ideas in a speech.

We are in a transitional period right now—*fascinating and exhilarating* times, learning to adjust to *changes and the choices* we—men and women—are facing. (Former first lady Barbara Bush)

Now is the time for *repentance, restitution, and reconciliation,* and I honor those three functions in the light of the great ethnic, racial diversity in our world today. (Maggie Kuhn, founder of the Gray Panthers)

antithesis
Placement of words and phrases in contrast or opposition to one another.

Antithesis. The word *antithesis* means "opposite." In a speech, you use **antithesis** when you place words and phrases in contrast or opposition to one another. One of the most famous uses of antithesis comes from John F. Kennedy's inaugural address in 1961: "And so, my fellow Americans: Ask *not what your country can do for you*—ask *what you can do for your country.*" With this simple phrase he caused those listening to think about their personal responsibility for preserving the freedoms many Americans had begun to take for granted. Kennedy offered a second example of antithesis in that same speech:

Let us never negotiate out of fear. But let us never fear to negotiate.

Antithesis is perhaps more complex than alliteration and parallelism, but it still is used with great success. As you put together the ideas in your speeches, see if you might be able to phrase them using antithesis. Here's how Werner used antithesis in his speech:

Some say that developmentally disabled people only *take from us,* but I say they actually *give to us.*

A number of other speakers have used antithesis with great impact:

We can do no *great things*—only *small things* with great love. (Mother Teresa, humanitarian and Nobel Peace Prize laureate)

Words cannot *be remote from reality* when they *create reality.* (John Cowper Powys, English novelist)

One of the things about equality is not just that you *be treated equally to a man,* but that you *treat yourself equally to the way you treat a man.* (Marlo Thomas, actress and equal rights activist)

If we don't teach our children *peace,* somebody else will teach them *violence.* (Colman McCarthy, journalist and founder of the Center for Teaching Peace)

Antithesis draws an audience into your speech, adding vitality and a pleasant tempo to your ideas. To see a particularly accomplished speaker's use of effective imagery, use your *Invitation to Public Speaking* CD-ROM to watch a video clip of Martin Luther King Jr.'s "I Have a Dream" speech, included under Speech Interactive.

These seven devices for engaging your audience in your ideas—simile, metaphor, personification, parallelism, repetition, alliteration, and antithesis—can help you create memorable images and ideas. Using your *Invitation to Public Speaking* CD-ROM, watch the video clip of Stacey under Speech Interactive. Note how she uses some of these devices in her speech. Used thoughtfully, they can help your audience recall sensations and experiences and remember your ideas. Keep in mind the importance of respecting cultural differences as well as including both women and men as you use these linguistic devices. Similarly, remember that language can be ambiguous, and your linguistic devices should clarify your ideas, not confuse your audience. If you create appropriate and engaging images, you will enhance the public dialogue.

John F. Kennedy is renowned for using eloquent language in his speeches. One of the techniques he's most known for is his use of antithesis. For your next speech, try to incorporate at least one example of antithesis.

List the subpoints of your speech. For each point, write at least three sentences that express these points with language that creates a pleasing rhythm (parallelism, repetition, alliteration, antithesis). Choose one or two of your sentences and incorporate them into your speech.

Chapter Summary

Language is the system of symbols we use to communicate with one another. Much of what we know comes to us through language rather than direct experiences. However, language is complex. Remember that the words we use can be ambiguous because each word has a denotative meaning and a connotative meaning. The denotative meaning is the dictionary definition of a word. The connotative meaning is its subjective meaning, based on our own experiences and beliefs. We can use the semantic triangle of meaning to understand how these two levels of meaning interact and how to explain our own meanings more clearly. The triangle illustrates the relationships among the symbol, the referent, and the thought (or reference) attached to the referent.

Our culture also affects our meaning. Different cultures and subcultures, because of their different geographies, experiences, and histories, name and view the world differently. To be audience centered, we need to use words that are not strictly tied to a single culture or to explain what is meant by words that are. Different cultures and subcultures also have preferences about how they are identified. As speakers, we need to learn the terms groups use for themselves in order to show respect for them. Similarly, we must try to use gender-inclusive terms and phrases to show respect for both men and women.

Accurate use of language communicates your credibility to your audiences, whereas inaccurate use of language can harm your credibility and cause unnecessary confusion. To ensure accuracy, check the definitions of keywords before you deliver your speech or improve your use of language by working with someone who has a strong command of the language or by taking a second language.

There are several differences between spoken and written language. Spoken language reflects an oral style that is more interactive, casual, and repetitive than written language. Because of these differences, avoid writing out your speech and reading it to your audience. Instead, work from an outline so you will deliver your speech in a conversational rather than written style.

To create vivid images and sensations, you can use seven different techniques. To create memorable images, use the following three techniques. *Similes* are explicit comparisons of two things, using the words *like* or *as*. *Metaphors* describe one thing in terms of another. *Personification* ascribes human characteristics to nonhuman objects or ideas.

To create a pleasing rhythm, use *parallelism, repetition, alliteration,* and *antithesis*. Parallelism balances related words, phrases, or sentences by giving them identical structures. Repetition emphasizes keywords or phrases at the beginning or ending of a sentence or clause. Alliteration is the repetition of a sound in a phrase or a sentence. Antithesis is the contrast of words or phrases.

The public dialogue depends on our careful and thoughtful use of language. When combined with a thoughtful delivery (Chapter 13) as well as careful research (Chapter 6) and organization (Chapter 9), you can enrich this dialogue and stimulate important discussions as you decide, are asked, or are required to speak publicly.

Invitation to Public Speaking Online

After reading this chapter, use your CD-ROM and the *Invitation to Public Speaking* Web site to review the following concepts, answer the review questions, and complete the suggested activities.

Key Concepts

language (276)
symbol (276)
referent (277)
thought, or reference (277)
concrete word (277)
abstract word (277)

idiom (278)
oral style (282)
simile (284)
metaphor (285)
mixed metaphor
  (286)
personification (286)

rhythm (287)
parallelism (287)
repetition (287)
alliteration (288)
mnemonic device
  (288)
antithesis (288)

Review Questions

1. Identify something you know about but have never experienced yourself. How did you learn about this thing? What kind of language was especially important in teaching you what you know?

2. Bring the newspaper to your next class. In groups select three or four especially complex or ambiguous words. Using the semantic triangle of meaning, identify the symbol, referent, and thought or reference you have for these words. Are your thoughts and references the same? Rewrite those parts of the article so you explain the ambiguous words more clearly and enhance the meaning of the article.

3. Look up five to seven keywords you will use in your next speech. Do they mean what you thought they meant? Have you been pronouncing them correctly? If you were using an incorrect word, replace it with a correct one.

4. Determine how you will refer to people in your speeches. Conduct a demographic analysis (Chapter 5) of your audience to find out what labels the people in your audience use or prefer. Remember to consider culture as well as gender.

5. In groups, converse with each other for a few minutes about a specific topic or just in general. Identify the idioms you used in your conversation. Do you think they could confuse someone who is not fluent in your language? Do they confuse those who are fluent? How might you rephrase these idioms to be clearer?

6. Using the same issue of the newspaper you used for question 2, look for language that is sensitive or insensitive to culture and gender. In what ways is the language appropriate or inappropriate? What mistakes do you think the authors of the articles make, if any? What are the implications of these mistakes? What are the implications of the appropriate choices the author made?

7. Bring a dictionary to class. Look up the following commonly confused pairs of words:

    accept/except, compose/comprise, nauseated/nauseous, adverse/averse, explicit/implicit, principal/principle, affect/effect, farther/further, poured/pored, anxious/eager, fewer/less, reign/rein, appraise/apprise, healthy/healthful, stationery/stationary, between/among, imply/infer, uninterested/disinterested, compliment/complement, lay/lie, who/whom

    How many of these words did you have confused before you began this exercise?

8. Select a topic for an imaginary speech. Write out your introduction or first main point for that speech. Now read that to a small audience. Put the paper aside and talk that part of your speech in an oral style. What differences do you notice? Is the oral style interactive, casual, and repetitive?

9. Divide into groups and select one of the following terms:

    smoking   greyhound racing   the draft
    Halloween   gasoline

    Using the seven devices for creating imagery (simile, metaphor, personification, parallelism, repetition, alliteration, antithesis), write statements about this topic. Share your results with the class. Which devices helped you do a particularly good job conveying your ideas? Why do you think so?

10. This chapter suggests that language is central to the public speaking process. Do you think this is true? Why or why not? What techniques have you learned from this chapter that will help you use effective language in your speeches?

The *Invitation to Public Speaking* Web Site

The *Invitation to Public Speaking* Web site features the review questions about the Web sites suggested on pages 276–277, and 281, the interactive activities suggested on pages 278, 280, and 286, and the InfoTrac College Edition exercises suggested on pages 282 and 284. You can access this site via your CD-ROM or at http://www.wadsworth.com/product/griffin. To access Speech Builder Express, you will need the username and password included under "Speech Builder Express" on your CD-ROM.

Web Links

12.1: Symbolic Interaction: Identity and the Internet (276)
12.2: I. A. Richards (277)
12.3: Oxford Dictionary's Words and Expressions Commonly Misused (281)
12.4: Merriam-Webster Online (281)

Interactive Activities

12.1: Exploring Idioms (278)
Purpose: To understand how we use idioms in our everyday communication.

12.2: Choosing Gender-Neutral Language (280)
Purpose: To learn how to use gender-neutral language.

12.3: Using Similes and Metaphors (286)
Purpose: To appreciate how similes and metaphors can create meaning for audiences.

 ## InfoTrac College Edition Exercises

12.1: Learning New Words (282)
Purpose: To explore the meanings of new words.

12.2: Comparing Written and Spoken Language (284)
Purpose: To compare and contrast written and spoken language.

Speech Interactive on the *Invitation to Public Speaking* CD-ROM

The following video clips of speeches, referenced in this chapter, are included under Speech Interactive on your *Invitation to Public Speaking* CD-ROM. After you have watched the clips, click on "Critique" to answer the questions for analysis.

Video Clip 1: Casual Style of Speaking: Brandi Lafferty (283). As you watch Brandi speak, pay attention to the casual style of language she uses. When would a more formal style of speaking be necessary? When is it appropriate for a speaker to be more casual?

Video Clip 2: Martin Luther King Jr.'s "I Have a Dream" (289). As you watch Martin Luther King Jr.'s "I

Have a Dream" speech, notice how he uses language. Find examples of parallelism, repetition, alliteration, and antithesis. What effect does this language have on your recall of lines from his speech? How does King's use of language give him credibility with his audience?

Video Clip 3: Language Techniques: Stacey Newman (289). As you watch Stacey speak, pay attention to the language techniques she uses. What are examples of the imagery she uses? Of the parallelism? Of the repetition? Do you think her use of language is effective? Why or why not?

Chapter Thirteen

Delivering Your Speech

In this chapter you will learn to

Identify and describe four different methods of delivering a speech

List and demonstrate the verbal components of delivery

List and demonstrate the nonverbal components of delivery

Identify at least three tips for effectively managing question-and-answer sessions

Advertising has made us hostages of quick-fix phrases. The media can only speak to us in bold headlines . . . . In so many ways it has eroded our ability to withstand language for any stretch of time. We rarely have the patience any longer to follow a complex argument. Yet when we hear a carefully honed and well-articulated speech we are instantly galvanized and transfixed. We all recognize an acute need for words when we hear it. We are all intelligent enough to distinguish between a sincere and an insincere use of language. We all hear the ring of truth when it is spoken.

—Patsy Rodenburg, *The Need for Words: Voice and the Text*, 1993[1]

delivery
Action and manner of speaking to an audience.

If you look up the word *delivery* in the dictionary, you will discover that it is defined as (1) the carrying of something to a particular person or address; (2) the process of giving birth; (3) the action and manner of throwing or tossing a ball or punch; (4) the rescue of someone from hardship; and (5) the action or manner in which somebody speaks to an audience. Although this chapter focuses on the fifth definition of **delivery**, the action and manner of speaking to an audience, the other four definitions are also relevant.

When we deliver our speeches, we do carry something to others—our message. Our delivery also gives birth to our ideas as we bring our hard work and thoughts to life for our audience. Similarly, when we enter the public dialogue, we throw or toss our ideas out to our audiences, hoping they will catch them. Depending on the speaking environment, our passion and engagement, and the beliefs of our audience, our ideas may even feel like a punch. Finally, when we share information others do not have or encourage them to change, we sometimes help them avoid hardship or confusion.

What these other definitions of *delivery* suggest is that delivery is more complex than simply "giving a speech." It is your way of connecting with your audience and sharing your ideas with them. Because of the importance of delivery, this chapter covers the verbal and nonverbal components of delivery that will help you present your ideas in just the way you want. In the discussion that follows, you will learn about four methods of delivery as well as the verbal and nonverbal components of delivery. You also will learn ways to prepare for and manage question-and-answer sessions.

Methods of Delivery

The four types of delivery you use as a public speaker are extemporaneous, impromptu, manuscript, and memorized.[2] Let's look at each of these methods of delivery and the reasons for using them.

Extemporaneous Delivery

extemporaneous speech
A speech that is carefully prepared and practiced from brief notes rather than from memory or a written manuscript.

Most of your speeches will be extemporaneous. When you give an **extemporaneous speech**, you present a carefully prepared and practiced speech from brief notes rather than from memory or a written manuscript. Because extemporaneous delivery tends to be more natural than other deliveries, it is one of the more common methods.

An extemporaneous delivery evolves as your speech evolves. That is, as you work from your preparation outline to your speaking outline, you are getting ready to deliver your speech extemporaneously. Recall from Chapter 11 that when you work with your preparation outline, you organize all the material you've thoroughly researched. As such, you come to know your speech in full detail. You then summarize that detail in the speaking outline. When you practice giving your speech from the speaking outline, words and phrases remind you of the full ideas on the preparation outline. Thus your speaking outline provides you with the brief notes you speak from. Because you don't need to read the full text of your speech to remember what you want to say, you can give your speech in a very natural way.

The advantages of extemporaneous deliveries are many. The speaking outline or speaking notes prompt your ideas but do not allow you to read every word to your audience. Your eye contact and gestures are natural and your tone is conversational. Finally, because extemporaneous deliveries encourage direct communication between the speaker and audience, you stay audience centered.

Tiffany

I enjoy the extemporaneous method of speaking. It allows you to have a brief outline of your speech in front of you, but it also gives you some freedom to deliver the speech naturally because it isn't written out word for word. You're able to have a more conversational tone with your audience.

Delivery tips. Beginning speakers sometimes find extemporaneous delivery intimidating—they fear they may forget their ideas. However, the solution isn't to write out every word. One solution is to add more keywords and phrases to your outline (not full sentences) so you have more cues to help you. Second, practice your speech often before you give it so you will feel more confident about what you will remember and want to say. Your goal isn't to eliminate your fear by reading your speech, but to give yourself tools so you can "talk" your speech. Consider the benefits and drawbacks of extemporaneous delivery by completing Interactive Activity 13.1, "Memorize, Read, or Extemporize?" online under Student Resources for Chapter 13 at the *Invitation to Public Speaking* Web site.

The difference between an extemporaneous delivery and a speech read to an audience is striking. With an extemporaneous delivery, your language follows an oral rather than a written style (Chapter 12). An extemporaneous delivery also follows a **conversational style,** which is more formal than everyday conversation but remains spontaneous and relaxed.[3] Additionally, with a conversational style your posture and gestures are relaxed and you make frequent eye contact with your audience. In contrast, because reading requires your full attention, you're less able to make eye contact and gesture spontaneously. Imagine if Dr. Martin Luther King Jr. or Barbara Bush had read their most famous speeches to their audiences. Their charisma and power would have disappeared. To compare the difference between a speech delivered in a conversational style and one that is read, watch the video clips of Shelley's and Eric's speeches under Speech Interactive on your *Invitation to Public Speaking* CD-ROM. Which style of delivery do you think is more effective?

conversational style
Speaking style that is more formal than everyday conversation but remains spontaneous and relaxed.

WEB SITE

Eric Daley

Impromptu Delivery

When you give an **impromptu speech,** you present a speech that you have not planned or prepared in advance. Although you may be wondering why anyone would do this, especially in light of the previous discussions about the importance of preparation, planning, and practice, impromptu speaking is quite common. It

impromptu speech
Speech that is not planned or prepared in advance.

American author and speaker Mark Twain joked, "It usually takes more than three weeks to prepare a good impromptu speech." This isn't true, of course, but with a few minutes of thoughtful organization, you can make it seem that you took three weeks to prepare your impromptu speech.

occurs in meetings or public gatherings when someone is asked to speak or feels the need to share her or his perspective. When you decide to speak, you have the advantage of having a moment or two to organize your ideas. If you suddenly are asked to speak, you may not be able to jot down notes, but you still can organize your ideas. Consider the following two scenarios:

As Lissette listened to the discussion, she knew she had some insights and information she wanted to share. She also wanted to raise two questions for the group to consider. As a colleague was finishing his explanation, she jotted down the three ideas she wanted to share. She also wrote her two questions as key phrases with question marks after them. When her colleague finished, she entered the discussion by previewing her three points. When she finished explaining them, she transitioned to her questions by saying she wanted to raise two questions that had occurred to her while she listened. Her impromptu speech was a success because she had organized her thoughts. She also raised questions and invited her colleagues to consider them with her.

As a senior at the university, José was having trouble registering for the courses he needed to graduate. Enrollment on his campus was at an all-time high, and the number of majors in his own department had grown enormously. As a result, classes filled early. He expressed his frustration to his adviser, who suggested José attend a campus open forum on graduation requirements. José's adviser facilitated the discussion, and during the question-and-answer session, he asked José if he would share his frustrating experiences with the audience. José paused and quickly organized his thoughts about his frustrations and how they related to the discussion. His speech was a success not only because it addressed the discussion directly but also because he was candid about his experiences.

Both speakers entered the public dialogue through impromptu speeches, and both took a few seconds or minutes to organize their thoughts. That quick organization gave them confidence and helped them deliver audience-centered speeches that were easy to follow. If you decide to give an impromptu speech, as Lissette did, take time to make a quick speaking outline and jot down key ideas and points. You may even have time to organize these points. If you have no time to make a few notes, as in José's case, you can quickly organize your ideas in your head before you begin to speak.

Delivery tips. Although you never have much time to prepare an impromptu speech, you can practice impromptu deliveries. In fact, your speech instructor likely will ask you to give several impromptu speeches during the semester. When you deliver an impromptu speech use the following guidelines:

1. Quickly but calmly decide on the main points you want to make.

2. Introduce your main points as you would in a speech you had time to prepare: offer a preview such as "the three things I'd like to cover are" and use signposts such as "first."

3. Support your main points with sub and sub-subpoints.

4. Summarize your main points in a brief conclusion.

If you find yourself in an impromptu situation, stay calm. The skills you learn in your public speaking course are invaluable for such situations. Even though you may be nervous, you have learned to organized ideas, relate them to the audience, and deliver various types of speeches. Remember, too, that when you give an impromptu speech, your audience does not expect elaborate source citation, fancy visual aids, or creative introductions. They are looking for immediate clarity or guidance. If you rely on the fundamental skills you have learned in your public

Think of a time when you were asked or decided to give an impromptu speech. Were you able to implement the tips recommended in this chapter? How do you think the tips will help when you give your next impromptu speech?

speaking course, you can handle impromptu speeches successfully. To learn more about giving impromptu speeches, see http://www.powerfulpresentations.net/article1015.html.

Manuscript Delivery

When you give a **manuscript speech**, you read to an audience from a written text. Although most speeches are best delivered extemporaneously, some speeches require a manuscript delivery:

manuscript speech
Speech that is read to an audience from a written text.

- When detailed and exact information must be reported carefully, such as to a professional board or a formal committee
- When your speech will be scrutinized word by word, archived, and referred to later (for example, the president's address to the nation)
- When your speech text will be used later for some other purpose (for example, a keynote address at a conference, which often is published)

A manuscript speech is one of the most challenging forms of delivery. Contrary to what most beginning public speakers think, speaking from a manuscript requires more preparation and skill than extemporaneous or impromptu speaking. Two problems are likely when a speaker is reading from the full text. First, the speech often sounds like a written text and not an oral text, or a speech that "reads" well but doesn't "talk" well. (Recall the differences between spoken and written language explained in Chapter 12.) Second, the speaker may be inclined to read to the audience rather than talk with them, which isn't conducive to a healthy public dialogue. Let's look at some solutions to these problems.

Delivery tips. When you write your speech in manuscript format, talk the speech aloud as you write it. Working from your preparation outline, sit at your desk and say the speech orally as you write down the words on your computer or paper. If you find yourself thinking the speech rather than saying it aloud, go back and speak the part you have just written. You usually will notice that you've slipped into a writer's style instead of a speaker's style. Change the language in these sections to reflect spoken ideas rather than written ones. Remember, your goal is to write a speech, not an essay.

The second problem with using a manuscript is the temptation to read the manuscript to the audience. First, your eye contact is greatly reduced because you are focusing on the manuscript and not the audience. Second, your words may sound wooden because you are not paying attention to their purpose or meaning. Third, your delivery may be too fast because you are not paying attention to the audience's reactions or are not thinking about what you are trying to say.

The solution to this second problem—reading your speech—is to practice speaking from the manuscript again and again. If you become familiar with your manuscript during practice, you will find your natural rhythm and conversational style. You will notice where you can make eye contact with your audience easily and for extended periods. Like your extemporaneous speeches, you will be able to deliver full ideas or subpoints without reading. You also will discover that you'll want to slow down because, even though the words are in front of you, you feel comfortable enough with them to speak them with feeling rather than rush through them. For more tips about speaking from a manuscript, go to http://home-pages.ius.edu/KBALDRID/manuspkg.htm.

To watch an example of an effective manuscript delivery, use your *Invitation to Public Speaking* CD-ROM. Watch the video clip of Hillary Rodham Clinton's address at the 2000 Democratic National Convention under Speech Interactive. Consider how she stays audience centered despite using a manuscript style of delivery.

Memorized Delivery

memorized speech
Speech that has been written out, committed to memory, and given word for word.

When you give a **memorized speech,** you present a speech that has been written out, committed to memory, and given word for word. With a memorized delivery, you give the speech without any notes. Orators two thousand years ago prided themselves on their ability to memorize speeches that were hours long. Today, memorized speeches are usually used only for toasts, blessings, acceptance speeches, sometimes for speeches of introduction, and sometimes in forensics. Use a memorized delivery in these situations:

* When your speech is very short

* When you want to say things in a very specific way

* When notes would be awkward or disruptive

The trick to a memorized delivery is to speak as naturally and conversationally as possible. Rather than focusing on remembering your words, focus on communicating your words to your audience. When you deliver a memorized speech, don't recite it, but rather deliver it as though you were talking to your audience.

Delivery tips. To commit a speech to memory, follow these steps:

1. Write a manuscript of the speech, using a spoken style and not a written one.

2. Begin with the first line or first part of the first line and read it aloud over and over.

3. When you are familiar with that first line, deliver it, or parts of it, without reading it. Do this over and over until you can deliver the full line by heart.

4. Now, holding your manuscript but not looking at it, deliver the line by memory, looking out at an imaginary audience.

5. Once you've committed that first line to memory, deliver it again from memory and then read the second line aloud. Do this again and again until this line is familiar.

6. Repeat steps 3 through 5 for the remaining lines of the speech. Every few lines, set the manuscript aside and practice them until you can deliver them naturally and with confidence.

7. Once you've learned the full speech, practice it over and over, reminding yourself to listen to the meaning of your words. Remember, you want to bring the words to life and connect with your audience.

If you are delivering a long memorized speech, keep your manuscript nearby, if you can, so you can find your place if you get lost. If you can't keep your manuscript near you, someone else may be able hold it and prompt you if you lose your place. If you lose your place and have no one to prompt you, continue extemporaneously, or pause, backtrack to the last line you remember, repeat it in your head, and you should be able remember what comes next. For tips to improve your memorization ability, go to the Website Memory Techniques at http://www.plu.edu/ ~aast/memory.html.

Although they do take practice, memorized deliveries have their place in your toolbox of delivery styles. If done properly, a memorized delivery can free you from your notes but give you the comfort of knowing you will say exactly what you planned to say.

See Table 13.1 to review the advantages and disadvantages of the four delivery methods. Using your *Invitation to Public Speaking* CD-ROM, watch the video clips of Brandi, Amy, Carol, and Hans under Speech Interactive. Each of these speakers used a different method of delivery for her or his speech. Which delivery method do you think was most effective?

Table 13.1

Advantages and Disadvantages of Each Delivery Method

	EXTEMPORANEOUS	IMPROMPTU	MANUSCRIPT	MEMORIZED
Definition	A speech that is carefully prepared and practiced from brief notes rather than from memory or a written manuscript.	A speech that is not planned or prepared in advance and uses few or no notes.	A speech that is written word for word and read to an audience.	A speech that is written word for word, memorized, and given word for word.
Advantages	Combines a conversational style with a speaking outline. Encourages careful organization.	Allows for a conversational style with few or no notes	Helps present very detailed or specific information exactly as the speaker wants.	Frees the speaker to move about the room. No need for notes.
Disadvantages	Requires practice time. Speakers may be tempted to memorize the speech.	Requires thinking and organizing ideas quickly. No time for preparation.	Requires a conversational style that can be hard to achieve because the speaker reads from a full text.	Requires careful memorization. Speaker must remember important points and details without notes.

Verbal Components of Delivery

vocal variety
Changes in the volume, rate, and pitch of a speaker's voice that affect the meaning of the words delivered.

Our audiences sit up and listen to our words, in part, because of our delivery of those words. A speech's ring of truth (discussed in the quote that opens this chapter) comes not only from its words, but also from how they are delivered. Speakers known for their delivery—for example, Elizabeth Dole, Ann Richards, and Martin Luther King Jr.—use **vocal variety**, or changes in the volume, rate, and pitch of a speaker's voice that affect the meaning of the words delivered. We achieve vocal variety by consciously using certain verbal components of delivery: volume, rate, pitch and inflection, and pauses. Proper articulation and pronunciation of words are also important verbal components of delivery.

Volume

volume
Loudness of a speaker's voice.

Volume is the loudness of the speaker's voice. Common sense tells us that we want to speak loudly enough for our audiences to hear us. However, knowing just how loud that is can be difficult because our own voice sounds louder to us than to the audience and because the appropriate volume varies with each situation. Culture affects loudness as do our intentions. For example, in some Mediterranean cultures, a loud voice signals sincerity and strength, whereas in some parts of the United States it may signal aggression or anger. In some Native American and Asian cultures, a soft voice signals education and good manners.[4] However, in some European cultures, a soft voice may signal femininity, secrecy, or even fear.

Pay attention to nonverbal cues from your audience to help you adjust your volume. If you are speaking without a microphone, watch the faces and postures of people in the back of the room as well as those in front as you begin to speak. If the people in the back seem to be confused, straining to hear, or are leaning forward intently, it's a signal to increase your volume. If the people in front move back in their seats and look uneasy, you likely are speaking too loudly. This is a signal to lower your volume. When you get these signals you can also make adjustments by explaining cultural differences (Chapter 5).

When you use a microphone, you still need to pay attention to your volume because naturally loud voices project more loudly than soft voices. Before you begin your speech, test your voice with the microphone. Make sure you are the proper distance from it (neither too far nor too close) so the audience can listen comfortably. Don't turn off or avoid a microphone because it makes you nervous or you think people can hear you without one. Microphones exist to help audiences listen comfortably. Stay audience centered and use the microphone.

Rate

Rate is the speed at which we speak. There is no formula for the proper rate at which to deliver a speech. For example, Dr. Martin Luther King Jr. began his "I Have a Dream" speech at a rate of 92 words per minute and finished it at a rate of 145.[5] The rate at which we speak conveys different feelings. When we speak quickly, we project a sense of urgency or excitement, or even haste. When we speak slowly, we convey seriousness, heaviness, or even uncertainty. Both a rapid rate and a slow rate have their place in a speech. However, too much of one or the other strains the audience's attention. If a speaker speaks too fast for too long, the audience will stop listening because they need a break from the rapid-fire presentation. If a speaker speaks too slowly, the audience is likely to become distracted

To check your rate, tape yourself for several minutes. Then play back the recording and assess your speed. If you are using a manuscript, each page (typed, double spaced, in a 12-point font) should take two minutes to deliver. If you are much faster or slower, adjust your rate accordingly. You can also use rhythm (Chapter 12) to help you monitor your rate. Arranging your words into patterns so the sounds of the words together enhance meaning can help you vary your rate in an appealing way. Remember, rate is an audience-centered concern. We want to engage our audience, and our rate of speaking helps us by communicating certain emotions or energies.

When members of your audience come from varied cultural backgrounds or speak your language as a second language, try to slow your rate so accents and unfamiliar words are easier to follow. Adjusting your rate in this way communicates an audience-centered stance and adds to your credibility.

rate
Speed at which a speaker speaks.

Pitch and Inflection

Pitch is the highness or lowness of a speaker's voice on the musical scale. **Inflection** is the manipulation of pitch to create certain meanings or moods. Pitch and inflection help us communicate emotions. They allow us to say "well," meaning joyful surprise; "well," meaning indecision; "well," meaning indignation; and "well," meaning pity. Although women tend to have higher voices than men, both manipulate their pitch to create meaning during their speeches. All of us alter our pitch to ask a question, express satisfaction or displeasure, convey confidence or confusion, or even communicate threats or aggression. Variations in pitch clarify meaning and help catch and keep our audience's attention.

Speakers who do not pay attention to their pitch and inflection risk losing their audience. Speakers who do not alter their pitch speak in what is called a **monotone**. An audience loses interest when there is no inflection or vocal variety. Other speakers may say everything in a high pitch, which communicates "excessive zeal."[6] When the pitch is too high for too long, every word is communicated with equal enthusiasm, and the audience begins to wonder which points are the most important. In contrast, when a speaker says everything in a low pitch, the audience senses a lack of interest or energy.

There are solutions to such problems. First, tape yourself so you can hear your pitch. If you speak in too high a pitch, practice breathing more deeply (from the abdomen rather than the throat) and relaxing your throat muscles as you speak. Speak from your diaphragm rather than your throat, and read aloud regularly to practice this technique until you can get your pitch to drop naturally. (Note that proper breathing also helps you increase the volume of your voice and project your voice farther.) If you speak in a monotone or in too low a pitch,

pitch
Highness or lowness of a speaker's voice on the musical scale.

inflection
Manipulation of pitch to create certain meanings or moods.

monotone
A way of speaking in which a speaker does not alter her or his pitch

practice delivering your speech (or reading something aloud) in an overly dramatic way, using inflection, exclamations, and vocal variation as much as possible. With practice, vocal variation will come naturally and carry over into public speaking situations.

Pauses

Pauses are hesitations and brief silences in speech or conversation. In speeches, they often are planned, and they serve several useful functions. Pauses give us time to breathe fully and to collect our thoughts during a speech or before we answer a question from the audience. Pauses also give audiences time to absorb and process information—they're like a rest stop, giving the audience a breather before continuing. Finally, pauses before or after a climactic word or an important point reinforce that word or point.

Pauses can also add clarity. Read the passage here without stopping to pause after any of the words.

> The back of the eye on which an image of the outside world is thrown and which corresponds to the eye of a camera is composed of a mosaic of rods and cones whose diameter is little more than the length of an average light wave.

Without pauses it's hard to understand what's being said here, isn't it? Now read the passage again and note where you would naturally pause. Does the meaning of the passage become clear?

The four pauses that make this passage easier to understand are after *eye*, *thrown*, *camera*, and *cones*.[7] These are places in written text where we would add commas to indicate meaning. In written text, pauses often are indicated by punctuation, but in speeches, audiences can't see the punctuation. Pause to punctuate your words, as well as to establish mood, indicate a transition of idea or argument, take time to reflect, or to make a particular impact. For example, in his speech on the pollution caused by using fossil fuels, Preston used a pause to make a particular impact: "In fact," Preston argued, "according to the Southern California Edison Electric Transportation Web site, updated only last month, running for half an hour in urban air pollution introduces as much carbon monoxide into your lungs as [pause]smoking a pack of cigarettes."

Learning the art of the pause takes time and practice. Before you become comfortable with the brief moments of silence necessary in a speech, you may have the urge to fill the silence. Avoid **vocalized pauses,** or pauses that speakers fill with words or sounds like "um," "er," or "uh." Vocalized pauses not only are irritating, but they can also create a negative impression of the speaker. When a speaker uses so many vocalized pauses that the audience begins to focus on them, the audience may view the speaker as less intelligent and even uncomfortable and uninteresting.[8] If you find you have a habit of vocalizing pauses, try the following process to eliminate them:

1. Listen for vocalized pauses in your daily speech.

2. When you hear one, anticipate the next one.

3. When you feel the urge to say "um" or "er" to fill space, bite your tongue and don't let the word escape.

4. Wait until your next word of substance is ready to come out and say it instead.

It may take time to eliminate vocalized pauses from your speech, and you may feel awkward with the silence, but the results are worth the effort. To practice varying

© Bob Daemmrich/The Image Works

your vocal style, complete Interactive Activity 13.2, "Improving Vocal Variety," online under Student Resources for Chapter 13 at the *Invitation to Public Speaking* Web site.

WEB SITE

Articulation

Articulation is the physical process of producing specific speech sounds in order to make language intelligible to our audiences. Our clarity depends on our articulation—whether we say words distinctly or whether we mumble and slur. Articulation depends on the accuracy of movement of our tongue, lips, jaws, and teeth. This movement produces either "didjago?' or "did you go?" In fact, scholars of performance and delivery argue that poor articulation is a current trend across all sectors of U.S. culture.[9] To learn how to articulate sounds correctly, complete Interactive Activity 13.3, "Practicing Articulation," online under Student Resources for Chapter 13 at the *Invitation to Public Speaking* Web site.

WEB SITE

articulation
Physical process of producing specific speech sounds in order to make language intelligible.

Audiences expect public speaking to be more clearly articulated than private conversation. Speakers with an audience-centered focus care about clear articulation. Clearly articulated words communicate that you want your audience to understand you and can add to your credibility. For your audience to understand your ideas, they must be able to decipher your words. To improve your articulation skills, try the following exercise:

1. Several days before your speech, select a part of your speech or a short written text you can read aloud.

2. Practice saying each word of your speech excerpt or text as slowly and clearly as possible, overexaggerating the clarity of each word.

3. Repeat this exercise once or twice each day before you give your speech.

This exercise will help you recognize how much you slur or mumble and teach you to speak more clearly when you give your speech. Don't worry—you won't speak in this overexaggerated way when you finally deliver your speech, but your words will be much clearer.

Pronunciation

Just as you would not turn in an essay you knew was filled with spelling errors, never deliver a speech filled with pronunciation errors. **Pronunciation** is the act of saying words correctly according to the accepted standards of a language. Pronunciation and articulation may seem similar, but pronunciation refers to how *correctly* a word is said, whereas articulation refers to how *clearly* a word is said. For example, saying the word *nuclear* as "nu-cle-ar" (correct) rather than "nu-cu-lar" (incorrect) has to do with pronunciation, and mumbling either pronunciation rather than clearly speaking it has to do with articulation.

pronunciation
Act of saying words correctly according to the accepted standards of a language.

Pronouncing words correctly communicates to your audience that you have listened carefully to the public dialogue going on around you. You have taken care to learn the common language and pronounce it correctly. (Recall from Chapter 12 that it is also important to use language accurately, to use the correct words to express your thoughts.) In addition, correct pronunciation of terms and names in a language other than your native one communicates your respect for that culture and enhances your credibility.

Dialect

dialect
Pattern of speech that is shared among ethnic groups or people from specific geographic locations.

A **dialect** is a pattern of speech shared among ethnic groups or people from specific geographic locations. Dialects include specific vocabulary that is unique to a group as well as styles of pronunciation shared by members of that group. All people have a dialect, and your own dialect comes from your ethnic heritage as well as the place you grew up. For example, do you say "wash" or "warsh" when you want something clean? How about "soda," "pop," or "coke" when you want a soft drink? Your choices reflect your dialect.

People who use a standard American dialect (the dialect newscasters use when they are on the air) often forget that they, too, have a dialect, and they sometimes view the dialect of others as inferior. For public speaking, a dialect is important not because one is better than another, but because a dialect is not generally shared by people outside a group. So speakers may use words that aren't familiar to their audience or may pronounce words in ways that sound odd or different.

If you know your dialect will be unfamiliar to your audience, try the following:

1. Acknowledge your region of birth or ethnic heritage.

2. Talk about how that shapes your use of language by giving examples of some of the differences you've encountered between your dialect and that of your audience.

3. Define terms that are unfamiliar to your audience.

4. Soften the accent associated with your dialect if that accent is fairly strong and might hinder understanding.

Speech Step 13.2 / Refine the Verbal Components of Your Delivery

Continue the preparation you began in Speech Step 13.1 by focusing on the verbal components of your delivery. As needed, adjust your volume and rate. Look for natural pauses and for pauses that add meaning, clarity, and emphasis to your ideas. Adjust your pitch and inflection as needed to add emphasis and maintain your audience's interest. Finally, make sure your articulation is clear and your pronunciation correct.

Nonverbal Components of Delivery

The nonverbal components of delivery are those aspects communicated through our bodies and faces. For public speakers, these include personal appearance, eye contact, facial expression, posture, gestures, and proxemics.[10]

Scholars of interpersonal communication recognize that nonverbal communication has a powerful impact on the meanings exchanged between people. Researchers suggest that between 65 and 93 percent of the total meaning of a message comes to us through nonverbal signals.[11] Additionally, when nonverbal signals contradict verbal signals (for example, you say you're glad to see someone but your nonverbal signals suggest you're not), people believe the nonverbal signals.[12] To consider the importance of nonverbal communication, complete InfoTrac College Edition Exercise 13.1, "Using Nonverbal Communication," online under Student Resources for Chapter 13.

For public speakers, nonverbal communication is especially important because it conveys meaning and it can either enhance or detract from the overall message. Let's look at how the components of nonverbal communication affect a speech.[13]

Personal Appearance

Personal appearance, or the way you dress, groom, and present yourself physically, is an important part of delivery. But how important? Consider the following sayings:

You can't judge a book by its cover.

Beauty is in the eye of the beholder.

Looks are everything.

Beauty is as beauty does.

You can never be too rich or too thin.

You can dress him up, but you still can't take him out.

Good-looking lawyers make more money.

Which statements are true? Does physical appearance matter or is it irrelevant? Studies show that, indeed, personal appearance matters quite a bit. People deemed "more attractive" earn more money than their "less attractive" peers, and personal grooming plays a large part in our perception of a person's attractiveness, for both men and women.[14] Attractive characteristics are defined as "those characteristics that make one person appear pleasing to another."[15] Even though we may say we shouldn't judge people by their looks, it seems that is exactly what we do.

Without a doubt, standards for attractiveness and beauty change with generations, as well as with cultures and subcultures. Despite these differences, though, there is a basic standard for acceptable personal grooming in public speaking situations.[16] That standard is the speaker's dress should be appropriate to the occasion. If the occasion is a formal one, the speaker is expected to dress formally.

Research suggests that a speaker's dress should be appropriate to the occasion. Actor Matt Dillon is shown here reading a farewell speech by baseball great Lou Gehrig at a New York Mets game to raise awareness about Lou Gehrig's disease. Do you think he is dressed appropriately given his audience and speaking situation? When you've given speeches in class, have you considered the importance of your appearance? What do you think is appropriate to wear for a classroom speech?

If the occasion is casual, the speaker's clothing should be less formal. A speaker who shows up at a formal occasion in a T-shirt and shorts not only displays a lack of audience analysis, but is likely to lose credibility. Similarly, wearing formal business attire to speak at a casual gathering is also inappropriate. In short, be sure your clothing matches the style and tone of the occasion.

Another standard for appropriate grooming in public speaking situations is to wear attire that is neither too revealing nor too restricting. As fashions change, standards for acceptability change. Over a hundred years ago, displaying bare skin in public was considered very unacceptable. Today, the amount of bare skin or body that can be exposed or accentuated is stunning, and many celebrities accept awards and make speeches wearing almost nothing at all. Because most of us aren't a movie star or a pop star, when giving a speech in public, we want the audience to be able to listen to our message and not be distracted by our appearance. Dressing simply and tastefully does more than help your audience pay attention to your message. It helps us move about comfortably and freely as we deliver our message.

Personal appearance is a complex combination of social norms, cultural and generational influences, and personal style. Your personal appearance should match your objective as a speaker, which is to have your words and ideas taken seriously in the public dialogue. Delivery begins the moment the audience sees you, so pay careful attention to your personal appearance and present yourself appropriately for the occasion at which you are speaking. For some additional pointers about personal appearance, go to the Web site Dress for Success at http://www.quintcareers.com/dress_for_success.html.

Eye Contact

eye contact
Visual contact with another person's eyes.

The second essential component of nonverbal delivery is **eye contact**, visual contact with another person's eyes. Like personal appearance, appropriate eye contact is affected by culture and gender. Most North Americans and western Europeans expect a speaker to make extensive eye contact. However, in Native American cultures, as in Japan and parts of Africa, extensive eye contact is considered invasive and disrespectful. Gender, too, affects the meaning of eye contact. For men, direct and extended eye contact with another man may be perceived as a challenge or threat. For women, direct and extended eye contact with a man may be interpreted as an invitation to flirt. So knowing what to do with our eyes as we deliver a speech depends on knowing who is in our audience.

Even though the nuances of eye contact are complex, most cultures expect at least some eye contact during a speech. Eye contact has three functions. First, it is a way to greet and acknowledge the audience before the speech begins. Second, eye contact is a way to gauge and keep our audience's interest. We use eye contact to monitor feedback from our audience and adjust our volume, rate, and tone accordingly. Third, eye contact is a way to communicate sincerity and honesty. Audiences rate speakers who make eye contact for less than half their speech as tentative, uncomfortable, and even as insincere and dishonest.[17] In contrast, speakers who make eye contact for more than half their speech are viewed as more credible and trustworthy.[18] For more tips on enhancing your credibility, complete InfoTrac College Edition Exercise 13.2, "Communicating Sincerity," online under Student Resources for Chapter 13.

For eye contact to be effective, try to do two things as you look out at your audience. First, make eye contact with many people in the audience rather than a few friendly faces. Make eye contact with people in all parts of the room, not just those immediately in front of you. Gather information about level of comprehension, interest, and agreement from as many people as you can.

Second, look with interest. Rather than scanning faces in the audience or looking over their heads to the back of the room, really look at individual people in the audience. Slow down your looking so you actually make a connection with them. Looking with interest communicates you are pleased to be speaking to your audience and are interested in their responses.

Facial Expression

Your face plays a central role in communicating with your audience, letting them know your attitudes, emotional states, and sometimes even your inner thoughts. Your face expresses these things through the manipulation of your eyes, eyebrows, and mouth. Actors are highly skilled at using their faces to communicate, and audiences appreciate this talent. Although you don't need to be as skilled as an actor, you do need to consider your facial expressions as you deliver your speech. A poker face, although useful in a card game, will not help you communicate your ideas.

You can use your facial expressions to communicate your own interest in your topic, your agreement or disagreement with a point, your openness to an idea, and even your feeling about an issue. Take some time to decide which facial expressions might be useful to include in your speech. If these expressions aren't coming naturally to you, practice them until you are comfortable delivering them.

Posture

Posture is the way we position and carry our bodies and, whether we realize it or not, people assign meaning to our posture. We are perceived as confident and relaxed or tense and insecure based, in part, on our posture. A confident speaker is often called "poised," which means to possess assurance, dignity, and a sense of calm. Nervousness can affect our posture, making us feel awkward and do things we'd never do in other situations: grip the podium with both hands, slouch over our speaking notes, pace back and forth, or stand stuck to one spot. These nervous reactions detract from our delivery and communicate a message we probably don't want to be sending.[19]

But by paying attention during practice to the way we carry our bodies, we can eliminate some nervous postures. To become aware of your posture during a speech, practice your speech in the way you actually will give it. That is, if you will deliver your speech standing, practice standing up. Devise a makeshift podium if need be. Or if you are to sit while giving the speech, practice the speech while sitting, with chairs beside you and your notes on a table in front of you. Similarly, if you will use a hand-held or attachable microphone, practice with something resembling it so you get the feel of speaking with a microphone.

By practicing the speech in the way you'll actually give it, you can correct your nervous habits before you give the speech. For example, if you find that you pace or grip the podium tightly, you can replace the bad habit with a better one. If you discover you stand immobilized when you practice, you can add cues to your speaking outline to remind you to move during your speech. If you slouch, you can practice sitting up straight and looking out at your audience. In sum, your posture during your speech should improve if you pay attention to your body during practice.

One final word about posture and delivery: Pay attention to the way you begin and end your speech. Wait until you are at the podium or have the microphone in your hand before you begin talking. Don't start speaking until you are facing your

posture
Way speakers position and carry their bodies.

audience and have made eye contact. Similarly, don't walk off the stage until you have finished the last word of your conclusion. Finishing your conclusion or your final answer before you leave the spotlight communicates confidence and a willingness to give every word the attention it deserves. These guidelines will help you remain audience centered. To read about how to stay audience centered for one type of audience, go to the ACPA Standing Committee for Disability Web site at http://www.acpa.nche.edu/comms/disab/tipscover.html#tips.

Gestures

Gestures are movements, usually of the hands but sometimes of the full body, that express meaning and emotion or offer clarity to a message. Students of rhetoric in ancient Greece and Rome spent hours learning specific gestures to accompany specific parts of their speeches. For example, certain gestures were used with transitions, and others signaled specific kinds of main points or ideas. These choreographed gestures were used until the eighteenth century.[20] Today, research on gestures in public speaking indicates that gestures should be as natural as possible rather than memorized.

However, beginning public speakers don't always know what gestures will appear natural in a speech. With only minor variations, natural gestures in a speech are the same as those you normally use in personal conversations to complement your ideas and bring your words to life. The same is true for public speeches. Gestures make our delivery lively, offer emphasis and clarity, and convey our passion and interest Use these tips to help you with gestures:

1. *Vary your gestures.* Try to use different kinds of gestures rather than only one gesture repeated over and over. Some gestures emphasize (a fist on the podium), clarify (counting first, second, third, on your fingers), or illustrate (drawing a shape with your hands in the air). Try to incorporate a variety of these gestures into your speech.

2. *Use gestures that fit your message.* Sometimes a point needs an extravagant gesture; at other times a more subtle gesture is much more effective. For example, use a relaxed pattern of movement of your hands as you explain a point but a larger more vigorous movement when you are emphasizing something quite important.

3. *Stay relaxed.* Your gestures should flow with your words. Try to keep your movements comfortable and effortless. If you find a gesture makes you tense, drop it from the speech and replace it with something more casual and familiar.

You will find that as you relax and gain experience speaking, you stop thinking about your gestures and simply use them as you normally do in conversation. Using your *Invitation to Public Speaking* CD-ROM, watch a video clip of President Ronald Reagan under Speech Interactive. Reagan was often called the "Great Communicator" because of his masterful delivery. Practice your own delivery by completing Interactive Activity 13.4, "Practicing Your Gestures," online under Student Resources for Chapter 13 at the *Invitation to Public Speaking* Web site.

WEB SITE

Proxemics

Effective speakers pay close attention to the use of space during communication, or **proxemics.** Pay attention to how far away you are from your audience, as well as how elevated you are from them (for example, on a platform or a podium). The farther away you are, the stronger the idea of separation. The higher up you are, the more the idea of power is communicated.

You can work with proxemics in your delivery. One of the strengths of speakers like Elizabeth Dole and Bill Clinton is their ability to move close to their audiences at key points during their speeches. Similarly, recall from Chapter 5 that the Dalai Lama worked without a lectern, sometimes even sitting down on stage. Although you don't want to remain too close to your audience throughout your speech, getting close to them at key points allows for greater connection and communicates a desire to be perceived as more of an equal. Try stepping from behind the lectern or down from the podium and moving closer to your audience. If you can't do this because you need a microphone or a place to put your notes, you might be able to move closer during a question-and-answer session. Doing so will help you communicate openness and a willingness to engage in conversation with your audience.

Rehearsing Your Speech

Although it may sound odd, the more you practice, the more natural you will sound. This is because you will be familiar with your speech on many levels. You'll not only know the ideas but will have some of the wording worked out. You also will be comfortable with the verbal and nonverbal components of your delivery. And you'll feel more confident during your question-and-answer session because you will have prepared and rehearsed the answers to questions you might be asked (discussed in the next section). Take a look at the following guidelines for rehearsing your delivery. If you follow them, your delivery will communicate your interest in participating in the public dialogue.

It can be tempting to leave the process of rehearsing your speech until the last minute. However, you'll get the best results if you give yourself plenty of time. What are your plans for rehearsing for your next speech?

1. Practice giving your speech aloud using your speaking outline (Chapter 11).

2. Practice all stories, quotations, statistics, and other evidence until you can deliver them exactly as you want.

3. When you are comfortable with your material, practice your speech in front of a mirror. Monitor your nonverbal communication and make adjustments as needed so you communicate your message clearly.

4. Now tape your speech and listen for vocal variety. Check your volume, rate, pitch and inflection, pauses, and how you articulate and pronounce words. If you think your dialect will hinder your delivery, make adjustments.

5. Practice your speech again, incorporating the verbal and nonverbal changes you worked out in steps 1 through 4.

6. Now practice a few times in front of a friend. Have the person ask you questions at the end of the speech, and practice answering them. Incorporate any useful feedback your friend may have for you.

7. Stage a dress rehearsal. Consider your personal appearance by wearing the clothing you will wear on the day you speak. Set up your practice area so it resembles the actual speaking situation as closely as possible. Consider proxemics and the space you want between you and the audience.

© Michael Newman/PhotoEdit

Question-and-Answer Sessions

Throughout this text, speaking in public has been framed as entering the public dialogue. This dialogue creates an environment in which we can explore issues and ideas. With our speeches, we not only add our own voice to the dialogue, but we also invite others to engage our ideas. Question-and-answer sessions provide an opportunity for our audience to explore our ideas in more detail, ask for clarity, and share their own perspectives. Question-and-answer sessions occur after speeches for several reasons:

- *The speaker stimulated thought.* The content of a speech caused an audience to think in new ways, challenged an audience, or raised numerous questions. All these are good outcomes, and they mean a question-and-answer session will be engaging and lively.

- *The speaker was able to explore only a part of an issue during the speech.* This happens because of time limitations, and a question-and-answer session gives both the audience and the speaker time to fill out an argument or position.

- *The speaker wants to hear the audience's perspectives and insights.* The purpose of the speech, especially an invitational speech, may be to encourage dialogue with the audience.

Even though you won't know for sure what to expect in a question-and-answer session, you can prepare for it. Your preparation can make the difference between a mediocre question-and-answer session and a stimulating one. Ensuring a good question-and-answer session has two steps: preparing for potential questions as you prepare your speech and managing the session itself.

Preparing for Questions

Before the speech, you can do several things to prepare for questions. First, take time to identify the questions you think your audience might ask. Then, prepare and practice your answers to those questions.

Identify potential questions. As you prepare for your question-and-answer session, first identify the questions you might be asked. Keep a log of the questions your research raises in your own mind. Chances are that if you've wondered about these questions, members of your audience have too. Second, pay attention to the controversies or disagreements that surround your speech topic. Some people in your audience are likely to want to discuss them. Finally, if you can practice your speech in front of people, they can help you identify likely audience questions. Add these to the log of questions you started during your research. Now you're ready to move to the next step—formulating the answers to these questions.

Formulate answers. After you've identified the questions you might be asked, prepare your answers as though they are a part of your actual speech. Write out your answers, outline them, and record pertinent quotes, statistics, examples, or other data that support your answer. Although this may seem like an extra step, the following example indicates its value:

> Sean had prepared his speech carefully and anticipated a lively question-and-answer session. He knew his topic was a controversial one, and he anticipated many questions in opposition to his position. He knew he might be asked how he could support the kinds of regulations he advocated, so he had prepared his answers carefully. He had collected statistics and testimony and recorded them on separate sheets of paper. During the question-and-answer session, one member of his audience challenged Sean's solution, arguing that the regulations he advocated would only cause more frustration and hostility. Pulling out a page of his notes, he was able to offer statistics and testimony that suggested otherwise. Although the audience member still disagreed, Sean's ability to provide a concrete response to the challenge won him respect from others in the audience.

If Sean had not taken time to prepare for that question, he likely would have been caught off guard. He would have known the evidence to counter the accusation existed, but not had that material at his fingertips.

Practice the answers. Your final pre-speech preparation step is to practice the answers you've formulated. Although you cannot always anticipate the exact questions you will receive, you often can come close. You should be able to answer a question that is similar to one you anticipated by making minor adjustments to the answer you formulated. If some of the questions you are asked are likely to be controversial, practice your answers in front of other people. They can help you with wording and organization as well as with adding or subtracting details.

As a rule, your answers to simple questions should be brief—between ten and sixty seconds. Answers to complex questions may take longer, but remember, you are answering questions, not giving another speech. Remember, too, that others are waiting to ask questions. If you spend all your time on one question, you will prevent others from raising important issues.

Managing the Question-and-Answer Session

Several techniques will help ensure a productive question-and-answer session. They can help you manage the flow of conversation as well as keep an audience-centered perspective.

Explain the format. It's a good idea to establish the format of the question-and-answer session during the introduction of your speech. You can preview the question-and-answer session as the final main point, for example, or simply say that at the end of the speech, you'll be happy to answer any questions from the audience. This lets the audience know you've planned time for questions, you're interested in the discussion that surrounds the topic, and you're prepared to facilitate that interaction. If you're inclined, you also can indicate you'll accept questions during the speech itself. But be sure you have planned a way to present all your material despite the time taken to answer questions.

Listen and clarify. One of your most important tasks is to listen to each question and to answer thoughtfully. This can be a difficult task if the question feels like an attack or challenge or if it is not clearly worded. When you are asked an unfocused question, try to listen carefully for the keywords and important points. Then, using this information, restate the question so it is clear to you, and ask the person if this is what he or she is asking you. Use such language as, "If I understand the question, you are asking me . . . is that correct?" or "I think what you're asking is . . . am I right?" If you simply cannot make sense of the question, you can always ask the person to repeat it for you.

When you are faced with a hostile question, it can be hard to really hear what the person is asking. Hostile questions usually come from someone who feels threatened or believes you have not addressed his or her needs and concerns. Sometimes you can respond to the content of the question as well as acknowledge the emotion. This takes practice. Here are some tips:

1. Don't take the hostility personally. Establish goodwill and common ground. If you can, identify points of agreement, shared experiences, or common background with your audience.

2. Display an audience-centered perspective, and communicate with civility (Chapter 1) as you respond. Responding civilly is more likely to decrease the hostility than an uncivil response.

3. Listen to the content as well as the emotional components of the questions being asked. Separate out the emotions, and determine the facts or information you are being asked to provide.

4. Begin your answer by addressing the content issue. Offer information that will clarify your ideas or position. This might be a good time to create an invitational environment (Chapter 16) so you can explore an issue and get as many perspectives as you can. Try to explain rather than argue.

5. Offer evidence for your position. Use the skills you learned in Chapter 7 to help you develop your ideas logically and with credibility. Sometimes the hostility in a question can be reduced with strong evidence and support.[21]

After you have tried these strategies, if you feel confident enough to do so, you can acknowledge the considerable emotion attached to the issue. You want to be careful here, though, because many people do not like to be told how they feel. If you say something like "I understand the anger attached to this issue," the person may either appreciate the recognition, or snap back with a retort about not being angry. As a rule, beginning speakers should use caution when answering emotionally charged questions.

Keep a positive mind-set. Some beginning speakers are uneasy about question-and-answer sessions. One way to feel more confident about this part of a speech is to frame it positively. Most questions from your audience are signs of interest and curiosity—they genuinely want to know more about your subject. Because a speech necessarily limits what you are able to say, the question-and-answer session gives audience members a chance to ask for additional information and you the opportunity to provide it. If you recognize that interest is the reason for most of the questions you receive, you can respond with poise.

AP/Wide World Photos

Secretary of State Colin Powell is often asked to address questions from the media. Regardless of the question, Powell stays calm, addresses the entire audience, and answers candidly. Do you think Powell follows the suggestions provided in this chapter for preparing for tough questions? What steps have you taken to prepare for your next question-and-answer session?

Address the entire audience. Even though a specific person in the audience has asked a question, keep your answer audience centered. First, restate the question so all the audience members can hear it. Second, deliver the answer to the entire audience, not just to the person asking the question. These two actions bring the full group into the conversation and help keep them interested.

Usually, a question asked by one audience member is a question that others have too. However, you occasionally receive a question whose answer applies only to the person asking it. When this happens, respond that the question seems to address the needs of only one person and you will be glad to speak with him or her after the presentation. In doing so, you acknowledge the importance of the person, but not at the expense of the larger group.

Answer with honesty. At some point in your speaking career, you will be asked a question for which you do not have an answer. Rather than trying to fake an answer or justify why you don't have one, be honest. Admit you don't know the answer. Then acknowledge the importance of the question and refer it to someone who may know the answer, or offer to try to find the answer after the speech, if it seems appropriate to do so.

Stay focused. Unlike a speech, which has a specific purpose and thesis statement, question-and-answer sessions can cover a wide range of ideas and perspectives, some of them only remotely related to your speech. Additionally, with many people asking questions, keeping track of time and flow of ideas is difficult. However, you can do several things to keep the dialogue focused.

- First, state how much time you have for the question-and-answer session. This will help your audience gauge the length and number of their questions and the amount of detail you can provide in your answers.

- Second, you occasionally will get a few audience members who seem to want to dominate the session. They take over either through repeated questions or an extended monologue. When you can regain the floor, thank those people for their interest and ideas, and explain it's important to hear from a variety of audience members. Then turn to other people with questions to keep the discussion moving.

• Third, keep track of time, marking the halfway point as well as when the session is nearing its end. At these points, you can refocus the discussion, stating, "We've had a number of questions related to [this aspect of the speech topic]. Do we have any questions on topics we haven't covered yet?" In this way, you can make a space for audience members who have not have been able to ask their questions.

WEB SITE Practice addressing difficult questions by completing Interactive Activity 13.5, "Answering Difficult Questions," online under Student Resources for Chapter 13 at the *Invitation to Public Speaking* Web site.

Speech Step 13.4 / Prepare for a Question-and-Answer Session

Write down the questions you think your audience will ask after your next speech. Then write your answers and practice delivering them, making notes to prompt you as needed. Determine how you will set up the question-and-answer session for your speech. Make note of your decisions on your speaking outline.

Chapter Summary

To deliver a speech to an audience is to share your hard work and well-planned ideas. There are four types of delivery: extemporaneous, impromptu, manuscript, and memorized. An extemporaneous speech is delivered from brief notes or an outline. An impromptu speech is delivered with little or no advance notice or time for preparation. A manuscript speech is written out word for word and read aloud. A memorized speech has been committed to memory and is delivered without notes.

As you deliver your speeches, pay attention to both verbal and nonverbal components. In order to achieve vocal variety, pay attention to verbal components: volume, rate, pitch and inflection, pauses, articulation, pronunciation, and dialect. In order to enhance your verbal message, pay attention to nonverbal components: personal appearance, eye contact, posture, and gestures.

As a speaker, you likely will be engaged in question-and-answer sessions during or after a speech. Although they can be unpredictable, there are ways you can prepare for them. As you prepare your speech, identify potential questions, formulate answers to them, and practice the answers out loud. You can manage these sessions by explaining their format and time limit, carefully listening to and clarifying questions that are asked, keeping a positive mind-set, and addressing the entire audience when you answer questions. Be honest when you don't know an answer, and stay focused so a range of topics and audience members are included in the session.

Although *delivery* can be defined as the action of speaking to an audience, this act has many components. When we hear or give that "carefully honed and well-articulated speech" mentioned in the opening quote of this chapter, we realize that delivery is the art of clarifying issues and engaging audiences.

Invitation to Public Speaking Online

After reading this chapter, use your CD-ROM and the *Invitation to Public Speaking* Web site to review the follow-ing concepts, answer the review questions, and complete the suggested activities.

Key Concepts

delivery (296)
extemporaneous speech (296)
conversational style (297)
impromptu speech (297)
manuscript speech (299)
memorized speech (300)
vocal variety (302)

volume (302)
rate (303)
pitch (303)
inflection (303)
monotone (303)
pauses (304)
vocalized pauses (304)
articulation (305)

pronunciation (305)
dialect (306)
personal appearance (307)
eye contact (308)
posture (309)
gestures (310)
proxemics (310)

Review Questions

1. Identify speakers you consider to have good delivery. What characteristics make their delivery strong? How many of these characteristics might you incorporate into your style of delivery?

2. Make several tapes of yourself in conversation with others (be sure to get their permission before you tape them). Tape yourself talking with someone you know well and someone you don't know well, in formal and informal situations. Compare your delivery in each. What aspects do you like and what would you like to change? Now tape yourself practicing your speech. Evaluate your delivery again, and determine your strengths and areas for possible improvement.

3. Which method of delivery will you choose for your next speech? Why? How will you make that method as audience centered as possible?

4. Which method of delivery do you prefer? Why do you feel most comfortable with it?

5. Review the discussion in Chapter 2 about nervous-ness. Are there any tips in Chapter 2 that you can incorporate into your delivery? Which ones? Why do you think they are useful?

6. Identify the differences among extemporaneous, impromptu, manuscript, and memorized deliveries. What are the strengths and weaknesses of each type of delivery?

7. Have each person in class write a quick speech. Now trade speeches with one another. In groups, give that speech as though it were a tragedy, a surprise, or a hilarious story. Or choose some other approach that will allow you to work on vocal variety. How well are you able to match the verbal aspects of your delivery to the mood you have selected?

8. Consider your next speech. What will you wear, and why did you choose that style and manner of clothing?

9. Share the topic and specific purpose of your next speech with the class. Let them ask you questions about your topic and purpose, and practice answering those questions as though you were conducting a question-and-answer session.

The *Invitation to Public Speaking* Web Site

The *Invitation to Public Speaking* Web site features the review questions about the Web sites suggested on pages 299–301, 308, and 310, the interactive activities suggested on pages 297, 305, 310, and 316, and the InfoTrac College Edition exercises suggested on pages 306 and 308. You can access this site via your CD-ROM or at http://www.wadsworth.com/product/griffin. To access Speech Builder Express, you will need the username and password included under "Speech Builder Express" on your CD-ROM.

Web Links

13.1: How to Give a Successful Impromptu Speech (299)
13.2: How to Prepare a Manuscript for Delivery (300)
13.3: Memory Techniques (301)
13.4: Dress for Success (308)
13.5: Presenting to People with Disabilities (310)

Interactive Activities

13.1: Memorize, Read, or Extemporize? (297)
Purpose: To consider delivery options.

13.2: Improving Vocal Variety (305)
Purpose: To improve your vocal variety.

13.3: Practicing Articulation (305)
Purpose: To learn and practice proper articulation.

13.4: Practicing Your Gestures (310)
Purpose: To practice effective gestures.

13.5: Answering Difficult Questions (316)
Purpose: To practice responding to difficult questions.

InfoTrac College Edition Exercises

13.1: Using Nonverbal Communication (306)
Purpose: To understand the importance of nonverbal communication.

13.2: Communicating Sincerity (308)
Purpose: To understand how speakers communicate sincerity.

Speech Interactive on the *Invitation to Public Speaking* CD-ROM

The following video clips of speeches, referenced in this chapter, are included under Speech Interactive on your *Invitation to Public Speaking* CD-ROM. After you have watched the clips, click on "Critique" to answer the questions for analysis.

Video Clip 1: Comparison of Conversational and Written Styles: Shelley Weibel and Eric Daley (297). Compare the delivery styles of Shelley and Eric. How can you tell that Shelley is using an extemporaneous style? What makes Eric's delivery look like he is reading from a manuscript? Which style do you think is more effective? Why? Are there times when an extemporaneous style is more appropriate than a manuscript style? Are there times when reading from a manuscript would be more effective than using an extemporaneous style?

Video Clip 2: Hillary Rodham Clinton's Address at 2000 Democratic National Convention (300). Watch Hillary Rodham Clinton's speech at the 2000 Democratic National Convention. How does her language reflect a written, rather than spoken, style? How does she make her speech delivery seem extemporaneous?

Video Clip 3: Comparison of Delivery Methods: Brandi Lafferty, Amy Wood, Carol Godart, and Hans Erian (301). Compare the delivery methods Brandi, Amy, Carol, and Hans used in their speeches. Which delivery method do you think is most effective? Why? Are there times when one method is more appropriate than another? In what speaking situations might you use the extemporaneous, impromptu, manuscript, or memorized method of delivery?

Video Clip 4: Ronald Reagan's Acceptance Speech at the 1980 Republican National Convention (310). Watch President Ronald Reagan, often called the "Great Communicator," speak at the 1980 Republican National Convention. As you watch the speech, watch for the elements of delivery we have discussed. How does Reagan use verbal elements, such as volume, pauses, and inflection? How does Reagan use nonverbal communication, such as eye contact, gestures, and posture? To what degree do you think Reagan connected with his audience because of his delivery?

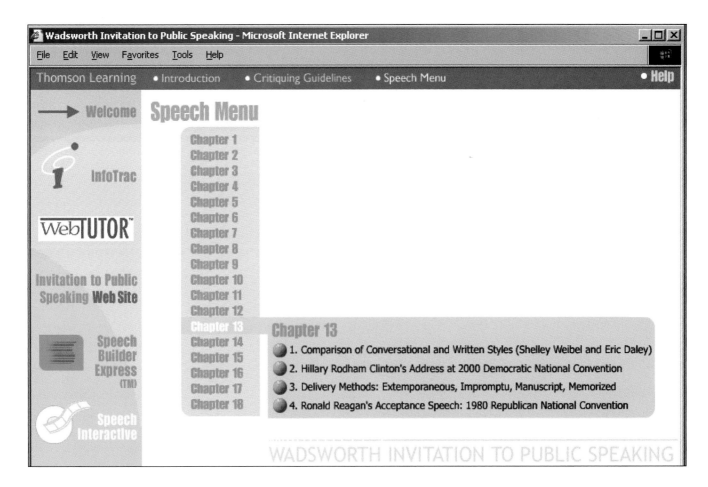

Chapter Fourteen

Visual Aids

In this chapter you will learn to

Discuss the importance of using visual aids

Identify and describe the different types of visual aids

Determine what to show on a visual aid

Format visual aids effectively

Identify the five guidelines for using visual aids

There is no doubt that images can be influential in affecting attitudes and beliefs. A single visual image can probably be more powerful than a single verbal assertion.

—J. Anthony Blair, "The Possibility and Actuality of Visual Arguments," 1996[1]

For people born in the 1960s or later, to say we live in a visual culture is to state the obvious. Bombarded by thousands of images every day of our lives, we have come to accept the information we get from visual messages as casually as we accept the sunrise. So prevalent are these images that when we are asked to listen without visual stimulus, we often lose interest and become restless. Although people once listened to music and politicians without accompanying images and visual distractions, now we are bored by performances that aren't stimulating to the eye as well as the ear.

What does our visual culture mean for beginning public speakers? In at least one of your speeches for your speech class, you probably will be asked to use some kind of visual aid. And in many of your speeches outside the classroom, you will want to display parts of your message visually. But how do you compete with the sophistication of the images in magazines and newspapers, on television and computer screens, and in live performances? How do you take advantage of technology to craft visual aids that not only enhance your message but also appeal to your audience?

Public speakers want, and often need, to design effective visual aids. To help you as a public speaker, this chapter discusses the reasons for using visual aids, various types of visual aids, what to show on a visual aid, formats for visual aids, and guidelines for using them.

Why Are Visual Aids Important?

You can certainly give an effective speech without visual aids. In fact, many of the speeches you've read about in this book were given without visual aids, including Martin Luther King Jr.'s famous "I Have a Dream" speech. Yet many types of speeches benefit from effective visual aids, especially those that describe a process, include complex information, or are intended to have great impact. Let's take a look at the very important functions of visual aids in a speech.

Visual Aids Help Gain and Maintain Audience Attention

In 1996 when attorney Johnny Cochran displayed the glove said to belong to accused murderer O. J. Simpson and told the jurors, "If it doesn't fit, you must acquit," he had his audience's full attention. Although his words were compelling and he used a memorable rhyme, the visual aid caught the jury's attention and kept them focused on his argument. A visual aid gives an audience something to focus on, and it reinforces your verbal message. If you want to capture your audience's attention, consider using a visual aid to complement your words.

Visual Aids Help Audiences Recall Information

One of the best known studies of visual aids in speeches assessed the amount of information the audience recalls because of visual aids. The researchers found that when a speech does not include visual aids, the audience recalls 70 percent of the information three hours after the speech. Three days later, they recall only 10 percent of the information. When the same message is delivered with visual aids only, the audience recalls 72 percent after three hours and about 35 percent after three days. When the message is delivered both in a speech and with visual aids, the recall after three hours is 85 percent and after three days 65 percent.[2] Clearly, visual aids assist with recall.

In another study, researchers asked people to examine a series of photographs and identify those that were repeated. With as many as two hundred photographs in a series, people still could pick out the repeat photographs.[3] However, when recall was tested by listening to series of numbers, people begin to forget which numbers were repeated in series of only six or seven numbers. Although common sense tells us that it often is more difficult to remember numbers, this study reinforces the previous one: visual information greatly improves audience recall. So one of the goals of your visual aids is to help your audience remember information.

Visual Aids Help Explain and Clarify Information

Research also suggests that visual aids can help you explain material and thus enhance the clarity of your information. Complex ideas and numbers can be hard to understand verbally but are much easier to sort out when displayed visually. Presenting an idea visually makes it more concrete. Visual aids such as handouts also increase the audience's continuity of thought—they can go back and check their understanding.[4] So the second goal of your visual aids is to help you explain or clarify your ideas.

Visual Aids May Increase Persuasiveness

Research also suggests that visual aids may increase your persuasiveness.[5] Visual aids not only clarify your message, but they can also help organize information, identify key points, and facilitate the reasoning process. In addition, images encourage audiences to make associations, so you can use both text and images to move your audiences toward a particular position. For example, a graph that displays a

Visual aids can be quite powerful and memorable. As such, they are often used in legal trials to help persuade juries of a defendant's guilt or innocence. What visual aids will you use in your next speech? How will they help you catch your audience's attention, help you be more persuasive, and enhance your credibility?

WEB SITE trend in people's attitudes is an excellent way to display the evidence you're using to back up a claim. Learn more about the power of visual images to persuade by completing Interactive Activity 14.1, "Persuading with the Flag," online under Student Resources for Chapter 14 at the *Invitation to Public Speaking* Web site.

Visual Aids May Enhance Credibility

Research also suggests that visual aids can add to your credibility by bringing a visual dimension to your speech.[6] Professional-looking and creative visual aids can energize your speech, causing you to seem more prepared, engaging, and lively. By helping you organize and clarify information, they also communicate an audience-centered perspective that contributes to your credibility. Using your *Invitation to Public Speaking* CD-ROM, watch a video clip of Carol's speech under Speech Interactive. Consider whether her visual aids helped her increase her persuasiveness and credibility.

Visual Aids May Reduce Nervousness

Finally, visual aids may help reduce your nervousness.[7] When you prepare effective visual aids, you pay more attention to the effectiveness of your speech's organization. Being better organized reduces your nervousness because you know your ideas are logical and carefully planned. Visual aids also can direct attention away from you and give you something to focus on other than your nervousness. Additionally, visual aids give you something to do with your hands, helping you relax in front of your audience. For example, in her speech on fitness, Jemma used a fit ball (a large rubber ball used to stretch and strengthen muscles) as a visual aid. A very nervous speaker, Jemma found that as she demonstrated how to use the ball, her attention was focused on explaining her ideas rather than on her nervousness. Not only was she more relaxed, but the audience learned a great deal from her demonstrations.

Types of Visual Aids

To make the most of a visual aid, let's look at the various kinds of visual aids you may be required or choose to use. Every type of visual aid has its strengths and weaknesses, so don't fix on any one kind until you've decided what you want to accomplish with the visual aspect of your speech.

Objects, Models, and Demonstrations

object
Something that can be seen or touched.

model
Copy of an object, usually built to scale, that represents an object in detail.

An **object** is something that can be seen or touched, and a **model** is a copy of an object, usually built to scale, that represents that object in detail. When you use objects and models, you help your audience understand certain ideas better than they could if you had merely described the idea verbally. Sometimes objects are impractical or impossible to bring to a speaking situation. For example, when you give a speech about the workings of a car, you could not easily bring a real engine to class. In such cases, models are ideal. Models can be smaller than the objects they represent (a model of a car engine), larger (a model of the mechanics of a wristwatch), or life size (a model of a human brain). In all these cases, the models allow you to show an object that otherwise would have been difficult to show.

Displaying an object or a model can engage an audience immediately, and many speeches lend themselves to this type of visual aid. For example, several of the speakers in Chapter 9 displayed objects. Cindy displayed a flag in her speech on flag etiquette. Molly displayed common household products that contain beef by-products in her speech on the invasion of beef by-products. Similarly, Jeret's speech on safe scuba diving ascents, Candice's speech on making a scrapbook, Brooke's speech on the chili pepper, and Martha's speech on batik all featured objects as visual aids.

Some of these speakers used their objects to demonstrate a process. A **demonstration** is a display of how something is done or how it works. For example, Cindy used her flag to demonstrate the process of folding a flag. Candice showed a scrapbook she'd created to demonstrate how to compile a scrapbook. Martha displayed various batik styles as she described how batik is produced. These speakers each used an object or a demonstration with that object to illustrate, clarify, and capture their audience's attention. Using your *Invitation to Public Speaking* CD-ROM, watch a video clip of Cindy's speech under Speech Interactive. Evaluate how effectively she uses the flag in her speech. When you display an object, display a model, or demonstrate a process, consider the following guidelines.

demonstration
Display of how something is done or how it works.

Cindy Gardner demonstrates the process of folding a flag.

Choose objects or models that help you illustrate or clarify a point.
Some objects or models may be intriguing, but they won't enhance your speech. Choose an object or a model that clarifies information. Remember, you want to use the object or model to help your audience understand your topic better. When Lee gave his speech on the Vietnam Veteran's Memorial, he wore a T-shirt he had purchased when he visited the memorial. Although the shirt was attractive, it did not help him clarify a point or illustrate the power of the memorial to evoke emotions. Lee would have been better off using an object (a replica of the item he left at the memorial, for example) to help him illustrate the power of the memorial on those who visit it.

Choose objects that are legal and nonthreatening.
Many interesting objects are illegal, threatening, or dangerous. Avoid displaying weapons, chemicals, drugs, or animals, all of which can be dangerous or difficult to handle. Although you may know how to handle these items outside a speech situation, you can't always predict what an animal, a dangerous substance, or other people will do during the speech.

Practice your demonstration before your speech.
Don't leave anything to chance with a demonstration. Rehearse it several times before the speech to be sure your equipment works correctly, your steps are smooth and effective, and your words explain what you are showing the audience. Recall Oscar's speech on the martial arts (Chapter 4). He practiced his demonstration in a small space, so he knew he could show his audience his martial arts moves without hurting someone or knocking things over. He also practiced when and how he would speak as he demonstrated various moves.

Make sure your demonstration enhances understanding.
Try to avoid demonstrations that are too complex, require a lot of equipment, or might make you look awkward or unprofessional. If your process is complex, simplify it for your demonstration or show only a part of the process. When Brock gave his speech on emergency rescue services, he wanted to talk about the importance of the equipment used and the knowledge that rescue workers need to use the equipment properly. To demonstrate some of the more complex knots rescue workers often use, Brock brought in ropes with knots already begun. He finished tying the

knots for his audience, demonstrating their strength as well as their complexity. Rather than take his audience through the entire process, he helped them understand that process by having a part of it prepared and set up before he began his speech.

Handouts

Business speakers often use handouts as visual aids. Examples include bound copies of business plans or year-end summaries; agency or product brochures; maps and photographs; and photocopies of graphs, charts, or articles. Handouts provide detailed information that the audience can refer to during a speech or read later and pass along to others. Handouts can elaborate on your message and help you spread it beyond your immediate audience. If you decide to use a handout, consider the following guidelines.

Mark the points you want to emphasize. One of the problems with handouts is that the audience sometimes has trouble finding the point you want them to focus on. To prevent this confusion, mark the points you want the audience to locate. Use letters or symbols or a more visual device such as color-coded plastic tabs. For example, if you want your audience to pay attention to one area on a graph or map, identify it with an arrow, symbol, or number. If you want them to turn to specific pages in a report, place tabs on those pages. Another way to help your audience locate specific spots in their handouts is to show the page, chart, or map on an overhead projector. Highlight the information or areas you will refer to, and direct their attention to those places as you speak.

Distribute the handout before or after a meeting. To avoid the disruption of passing out material during your speech, distribute your handouts, facedown, before the meeting begins or your speech starts. Angela (Chapter 4) distributed her handouts before her presentation. When she was ready to refer to the handout, she asked the audience to turn it over. She also had information she wanted her audience to review later—she distributed it after she finished speaking so the audience could refer to it later.

Remember that the handout supplements the message. A handout should add information to your speech and not become its text. Do not read lengthy passages from the handout aloud. Just refer to key points in it during your speech so your audience will be sure to note them when they read the handout after your speech. To avoid depending on the handout too much, outline its key points in your notes. And to keep your delivery extemporaneous, refer to the outline rather than to the handout itself.

Chalkboards and White Boards

Available in many offices and classrooms, chalkboards and white boards are convenient when you need to create a visual aid as you speak, clarify concepts during your speech, or keep track of ideas generated during discussions. Although you'll want to prepare your visual aids beforehand for most speeches, a chalkboard or white board may come in handy when you need to respond immediately to audience confusion or questions. They also allow you to keep information in front of the audience rather than having to remove it to make space for new information.

With some high-tech boards, you can even duplicate what you write on them and make a handout for the audience at the end of your speech.[8] One such board is called the SmartBoard. Go to http://www.smarttech.com/products/smartboard/inuse.asp to read about how communicators use this type of board. Used in these ways, chalkboards and white boards can help you stay audience centered throughout your speech. If you use a chalkboard or white board during a speech, consider the following guidelines.

Write neatly and legibly. Because your visual aid is not prepared ahead of time, what you write on the board may not be as neat as it would be on a prepared visual aid. It also hasn't been proofread for errors in spelling and grammar. So take care to write clearly, use a systematic organizational framework (such as an outline), and watch for spelling errors.

Talk to the audience and not the board. We sometimes talk while we are writing on the board because we're trying to stay within our time limit and because we're involved in the speech and want to keep the momentum going. However, this means our back is to the audience while we're talking. To avoid this problem, stop talking when you turn to the board to write. When you've finished writing, turn back to the audience and begin talking again. Although this pause may feel awkward the first few times, your audience will notice and appreciate your care to speak to them directly.

Poster Boards and Flip Charts

Poster boards and flip charts are durable and can be reused, so they are a good choice for speeches you will deliver more than once (such as sales presentations). If you want, you can write or draw your information lightly in pencil beforehand and then trace over your words and images as you speak, creating the visual as you go but ensuring neatness and correct spelling. In addition, you can use flip charts like chalkboards and white boards to record information during your speech, which is convenient for speaking in groups when brainstorming is a part of your process.

Because of their size (about 24 by 36), poster boards and flip charts are not suitable for large audiences. Use them for small groups where everyone will be sitting near enough to read them. If you use a poster board or flip chart as a visual aid, consider the following guidelines.

Make the design as professional as possible. Take time to display your ideas neatly and professionally. Don't just throw something together. Instead, think carefully about what you want to include on the poster board and flip chart. Use color and images to attract interest and attention. Use rulers and guides to ensure straight lines for words and sentences. Print neatly and clearly. If your writing isn't suitable, find someone who can do the lettering for you, or use stencils or stick-on letters for a professional look. If you will be using the poster board or flip chart again and again, consider having it professionally designed.

Display it professionally. Make sure you will have an easel or stand for placing the poster board or flip chart. Many speakers carry their own tabletop easel. If you plan to hang the visual aids, bring pins or tape with you (make sure ahead of time that pins or tape won't damage the walls). Think ahead about where you will display the poster board or flip chart so everyone can see it. Consider where you will put poster boards you've finished discussing, and practice flipping the pages of your flip chart so you do not tear them or tip the stand over.

Speak to the audience, not the poster board or flip chart. As with chalkboards or white boards, you may sometimes find yourself speaking to the poster board or flip chart rather than the audience. To avoid this problem, practice your speech with the visual aid so you are able to glance at or point to it but talk to the audience. Note that the students speaking on affordable housing (Chapter 7) not only prepared visual aids that looked professional so they could present their statistics clearly, they practiced using the poster boards so they were speaking to their audience rather than to the visual aid. They also worked in teams with one student pointing to the visual aids while a second student explained the significance of the numbers.

Transport and store poster boards and flip charts with care. Because they are durable, you can use these visual aids many times over. To protect them, store them in a safe place, wrapped or secured carefully. Transport them either in a case or inside protective materials, like plastic, or even between two blank poster boards. Using your *Invitation to Public speaking* CD-ROM, watch the video clip of Tony displaying an image with a poster board. How effectively do you think Tony used his visual aid?

Overhead Projectors

Although some may think overhead projectors are old-fashioned, they are an excellent choice for incorporating visual aids into a speech. They require little technological expertise, you can move or reposition them easily, and the transparencies are inexpensive and easy to prepare and store. Overhead projectors are appropriate for large audiences because they display material on a screen or a wall so everyone can see it clearly. Overhead projectors have other advantages too. Unlike chalkboards and white boards, you can work with an overhead projector and transparencies without having to turn your back to the audience. And, unlike some of the more sophisticated technology discussed later, less can go wrong with an overhead projector. The only skill you need is to position the transparency correctly on the projector. If you use an overhead projector, consider the following guidelines.

Prepare your transparencies in advance. Use a copy machine, printer, or a professional copy service to prepare your transparencies in advance. Design your visual message to enhance (not replace) your verbal message. Courtney (Chapter 15) used them to help her show her audience how to identify the various constellations in the night sky, adding to her descriptions rather than replacing them. Proofread your transparencies for spelling and punctuation errors. Check for clarity of font and font size (see the discussion of fonts later in the chapter). Check for consistency from transparency to transparency. For example, number your points consecutively (I., II., III., and so on), or outline your points using the standard format for outlines. Finally, peel off the protective paper before your speech rather than during it.

Check your equipment in advance. Before your speech, turn on the overhead projector, position it where you want it, and adjust the focus. Then turn off the machine until you are ready to use it. This gives you a chance to troubleshoot before the speech, replacing light bulbs or cleaning dust from the machine, so you can use your transparencies smoothly during your speech. The bulb in an overhead projector may go out at any time. If you use transparencies often, try to bring your own replacement bulb with you.

Consider how you will display your transparencies. One of the advantages of transparencies is that you can use them strategically. You can display the whole transparency (for example, a graph or chart) at once. Or you can cover it with a piece of paper as you begin speaking, uncovering it part by part as you speak. You can layer transparencies, adding new information by putting transparencies on top of each other (Courtney did this as she neared the end of her speech to show her audience the full night sky), and mark on transparencies with erasable markers. Practice your speech with your transparencies so you will feel confident when you display them to the audience.

Talk to the audience, not to the overhead projector or screen. When you use an overhead projector, your audience may be looking at the screen behind you rather than directly at you. You may be tempted to follow their gaze and turn around. Or you may be tempted to look down at the transparency rather than out at the audience. Keep your notes in front of you so you can speak from them rather than from the transparency or the material on the screen. To avoid being distracted by the transparency when you are through discussing it, remove it, turn off the projector, or cover the transparency. Remember, your goal is to keep your focus on the audience. For additional tips on using overhead projectors, go to http://www.ljlseminars.com/transp.htm.

Slides

Slides are another excellent visual aid for large audiences. Use them to display photographs that help you explain or reinforce a point. They can add color, detail, and a real-life atmosphere to your speech. You can add a bit of drama or even a personal touch by telling a story about the image on the slide. You can buy premade slides (reproductions of fine art, for example), ask a professional to take photos for you and have them made into slides, or have slides made from your own photographs. The biggest disadvantage of slides is that they require a darkened room, so be sure the room can be darkened (with window shades, for example), the audience does not need to take extensive notes, and you don't need to rely on your speaking outline or notes. Slides take time to organize and practice to deliver effectively, so if you select this form of visual aid, consider the following guidelines.

Prepare and organize your slides in advance. Whether you use slides created by a professional or slides made from your own photographs, start preparing early. Professional slides take time to produce and so does taking your own photographs and having them developed. In addition, you need time to retake any shots that did not come out well and to add slides to fill out your presentation, if necessary. You also need time to organize and reorganize your images as you develop your speech so the sequence of slides makes sense to both you and your audience.

Practice the wording of your descriptions. If you use images to help you tell a story, personalize an idea, describe a process, or illustrate an event, work out your wording before your speech. Practice your descriptions and narratives so you can deliver them extemporaneously. Practice will also help you remember when to advance to the next slide. Your speech will flow better if you don't have to go back to a previous slide to add a detail you forgot. Practice also gives you confidence to laugh at the unexpected—like accidentally pressing the reverse button on the remote rather than the advance.

Check the equipment. Equipment failure is probably the most common problem for speakers using slides. Your slide carousel may not fit the projector, the projector bulb may have burned out, the remote control may be missing, or the plug may not reach the outlet without an extension cord. Many speakers (like Landon in Chapter 5) find they have to reload their slides into a different carousel moments before their speech or have to send people hurrying around to find a bulb or an extension cord. To avoid these last-minute stresses, check the equipment well before your speech so you have time to fix anything that isn't working. If you can, bring a replacement bulb and extension cord with you, and be sure the carousel in which you've assembled your slides fits the projector.

Videotapes and Audiotapes

Videotapes and audiotapes allow you to show your audience images and to hear the sounds of what you are describing. They can bring a place or an event to life. If your audience is not likely to have seen or heard what you're talking about, a videotape or audiotape is an excellent way to introduce them. If you decide to use a tape, consider the following guidelines.

Keep your clip brief. Because speeches usually have a tight time limit, you don't want your video or audio segment to take up too much of your time. For example, if you have five minutes for a speech, a one-minute video or audio clip would leave you with four minutes for your speech. And after you subtract the time for your introduction and conclusion, you'll have less than three minutes to make your main points. Occasionally, you may talk over a video or audio clip. However, this tends to distract audiences, who have to struggle to listen to both you and the clip, so it's usually better to wait until the segment is done before speaking again. The shorter your speech, the shorter your video or audio clip should be. Use the clip to familiarize your audience with a new experience. Don't let the videotape or audiotape take over the speech.

Cue and edit your video or audio segment. If you are using only one segment of a tape, cue up that segment before your speech. Then, when you deliver your speech, you only need to push "play" to get the exact segment you want. If you are using more than one segment, make a master tape so they are on a single tape, eliminating the need to switch tapes or find a segment by fast-forwarding.

Today's computer technology makes it easier than ever to create professional quality videotapes on your home computer. One of the simplest programs to use is Apple's iMovie. To learn about creating high-quality videotapes for your next speech, complete Interactive Activity 14.2, "iMovie Tutorials," **WEB SITE** online under Student Resources for Chapter 14 at the *Invitation to Public Speaking* Web site.

Computer-Projected Technology

Commonly called PowerPoint (because of the popularity of Microsoft's PowerPoint program), computer-projected technology allows you to attach a computer monitor to a projection system and display your computer-generated visual aids on a screen. The images are stored, like a series of slides, on a floppy disk or a CD ROM. You insert the disk or CD into the computer, and it does the work of projecting the images on the screen. Like overhead projectors, this technology is excellent for large audiences but also very popular among speakers who address small audiences. You can design your slides with color and other graphic techniques, such as fade-ins, fade-outs, and overlays. Then, with a click of the mouse or a touch of a key, you can project your text, images, and graphics. Practice using Microsoft PowerPoint by completing Interactive Activity 14.3, "Creating a PowerPoint Presentation," located online under Student Resources for Chapter 14 at the *Invitation to Public Speaking* Web site.

WEB SITE

Computer-projected technology requires sophisticated equipment, but if it is available, it can enhance your speech. However, as with all visual aids, think about what you want to display visually and the best format for that material. It may be tempting to use the latest in technology, but if those bells and whistles don't help your audience understand and recall your message, your efforts are wasted. To consider some possible disadvantages of using PowerPoint, complete InfoTrac College Edition Exercise 14.1, "Thinking Critically About PowerPoint," online under Student Resources for Chapter 14 at the *Invitation to Public Speaking* Web site. If computer-projected technology will enhance your ideas, it is an excellent visual aid to use. When you are using computer-projected technology, consider the following guidelines.

Familiarize yourself with the technology. In order to use computer-projected technology to its fullest, become familiar with the technology and what it can do for you. You can get this information either from your speech instructor or from manuals that come with the software program. Make sure you understand the strengths as well as the limitations of the program so you can design effective visual aids.

Understand the purpose of a visual aid. Even though computer-projected technology offers a wide variety of design options (such as graphics, overlays, fade-outs, and sound), you don't need to use them all. Use only those that will help you focus, clarify, and organize your speech. Don't distract from your message with too many fancy techniques and moving images. Using your *Invitation to Public Speaking* CD-ROM, watch a slide show of Carol's PowerPoint presentation. Evaluate the effectiveness of her PowerPoint slides.

Jordan

I chose my visual aid by comparing my options. I could have used either photographs, overhead transparencies, poster boards, or PowerPoint. I finally decided on PowerPoint because I felt the flow of PowerPoint best matched my topic. My PowerPoint presentation took me almost four days to create. The part that took the most time was finding the pictures to use on the slides. Then I prepared by going through my speech and matching up the slides so my speech flowed with the images. It turned out to be very effective—during my speech there were no problems. I think PowerPoint is very effective; it can be entertaining, informative, and interesting.

Prepare and practice in advance. As with any visual aid, take time to prepare your slides and the accompanying descriptions. Give yourself enough time to reorganize, add additional slides, and eliminate those that don't seem to add to your speech. Use your preparation time to decide which points (if any) lend themselves to fades, overlays, graphics, or sound. And don't forget to save time to check for spelling and grammar errors once you've designed your slides. Additionally, practice using and describing your slides so your delivery is fluid and extemporaneous. To read about additional ways to avoid technological problems, read Claudyne Wilder's article "Technology: Make Sure It Works" at http://www.presentersuniversity. com/courses/show_vausing.cfm?RecordID=189.

Speech Step 14.1 / Identify Visual Aids to Use in Your Speech

Consider the eight different options for visual aids discussed in this section. Identify the types of visual aids that might enhance your next speech. Given your speaking goals, environment, and the available equipment, select one or two of these visual aids to use with your speech. Access Speech Builder Express for activity questions and Web links to help you develop your visual aids and incorporate reference to those aids in your speaking outline.

What to Show on a Visual Aid

Choosing the best type of visual aid to enhance your speech is your first step in using visual aids effectively. The second is deciding just what to show on your visual aids. Remember the purpose of visual aids: to clarify, enhance, and illustrate your ideas as well as help your audience remember your key points. You can accomplish your purpose by using visual aids that are based on text (lists), diagrams (charts and graphs), or images (drawings, photographs, and maps).

Lists

list
Series of words or phrases that organize ideas one after the other.

A **list** is a series of words or phrases that organize ideas one after the other. Lists are text-based visual aids, meaning they rely on the written word rather than on images to convey meaning. Use lists when your material lends itself to itemizing a group or a series, such as names, key features, or procedures. Lists help audiences keep track of material and identify the main points of a speech or discussion. The types of visual media best suited to lists are chalkboards and white boards, flip charts, poster boards, overheads, and computer-projected technology. When you use lists, consider the following guidelines.

Make your list brief. A list is a synopsis, so keep your lists brief. Use key-words or phrases rather than full sentences. Your goal is to prompt the memory of your audience members, not to have them read your full text. Here are some examples showing how to shorten sentences to words or phrases:

Incorrect	*Correct*
Visual aids help audiences recall more information.	Recall
Visual aids help explain and clarify information.	Explain
Visual aids can enhance a speaker's persuasiveness.	Persuade
Visual aids can enhance a speaker's credibility.	Enhance credibility
Visual aids can reduce a speaker's nervousness.	Reduce nervousness

Follow the six-word/six-line rule, which suggests you use no more than six words per line and no more than six items per list.[9] Remember, you goal is to cue your audience visually, not overload them with text.

Balance your wording. Audiences recall lists best if the items are parallel (Chapter 12). As you develop your lists, try to find balance or symmetry in the wording. For example, in a list of tips for using objects as visual aids, here's how you could balance your wording:

Incorrect	*Correct*
Use objects that illustrate or clarify.	Illustrate and clarify
Illegal and threatening objects may harm or frighten your audience.	Legal and nonthreatening

Include a heading. To help the audience keep track of your ideas, put a heading in boldface type at the top of your list. Because your audience can't go back and reread your written material, as they can with a full text, help them with recall by naming each list.[10] Here's an example:

The Importance of Visual Aids
- Recall
- Explain
- Persuade
- Enhance credibility
- Reduce nervousness

Charts

Charts can help you show steps in a process or parts of a concept. This helps an audience understand the relationship among the steps or parts and how they relate to the whole process or concept. The two most common charts used as visual aids are the flow chart and the organizational chart. A **flow chart** illustrates direction or motion—for example, the unfolding of a process or the steps to a

flow chart
A chart that illustrates direction or motion.

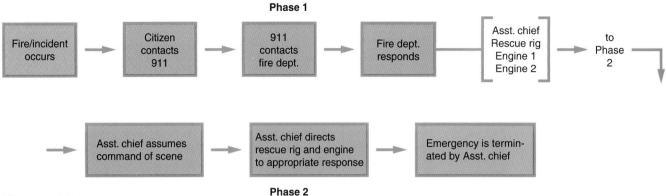

Phase 1

Fire/incident occurs → Citizen contacts 911 → 911 contacts fire dept. → Fire dept. responds → Asst. chief / Rescue rig / Engine 1 / Engine 2 → to Phase 2

→ Asst. chief assumes command of scene → Asst. chief directs rescue rig and engine to appropriate response → Emergency is terminated by Asst. chief

Phase 2

Figure 14.1
Flow Chart

organizational chart
A chart that illustrates the makeup of groups.

goal. An **organizational chart** illustrates the makeup of groups, such as organizations or places of business. Use a chart as a visual aid when you want to represent the parts of a whole or to simplify a complex process. Because charts are usually drawn in advance, the types of visual media best suited to them are handouts, overhead projectors, poster boards, and computer-generated visual aids. If you select a chart as your visual aid, consider the following guidelines.

Emphasize the visual image. When you create a chart, make the visual element primary and the text secondary. Use single words or short labels for titles and positions and as few words as possible to describe the steps of a process. You want your audience to visualize a process or the parts of a whole quickly and clearly, so keep it simple. For example, in Figure 14.1 each row of boxes indicates a separate phase of a fire department's response to an emergency—before and after a rescue crew arrives on the scene. Figure 14.2 is organized into a loose pyramid that places the head of a fire department's operations unit (the fire chief) at the top of the chart. The level of each employee's supervisory responsibility is

Figure 14.2
Organizational Chart

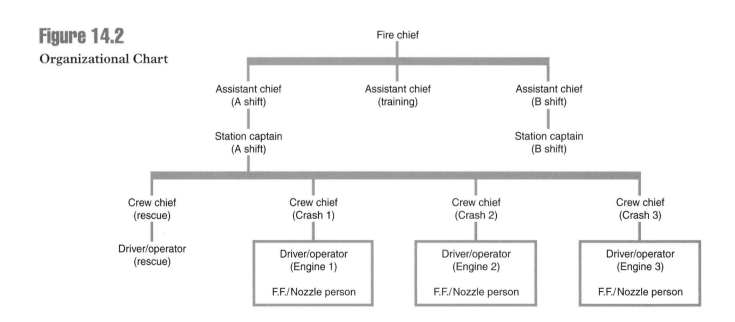

Fire chief

Assistant chief (A shift) — Assistant chief (training) — Assistant chief (B shift)

Station captain (A shift)   Station captain (B shift)

Crew chief (rescue) — Crew chief (Crash 1) — Crew chief (Crash 2) — Crew chief (Crash 3)

Driver/operator (rescue)

Driver/operator (Engine 1) / F.F./Nozzle person

Driver/operator (Engine 2) / F.F./Nozzle person

Driver/operator (Engine 3) / F.F./Nozzle person

then indicated by each layer of the pyramid—those with the highest levels are indicated in the top layers, those with the least in the bottom layers.

Use lines, arrows, shading, and color to show relationships and direction. To keep the audience's attention moving in the direction you want, use lines, arrows, shading, or color to help them follow your points as you explain the steps in a process or the structure of an organization. For example, in Figure 14.1 the blue boxes show the beginning and the end of a fire department's response to an emergency, the green boxes indicate each step of the response process, and the arrows indicate the progression of the steps from beginning to end.

Graphs

When you want to compare numbers or quantities, graphs are excellent visual aids. A **graph** is a visual comparison of amounts or quantities and it helps audiences see growth, size, proportions, or relationships. Use graphs when you are presenting numbers and statistics and want your audience to see the relationship between them. There are different kinds of graphs you can use for different purposes. **Bar graphs** compare quantities at a specific moment in time. **Line graphs** show trends over time. **Pie graphs** show the relative proportions of parts of a whole. **Picture graphs** present information in pictures or images. Figures 14.3, 14.4, 14.5, and 14.6 show how data from the U.S. census of 2000 could be represented for different purposes.

graph
Visual comparison of amounts or quantities that show growth, size, proportions, or relationships.

bar graph
A graph that compares quantities at a specific moment in time.

line graph
A graph that shows trends over time.

pie graph
A graph that shows the relative proportions of parts of a whole.

picture graph
A graph that presents information in pictures or images.

Figure 14.3

Bar Graph

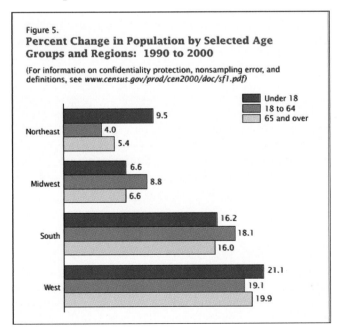

Source: U.S. Census Bureau, Census 2000 Summary File 1; 1990 Census of Population, *General Population Characteristics, United States* (1990 CP-1-1).

Figure 14.4

Line Graph

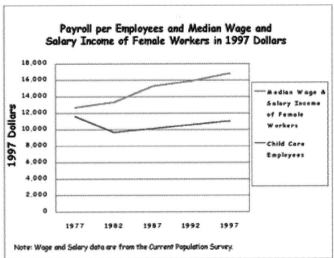

Source: U.S. Census Bureau, Population Division, Fertility and Family Statistics Branch. Maintained by Laura K. Yax (Population Division). Last revised: August 16, 2001 at 02:47:52 PM. Census 2000 & nb.

Figure 14.5

Pie Graph

Source: U.S. Census Bureau, Census 2000 (http://www.census.gov/prod/cen2000/dp1/2Kh00.pdf, page 3).

Racial Profile of the United States, 2000

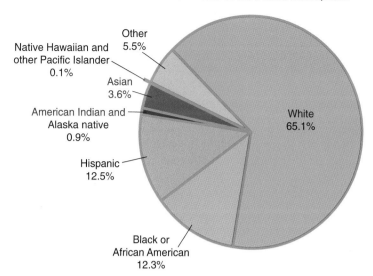

Figure 14.6

Picture Graph

Total U.S. Population: 1960 to 2050

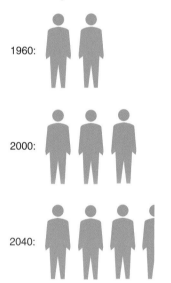

1960:

2000:

2040:

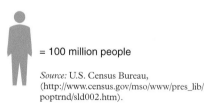

= 100 million people

Source: U.S. Census Bureau, (http://www.census.gov/mso/www/pres_lib/poptrnd/sld002.htm).

drawing
Diagram sketch of someone or something.

Like charts, graphs usually are prepared in advance and suited to handouts, overhead projectors, poster boards, flip charts, and computer-projected technology. To read more about how effective graphs can be in displaying numerical information, complete InfoTrac College Edition Exercise 14.2, "Using Graphs," online under Student Resources for Chapter 14 at the *Invitation to Public Speaking* Web site. When you decide to display the figures you present in a chart, consider the following guidelines.

Use clear and consistent labels. Label the horizontal and vertical axes with descriptive words such as "Year" and "Percentage." Mark equal intervals in the graph's grid—for example, numbers by tens, hundreds, or thousands, and dates by decades or centuries. Show the numbers of those intervals on the horizontal and vertical axes. For example, the vertical axis in Figure 14.4 indicates 1997 dollars earned in intervals of two thousand dollars. The horizontal axis indicates time in intervals of five years.

Use a computer to design your graph. Because graphs display amounts, relationships, and proportions, presenting this information accurately is important. A computer can help you represent this information cleanly and precisely, drawing images to scale and marking points on a graph clearly. Using a computer program, simply plug in the numbers and labels on the Excel table (or its equivalent), and the computer does the work for you. You can even experiment with different kinds of graphs and how they show your information.

Drawings

Drawings are diagrams and sketches of someone or something. They add clarity to your presentation because they help you show your audience what something looks like. You can draw your own images; photocopy, photograph, or scan images from books and magazines; or use computer clip art. The best visual media for drawings are handouts, overhead transparencies, flip charts, poster boards, and computer-projected technology. Simple images can be drawn on a chalkboard or a white board. If you decide to show your audience what you are discussing through drawings, consider the following guidelines.

Simple is best. According to many graphic arts texts, people seem to remember the outline of an image more than its details.[11] These texts advise you to keep your drawings simple. Use line drawings, symbolic representations rather than realistic drawings, simple clip art, photocopies of simple images, and even children's art. When Cory gave a speech about the process of knitting a wool sweater, she used simple line drawings to illustrate how the wool from a sheep is processed into yarn (see Figure 14.7). Remember, your goal is to represent your verbal message visually and not to use or create a great work of art. Learn how to create simple, professional-looking drawings with a computer by completing Interactive Activity 14.4, "Creating Images and Drawings," online under Student Resources for Chapter 14 at the *Invitation to Public Speaking* Web site.

WEB SITE

Figure 14.7

Simple Line Drawing

(From www.straw.com/clipart. Used with permission.)

Make sure the drawing clarifies the verbal message. Although drawings can be used to set the tone or communicate emotion, more often you will use them to explain your ideas and articulate your message clearly. Use drawings to clarify shapes (animals, buildings, symbols, and patterns, for example) and to show your audience the details of something (for example, what someone with dyslexia sees, or acupressure points on the body). Before you add a drawing to your speech, think about how it helps communicate your message. Does it clarify a concept? Does it illustrate something your audience may not have seen before? Does it simplify something that is complex? Be sure the drawing will enhance understanding for the audience.

Use audience-centered humor. You can use cartoons and funny or unusual drawings to make a humorous statement. However, first consider how your audience might react to the message sent by a visual aid you find humorous. Consider master statuses and the standpoints, attitudes, beliefs, and values (Chapter 5) of your audience members. Be certain a humorous drawing will be funny to everyone and not offensive. Reject those you think might insult members of your audience. For more on the topic of humor in speeches, see Chapter 19.

Photographs

Photographs help you show your audience what something really looks like or what really happened. They can also add color and drama to your speech. Photographs are most often shown on slides or computer-projected images, but you can also photocopy them onto a transparency or a handout. Note that a regular 3 x 5 or 4 x 6 photograph is too small for most audiences to see if you hold it up from the podium. In general, if you want to use photographs, project them on a screen so the entire audience can see them. A good Web source for presentation photos is Bizpresenter.com, located at http://www.bizpresenter.com/. If you think a photograph will help you clarify your ideas or make your point, consider the following guidelines.

Describe the photograph. To use a photograph successfully, you need to tell the audience what they are seeing. Call their attention to certain aspects of the photograph by describing them or explaining the action captured by the photograph. Don't be tempted to let the image speak for itself. Use the photograph to help you make your point by talking with the audience about it. For example, when Demetrious used photographs to describe the five villages of the Cinque Terre (Chapter 9), he pointed out the unique aspects of each village to help the audience distinguish them.

Don't pass out photographs. Rather than passing out original photographs to your audience during your speech, copy them and distribute them as a handout before the speech. When you are ready to refer to a photograph, call the audience's attention to the handout (in Chapter 8, Kameron did this to illustrate a zebra mussel colony on a buoy). Passing out individual photographs poses several problems: Original photographs are much more expensive than photocopies, especially if you are reproducing them for a large audience. Your audience will be distracted by them and by the process of passing them around the room. And by the time the last rows get the photographs, you will probably have introduced several new points.

Do not display photos in a book. It can seem time and cost efficient to simply stand in front of an audience and show them photos from books. However, images in books are too small to be seen by anyone but those sitting right in front of you. Instead of showing the picture in the book, reproduce it on a slide or a transparency, or scan it so you can show it with computer-projected technology. Your audience will appreciate your effort to include everyone in the presentation, not just those in the front rows. If for some reason you cannot reproduce images from a particular book or you want to show the entire book as well as the images it contains, display the book after the speech so the audience can get close to the images and even talk with you about them.

Maps

map
Visual representation of geographic features, urban areas, roads, stars and planets, and the like.

Maps are visual representations of geographic features, urban areas, roads, stars and planets, and the like. Maps can help you show your audience the physical layout and characteristics of a place, its location in relation to other places, and the route between places. Use a map to show your audience physical details that are best understood when presented both verbally and visually. The best visual media for maps are overhead transparencies, poster boards, and handouts. If you decide to incorporate a map into your speech, consider the following guidelines.

Draw your map to scale. Because maps help audiences understand relationships, draw the map to scale so the relative distances are accurate. Put your scale of measurement on a corner of your map so your audience can gauge the actual distances. For example, in drawing a map of a certain neighborhood, the students from Chapter 7 used the scale of 4 inches = 1 city block. This kind of scale doesn't require precise measurements because the students were mapping out something generally. Of course, a speaker would likely use a published map to illustrate specific geographic or astronomical features.

Include the most important details. When you copy a map or draw one yourself, follow the design principle for drawings: simple is best. Eliminate unnecessary details so the most important features will stand out. This will help the audience focus on your points and not get distracted by unnecessary details. Just as you would when you draw a map for a friend, give your audience only the key points or markers to help them find their way or understand the path they should follow.

Mark the spots you want to emphasize. To help your audience find the most important spots on your map, mark them with clear identifying features such as arrows, circles, or color. If you are giving directions or explaining a movement, such as the migration of birds, mark the path with numbers or arrows (you

Figure 14.8

Map of the Cinque Terre Region in Italy

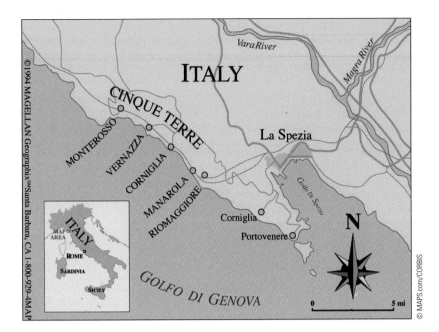

can do this beforehand, or you can draw on the map with markers as you describe the path). This will help keep your audience focused where you want them. For example, in Demetrious's speech about the Cinque Terre region in Italy, as he described them, he could have circled each village on the map to help the audience see where the villages of the Cinque Terre region are in relation to one another (see Figure 14.8).

If you hand out a map, show a larger visual aid of that same map. Use an overhead projector or poster board to explain a handout map to your audience. This way, you can point to or mark areas of the map rather than trying to describe them with words alone. This technique is especially useful when you want to point out several areas of a map and a handout would help your audience follow your discussion.

Talk to the audience, not to the map. As you describe your map, make eye contact with the audience rather than looking at the map. In terms of eye contact, maps may be the most challenging visual aid because we usually want to follow the map with our eyes as we describe it. To prevent this, keep your notes in front of you and refer to places on the map by the number or color you used to highlight them or by pointing briefly to the map and then returning to your notes.

Once you've decided on the type of visual aid you want to use and what you want to show on it, follow some basic principles regarding format, which is discussed next. These principles will help you design a visual aid that is easy to see and communicates your ideas effectively.

Speech Step 14.2 / Identify What You Want to Show on Your Visual Aids

Identify the material you want to show on the visual aids you selected in Speech Step 14.1. What type of material will help your audience with clarity and recall? What type will help you increase your credibility and give an audience-centered speech?

Formats for Visual Aids

Some speakers create their visual aids using computer programs and their own artistic skills. Others decide to have their visual aids professionally designed. Understanding a few basic design principles will help you develop a professional-looking visual aid or work with a graphic designer to create them. A few simple techniques will help you create visual aids that will enhance your verbal message.

Note that if you decide to create visual aids with Microsoft PowerPoint, you have access to many templates that incorporate the ideas discussed in this section. However, some of these templates don't follow the formatting advice offered here and so can detract from your message. Be sure to review the templates provided by PowerPoint before you use them. Or find additional templates at http://presenters university.com/scripts/pptregform.cfm?link_to=powerpoint.

Font Style and Size

font
Type or style of print.

A **font** is a type or style of print. Fonts range from simple to elaborate. As a rule of thumb, choose a simple font over a fancy one. Select a *serif font,* which shows small finishing strokes at the ends of the strokes of the letters. (The font you're reading now is a serif font.) Serif fonts create a baseline for the reader's eyes, leading them easily from letter to letter. Most newspapers and books use serif fonts, and if your visual aid contains a lot of text, this is an excellent font to use. To emphasize words, use a boldface version of your font to make the letters heavier and darker. Some common serif fonts are illustrated here, and you will find others on your own computer program.

Times New Roman	**Times New Roman (bold)**
Bookman	**Bookman (bold)**
Palatino	**Palatino (bold)**
Courier	**Courier (bold)**

Graphic artists suggest you can add variety to your visual aids by using different fonts in your titles or headings. To do this, use *sans serif fonts,* or fonts without the finishing strokes at the ends of the letter strokes.[12] Because of their straight lines, sans serif fonts create a bold, crisp look. As such, they tend to mark titles or headings as more prominent than the text in serif fonts that follow them. Some common sans serif fonts are shown here, and you will find others on your own computer:

Helvetica	**Helvetica (bold)**
Lucida Sans	**Lucida Sans (bold)**
Univers	**Univers (bold)**

When you create your visual aids, avoid elaborate font styles. Although they look fun and interesting, they are more difficult to read and create extra work for your audience. Notice how your eyes have to slow down to identify each letter in the samples here:

Mistral	*Zaph Chancery*
Lucida Serif	Handwriting
Goudy	

Save fancy styles for other projects, and keep your visual aids simple and easy to read.

Font size is the size of the letters and measured in *points*. The general rules for font size on visual aids like transparencies and computer-projected images are as follows. Note the size for headings, main points, and subpoints:

font size

Size of the letters in a particular font, measured in *points*.

Headings: 30- to 36-point font

Main points: 24-point font

Subpoints: 18-point font

By varying your font size, you help your audience identify your main and subordinate points. Unless your audience will all be sitting close to the screen, don't use smaller fonts than these because they are hard to read from a distance. If people struggle to see your text, your ideas become difficult to follow. Note that most audiences start sitting at about two or three feet from the speaker. To test whether your audience will be able to read the text on a projected visual aid, view it from about six feet away. If you have to strain to read it, you audience probably will too.

Color

When you add color to your visual aids, you tap into several design principles. First, color helps an audience make associations. For example, soft tones tend to set a calm, soothing mood, whereas bright colors tend to set an exciting mood. Note that the meanings of color, and the moods they evoke, vary across cultures. For example, in Western traditions, red can bring to mind anger or sinful activity. But in China, red often symbolizes good fortune, and in ancient Mexico, red symbolized the sun and its awesome power.[13] Second, different colors help your audience differentiate objects or items in a list. Finally, color creates hierarchies. For example, darker to lighter progressions indicate the level of importance, with the darkest the most important. You can use these three design principles to their advantage in your visual aids.

Notice how the addition of color to a visual aid can create a particular mood. Recall Silas's speech about melanoma from Chapter 12. He used Figure 14.9 when he discussed the dangers of spending too much unprotected time in the sun. The reds and oranges create an irritating, uncomfortable mood, implying the burning effects of the sun. He used Figure 14.10 with the same basic image, but with blues and greens to create a cooler, soothing mood that implies shade and protection.

In Figure 14.11, Jennifer used color to help her audience differentiate items in a list. The dark color (red) indicates the main point of her argument, and the light color (yellow) indicates the subpoints.

Recall Terri's speech in Chapter 9 about healthy eating. In her drawing of the food pyramid, she created a visual hierarchy by using darker colors to show which foods we want to eat more of during the day, lighter colors to show the foods we want to eat sparingly (see Figure 14.12).

When you use color in visual aids, establish a contrast between the text and the background so the text is legible. Avoid combinations of colors that are hard to read, such as bright red on dark green, or white on light beige. Also, be careful not

Figures 14.9
Beach-Goer in Hot Colors

Figures 14.10
Beach-Goer in Cool Colors

to overwhelm your audience with too much color. To find the balance you need, follow these suggestions:

Cool Colors: Blue, purple, green. Cool colors are calm and relaxing for most people, and they tend to be easier on the eyes. Use no more than two of these colors per page. Use them for text or graphics (as alternatives to using black and brown).

Hot Colors: Fuchsia, orange, red. Hot colors are stimulating and grab the audience's attention. Use them sparingly to identify keywords, bullet points, create emphasis, or draw the audience's attention to one particular item.

Figure 14.11
PowerPoint Slide That Uses Color to Indicate Hierarchy of Points

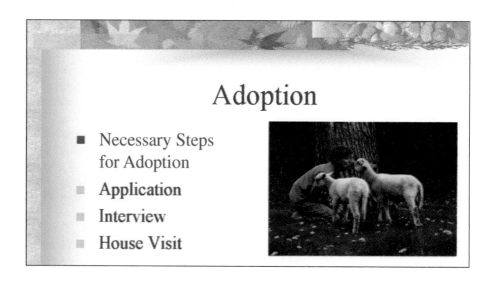

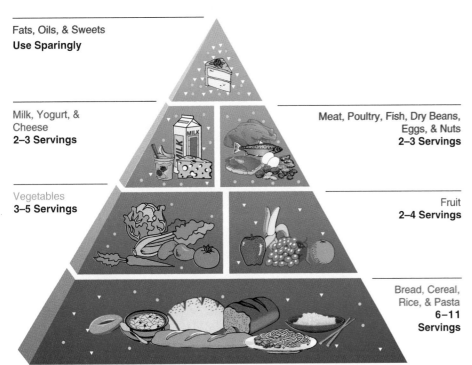

Fats, Oils, & Sweets
Use Sparingly

Milk, Yogurt, & Cheese
2–3 Servings

Meat, Poultry, Fish, Dry Beans, Eggs, & Nuts
2–3 Servings

Vegetables
3–5 Servings

Fruit
2–4 Servings

Bread, Cereal, Rice, & Pasta
6–11 Servings

Background Colors: Soft yellow, light blue, lavender, light green, soft orange, and beige. Background colors are soft colors that create backgrounds and borders. They also fill in solid areas that otherwise would have no color. Use them to add interest without grabbing the audience's attention. Use these background colors to help the audience clarify and focus on the foreground elements, like letters or images.

Balance

Balance is the relationship of the items on your visual aid to one another. You establish balance by the way you use space to arrange your ideas. A balanced visual aid helps your audience find information easily and not feel like their eyes are tipping in a certain direction. With text, it is easy to achieve balance by using bullets and indentation:

balance
Relationship of the items on a visual aid to one another.

Heading
- First point
- Second point
- Third point

You also can achieve balance by dividing your page (or screen) down the center with an imaginary line. The images on both sides should look similar. Figures 14.13 and 14.14 show how this can be done.

Consider the placement of your information carefully. A balanced visual aid sets the audience at ease and makes listening easier. It also helps you communicate your message clearly.

Figure 14.13
Imbalanced Page

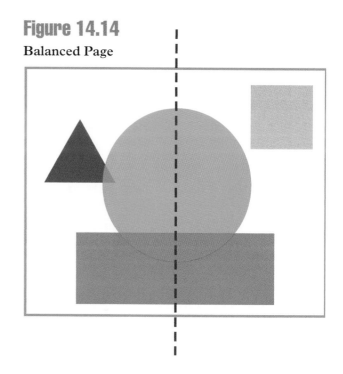

Figure 14.14
Balanced Page

 Using your *Invitation to Public Speaking* CD-ROM, analyze Carol Godart's PowerPoint presentation based on what you have read in this chapter under Speech Interactive.

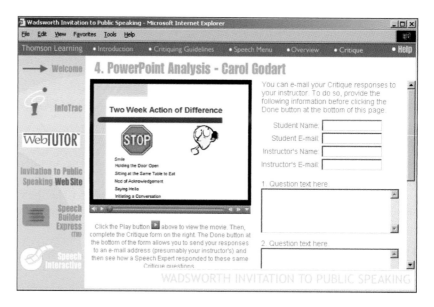

Speech Step 14.3 / Design Your Visual Aids

Begin designing your visual aids for your next speech. Make sure your visual aids follow the basic design principles of font style and size, color, and balance. Prepare at least a couple of drafts for each of your visual aids, and then check with friends or classmates about which are most effective in helping with recall, explaining information, and clarifying information.

Guidelines for Effective Visual Aids

No doubt you will use many different types of visual aids during your speech class and in your speaking career. There are several guidelines to follow to help you use those visual aids most effectively, no matter what kind you use.

Prepare in Advance

As with every other aspect of your speech, give yourself plenty of time to prepare your visual aids. Using the principles and guidelines discussed in this chapter, create visual aids that look professional and communicate your message clearly. Give yourself enough time to make adjustments and additions to your visual aids. By taking time to prepare, you will avoid last-minute pressure and have visual aids you can be proud of.

Practice in Advance

No matter how well you think you know your visual aids or how familiar you are with the equipment, practice your speech several times using the visual aids. When you use demonstrations, technology, and props like stands and easels, you have more to manage in your speech. Practicing allows you to check the time (how long is that demonstration or video, really?) and to work out any glitches with overhead transparencies or computer-projected images. It also lets you change the order of the visuals, if you need to, and practice talking about them while still making eye contact with the audience. As with the verbal component, you want to be sure you can deliver the visual component with confidence and skill.

Use Your Visual Aids Only When You Discuss Them

A visual aid is a tool to clarify and reinforce an idea. This means the length of time you use a visual aid will vary. However, use the visual aid only when you are discussing the idea to which the visual aid relates. When you're through discussing the idea, put the visual aid away, cover it with a piece of paper, or click to a blank slide in the carousel or computer images. This will draw your audience's attention back to you and your next point.

Explain What Is Shown on Each Visual Aid

Even though the image is directly in front of the audience, always tell them what they are seeing. Identify the key components of lists, graphs, charts, and images. Fill in the words left out of an outline, and take the time to point out the key points of an audiotape or videotape before you play it. Use each visual aid to its fullest rather than showing it quickly and moving on. You've taken time to develop your visual aids, so give them the time they deserve in your speech. Not only do audiences appreciate having the visual aids explained, but you benefit by making the most of your visual aids.

Talk to the Audience, Not the Visual Aid

Although it is tempting to look where the audience is looking (at the visual aid), remember to make eye contact with them as you talk about the visual aid.

Practicing the speech with the visual aid helps you keep eye contact with your audience. Because audiences look at visual aids for a short while before turning back to the speaker, you want to be ready for them. Your practice making eye contact as you work with your visual aids ensures that you will.

As you think about how you can use these guidelines to create effective visual aids, use your *Invitation to Public Speaking* CD-ROM to watch a video clip of Ross Perot under Speech Interactive. Evaluate how effectively he used his visual aids.

Chapter Summary

Visual aids have five purposes. First, they help audiences recall information. Second, they help you explain and clarify information. Third, they can increase your persuasiveness. Fourth, they can enhance your credibility. Fifth, they may reduce your nervousness. You have a choice of a variety of visual aids:

• Objects, models, and demonstrations

• Handouts

• Chalkboards and white boards

• Poster boards and flip charts

• Overhead projectors

• Slides

• Videotapes and audiotapes

• Computer-projected technology

You can show six different kinds of information on your visual aids to clarify, enhance, and illustrate your ideas. Lists of keywords and phrases help you organize ideas sequentially. Charts help you break ideas into separate parts. Graphs allow you to compare quantities and amounts. Drawings show diagrams and sketches of people and things. Photographs show audiences how things look in real life. Maps help audiences see places geographically and spatially. When using any of these different kinds of information on visual aids, pay careful attention to their formatting—font styles and sizes, color, and visual balance.

There are several guidelines for using visual aids in speeches. First, prepare the visual aid in advance. This allows you to make sure the design communicates clearly and effectively and to make any necessary changes before the speech. Second, always practice your full speech with your visual aids so you become comfortable using them. Third, when you are finished talking about the visual aid, put it away or cover it so your audience will return their attention to you. Fourth, always explain each visual aid to your audience so its meaning is clear. Finally, talk to the audience when using visual aids so your attention is on them rather than the visual aid.

Audiences have come to depend on visual images for both information and entertainment. Using simple visual aids in your speech responds to this expectation and helps you clarify and communicate your message for and to your audience. In the public dialogue, visual messages are as welcome as verbal ones, and by following basic principles and guidelines, visual aids can become a part of many of the speeches you give.

Invitation to Public Speaking Online

After reading this chapter, use your CD-ROM and the *Invitation to Public Speaking* Web site to review the following concepts, answer the review questions, and complete the suggested activities.

Key Concepts

object (324)
model (324)
demonstration (325)
list (332)
flow chart (333)

organizational chart (334)
graph (335)
bar graph (335)
line graph (335)
pie graph (336)

picture graph (336)
drawing (336)
map (338)
font (340)
font size (341)
balance (343)

Review Questions

1. Watch a few speakers outside of class, live or taped, give speeches. Which speakers incorporate visual aids and which do not? What are the strengths and weaknesses of each approach?

2. Bring an object or a model to class and practice describing it to your classmates. Try holding it, displaying it, and passing it around. Which techniques work well for you and which do not? Why and why not?

3. Many students believe computer-projected visual aids are superior to other types of visual aids. Additionally, many employers want employees to be familiar with this technology. In light of this emphasis on a single type of visual aid, identify the strengths of computer-projected visual aids. What kind of material is best suited to this form of presentation? Although you may use this type of visual aid in your future workplace, what other types of visual aids might you also use?

4. Incorporating font style, font sizes, color, and the principles of balance, create several drafts of your visual aids and bring them to class. In groups, select those that are most effective. Why are they effective? Why are the visual aids that you didn't choose ineffective?

5. Review the material you have gathered for your next speech. Which of your main points lend themselves to support by visual aids? What types of visual aids might you use? Assess the strengths and weaknesses of each type.

6. Select one of the following speech topics. Generate ideas for visual aids you could use for an informative, invitational, or persuasive speech on the topic.

   travel by light rail rather than by air

   musical instruments

   bubble gum

   retirement plans

   Alexander Graham Bell

The *Invitation to Public Speaking* Web Site

The *Invitation to Public Speaking* Web site features the review questions about the Web sites suggested on pages 327, 329, 332, 337, and 340, the interactive activities suggested on pages 324, 330, 331, and 337, and the InfoTrac College Edition exercises suggested on pages 331 and 336.

You can access this site via your CD-ROM or at http://www.wadsworth.com/product/griffin. To access Speech Builder Express in order to complete Speech Steps 14.1 and 14.3, you will need the username and password included under "Speech Builder Express" on your CD-ROM.

Web Links

14.1: SmartBoard in Use (327)
14.2: Using Overhead Projectors (329)
14.3: Technology: Make Sure It Works (332)
14.4: Bizpresenter.com (337)
14.5: PowerPoint Templates (340)

Interactive Activities

14.1: Persuading with the Flag (324)
Purpose: To consider the power of photographs in persuasion.

14.2: iMovie Tutorials (330)
Purpose: To learn basic video editing techniques.

14.3: Creating a PowerPoint Presentation (331)
Purpose: To create a PowerPoint presentation.

14.4: Creating Images and Drawings (337)
Purpose: To create diagrams for your next speech.

InfoTrac College Edition Exercises

14.1: **Thinking Critically About PowerPoint** (331)
Purpose: To understand the limitations of using PowerPoint.

14.2: **Using Graphs** (326)
Purpose: To learn about graphs and how they may be used effectively.

Speech Interactive on the *Invitation to Public Speaking* CD-ROM

The following video clips of speeches, referenced in this chapter, are included under Speech Interactive on your *Invitation to Public Speaking* CD-ROM. After you have watched the clips, click on "Critique" to answer the questions for analysis.

Video Clip 1: Enhanced Credibility through Visual Aids: Carol Godart (324). As you watch the conclusion of Carol's speech, pay close attention to the final image included on her PowerPoint presentation. How effective was this photograph? Did it enhance her credibility as a speaker?

Video Clip 2: Effective Use of Object as Visual Aid: Cindy Gardner (325). As you watch Cindy's speech on flag etiquette, pay close attention to how she uses the flag as a visual aid. How effective was her speech? How did using the flag add to the clarity of her speech? What might she have done differently to deliver a more effective speech?

Video Clip 3: Effective Use of a Poster as Visual Aid: Tony D'Amico (328). Evaluate Tony's use of a poster as a

visual aid in the speech he gave at a forensics tournament. Was his poster professionally displayed? Did he speak to the audience and not the poster?

Video Clip 4: Analysis of PowerPoint Presentation: Carol Godart (331 and 344). Based on the principles you learned in this chapter for creating visual aids, analyze the PowerPoint presentation Carol Godart created for her persuasive speech on "Fat Discrimination." Did Carol's slides follow the guidelines for font style and size, color, and balance?

Video Clip 5: Ross Perot's 1992 Campaign Speech (346). Ross Perot gained a great deal of attention during the 1992 presidential campaign for his arguments and speaking style. One characteristic of his style was the use of visual aids. After you understand how to use visual aids effectively, watch the clip of Perot's speech. Do Perot's charts appear professional? Does he use them only when discussing them? Does Perot explain each chart adequately? Does he keep eye contact with the audience?

Chapter Fifteen

Informative Speaking

In this chapter you will learn to

Describe the five types of informative speeches

Apply the four most common patterns of organization for informative speeches

Identify three tips for giving effective informative speeches

Identify three principles for giving ethical informative speeches

Sometimes, people just need more information. Like the time my friends asked me, "Why can't I just leave my trash here? Isn't that what the staff is paid for, to pick up my trash?" or when they said, "Why does it matter if we lose certain species? I'll never see that animal anyway." I knew then that they didn't need persuasion or invitation; they really didn't know why it mattered. They needed information.

—Jennifer McMartin, student at Colorado State University, 2001[1]

informative speech
Speech that communicates knowledge and understanding about a process, an event, a person or place, an object, or a concept.

informative speaking environment
Environment in which a speaker has expertise or knowledge that an audience needs but doesn't already have.

Although our days are often flooded with information—ideas, stories, data, facts, and more—we don't always receive the full story. We may receive snippets of useful information, but we don't always have enough to fully understand an important process, circumstance, or issue. Sometimes the part of the story we have is inaccurate or incomplete, so our assumptions are skewed, as this chapter's opening quote illustrates.

To fully understand the world we live in, we need a dependable flow of complete and accurate information. To meet that need, speakers in the workplace, the classroom, and in our communities, often speak informatively. An **informative speech** communicates knowledge and understanding about a process, an event, a person or place, an object, or a concept. Informative speakers share what they know or have researched in order to familiarize an audience with a topic the speaker thinks they should understand or that an audience itself wants or needs to understand.

Informative speakers create **informative speaking environments**, or environments in which a speaker has expertise or knowledge that an audience needs but doesn't already have. When speakers create informative environments, their goal is not to invite (Chapter 16) or persuade (Chapter 17) but rather to illustrate for an audience the importance and relevance of a topic. Informative speakers attempt to enhance an audience's understanding of how some part of the world works.

As you enter the public dialogue, you will give informative speeches quite often.[2] In fact, in a 1994 survey, people working in businesses and organizations responded that because "information must be disseminated, and not just in written reports and computer files," public communication skills are essential.[3] We place such emphasis on informative speaking because we need information every day in order to, for example, understand how a new medication will affect us, learn how to parallel-park, deliberate over the governor's proposal for spending a budget surplus, or complete the complex assignment our boss just gave us. To learn more about the importance of informative speaking in your life, complete

WEB SITE Interactive Activity 15.1, "Communicating Information in Your Career," online under Student Resources for Chapter 15 at the *Invitation to Public Speaking* Web site.

Types of Informative Speeches

The five types of informative speeches you will give most often in your public speaking class and in the workplace are speeches about processes, events, places and people, objects, and concepts. Each type of speech has a different focus, and each is suited to a different occasion.

Speeches About Processes

Commonly called a how-to or a demonstration speech, **speeches about processes** describe how something is done, how something comes to be, or how something works. Process speeches help an audience learn how to complete a task, understand how something develops over time, or comprehend how a process unfolds. The fundamental goal of a process speech is to show your audience how to *perform* a process or how to better *understand* a process. Some sample topics for process speeches are

speech about a process
Informative speech that describes how something is done, how something comes to be, or how something works.

How to create a PowerPoint presentation

How to use priceline.com

How to catch, land, and release fish without hurting them

How to make an envelope from paper you have around the house

How the Electoral College works

How trees are processed into the products we use every day

How women used different designs on quilts to give directions secretly to runaway slaves along the Underground Railroad

Process speeches are common because most people are constantly learning how to perform new tasks. Speakers are often asked or required to speak about processes. For example, your boss may ask you to explain to a colleague how to fill out and submit an expense report. Or you may be asked to explain to new staff how an employee incentive program came to be implemented, especially if you have a history with that particular program. In the classroom, you may be required to speak about a process that your fellow students will benefit from learning more about.

The following three examples illustrate process speeches about a very familiar topic: coffee. In the first example, Tracee describes how to brew and drink an espresso.

Specific purpose: To inform my audience how to make and drink an excellent cup of espresso.

Thesis statement: There are three steps to making and drinking a great cup of espresso.

Main points:
I. The first step is to select the right beans and grind.
II. The second step is to use the espresso machine properly.
III. The third step is to use the proper espresso cup and follow the proper style of drinking an espresso.

In the second example, Tracee describes how coffee came to be a popular drink in North America.

Specific purpose: To inform my audience how coffee became one of the most popular drinks in North America.

Thesis statement: Through a series of historical events beginning in the 1500s, coffee replaced tea as one of the most popular drinks in North America.

Main points:
I. Coffee found its way to North America in the 1500s when trade routes opened between coffee-growing countries and Europe, then expanded to North America.
II. Coffee began to gain in popularity as tensions with England accelerated in the 1700s and imports of tea decreased.

III. By the 1900s, international commerce, marketing techniques, and individual lifestyles made coffee one of the most popular drinks in North America.

In the third example, Tracee describes how the process of growing and harvesting coffee works.

Specific purpose: To inform my audience how shade-grown coffee is grown and harvested.

Thesis statement: The process of growing and harvesting shade-grown coffee differs from the process used by coffee plantations in three significant ways.

Main points:
    I. Shade-grown coffee is grown in small plots, quite unlike the more familiar coffee plantation method.

    II. As the plants grow, these plots provide nonchemical forms of fertilizer and pest control.

    III. When the coffee beans are mature, they are harvested and stored in ecologically friendly ways.

Notice how each of these speeches follows a progression of steps, from first, to second, to third. Because process speeches describe step-by-step progressions, they are almost always organized chronologically. Recall from Chapter 9 that the chronological pattern traces a development or evolution over time. A chronological organizational pattern allows you to develop your speech from the first step to the last, or from the earliest signs to the most recent examples. (Later in this chapter you'll explore organizational patterns for informative speeches more fully.) To better understand the importance of presenting information clearly and chronologically, complete Interactive Activity 15.2, "Evaluating a Process Speech," online under Student Resources for Chapter 15 at the *Invitation to Public Speaking* Web site.

WEB SITE

Danielle

I enjoyed presenting the informative speech the most because I felt I had more options to choose from. When I learned the speech could be a speech about processes, I knew I wanted to give a speech on how the clarinet has progressed over time and then play part of a piece for the class. I chose the chronological pattern of organization to discuss the evolution of the modern-day clarinet. I think it went well, and the class said they enjoyed hearing me play.

Speeches About Events

speech about an event
Informative speech that describes or explains a significant, interesting, or unusual occurrence.

Speeches about events are speeches that describe or explain significant, interesting, or unusual occurrences. Speeches about events help an audience understand what happened, why it happened, and what effect it had. Just as we often describe what happens in our personal lives so we can better understand how events influence our lives, public speakers share what happens with audiences to help them understand a significant event in the context of history or society or community. In some ways, speeches about events are mini history lessons that educate audiences about key moments. Some sample topics for speeches about events are

The student protests at Tiananmen Square

Lighting the torch at the Olympic games

The most recent space flight

New York's Saint Patrick's Day Parade

The assassination of Dr. Martin Luther King Jr.

The discovery of penicillin

Speakers are often asked to speak about events, usually in professional settings. Consider Jackson, whose boss asks him to speak to his fellow employees about what he learned at a recent trade show.

Specific purpose: To inform our staff of last week's athletic equipment trade show.

Thesis statement: The About Athletes trade show displayed the newest and most popular pieces of sporting equipment, promoted exercise as a part of a healthy lifestyle, and featured presentations about the latest trends in athletics.

In a community setting, people may decide to speak about events in their community as a way to inform councils, planning boards, or community service agencies and perhaps assist them with the decisions they make.

Specific purpose: To inform the city council about the high rate of accidents at the corner of College and Main Streets.

Thesis statement: The intersection of College and Main is the site of an unusually high rate of accidents during certain hours of the day.

When you are required to speak about an event, such as when you are assigned an informative speech in class, select a topic your audience will find interesting and relevant. For example, inform your classmates of an event that affects your own campus (a public hearing to improve public transportation to the campus), the community that houses your campus (an annual jazz festival that showcases successful musicians from the community), or your state or region (a recognition ceremony for local volunteers who helped battle forest fires throughout the

Historical events are often interesting topics for informative speeches, especially if they relate somehow to an audience's current experience. For example, the invention of the ENIAC computer in 1945 marked the beginning of a revolution in how we distribute, process, and store information. What historical events do you think might make a good topic for an informative speech?

© Bettmann/CORBIS

state). To read about an interesting event that would be a good topic for an informative speech, complete Interactive Activity 15.3, "Describing the Race of a Lifetime," online under Student Resources for Chapter 15 at the *Invitation to Public Speaking* Web site.

Most speeches about events, especially historical events, are arranged chronologically. However, if the way in which an event unfolds is not the focus of your speech, you can organize your speech topically. Or if you want to analyze why an event occurred and what effect it had, you can use a causal organizational pattern.

Speeches About Places and People

speech about a place or a person
Informative speech that describes a significant, interesting, or unusual place or person.

Speeches about places and people describe significant, interesting, or unusual places or people. Speeches about places and people can be fun to give in a classroom because you can share your experiences with places and people you've visited or have found fascinating. In the workplace or the community, speeches about places and people help audiences understand the importance, nature, appeal, charm, or integrity of a particular place or person, or the contributions a particular person has made to an organization or a community. An excellent source of topics and information about people is A&E's *Biography* Web site, found at http://www.biography.com. Some sample topics for speeches about places and people are

Service agencies in your community	Langston Hughes
Natural history museums	Elizabeth Dole
Greenwich Village	Ellen DeGeneres

Because you won't have time in a speech to discuss all there is to know about a place or a person, the goal of this type of speech is to capture the *spirit* of that place or person. You want your audience to understand why this place or person is important or useful to them or their community, important historically, or just interesting and worth learning about. Let's look at an example of a speech that Pia, an outreach coordinator, gave to students in a sociology course.

Specific purpose: To inform my audience about Crossroads, the safe house for battered women and children in our community.

Thesis statement: Crossroads shelters battered women and children so they feel safe as they get on their feet and begin to reestablish their lives.

In the next example, Rhonda informs her classmates about a significant person who attended their university and who represents a part of their history.

Specific purpose: To inform my classmates of John Jones, one of the first African American students to attend this university.

Thesis statement: When Jones first came to this university as a student in 1950, he faced prejudice and segregation, in part because of the racism in society at the time and in part because the university was not fully prepared to accommodate an integrated student body.

Speeches about places or people can be organized topically (each of the services Crossroads offers its clients), chronologically (significant experiences in John Jones's university career from his freshman year through his senior year), or spatially (Big Bend National Park in Texas features recreational areas in the mountains, the desert, and at the Rio Grande River). To consider how information about a person can be presented to an audience, complete Interactive Activity 15.4, "Meet Winona LaDuke," online under Student Resources for Chapter 15 at the *Invitation to Public Speaking* Web site.

WEB SITE

Speeches About Objects

Speeches about objects are speeches about anything that is tangible, that can be perceived by the senses. When we speak informatively about objects, we describe the components or characteristics of something so an audience can better understand it and why it might be important or valued. Some sample topics for speeches about objects are

speech about an object
Informative speech about anything that is tangible, that can be perceived by the senses.

The largest or oldest tree in the world	The features of cell phones
The fastest automobile	Albino leopards
Buildings on the historical register	Poisonous frogs

Speeches about objects are common in the working world. For example, a product development coordinator might speak regularly to her colleagues about new products that come across her desk, describing their qualities, uses, and appeal. Similarly, tour guides often speak about local objects of importance or interest, describing buildings, sculptures, and pieces of art. For a required classroom speech about an object, you might describe an object that is useful, rare, or of interest to a speech class audience. For example, Jun Lee gave a speech about Mona Lisa's mysterious smile:

Specific purpose: To inform my audience about the Mona Lisa and the many theories about her famous smile.

Thesis statement: One of the most famous paintings of all time, the Mona Lisa has inspired several theories about the reason behind her mysterious smile.

A very popular topic for speeches about *animate* objects is animals and their behaviors, habitats, and ways of interacting with humans and other animals. Here is a sample specific purpose and a thesis statement for a speech about the communication patterns of African elephants.

Specific purpose: To inform my audience of the sophisticated communication behaviors of the African elephant.

Thesis statement: African elephants are known to send messages to one another across great distances and to communicate tremendous grief at the loss of a member of their family or community.

To learn more about how to present information about animals effectively, complete InfoTrac College Edition Exercise 15.1, "Learning About Pandas," online under Student Resources for Chapter 15. To find pictures of animals you can use for free as visual aids for your speech, go to http://www.fotoclipart.com/frame/animals.htm.

Many speeches about objects are organized topically (the characteristics of the poisonous frog). Others are organized spatially (the features of the cell phone), and sometimes a speech about an object can be organized chronologically (the buildings on the historical register, from oldest to youngest). Be sure to select the pattern that helps you express your ideas clearly and efficiently.

Speeches About Concepts

speech about a concept
Informative speech about an abstraction, such as an idea, a theory, a principle, a worldview, or a belief.

Speeches about concepts are speeches about abstractions, such as ideas, theories, principles, worldviews, or beliefs. The goal of a speech about a concept is to help your audience understand a concept, its history, its characteristics, and its effect on societies or individuals. A concept is something you can't perceive with your senses, such as socialized medicine, theories about how the world began, individualism, democracy, equality, and Christianity. Some sample topics for speeches about concepts are

Philosophies about reincarnation	Social equality
Adult literacy	Theories of child development
Principles of modern art	Poverty in the rural United States

In the workplace, community, or classroom, when you give speeches about concepts you help audiences more fully understand or appreciate issues, principles, systems, and the like. Consider Mallori's speech about the benefits of a sustainably designed home.

Specific purpose: To inform my audience about the benefits of a sustainably designed home.

Thesis statement: Many people think sustainable designs will result in an unattractive or expensive home, but sustainable designs are often attractive and affordable.

Speeches about concepts can be challenging because sometimes it is difficult to explain an abstraction clearly. However, this type of speech is also very helpful because sometimes audiences need to understand concepts before they can understand how something works or why a person is significant. Consider again Mallori's speech about sustainable design. Her audience may not have appreciated a speech about how to build a sustainably designed home if she had not first informed them of the nature and qualities of sustainable design.

Speeches about concepts are often organized topically (the principles of modern art) or chronologically (early theories of child development to the most recent ones). Sometimes a speech about a concept can be organized causally (the causes of poverty in the rural United States).

 Speech Step 15.1 / Select an Informative Speech Type

For your next informative speech, decide whether you will speak about a process, an event, a place or a person, an object, or a concept. Use the assignment given to you by your instructor and review the descriptions of each type of speech in this section to help you make your decision.

Organizational Patterns for Informative Speeches

Informative speeches can be organized in a variety of ways, and you will probably use a wide range of organizational patterns as you become a proficient public speaker. As a beginning speaker, practice using the most common patterns, discussed in Chapter 9 generally and in this section specifically. These organizational patterns are the chronological, spatial, causal, and topical patterns. Note that these patterns are effective in part because they help you organize your main points logically.

Chronological Organizational Pattern

With a chronological pattern, you can organize your main points to illustrate how a topic has developed over time or what steps an audience must take to do some task. Most of us are familiar with the chronological pattern because it is the pattern many stories use to describe developments over time. Chronological patterns are especially effective for process speeches, but as you learned earlier in this chapter, they also are well suited for other kinds of informative speeches. In the following example, Courtney gives a process speech to explain how her audience can identify major constellations in the sky.

Specific purpose:	To inform my audience how to identify some of the major constellations in the night sky.
Thesis statement:	Several constellations are easy to locate with simple equipment and the use of a step-by-step process in which using stars in one constellation helps you find other constellations.
Main points:	I. The first and easiest constellation to identify is Ursa Minor, or Little Bear.
	II. Once you find Little Bear, you can find the Little Dipper within it.
	III. After you've found these two constellations, you can find Ursa Major and the Big Dipper.
	IV. From the Big Dipper, you then can find another constellation, Cassiopeia.

Courtney takes her audience through a four-step process of first finding the easiest constellations and then the constellations that are harder to locate. By using this pattern, she provides her audience with basic information they can then build on as she progresses through her speech. Note that she could have used the spatial organization pattern instead, moving east to west across the sky. However, for an audience unfamiliar with stargazing, she felt that organizing her ideas chronologically would make her speech easier to follow.

The next example illustrates how Joseph used the chronological pattern to trace the evolution of a concept. He described a spiritual belief system, its evolution, and the ways in which the system is integrated into every aspect of life.

Specific purpose:	To inform my audience how the Kemetic civilizations of ancient Egypt created a holistic view of existence.
Thesis statement:	Even though African civilizations are often thought of as pagan, the Kemetic civilizations of ancient Egypt created a holistic view of existence in which a monotheistic spiritual belief system was integrated into every aspect of life, including architecture and astronomy.
Main points:	I. This religious belief system began with the observation of heavenly bodies.
	II. The Kemites began to integrate their knowledge of celestial cycles into their religious beliefs and identified many deities, each worshiped as different aspects of one God.

Many topics of informative speeches can be organized in several different ways. For example, a speech about pollution and the environment could be organized chronologically (pollution during the agricultural age, the industrial age, and the information age) or spatially (pollution in the air, on land, and in water). This photograph depicts the cleanup of a 10,000-gallon industrial oil spill in Michigan's Rouge River. How do you think you could organize this topic topically and causally?

© Bill Pugliano/Getty Images

III. As the Kemites' body of knowledge increased, their society began to integrate their religious beliefs into every aspect of life.

Joseph takes the audience through an evolutionary process, tracing and describing the development of a belief system from its origins to its full development.

Spatial Organizational Pattern

The spatial organizational pattern allows you to address topics logically in terms of location or direction. Recall from Chapter 9 that with this pattern you can arrange your main points by the position they represent within a physical space. You can use this pattern to inform your audience of the places that relate to your topic, the activities that occur in those places, or the activities that are necessary to the functioning of your topic. In the following example, Lehla uses a spatial pattern to describe the animal shelter she works for.

Specific purpose: To inform my audience about the animal shelter and the various kinds of animals we care for there.

Thesis statement: Although we care for dogs and cats at the shelter, we also have the capability to care for animals ranging from livestock to fish.

Main points:
    I. Dogs and cats, which make up most of our clientele, are housed closest to the entrance for ease of care and visitation.

    II. In the cages and containers behind the dogs and cats, we have birds, fish, and small reptiles.

    III. Outside, in back of the shelter, we house the livestock, which need more space and open air.

    IV. At the furthest border of the property, and under tight lock and key, we keep the large reptiles.

By addressing her topic spatially, Lehla guides her audience around the various parts of the shelter. They learn something about the shelter itself as well as about the animals, which was one of her primary speech goals.

In the next example, Tye uses a spatial pattern to describe four popular sculptures in the central park of his city.

Specific purpose: To inform my audience of the four sculptures displayed in the park, all created by local artists.

Thesis statement: There are four sculptures in our downtown park, each created by a different local artist and each representing a different aspect of our community.

Main points:

I. When we enter from the north side, which links us to the museum and the performing arts center, the first sculpture we find is called, of course, *Encore*.

II. Following a route toward the east, where the playgrounds are always full of busy children, the second sculpture is known as *L'Chaim*, the Hebrew expression meaning "for life" or "to your life."

III. Near the south entrance, the third sculpture is called *Arboleda*, the Spanish word for "grove of trees," and it represents the botanical gardens in that part of the park as well as the efforts to preserve a very old stand of trees within our city.

IV. At the west entrance, our commitment to community is expressed in the fourth sculpture, called *Nommo*, which is an African term for the power of the spoken word to bring people together and sustain them in all kinds of circumstances.

Describing the sculptures spatially allowed Tye to address each sculpture in a logical progression through the park. This organization also allowed him to explain how each part of the park represents the principles the community is attempting to celebrate.

Causal Organizational Pattern

Causal organizational patterns highlight cause-and-effect relationships. A cause is an event that makes something happen, and an effect is the response, impression, or change that results from that cause. When you use causal patterns, you inform your audience about what causes certain events, places, objects, or concepts to come into being.

In the following example, Erin addressed the issue of school violence, particularly as it affected her—she was one of the students at Columbine High School in Colorado on April 20, 1999, when two students killed thirteen fellow students and one teacher. Erin's use of a causal pattern helped her explain why school violence is becoming more common.

Specific purpose: To inform my audience about some of the causes of school violence.

Thesis statement: Experts agree that school violence is caused by several factors: frustration, manipulation, retaliation, and the misconception that violence is an appropriate response.

Main points:	I. Some students turn to violence because they lack a constructive outlet to express their frustration.
	II. Some students lash out when they are manipulated by other students.
	III. Some students seek retaliation against perceived wrongs or insults.
	IV. Some students have learned that responding to certain situations with violence is appropriate.

Erin did not try to persuade or to invite her audience into her world. Rather, she provided information about a difficult issue, helping her audience understand, as she had come to understand, how the violence at Columbine could have happened. By using the causal pattern, she helped her audience understand what causes some students to resort to violence, and in a later speech, Erin discussed with them possible solutions to school violence.

Topical Organizational Pattern

The topical organizational pattern allows a speaker to address different aspects of a topic. For example, the topic of elephants can be organized according to their habitats, favorite foods, and interactions with other elephants. Topical patterns work well in informative speeches whose topics can be easily and logically divided into subtopics. Using a topical pattern, you can highlight the aspects of a topic that are most useful and important for an audience to understand. Let's look again at Pia's speech about the Crossroads safe house and how she could have used a topical pattern to discuss its characteristics and services.

Specific purpose:	To inform my audience about Crossroads, the safe house for battered women and children in our community.
Thesis statement:	Crossroads shelters battered women and children so they feel safe as they get on their feet and begin to reestablish their lives.
Main points:	I. A "safe house" is a secret location where battered women and their children can live without fear of being found by their abusers.
	II. The typical family at Crossroads is a woman and her children who are seeking respite from an abusive husband or boyfriend.
	III. To help women and their children get back on their feet, Crossroads provides temporary housing, clothing, job placement services, counseling, and, above all, safety.

Cindy Gardner

By using this organizational pattern, Pia could have highlighted the different features of Crossroads and educated an audience about the purpose of safe houses, the families that stay at Crossroads, and the services provided there.

To evaluate the organizational patterns used by a magazine writer in an informative article about a personal digital assistant, complete InfoTrac College Edition Activity 15.2, "Identifying Organizational Patterns," online under Student Resources for Chapter 15. And to watch a video clip of Cindy giving her informative speech, use your *Invitation to Public Speaking* CD-ROM to access Speech Interactive. (Recall that you saw Cindy using the flag as a visual aid in Chapter 14.) Consider the effectiveness of the organizational pattern she uses for her speech. You can read the full text of Cindy's speech at the end of this chapter.

An informative speech topic can be organized chronologically, spatially, causally, and topically. Consider your next informative speech and select the pattern that helps you explain your topic clearly and in a way your audience will find useful and interesting. Speech Builder Express helps you outline your informative speech once you've selected an organizational pattern. Access Speech Builder Express online by using the username and password included under "Speech Builder Express" on your *Invitation to Public Speaking* CD-ROM.

Tips for Giving Effective Informative Speeches

In an informative speaking environment, you contribute to the public dialogue by sharing your knowledge with audiences. As an informative speaker, you fill in the gaps in an audience's base of knowledge, illustrating with clarity and detail the relevance and importance of that knowledge. Three tips that will help you create informative speaking environments and give effective informative speeches are (1) bring your topic to life, (2) manage your information, and (3) use language that is clear and unbiased.

Bring Topics to Life

Although the purpose of an informative speech is to provide information, audiences want more than a dry list of facts or an endless stream of data. They want information that will help them understand your topic in a more complex and dynamic way. Effective informative speakers bring a subject to life for an audience, engaging them so they appreciate the information they receive. As such, take careful stock of your topic and your audience so you can be sure to share information that is *engaging* and *relevant*. Engaging material draws an audience in and excites or interests them. Relevant material is material an audience finds useful or they must know in order to do their jobs, live in a community, or make informed decisions. In short, present information in a way that doesn't bore or confuse an audience but rather holds their attention and interest.

One of the most audience-centered ways to bring a topic to life is to relate the material of your speech to your audience. As you craft your speech, continually ask yourself how your overall topic, main points, and subpoints relate to your audience. What does the audience need to know? How will they use the information you present? How can you make the information clear? If you keep these questions in mind throughout your preparation process, you will be more likely to present your material in a relevant and engaging way. For example, in the speech about school violence, Erin brought her second point, manipulation by other students, to life by asking her audience a rhetorical question: "Think back to high school. How many examples of manipulative behavior can you think of? Probably too many. In my junior year I remember one group of students who constantly picked on my friends and me. It felt like no matter what we did, we were the brunt of their jokes and the focus of their hostility." By sharing her own experience of manipulation, she touched on an experience common to many members of her audience.

Another way to bring your topic to life is to share not only details, facts, and figures, but also the human side of your topic. If you are presenting technical information, providing a lot of detail and descriptions, or carefully outlining a

Finding a way to bring a topic to life can mean the difference between a good speech and a great speech. You can probably think of speakers you've heard or seen who were especially good at making even a complex or technical topic seem interesting and relevant. What language, support materials, or visual aids can you use to bring your informative speech to life?

process, try also to use examples, images, and descriptions that help your audience connect to your topic personally. As one student asked after hearing an informative speech about electromagnetic waves and their relationship to cancer, "What do all those formulas and fancy names mean for me personally?" As you prepare your speech, anticipate this kind of question and look for opportunities to relate your information to the human experience. For example, in a speech on modern art, you might personalize different techniques and styles by drawing parallels to skills learned in art classes at your school or by asking your audience to attempt the techniques on their own as you describe them.

Tailor Your Information to Your Audience

Recall from Chapter 6 the discussion of information overload. Just as we can feel overwhelmed by the abundance of information we find in our research, so too can audiences be overwhelmed by more information than they can process—no matter how lively that information is presented. As an informative speaker, one of your most challenging tasks is to decide how much information to include in a speech and how much to leave out.

When you present too much information, you run the risk of overwhelming an audience. However, when you present too little information, you run the risk of boring them. Similarly, material that is too technical, detailed, and complicated is hard to follow, and material that is too simple makes an audience feel as though you are talking down to them. The best way to tailor your information to your audience is to stay audience centered throughout the speech process. As you develop and present your speech, continually reflect on the needs and interests of your audience. Include information that you think would be most educational for your audience, and adjust your content so it matches their level of knowledge, expertise, and experience.

The decisions about what information to include or exclude can seem very subjective, but if you follow the principles of effective listening and interference caused by too much information (Chapter 3), audience centeredness (Chapter 5), and organizing your speech for clarity (Chapter 9), you will find it easier to determine how much information to include in your speech.

Speakers often give too much information in process speeches. For example, in a speech on how to create a PowerPoint presentation, you could easily give extensive detail about theories of design and slide preparation, detailed procedures explaining how to use the equipment, step-by-step techniques for showing the slides and interacting with the audience, and so on. In order to reduce the amount of information so it is appropriate for the time available, ask yourself what the most important aspects of creating a PowerPoint presentation are. Then focus your main points on those aspects, omitting the details that may be of interest to you but are more specific than your audience needs.

Using your *Invitation to Public Speaking* CD-ROM, watch the video clip of President George W. Bush's speech about stem cell research. As you watch his speech, consider how he tailored his information to his audience.

Demonstration speeches are often very engaging because they provide audiences with especially relevant, useful information. When you give this type of speech, remember to avoid overwhelming your audience with *too much* information. Consider a demonstration speech you might like to give. What is the most important information you think your audience would need?

Use Language That Is Clear and Unbiased

Because informative speeches focus on describing, defining, and explaining, use language that is descriptive and instructive: define new terminology, break complicated processes into steps an audience can easily follow, and explain terms or phrases specific to a particular field or activity. For example, when Tracee spoke about shade-grown coffee, she explained what the terms *shade grown, fair trade, organic,* and *sustainable* mean. Similarly, when Jackson spoke to his colleagues about the About Athletes trade show, he made sure his audience understood the jargon his company uses to discuss marketing strategies and the competition. Similarly, make a point of explaining familiar words you use in new ways. For example, the terms *safe, house,* and *client* are common terms, used in various industries and circumstances, but they had a specific meaning when Pia used them in the context of the Crossroads shelter.

The Internet features many sites that can help you identify and explain words that have specialized meanings. One useful site is Jon Storm's dictionary of computer jargon, found at http://www.jonstorm.com/glossary. As you review this site, consider the terms you would want to define and explain for your audience if you were giving an informative speech on some aspect of computers.

Informative language helps you speak as objectively as possible about your topic. This helps you focus on clearly expressing your information rather than on fully expressing your own view (as in invitational speaking) or swaying your audience (as in persuasive speaking). Remember that the goal of informative speaking is to pass along information your audience needs or wants or you think they should have. As such, make sure the language of your speech is as fair and unbiased as possible. Informative language is slightly more detached than invitational or persuasive language, so phrases like "my research indicates that" or "according to the experts" are more common than "I hope I've convinced you this is the best way" or "you should do this because."

Similarly, when you incorporate personal knowledge into an informative speech, which is common when you describe or explain something you have experience with, make sure the language you use reflects your *experience,* not your biases or preferences. For example, phrases like "after seven years with these machines, I'd recommend the following steps" and "I've been involved with this issue since I began with this agency, so I can give you some background and details" are more informative than persuasive.

These differences in language are slight, but they are important because they set informative speaking apart from other kinds of speaking. For more information on the effective use of language, see Chapter 3 (how language affects listening) and Chapter 12 (language style).

Ethical Informative Speaking

Ethical informative speakers make sure their speeches are based on careful research, unbiased information, and the honest presentation of information. Let's take a look at each of these components of ethical informative speaking.

First, when we present information to audiences, they expect we have taken the time to find information that is accurate and complete. Thus our research must be careful and detailed so we can provide the full story to our audiences in our speeches. If we haven't researched our topic carefully, we may be giving our audiences inaccurate or incomplete information. (See Chapter 6 for tips on how to gather accurate and complete supporting materials for your speech.)

Second, as an informative speaker, try to present as unbiased a perspective as possible. Recall from Chapter 5 that although we all hold biases, we can take steps to minimize them. Minimize biases by presenting your examples, statistics, testimony, and such, as fairly and as neutrally as possible, regardless of your own personal positions. Save your preferences for your persuasive speeches; use your informative speeches to help your audiences gain a full understanding of your topic. To evaluate an example of how objectively information can be presented, complete InfoTrac College Edition Exercise 15.3, "Discussing Human Cloning," online under Student Resources for Chapter 15 at the *Invitation to Public Speaking* Web site.

Finally, present your information honestly. Don't distort your evidence or make up supporting material as you need it. A healthy public dialogue depends on accuracy. If you misrepresent your speech topic, your audience will come away with an inaccurate view of important issues and situations. Ethical informative speaking relies on the truthful distribution of information, which can only happen if that information is presented truthfully.

Student Speech with Commentary

U. S. Flag Etiquette *by Cindy Gardner*

Specific purpose: To inform my audience about the rules and regulations for handling the U. S. flag.

Thesis statement: The flag, a symbol of much that is great about this nation, should be hung, handled, and folded in a specific manner.

You may have already given an informative speech in your class. Whether you have, or whether this is the first time you've spoken informatively, you can use the following speech as a model. You can see the outline for this speech under Student Resources for Chapter 15 at the Invitation to Public Speaking *Web site. Also, you can use your* Invitation to Public Speaking *CD-ROM to watch a video clip of Cindy Gardner's speech, which she gave in an introductory public speaking class. The assignment was to give a four- to six-minute speech, with a minimum of four sources cited. Students were also asked to create a preparation outline that included a works cited section, and to use at least one visual aid in their speech*

"The flag is the symbol of our national endeavor, our aspiration, our unity. The flag tells of the struggle for independence, for our union preserved, and for the sacrifices of brave men and women to whom the ideals and honor have been dearer than life." This is a quote from Charles Hughes, a teacher of flag etiquette.

For many Americans, the U.S. flag is more than just a piece of material; it stands for all that is great in this nation. In the wake of the tragedies in New York City and Washington, D.C., on September 11, 2001, more people than ever feel that the flag is a symbol of humanity, liberty, and justice. Today I would like to educate you on how to display the flag, some important rules to remember when using the flag, and how to fold it.

Each part of the flag has a specific meaning dedicated to symbolizing patriotic ideas. The thirteen red stripes symbolize blood and the fearless courage of the men and boys who gave their lives for our country. The white stripes represent purity and faith. The blue behind the stars represents heaven and our courage for our country. And lastly, each star on the flag represents one state of our union.

Since the birth of our flag, there have been many rules and regulations regarding how to hang and use it. When hanging a flag, it is important to keep its significance in mind. When hanging a flag that is not on a staff but just on a wall, you must place the union at the uppermost left corner. The union is the part of the flag that features the stars and blue background. If you hang a flag from the side of the building in a diagonal angle, you must put the union to the top of the staff. In this case, you want to place the union at the top of the pole unless it is at half-staff. Sometimes other flags are flown on the same staff as the United States flag. In this case, the U.S. flag would be the uppermost flag. The biggest mistake people make when displaying the flag is that they place it to the wrong side of a speaker. It should always be to the speaker's right. If you'll notice in this room, the flag is to my left, which is wrong.

(continued on next page)

Commentary

Cindy begins with a quote and then identifies the source of the quote, leading her audience into to the topic of her speech. She then clearly reveals her topic and purpose, and she previews the main points of her speech. Notice that the language Cindy uses in her introduction draws her audience in emotionally.

Cindy's brief description of the flag's symbolism sets up her first main point, how to display the flag. She provides this context so her descriptions of how to display the flag have greater meaning for her audience. Note that she organizes this main point spatially.

Cindy uses an internal summary and preview to begin her second main point, and she cites two separate sources to build her argument and her credibility. She closes this point with an internal summary and another preview.

I have given you tips on how to hang the flag, and now I would like to explain some rules regarding its use. Flag etiquette is more than just stories told from generation to generation. The United States has actually developed a code regarding its use: Title 36, Chapter 10. According to the U.S. Code, when a flag is no longer fit for display, it should be disposed of in a dignified way—burning is preferred. According to the *Rocky Mountain News,* "The flag should only be displayed from sunrise to sunset unless you have a spotlight on it." Also, it should never be used as a piece of clothing or costume. In honor of the flag, we place our right hand over our heart and face the flag when the national anthem is sung. Now that I have explained some rules regarding the flag, you might be wondering what to do when you are done using it.

As she demonstrates how to fold a flag, Cindy uses numerous signposts. Notice how "first" and "second" help her audience keep track of the folds and the reasons for them. Although she uses the word "next" several times, she then uses "second to the last" and "lastly" to signal the end of the folding process.

When putting the flag away, you fold it in a specific manner. Each fold in the flag represents something different. The first fold represents life. The second fold represents eternal life. Then you begin to fold the flag in a triangle. The first fold represents remembrance of our veterans. The second one represents our trust in God. The third one is a tribute to our country. The fourth one is where our heart lies when we say the Pledge of Allegiance. The next one is a tribute to those in our armed forces. The next one is a tribute to the one who entered into the valley of the shadow of death. The next is a tribute to womanhood, the people who have given us our sons and daughters. The next is to the fathers of our country. The second to the last one is to the eyes of the Hebrew citizens, and the last one is a tribute to all the Christians and their eyes to the Father, the Son, and the Holy Ghost. Lastly, you tuck the flag in to show four stars remaining on the front. This symbolizes the motto "In God we trust."

I hope you have found some valuable information in my speech. When we look at the flag, it is important to remember the rules and regulations regarding it and why they are there.

Cindy transitions into her conclusion with an internal summary and then explicitly summarizes her three main points. She ends with a quote whose language and imagery draws her audience in emotionally and reinforces her thesis.

The flag stands for something different for each and every one of us, and that is why it is to be respected. Today I talked about how to hang the flag—the union and its position are most important when hanging it. I also talked about how to follow the rules to respect the flag—the U.S. Code is helpful when deciding how to use it. Lastly, I discussed how to fold the flag—each fold represents something different. I would like to end with a quote from the poem *My Name Is Old Glory:* "But my finest hour comes when I am torn into strips to be used [as] bandages for my wounded comrades on the field of battle, and when I lie in the trembling arms of a grieving mother at the grave site of her fallen son [or daughter]."

Chapter Summary

Informative speaking may be the most common form of public speaking. To speak informatively is to share knowledge with an audience in order to increase their understanding of a particular topic. To create an informative speaking environment is to bring a topic to life for an audience, to illustrate its significance and relevance so an audience better understands it and its impact on their world.

The five types of informative speeches are speeches about processes, events, places and people, objects, and concepts. Process speeches describe how something is done, how something comes to be, or how something works. Speeches about events describe or explain a significant, interesting, or unusual occurrence. When you give speeches about places and people, you want to describe a significant, interesting, or unusual place or person. In speeches about objects, you inform your audiences about anything that can be perceived by the senses. Finally, speeches about concepts help you describe or explain abstractions, such as ideas, theories, principles, worldviews, or beliefs.

These five different types of informative speeches can be organized chronologically, spatially, causally, or topically. Chronological organizational patterns illustrate the development of an event or a concept or describe the steps necessary for completing a task. A spatial pattern helps you show an audience how the topic is related to various locations or that activities related to a topic occur in a specific location. Casual patterns are useful when you want to show important cause-and-effect relationships or clarify how ideas or behaviors relate to one another. A topical organizational pattern allows you to highlight the different facets or characteristics of a topic for an audience. These patterns can apply to many different topics, so choose a pattern that best suits your speech by considering your audience's goals, your specific purpose, and your thesis statement.

Three tips that can help you give as effective a speech as possible are (1) bring your subject to life, (2) tailor your information to your audience, and (3) use language that is clear and unbiased. When you bring your subjects to life, you relate your topic to your audience by sharing the human side of that topic, avoiding dry, fact-driven presentations. When you tailor your information to your audience, you remain audience centered so you can determine how much an audience knows about a topic and thus how much information to present. Additionally, as an effective informative speaker you use language that focuses on descriptions, definitions, and explanations so audiences can more easily learn new information. The use of this type of language sets informative speaking apart from invitational and persuasive speaking. Additionally, make a point to commit to the principles of ethical public speaking. Informative speaking involves careful research and the unbiased, honest presentation of information.

Throughout your life, informative speaking will probably be one of the most common forms of public speaking you do. In your career and personal life, you will have many opportunities to communicate information you know from experience or have gathered for a particular purpose. With what you've learned in this chapter, you can enter the public dialogue via informative speeches, bringing your knowledge and expertise to life for an audience.

Invitation to Public Speaking Online

After reading this chapter, use your CD-ROM and the *Invitation to Public Speaking* Web site to review the following concepts, answer the review questions, and complete the suggested activities.

Key Concepts

informative speech (352)

informative speaking environment (352)

speech about a process (353)

speech about an event (354)

speech about a place or a person (356)

speech about an object (357)

speech about a concept (358)

Review Questions

1. Consider the following topics as possible informative speaking topics for your next assigned speech:

carpets	making pizza
rocks	religion
Marilyn Manson	subways

   How many different kinds of informative speeches could you give on each topic? What would be the strengths or advantages of choosing one type of speech over another for these topics?

2. Create a preparation outline for an informative speech on the topic of Pearl Harbor. How many different organizational patterns could you use for this topic? How would each pattern highlight a different aspect of this topic?

3. Have you ever listened to an informative speech in which you left confused, sometimes more confused than you were before the speech? Why do you think you left confused? What could or should the speaker have done to be clearer during the presentation?

4. In groups or as a class, identify five or six of the most commonly used, but poorly defined, terms you hear. Use informative language to define those terms for your classmates. Some terms to define might be

feminism	affirmative action
sexism	free speech
discrimination	hate speech

5. Select one of the topics from question 1 and write a specific purpose and thesis statement for that speech. Next choose your organizational pattern and develop the main points for this speech. How might you bring this topic to life and manage the information you have about this topic so it is relevant to the audience?

The *Invitation to Public Speaking* Web Site

The *Invitation to Public Speaking* Web site features the review questions about the Web sites suggested on pages 356, 357, and 365, the interactive activities suggested on pages 352, 354, 356, and 357, and the InfoTrac College Edition exercises suggested on pages 357, 362, and 366.

You can access this site via your CD-ROM or at http://www.wadsworth.com/product/griffin. To access Speech Builder Express in order to complete Speech Step 15.2, you will need the username and password included under "Speech Builder Express" on your CD-ROM.

Web Links

15.1: A&E's Biography (356)
15.2: Animal Art (357)
15.3: Dictionary of Computer Jargon (365)

Interactive Activities

15.1: Communicating Information in Your Career (352)
Purpose: To learn about the importance of informative speaking in a career.

15.2: Evaluating a Process Speech (354)
Purpose: To consider how processes can be clearly explained.

15.3: Describing the Race of a Lifetime (356)
Purpose: To learn how examples can bring informative speeches about events to life.

15.4: Meet Winona LaDuke (357)
Purpose: To think critically about how information about a person can be presented to an audience.

15.1: Learning About Pandas (357)
Purpose: To consider carefully how information about animals is presented.

15.2: Identifying Organizational Patterns (362)
Purpose: To identify and assess the effectiveness of organizational patterns.

15.3: Discussing Human Cloning (366)
Purpose: To evaluate how objectively the information about a concept can be presented.

Speech Interactive on the *Invitation to Public Speaking* CD-ROM

The following video clips of speeches, referenced in this chapter, are included under Speech Interactive on your *Invitation to Public Speaking* CD-ROM. After you have watched the clips, click on "Critique" to answer the questions for analysis.

Video Clip 1: Informative Speech: Cindy Gardner (362). As you watch Cindy's speech about folding a flag, consider how she organized her speech. What type of informative speech does she present? Which organizational pattern does she use? Was her choice of pattern effective? What other organizational patterns might she have used?

Video Clip 2: President George W. Bush's Stem Cell Decision Speech (364). In 2001, President George W. Bush announced his decision regarding the use of federal funds for stem cell research. This research is controversial and complicated, so before revealing his decision, President Bush presented both sides of the issue and explained the controversy. As you watch his speech, consider how he tailored his information to his audience. Did he provide enough information for viewers to understand the issue? Did he provide too much information? What else might he have said?

Chapter Sixteen

Invitational Speaking

In this chapter you will learn to

Identify the three conditions for an invitational speaking environment

Describe the two types of invitational speeches

Apply the four most common patterns of organization for invitational speeches

Identify three tips for giving effective invitational speeches

Identify two principles for giving ethical invitational speeches

I do not believe that we should put aside the argument model of public discourse entirely, but we need to rethink whether this is the only way, or always the best way, to carry out our affairs . . . . Instead of asking "What's the other side?" we might ask instead, "What are the other sides?" Instead of insisting on hearing "both sides," we might insist on hearing "all sides."

—Deborah Tannen, *The Argument Culture: Stopping America's War of Words*, 1999[1]

The diversity of people and perspectives we encounter in our daily lives is both a gift and a challenge. On the one hand, our communities, workplaces, and schools are enriched by the range of perspectives of the people in them. We learn new things and see situations in new ways because of this variety of perspectives. On the other hand, different perspectives can be challenging. People may offer solutions we do not agree with, take positions that go against our values and beliefs, or ask us to implement policies we feel we cannot support. The extensive diversity of thought in the United States, as well as of the "global village" of the world, not only enhances our lives but also exposes us to people who are different from us.

We probably have all encountered people whose positions on social and political issues are not at all like ours. In such cases, we're not likely to change each other's views, no matter how hard we try. In fact, in many situations, such as business meetings or community forums, trying to persuade someone that our view is the best is not only unrealistic, but it is also inappropriate, especially in a situation where mutual problem solving is the goal. Trying to persuade someone to change can also be inappropriate when we do not have enough information to know what is best for another person, or when someone's position is so personal that it is not our place to ask them to change. For example, issues such as the death penalty, animal rights, and cloning are tied to deeply held personal beliefs about politics, economics, and religion that are far beyond any speaker's area of expertise.

So what should we do in these types of situations? Do we simply give up when our audience sees things differently than we do? Do we forge ahead with our attempts to persuade them even though we do not really understand their perspectives? Or could we, as the quote that opens this chapter advocates, try a different kind of interaction, one that encourages the audience to share their perspectives with us? Could we avoid common stereotypes (for example, Republicans see Democrats as foolish, and Democrats see Republicans as greedy), asking instead, "What are the various positions possible?" Could we try to understand those various positions more fully, perhaps without arriving at a clear-cut solution or course of action?

This chapter suggests that even though we may not be able to change our audience, or even want to change them, we can still enter the public dialogue. We can engage in **invitational speaking**, a type of public speaking in which a speaker enters into a dialogue with an audience in order to clarify positions, explore issues and ideas, or articulate beliefs and values. To speak invitationally is to do something other than inform or persuade. To speak invitationally is to decide to continue the public dialogue and seek mutual recognition, despite firm differences in opinions, values, and beliefs.

Let's look at an example that illustrates the difference between informative, invitational, and persuasive speaking. An informative speaker might inform an audience that ethical hunting can help control wildlife populations, and he would stop there. He wouldn't ask the audience to accept his position on the topic. An

invitational speaking
A type of public speaking in which a speaker enters into a dialogue with an audience in order to clarify positions, explore issues and ideas, or articulate beliefs and values.

invitational speaker might explain why he supports ethical hunting, ask the audience to try to understand his position, and then lead a discussion with the goal of understanding opposing opinions raised by the audience. A persuasive speaker might ask the audience to support ethical hunting and possibly take a course of action, such as supporting a local initiative to extend the hunting season in a community. Although a persuasive speaker might also be interested in opposing opinions, his goal as a speaker would be to advocate his own position over others.

In summary, to speak invitationally is to engage an audience in the investigation of a topic and give voice to its complexities. Your purpose is not simply to inform others, and it is not to try to persuade your audience to see things as you do. Instead, your purpose is to try to understand why your audience sees things as they do by exploring a topic civilly and with openness.[2] To help you identify the components of an invitational speech, complete InfoTrac College Edition Exercise 16.1, "Identifying Invitational Speeches," online under Student Resources for Chapter 16.

AP/Wide World Photos

Some topics tap into deeply held attitudes, values, and beliefs that audiences don't want to be persuaded to change. Yet an audience may be interested in exploring different aspects of an issue with a speaker to gain understanding or clarify their own positions. What are some topics you'd like to explore with an audience by giving an invitational speech?

The Invitational Speaking Environment

In order to speak invitationally, you need to try to create an **invitational environment,** or one in which understanding, respecting, and appreciating the range of positions that are possible on an issue, even if those positions are quite different from the speaker's own, is the highest priority. Although all speakers want to create an environment of respect, this is especially important in invitational speaking because you want to begin a dialogue with your audience. In this dialogue you offer your position as one viable stance and encourage your audience to express their positions so that everyone might come to a fuller understanding of the different positions. Note that because invitational speaking allows for this type of dialogue, it is often best suited for situations in which speakers have some time with an audience to allow for the fullest expression of the various positions possible. For specific techniques on leading discussions and encouraging dialogue with audiences, see Chapter 13 and look under Student Resources for Chapter 5 at the *Invitation to Public Speaking* Web site.

One of the keys to creating a successful invitational environment is by altering the traditional roles of the speaker and the audience. Rather than taking on the

invitational environment
Environment in which understanding, respecting, and appreciating the range of positions possible on an issue, even if those positions are quite different from the speaker's own, is the highest priority.

WEB SITE

role of the "expert" and assigning the role of the "listener" to the audience, you consider yourself and the audience as both the experts and the listeners. By not only expressing your views, but also listening carefully to your audience's views and facilitating a discussion of them, the speaking environment becomes more than a speech given by one person to an audience. The traditional distance between the speaker and the audience is replaced with a feeling that everyone is free to express their views without risk of attack or ridicule. This type of environment is often called a *supportive climate*. To learn more about supportive climates,

WEB SITE complete Interactive Activity 16.1, "Building a Supportive Climate," online under Student Resources for Chapter 16 at the *Invitation to Public Speaking* Web site.

In order to create this invitational environment, you must create three conditions: equality, value, and self-determination. These conditions allow you and your audience to see one another as knowledgeable and capable, although perhaps in different ways. Although these three conditions are interrelated, they are presented separately here in order to clarify each condition and its goal. However, all of these conditions help you create an atmosphere of mutual respect, understanding, and exploration. They help you communicate effectively with people who hold positions quite different from your own.[3]

The Condition of Equality

condition of equality
Condition of an invitational speech that requires the speaker sees audience members as holding equally valid perspectives and positions that are worthy of exploration.

When you create the **condition of equality**, you see audience members as holding valid perspectives and positions that are worthy of exploration. You use language, delivery, and presentation of ideas to let your audience know that you recognize them as people whose knowledge, experiences, and perspectives are as valid for them as yours are for you. Because you and your audience are equal in this sense (although you still give the speech and lead the discussion), your audience is able to offer their perspectives, share their experiences, and even question you—in the same way you do with the audience. Using your *Invitation to Public Speaking* CD-ROM, watch a video clip of Shelley under Speech Interactive. How does she create a condition of equality?

The Condition of Value

condition of value
Condition of an invitational speech that requires the speaker recognizes that the views of the members of the audience, although they may differ from the speaker's, have inherent value.

Shelley Weibel

You create the **condition of value** by recognizing that the views of the audience, although different from the speaker's, have inherent value. You let your audience know they will be encouraged to express their views and opinions, even if they are vastly different from yours. In creating the condition of value, you encourage your audience to express their differing views and opinions, and communicate that those differences will be explored in a spirit of mutual understanding, without judgment or attempts at persuasion. In fact, in creating the condition of value, you communicate that you will try to step outside your own standpoint (Chapter 5) in order to understand another perspective and see the world as your audience sees it. So when an audience member shares an opposing perspective (for example, on the traditional practice of female circumcision in certain cultures), you might disagree, but you would try to understand the opposing position and the reasons (cultural and personal) why that person holds those views.

The Condition of Self-Determination

Because invitational speaking offers us a way to enter the public dialogue when we know we can't or don't want to change our audience, you need to create the

condition of self-determination. You create this condition by recognizing that the members of your audience are experts in their own lives—that people know what is best for them and have the right to make choices about their lives based on this knowledge. Although their choices may not be the ones you would make, the members of your audience are free to decide for themselves how to think, feel, and act. The condition of self-determination means you won't close off conversation or try to persuade your audience to do something they may not feel inclined to do. Rather, you will create an atmosphere in which the members of the audience feel in control of their choices and are respected for their ability to make them. Using your *Invitation to Public Speaking* CD-ROM, watch a video clip of Melissa under Speech Interactive. How does she create a condition of self-determination?

In our increasingly diverse and complicated world, invitational speaking is a useful tool in some of the most difficult of public conversations and exchanges. When you choose to speak invitationally, you are seeking a full and open exchange of ideas and positions. Creating these three conditions—equality, value, and self-determination—helps you succeed in this exchange. Remember, the goal of invitational speaking is to go beyond informing and to steer clear of trying to change the audience. Instead, when you speak invitationally, you try to explore issues in a spirit of acceptance and openness.

condition of self-determination
Condition of an invitational speech that requires the speaker recognizes that people know what is best for them and have the right to make choices about their lives based on this knowledge.

Types of Invitational Speeches

The two types of invitational speaking are to articulate a position and to explore an issue. In the first, you hold a fairly well-defined position, and your goal is to explain your position, then discuss it with your audience so that they might understand you and your position more fully. In the process, you may better understand the positions of your audience members as well. In the second, you have some tentative thoughts about an issue or a plan, but you want to discover what your audience thinks; your goal is to understand your audience's views so you might understand your own position more fully or develop a course of action that more fully accounts for their differing positions. Let's take a closer look at each type of invitational speaking.

Speeches to Articulate a Position

When you hold a fairly well-developed perspective on a subject and want to explore your perspective with others, you may want to give an invitational speech to articulate a position. When speaking to **articulate a position,** you invite an audience to see the world as you do and to understand issues from your perspective. This type of invitational speaking is similar to informative speaking in that you share information with an audience. But it is different because you are also open to conversation with the audience about *their* views on the topic. The result is that both you and your audience leave the exchange with a richer understanding of a complex issue.

Let's look at two examples of invitational speeches to articulate a perspective and how they differ from informative and persuasive speeches. In the first example, Paul asked his audience to consider the controversial Equal Rights Amendment (ERA), which was written to ensure the rights of women in the United States. This amendment to the Constitution has been introduced into Congress every year since the early 1900s, but it has never been ratified. If Paul had given an *informative* speech on the Equal Rights Amendment, he could have

speech to articulate a position
Invitational speech for which the speaker invites an audience to see the world as she or he does and to understand issues from her or his perspective.

organized it so the audience learned something about the amendment, its history, the reasons for its defeat, and its impact on society. However, because Paul decided to give an *invitational* speech, he personalized his presentation by explaining why he supported the amendment, describing how he came to feel the way he did, and trying to understand why people in his audience had different views. His specific purpose, thesis statement, and main points looked like this:

Specific purpose: To invite my audience to understand the powerful impact that ratifying the Equal Rights Amendment could have on all our lives.

Thesis statement: For over seventy years, my grandmother, mother, and sisters have worked to see the Equal Rights Amendment ratified, and I have learned from them the importance of the amendment and the significant impact it could have on our lives if ratified.

Main points:

I.   The Equal Rights Amendment has a long, intriguing history.

II.   For over seventy years, the women in my family have played a role in the effort to see the amendment pass.

III.   I've learned many important lessons from watching and hearing about their efforts, including how important the Equal Rights Amendment is.

IV.   I personally believe the amendment could significantly advance the status of both women and men in our society.

V.   I'd like to discuss my position with my audience and learn about their views of the amendment.

Paul provided information not only to educate his audience, but also so they could give full, well-informed expression to their own views. In addition, he invited the audience into his world so they could see the issue as he did and so he could see the world as they do.

In the second example, from a speech on gun control, Jean could have chosen a persuasive tack to persuade her audience that the United States does not need stricter gun control laws. Instead, she chose an invitational approach because she knew that many in her audience strongly supported stricter regulations. Jean knew that changing their minds was not only unrealistic, but could lead to angry interactions. So she chose to invite the audience into her world to see the issue of guns from another perspective. In doing so, she created an atmosphere of openness so people could voice their concerns, frustrations, and even anger without judgment. Jean's specific purpose, thesis statement, and main points looked as follows:

Specific purpose: To invite my audience to consider some of the positive lessons that can be taught with the ethical use of guns.

Thesis statement: Although many people fear guns, two hunting experiences in my childhood taught me to use guns responsibly and ethically, and I believe the lessons I learned have been invaluable in my life.

Main points:

I.   People fear guns for a number of reasons.

II.   I had two memorable hunting experiences during my childhood, one positive and the other negative.

III.   Those experiences have proved to be invaluable in my life and shaped my current views on the responsible and ethical use of guns in our society.

The value of controlling access to guns is a much debated topic, especially in light of several gun-related tragedies in recent years. How would you articulate your position about this topic in an invitational speech to your classmates?

© A. Ramey/Woodfin Camp & Associates

> IV. I'd like to explore with my audience ways in which the ethical use of guns could be a healthy part of our lives.

In a persuasive speech, Jean would have tried to convince the audience that guns actually aren't as bad as some people think. However, in this invitational speech, she was more interested in sharing positions than changing minds. Her goal was to facilitate understanding and exchange on gun control, a very controversial topic.

When you articulate a position, you try to develop that position as fully and openly as possible. You invite your audience to enter your world for a moment, and you return the gesture by entering their world during the discussion. Your goal is not change or the simple exchange of information, although both of these things might happen. Your goal is that both you and members of your audience will gain a better understanding of different views and frame the issues in more complete and inclusive ways in the future. To assess one speaker's attempt at articulating a position, complete InfoTrac College Edition Exercise 16.2, "Articulating a Position," online under Student Resources for Chapter 16.

Speeches to Explore an Issue

When you give invitational speeches to **explore an issue,** you attempt to engage your audience in a discussion about an idea, concern, topic, or plan of action. Your goal is to gather information from your audience so you might understand the subject more fully and from the audience's perspectives. Quite often, you use this information to solve problems or plan courses of action because, even though you may have a position of your own, you also want to take into consideration the positions of an audience.

You often begin these types of invitational speeches by stating your intent to explore the issue. Then you might lay out the positions on an issue. Or you may share your opinions, even if they are tentative ones, about the issue. With either approach, you are laying the groundwork for an open dialogue, one rooted in equality, value, and self-determination and one in which people feel heard and respected by one another.

speech to explore an issue
Invitational speech for which the speaker attempts to engage an audience in a discussion about an idea, concern, topic, or plan of action.

The following two examples illustrate invitational speeches to explore issues. In the first example, Cara framed the issue of teaching evolution and creationism in public schools invitationally because she knew the issue is a controversial one. Her goal was to get her audience thinking about exactly what information belongs in the public school curriculum and to help her clarify her own thoughts about the issue.

Specific purpose: To invite my audience to explore, and to explore myself, three theories of evolution and creation and their role in public education.

Thesis statement: I'd like to describe for my audience the controversy over three theories of how the universe was created—creationism, the big bang theory, and intelligent design—then explore which theory should be taught in our schools.

Main points:
I. The debate between evolution and creationism has existed since the theory of evolution was proposed by Darwin and brought to the public's attention in the Scopes "Monkey Trial" in 1925.

II. The creationist theory holds that God created the universe and all living things, including humans, whom God made in his image.

III. The theory of evolution, also known as the big bang theory, argues that the universe was created through a compression of matter and intense heat.

IV. A new theory, known as the intelligent design theory, accounts for the origins of RNA and DNA and recently has become a part of this debate.

V. Discussion about the appropriateness of each theory in public schools would help us make decisions about what to teach our children in our classrooms.

In this speech, Cara states which theory she'd prefer to be taught in public schools, but she gives all three theories a fair presentation, describing their strengths and weaknesses. She then opens the discussion, knowing that her audience will have strong views. However, at the beginning of her speech she set the stage for an invitational discussion in which her audience could feel free to share their views and help her clarify her position on this issue. Using your *Invitation to Public Speaking* CD-ROM, watch a video clip of Cara giving her speech under Speech Interactive. You can also read the full text of Cara's speech at the end of this chapter. How fairly does she present all three theories of evolution and creationism, given that she favors only one of them?

In the next example, Shelley proposes cloning as an alternative to the problem of endangered species. She comes to the speech with her own values and beliefs, but not with a predetermined position. She speaks to engage her audience in a discussion in order to clarify her own views. Because she provides her audience with the background of this issue, they are better able to discuss it with her and share their own views.

Cara Buckley-Ott

Specific purpose: To invite my audience to explore, and to explore myself, the positive and negative aspects associated with cloning endangered animals.

Thesis statement: Given opinion polls that show more people are in favor of cloning than not, the three primary benefits and three primary negative aspects of cloning endangered animals merit discussion.

Main points:

    I. Three main benefits are associated with cloning endangered animals.

        A. Cloning may be able to bring back once extinct animals.

        B. Cloning is less expensive than protecting endangered animals.

        C. Cloning provides an option for those animals that do not breed well in captivity.

    II. There are also three negative aspects to cloning endangered animals.

        A. Many people feel that cloning places us in the role of God and are uncomfortable with this.

        B. Cloning does not encourage us to solve the reasons these animals are endangered—the loss of habitat.

        C. Animals must be removed from the wild in order to clone them.

    III. Opinion polls show that more people are in favor of cloning than not, and I'd like to know how my audience feels about this topic.

In this example, Shelley presented the controversy fairly and openly. Because she did not have a firm position on the issue, she asked her audience to share their views with her as she sorted out her own, knowing that their various beliefs and values would help her formulate her views. She created an environment in which both she and her audience felt free to express their views as openly as possible. To read about how talk-show host Oprah Winfrey creates an invitational environment by using "rapport talk," go to http://www.time.com/time/time100/artists/profile/winfrey.html.

    Speaking invitationally, like any form of speaking, has its challenges and rewards. Remember, people feel most free to share their positions when the conditions of equality, value, and self-determination are met, and these conditions can take time to develop, especially among strangers or when issues are hotly contested.

Today's new technologies are quickly leading to advances in a number of fields. However, the ethical implications raised by some advances, such as stem cell therapies, are not always clear. Invitational speeches are well suited to exploring the pros and cons of issues like these. As an audience member, how might you express your concerns about an issue in an invitational way?

© Bill Varie/CORBIS

You can create the conditions from the very beginning of a speech (Chapter 9) and through your delivery (Chapter 11). You also create them through the organizational patterns you choose. The patterns best suited for invitational speaking are discussed next.

 Speech Step 16.1 / Select an Invitational Speech Type

Make a list of possible speech topics for your next invitational speech. Which topics seem suited to articulating a position? Which seem suited for exploring an issue? Select one topic for each type of speech. For which topic could you most effectively create conditions of equality, value, and self-determination? Select that topic for your next invitational speech.

Organizational Patterns for Invitational Speeches

As with informative and persuasive speaking, many organizational patterns are suitable for invitational speaking. The easiest for beginning speakers are the familiar chronological, spatial, and topical, as well as a new pattern especially appropriate for speeches to explore an issue, multiple perspectives. As your skill at invitational speaking develops, you can modify these patterns and adapt to your audiences and speaking situations as needed.

Chronological Organizational Pattern

Recall from Chapter 9 that a chronological pattern allows you to trace a sequence of events or ideas. This pattern works well for both speeches to articulate a position and speeches to explore an issue. In the next example, Eric uses this pattern to explore an issue. He develops the issue, and his position on that issue, as they have developed over time.

Specific purpose:	To invite my audience to consider the damage done to trails by mountain bikers and to explore possible solutions to this problem.
Thesis statement:	An avid mountain biker, I've recently discovered the damage that mountain bikers can do to trails, and I'd like to hear my audience's view on this problem and explore possible solutions with them.
Main points:	I. An avid mountain biker since I was a teenager, last year I began to research the damage often done to trails by bikers like me.
	II. Additionally, just recently I returned to my early routes and saw with new eyes the impact of mountain bikers on these trails.
	III. I'm not willing to give up riding, but I wonder if there are solutions to the problems caused by mountain bikers.

Eric used the chronological pattern and traced his evolution as a mountain biker, as well as his evolving consciousness. In the discussion with his audience, he considered such suggestions as closing trails to mountain bikers completely, encouraging bikers to adopt different riding practices, and finding ways to increase the maintenance of existing trails. Eric's audience learned about the attraction of mountain biking, and he learned of their concerns for the environment and frustrations with mountain bikers. Together they explored solutions that could work for the whole community rather than just one group.

The next example illustrates how the chronological pattern might work in a business setting. In this example, Shalon addressed colleagues about proposed changes in a parental leave policy in order to explore whether those changes would work for the employees.

Specific purpose: To invite my audience to work with me to develop a parental leave policy that benefits all employees.

Thesis statement: A discussion with my coworkers could help us develop a parental leave policy that may be more comprehensive, and thus more advantageous to more employees, than the company's original policy, current policy, and the new policy proposed by our employers.

Main points:

I. Our company's original parental leave policy is one of the earliest policies and had both strengths and weaknesses.

   A. The policy reflected the demographics of the workplace as well as the politics of the time.

   B. This early policy had many advantages and disadvantages.

II. Our current policy reflects that fact that the company made changes to this early policy as a result of employee need.

   A. The changes affected women in certain ways.

   B. The changes affected men in certain ways.

   C. The changes also affected our company as a whole.

III. The parental leave policy currently proposed by our employers is both similar and different to previous policies.

   A. In many ways, the proposed plan is similar to the previous plans.

   B. However, the proposed plan includes key differences.

IV. Given the history of the plan and the new proposal, I'd like to explore with my coworkers the changes we might want to suggest to the proposed plan.

Shalon described past parental leave policies not to bias or sway her colleagues, nor to simply educate them, but rather to collect information, stimulate open discussion, and foster self-determination. With this history, her audience could see more clearly how the proposed changes could affect them and could develop an alternative proposal to present to management.

A chronological organizational pattern allows you to share history and offer background information that may help audience members enter a discussion. In the first example, the background information helped Eric's audience understand his position more fully and explore possible solutions. In the second, it helped Shalon's audience propose changes that would be in their best interest. By tracing the evolution of your perspective or an issue over time, you establish common ground as well as openness to seeing how the perspective or issue might continue to evolve.

Spatial Organizational Pattern

Recall from Chapter 9 that the spatial pattern of organization can help you organize your ideas according to location or geography. You can use this pattern to articulate your position or explore an issue. This pattern is useful when you want to discuss what a topic has in common, or how it differs, across countries, nations, states, or cities. Riley used a spatial pattern to describe the ways communities have responded to hate crimes and to explore how his community might begin to heal from such a crime.

Specific purpose: To invite my audience to visit the scene of several hate crimes committed across the country so we might know how to begin to heal from what happened in our own town.

Thesis statement: Trying to understand the response to the many hate crimes that have been committed in other communities across the United States might help my own community heal from our recent tragedy.

Main points:

    I. The response of a Texas community to the hate crime against James Byrd Jr. involved both public and private actions.

    II. Similarly, the response of a Wyoming community to the hate crime against Matthew Shepard was both private and public, bringing in the surrounding areas as well.

    III. The response of a California community to the hate crime against a church with a largely Middle Eastern congregation was far more public in nature.

    IV. With these responses in mind, I'd like to invite the audience to discuss ways in which we might respond to our own recent tragedy.

By describing how other communities responded to hate crimes, Riley stimulated and encouraged discussion with his audience about the needs of the community and how they felt they needed to respond to their own tragedy. By exploring this issue, both he and his audience began to formulate a plan of action that helped the community come to terms with a painful event.

You can use a spatial organizational pattern to invite your audience to see how other localities have dealt with many types of public issues, such as transportation, health, poverty, crime, education, and pollution. You can also use this pattern in business speeches to compare how other businesses have dealt with a problem. This pattern allows you to connect your position to others or to help your audience explore an issue using information from other places.

Topical Organizational Pattern

When you articulate a position, topical organization is an effective pattern. Recall from Chapter 9 that this pattern allows you to discuss the aspects of your topic, point by point. Jean's speech on gun control discussed earlier in this chapter uses the topical pattern. In that speech, Jean addressed audience fears about guns, her own experiences with guns, and the lessons she learned from those experiences. She then initiated a discussion with the audience about her position. Here is an example of the topical pattern from Kip's speech articulating his position about integrating more women into history courses and textbooks:

Specific purpose:	To invite my audience to consider the idea that women pioneers should be represented in history textbooks.
Thesis statement:	A discussion about three important women in history will open up a conversation about the fact that women are a rich and important part of our history but are rarely included in history textbooks in any significant way.
Main points:	I. Current history textbooks tell the story of kings, presidents, emperors, and generals.
	II. Three women who are not, or are rarely, mentioned in history textbooks make me want to learn more about many, many other women in history.
	A. Clara Brown is reported to be the first African American woman to cross the Plains during the Gold Rush, and she helped many other African Americans come west.
	B. Frances Wisebart Jacob established the first kindergarten in Denver, Colorado, and established the United Way.
	C. Mary Harris Jones, known as "Mother Jones," is considered the founder of the labor movement and successfully organized to abolish child labor and improve conditions for miners.
	III. Although acknowledging the contributions of women like these would require changes to our history textbooks, women helped make our nation what it is today, and I think we should teach our children about their strength and ambition.
	IV. I'd like to invite my audience to discuss what they think about adding more information about women to our history textbooks.

Using the topical organizational pattern, Kip shared three examples of women he had read about on his own. However, he did more than inform his audience about these women; he shared his perspectives on their importance in understanding history. During the discussion, Kip remained open to alternatives, new information, and concerns about how adding new material to current history textbooks might affect the history that students learn in classrooms today.

Multiple Perspectives Organizational Pattern

Although you can use this organizational pattern in other types of speeches, it is especially suited for invitational speeches. The **multiple perspectives pattern** allows you to address the many sides and positions of an issue. You can go beyond dividing an issue into only two opposing sides and illustrate the multiple perspectives possible on it. This approach not only respects a diversity of opinions, but also invites your audience to consider even more views than those you covered and make room for additional perspectives from your audience.

This organizational pattern works well when you want to speak to explore an issue with an audience. Recall Cara, who invited her audience to explore what to teach in schools about the creation of the universe. She used the multiple perspectives pattern for her speech, but she could have gone beyond the creationist, big

multiple perspectives pattern
Organizational pattern that allows the speaker to address the many sides and positions of an issue.

Teachers often frame topics with the multiple perspective patterns in order to encourage students to think about an issue in more than one way. Could you use this organizational pattern in your next speech?

© Michael Newman/PhotoEdit

bang, and intelligent design theories to explore the many other views on creation. She could have invited her audience to consider how all those views might fit into a public school education. If she had chosen this pattern, the basic outline of her speech might have looked as follows:

Specific purpose: To invite my audience to explore the many theories of creation and their role in public education.

Thesis statement: Perhaps some of the many theories throughout time and across cultures that explain how the universe was created—particularly creationism, the big bang theory, intelligent design, ancient Egyptian and African theories, and Native American theories—could be taught in our public schools.

Main points:
I. One of the modern theories of how the universe was created, that God created the universe, comes from the Judeo-Christian tradition.

II. A second theory, proposed by the Greek philosopher Democritus in 400 B.C., set the stage for the big bang theory of creation proposed by most scientists today.

III. A third theory, known as the intelligent design theory, accounts for the origins of RNA and DNA and could add yet another perspective to our children's education.

IV. A fourth theory, offered by ancient Egyptian and African civilizations, presents a holistic view of existence in which many deities are worshiped as different aspects of God.

V. Yet another theory, advocated by many Native American peoples, suggests that the creator of all, sometimes known as Thought Woman, has both female and male aspects and "thinks" all things into being.

VI. I'd like to discuss with my audience the possibility that all of these creation theories be taught in public schools to create a more inclusive curriculum.

The next example illustrates how the multiple perspectives pattern can be used in community presentations. In this example, Marko addressed businesspeople and articulated his perspective on donating to the United Way.[4]

Specific purpose: To invite my audience to consider the various benefits of donating to the United Way and to value the ways they already give back to their community.

Thesis statement: The United Way, with its overarching view of the community and its needs, is but one of many excellent ways to give back to a community.

Main points:
    I. Because of its holistic view, contributing to the United Way is a great way to give back to the community.
        A. The United Way brings together key public and private entities to address many of the social ills of our community.
        B. One contribution to the United Way supports forty-one different agencies and projects in this community.
        C. Those who donate can feel confident that their contributions will be wisely distributed, because the advisory committee that determines the distribution formula is composed of volunteers from our own community.
    II. The United Way also supports other avenues of giving to the community.
        A. Donations to individual agencies and projects are excellent ways to give to the community.
        B. Volunteering is yet another way to support these agencies and projects.
        C. When time or money are tight, simply speaking highly of the United Way and other forms of giving is a third positive act.
    III. I'd like to discuss with my audience the idea of donating to the United Way and to other community-based agencies.

Although a persuasive speech might seem the most appropriate speech to use to solicit donations, Marko uses an invitational approach with great success. He uses the multiple perspectives pattern in a unique way. Not only does he articulate his position on why he believes the United Way is a fine agency to contribute to, but he addresses the "other sides" as well. In arranging his ideas to show the multiple perspectives, Marko is able to validate the different situations among the members of his audience and encourage self-determination. They get to choose which method of giving works best for them because he has used a multiple perspectives pattern and opened up the dialogue to numerous possibilities for giving back to one's community.

To use a multiple perspectives organizational pattern, you must follow three guidelines. First, do your research so you can explain the various sides to your audience. Second, present each perspective fairly so the audience members can make their own assessment of the different perspectives. Third, make room for even more perspectives to be offered from the audience. These three guidelines will facilitate understanding as well as dialogue.

In this diverse world, invitational speaking is an option that allows you to continue the public dialogue even about the most controversial issues. With effort and respect, you can establish the conditions of equality, value, and self-determination even in the most controversial exchanges. These three conditions become increasingly important because, as cultural critic bell hooks explains, if "a person makes a unilateral decision that does not account for *me*, then I feel exploited by that decision because my needs haven't been considered. But if that person is willing to pause, then at that moment of pause there is an opportunity for mutual recognition because they have at least listened to and considered, honestly, my position."[5]

Speech Step 16.2 / Select an Organizational Pattern for Your Invitational Speech

An invitational speech can be organized chronologically, spatially, topically, or according to the multiple perspectives pattern. Select an organizational pattern for your speech that will allow you to articulate a position or explore an issue effectively. Speech Builder Express helps you outline your invitational speech once you've selected an organizational pattern. Access Speech Builder Express online by using the username and password included under "Speech Builder Express" on your *Invitation to Public Speaking* CD-ROM.

Tips for Invitational Speaking

Like informative and persuasive speaking, invitational speaking has specific guidelines to follow so you can give a more effective speech. Three tips will help you give effective invitational speeches and create a speaking environment of equality, value, and self-determination: (1) know your position, (2) use invitational language, and (3) allow time for discussion.

Know Your Own Position

One of the most important aspects of invitational speaking, especially when articulating a position, is to take time before you begin to put your speech together to figure out how you really feel about the issue and why you feel as you do. This means you must research an invitational speech as thoroughly as you would any other type of speech. You must support your main ideas with evidence as well as personal opinion. To articulate your position fully and with respect for others, you cannot just ramble on about an issue you haven't given much thought to. You must take time to determine what your position is and why you hold it, why it is correct for you. You will discover that your attempts to create conditions of value and self-determination will be enhanced if you speak with accuracy, clarity, and detail about your views and

WEB SITE their place in your life. To help you understand and clarify your own position on various issues, complete Interactive Activity 16.2, "Thinking About Attitudes," online under Student Resources for Chapter 16 at the *Invitation to Public Speaking* Web site.

Tiffany

I absolutely loved the invitational speech round. This type of speech is so different from the other speeches given in class. It's not just all about you being the authority on your topic—it's okay if you aren't sure about everything. And the environment is a lot more relaxed when you get to interact with the audience. I can see this type of speech relating to everyone outside of class—if not now, then when we join the work force. This is a perfect preparation for being the head of a company meeting, teaching people something, or holding a discussion group. There are so many different venues that a speech like this can be used for, and I think giving this type of speech is great preparation for activities now and in the future.

Use Invitational Language

A second tip for creating effective invitational speaking environments is to use invitational language. Phrases like "you should," "the only correct position is," "anyone can see," that advocate your position over others only reduce your chances of creating the condition of equality. Equality means that all positions have merit—they are viable for the people who hold them, even if they may not be for you. Invitational language offers your view as one possible view, but not as "the best" view.

Phrases such as "I came to this view because," "for me, this position makes sense because," "because of that experience, I began to see this issue as," and "although this may not work for all of you, this is the position I hold" communicate to your audience that you are trying to explain your view without imposing it on others. Try to use phrases that display respect for and openness to other positions throughout your speech. To think more about how you can use invitational language effectively to show respect and openness, complete InfoTrac College Edition Exercise 16.3, "Using Invitational Language," online under Student Resources for Chapter 16.

During discussions with your audience, invitational language is also important. In discussions, people may offer views different from yours or even the opposite of yours. Rather than silencing or censoring those views, encourage dialogue about those differences and disagreements. Offer positive reinforcement to the ideas of others so the dialogue can develop openly and freely. Instead of responding with "that's not a good idea," or "I doubt that would work," use phrases like "can you elaborate on that idea?" "how might that work?" "why do you think so?" "can you explain why you prefer that solution?" and "what benefits do you see with that position?" As you engage audiences in an exploration of an issue, draw them out and get them to elaborate on their views. When the discussion gets heated, keep track of ideas you want to return to later by writing them on a white board or flip chart. In an invitational setting, you are asking your audience to articulate their position as fully as you try to articulate your own. Your language and validation of ideas can help you open up the dialogue rather than limit it.

Finally, if you encounter a hostile audience member, your language can help manage and even reduce some of that hostility. When audience members respond with anger, the reason usually is that the speaker has touched a sensitive nerve. But your language can diffuse the situation and reestablish value. Use words and phrases that acknowledge your audience member's position, express your desire to understand that position more fully, and even apologize for upsetting that person. Rather than responding with angry words or denying that the person has reason to be angry, use language that communicates your respect for his or her as someone with views that may be different from yours. For more tips on how to deal with hostile audience members, go to the Web site Hecklers, Hardliners, and Heavy Questions: Handling Difficult Questions and Questioners with Eloquence and Ease at http://www.craigspeaks.com/DifficultQ.html.

Allow Time for Discussion

Articulating positions and exploring ideas with an audience take time. This means you must be patient, not rush through your part of the presentation or hurry your audience through the discussion. If we are to create the conditions of equality, value, and self-determination and make a space for others in the public dialogue, we must be willing to take the time necessary to do so. Sometimes this seems inefficient. Western culture encourages us to get things done quickly and to make decisions without delay. Efficient presentations are often seen as brief, to the point, and very tightly organized. However, in invitational speaking, brevity and efficiency may work against you if you become overly controlling and unwilling to explore someone's position. Invitational speakers must allow time for the dialogue about ideas. To read about how other cultures view time, visit the Web page The Cultural Rhythms of Time, located at http://www.trinity.edu/~mkearl/time-c.html.

In classrooms, where the time for speeches is limited, allowing time for invitational speeches can be a problem. It may be a problem in other settings as well. For example, if you are required or choose to speak invitationally, there is a solution to these time constraints. Begin by considering your time frame carefully. If you have only a small amount of time, reduce the scope of your presentation. Decide what you can address in a shorter amount of time and restructure your invitation. Instead of covering three forgotten women in history, Kip could have invited the audience to name ten famous women in history, then explore why so few women are included in history textbooks and what that does to our concept of history. With this reduced scope, Kip still could have offered an invitation, just not the more detailed presentation he first chose. By reducing the scope of your presentation, you respect the opinions of the audience and make it possible to engage in a discussion of the larger issue.

These three guidelines—know your position, use invitational language, and allow time for discussion—will assist you in creating the three conditions of equality, value, and self-determination. They also will help you organize your ideas and keep your focus on inviting an audience to understand and explore an issue with you.

Ethical Invitational Speaking

Ethical invitational speakers must be sure they are speaking on a topic that they are open to discussing and that their purpose is mutual understanding. Let's look at these two components of ethical invitational speaking.

When you choose to speak invitationally, you choose to share your perspective and listen fully to the perspectives of others. If you are not able to listen to perspectives that are incompatible with your own or to grant them value, then you are being unethical if you give an invitational speech. Ethical speakers stay true to their beliefs and values, and they do not pretend they are open to views when they are not. Thus your topic in an invitational speech must be one about which you truly are open. This doesn't mean you have to be willing to change your view, but it does mean you have to be willing to listen with respect to other views. If you cannot grant value and self-determination to someone who disagrees with you, then it would be more ethical for you to give an informative or a persuasive speech on that topic. Religion, sexuality, and forms of oppression are three topics that may be especially difficult for invitational speeches because people have such strong beliefs about them. To read more about why it is important to keep an open mind while discussing difficult topics, go to http://www.mendosa.com/openmind.htm.

Your second ethical responsibility as an invitational speaker is to stay true to your purpose. It is tempting to try to invite an audience to consider your perspective with the underlying goal of persuading them that your view really is best. To speak ethically, you truly must have invitation as your goal. Although you can create the three conditions of equality, value, and self-determination in other types of speaking, in invitational speaking you create these conditions because your fundamental goal is the exchange and appreciation of perspectives, not persuasion. If you really want to change your audience, do not pretend you are offering an invitational approach—give a persuasive speech instead. To explore the dangers of

WEB SITE hidden agendas and how you can identify and avoid them, complete Interactive Activity 16.3, "Detecting Hidden Agendas," online under Student Resources for Chapter 16 at the *Invitation to Public Speaking* Web site.

Student Speech with Commentary
Creationism Versus the Big Bang Theory *by Cara Buckley-Ott*

Specific purpose: To invite my audience to explore, and to explore myself, three theories of evolution and creation and their role in public education.

Thesis statement: I'd like to describe for my audience the controversy over three theories of how the universe was created—creationism, the big bang theory, and intelligent design—then explore which theory should be taught in our schools.

Are you ready to give an invitational speech? You can use the following speech as a model. You can see the outline for this speech and read the discussion that accompanied the speech under Student Resources for Chapter 16 at the Invitation to Public Speaking *Web site. Also, you can use your* Invitation to Public Speaking *CD-ROM to watch a video clip of Cara Buckley-Ott's speech, which she gave in an introductory public speaking class. The assignment was to give a five- to seven-minute invitational speech, manage a five- to seven-minute dialogue with the audience, and wrap up with a one-minute conclusion. As you'll see, Cara's speech and discussion went over time. However, she fulfilled the other requirements of the assignment, which were to provide at least four sources, meet the objectives of an effective introduction and conclusion, and provide relevant information. She also created the conditions of equality, value, and self-determination, and she remained invitational throughout her dialogue with the audience.*

Commentary

By the end of a toothbrush's life, usually one to three months, there is more microscopic bacteria collected within its bristles than in the average public toilet. Thinking of investing in a new toothbrush? Well maybe you should think again, because according to popular belief, these microscopic mouth-invaders are really nothing more than distant relatives of everyone in this room today. This belief, of course, is the belief in the theory of evolution—the idea that microscopic organisms created at the big bang, or the creation of the earth, have evolved over time to form human beings. But this is not the only theory about the creation of the earth. In fact, the theory of evolution has been debated for years, along with the theory of creationism. And recently a new theory has been added to this mix, making the debate even more complicated. For this reason, it's my belief that we need to come to a better understanding of all three theories in order to help us decide which theory should be taught in public schools.

So the first thing I want to do today is give you a little history about the debate over teaching the theories of evolution and creationism. The next thing I want to do is give you a detailed explanation of these two theories. And finally, I want to talk to you about a new theory, intelligent design, so we can all have a better understanding of how it relates to the two traditional theories. After I've discussed these three points, I'd like to have a discussion with the class about what our thoughts and opinions are about

(continued on next page)

Cara begins with a startling statement that quickly draws her audience into her topic while at the same time revealing the topic of her speech. She sets the stage for three theories, acknowledging that all of them are under debate. She then states her own position clearly, that we must better understand all three theories to help us make a decision about what should be taught in public schools.

Cara previews her speech and explains to her audience that she's not sure of her own position. She invites the audience to discuss with her the ideas she presents so that both she and they can come to a better informed decision about their views. Notice that she uses invitational terms like "I'm not yet decided," "hopefully," and "feel free to voice opinions and ask questions."

which theory should be taught in public school classrooms. I think this is important because this issue affects all of us potentially. Also, given the fact that I'm not yet decided on how this issue should be resolved, it would be really helpful to me to hear other opinions and gather some thoughts from the class. Hopefully, this discussion will be helpful to you too. Although I have planned for time in this speech when you can ask questions, feel free to voice opinions or ask questions at any time if you feel it will help clarify this issue. As you'll see, the answer to the question of what to teach about how the earth was created is nowhere near decided at this point.

Because of her research, Cara is able to cite sources and provide little-known facts in her first main point to describe the history of the debate over creationism. Note that her speech is organized chronologically, and that she remains audience centered throughout by presenting each position carefully and with excellent detail.

According to the *Plain Dealer* of March 12, 2002, although the debate about evolution and creationism has been ongoing since Darwin first proposed the theory of evolution, the debate about which theory to teach in schools began with what's known as the Scopes Monkey Trial. John Scopes was a science teacher at a high school in Tennessee, and he was arrested for teaching evolution, which was illegal in the state at the time. What a lot of people don't realize about John Scopes is that he didn't just decide one day to teach evolution in his classroom. He had been approached by Clarence Darrow, a proponent of evolution, who asked Scopes to teach the theory in his classroom so he would be arrested. The subsequent trial would then bring attention to the issue. However, the trial became a larger public spectacle than anyone had expected, mostly because of the high profile of the two lawyers involved: Clarence Darrow defended John Scopes, and William Jennings Bryant prosecuted him. John Scopes was convicted of teaching evolution in the classroom, although that conviction was overturned a year later. It took another forty-three years for the Supreme Court to declare it unconstitutional to criminalize teaching evolution in classrooms. Because it became legal to teach evolution, and because teaching creationism was declared unconstitutional due to the separation of church and state, evolution has become the dominant theory taught in our classrooms.

Beginning with a transition, Cara previews her second main point. She develops this point by using several examples and language that allows her audience to see each example as legitimate and reasonable. Again, her research enables her to provide her audience with useful information that will help them discuss the issues in the question-and-answer session of the speech.

Now that you have a better understanding of the history of this debate, I want to describe some of the intricacies of the two theories that have fueled it. I'd like to begin with creationism because that is the oldest theory about how the world was created. According to Robert Pennock's 1999 book, *Tower of Babel,* creationism reflects the belief that God created the universe and all living things—including humans, whom God made in his image. Most people don't realize that there are many versions of the theory of creationism. For example, new earth creationism is the literal belief that God created the earth in six 24-hour days. Another theory, old earth creationism, says yes, God did create the universe in six days. However, at that time the days were much longer, which allows the earth to be millions of years old, as has been proven by modern science. Some creationists believe that God set evolution in motion, saying, "Okay, I'm just going to give you the rules and boundaries, and then I'm going to let it go from there." Whatever the creationists believe, all of them believe that God created the universe and that he created humans to serve him.

Many believe that teaching evolution in classrooms without also teaching creationism leads to many of the problems we have in our society, such as school violence. This view was expressed by a student at a high school that teaches creationism in the classroom, quoted in *Newsday,* March 11, 2002. The student, Jordon Reed Thomas, said, "Evolution teaches us that we're animals, so who cares if we do something that's wrong or right?" That's the belief fueling much of the argument today for teaching creationism in classrooms and teaching that there is someone up there watching what we're doing. Teaching these beliefs is what the creationists are after.

She then introduces the controversy about teaching evolution versus creationism, using testimony to explain it. She discusses her own position, using invitational phrases to introduce her own doubts. She also reasons deductively—if many races, cultures, and religions make up our society, why teach only one perspective about the creation of the earth? Although her own view on this issue is fairly strong, she remains open to other perspectives as she begins her third main point.

I absolutely believe that people from every religion and every culture have the right to teach their children whatever they want to about the creation of the universe. However, I strongly believe that the classroom, especially the public school classroom, is not the place to teach the theory of creationism. Our society includes so many different races, cultures, and religions—it seems wrong to me that we would teach from only one of those religious systems in a classroom. Basically it's a way of indoctrinating children with only one way of thinking.

On the other side of the debate is the theory of evolution. This theory supports the idea of the big bang. According to the *Plain Dealer,* February 24, 2002, the big bang theory states that from a point in the universe where there was basically nothingness, a huge compression of matter and heat led to a giant explosion, or bang. And from that explosion came a life-creating element that enabled new life to form on this planet. Life here started with single-celled organism that slowly, over time, evolved into more complex multi-celled organisms. And these more complex organisms eventually evolved into human beings. The theory of evolution contends that there is overwhelming evidence all living creatures on earth came from the same background—they all share a common ancestor. Many evolutionists support this claim by citing the fossil record, the genetic code, and the wide distribution of life on earth. Even comparative studies in anatomy and biology have pointed to the fact that every creature, from slugs to human beings, comes from a common ancestor.

Cara develops her third main point by citing sources, using examples, and using cause-and-effect reasoning. Notice again how she remains audience centered and invitational by presenting the theory of evolution openly and fairly.

(continued on next page)

Cara gives fairly extensive detail about her Walczack source. (As you watch Cara on the Invitation to Public Speaking *CD-ROM, you'll also notice that she pronounces the source's name correctly). This, along with her careful research, helps her establish her own credibility as well as the credibility of the source. She then acknowledges her own position but doesn't privilege it over others. Rather, she presents it as the one that works best for her but not necessarily for others. She then invites her audience to consider a third option.*

She acknowledges a weakness in the theory of evolution, providing new information that will stimulate discussion about the theory during her question-and-answer session. She then explains the theory of intelligent design, describing one of its strengths, that it doesn't specify a "designer" but leaves this open to the individual.

Cara affirms her invitational purpose, indicating that she has some preferences and doubts, and that she remains undecided on this complex issue.

Evolutionists further contend that it's immoral of us to teach creationism in classrooms because this theory doesn't speak to children of all cultural and religious backgrounds. The theory of evolution doesn't stem from culture or religion; it's truly based on scientific facts. Vic Walczack, the executive director of the Pittsburgh chapter of the ACLU, pointed out in the *Pittsburgh Post Gazette* of March 17, 2002, that "we live in too pluralistic a society for the public schools to be indoctrinating children with a particular faith." Personally, I have always ascribed to the theory of evolution. I think it is sufficiently neutral religiously, which makes it usable in a public school classroom. And I believe there's strong scientific evidence that supports this theory. However, when I researched this speech, I came across a third theory, which I'm going to talk about next.

In recent years, a new theory of evolution called the intelligent design theory has gained some acceptance. I honestly feel there's value in this theory. According to the people who proposed the intelligent design theory, it fills a gap left by the theory of evolution. The gap is that we still don't know the origins of our ancestor's RNA and DNA, the microscopic building blocks of all life on earth, and we cannot replicate them in a scientific study. Intelligent designers say that because RNA and DNA are so complex in nature, it only makes sense that an intelligent designer—someone or something—created them. People who believe in intelligent design say they feel "the complexity of biological structures within our culture require an intelligent creator"— that's from the *Columbus Dispatch* of March 17, 2002. One of the key aspects of the intelligent design theory is that it is religiously neutral. Instead of saying the intelligent designer was God or Allah or Yahweh, proponents of this theory say the designer could have been anything—aliens could have created the human race. The idea behind teaching the theory of intelligent design in the classroom is that it could be taught in a completely neutral way religiously. No specific deity or being would be credited as the intelligent designer.

Personally, I continue to see the merit of the big bang theory and evolution. However, I'm willing to believe that it's possible life began with some sort of intelligent designer. I think I would be comfortable seeing the theory of intelligent design introduced into classrooms as long as it was taught with religious neutrality. However, I'm not sure it would be possible for some teachers to remain religiously neutral, and I'm also not sure how some scientifically minded teachers would respond if this theory were introduced into science classrooms. That's why I remain undecided on this issue.

Before I open up the floor to discussion, let me just explain to you why I think it's so important that we discuss this issue. The number one reason is that recently this has been an issue in public school systems across the country. Ohio was the state most recently affected. There someone approached a school board and said, "Look, I think you should introduce the theory of intelligent design into your classrooms." Ohio eventually said no, we're not going to change what we currently teach; we're going to continue teaching evolution. But it seems to me that more and more school boards are going to be faced with this issue. And considering that schools boards will be influenced by local citizens, I think it's important that those citizens be well informed about this issue and able to make a good decision about whether we want to teach intelligent design in our classrooms.

Furthermore, all of us are products of the U.S. education system. Someday we'll have children that will also be products of that system. We all have cousins, nieces, and nephews who are products of that system. We all have something to gain; we all have a vested interest in our education and what is taught in schools. That's why I think it's important we have a better understanding of this issue, and I'd like to gather your opinions and thoughts about it. I'll begin the discussion by asking you a question: Do you think the theory of intelligent design should be taught in public schools?

Cara and her audience discussed the pros and cons of teaching the theories of creationism, evolution, and intelligent design in the public school classroom. When the discussion was over, Cara concluded her speech.

Thank you all for your input. I really appreciate that. I hope you've come to a better understanding of my topic today—I certainly feel like I have. I've discussed the history of the debate over the creation of the earth, I've described the differences between the theories of creationism and evolution, I've introduced the theory of intelligent design, and we've discussed whether intelligent design should be taught in public schools. I hope you now feel you can have an intelligent conversation with someone else about this issue if it comes up in conversation! And maybe the next time you look at your toothbrush and think about all those bacteria, you'll be undecided about whether you should throw it away or throw a family reunion.

At this point she indicates she is about to open up a discussion, giving her audience time to prepare their thoughts and questions. She adds that this issue is being discussed in school systems across the country and, as such, is an important one for her audience to discuss before it comes up in their own school system. This claim reinforces her invitational position—that each person must sort out for herself or hisself what she or he believes, and that as a group they can help one another do just that.

Cara reinforces the importance of her topic by reminding her audience that someday they may also have children affected by the choices school boards make. She then opens the discussion with a question, indicating her desire to hear her audience's views and sort out the issue with them.

Stating the benefit she feels from discussing her topic with her audience, Cara closes by summarizing her main points. She also states her hope that her audience now has a better understanding of the issues they've discussed, then ends on a light note by returning to the startling statement she used to open her speech.

Chapter Summary

To speak invitationally is to articulate your position or explore an issue with your audience. It is to engage in a dialogue about differences and to offer and seek mutual recognition of the variety of positions possible on an issue. When you speak invitationally, you decide to do something other than inform or persuade your audience. You want to explore the many sides of an issue and continue the public dialogue, even when seemingly insurmountable differences of opinion, value, and belief exist.

Invitational speakers create a speaking environment in which priority is given to understanding, respecting, and appreciating the range of positions possible on an issue. You create this environment by developing conditions of equality, value, and self-determination in your speeches. The condition of equality means you recognize that your audience holds valid perspectives that are important to explore. The condition of value means that you recognize their positions have merit. The condition of self-determination means that you recognize that your audience members have the right to choose what is best for them, even if those choices are not the ones you would have made.

You can use two types of invitational speeches. You give speeches to articulate a position when you want to invite an audience to see the world as you do and to understand issues from your perspective. You give speeches to explore an issue when you want to engage your audience in a discussion about an issue or plan of action so you can clarify your own views or develop a course of action that takes your audience's view into account. You can use several organizational patterns to give these two types of invitational speeches. Chronological, spatial, topical, and multiple perspectives are four commonly used organizational patterns for beginning invitational speakers.

Three tips are useful for invitational speakers. First, research your topic to understand your own position and why you hold it so you can give the fullest expression of your views possible. Second, use invitational language that encourages the respect and expression of different views and that helps you have an open discussion of those views. Third, allow time for dialogue and discussion in your speeches. Remember, invitational speakers must be ethical and choose topics about which they truly want to exchange perspectives rather than inform or persuade their audience.

Invitational speaking (like informative and persuasive speaking) is not appropriate for every situation. But, because invitational speeches stimulate thinking, offer alternatives on issues, provide solutions to complex issues, and keep the public dialogue going even about controversial issues, they have their place in any beginning speaker's repertory.

After reading this chapter, use your CD-ROM and the *Invitation to Public Speaking* Web site to review the follow-ing concepts, answer the review questions, and complete the suggested activities.

Key Concepts

invitational speaking (374)
invitational environment (375)
condition of equality (376)

condition of value (376)
condition of self-determination (377)
speech to articulate a position (377)

speech to explore an issue (379)
multiple perspectives pattern (385)

Review Questions

1. Can you identify situations in which you might have preferred giving an invitational speech but gave another type instead? What might have been different if you had given an invitational speech rather than the type of speech you did give?

2. Imagine you are giving an invitational speech on the subject of gays and lesbians being drafted into the army. How might you create conditions of equality, value, and self-determination in this speech?

3. Identify a person or a group with whom you strongly disagree. Consider whether you might speak invitationally with that person or group and what benefits or disadvantages might result from such an interaction.

4. Develop an invitational speech to give to the person or group you identified in question 3. Would you prefer to articulate a position or explore an issue with them? What is it about your position that you would like them to understand, and what aspect of their position would you like to explore? Did you allow time for these types of interactions in your speech?

5. During the speech you are giving in question 4, a member of your audience strongly disagrees with the position you articulate and shares a story of his daughter's experiences in the military during the Gulf War. What kind of language could you use to acknowledge his anger and frustration but also continue to have a productive dialogue with him and other members of the audience? (You might role-play this scenario with members of your class.)

The *Invitation to Public Speaking* Web Site

The *Invitation to Public Speaking* Web site features the review questions about the Web sites suggested on pages 381, 389, and 390, the interactive activities suggested on pages 376, 388, and 390, and the InfoTrac College Edition exercises suggested on pages 375, 379, and 389. You can

access this site via your CD-ROM or at http://www.wadsworth.com/product/griffin. To access Speech Builder Express in order to complete Speech Steps 16.1 and 16.2, you will need the username and password included under "Speech Builder Express" on your CD-ROM.

Web Links

16.1: Report versus Rapport (381)
16.2: Hecklers, Hardliners, and Heavy Questions (389)
16.3: Cultural Rhythms (390)
16.4: Keeping an Open Mind (390)

Interactive Activities

16.1: Building a Supportive Climate (376)
Purpose: To assess a communication climate.

16.2: Thinking about Attitudes (389)
Purpose: To think critically about attitude formation.

16.3: Detecting Hidden Agendas (390)
Purpose: To understand the effects of hidden agendas.

InfoTrac College Edition Exercises

16.1: **Identifying Invitational Speeches** (375)
Purpose: To learn how to identify invitational speeches.

16.2: **Articulating a Position** (379)
Purpose: To understand a speech to articulate a position.

16.3: **Using Invitational Language** (389)
Purpose: To appreciate the importance of using invitational language.

Speech Interactive on the *Invitation to Public Speaking* CD-ROM

The following video clips of speeches, referenced in this chapter, are included under Speech Interactive on your *Invitation to Public Speaking* CD-ROM. After you have watched the clips, click on "Critique" to answer the questions for analysis.

Video Clip 1: Condition of Equality: Shelley Weibel (376). How does Shelley create a condition of equality as she's giving her speech? Do you think she does so effectively? As an audience member listening to her speech, would you be willing to offer your perspective or experience on the subject? Why or why not?

Video Clip 2: Condition of Self-Determination: Melissa Carroll (377). How does Melissa create a condi-

tion of self-determination as she's giving her speech? Do you think she does so effectively? As an audience member listening to her speech, would you think Melissa recognized that you knew what was best for you and had the right to make choices about your life? Why or why not?

Video Clip 3: Invitational Speech: Cara Buckley-Ott (380). How fairly does Cara present the three theories of evolution and creationism, given that she favors only one of them? How do you think her discussion with her audience helps her clarify her own position and understand the positions of people in her audience? Do you think her invitational speech was effective? Why or why not?

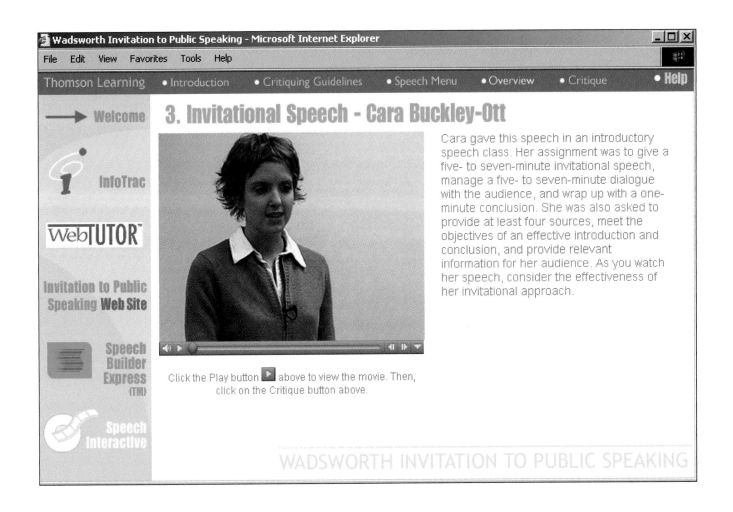

Chapter Seventeen

Persuasive Speaking

In this chapter you will learn to

Describe the three types of persuasive speeches

Apply the four most common patterns of organization patterns for persuasive speeches

Identify three tips for effective persuasive speeches

Identify the principles for giving ethical persuasive speeches

[Some of the] oldest surviving documents on persuasion are those written by Greeks and Romans more than 2000 years ago. Plato, Socrates, Aristotle, Cicero, Quintillian, and many others like them, have established the long history of the study and practice of persuasive speaking. Their ideas and traditions have found their way into court rooms, churches, political arenas, advertising campaigns, business deals, entertainment venues, and of course, public speaking classrooms. So powerful is persuasion that it has been described as "constantly remaking us into persons who are measurably changed. Sometimes imperceptibly—oftentimes dramatically.

—Timothy C. Brock, Sharon Shavitt, and Laura A. Brannon, "Getting a Handle on the Axe of Persuasion," 1994[1]

or over two thousand years, people have given persuasive speeches in political arenas, courtrooms, workplaces, community settings, social gatherings, and classrooms. Throughout history, persuasive speech has been used in the public dialogue to influence and alter the perspectives, positions, and even lives of others. When you understand the principles of persuasive speaking, you too can add your voice to the public dialogue as a persuasive speaker, whether you decide to speak, are asked to speak, or are required to speak.

Persuasion is so common that many people cannot imagine going through a day without encountering some sort of persuasive communication. For example, as you drive to school in the morning, a radio advertisement tries to convince you that you'll have the time of your life if you attend an upcoming concert. At lunch you try to convince your friends to eat at the campus cafeteria because it's cheaper than eating at a restaurant off campus. And in the evening your roommate tries to convince you to go out to a campus demonstration even though you have to get up early for work the next morning. As such, the study of persuasion has become prevalent, as this chapter's opening quote illustrates. To be persuasive is to influence another person's thinking or behavior. A **persuasive speech** is a speech whose message attempts to change or reinforce an audience's thoughts, feelings, or actions.

To ask an audience to see things the way we do is quite different from speaking informatively (Chapter 15) or invitationally (Chapter 16). When we speak to inform, we share our knowledge or expertise with an audience, helping them better understand a topic by providing information. When we speak to invite, we set the stage for an exploration of a topic, encouraging an open discussion that welcomes different perspectives. In contrast, when we speak to persuade, we ask an audience to think as we do about a topic, to adopt our position, or to support and mirror our actions and beliefs. In that sense, we act as advocates for a particular issue, belief, or course of action.

This chapter discusses several aspects of speaking that are central to persuasion. You will explore the three major types of persuasive speeches, the organizational patterns best suited to persuasive speeches, some strategies for gaining audience support, and some of the common challenges and ethical considerations that persuasive speaking presents.

persuasive speech
Speech whose message attempts to change or reinforce an audience's thoughts, feelings, or actions.

Types of Persuasive Speeches

Attempts at persuasion generally fall into three categories: questions of fact, value, and policy. Each category focuses on a different type of change. Knowing which type of change you want to request helps you develop a listenable message.

Questions of Fact

When we want to persuade an audience about what is or isn't true, we are speaking about questions of fact. A **question of fact** is a question that addresses whether something is true or not. For example, we can determine with certainty who ran the fastest marathon at last summer's Olympic games by consulting a yearbook or looking up Olympic records online. But we cannot absolutely determine the training schedule that will produce the fastest Olympic marathon runners. That fact is open to dispute, and an audience can be persuaded to accept one fact or another by a speaker's use of arguments, evidence, and reasoning (Chapters 8 and 18).

Similarly, the reasons dinosaurs became extinct, the original purpose of Stonehenge, the techniques used to construct the Egyptian pyramids, the cure for cancer, or the guilt of someone charged with a crime cannot be verified absolutely. The facts about these issues are inconclusive and raise many questions. As such they are often topics for speeches in which you try to persuade audiences that you have the correct answers.

Questions of Value

When we want to persuade an audience about what is good or bad, right or wrong, we are speaking about questions of value. A **question of value** is a question that addresses the merit or morality of an object, action, or belief. Are old-growth forests worth saving from logging? Is it moral to punish certain crimes with death? Is it possible to raise children to be ethical adults if you don't also encourage them to be religious? These are questions of value, as are debates over what constitutes "good" and "bad" art, music, or theater.

When you attempt to persuade your audiences about questions of value, you move from asserting that something is true or false to advocating that one thing is better or worse than another. Questions of value cannot be answered simply by analyzing facts. Rather, they are grounded in what people believe is right, good, appropriate, worthy, and ethically sound. As such, it can be difficult to persuade audiences about questions of value. This is because when we speak on questions of value, we must *justify* our claims. We must provide acceptable reasons for accepting a particular action or view. When we justify a claim, we set *standards* and we argue that our view satisfies certain principles or values generally regarded as correct and valid by most people. So when we try to persuade an audience to save old-growth forests, we justify that claim by arguing that a stand of old-growth trees meets a certain standard for protection. Or, when we attempt to persuade our audience that it is moral to punish certain crimes with death, we try to justify our claim on the basis of a particular standard: that certain actions fall into a specific category that warrants this kind of punishment.

To find links to Web sites that discuss standards by which we can judge values, go to Rutgers University's Virtual Religion Index at http://religion.rutgers.edu/vri/ethics.html.

Questions of Policy

When we want to persuade an audience about the best way to act or solve a problem, we are speaking about questions of policy. A **question of policy** is a question that addresses the best course of action or the best solution to a problem. What form of support should employers provide for veterans with disabilities? How should the federal government implement mandatory drug testing? How many

Persuasive speakers often ask audiences to take a course of action that will solve a problem or otherwise benefit a particular community. What problem do you feel needs to be addressed in your community? What course of action could you suggest that would motivate an audience to help you address that problem?

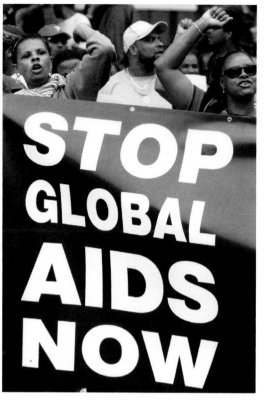

© AFP/CORBIS

credits for graduation should the university require? At what age should people be allowed to drink legally? Each of these questions focuses on an issue that cannot be resolved solely by answering a question of absolute fact or debating the morality of an issue.

Although questions of policy might address the facts about the contributions veterans make in the workplace or the morality of mandatory testing, they go beyond these questions to offer solutions and plans of action. In sum, speeches about questions of policy present an audience with a specific solution or plan to a problem and try to persuade them that the solution or plan will eliminate the problem satisfactorily. To read an article about a useful way to think about policy speeches, go to professional problem solver Hidetoshi Shibata's Web site, Problem Solving: Definition, Terminology, and Patterns at http://www.mediafrontier.com/ info/problem.htm.

To learn more about how to distinguish among fact, value, and policy speeches, complete InfoTrac College Edition Exercise 17.1, "Fact, Value, or Policy Speech?" featured at the end of this chapter and online under Student Resources for Chapter 17. And to find topics for persuasive speeches, visit the Yahoo! directory Web page on issues and causes at http://dir.yahoo.com/Society_and_Culture Issues_and_Causes/.

Because each type of persuasive speech—questions of fact, value, or policy—focuses on different issues and goals for change, each requires a different type of organizational pattern in order to be most effective. Many persuasive speeches can be organized according to the patterns discussed in Chapter 9, particularly speeches about questions of fact and value. However, because speeches about questions of policy often call on an audience to take a specific action, they sometimes require unique organizational patterns. Let's explore organizational patterns for speeches on questions of fact and value and then move on to the special organizational patterns for speeches on questions of policy.

 Speech Step 17.1 / Select a Persuasive Speech Type

For your next persuasive speech, decide whether you will try to persuade your audience about a question of fact, value, or policy. Use the assignment given to you by your instructor and review the descriptions of each type of speech in this section to help you make your decision.

Organization of Speeches on Questions of Fact

Speeches on questions of fact can be organized chronologically, spatially, and topically. To help you decide which organizational pattern is best to use, ask yourself the following questions: Can you achieve your goals best by describing the issue as it developed over time, by describing a spatial arrangement, or by covering distinct topics? In the following example, Kendra traces fifty years' worth of data about aerobic exercise to build a case for the benefits of aerobic exercise.

Specific purpose:	To persuade my audience that regular aerobic exercise is the best way to enhance their quality of life.
Thesis statement:	Over the past fifty years, research on aerobic exercise indicates that regular aerobic exercise significantly enhances a person's quality of life in ways other forms of exercise do not.

Main points:

I. Recognition of the importance of aerobic exercise and its impact on the quality of life began in the 1950s.

II. In the 1970s, "new" findings on aerobic exercise and its impact on the quality of life prompted the aerobics craze most of us are familiar with.

III. In the 1990s, additional research on the link between aerobic exercise and the quality of life revealed that this form of exercise is more beneficial than other forms, such as strength training.

IV. Sports scientists continue to recognize the superior benefits of aerobic exercise and to tinker with the "perfect" aerobic workout for the current era.

Occasionally questions of fact can be organized spatially. In the following example from a speech about campus lighting, Thomas traces the layout of the campus from its center to its perimeter to make the case that it is not adequately lit for safety.

Specific purpose:	To persuade my audience that the lighting on campus is not adequate.
Thesis statement:	From the library to the farthest parking lot, the lighting on campus is not adequate to ensure safety after dark.

Main points:

I. Lighting near the center of the campus casts many shadows in which someone can hide.

II. Around the perimeter of this center, the lighting is spaced too far apart to offer adequate protection.

III. The lighting in the parking lots that border the campus should be much brighter than it currently is.

In the next example, Evan used the topical pattern to develop his speech about the best treatment of attention deficit disorder.

Specific purpose:	To persuade my audience that attention deficit disorder can be treated effectively without the use of medication.
Thesis statement:	Diet and exercise alone can be used to treat attention deficit disorder effectively.

Main points:

I. A diet low in sugar and processed foods is the first part of an effective treatment for attention deficit disorder.

II. A regular program of exercise is the second part of an effective treatment for attention deficit disorder.

By organizing his speech topically, Evan was able to use his main points to identify key issues that are open to dispute.

Organization of Speeches on Questions of Value

Like speeches on questions of fact, speeches on questions of value can be organized chronologically, spatially, or topically. In the following example, Eiji used the chronological pattern to develop her speech about the value of encouraging girls to participate in the sciences.

Specific purpose: To persuade my audience that encouraging girls to participate in the sciences is of value to us all.

Thesis statement: Throughout history, when women have been encouraged to participate in the traditionally male-dominated world of science, they have made significant contributions that have benefited all of us.

Main points:
I. In the late 1700s, Caroline Lucretia Hershel's father and brother encouraged her interest in astronomy, and she developed the modern mathematical approach to astronomy.

II. In the late 1800s, with the support of her husband and colleagues, botanist Elizabeth Knight Britton built impressive botanical collections and is said to be the first person to suggest the establishment of the New York Botanical Gardens.

III. In the early 1900s, Maria Goeppert-Mayer was encouraged by her university professors to pursue her interest in science, which led to her winning the 1963 Nobel Prize in Physics for her groundbreaking work in modeling the nuclei of atoms.

The next example illustrates a question of value organized spatially. In this speech, Trevor arranged his main points so they followed specific locations within a city.

Specific purpose: To persuade my audience that the preservation of open space within and between communities should take priority in city planning.

Thesis statement: Open space both within and along the perimeter of a city is crucial for a healthy community.

Main points:
I. Open space in the heart of a city creates a friendlier, more relaxed city center.

II. Open space in identifiable areas or districts within a city brings people together, resulting in more familiarity with one's neighbors and safer neighborhoods.

III. Open space between two cities reduces urban sprawl and strengthens people's attachment to their own city.

In the next example, Ted used the topical pattern to organize his speech about the value of spending equal time teaching students the history of minority groups in the United States.

Specific purpose: To persuade my audience that the history of minority groups in the United States is as important as the history of the dominant cultural groups.

Thesis statement: Minority groups within the United States have a rich and varied past that should be taught to students in elementary and high school history courses.

Main points:
I. The people and cultures currently described in popular history texts offer students a limited story of the contributions that have been made throughout history.

II. People from minority cultures and groups have made significant contributions to society throughout history.

III. Including the contributions of people from minority groups and cultures in these texts would offer a more comprehensive story.

When we give persuasive speeches on questions of fact or policy, we may ask our audience to change their view or agree on what is right or wrong, but we do not ask them to do anything. As such, the chronological, spatial, and topical patterns work well for these types of speeches. However, for persuasive speeches about questions of policy, we also ask our audience to agree on what must be done to solve a problem. As such, we must rely on different types of organizational patterns.

Persuading an audience on a question of value can be a challenge, especially if audience members have different opinions about what is good or moral. As such, selecting an effective organizational pattern is important. For example, would it be more effective to persuade a group of teenagers that smoking is dangerous by discussing the diseases that smokers typically die of (topical) or by discussing the debilitating progression of a particular disease (chronological)?

Organization of Speeches on Questions of Policy

Persuasive speeches about questions of policy usually require organizational patterns that clearly define a problem and then offer a well-developed solution. The most effective type of organizational pattern for your speech depends on the kind of change you are hoping to get from your audience: *immediate action* or *passive agreement*. The differences between the two are simple, yet the impact they have on a speech is significant.

When you attempt to **gain immediate action**, your goal is to motivate an audience to engage in a specific behavior or take a specific action. You want to move beyond simply asking your audience to alter a belief. When you seek immediate action, you want to be as specific as possible in stating what it is you want your audience to do. You will need a clear **call to action**, a request that an audience engage in some clearly stated behavior. For example, rather than asking your audience to simply agree with you that the lighting on campus is inadequate, ask them to contact the school administration and urge them to add money to next year's budget to improve campus lighting.

In contrast, when you want to **gain passive agreement**, you goal is to ask an audience to adopt a new position without also asking them to act in support of that position. When you seek passive agreement, you still advocate a solution to a problem, but you don't call your audience to action. Instead, you simply encourage

gain immediate action
Motivate an audience to engage in a specific behavior or take a specific action.

call to action
Request that an audience engage in some clearly stated behavior.

gain passive agreement
Ask an audience to adopt a new position without also asking them to act in support of that position.

them to adopt a new position or perspective. Consider the differences between requesting immediate action and passive agreement in the following specific purpose statements:

Immediate action

To persuade my audience to attend the next city council meeting in support of open-space measures.

To persuade my audience to vote for school board members who support history textbooks that include more material about the contributions of minority groups in the United States.

To persuade my audience to adopt my aerobics training program.

Passive agreement

To persuade my audience that open space in a city benefits that city and its residents by making it more attractive and livable.

To persuade my audience that elementary and high school students would receive a richer education if the material in their history courses reflected more diversity.

To persuade my audience that aerobic exercise is fun and significantly enhances a person's quality of life.

Notice how the requests for immediate action focus on asking an audience to do something specific, whereas the requests for passive agreement simply ask an audience to alter a belief. To explore more about identifying the differences between immediate action and passive agreement speeches, complete Interactive Activity 17.1, "Calling for Action in Congress," online under Student Resources for Chapter 17 at the *Invitation to Public Speaking* Web site. Let's look at some organizational patterns that will help you meet your speech goals whether you request immediate action or passive agreement.

WEB SITE

Problem-Solution Organization

problem-solution organization
Organizational pattern that focuses on persuading an audience that a specific problem exists and can be solved or minimized by a specific solution.

Speeches that follow a **problem-solution organization** focus on persuading an audience that a specific problem exists and can be solved or minimized by a specific solution. These types of persuasive speeches are generally organized into two main points. The first point specifies a problem, and the second proposes a solution to that problem. In the problem component of your speech, you must define a problem clearly and the problem must be relevant to your audience. In the solution component, you must offer a solution that really does help solve the problem and that an audience can reasonably support and implement.

Consider the following examples of problem-solution speeches, given by Courtney and Brent. Notice how they used their thesis statements to state a problem clearly, then how they communicated that problem to their audiences in their first main points. Also notice how they related the problem to their audiences directly and personally. In the first example, Courtney spoke about the issue of light pollution.

Specific purpose: To persuade my audience that although light pollution is a problem that affects us increasingly every day, we can implement simple solutions to reduce the effects of this pollution.

Thesis statement: Light pollution disrupts ground-based astronomy, is a costly energy waste, and affects our health and safety, but there are simple solutions to the problem of light pollution.

Main points: I. Light pollution poses three significant problems.

      A. In cities, light pollution causes urban sky glow, which disrupts ground-based telescopes.

      B. Light pollution represents an extreme waste of energy, and that waste is costly to all of us.

      C. Light pollution causes mild to severe medical conditions and so is unsafe for our communities.

    II. The problem of light pollution can be alleviated in two ways.

      A. Light pollution can be controlled through government regulations, such as light codes, which are similar to noise codes.

      B. Light pollution can be reduced through personal actions, such as using less unnecessary light and purchasing equipment that reduces light directed toward the sky.

Courtney Stillman

Notice how Courtney's first main point clearly defines the specific problems created by light pollution and how her second main point offers reasonable solutions. Also note that she requests both passive agreement and immediate action—she asks for passive agreement when she states that supporting government regulations is a good idea, and she asks for active agreement when she suggests her audience modify the lights in their homes. Using your *Invitation to Public Speaking* CD-ROM, watch the video clip of Courtney giving her persuasive speech. Consider the effectiveness of the organizational pattern she uses for her speech.

In the next example, Brent urges active agreement—he wants his audience to hike responsibly when they are seeking the perfect nature photo.

Specific purpose: To persuade my audience to stay on designated trails and roadways while photographing nature in national parks and recreation areas.

Thesis statement: When nature photographers stray off trails, they place themselves at risk and damage the ecosystem, but by following some simple tips, photographers can easily remain on designated trails and still take memorable photographs.

Main points: I. When you stray off trails while scouting a good photograph, it is easier to get into dangerous situations and to damage fragile ecosystems.

      A. Trails are designed to keep you from getting lost and to help you avoid hazardous terrain.

      B. The damage caused by new trails you create on your own and by one adult foot in a hiking boot is extensive.

    II. While searching for the perfect shot in national parks and recreation areas, follow four simple guidelines to stay safe and protect the environment.

      A. Stay alert and pay attention to your surroundings.

      B. Read all signs, postings, and trail markers when entering parks or recreational areas and when you're on hiking trails.

C. If you're on a hike in the evening, carry a flashlight so you can see the trails.

D. If you do get lost, stay put to avoid damage to yourself and to the ecosystem.

Brent illustrated the damages caused by irresponsible hiking. He also offered viable solutions that suited his problem and that his audience could easily implement. Using your *Invitation to Public Speaking* CD-ROM, watch a video clip of Brent giving his persuasive speech under Speech Interactive. Pay attention to the solutions he proposes. Could you implement them?

Because problem-solution speeches pose a problem while simultaneously offering a solution, they are excellent vehicles for persuading an audience to support a cause or take an action. When you use a problem-solution organizational pattern, be sure to remember the following:

- Pose a clearly defined problem.
- Pose a relevant problem.
- Offer a solution that remedies the problem.
- Offer a solution that is appropriate to the audience.

Brent Erb

problem-cause-solution organization
Organizational pattern that focuses on identifying a specific problem, the causes of that problem, and a solution for the problem.

Problem-Cause-Solution Organization

The problem-cause-solution pattern of organization is a slight variation of the problem-solution pattern. Speeches that follow a **problem-cause-solution organization** focus on identifying a specific problem, the causes of that problem, and a solution for the problem. This type of speech is especially effective when you think you will be more persuasive if you explain how a problem came about. Explaining the causes of a problem can help your audience better see the merits of a proposed solution. Describing causes also allows you to explain how an audience came to believe what they do and to clarify any misconceptions about a topic. In either case, you are sometimes more persuasive if you provide an audience with more information about a problem.

Problem-cause-solution speeches generally have three main points—the first identifies the problem, the second identifies the causes of that problem, and the third details the solution to the problem. Two examples illustrate this pattern of organization:

Specific purpose: To persuade my audience that the problems caused by feeding big game wildlife can be easily solved.

Thesis statement: The problems of wildlife overpopulation, the spread of disease, and other negative consequences caused by feeding big game wildlife can be solved by keeping food away from wild animals.

Main points:
  I. In many areas where people and big game wildlife live near each other, there is overpopulation in certain species, outbreaks of disease, and a decrease in our acceptance of hunters and hunting.

  II. These problems are caused by well-meaning people leaving food out for wildlife in the winter and by campers who are not careful to keep their food and food smells away from wild animals.

  III. These problems can be solved by simply not feeding wildlife; by protecting our food, washing our dishes, and washing our faces and hands when camping; and by putting our garbage in sealed containers.

The screenshot at the top of the page:

Thomson Learning • Introduction • Critiquing Guidelines • Speech Menu • Overview • Critique • Help

Welcome

InfoTrac

WebTUTOR

Invitation to Public Speaking Web Site

Speech Builder Express (TM)

Speech Interactive

3. Causes - Brandi Lafferty

RealOne Player   File » ⊚   _ □ X
www.wadsworthmedia.com   0:14 / 6:51

Then, complete the Critique form on the right. The Done button at the bottom of the form sends your responses to an e-mail address (presumably your instructor's) and then shows how a Public Speaking expert responded.

You can e-mail your Critique responses to your instructor. To do so, provide the following information before clicking the Done button at the bottom of this page.

Student Name:
Student E-mail:
Instructor's Name:
Instructor's E-mail:

Causes

Watch Brandi's speech.

1. Does she clearly describe why the problem exists? How does knowing the cause of a problem help a speaker convince an audience the problem can be solved? Did Brandi's decision to include a discussion of the problem's cause make for a more effective speech?

WADSWORTH INVITATION TO PUBLIC SPEAKING

Notice how Brandi was able to make a stronger case for her solution by identifying the specific causes of wildlife overpopulation, the spread of disease, and other wildlife-related problems. Once her audience knew the reasons for the problems, they could see the merits of a solution that might have seemed too simple to be effective. Using your *Invitation to Public Speaking* CD-ROM, watch the video clip of Brandi giving her persuasive speech under Speech Interactive. Did her decision to include a discussion of the problem's cause make for a more effective speech?

A second example illustrates a different purpose for addressing a cause of a problem:

Brandi Lafferty

Specific purpose: To persuade my audience that wildfires should be allowed to burn, because they are an important and natural part of the ecosystem.

Thesis statement: By letting wildfires burn, supporting prescribed burns, and allowing clear-cutting, we can prevent unnecessary forest fires caused by a century-long policy of fire suppression.

Main points: I. Aggressively suppressing or putting out fires interferes with a necessary environmental cycle and leads to an unnatural state in the forest.

II. A century-long policy of "fight all fires" has created this imbalance and has confused the public about the purpose of fire in the forests.

III. Letting fires burn themselves out, prescribing burns in certain safe areas, and thinning forests manually could help right the imbalance we now face.

In this example, Tony addressed the cause of the forest fire problem so his audience could better understand their beliefs about wildfires and how they start. By addressing this cause, Tony illustrated some of the unintended outcomes of the fire suppression campaign and helped people adjust their beliefs about fire and its effects.

Problem-cause-solution organizational patterns are useful when you think that providing information about the cause of a problem will help persuade your audience to change their views or beliefs. When you use a problem-cause-solution pattern, be sure you

- Identify a clear and relevant problem
- Identify a relevant cause of the problem
- Offer a clear and appropriate solution to the problem

Comparative Advantages Organization

comparative advantages organization
Organizational pattern that illustrates the advantages of one solution over others.

When your audience agrees with you about a problem but feels the solution is up for debate, a comparative advantages speech is often an excellent choice. Speeches that follow a **comparative advantages organization** illustrate the advantages of one solution over others. In this type of speech, use each main point to explain why your solution is preferable to other possible solutions. If you must criticize alternative solutions in order to strengthen your explanations, simply explain why the alternatives will not work, taking care not to degrade or belittle them. (See the Tips for Effective Persuasive Speaking section for reasons why your criticisms should be offered with care.)

Consider Angela from Chapter 4. Her coworkers and bosses already knew a problem existed—sales were down and they were beginning to lose what had once been faithful customers. As such, Angela chose to give a comparative advantages speech so she could focus on illustrating the strengths of her proposed training program.

Specific purpose: To persuade my coworkers that my new training program will increase our sales and enhance our public profile.

Thesis statement: My proposed training program—which includes a longer initial training period, a more detailed assessment and understanding of the strengths of our products, and a stronger mentoring component than our current program—will turn our sales around.

Main points:
I. A longer initial training program will give our staff more time than our current program allows to develop a working knowledge and appreciation of the company and its mission.

II. A more detailed knowledge of our products and their value will enable our staff to work with our clientele more expertly than our current training allows.

III. A stronger mentoring program will improve the communication style of our new sales staff and help them respond to unfamiliar situations more effectively than our current mentoring program does.

Angela did not spend time outlining the problem because her audience already knew the training program needed improvement. Instead, she compared the advantages of her program to the weaknesses of the company's current program. She was careful to avoid criticizing the current program too heavily, because her boss had been instrumental in bringing that model to the company. Rather, she simply said, "Our current program no longer is meeting our needs. If we make these changes, we'll be back on top."

When you select a comparative advantages organizational pattern, be sure you

- Discuss the problem you are solving only briefly, spending the bulk of your time explaining your solutions
- Illustrate the advantages of your solution over other options

Monroe's Motivated Sequence

Monroe's motivated sequence
Sequential process used to persuade audiences by gaining attention, demonstrating a need, satisfying that need, visualizing beneficial results, and calling for action.

Monroe's motivated sequence is an organizational pattern that helps you address an audience's motives and how those motives could translate to action. Developed in 1935 by Alan Monroe, **Monroe's motivated sequence** is a sequential process used to persuade audiences by gaining attention, demonstrating a need, satisfying that need, visualizing beneficial results, and calling for action. Monroe maintained that this pattern satisfies an audience's desire for order and helps a speaker focus on what motivates an audience to action. Monroe's motivated sequence organizes the entire speech, not just the body, and takes listeners through a step-by-step process of identifying a problem and resolving to help solve that problem.[2]

1. **Attention.** In this step, you catch the audience's interest so they take notice of an issue. Your goal in this step is to motivate the audience to listen and see the personal connection they have to a topic.

2. **Need.** In the second step, you identify the need for a change, meaning a problem that can be solved. You define the problem and how it directly or indirectly affects the audience. In this step, your goal is to encourage your audience to become invested in the problem, feel affected by it, and want to find a solution.

3. **Satisfaction.** In this step, you define what the specific solution is and why it solves the problem. In doing so, you show the audience how their "need" is "satisfied."

4. **Visualization.** In this step, you describe the benefits that will result from the audience's need being satisfied. You can describe what life will be like once the solution is in place, or you can remind the audience what it would be like if the solution were not implemented. Either way, you help the audience visualize how the solution will benefit them.

5. **Action.** In this final step, you outline exactly what the audience should do. This is your call to action, the plea for the audience to take immediate action or make a personal commitment to support the changes you're advocating.

For a detailed summary and examples of the Monroe's motivated sequence pattern of organization, go to http://www.ridgeweb1.mnscu.edu/~keith_g/121/monroes.htm.

To explore how Martin Luther King Jr. used organization to create an effective message, complete Interactive Activity 17.2, "Persuading an Audience to Follow a Dream," online under Student Resources for Chapter 17 at the *Invitation to Public Speaking* Web site.   **WEB SITE**

Speech Step 17.2 / Select an Organizational Pattern for Your Persuasive Speech

A persuasive speech topic can be organized in many ways. You can use a chronological, spatial, or topical pattern of organization. Or you can use an organizational pattern that proposes a solution to a problem: problem-solution, problem-cause-solution, comparative advantages, or Monroe's motivated sequence. Select the pattern that helps you persuade your audience to take action or modify their thinking about a topic. Speech Builder Express helps you outline your persuasive speech once you've selected an organizational pattern. Access Speech Builder Express online to outline your speech.

Tips for Effective Persuasive Speaking

Consider the many times you've wanted to convince others to join with you, think like you, or support you. You may have wanted them to do something as simple as go to a movie or eat a new kind of food, or as complicated as join a particular organization or share your passionate social views. Most people are deeply committed to certain things in life, such as a spiritual or political path. Or, because of deeply held beliefs, they feel a strong sense of right and wrong about certain issues, such as whether women should participate in active combat. It's natural to want others to share in our commitments and beliefs, and most of us can think of many times when we wanted to convince others to think, feel, and act as we do.

To help you give persuasive speeches, remember the following tips: (1) increase your chances for successful persuasion by being realistic about changing your audience's views, (2) use your evidence fairly and strategically for best results, and (3) use language that respectfully motivates your audience to change.

Be Realistic About Changing Your Audience's Views

Researchers generally agree that successful persuasion involves an audience that is open to change. If an audience is not open to change, even your best persuasive efforts are likely to fail. This means you must consider your audience's perspectives carefully and frame your persuasive attempts around issues that your audience will be open to considering. If you know your audience believes something quite strongly and isn't open to change (views on religion often fall into this category), you probably won't be successful in convincing them to change that view no matter how well reasoned or researched your speech is. However, if the audience is open to considering an alternative perspective (for example, that there is a place in our society for different religious practices), your persuasive efforts are more likely to be successful.

This means you must think carefully about the position your audience holds and choose a realistic argument before you attempt to change their views. It is often tempting to ask an audience to change their views completely, especially if you don't agree with those views. However, successful persuasion involves advocating a position, or some *aspect* of a position, that your audience can be open about. For example, it may be unrealistic to think you can change your audience's views on legalizing certain drugs if your audience has had bad experiences with

Be realistic about what you can or cannot persuade an audience to think, feel, or do. For very personal issues, such as politics, focus on some aspect of an issue that an audience could reasonably consider. How can you frame the topic of your next persuasive speech in order to be realistic about asking your audience to change?

drugs or people who use drugs. But you may be able to persuade them to see the benefits that some of these drugs offer in medical treatments. In other words, you may be able to persuade them to reconsider some part of their position rather than undertake a radical change.[3]

Your attempts at persuasion will likely be more successful if you take a realistic, audience-centered approach to changing others. Rather than asking for radical changes, approach your speech goals and your audience with some restraint. Remember, audiences hold particular beliefs and positions because of their experiences and worldviews. If you respect those positions and experiences as you ask your audience to change, you'll be more likely to give a successful speech. To help you better understand your classroom audience and the attitudes they may have about your topic, complete InfoTrac College Edition Exercise 17.2, "Analyzing Your Audience," under Student Resources for Chapter 17.

Use Evidence Fairly and Strategically

Research on evidence and persuasion suggests that besides carefully researching, organizing, and delivering your speech, there are some strategies you can use to help you construct effective persuasive arguments. These strategies involve two-sided messages, counterarguments, and fear appeals.

Because persuasive speakers advocate one position over others, they often frame an issue as two sided, even if there are multiple perspectives on the issue (Chapter 16). A **two-sided message** addresses two sides of an issue, refuting one side to prove the other is better. Research suggests that when speakers discuss two sides of an issue, they are more persuasive when they offer a rebuttal to the side they oppose rather than simply mentioning it and then ignoring it.[4]

Similarly, addressing **counterarguments**, arguments against the speaker's own position, enhances a speaker's position. For example, when Tony advocated a policy of controlled burns to prevent forest fires, he increased his believability when he also discussed the argument that controlled burns can get out of control and cause major damage. By acknowledging this counterargument, Tony illustrated why the concerns it raises are unfounded, strengthening his position that controlled burns prevent other fires from burning out of control.

Note, however, that you must use two-sided messages and counterarguments with care. In persuasion, credibility is important (Chapters 8 and 18), and you must take care that your rebuttals are not too judgmental or inflammatory. If you unfairly attack someone else's view or refute an opposing position too harshly, audiences may perceive you as less likable—and audiences are less likely to be persuaded by unlikable speakers. Additionally, the audience will focus their attention on assessing the merit of your judgmental claim rather than attending to the rest of your message.[5] So when Tony advocated for controlled burns, he avoided saying, "That's stupid. Anyone knows that the fear of out-of-control prescribed burns is as ridiculous as fearing you'll burn down your house by lighting your barbecue!" Instead, he clearly and directly illustrated why the fear is unfounded—but not stupid—and why his policy is preferable.

Speakers also often use fear appeals to persuade audiences to change or take action. For example, in political ads, politicians often use fear appeals as a way to motivate voters. A **fear appeal** is the threat of something undesirable happening if change does not occur. Research suggests that fear appeals may motivate audiences who are not initially invested in your topic to *become* invested.[6] A fear appeal causes an audience to take notice of an issue and see how it relates to them personally. When audiences already feel connected to the topic, fear appeals simply reinforce that connection. However, if a fear appeal is so extreme that audiences

two-sided message
Persuasive strategy that addresses both sides of an issue, refuting one side to prove the other is better.

counterarguments
Arguments against the speaker's own position.

fear appeal
Threat of something undesirable happening if change does not occur.

feel immobilized, that there is nothing they can do to solve the problem, they may simply avoid or deny the problem.[7] Thus, if you use fear appeals, temper them so your audience feels there is a solution to the problem they fear and that the solution will actually work. For example, if your speech is about the risk of leukemia in your community, speak honestly about it but do not exaggerate it. Then offer practical steps your audience can take to reduce their risk so they feel hopeful and empowered rather than defeated. To read an article that illustrates how using too much fear can make an audiences feel they can do nothing about a problem, go to the Web site Fear Advertising—It Doesn't Work! at http://www.mecca.org/~crights/dream.html.

Use Language That Encourages an Audience to Change

Just as informative speaking relies on language that is clear and unbiased, and invitational speaking relies on language that fosters openness and a desire to explore an issue, persuasive speaking relies on language that will motivate an audience to think or act differently. The most obvious examples of persuasive language are words and phrases that indicate what an audience "should do," what the "best" solution would be, or how something is "better than" something else. Persuasive language often appeals to emotions, as in "wouldn't it be tragic if we failed to respond appropriately to this situation?" (See Chapter 18 for more about emotional appeals.) Additionally, audiences should hear strong calls to action such as, "I'm asking each one of you to attend the rally tonight" or appeals such as "Imagine what our national park would look like with power lines running through it." However, research indicates that the more invested people are in a position, the less effective phrases such as "Today I'll persuade you that" or "I'm here to convince you that" are, especially in your introduction.[8] When you tell an audience you will persuade them, they tend to hold more firmly to their positions.

WEB SITE To evaluate the effectiveness of persuasive language, complete Interactive Activity 17.3, "Assessing the Persuasiveness of Newspaper Editorial Page," online under Student Resources for Chapter 17 at the *Invitation to Public Speaking* Web site.

Research on persuasion in conversations suggests that speakers who use words and phrases that show they understand the feelings and motivations of others are generally more persuasive than speakers who don't.[9] This means your language should reflect an appreciation for the positions audience members hold. Use language that helps you clarify your position and its merits without casting a negative light on the views of others. Although persuasive speeches are sometimes used to attack or argue, when you enter the public dialogue you can avoid this unnecessary sort of speech by using respectful language, even if you and your audiences disagree.

Using this type of language does not mean you should not try to motivate your audiences to change. On the contrary, the goal of persuasive speaking is to encourage an audience to think or act differently, and your language should reflect this challenge. Phrases like "Perhaps you've never thought about the impact of," "I encourage you to consider this evidence carefully," and "How can we let this kind of damage continue?" are phrases that do not attack or demand but instead urge audiences to reevaluate their positions. Some of our best efforts at persuasion have resulted in speeches that respectfully challenged an audience to think in new ways.

WEB SITE To further explore the idea that you can use respectful persuasive language, complete Interactive Activity 17.4, "Persuading While Conceding," online under Student Resources for Chapter 17 at the *Invitation to Public Speaking* Web site.

Ethical Persuasive Speaking

Have you ever noticed that sometimes when you try to change someone, that person regularly resists your attempts?[10] Can you recall the times when your parents tried to persuade you to do (or not to do) something, like dress a certain way, date a certain kind of person, or attend a certain function? For many people, as soon as the persuasion began, so did the resistance. Why is this so when our parents likely had our best interests at heart?

Research and personal experience tell us that when others try to persuade us, we feel our freedom to choose our own path is threatened. In the United States especially, the freedom to choose often resides at the heart of our sense of self. When someone tries to convince us to think, feel, or do something new or different, many people dig their heels in and hold on to their positions even more firmly.

The issues we try to persuade others about are also complicated, making the process of persuasion even more challenging. Questions of fact, value, and policy are rarely simple or clear cut. When feelings, preferences, experiences, and habits come into play, these questions can get clouded and emotional, and people often invest in particular outcomes. Additionally, persuasion inherently relies on uncertainty or differences, so the issues you want to persuade an audience about are grounded in this uncertainty and difference.

Given these characteristics of persuasion, be sure you request change ethically. To persuade ethically is to persuade others without threatening or challenging their sense of self-determination and freedom to choose what is best for them. Remember, when you persuade, you act as advocate for a particular position, not a bully who tries to force or threaten an audience to see things your way. Ethical persuasion also requires you to recognize the complexity of the issues you speak about and the possible impact of your proposed solutions on your audience. As you prepare your persuasive speech, keep the following four questions in mind—the first three address the complexity of audiences and issues, and the fourth helps you consider the effect of the changes you request.

- What is my position on this topic and why do I hold this position?

- What is my audience's position on this topic and why do they hold this position?

- Why am I qualified to try to persuade my audience on this issue?

- Is my request reasonable for my audience, and how will they be affected by the change?

As an ethical persuasive speaker, you must understand your own positions as well as the positions of your audiences. Acknowledge your own master statuses, standpoints, and unique experiences as well as those of each member of your audience.

Similarly, ethical persuasive speaking requires you to *present information* in an ethical way. This means you must tell the truth, avoid distorting or manipulating evidence, and present information accurately and completely. To ensure that you present your evidence ethically, review the research tips in Chapter 6. Remember, audiences dislike being manipulated and lied to. Even if a speaker gains support through the unethical manipulation of evidence or ideas, that support is usually lost as soon as the audience discovers the deceit. Gaining support through ethical means will only increase your credibility. To explore an example of a business that used unethical methods of persuasion, complete Info-Trac College Edition Exercise 17.3, "Persuasion and Ethics," online under Student Resources for Chapter 17.

Because you are asking audiences to alter their attitudes, values, and beliefs when you give a persuasive speech, take an ethical approach to this type of speaking. Because of his strong commitment to social justice, Jimmy Carter is considered a highly ethical speaker. Who do you consider to be an ethical speaker?

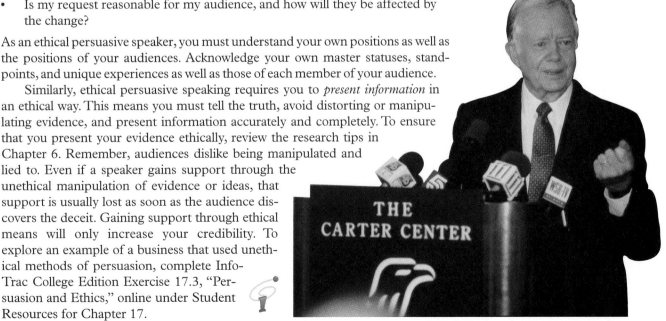

Specific purpose: To persuade my audience to decrease their sugar intake and so live healthier lives.

Thesis statement: The health problems that many Americans have as a result of misconceptions about the effect of too much sugar in their diets can be alleviated by taking action at the national level and on a personal level.

Are you ready to practice your powers of persuasion by giving an effective persuasive speech? Use the following speech as a model. You can see the outline for this speech under Student Resources for Chapter 17 at the Invitation to Public Speaking *Web site. Also, you can use your* Invitation to Public Speaking *CD-ROM to watch a video clip of Hans Erian's speech, which he gave at the 2002 Phi Rho Pi National Tournament. (Phi Rho Pi is a national honor society for speech competitors in two-year colleges in the United States. For more information about this organization, go to http://www.phirhopi.org/). Contestants at the tournament were required to give a memorized speech no longer than ten minutes in length, and to provide a preparation outline that included a section of works cited.*

Hans begins his introduction with an interesting story to catch his audience's attention. He also cites two sources to establish his credibility and uses examples to illustrate what he means by "life-threatening complications."

Arnell Scott was fifteen years old and weighed over 300 pounds. One day his mother noticed that he was losing weight rapidly and was constantly thirsty, so she took him to the hospital. There the doctors diagnosed this fifteen-year-old with Type 2 Diabetes. According to *Newsday,* July 20, 1999, Type 2 Diabetes—which is usually associated with adults—is now increasing at an alarming rate in children, leaving them open to life-threatening complications like blindness, kidney disease, heart disease, and stroke at ages as young as thirty. Dr. Barbara Linder of the National Institute of Diabetes and Digestion and Kidney Diseases attributes this rise in Type 2 Diabetes to a rise in obesity, and obesity is on the rise because of sugar.

In introducing his topic, Hans translates his statistics so that his audience gets a better sense of how much 50 percent is. He then links the statistics to the problem he addresses, revealing the topic of his speech and previewing what he will discuss. He uses the signposts "next" and "finally" to help his audience follow his preview.

According to the *New York Times* of February 16, 2001, of the top ten most bought foods at supermarkets, most are sugar-rich junk foods. A Georgetown University study shows that 25 percent of the calories adults consume are from sugar, but for kids it's closer to 50 percent. That means that the average person in this room consumes about 125 to 150 pounds of sugar per year. *Consumer Reports on Health* of August 2001, says that when blood sugar levels rise, so does the risk of disease and even death. Americans are consuming too much sugar, and it's destroying our health but most don't even realize it. Today we'll look at the misconceptions average Americans have regarding their intake of sugar. Next, we'll look at what these misconceptions lead to. And, finally, we'll explore some ways you can overcome your lethal sweet tooth.

He begins his first main point with a rhetorical question and then previews his subpoints with the phrase "the two main reasons." Hans also uses interesting language, "linguistic tug-of-war," to bring the controversy to light for his audience.

So why are Americans consuming all of this sugar? The two main reasons are ignorance and an increased consumption of soda pop. We often consume sugar without even realizing it. This is partly due to the food labeling process. The FDA and the Sugar Association have been fighting a linguistic tug-of-war since about 1970 over the definition of sugar. Let's look at the basics: Fructose is good sugar that you find in fruits and vegetables. Bad sugar is what you find in most of the items you eat, and these types of sugar go by many different names, including sucrose, dextrose, corn syrup, and high fructose corn syrup. The last one, high fructose corn syrup, may cause some confusion at first because it has the word fructose in it, but don't be fooled! This is just another type of refined sugar.

Now, let's take a look at a few common items that you can find at any local Safeway to see the confusion in action. Here we have a cranberry tangerine mix—a juice that we expect to be healthy for us—but notice that the second ingredient is high fructose corn syrup. Now let's take a look at Wheaties, supposedly one of the healthiest breakfast cereals on the market—even their slogan promotes health. Let's look at the ingredients: number one is whole wheat, and number two is sugar. And we also have corn syrup (another bad sugar) and brown sugar syrup (another bad sugar). All of this sugar can't be in the breakfast of champions! These are the kinds of "health foods" that we put into our bodies daily, and we assume that they are healthy for us but they're not.

Hans uses an extended example to illustrate the difficulty people have in sorting out the different sugars, taking his audience on a "virtual" shopping trip to point out the hidden sugars in specific products.

The other reason Americans consume so much sugar is because of the increased consumption of soda pop. Let's take a look at Coca-Cola. Notice that its second ingredient is high fructose corn syrup and/or sucrose. (Here the manufacturer used the chemical name for sugar, sucrose.) The average can of Coke has about ten teaspoons of sugar. According to the *San Jose Mercury News,* of January 17, 1999, since the mid-80s, U.S. soda pop consumption has increased by 43 percent to more to eighty-five gallons per American per year. That's 555 cans annually for every American. How much soda do you drink?

Hans begins is second subpoint with a signpost: "the other reason." In developing this point he again uses statistics (notice how much detail he provides about his sources), translates those statistics for his audience (555 cans annually), and closes this point with a direct question to his audience, drawing them personally into his argument.

Now that we've seen that Americans are consuming too much sugar due to ignorance and an increased consumption of soda pop, let's look at how all this sugar has had a negative impact on our health. The *New York Times* of September 9, 2001, says that there is convincing new evidence about the relationship between weight gain in children and soda pop consumption. The *New York Times* goes on to say that obesity is directly linked to soda pop consumption, regardless of the amount of food you eat or the lack of exercise. Part of the explanation for this may be that the body has trouble adapting to such intense concentrations of sugar taken in liquid form. Obesity has been linked to high blood pressure, high cholesterol, and heart disease. Obesity is also linked to cancer. In fact, obesity is now considered the number-two killer in the United States because of its link to cancer, according to the *New York Times* of October 9, 2001. The *Hindu* of April 26, 2001, says that obese people are 70 percent more likely to get pancreatic cancer, which has a 95 percent mortality rate. The U.S. Department of Health affirms the claim that obesity causes several types of cancer, including post-menopausal breast cancer and colon cancer.

Hans introduces his second main point with an internal summary and preview. He uses cause-and-effect reasoning to suggest that soda causes obesity and that obesity causes significant health problems. He then concludes with specific examples of the health problems obesity can cause—cancer and diabetes. Note his use of creative language: the metaphors "tidal wave of suffering" and "avalanche of healthcare bills."

(continued on next page)

Again, Hans provides his audience with an internal summary, using simple but creative language ("one bite or sip at a time"). He then previews solutions to the problem he has just discussed, one at the national level and one at the personal level. To support his solution, he uses testimony from a source most audiences will find credible and then reasons by analogy, suggesting that what is working in other parts of the nation will also work for the members of his audience.

Hans moves to the second part of his solution, addressing the personal commitment people must make to decrease their sugar intake. He makes a direct call to action, suggesting three simple behavior changes the members of his audience can make. His solution is realistic, not drastic or hard to accomplish, and thus is easier for his audience to implement—rather than cutting out all sugar, they can simply drink one less soda a day, eat fruits or vegetables rather than sweets, and read labels for hidden sugars.

In his conclusion, Hans summarizes his main ideas and ends simply by returning to the story of the young boy from his introduction. Thus he is able to draw his audience in emotionally without exaggeration or extreme appeals to pathos.

Along with causing cancer, obesity is also a key cause of diabetes. According to the *Hartford Chronicle* of September 9, 2001, since 1991 adult obesity has increased by 60 percent and the percentage of overweight kids has doubled in the last decade, helping to put significant numbers of children and adolescents among the ranks of Type 2 diabetics. Type 2 Diabetes usually comes on after the age of 45. Dr. Gerald Bernstein predicts that left unchecked, the onset of more diabetes could have a huge impact, with more than 500 million diabetics worldwide in twenty-five years. We're looking at a tidal wave of suffering and an avalanche of healthcare bills if people don't change their ways.

Now we've seen that Americans are consuming too much sugar, and its destroying their health, one bite or sip at a time. We obviously need to decrease our sugar intake. So now we'll look at what we could do at a national level. Next, we'll look at what we can do as individuals. On a national level, we need to do two things: increase awareness and decrease soda pop consumption. Kelly Brownwell, director of Yale University's Eating and Weight Disorders, has suggested that we regulate food advertisements directed at children to provide equal time for pro-nutrition and physical activity messages. She also suggests that we change the price of foods to make healthier foods less expensive. Nationwide, schools should mimic what nearly a dozen states are already considering, and that is to turn off school vending machines during class time, stripping them of sweets, or to impose new taxes on soda pop machines. The *New York Times* of February 16, 2001, says that taking these actions will discourage kids from buying sweets. We can even take this proposal one step further and not only impose taxes on school vending machines but also on soft drinks in general. These are a few ways we can create incentives for people to eat healthily and decrease their sugar intake.

Now, we would all like someone else to make us healthy, but what is really needed is a personal commitment to health. You know the answer to the question "How do I get rid of my sugar addiction?" Simple. Start off slow and follow Dr. Ralph Gowen's advice: moderation. The author of *Optimal Wellness* has suggested that dessert a few times a week or a can of pop once or twice a week isn't going to hurt anyone's health. In fact, the World Health Organization has suggested that between 0 to 10 percent of your daily calories can come from sugar and this will still be considered within a safe range. Try to stick to good foods, though, like fruits, vegetables, and fruit juices that don't have any added sugar. Become a label reader and be aware of what you're eating.

Today we've looked at the misconceptions about sugar, looked at where these misconceptions lead, and have found some solutions to our sugar addiction. Americans have become unhealthy because they're eating too much sugar. Americans need to decrease their sugar intake before more of them end up like fifteen-year-old Arnell Scott, having to take daily insulin injections just to stay alive.

Chapter Summary

Persuasive speeches generally fall into three categories: questions of fact, questions of value, and questions of policy. Questions of fact address the correctness of an issue. Questions of value refer to the appropriateness of an action or belief. Questions of policy focus on the best solution to a problem. Whichever kind of question you take up for your persuasive speech, your goal is to alter or influence an audience's thoughts, feelings, or actions about issues that are not easily resolved.

There are many organizational options for persuasive speeches: chronological, spatial, topical, problem-solution, problem-cause-solution, comparative advantages, and Monroe's motivated sequence. All of these organizational patterns allow you to present information about a problem and proposed solutions differently, and which of these patterns you use depends on your audience and your speech goals. With any of these patterns, you can request immediate action or passive agreement. When you seek to gain immediate action, you try to persuade an audience to act in a specific way about an issue. When you seek passive agreement, you try to persuade an audience to adopt a new position or perspective.

Because as a persuasive speaker you often address questions that are complex and not easily resolved, remember three important tips: (1) Use persuasion realistically. Don't ask for radical changes if an audience isn't likely to support your proposals. Adapt your request for change to your audience's ability to make those changes. (2) Use evidence fairly and strategically to strengthen your arguments and increase your chances for audience support. Address complex issues with two-sided messages and counterarguments so you can refute, not attack, alternate positions and arguments in order to bolster your own positions and arguments. Similarly, use fear appeals to motivate your audience to change and so avoid an undesirable outcome, but don't overuse this strategy and frighten your audience so much they deny a problem exists or feel immobilized by fear. (3) Use language that will motivate your audience to change but will not threaten or insult them.

Finally, do your best to give ethical persuasive speeches. Request change without threatening or manipulating your audience, make an effort to understand your own position on an issue as well as the position of your audience, and present information that is honest, accurate, and fair.

Invitation to Public Speaking Online

After reading this chapter, use your CD-ROM and the *Invitation to Public Speaking* Web site to review the following concepts, answer the review questions, and complete the suggested activities.

Key Concepts

persuasive speech (402)
question of fact (403)
question of value (403)
question of policy (403)
gain immediate action (407)

call to action (407)
gain passive agreement (407)
problem-solution organization (408)
problem-cause-solution organization (410)

comparative advantages organization (412)
Monroe's motivated sequence (412)
two-sided message (415)
counterarguments (415)
fear appeal (415)

Review Questions

1. With other members of your class, develop an imaginary speech to persuade lawmakers to lower the voting age to 16 years old. As you develop this speech, consider the implications of the requested change for as many constituencies as possible: 16-year-olds, parents, lawmakers, voter registration workers, voting sites, mail ballots, candidates, teachers, the structure of education, and the like. What are the implications of this persuasive request?

2. You have just been informed you have only ten minutes of the legislator's time to present your persuasive appeal developed in question 1. What do you keep in and what do you leave out? How do you decide?

3. Consider the speeches you have heard that changed your mind or actions regarding an issue. What caused you to be persuaded? Can you incorporate these components into your persuasive speech?

4. Your topic is public transportation. Develop a specific purpose statement, thesis statement and main points for the following three types of persuasive speeches: a question of fact, a question of value, a question of policy. Use the material in this chapter about organizational patterns to help you organize your speech.

5. Write an outline of a persuasive speech organized according to Monroe's motivated sequence for a speech about physical education in schools. Pay careful attention to each of the steps in this organizational pattern. What are the advantages of this pattern over, say, a comparative advantages speech or a problem-solution speech? What are the disadvantages?

6. Log on to this Web site: www.thetruth.com. Are the fear appeals used in this antismoking campaign legitimate? Do they motivate an audience to action, or are they so strong that they immobilize an audience? Why?

7. Discuss with your class the differences among informative, invitational, and persuasive speaking. How are they different? How are they similar? For what situations are each best suited? Do you have a preference for one kind of speaking? Why or why not?

The *Invitation to Public Speaking* Web Site

The *Invitation to Public Speaking* Web site features the review questions about the Web sites suggested on pages 403, 404, 413, and 416, the interactive activities suggested on pages 408, 413, and 416, and the InfoTrac College Edition exercises suggested on pages 404, 415, and 417.

You can access this site via your CD-ROM or at http://www.wadsworth.com/product/griffin. To access Speech Builder Express in order to complete Speech Step 17.2, you will need the username and password included under "Speech Builder Express" on your CD-ROM.

Web Links

17.1: Virtual Religion Index (403)
17.2: Problem Solving: Definition, Terminology, and Patterns (404)
17.3: Yahoo and Persuasive Topics (404)
17.4: Monroe's Motivated Sequence (413)
17.5: Fear Appeals (416)

Interactive Activities

17.1: Calling for Action in Congress (408)
Purpose: To understand the differences between immediate action and passive agreement.

17.2: Persuading an Audience to Follow a Dream (413)
Purpose: To investigate how a speaker can use an organizational pattern to create an effective message.

17.3: Assessing the Persuasiveness of Newspaper Editorial Pages (416)
Purpose: To evaluate the persuasiveness of letters to the editor and newspaper editorials.

17.4: Persuading While Conceding (416)
Purpose: To further explore how persuasive language can be used respectfully.

 InfoTrac College Edition Exercises

17.1: Fact, Value, or Policy Speech? (404)
Purpose: To distinguish among fact, value, and policy speeches.

17.2: Analyzing Your Audience (415)
Purpose: To better understand the attitudes of your classroom audience.

17.3: Persuasion and Ethics (417)
Purpose: To learn how ethical judgments about persuasion are made.

Speech Interactive on the *Invitation to Public Speaking* CD-ROM

The following video clips of speeches, referenced in this chapter, are included under Speech Interactive on your *Invitation to Public Speaking* CD-ROM. After you have watched the clips, click on "Critique" to answer the questions for analysis.

Video Clip 1: Persuasive Organizational Patterns: Courtney Stillman (409). As you watch Courtney's speech, notice how she organized it. What techniques did she use to illustrate the problem? How did she connect the problem to her audience?

Video Clip 2: Solutions: Brent Erb (410). As you watch Brent's speech, pay attention to the solutions he proposed. Could you implement them? What additional solutions might he have advocated?

Video Clip 3: Causes: Brandi Lafferty (411). Watch Brandi's speech. Does she clearly describe why the problem exists? How does knowing the cause of a problem help a speaker convince an audience the problem can be solved? Did Brandi's decision to include a discussion of the problem's cause make for a more effective speech?

Video Clip 4: Persuasive Speech: Hans Erian (418). As you watch Hans's speech about diabetes, consider how he organized his speech. What type of persuasive speech does he present? Which organizational pattern does he use? Was his choice of pattern effective? How effective are Hans's visual aids? Did he use evidence fairly and persuasively?

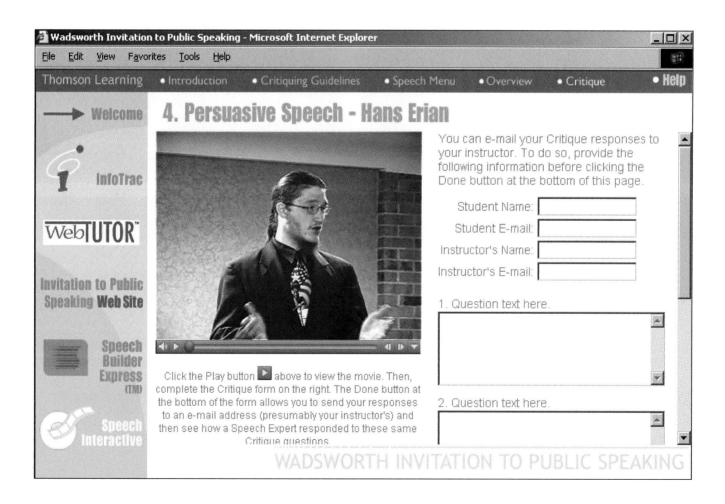

Chapter Eighteen

Persuasion and Reasoning

In this chapter you will learn to

Use evidence effectively in a persuasive speech

Enhance your credibility before, during, and at the end of your speech

Use emotional appeals effectively and ethically to persuade your audience

Appeal to mythos effectively and ethically to persuade your audience

Avoid five of the most common fallacies in persuasive arguments

Persuasion does indeed involve moving people to a position they don't currently hold, but not by begging or cajoling. Instead, it involves careful preparation, the proper framing of arguments, the presentation of vivid supporting evidence, a speaker's credibility, and the effort to find the correct emotional match with your audience.

—Adapted from Jay A. Conger, "The Necessary Art of Persuasion," 1998[1]

logos
The word Aristotle used to refer to logical arrangement of evidence in a speech.

ethos
The word Aristotle used to refer to the speaker's credibility.

pathos
The word Aristotle used to refer to emotional appeals made by a speaker.

The last thing a 25-year-old Pennsylvania woman expected was to be victimized by insurance companies for being a victim. But that's exactly what happened when Charlotte (not her real name) sought medical care after her husband shoved her into some furniture during an argument, injuring one of her hips. Encouraged by a battered women's group to report the injury, and others before it, two national companies denied Charlotte insurance, citing the single episode of abuse. As one company representative said, covering battered women is like "covering diabetics who refuse to take their insulin." U.S. representative Constance A. Morella (D-Md.) told a Senate committee hearing on insurance discrimination in July, "domestic violence has now become a pre-existing medical condition."[2] Although some insurance companies find the analogy made in this true story valid and use it as a way to keep costs down, other groups, especially those that offer services to women battered by their spouses or partners, may not. Is the reasoning accurate and can we claim that being a victim of a crime is the same as a preexisting medical condition? Whatever your reaction to this story, it is a powerful example of the use of an analogy and the way we reason to justify or make our claims.

The arguments in this story, and the ones you will use in your speeches, are based on reasoning. Recall from Chapter 8 that speakers accomplish sound reasoning when they use logos, ethos, and pathos. **Logos** is the logical arrangement of evidence in a speech, **ethos** refers to the speaker's credibility, and **pathos** refers to the emotional appeals made by a speaker.[3] You read about logos and ethos in Chapter 8, and in this chapter you'll learn more about them, as well as about pathos. You'll also learn about two additional components of reasoning: *mythos* and fallacies of reasoning. Speakers appeal to mythos when they want to tap into common cultural beliefs and attitudes in order to persuade their audience. Fallacies are the errors in logic and reasoning commonly made in persuasive speaking.

In persuasive speeches, your arguments are either strengthened or weakened by your logical use of evidence, your appeals to credibility, and your appeals to emotion. The three work together to help you move an audience toward a particular position. They help you introduce an issue and increase the audience's awareness of its implications. They also help you secure your audience's agreement and encourage them to take action. Finally, the effective use of reasoning helps your audience integrate their new awareness into their daily lives.[4] The next three sections discuss how you can incorporate evidence, credibility, and emotion successfully in your persuasive speeches.

Evidence and Persuasion

When you speak persuasively, you will use evidence in much the same way you use it in other types of speeches. However, for persuasive speeches, three aspects of the effective use of evidence are especially important: the use of specific evidence, novel information, and credible sources.

Use Specific Evidence

When you want to convince your audience that something is true, good, or appropriate, you will be more successful if you use evidence that is *specific* rather than *general*.[5] Your evidence should support your claims as explicitly as possible. For example, in a speech persuading her audience not to smoke, Shannan used the following specific evidence to describe the toxic ingredients in cigarettes:

> You want to make a cigarette? According to Dr. Roger Morrisette of Farmington State College, a single cigarette contains over four thousand chemicals. If you want the recipe, well, this is what you'll need. You'll need some carcinogens, or cancer-causing agents; some formaldehyde, or embalming fluid; some acetone, which is paint stripper or fingernail remover; benzene or arsenic; pesticides such as fungicides, herbicides, and insecticides; and toxins like hydrogen cyanide, ammonia, and nicotine.

Shannan could have argued "Cigarettes are toxic and contain thousands of poisonous chemicals," but that is far less specific than her list of ingredients. She is more persuasive because she uses specific evidence rather than simply making a general claim.

Present Novel Information

When we try to persuade our audiences, we are trying to get them to change their views. This can be difficult to accomplish in this age of information overload because audiences already have been exposed to so much information. They have heard, it seems, "all the reasons" to do something (or not to do something). Still, research indicates that you will be more persuasive when you present new, rather than well known, information to your audience.[6] When you go beyond what your audience already knows, you capture their attention and cause them to listen more carefully to your ideas.

In a speech on pet overpopulation, Malachi produced new information that was quite persuasive. His audience already knew that unspayed animals are the cause of pet overpopulation, so he presented some novel information on this familiar topic: "According to the Humane Society of the United States," Malachi stated, "in seven years, one unspayed female cat and her unspayed offspring can theoretically produce 420,000 cats. In six years, one unspayed female dog and her offspring can produce 67,000 dogs." Malachi used information that was new to his audience as well as specific evidence (the exact figures). He took a familiar topic, pet overpopulation, and helped his audience take notice in new ways. To consider another speaker's use of specific evidence and novel information, complete InfoTrac College Edition Exercise 18.1, "Using Specific Evidence," online under Student Resources for Chapter 18.

Use Credible Sources

Recall that in research, credibility relates to the potential bias of a source, whereas in reasoning it relates to the trustworthiness of the source. When you want to persuade your audience, you must use evidence that comes from dependable sources. If you don't, you will be less effective in convincing your audience of your position. To read a discussion about how to evaluate the credibility of Web sources, go to Julie Eckerle and Nancy Foreman's Web page at http://www.uky.edu/ArtsSciences/English/wc/credibility.html.

There are two guidelines for using credible sources persuasively. First, provide enough information about your source that your audience can assess its credibility.[7] This means you must provide dates, credentials, and other significant

Sources that are well respected and perceived as being trustworthy and fair are also perceived as being credible. What evidence from a well-respected source could you use to lend credibility to your next speech?

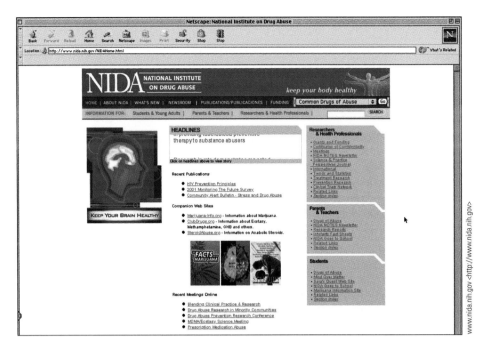

information. In the following example, Brian's credibility is weakened because he does not provide this information: "Numerous articles have been published explaining the benefits of this laser eye surgery. According to one, this procedure is the safest of all available." How many is "numerous"? Who wrote these articles? When were they written? Brian offered no dates, sources of publication, and no credentials. Although the evidence might be legitimate, the audience has no way of determining if it is. They are less likely to be persuaded than if Brian had offered concrete information about dates, authors, and publications (see Chapter 6 for citing sources in speeches).

Second, select sources your audience will see as trustworthy and fair. Although every source has a perspective, use sources your audience will see as relatively unbiased. For example, even though the Humane Society has a position on animal overpopulation, it also has a reputation for being credible and fair. To be persuasive, choose sources that are reliable and known for expertise in your subject; avoid sources that may be seen as extreme or overly biased. Similarly, select sources that are known to your audience or have a positive record in your field so that your audience will be more open to considering your evidence and your persuasive arguments. One well-respected source, the Gallup Organization, conducts numerous polls. In one of their annual polls, they try to determine who the most admired man and woman in the world are. To check out the results from 2000, go to http://www.adherents.com/misc/poll_GallupAdmired.html.

Your audience is more likely to consider your persuasive arguments when you strengthen your reasoning with specific, novel evidence and credible sources. However, you must go beyond using evidence effectively in a persuasive speech. You must also make appropriate use of ethos, or your credibility as a speaker.

Credibility and Persuasion

Two speakers hold similar views, address an audience in similar ways, present similar data, and speak for a similar amount of time, yet one speaker is more credible than the other. Why? Why does an audience see one person as more believable than another? These differences in perception can be explained by each speaker's

credibility, or the audience's perception of a speaker's competence and character. As you learned in Chapter 8, the most important aspect of credibility is that an audience attributes it to a speaker. No matter how talented, prepared, or polished a speaker you are, if the audience does not *see* you as credible, you simply aren't credible.[8]

Credibility, like evidence and emotion, is one of the linchpins of persuasive speaking. Without it, you'll have a hard time persuading an audience of much of anything, regardless of other appeals you make. Audiences might be entertained, or even informed, but they will not be persuaded if you lack credibility. Politicians are perhaps the most obvious examples of the effect of weak credibility on persuasive appeals. Voters who perceive a politician as lacking competence and character will not be persuaded by her or his arguments, regardless of the claims and appeals used.

But what causes an audience to perceive a speaker as credible? Several factors come into play, among them sociability (are you friendly and pleasant?), dynamism (are you energized and expressive?), physical attractiveness (are you well groomed and well dressed?), and perceived similarity between the speaker and the audience (are your values and views similar to your audience's?). However, the two most important factors in credibility are the audience's perception of your competence and character. As you learned in Chapter 8, **competence** is the audience's view of a speaker's intelligence, expertise, and knowledge of a subject, and **character** is the audience's view of a speaker's sincerity, trustworthiness, and concern for the well-being of the audience.[9]

You express your competence through your research, your organization, and your delivery. If you have taken time to prepare and practice your speech, you are more likely to be viewed as competent. Competence also comes from your personal talents and expertise, the experience and knowledge you bring to the speech before your research. You communicate your character by taking the time to analyze your audience and tailor your speech to meet their needs, using inclusive language, and using well-prepared logic to express your integrity, values, principles, and attitudes toward others. These actions let your audience know you care about them and can be trusted to give a speech that is well thought out and worth listening to.

You can manage your credibility by understanding the types of credibility and when you establish them in a speech, and by knowing how you can enhance your credibility.

Types of Credibility

Three types of credibility exist in any speech: initial, derived, and terminal. **Initial credibility** is the credibility a speaker has before giving a speech, **derived credibility** is the credibility a speaker develops during a speech, and **terminal credibility** is the credibility given to the speaker at the end of a speech. Read the following scenario to understand how these three types of credibility develop in a speech:

> You've been assigned to speak to a group of high school students and persuade them to volunteer in their community. When you arrive at the high school auditorium to speak, you've brought your *initial credibility* with you, what the students think about you before you even begin your speech. Their impression might be based on very little information (you're some college student) or on some specific information (their teachers told them who you are, why you're coming to speak, and what you'll be talking about).
>
> You begin your speech. It's well researched and you've thought carefully about your audience and how your topic is relevant to them. You've developed a style of delivery

credibility
Audience's perception of a speaker's competence and character.

competence
Audience's view of a speaker's intelligence, expertise, and knowledge of a subject.

character
Audience's view of a speaker's sincerity, trustworthiness, and concern for the well-being of the audience.

initial credibility
Credibility a speaker has before giving a speech.

derived credibility
Credibility a speaker develops during a speech.

terminal credibility
Credibility given to the speaker at the end of a speech.

that you think the students will appreciate. You've worked hard on your introduction, knowing you need to catch their attention right away. You've also decided to share your own volunteer experiences with them. As you give your speech, you are establishing *derived credibility*, what you say and do throughout your speech to cause students to see you as competent and trustworthy.

You finish your speech and open up the floor for questions and discussion. At the end of your time with the students, you close your presentation and say good-bye. When the students leave their interaction with you, they've assigned what's called *terminal credibility*—they walk away with some conception of your level of knowledge, expertise, sincerity, and trustworthiness.

As you can see from this scenario, credibility evolves during a speech. You may start with high credibility but do something that offends an audience and see your credibility drop. Or you may begin with low credibility because an audience does not know you and then end with excellent credibility because of what you said and how you said it. Because credibility is a process, how to enhance it, or keep it high, is the subject of the next section.

Enhancing Your Credibility

If you begin a speech with little initial credibility because the audience does not know you, you need to build credibility during the speech. You can build your credibility in three ways: explain your competence as you begin your speech, establish common ground with your audience, and deliver your speech fluently, with expression and conviction.

Your introduction (Chapter 10) is an effective place to establish your competence. You can reveal your credentials, training, or experiences that make you competent to speak on the topic. Or you can explain that although you may not be specifically trained, you have done extensive research on the topic. Throughout the speech, you can increase your credibility by citing sources, sharing your experiences, and offering your insights based on your background and research. To enhance her credibility right away, Katrina began a speech by explaining her qualifications immediately.

> I come from a family of dancers. Both my father and mother danced with the San Francisco Ballet. They taught dancing after they retired and, at the age of 3, I was already dancing around the living room with them. At 5, I took my first formal ballet lesson. At 7 I began tap. I won't bore you with the details, but for the next ten years I took every kind of lesson possible and helped my folks out in their studio. When I went to college, I kept on dancing. Needless to say, if it's dance, I know it.

At first, Katrina had little initial credibility and seemed to be just another speaker. But within minutes she had stated her credentials and increased her credibility quite efficiently.

A second way to build your credibility is to establish common ground with your audience. To establish **common ground** is to identify similarities, shared interests, and mutual perspectives with an audience. You can establish common ground by showing the audience you share values, experiences, and group memberships with them.[10] You can do so by simply stating that you belong to similar organizations, appreciate the same activities, or hold certain values as important. You can also establish common ground when you explain your views and positions and why they are in harmony with those held by audience members. When you take time to establish a friendly bond (often called rapport) with your audience, they will begin to like, trust, and respect you. Audiences attach higher credibility to speakers they see as similar to them.

common ground
Similarities, shared interests, and mutual perspectives a speaker has with an audience.

Barbara Bush is a speaker who is well known for establishing common ground in one notable speech. In 1990, Bush was asked to give the commencement speech by the senior class of Wellesley College when they found their first choice, author Alice Walker, could not attend. About a quarter of the graduating class protested, claiming that because Bush was famous not for her own accomplishments but because of the man she married, she was not a good role model for the career-oriented students of Wellesley. Knowing how her audience perceived her, Bush established common ground by acknowledging their interest in Walker and relating that interest to their college experience:

> Now I know your first choice today was Alice Walker, known for *The Color Purple*. Instead you got me—known for the color of my hair! Alice's Walker's book has a special resonance here. At Wellesley, each class is known by a special color. For four years the class of '90 has worn the color purple. Today you meet on Severance Green to say good-bye to all of that, to begin a new and a very personal journey to search for your own true colors.

To assess how another speaker effectively established her credibility and common ground with her audience, complete the InfoTrac College Edition Exercise 18.2, "Establishing Credibility," online under Student Resources for Chapter 18.

A third way to enhance your credibility is through your delivery. Research indicates that speakers who are prepared, energetic, speak moderately fast, and who appear comfortable in front of their audience are seen as credible.[11] If you practice your speech and work on your delivery (Chapters 1 and 13), your credibility should increase. Here's how one student enhanced his credibility through delivery.

> Kip knew his initial credibility for his speech would be low. He'd blown his first speech for the class and this was the second round. Not only that, he was the only minority in the course, a member of the football team, and he'd missed some classes because of travel to games. He knew the other students thought he was just a "dumb football player" who didn't care about the class.

> However, Kip wanted to get his degree and teach history at a high school. He knew the importance of public speaking and communication skills in his future profession. So he chose a topic he felt really connected to, worked hard on putting his speech together, and practiced delivering his speech as many times as he could before the

Do you see this speaker as being credible? Do you think his audience sees him as being credible? What do you think this speaker can do to establish common ground with his audience?

speaking day. He worked on his speaking rate because he knew he talked too fast when he was nervous. He worked on his eye contact so he could connect with his classmates nonverbally as well as verbally. He was enthusiastic about the topic and found ways to convey that enthusiasm in his delivery and his language. He also wanted to appear comfortable (even though he was really nervous), so he worked on his introduction until he had it just perfect.

On the day of the speech, Kip appeared confident, prepared, and quite engaged with his material and the audience. He went from being a "dumb football player" in the eyes of his classmates to a very credible speaker.

Remember that the audience assigns credibility to a speaker. Speakers with high credibility tend to be more persuasive than those with low credibility do, so give this component of your speech careful consideration. You can also strengthen your persuasive message by making appropriate use of pathos, or appeals to emotion.

Emotion and Persuasion

Emotional appeals, or pathos, can be one of the most challenging aspects of persuasion. On the one hand, research suggests that speakers persuade only when they appeal to emotions. Appeals to emotions can be powerful because they encourage your audience to relate to an issue on an internal, personal level. On the other hand, because emotions are so personal and powerful, research also suggests that an inappropriate appeal to emotions can cause your audience to shut down in an instant.[12] Appeals to emotions can be complicated, so it's useful to understand what emotions are and which emotions people most commonly experience.

Emotions are "internal mental states" that focus primarily on feelings. Research distinguishes emotions (internal states such as fear, anger, sadness) from three other states: bodily states (tiredness, hunger), cognitive states (confusion, uncertainty), and behavioral states (timidity, aggressiveness).[13] Communication research has identified six primary emotions that tend to be expressed similarly across cultures and three secondary emotions that are expressed differently depending on age, gender, and culture.[14] The primary emotions are

- *Fear:* an unpleasant feeling of apprehension or distress; the anticipation of danger or threat
- *Anger:* a feeling of annoyance, irritation, or rage
- *Surprise:* a feeling of sudden wonder or amazement, especially because of something unexpected
- *Sadness:* a feeling of unhappiness, grief, or sorrow
- *Disgust:* a feeling of horrified or sickened distaste for something
- *Happiness:* a feeling of pleasure, contentment, or joy

The secondary emotions are

- *Pride:* exhibiting an appropriate level of respect for a person, character trait, accomplishment, experience, or value; feeling pleased or delighted
- *Guilt:* an awareness of having done wrong, accompanied by feelings of shame and regret
- *Shame:* a feeling of dishonor, unworthiness, and embarrassment

Another emotion common to persuasive speeches but not identified among the primary or secondary emotions is

- *Reverence:* feelings of deep respect, awe, or devotion

Speakers often use figures of speech to call on these emotions. To learn more about using figures of speech effectively, visit Gideon Burton's Web site at http://humanities.byu.edu/rhetoric/Figures/Groupings/OF%20PATHOS.HTM.

In persuasive speaking, you make appeals to emotions in order to accomplish the following goals:

Gain attention and motivate listening: You often catch an audience's attention and motivate them to listen by appealing to their emotions with a compelling short story, testimony, or examples.

Reinforce points: You can use emotional appeals to reinforce main or subpoints. For example, when you support a point with a statistic, then reinforce the statistic with an example of how some aspect of the statistic has affected a specific person, an audience can understand your point on a more personal level.

Express personal commitment: When you care deeply about an issue and want your audiences to recognize this depth of commitment, you may appeal to emotions by shifting your delivery to a more passionate or intense tone, or you may personalize your claims and arguments.

Call to action or conclude memorably: You can often move an audience to action by asking them to envision the result of that action and how it could affect them personally. You might end your speech with a compelling story or quote, and so conclude memorably.

To see a particularly effective use of emotional appeal in a persuasive speech, use your *Invitation to Public Speaking* CD-ROM to watch the video clip of Mary Fisher's speech to the 1992 Republican National Convention, included under Speech Interactive. Consider how she appealed to emotions in each of the four ways just described.

Because emotional appeals engage an audience personally, you'll want to consider a few aspects of emotional appeals in order to use them effectively: audience centeredness, vivid language, and a balance of emotion and reason.

Stay Audience Centered

Perhaps the most important component of a persuasive emotional appeal is how appropriate that appeal is for the audience. Consider your audience very carefully before you decide what kinds of appeals to use. For example, almost every element of our master status (Chapter 5) affects how we respond to the emotional side of an issue—our age, sex, physical ability, religion, ethnicity, and culture greatly influence how we see an issue and thus the acceptability of an emotional appeal. As you consider the emotional appeals you want to make to your audience, ask yourself the following questions: Will the members of your audience have firsthand experience with your topic, or will it feel distant to them? What kinds of experiences will they have had? What emotions might be associated with those experiences? If they haven't had direct experiences, why not? In what ways might you be able to draw them into your topic emotionally without being inappropriate?

Although no speaker can predict with total accuracy how an audience will respond to an emotional appeal, you can consider your audience carefully and select those appeals to emotions that seem most appropriate. When speakers misjudge the appropriateness of an appeal to an emotion, they generally make one of three errors.

Overly graphic and violent appeals. A visual or verbal appeal that describes wounds and injuries, deaths, attacks, or harm to another being in extensive detail is overly graphic. The speaker generally is hoping to impress the audience with the horror of an act, but carries the description too far and causes the audience to shut down or feel overwhelming revulsion. To watch examples of a particularly aggressive advertising campaign that some consider overly graphic, go to http://thetruth.com, the Web site maintained by truth, the antismoking organization.

Overly frightening or threatening appeals. When a speaker describes something so frightening or threatening that the audience feels helpless or panicked, they will stop listening or they will feel immobilized. These kinds of appeals tend to stay with an audience long after a speech is over and cause them to feel unnecessarily fearful. In contrast, an appropriate fear appeal is one that moves the audience to act but does not immobilize or terrorize them (Chapter 17). A common overly frightening appeal is one in which a speaker argues that if the audience doesn't prevent something from happening or stop some behavior, they or someone they care about will die.

Overly manipulative appeals. An appeal to an emotion, either positive or negative, that relies on theatrics, melodrama, and sensation rather than on fact and research is overly manipulative. Such appeals encourage the audience to feel pity, shame, guilt, or humiliation about something or to become overly excited or enthusiastic. Speakers may make overly manipulative appeals when they want their audience to see a person in a certain way, donate time or money to a cause, or do something they might not normally do. For example, in a speech asking an audience to give to a charitable organization, Jade showed images of children with cerebral palsy. She asked her audience questions to engage them, then created sad stories about the children based on the answers they gave. Although she received donations, she manipulated her audience's emotions with hypothetical stories to get them to give money rather than relying on true stories or research.

SPEECH INTERACTIVE

WEB SITE

By staying audience centered, you can make appropriate appeals to emotions. If you keep your audience in the front of your mind, you will recognize which appeals are appropriate for them and which ones aren't. Take another look at Mary Fisher's speech to the 1992 Republican National Convention under Speech Interactive, or go to the *Invitation to Public Speaking* Web site to read the text of the speech. Notice how she appeals to the emotions that accompany illness, loss, death, HIV and AIDS, conceptions of evil, risk and safety, and love and care for one another. Although her appeals are powerful, they are appropriate to her audience and not overly graphic, frightening, or manipulative. Fisher is an example of an audience-centered speaker who uses pathos to make compelling emotional appeals without misusing the audience's feelings.

Use Vivid Language

Appeals to emotions ask an audience to recall some of their most profound experiences. You can use vivid descriptions and examples to help your audience connect with those experiences. One of the reasons that Martin Luther King Jr. is considered one of the most influential speakers of the twentieth century is the vivid language he used to create images for his audiences. In his "I Have a Dream" speech on the steps of the Lincoln Memorial, his language helped his audience "see" his vision and connect to it emotionally as well as rationally. When he spoke of freedom, he described the "chains of discrimination" and the "manacles of segregation" that "crippled." He used evocative words and phrases, such as "languishing" and "exile," the "magnificent words of the Constitution," and a "promise to all" for the "riches of freedom."[15] You can watch King's speech under Speech Interactive on your *Invitation to Public Speaking* CD-ROM. While watching the video clip, notice the vivid images he calls forth and how he uses the emotion evoked by these images to appeal to his audience.

The world's most profound speakers have been trained to make the most of vivid language, but even novice speakers can use language to move and inspire. In a speech on American veterans that was both persuasive and commemorative, Darrin created the following emotional appeal through his vivid language:

> Imagine sitting down to a peaceful meal with your wife, husband, or children. A "ring," "ring," "ring" is heard, interrupting you like an unwanted guest. The distinct sound of this ring suspends all talk. It's like this illusionary figure drifts across the room, touching the souls of those dear to you. Even before you pick it up, you know your country has gone to war, and this is your call to duty.

Vivid language helps your listeners create images that are rich with feeling. When you speak persuasively, try to find words and phrases that tap into your audience's memories. If you do so, you will have an easier time drawing your audience in emotionally to your claims and arguments.

Martin Luther King Jr. is particularly well known for his powerful use of language to inspire and motivate his audiences. Consider your next persuasive speech. What are some images you can use to help your audience see what you're talking about and make an emotional connection to your topic?

AP/Wide World Photos

Balance Emotion and Reason

When you speak persuasively, try to find a balance between your use of reason and emotion. Overly emotional speeches may stimulate your audience, but without sound reasoning, they are less likely to be persuaded by your arguments.

Use appeals to emotion to elaborate on your reasons or to show the more personal side of your evidence. If you make a claim with statistics or offer an example of the impact of a plan, support it by drawing out the emotional aspects. Similarly, if you make an appeal to emotions, back it up with sound reasoning. When you balance emotion and reason, your audience will see more than one dimension of your persuasive appeals and will be persuaded on more than one level.

Appeals to emotion are necessary parts of persuasive speeches. If you can avoid overly graphic, frightening, or manipulative appeals, you can tap into powerful emotions. By staying audience centered, paying careful attention to your language, and balancing reason and emotion, you will be able to craft persuasive arguments that encourage your audience to think differently about issues.

Sam

It was really hard trying to find resources on my persuasive topic of domestic violence. All the topics on the Internet seemed to be biased and overly emotional, and I didn't really want to use them. Instead, I looked on the library databases and reserved some books and decided to use those. I was also able to use personal testimony from women who have been in a domestic violence situation. I think this established an emotion of sadness. Then when I gave a call to action, I think my audience was ready to help.

Mythos and Persuasion

mythos
Interrelated set of beliefs, attitudes, values, and feelings held by members of a particular society or culture.

"No one is immune to the folk knowledge of their culture," state Marian Friestad and Peter Wright, marketing and psychology researchers at the University of Oregon.[16] The folk knowledge of a culture is **mythos**, the interrelated set of beliefs, attitudes, values, and feelings held by members of a particular society or culture. Friestad and Wright explain that we learn mythos not through any formal training, but rather through the "whisperings of Mother culture."[17] We listen to these whisperings as children, adolescents, young adults, and adults. They come through anecdotes and customs, as well as through events and accepted norms for behavior.

Whether you have grown up in the United States or another culture, you're likely familiar with the cultural myths of the United States. These cultural narratives stress the importance of freedom and democracy. They describe the United States as the land of opportunity and tell of journeys from rags to riches. They emphasize the value of progress and the exploration of new frontiers. They celebrate heroes and heroines who have made the United States a world leader. In any culture, its mythos communicates who the people are and what they will become.

Mythos and persuasion are tightly interconnected. When we appeal to mythos, we call to mind history, tradition, faith, feelings, common sense, and membership in a community or culture. In doing so, we tap into a rich reservoir of emotions, attitudes, and values. We encourage our audience to accept our claims based on stories told over generations. We personalize an argument beyond making an appeal to an emotion: we tap into larger stories about "the way things are" and "the way things should be." Because mythos is an important part of the persuasive process, consider a few guidelines when you use this appeal in your speeches.

A Part of the Story Can Tell the Whole Story

To tap into the mythos of a culture, you rarely need to tell the full story to the audience. In the 1960s, John F. Kennedy referred to the mythos of the American frontier in many of his speeches, calling forth the complete myth with just a few words:

> The New Frontier of which I speak is not a set of promises—it is a set of challenges. It sums up not what I intend to offer the American people, but what I intend to ask of them.

With these few words, Kennedy was able to call to mind the stories of settling the West, of overcoming odds, and of hard work. With the phrase "New Frontier," he transferred the myths of the "old frontier" to his presidency and drew people into the adventure and its challenges. Similarly, when Martin Luther King Jr. spoke of freedom in his "I Have a Dream" speech, he did not detail the full story of freedom in the United States. Instead, he referred to elements of that story to call forth the full mythos of freedom in a democratic society for his audience:

> In a sense we've come to our nation's Capitol to cash a check. When the architects of our republic wrote the magnificent words of the Constitution and the Declaration of Independence, they were signing a promissory note to which every American was to fall heir. This note was a promise that all men—yes, black men as well as white men—would be guaranteed the unalienable rights of life, liberty, and the pursuit of happiness.

When speakers rely on mythos, they don't tell just any story. They refer to an intensely familiar story, one that has been repeated over the years and is part of the common sense of a culture.

Mythos Has a Logic

Although a culture's myths may be as much legend as fact, they do contain a logic that rings true for that culture. They're like the fairy tales, folklore, and science fiction we grow up with. Although these myths are filled with larger-than-life heroes and villains, incredible adventures, death-defying feats, and supernatural powers, they reflect the logic, or common sense, of their culture. For example, consider the story of George Washington and the cherry tree. We now know that Washington probably never chopped down a cherry tree, but the logic of the story rings true: it is wrong to tell lies.

The power of mythos in a persuasive speech is that it allows you to tap into the logic of a culture. When you use mythos, think carefully about what logic you are appealing to and how that logic "makes sense" to your audience.[18] To learn how President George W. Bush appeals to U.S. cultural beliefs and values, complete the InfoTrac College Edition Exercise 18.3, "Drawing on Mythos," online under Student Resources for Chapter 18.

Different Cultures Have Different Myths

Because all cultures have a unique history, they all have unique myths. When you appeal to mythos in a speech, stay audience centered and keep in mind that members of your audience may have different cultural myths.

For example, Native Americans recognize communication with nonhuman entities, such as the rivers or the wind, as completely normal, and even necessary for human survival. However, people from other traditions may have difficulty accepting this perspective. Similarly, many African Americans tell a story of two worlds, one in which African Americans live and another inhabited by white people. In contrast, many white people tell a story of only one world, inhabited equally by all, in which all are equally free to move about and make choices. Each culture has a different mythos, and you must recognize these differences or risk alienating rather than persuading your audiences.

Entrepreneurs often appeal to mythos in order to sell products. For example, home-and-garden expert Martha Stewart appeals to cultural beliefs and values in her line of household goods and in her media empire. To evaluate her appeals, complete Interactive Activity 18.1, "Identifying Cultural Beliefs," online under Student Resources for Chapter 18 at the *Invitation to Public Speaking* Web site.

WEB SITE

AP/Wide World Photos

American labor leader Cesar Chavez often appealed to mythos to inspire and persuade his audiences. For example, he related the Mexican American mythos of pilgrimage, penance, and revolution to the fight for the rights of the poor. What cultural mythos could you refer to that would help you appeal to the beliefs and values of your audience?

Using evidence effectively and appealing to credibility, emotion, and mythos will help you build a strong case for your position. Another strategy that will help you craft persuasive messages is to build sound arguments. By avoiding the five common fallacies in reasoning discussed next, you can make sure your arguments are accurate and strong.

Fallacies

Whether intentional or not, you can make inaccurate arguments, called fallacies. A **fallacy** is an argument that seems valid but is flawed because of unsound evidence or reasoning. Fallacies are a problem in persuasive speeches not only because they are incorrect arguments but also because they can be quite persuasive. Fallacies can seem reasonable and acceptable on the surface, but when we analyze them we see the logic is flawed (Toulmin's model of reasoning from Chapter 8 is an excellent tool for analyzing arguments). Although there are over 125 different fallacies, a description of five of the most common ones is adequate for beginning public speakers: ad hominem, bandwagon, either-or, red herring, and slippery slope.[19]

Ad Hominem: Against the Person

Ad hominem is a Latin term that means "against the person." Perhaps one of the most familiar fallacies, an **ad hominem fallacy** is an argument in which a speaker attacks a person rather than that person's arguments. By portraying someone with an opposing position as incompetent, unreliable, or even stupid, you effectively silence that person and discredit her or his arguments or ideas. (Can you see the ad hominem argument in the story that opens this chapter?) Here are some other examples of ad hominem fallacies:

> Well, I wonder if we can even take this idea seriously. After all, hasn't this person been labeled a "tree hugger" by most of our nation's newspapers?

> Well, sure, Bush wants to open up lands for drilling. Isn't that how he got into office, with the financial support of his oil buddies?

Ad hominem fallacies are persuasive because they turn the audience's attention away from the content of an argument and toward the character and credibility of the person offering that argument. They cloud an issue, making it hard for an audience to evaluate the ideas the speaker challenges. But more importantly, ad

fallacy
Argument that seems valid but is flawed because of unsound evidence or reasoning.

ad hominen fallacy
Argument in which a speaker attacks a person rather than that person's arguments.

hominem fallacies make erroneous claims. The fact that someone has been labeled a "tree hugger" does not mean she or he is unintelligent or poorly informed. Similarly, Bush may have indeed received campaign financing from oil companies, but that fact does not prove his drilling policy is suspect.

Listen carefully for arguments against a person's character and avoid them in your own speeches. They do little to build your own credibility or help your audience see that your ideas are preferable to someone else's.

Bandwagon: Everyone Else Agrees

When you fall prey to the **bandwagon fallacy**, you are suggesting that something is correct or good because everyone else agrees with it or is doing it. In public speaking this translates to making statements like this:

> Many other communities are adopting this nonsmoking ordinance in restaurants. It's a perfect solution for us as well.

> How can we allow gays and lesbians in our organization? They've not been allowed in the military or scouting organizations, so why should we accept them in ours?

The bandwagon fallacy works a little like group pressure—it's hard to say no to something everyone else is doing. But the logic of the bandwagon is flawed for two reasons. First, even though a solution or a plan might work well for some, it might not be the best solution for your audience. You need to do more than argue "it will work for you because it worked for others." You need to explain exactly why a plan might work for a particular group of people, community, or organization. Second, just because "lots of others agree" does not make something "good." Large groups of people agree about many things, but those things aren't necessarily appropriate for everyone. When you hear the bandwagon fallacy, ask yourself two things: If it is good for them, is it good for *me*? Even if many others are doing something, is it something I support?

bandwagon fallacy
Argument that something is correct or good because everyone else agrees with it or is doing it.

The idea that something is good because everyone is doing it is a powerful one. As such, the bandwagon fallacy can be tough to spot in an argument. Take a careful look at your next persuasive speech. Can you spot any fallacies in your reasoning?

Either-Or: A False Dilemma

A dilemma is a situation that requires you to choose from options that are all unpleasant or that are mutually exclusive. When we're facing a dilemma, we feel we must make a choice even if it is not to our liking. In persuasive speeches, an **either-or fallacy**, sometimes called a *false dilemma*, is an argument in which a speaker claims our options are "either A or B," when actually more than two options exist. To identify a false dilemma, listen for the words "either-or" as a speaker presents an argument. Consider these two examples:

> Either we increase access to our before- and after-school meal programs or our students will continue to fail.

> Either we increase the size of our facility or we turn clients out on the streets.

In both examples the audience is presented with a false dilemma. But intuitively we know there must be other options. In the first, there are other ways to respond to poor student performance—better nutrition is only one part of the solution. In the second, there likely are other facilities and services available to the clients. Sometimes it's hard to see the other options immediately, but they usually are there.

Either-or arguments are fallacious because they oversimplify complex issues. Usually the speaker has created an atmosphere in which the audience feels pressured to select one of the two options presented. Even if those options may be good choices, an either-or argument prevents us from considering others that may be even better.

Red Herring: Raising an Irrelevant Issue

The term *red herring* comes from the fox hunting tradition in England. Before a hunt began, farmers often dragged a smoked herring around the perimeter of their fields. The strong odor from the fish masked the scent of the fox and threw the hounds off its trail, keeping the hounds from trampling the farmer's crops. Although this worked well for the farmers, trailing the equivalent of a red herring around an argument is not such a good idea. When we make use of the **red herring fallacy**, we introduce irrelevant information into an argument in order to distract an audience from the real issue. The following examples illustrate the red herring fallacy:

> How can we worry about the few cases of AIDS in our town of only 50,000 when thousands and thousands of children are dying of AIDS and AIDS-related illnesses in other countries?

> Admittedly, women are beaten by their husbands. But what about those men who are battered by their wives or girlfriends? With the code of masculinity and toughness in today's society, we should be working toward assistance for the men, not more money for women.

In the first example, the speaker turns the argument away from her own community and toward the international problem of AIDS. The audience then becomes more concerned about AIDS in other countries. Undoubtedly, this is an important issue, but not the one under discussion, which is equally important. Because of the red herring, the audience is less inclined to move toward a solution for the local situation. In the second example, the speaker does not want to address the issue of inadequate assistance for battered women. Rather than addressing that issue, he brings up the issue of battered men, deflecting the audience's attention. Although violence against anyone is a serious issue, the red herring of violence against men prevents the conversation from focusing on women and the need for increased assistance.

Red herring arguments are fallacious because they turn the audience's attention from one issue to another. This type of fallacy can be hard to spot because both issues usually are important but the audience feels pulled toward the most recently raised issue. As an audience member, listen carefully when a speaker introduces a new and important topic in a persuasive speech; you might be hearing a red herring fallacy.

Slippery Slope: The Second Step Is Inevitable

A **slippery slope fallacy** is an argument in which a speaker claims that taking a first step in one direction will inevitably lead to undesirable further steps. Like a skier speeding down a hill without being able to stop, a slippery slope fallacy suggests the momentum of one decision or action will cause others to follow. Here are two examples of slippery slope fallacies:

> If we allow our children to dress in any way they want at school, they soon will be wearing more and more outrageous clothing. They'll start trying to outdress one another. Then it'll be increasingly outrageous behaviors inside and outside the classrooms. Soon they'll turn to other violence as they try to top one another.

> If we don't address the traffic problems now, we'll soon find ourselves plagued with the traffic problems of a larger city. Our streets will be clogged and noisy. We'll have to build more roadways, which will ruin the image of our city. We'll go from being a choice city to just another ugly, overcrowded example of urban sprawl.

Each of these speakers makes a slippery slope argument. They suggest that if one unwanted thing happens, others certainly will follow. The audience gets caught up in the momentum of this "snowball" argument. Slippery slope arguments can be persuasive because the speaker relates the first claim (for example, the dress codes) to a larger issue (violence) when the two may not even be linked. Before you accept the full claim being made with a slippery slope argument, stop and consider whether the chain of effects really is inevitable.

As you listen to speeches, and as you put your own arguments together, keep in mind that a fallacy is an error in logic. When we persuade others, we want to be sure our logic is sound and not based on error or deception. The fallacies that commonly occur in persuasive speeches are easy to spot if you understand how they work. Those presented in this chapter, as well as the errors in reasoning identified in Chapter 8, are easy to avoid if you take time to lay out your arguments carefully. To put into practice the critical thinking skills necessary to protect yourself from using fallacies—and from being used by them—complete Interactive Activity 18.2, "Identifying Fallacies," online under Student Resources for Chapter 18 at the *Invitation to Public Speaking* Web site. In avoiding fallacies, you will enhance your persuasive efforts, increase your credibility, and contribute positively to the public dialogue.

slippery slope fallacy
Argument in which a speaker claims that taking a first step in one direction will lead to inevitable and undesirable further steps.

WEB SITE

Speech Step 18.2 / Check Your Persuasive Speech for Fallacies

Look through your persuasive speech to make sure it doesn't include any of the fallacies discussed in this section. Can you find any examples of ad hominem, bandwagon, either-or, red herring, or slippery slope arguments? If you can, take a moment to adjust these arguments so your reasoning is sound.

Fat Discrimination *by Carol Godart*

Specific purpose: To persuade my audience to help eliminate the prejudice against overweight people.

Thesis statement: Fat discrimination exists because of stereotyping, misconceptions, and fear, but through education and awareness, we can each help break down the prejudice against overweight people afflicted with the disease of compulsive eating.

Commentary

Now that you've explored persuasive speaking and the strategies you can use to persuade audiences effectively and ethically, build your own persuasive speech. Use the following speech as a model. You can see the outline for this speech under Student Resources for Chapter 18 at the Invitation to Public Speaking *Web site. Also, you can use your* Invitation to Public Speaking *CD-ROM to watch a video clip of Carol Godart's speech, which she gave in an introductory public speaking class. The assignment was to give an eight- to ten-minute persuasive speech that focused on a question of policy, followed the problem-solution pattern of organization, and urged the audience to immediate action. She was also asked to cite seven sources.*

Carol begins her speech with a compelling story, drawing her audience in and establishing her own credibility. She reveals how common fat prejudice is and uses her personal experiences with this form of discrimination to deliver an introduction that immediately catches the attention of her audience.

Let me tell you a true story. After I had been in weight-loss recovery for a couple of years and had lost the majority of my excess weight, I attended a convention. During the opening session, I noticed a man who weighed approximately 400 pounds. In my mind, I condemned him for not working harder on his weight problem. He was the keynote speaker at the session, and I thought, "That must be a mistake, because he couldn't possibly be in recovery if he is that obese." As he began his speech, he said his name, that he'd been abstinent for over a year, and that he had lost approximately 250 pounds. I sat humbled in my seat, for I knew that I was still fat-prejudiced—I had judged him because he didn't look the way I thought he should. I share this information because I have been on both sides of fat prejudice. I have been discriminated against for being fat, and I have been the perpetrator of the very same discrimination.

Carol clearly identifies the topic of her speech and uses statistics to establish the prevalence of this type of discrimination. She asks her audience a rhetorical question, drawing them further into her topic and emphasizing how subtle this discrimination can be.

Fat discrimination is one of the last acceptable prejudices in this society, and like me, most of us have some kind of judgmental thought about the weight of other people or how their bodies appeared. You may think this is an exaggeration, but if how we look weren't such an issue for most of us, then why, according to the research I will present later, do the figures demonstrate that today three or four women and three men in this room are probably on a diet right now? That's approximately 35 percent of this room who are eating salads, counting calories, or using some other diet plan to lose weight.

In previewing her speech, Carol clearly states her two main points. Notice how these points are also stated in her thesis statement. Also notice that she uses the signposts "first" and "second" to signal her

When any prejudice exists, it stifles the avenues that help us heal regarding an issue, and I am here to persuade you to open your minds to the issues of fat discrimination so we can start to heal the disease of compulsive overeating that leads to obesity. First, I will convince you that fat discrimination exists because of stereotyping, misconceptions, and fear. Second, I will persuade you that compulsive overeating is a disease, but through education and awareness, we can break down the barriers of prejudice to allow the people afflicted to find the help they need and deserve.

Fat discrimination exists. Although there is controversy over how much the media really influences our behavior, the media's stereotype of an ideally thin female body is prevalent in our society today. According to the 2001 text *Mass Media/Mass Culture* by James and Roy Wilson, in 1995 American television was introduced to the island of Fiji, "where eating was thought of as a cultural norm, and big was considered beautiful for women." A little more than three years later, after having been exposed to television shows like *Melrose Place, The Bold and the Beautiful,* and *Seinfeld,* "studies showed that teens at risk from eating disorders had more than doubled, and the number of high school girls who vomited for weight control went up five times." Again, it's inconclusive whether the media's effect on viewers was the cause of this situation, but stereotyping people with such a narrow focus creates barriers of exclusion for the majority of a population.

As I have shown, stereotyping can be very harmful, and stereotyping stems from the miscommunication of information. One of the greatest misconceptions people have when they see someone overweight is that somehow that person should control her or his weight. I couldn't control my own eating or weight, and I can assure you it wasn't for lack of trying. I tried most of the diets that crossed my path, starting with my first one, unsupervised, at the age of nine. And as I stated earlier, 35 percent of this class could be on a diet right now according to the statistics I obtained on October 20, 2001, at www.ephedrafacts.com from a recently released study by the U.S. Center for Disease Control and Prevention. This study shows that 25 to 30 percent of adult American women and 20 to 24 percent of adult American men are trying to lose weight at any given time. That does not count the people who have just gotten off a diet, want to diet, plan on dieting, or will diet. If we could control our compulsive overeating, don't you think we would? Jerome Hass, our classmate and a diabetic, said in a personal interview on November 5, 2001, that he can't control his disease, but with education and daily treatment, he can and does maintain a fairly normal life.

Misconceptions and stereotyping seem to generate from the emotional response of fear. According to the 1999 textbook *Interpersonal Communication: Everyday Encounters* by Julia T. Wood, one of the most

main points and let her audience know that she is following a problem-solution organizational pattern.

Citing her sources by author, title, and date, Carol uses cause-and-effect reasoning in the first subpoint of her first main point to establish that stereotyping causes fat discrimination. She also uses the example about the shift in the perception of the ideal woman's body in Fiji, which resulted in increased levels of discrimination. However, at the same time she acknowledges the problems with blaming the media solely for perpetuating stereotypes of the ideal female figure.

In her second subpoint—stereotyping stems from misconceptions— Carol builds her argument by weaving together a brief personal narrative, statistics, examples, and testimony from an interview she conducted with a classmate. (Although she uses personal testimony here and in other parts of the speech, note that she also uses many other forms of evidence to support her arguments about the problem of fat discrimination.)

Carol concludes her first main point with the argument that misconceptions and stereotyping stem from fear. In this third subpoint, she

Persuasion and Reasoning   443

builds her point by using quotations from her research, explaining how the quotes relate to the fear of obesity, and providing more testimony from her interview. She cites thorough research from three different sources in this subpoint—a book, a Web site, and an interview—revealing that she can offer her audience the most comprehensive picture of the problem she discusses.

A simple transition lets her audience know that she is turning to the solution to the problem. The use of "first" signals to her audience that she is beginning to discuss the solution. She reasons by analogy here, comparing the addiction of alcohol to the addiction of overeating.

Using the signpost "second," Carol argues that everyone must be educated because education changes people's views on issues. She again reasons by analogy, using the example of Ryan White to suggest that if education worked to lessen prejudice about AIDS, it could also work to lessen prejudice about compulsive overeating.

Carol makes a specific call to action, asking her audience to change their behaviors for the next two weeks. She uses compelling language in this subpoint ("smallest of efforts," "no gesture is too small or too large") and translates her

basic human needs is self-esteem as depicted in Maslow's hierarchy of needs, which "needs to be satisfied before we can focus on those [needs] that are more abstract." The text states that "we gain our first sense of self from the others who communicate how they see us." When we are educated about differences in others, we see that obesity is not a threat to our basic needs and we can show compassion and not react with prejudice. Jerome Hass stated that the basic reaction of people who find out he has diabetes is sympathy. That's because the general population has been educated enough to understand the basic facts about his disease. As Edmund Burke, a famous seventeenth-century philosopher quoted on the Web site http://www.blu-pete.com, accessed November 30, 2001, said, "No passion so effectively robs the mind of all its powers of acting and reasoning as fear."

Now that I have identified the problem, I will focus on the solution. To minimize fat prejudice, we must rely on what history has proved—that understanding, education, and awareness are the keys to change. First, it is important to understand that compulsive overeating is a disease. According to the 1939 book *Alcoholics Anonymous,* "We believe . . . that the action of alcohol on the chronic alcoholics is manifestation of an allergy; that the phenomenon of craving is limited to this class and never occurs in the average temperate drinker." The same can be said for compulsive overeaters because we are dealing with the allergy of addiction, whether the substance is food, drugs, alcohol, gambling, or any other manifestation.

Second, when both the people who suffer from this disease and the general population speak out, fat discrimination can be greatly minimized through education, one person at a time. According to the article "The Ryan White Story: A Shift From Confusion, Fear, and Ignorance to Acceptance and New-Found Knowledge of AIDS" by Deepa Channiah, obtained on November 10, 2001 at www.engl.virginia.edu, in just a short time, Ryan White, one of the first well-known AIDS cases in the early '80s, "played a major role in changing people's views concerning the disease and AIDS patients." The author continues, "Education and behavior change [were] our only weapons."

Third, with awareness of how each of us might be contributing to the problem, we can instead help create the solution. Awareness takes practice. For the next two weeks, I'd like each of us to be aware of the thoughts, feelings, and behaviors we have when encountering obese or overweight people. For example, when we walk into the grocery store to pick up some items and we see an overweight person, let's stop for a moment and focus on the automatic thoughts and reactions we may be having, then shift them into positive actions. We can do this by reaching out to that person with what may seem the smallest of efforts, such as smiling, holding the door open, sitting at the same table to eat, giving an acknowledgment, saying hello, or to even initiating a conversation. No gesture is too small or too large if it is different than it will have been prior to the next two weeks. That is the point—difference. Doing something differently is what makes change. The Ephedra statistics show that 58 million of our adult population is overweight. Each of us in here can feasibly touch one person a day differently for fourteen days—that would mean a total of 300 people affected in just a short time. With awareness, change will happen.

statistics for her audience (one person for fourteen days equals 300 people). Her call to action is a simple one. Note that she isn't asking her audience for enormous changes, but rather for simple changes that are easy to implement.

Fat prejudice and discrimination must be addressed in order for those afflicted to reach the help they need and deserve. There are two main points I discussed in my speech today. I discussed how fat discrimination exists through stereotyping, misconceptions, and fear. I also discussed that each of us can have an impact on solving the problem through education and the awareness that compulsive overeating is a disease, that one person can make a difference, and that we can turn our prejudicial behavior around. I remind you of my story about the obese man I encountered at the convention. If you had walked into this classroom today and had seen this person, how you would have treated him? My hope is that you would have treated him just like anyone else, with a soft smile, a friendly hello, or a touch of kindness. My experience tells me that usually such treatment is not the norm. More often there is silent condemnation of overweight people, self-righteous judgment, and hurtful discrimination—I can say this is because prior to recovery, I was one of those overweight people.

Carol offers a brief summary of her two main points as she begins the conclusion of her speech. She then returns to the story from her introduction, bringing her speech full circle. She also restates her thesis and draws her audience into her topic emotionally so her proposed solution will be even more compelling.

Chapter Summary

Persuasive speaking requires carefully preparing and framing your arguments so you respectfully request change rather than badger or manipulate your audience into agreeing with you. When you use persuasion ethically, you frame your arguments using evidence, credibility, emotion, and mythos. When you use evidence in your persuasive speeches, you want to use evidence that is as specific as possible, present information that is new to the audience, and use credible sources.

When you use an appeal to credibility, you are asking your audience to see you as competent and of good character. Credibility, which the audience attributes to a speaker, evolves during a speech. You can add to your initial credibility by explaining your competence to the audience and establishing common ground with them. You can build derived credibility through your delivery, which should be energetic, moderately fast, and comfortable. If you are successful, you will end with high terminal credibility.

When you appeal to emotions, remember the six primary emotions (fear, anger, surprise, sadness, disgust, and happiness) are expressed similarly across cultures, but the three secondary emotions (pride, guilt, and shame) are expressed differently across age, gender, and culture. One additional emotion appealed to in persuasive speaking is reverence. Appeals to emotions help you catch your audience's attention, reinforce an idea, move your audience to action, or show your audience how deeply you feel about the topic. When you appeal to emotions in persuasive speeches, stay audience centered in order to avoid overly graphic and violent appeals, overly frightening or threatening appeals, and overly manipulative appeals. In addition, present your appeals to emotion with vivid language. Finally, balance your appeals to emotion with appeals to reason so your audience is exposed to both aspects of the issue.

Persuasive speakers also appeal to mythos—the stories told in a culture that reflect its folk knowledge and ideals. Appeals to mythos tap into a culture's common sense and call to mind its shared values, attitudes, and patterns of behavior. When we appeal to mythos, we rely on a story, or myth, that reminds our audience of important principles. Although our culture's myths may not be factually true, there is a logic embedded in them. Keep in mind that different cultures have different myths based on their different experiences and histories. Stay audience centered and use stories that speak to your audience's shared beliefs and values.

Fallacies are errors in an argument that result from flawed or inaccurate reasoning. The five most common fallacies are ad hominem (against the person), bandwagon (everyone else is doing it), either-or (a false dilemma), red herring (raising a distracting new issue), and slippery slope (one step will lead to others).

Fallacies are unethical and confusing for audiences because they cloud the central argument. Manipulating an audience's emotions through threats or overly graphic images is also unethical. The public dialogue stays healthy when we address complex issues honestly and fairly. Logos—the careful use of evidence, credibility, and emotion—and mythos—stories that draw on strong cultural beliefs and values—are two ethical ways to enhance this very important dialogue.

Invitation to Public Speaking Online

After reading this chapter, use your CD-ROM and the *Invitation to Public Speaking* Web site to review the following concepts, answer the review questions, and complete the suggested activities.

Key Concepts

logos (426)
ethos (426)
pathos (426)
credibility (429)
competence (429)

character (429)
initial credibility (429)
derived credibility (429)
terminal credibility (429)
common ground (430)
mythos (436)

fallacy (438)
ad hominem fallacy (438)
bandwagon fallacy (439)
either-or fallacy (440)
red herring fallacy (440)
slippery slope fallacy (441)

Review Questions

1. You have been asked to give a speech on the topic of living wills to your classmates. Your position is that living wills are good and you want to persuade audience members to have living wills, regardless of their age. How will you establish ethos, or credibility, on this topic? How will you make appeals to emotion, or pathos? What ethical considerations do you think you'll have to grapple with in this speech?

2. You have been asked to speak to residents of the dormitories on your campus on the very familiar topic of recycling. How might you make this topic engaging and persuade the audience to support recycling by bringing in new evidence? If you are not familiar with the arguments supporting recycling, choose another topic that is very familiar to most dorm residents (locking bicycles, getting up for early morning classes, and the like). How will you make your evidence new for them so you might be more persuasive?

3. Using the topic you have selected for your in-class persuasive speech, review Chapter 8 to identify three of the five possible types of arguments you might make in a persuasive speech (inductive, deductive, cause, analogy, and sign). Then use the suggestions from this chapter's section on evidence and persuasion to find ways you might make these patterns of reasoning more effective.

4. Identify five topics on which you will have high credibility with your classmates or service learning audience. Choose one of these topics and explain how you will share your competence with your audience in the introduction of your speech.

5. Using the topic you have selected for your in-class persuasive speech, make a list of the appeals to mythos you might make in the speech. After you've identified these appeals, consider your audience carefully. Determine which appeals likely will resonate strongly with your audience and which may not be appropriate given their cultural backgrounds.

6. Bring a copy of the morning newspaper or your favorite magazine to class. In groups, identify as many different types of fallacies as you can find. Label them as ad hominem, bandwagon, either-or, red herring, and slippery slope fallacies as appropriate. Now that you recognize these fallacies, evaluate the strength of the argument being advanced.

7. As a class, select a topic that is being given considerable attention nationally or locally. Identify several positions or perspectives on this issue and divide the class into groups, assigning each a different position or perspective. In these groups, develop five fallacious arguments in support of your position (ad hominem, bandwagon, either-or, red herring, and slippery slope). Present these to the class and see if they can find the fallacies and identify or name the type you are using.

The *Invitation to Public Speaking* Web Site

The *Invitation to Public Speaking* Web site features the review questions about the Web sites suggested on pages 427, 428, 433, and 434, the interactive activities suggested on pages 437 and 441, and the InfoTrac College Edition exercises suggested on pages 427, 431, and 437. You can access this site via your CD-ROM or at .

Web Links

18.1: Credible Internet Sites (427)
18.2: Most Admired Person (428)
18.3: Statements Used to Provoke Pathos (433)
18.4: Graphic Appeal to Emotion (434)

Interactive Activities

18.1: Identifying Cultural Beliefs (437)
Purpose: To understand how speakers use mythos to appeal to a culture's beliefs and values.

18:2: Identifying Fallacies (441)
Purpose: To learn the basic fallacies of reasoning and how to identify them in a speaker's argument.

InfoTrac College Edition Exercises

18.1: **Using Specific Evidence** (427)
Purpose: To appreciate the impact of using specific evidence.

18.2: **Establishing Credibility** (431)
Purpose: To understand how a speaker establishes credibility.

18.3: **Drawing on Mythos** (437)
Purpose: To understand how speakers use mythos to appeal to a culture's logic.

Speech Interactive on the *Invitation to Public Speaking* CD-ROM

The following video clips of speeches, referenced in this chapter, are included under Speech Interactive on your *Invitation to Public Speaking* CD-ROM. After you have watched the clips, click on "Critique" to answer the questions for analysis.

Video Clip 1: Mary Fisher's Speech to the Republican National Convention (433). As you watch Mary Fisher's speech to the 1992 Republican National Convention, consider how she uses emotional appeals. How does she use emotion to gain her audience's attention? How does she use emotion to reinforce her main points? How does she move the audience to action? How does she demonstrate her commitment to her topic?

Video Clip 2: Martin Luther King Jr's "I Have a Dream" (435). As you watch Martin Luther King Jr's "I Have a Dream" speech, notice how he uses vivid images. Do these images evoke emotion? Does he use emotion to reinforce his main points? Does he use emotion to appeal to his audience?

Video Clip 3: Persuasive Speech: Carol Godart (442). As you watch Carol's speech about fat discrimination, consider her use of evidence and appeal to mythos. Did these reasoning strategies help her persuade her audience? Recall that you saw Carol use source citations in Chapter 6 and visual aids in Chapter 14.

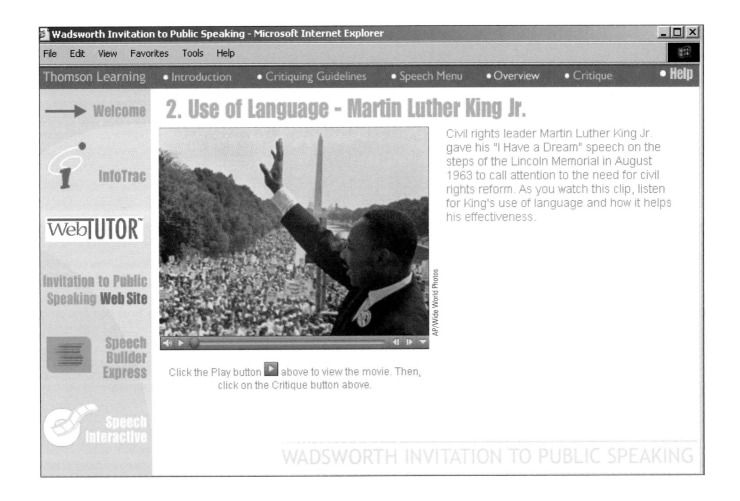

CHAPTER 19

Speaking on Special Occasions

So, I'm standing here in a strange hat and a strange, flowing gown in front of what looks very much like an audience, and I'm about to do something that I don't do very often, which is to make speeches in public. And I'm asking myself how I managed to end up here? This was never in any plan I'd outlined for myself. . . . And I have to say I'm a little bit nervous. You might think this is strange for a man who makes his living playing in stadiums, but I often stand in the middle of a stadium full of people and ask myself the same question.

—Sting, commencement address at Berklee College of Music, May 15, 1994[1]

People give special occasion speeches when they come together to celebrate, reflect, and remember or to establish a common purpose or goal. We give these speeches when we want to acknowledge someone's accomplishments or celebrate events or transitions. We also give them when we come together after difficult events. Such occasions are weddings, awards ceremonies, banquets, and memorials. Special occasion speeches often bring an audience together, reminding people of what they share in common. They also mark certain occasions as special, as unique from the familiar events of our lives.

This appendix introduces you to four types of special occasion speeches—speeches of introduction, commemoration, acceptance, and speeches to entertain. In Chapter 2 you were introduced to the first three types of speeches: introduction, commemoration, and acceptance. Here you will learn more about these speeches, and you'll be introduced to speeches to entertain. Speeches to entertain are less common than the other types of special occasion speeches, but there certainly are times when we are asked, decide to, or are required to give speeches to entertain. Each of these speeches recognizes a different kind of special occasion. As such, each has a slightly different goal. You will learn about these different goals as well as specific guidelines to help you prepare and deliver effective special occasion speeches.

Speeches of Introduction

introductory speech
introductory speech
Speech that gives the audience a sense of the unique perspective of the person introduced or that welcomes and familiarizes the audience with an event.

When you give an **introductory speech,** you give the audience a sense of the unique perspective of the person you are introducing or you welcome and make the audience familiar with an event. Introductory speeches are given for three reasons. You introduce yourself, such as at a job interview or in a newly formed group. You introduce someone else, usually at a formal event before that person gives a speech. And you introduce an event, often at conferences, workshops, or community events. Regardless of who or what you're introducing, introductory speeches tend to be brief and very tightly organized. The principle of "less is more" applies in that the audience does not want to hear lengthy monologues. Instead, they want you to be brief and give specific, interesting, and useful information.

Introductory speeches are organized around three goals:

- Acquaint the audience with a person, event, or both.
- Establish the credibility of the person or event being introduced.
- Generate enthusiasm for the person, event, or both.

To accomplish these goals, speeches of introduction should do the following:

Introducing Yourself

- State your name and any of your credentials or titles.
- Identify any qualifications, experiences, or expertise you possess that relate directly to why you're giving your speech. ("I've worked in the insurance business for four years as a . . . during which I learned . . . ")
- State your pleasure at being invited or able to participate in the task at hand.

To consider how professional speakers introduce themselves to audiences, complete InfoTrac College Edition Exercise 19.1, "Introducing Yourself," online under Student Resources for Chapter 19 at the *Invitation to Public Speaking* Web site.

Introducing Another Person

- State your own name and credentials. ("Hello, I'm Mary Brown, director of the Office of Volunteer Programs.")
- Indicate that you will introduce the other person. (For example, "It is my privilege tonight to introduce our speaker, Dr. Robert Gonzales.")
- Provide accurate, relevant details about the person, including credentials, accomplishments, activities, personality traits, personal stories, or even a quote from something the person has said. ("Dr. Gonzales holds a Ph.D. from Harvard University and currently is working as a consultant for . . . He also has experience in . . . He has received numerous awards, some of which include . . . He describes his life as . . . ")
- Identify the topic of the person's speech by describing the general topic or simply giving the title of the presentation. ("The title of Dr. Gonzales's presentation this evening is . . . He plans to share with us some highlights of his most recent research in . . . ")
- Provide closure to your remarks and welcome the person to the podium or the front of the room. ("Please join me in welcoming Dr. Robert Gonzales.")

WEB SITE To apply these tips to an introductory speech given by Laura Bush at the 2000 Republican National Convention, complete Interactive Activity 19.1, "Introducing the Future President," online under Student Resources for Chapter 19 at the *Invitation to Public Speaking* Web site.

Introducing an Event

- Identify yourself and your credentials.
- Welcome the audience to the event and thank them for attending.
- Thank or acknowledge important sponsors or people associated with the event.
- Explain the goals of the event.
- Identify any unusual, important, or special aspects of the event.
- Introduce key people who can answer questions or offer help.
- Identify key locations (for example, first aid, rest rooms, cafeterias).
- Inform audience of their next steps. ("After you've heard our keynote speaker present, you'll have about fifteen minutes to find the seminar room assigned to your group.")

Additionally, because we often give introductory speeches at formal events, use language that reflects this formality. When you give a speech of introduction, use language that is clear and concise, appropriate to the audience and the occasion, appropriate to the speaker, and enhances the speaker's credibility. In the next example of an introduction, notice the clarity of the language and how it lends credibility to the speaker being introduced.

> Hello, I'm Mary Brown, director of the Office of Volunteer Programs. It is my privilege tonight to introduce our speaker, Dr. Robert Gonzales. Dr. Gonzales holds a Ph.D. from Harvard University and currently is working as a consultant for HarpCor International, located in Chicago. He also holds the position of professor emeritus at Northwestern University and has taught there for over twenty-five years.

Compare this example with an informal version of the same introduction.

> Hi, I'm Mary Brown and I'd like to introduce Robert Gonzales. Robert holds a degree from Harvard and now works for HarpCor International. He's taught at Northwestern for many years.

Although the second example is shorter, it lacks the specificity of the first. It shares the same essential information (name, credentials, and such) but without

When introducing an event, describe its goals and generate an audience's enthusiasm for it. What sort of event do you think you'd like to introduce? What could you say in your speech to help your audience get excited about the event and make the most of it?

the clarity of the first, resulting in less credibility for the speaker being introduced. It also makes Professor Gonzales seem less interesting. So when you follow the "less is more" principle in your introductory speech, be certain you don't pare down your introduction so much that you fail to provide relevant and interesting details.

Consider the effectiveness of the next example, an introduction of Christopher Reeve before he spoke at the Society for Neuroscience Presidential Symposium:

> It's a special privilege for the Society for Neuroscience to hear a personal perspective from actor and director, Christopher Reeve. Christopher Reeve sustained, unfortunately, a spinal cord injury in 1995, but with unbelievable courage and determination, has overcome the limitations of his personal misfortune and turned his fantastic energy and fantastic skills at communication to become an advocate for all those who are living with diseases of the brain or spinal cord. It is not an exaggeration to say that his efforts and personal effectiveness have single-handedly raised public awareness of the need to increase basic research into the neurosciences. He's put a human face on spinal cord injury, but with wonderful intelligence and generosity on all diseases of the brain and spinal cord. He's a person who I admire deeply, and hence I am very pleased that he accepted my invitation to come here and speak tonight. I'd like to give you Christopher Reeve.[2]

When you introduce yourself, another person, or an event, your goal is to create a sense of respect, an eagerness to hear more, and an understanding of what to expect. To give an effective speech of introduction, consider the following guidelines.

Be Brief

When you introduce yourself, be brief and concise. It can be tempting to share a lot of details about yourself and your life, recount past experiences, and tell personal stories, but doing so can take a lot of time. A successful introductory speech rarely lasts more than three to four minutes. If you do opt to share a past experience or personal story, make sure you can tell it within a minute or two and it clearly relates to the point you are making.

When you introduce another person or an event, remember you are giving an introduction, not a full-length speech. As when you introduce yourself, avoid lengthy stories and drawn-out explanations. Try, instead, to share enough information so the audience is eager to hear from the speaker, but not so much that they feel overwhelmed with information. Remember, the audience is anxious to hear the guest speaker or move into the heart of the event.

Be Accurate

Introductory speeches require considerable personal experience with the speaker or the event, or they require careful research. If you must research a person or an event, you can do your research on the Internet or at the library, interview the person you are introducing or obtain a copy of his or her resume, or interview the people who are organizing the event. Being accurate in your speech means that you state all dates, titles, and awards the person has received correctly and you cite the original source of all quotes and personal stories. Being accurate also means you pronounce all information correctly, right down to the speaker's own name. Take time to get your details correct and you not only will show respect for the person you introduced, you also will enhance your own credibility.

Be Appropriate

Use your skills at analyzing an audience to present a speech that is appropriate to the occasion. Remember, your goal is to enhance the speaker's credibility and build enthusiasm for what's to come. If your remarks are too personal, irrelevant to the occasion, or too informal, you will affect not only your own image, but damage the speaker's credibility as well. As such, share only information that is fitting to the occasion.

Ask for permission before you share anything personal about the person you are introducing. What may seem trivial or like an interesting human interest anecdote to you may make the person you introduce feel exposed and uncomfortable. If the person asks you not to share that information, don't do so, even if it's one of your favorite stories.

Speeches of Commemoration

Commemorative speeches praise, honor, recognize, or pay tribute to a person, an event, an idea, or institution. The two most common types of commemorative speeches are speeches of tribute and speeches of award. A **speech of tribute** is a speech given to honor someone. A **speech of award** is a speech given to present a specific award to someone and describe why that person is receiving the award. Both highlight a person's exceptional value, qualities, contributions, or accomplishments. Recall from Chapter 2 that commemorative speeches are usually given in formal and very ritualized settings, such as banquets, receptions, retirement parties, special birthdays, memorial services, and rallies.

Speeches of commemoration are organized around two goals:

- Help an audience appreciate the importance of a person, an event, an idea, or an institution.

- Illustrate for an audience a person's unique achievements or the special impact of an event, idea, or institution.

To accomplish these goals, a speech of commemoration should do the following:

- Identify who or what you are commemorating. Name the person, event, idea, or institution and the occasion being celebrated.

- Identify and describe the quality or activity that makes this person, event, idea, or institution special. Clearly state the unique characteristics or actions being commemorated.

- Identify and describe the contributions or impact the person, event, idea, or institution has had on others or on society.

- Identify and describe any obstacles that a person had to overcome in order to accomplish what he or she did, or that an event, idea, or institution had to get past in order to come to fruition.

- Identify and describe your relationship to the person, event, idea, or institution being commemorated.

To assess an induction speech at the Pro Football Hall of Fame, complete Interactive Activity 19.2, "Assessing Hall of Fame Induction Speeches," online under Student Resources for Chapter 19 at the *Invitation to Public Speaking* Web site.

Effective commemorative speeches also include a specific kind of language. Commemorative speakers tell compelling stories and anecdotes, use rich language

WEB SITE

commemorative speech
Speech that praises, honors, recognizes, or pays tribute to a person, an event, an idea, or an institution.

speech of tribute
Speech given to honor someone.

speech of award
Speech given to present a specific award to someone and describe why that person is receiving the award.

© Frank Siteman/Stock Boston

that brings to mind vivid images, and, when appropriate, expresses deep emotion. They also recite special phrases, sayings, or quotations used by the person being commemorated or that are attributed to an event, idea, or institution.

In the next example, note how South African activist Nelson Mandela uses the occasion of his release from prison in 1990 to pay tribute to those who have assisted him. Although the second part of the speech (not included here) is a call to action, Mandela begins the speech by commemorating the people and institutions that supported him during his thirty-year imprisonment in South Africa:

> On this day of my release, I extend my sincere and warmest gratitude to the millions of my compatriots and those in every corner of the globe who have campaigned tirelessly for my release.
>
> I extend special greetings to the people of Cape Town, the city which has been my home for three decades. Your mass marches and other forms of struggle have served as a constant source of strength to all political prisoners.

Commencement speeches are a common type of commemorative speech used to congratulate students on their accomplishments, welcome them to a new phase of their lives, and inspire them to strive for new goals. Think about a particularly good commencement speech you've heard. What about it was special and inspirational? What would you like to hear in the commencement speech given at your own future graduation?

> I salute the African National Congress. It has fulfilled our every expectation in its role as leader of the great march to freedom.
>
> I salute our president, Comrade Oliver Tambo, for leading the ANC even under the most difficult circumstances.
>
> I salute the rank-and-file members of the ANC. You have sacrificed life and limb in the pursuit of the noble cause of our struggle.[3]

Throughout this excerpt, Mandela uses vivid imagery to commemorate the specific contributions of those who assisted him in his long struggle for freedom. In the next excerpt, notice that he also uses simple, yet deeply emotional, language to pay tribute to his family:

> My salutations will be incomplete without expressing my deep appreciation for the strength given me during my long and lonely years in prison by my beloved wife and family. I am convinced that your pain and suffering was far greater than my own.[4]

This simple use of emotional language ("deep appreciation," "long and lonely years," "beloved wife and family," "pain and suffering") is very effective in allowing Mandela to express his feelings clearly and appropriately.

The next example illustrates a speech of award. In 1999 Representative Bobby Rush, a U.S. congressman from Chicago and a former Black Panther, encouraged his audience to support legislation to award the Congressional Gold Medal to Rosa Parks for her remarkable role in the civil rights movement.

> Mr. Speaker, I rise today in support of legislation to award a Congressional Gold Medal to Rosa Parks.
>
> Occasionally in our nation's history there are pivotal moments and indispensable individuals that move America away from its divisive past and closer to its imagined promise. December 1, 1955, produced such a moment and such a person.

Invitation to Service Learning / Patrick

Photo courtesy of Marilyn Striffler

I chose to do my service learning at Columbine Care Center West, a nursing home facility, because I have a special place in my heart for the elderly. I feel that you can learn so much from them, and all they want is someone who is there to listen. I was more than glad to provide that service.

My responsibilities at Columbine were hardly responsibilities at all. I would just come for an hour or two a day and hang out with Ruth. We would either read, get involved with the activities that Columbine had going on that day, like bingo or puzzles, or I would listen to her tell me about her ranching days.

I decided to finish my service learning by giving a commemorative speech on Ruth. I chose this speech topic because Ruth is such an interesting woman and I thought it would be cool to share some information about her with her friends at Columbine. The speech went great! I had the most attentive audience I've ever had in my life. There were no problems at all, and I received a lot of positive responses afterward.

I thought that my service learning project was a great opportunity. It gave me the chance to really get to know a wonderful woman, and it really helped me with the information we were learning in class.

Rosa Parks grew up in segregation. Every day she was forced to deal with the violation of America's constitutional guarantees. On December 1, 1955, this American woman exacted of this country the freedom and equality the Constitution promises.

Tired, like most citizens after a hard day's work, Rosa Parks refused to obey a shameful law that required her to sit at the back of a Montgomery, Alabama, bus. Her actions set the stage for the civil rights movement of a people who were unfairly and unjustly living under racist law.

Because of this brave American woman, segregation laws around the nation began to crumble and our nation began to respond to the call for African-American equality.

Because of her invaluable contribution to our nation, every American lives a better life today. For that reason, it is quite appropriate that Mrs. Rosa Parks receive the Congressional Gold Medal.

But I must add, Mr. Speaker, that today, our nation continues to call for equality and freedom. There are still issues in our America that were issues in 1955. There are still Americans who do not enjoy the promises enumerated in the Constitution.

So, if we are to truly honor this great woman, we must do so, not only with a Gold Medal, but also with actions that further her purpose. We must all become individuals working to end the discrimination and inequalities that exist in our great nation.

I urge my colleagues to support this legislation and honor the mother of the civil rights movement, Mrs. Rosa Parks. Thank you.[5]

When you give commemorative speeches, you become responsible for conveying the significance of a person, event, idea, or institution to an audience. And if you're commemorating a person, you also want him or her to feel a sense of pride for having been praised and commemorated. To give an effective commemorative speech, consider the following guidelines.

Share What Is Unique and Special

Do not assume the audience already knows what makes who or what you are commemorating exceptional. Instead, offer specific praise and representative examples of successes, talents, accomplishments, special characteristics, and significant impacts. Be specific about the importance and meaning of who or what you are commemorating.

Express Sincere Appreciation

Express sincere appreciation for all that a person, event, idea, or institution has given or made possible. Speeches of commemoration, whether tributes or awards, praise and honor some person or some thing. Include in your speech sincere recognition of the ways in which who or what you're commemorating has affected a community. Your words should be genuine and express respect and gratitude. Using your *Invitation to Public Speaking* CD-ROM, watch Stacey's speech commemorating fallen U.S. soldiers under Speech Interactive for Chapter 12. Does she convey sincere appreciation for her subject?

Tell the Truth

Be certain your facts are correct, your stories accurate, and the traits you attribute to a person, event, idea, or institution are representative. Do not alter the truth to make a story more exciting. Instead, make an effort to find unique and special qualities and experiences that make your story especially compelling.

When you commemorate a person, you generally know him or her quite well. In your speech, share your personal experience with that person so your audience can appreciate his or her exceptional qualities. When you commemorate an event, idea, or institution, share the characteristics that make it special in a way that appeals to your audience. Remember, when you give a commemorative speech, you want your audience to feel inspired and appreciative and to respect and admire who or what you are honoring. For advice about giving a common type of commemorative speech, a wedding toast, go to http://www.usabride.com/wedplan/a_making_toasts.html.

Speech Step 19.1 / Design a Speech of Commemoration

Identify a person, event, idea, or institution you would like to commemorate. Then design a speech of commemoration. Make a list of the accomplishments, qualities, or influences you wish to recognize. Practice describing these characteristics, paying special attention to the language you use. Be sure your descriptions and praise are specific, your speech expresses sincere appreciation and respect, and your facts are accurate.

Speeches of Acceptance

acceptance speech
Speech that acknowledges gratitude, appreciation, and pleasure at receiving an honor or a gift.

In an **acceptance speech,** you acknowledge your gratitude, appreciation, and pleasure at receiving an honor or a gift. Speeches of acceptance are organized around three goals:

* Thank an audience for the award.

* Show your awareness of the significance of the award.

* Acknowledge the people who helped you accomplish what you're being honored for.

In the next example, notice how Guatemalan human rights activist Rigoberta Menchú Tum conveyed her understanding of the significance of receiving the Nobel Peace Prize in 1992:

Please allow me to convey to you all what this prize means to me. In my opinion, the Nobel Peace Prize calls upon us to act in accordance with what it represents and the great significance it has worldwide. In addition to being a priceless treasure, it is an instrument with which to fight for peace, for justice, for the rights of those who suffer the abysmal economic, social, cultural, and political disparities, typical of the order of the world in which we live.[6]

Sometimes speakers use the significance of an award to call attention to a larger issue. For example, Adam Horovitz, member of the musical group Beastie Boys, included in his acceptance of the 1999 MTV Video Vanguard Award a call to address the serious problem of sexual assault at some large music festivals, particularly the 1999 Woodstock festival. "They [the sexual assaults at the festival] made me feel really sad and angry," he said as he accepted the award. "I'm talking to all the musicians here—I think we can talk to the promoters and make sure they do something about the safety of all the women and girls who come to all of our shows."[7]

Although the main focus of a speech of acceptance is to express your thanks for receiving an award or a gift, it has other purposes as well. To give an effective speech of acceptance, consider the following guidelines.

Understand the Purpose of the Award

Be familiar with the background, history, and unique characteristics of the award. To receive an award is to receive an honor. Be certain you understand the honor you are receiving so you can speak intelligently about what the award means to you. You may even choose to organize your acceptance speech around the specific qualities of the award, as Menchú did. Similarly, you can use your understanding of the meaning and purpose of the award to encourage others to act, to remind the audience of larger social issues, or simply to reinforce shared values and principles.

Recognize Others

Although you are being recognized as an outstanding individual, give credit and thanks to those who have contributed to your success. Verbally acknowledge their influence, support, and the ways in which they helped you succeed. Use caution here, because it is tempting to try to thank everyone to whom you are close. Avoid this pitfall and thank only those people or groups who have been especially supportive, helpful, or pivotal to your success.

Respect the Time Limitations

The length of your acceptance speech will vary, depending on the situation. Some acceptance speeches are quite short, lasting only a minute or two. Others, like Menchú's Nobel Peace Prize acceptance speech, last longer. When you are invited to receive an award and give a speech, ask how long your speech should be. If the award committee requests a short speech, plan to be brief. If they want a longer speech, respect this request. A longer speech suggests your audience is interested in hearing a little more about you. For example, they may want to hear what you plan to do with the award (such as a monetary award) or what your future plans are.

Speech Step 19.2 / Design a Speech of Acceptance

Identify an award you've received in the past, one you've been chosen to receive soon, or one you imagine you'd like to receive. Design a short speech of acceptance. Consider why you're being given the award. What is the significance of the award? Who has helped you succeed? Outline an acceptance speech that incorporates these elements and fits within an appropriate length of time.

Speeches to Entertain

Sometimes called *after-dinner speeches*, speeches to entertain are often given after a meal, usually a dinner, but also after a lunch or even breakfast meeting.[8] Speakers who give speeches to entertain usually are more experienced at speaking. However, you may find as a novice speaker that you are asked to speak at a luncheon for a service group or after a formal dinner at a club to which you might belong. **Speeches to entertain** are lighthearted speeches that address issues or ideas in a humorous way. But note that they are not comedic acts. They do more than just provide the audience with a series of jokes—they follow many of the basic principles of other special occasion speeches. Speeches to entertain are organized speeches with a specific purpose, thesis statement, and main points. A speech to entertain may be informative, invitational, or persuasive and is organized around two goals:

- Entertain the audience.
- Make the audience think.

When you give a speech to entertain, you want to make the audience laugh and smile as you give your speech. You also want the audience to "entertain" the issue—to look at it carefully and explore its implications. This balance between humor and presenting issues can be a tricky one. Let's take a closer look at each of these components of a speech to entertain.

Humor is perhaps one of the most complicated communication phenomena. On the one hand, humor is highly personal—what is funny to one person isn't always funny to another. You tell a joke or story to two people and only one laughs. On the other hand, there are times when you tell a joke and everyone in the room thinks it's funny. Then you repeat that joke in a different context and no one finds it the least bit amusing. And, if those two issues weren't enough, if you rearrange the wording or forget to tell a line of a joke, no one even chuckles or understands what is supposed to be so funny. Predicting what will make people laugh is a bit like predicting the weather—we're often wrong. However, research tells us that what makes something funny is a combination of these elements:

- Timing
- Your objective in telling the joke
- The members of your audience

Timing is the way you use pauses and delivery for maximum effect. Research suggests that timing is a critical element in humor.[9] Personal experiences also tell us that timing is integral to how a joke is received and understood. Pauses to set a mood, before punch lines, or before key phrases can make the difference between

speech to entertain
Lighthearted speech that addresses issues or ideas in a humorous way.

timing
Way a speaker uses pauses and delivery for maximum effect.

When giving a speech to entertain, carefully consider how your humor will be received by your audience. San Francisco mayor Willie Brown, shown here speaking at a mayor's conference breakfast, must use humor that appeals to a widely diverse group of people. How could you incorporate humor into a speech to entertain so it would be well received by your audience?

© Karen Preuss/The Image Works

a successful joke and one that doesn't get the response you want. In a now famous joke, Barbara Bush, in her 1990 speech to the graduating class of Wellesley College, told her audience, "Who knows, somewhere out in this audience may even be someone who will one day follow in my footsteps and preside over the White House as the president's spouse." She paused, and added, "I wish him well."

The second aspect of successful humor is the objective of the joke. Jokes are told to make light of something, to remind us of our humanity, to highlight the silly or the bizarre, to tease others playfully, and even to relieve tension in difficult times. Humor also is used to belittle others, make fun of them, and put them down.[10] Avoid this type of negative humor in your speeches to entertain. Negative humor often offends members of an audience. Instead, rely on humor that brings relief to a tense situation, shows the lighter side of life, or gently teases someone and reminds us of our human side. This kind of humor stands a greater chance of truly entertaining the audience.

The third component of successful humor is the audience. Of course, different audiences will find different kinds of humor funny. And when you know the members of an audience quite well, you know better what the audience will find funny. However, one of the most common reasons a joke backfires is that you may have failed to consider the group memberships as well as the individual or collective experiences of your audience.[11] You tell a joke that "isn't funny" or that "goes too far" for the members of your audience.[12] So before you select the amusing stories you will tell and the jokes you will share, consider the master statuses and standpoints (Chapter 5) of your audience carefully.[13]

Research over the past twenty-five years suggests a number of interesting differences related to master statuses. Although men often find disparaging humor (humor that shows contempt or disapproval) directed at others funny, women are far less likely to appreciate these jokes. In contrast, women tend to find self-directed humor (humor about one's self) funnier than do men—but not when it's disparaging. Additionally, ethnic minorities may enjoy in-group humor but often take offense at out-group humor. That is, when people from a particular group make jokes about their own group, those jokes may be seen as funny. However, when people outside that group make jokes about the group, those jokes are far less likely to be perceived as funny.[14] As a rule, then, when the master statuses of your audiences are quite varied, try to avoid jokes that make fun of people or groups in harsh or mean-spirited ways. To learn how to incorporate humor successfully in your next speech, visit the Web site Humor Matters at http://www.humormatters.com/.

Although funny, speeches to entertain are also about issues that are relevant to a particular audience or community. Some issues that might be relevant to audiences today are how the government spends, or doesn't spend, tax dollars; the environment; and family life in the new millennium. Speeches to entertain help an audience make sense of what is happening around them or come to terms with issues and dilemmas that affect their lives.[15] They often put things into a new perspective and add humor to situations that may have been difficult or drawn out. They also can introduce new ideas, giving the audience something to think about that may not have occurred to them before. For example, politicians often use humor to address issues for particular audiences. To evaluate President Bush's humor at a White House correspondents' dinner, complete Interactive Activity

WEB SITE 19.3, "Using Humor in Politics," online under Student Resources for Chapter 19 at the *Invitation to Public Speaking* Web site.

As you consider the issues you might address in your speech to entertain, identify those topics that may be particularly relevant to the members of the audience. Once you've identified several possibilities, narrow these general topics and formulate a thesis statement. Check to be sure your approach has a humorous side to it and will appeal to your audience. From there, you can begin to develop the main points of your speech.

To help you balance humor and important issues and to give a speech that entertains rather than offends or bores, consider the following guidelines.

Use Humor Carefully

Always err on the side of caution as you incorporate humor into your speech. Although it is easy to get caught up in the moment, keep in mind that jokes often have more than one interpretation.[16] For those on the downside of the joke, the humor is rarely evident. If you think a joke might offend or put someone down, leave it out of the speech. Remember, your goal is to entertain, not alienate, the audience. When you offend an audience you lose credibility and respect, which are difficult to regain. To explore some of the advantages and risks of using humor in public settings, read the article "The Risky Business of Using Humor" online at http://www.asne.org/kiosk/editor/00.aug/horowitz1.htm.

Speak About Meaningful Issues

Remember, a speech to entertain is also about issues. Although it is meant to be funny, your goal is not to provide the audience with a continual stream of jokes. Rather, your goal is to develop an argument or an idea in an amusing way. As you select your topic and decide how you will frame it, consider your audience carefully. Although they do want to be entertained, they also want to hear a speech that is interesting and insightful. Before you finalize the topic of your speech, make sure it truly is relevant, appropriate, and will hold the interest of your audience.

Pay Careful Attention to Your Delivery

Although delivery is a key component of any speech, a skilled delivery is paramount in a speech to entertain. Practice your speech many times so you can deliver your stories, jokes, and anecdotes smoothly and without flaws. Work out the timing of your jokes well in advance and practice them until they feel like second nature. Your words and ideas will be even funnier if you can deliver your humor eloquently, in a relaxed style, and with the exact timing you want.[17] To explore two important elements of timing, read the article "A Theory of Humor" online at http://www.tomveatch.com/else/humor/paper/node17.html.

 Speech Step 19.3 / Design a Speech to Entertain

Identify three local or national issues that you think you'd like to speak about. Now consider the lighter side of these topics. Is there something that makes them humorous or could put them in a humorous light? Now consider a possible audience for each topic. Be sure that what you find humorous about these topics also will be funny to the audience. Now pick the topic you think would be the basis for a successful speech. Formulate a thesis statement and develop a short speech to entertain.

Invitation to Public Speaking Online

After reading this chapter, use your CD-ROM and the *Invitation to Public Speaking* Web site to review the key concepts, access the online review questions, and complete the suggested Web Link questions, Interactive Activities, and InfoTrac College Edition Exercises. You can access the book's Web site via your CD-ROM or at http://www.wadsworth.com/product/griffin.

Key Concepts

introductory speech (452)
commemorative speech (455)
speech of tribute (455)
speech of award (455)
acceptance speech (458)
speech to entertain (460)
timing (460)

Web Links

19.1: Tips for Making a Wedding Toast (458)
19.2: Humor Matters (462)
19.3: The Risky Business of Using Humor (462)
19.4: A Theory of Humor (463)

InfoTrac College Edition Exercises

19.1: Introducing Yourself (452)
Purpose: To study how a speaker has introduced himself or herself.

Interactive Activities

19.1: Introducing the Future President (452)
Purpose: To study a famous speech of introduction.

19.2: Assessing Hall of Fame Induction Speeches (455)
Purpose: To assess a speech of award.

19.3: Using Humor in Politics (462)
Purpose: To understand political uses of humor.

Chapter 20

Speaking in Small Groups

Never doubt that a small group of thoughtful, committed citizens can change the world. Indeed, it's the only thing that ever has.

—Margaret Mead, American anthropologist, 1928

A great deal of the public dialogue occurs in small group settings. Consider these examples:

- Local activist groups often start as small groups of people concerned about some aspect of their community. Through discussions, planning, and presentations, they can use their voices to influence issues and policies.

- In business settings, teams of coworkers pool their abilities to complete projects. As they work together, they use their voices to communicate ideas and ways of implementing their ideas.

- Although we think of our government as a large, monolithic entity, much of the government's work takes place when people speak in small groups. For instance, congressional committee members hear testimony from experts, deliberate about policy options, and use their voices to vote for the policy they think will work best. Local city councils hear concerns from residents, discuss those concerns, and then make decisions they hope are in the best interest of the community.

As you can see from these three examples, small group speaking is an important part of the public dialogue. **Small group speaking** is speaking to give a presentation to a small collection of individuals or speaking as part of a small group of people. We all are members of groups. We have families and friends; are members of churches, synagogues, or other religious organizations; take classes and attend seminars and workshops; contribute to our communities, and work with other people in our jobs. In each of these groups, we sometimes face challenges as we

small group speaking
Speaking to give a presentation to a small collection of individuals or speaking as part of a small group of people.

Speaking to or as part of your local city council is one way to enter the public dialogue with purpose. City councils are groups of elected officials that regularly hear concerns from the community and then work to address those concerns. How could you use your public speaking skills to influence this type of group?

© Owen Franken/CORBIS

try to communicate with others in that group. We might also be asked to communicate with people outside the group, sharing our ideas or findings with those who do not belong to the group. In order to give effective speeches in groups, we have to understand group dynamics and the ways groups work. In this appendix, we discuss these dynamics, covering the communication that occurs in groups; how group members use speech to lead groups, participate in groups, and solve problems; and how groups present their ideas to audiences.

Small Groups and the Public Dialogue

Throughout this text, we have explored types of public speaking for which one person is responsible for topic selection, organization, presentation, and responding to audience questions and feedback. Now we examine how people join with others to accomplish these same tasks. When we join groups, we become responsible for more than ourselves; we have to also pay attention to group goals, tasks, leadership, member roles, group structure, and even group conflict. And, although a public presentation may not be the final product of all groups, we also are responsible for helping the group think about speech topics, organization, and delivery. To begin, let's discuss what is meant by a "small group" and why people speak in groups.

Defining Small Groups

small group
Three to fifteen people who must work together to achieve a common goal and who have the ability to influence one another through verbal and nonverbal communication.

Researchers suggest that a **small group** consists of three to fifteen people who must work together to achieve a common goal and who have the ability to influence one another through verbal and nonverbal communication. Several characteristics distinguish small groups from other groups of people. Let's take a look at these characteristics.

First, the group must include at least three and not more than fifteen people. From your experiences, you probably know that interacting in a group of three is much different from interacting with just one other person—two people can pair up and influence the actions of the third, single person. In addition, in a group that has more than fifteen members, it is very hard to interact with one another. Consider classes you've had that are small and those that are large. In small classes, you can interact more easily with your classmates, learn their names, and get to know them. In larger classes, you don't always know who everyone is and it is much harder to get to know them. The upper limit on small groups is not clearly defined, but when a group has more than fifteen members, it changes significantly.

Second, group members have the ability to influence each other. An important characteristic of a small group is the flow of discussion that takes place among the members of the group. Although there may be a leader who guides the group's interaction, each group member should be able to express his or her ideas freely. Group members must also be able to see, hear, and communicate with each other.

Third, in a small group, nonverbal communication is quite important. Gestures, facial expressions, and even a person's unique habits and styles are just as important as the words that are said. Group members sometimes get the wrong idea about another person's nonverbal communication, which can affect the group negatively. To complicate matters, today much group interaction takes place through a mediated channel, such as videoconferencing, Internet chat, or satellite television. Thus, as technology is used more and more, groups will have to use more effective verbal communication to compensate for the lack of nonverbal communication.

Finally, small groups have a common goal that they must work together to achieve. This common goal binds the group together and keeps them communicating with each other. Ideally, members of a group must think of themselves as a group rather than as separate people. Thus group members must recognize that the group can achieve more as a group than if the individual members were working alone.

Why Do People Speak in Groups?

As we discussed in Chapters 1 and 4, public speaking occurs in different contexts. Speakers decide to speak, are asked to speak, or are required to speak. These same contexts influence public speaking in groups.

Deciding to speak in groups. Important issues can motivate us to speak individually (recall Lois Gibbs in Chapter 1), but they also can cause us to decide to speak in groups. Sometimes an issue is so important that we join with people who also have decided to speak out about an important matter. For example, Susan Love, Susan Hester, and Amy Langer joined together in 1991 to create the National Breast Cancer Coalition (NCBL).[1] Although each had been speaking about breast cancer alone, by joining together they found they had more influence and were successful in getting Congress to approve funding for breast cancer research. Love, Hester, and Langer spoke on television shows, testified at congressional hearings, and addressed survivor and activist groups. Today, the NBCL oversees more than six hundred organizations interested in breast cancer advocacy. You can learn more about this organization by visiting its Web site at http://www.natlbcc.org/.

Being asked to speak in groups. You might also be asked to speak as a member of a group because you have experiences or expertise in a particular area. In the workplace, you might be asked to give a speech because you have certain experiences or training that others want to hear about. You might also be asked to speak in an informal group (for example, a club) in order to provide information or new insights. Similarly, members of Congress are often asked to join committees because they have experience in a particular area. For example, the U.S. Senate Committee on Agriculture, Nutrition, and Forestry includes members who come from agricultural states and have experience with agricultural issues. Senators who join this group have experiences and expertise they wish to use to shape the nation's farming and forestry policies. They speak in small groups to other members of Congress, the media, and even their own constituents.

Being required to speak in groups. Finally, you might be required to communicate in a group context. The most common setting in which you might be required to speak in a group is in your work setting. In today's workplace, a great deal of work is done in small groups. In this setting, people meet frequently to give speeches about their ideas, research, or other findings. Additionally, today's workplace often involves teleconferencing and videoconferencing, and workers often find themselves giving speeches in these contexts. Thus, in addition to being required to give a speech in the actual work setting, you are also often required to give speeches via mediated communication.

Whether you decide, are asked, or are required to speak in a group, you will find that a particular structure for leadership is built into a group, and this structure affects all members of the group. In the following sections, you will learn about this leadership structure. You also will learn about how groups manage tasks and the types of presentations you may give in a group. Let's examine the structure of groups by discussing leadership and group roles.

Communicating Leadership

roles
Positions members of a group must fill in order for the group to accomplish its goals.

Members of a group can take on many **roles**, the positions they must fill in order for the group to accomplish its goals. Quite often, these roles are not formally determined; group members simply find themselves taking on roles or the roles develop because of the group's need to accomplish a certain task. We'll discuss many of these roles later, but for now let's focus on one of the most prominent group roles, that of the leader.

There are four different ways you can become a group leader. You might volunteer to be the leader of a group, in which case you would *choose* to be the leader. Or you might run formally for the position of leader and be *elected* to become a leader. People often do this when they are motivated by some issue or when they feel they have a vision that can help the group. You also may be *appointed* as a leader. For instance, a jury usually selects a foreperson who will poll the group's position on the verdict, guide deliberations, and announce the verdict in court. Similarly, a work group might ask you to lead the group because they look to you for direction and think you would give effective speeches for the group. Finally, you might *emerge* as the leader of a group. You may find that in certain groups you have some special expertise or skills appropriate to lead a group. In these situations, you may not be appointed or choose to be a leader, but you will become a group leader because of your skills or knowledge. In any case, it is important to understand the types of communication that make leaders effective.

What Types of Communication Make an Effective Leader?

Leaders help a group accomplish its goals. An effective leader helps a group make sense of the tasks it has been assigned and take action so the group can accomplish what it has set out to do. The leader of a group helps the group set goals, understand and evaluate information, overcome obstacles, and plan and select actions. Thus a leader does not necessarily rely on a specific set of traits or one particular style of communication because all groups are different. In fact, the more complicated the group's task, the more complex the leadership style will be because more complex tasks usually demand more complex styles of communication. However, all leaders exhibit certain **leadership behaviors** that involve making sense of information and problem solving.[2]

One of the key attributes of a leader is to make sense of information the group encounters. Groups receive information about their task from a variety of sources. For example, a group of employees may receive information from supervisors, customers, or government agencies.

- From its supervisors a group may receive information related to sales projections
- From customers, a group may receive information about needs and preferences
- From government agencies or management, a group may receive information about future policy considerations

Leaders assist the group in sorting through this information and in making sense of it. Leaders also help a group gather information. For example, the leader might

- Invite an expert on a subject to a group meeting to share information that is necessary for the group to complete its task
- Observe situations related to the group's task and gain information from these observations
- Attend meetings of company executives to learn about economic forecasts, company initiatives, and competitor goals

From here, the leader can share the information gathered and work with the group to evaluate that information and make future plans. Leaders also help the group overcome problems that keep them from achieving their goals. These problems are called *constraints*, and groups typically face two types of constraints.[3]

- Problems that affect how a group thinks about its task are called **cognitive constraints.** Cognitive constraints occur when group members do not have enough information, have faulty information, or reason incorrectly from the information they do have. Leaders help a group avoid these problems by providing more information, identifying sources that can provide more information, bringing in an expert to clarify or help the group, and helping the group reason correctly about the information they do have.

- Problems that come about as a result of power dynamics are called **affiliative constraints** and **egocentric constraints.** When people work with others, they are affiliated with and connected to each other. Because of this connection, and because of personality, culture, master status (Chapter 5), personal goals and needs, and a host of other factors, they can find themselves in conflict with one another. This type of conflict comes about as a result of affiliative constraints—the connections and affiliations within the group are causing problems for the members of the group. Egocentric constraints occur when a person puts herself or himself ahead of the group. Conflict occurs because someone forgets to work for the benefit of the group and, instead, works for the benefit of themselves. Leaders must manage these power dynamics by implementing procedures to resolve conflict and by encouraging group members to share feelings and discuss problems openly and productively.

leadership behaviors
The ability to make sense of information and solve problems.

cognitive constraints
Problems that affect how a group thinks about its tasks.

affiliative constraints
Problems that come about as a result of power dynamics in a group, particularly when the connections and affiliations within a group are causing problems for the members of the group.

egocentric constraints
Problems that come about when a person puts herself or himself ahead of the group.

By gaining and evaluating information and by helping the group overcome cognitive, affiliative, and egocentric constraints, leaders can help their group accomplish their task. Leaders use informative, invitational, and persuasive speaking in this process. They use informative speaking to present new information to their group members. They use invitational speaking to present perspectives, explore issues, and to promote a climate of respect and openness. Finally, they use persuasion to influence both members of the group and members of the larger community to accept the group's decisions or proposals.

Tips for Being an Effective Leader

The following tips can help you become an effective group leader.

*   *Ask questions.* At times, open-ended questions that facilitate the exchange of ideas and opinions are important ways to generate discussion. At other times, asking yes-or-no questions can help the group arrive at decisions.

*   *Summarize discussion at key times.* When discussion of one topic dies down, summarize the ideas that have been discussed before moving to a new topic. At the end of meetings, summarize what was discussed and set goals for future meetings.

*   *Involve everyone in discussions.* Some group members will be more willing to share their ideas than others; some groups will be very quiet during discussions. Involve everyone in a discussion by creating an environment in which all members are comfortable expressing their ideas. Invitational speaking may be very helpful here.

*   *Keep the group on task.* By reminding group members of the task at hand and by using statements that direct the group to discuss the issues related to their task purpose, you can help groups move efficiently toward problem solving.

 To learn additional information about cultivating leadership skills, complete InfoTrac College Edition Exercise 20.1, "Improving Leadership," online under Student Resources for Chapter 20 at the *Invitation to Public Speaking* Web site.

Participating in Groups

Sometimes you are a participant in a group, not the leader. In this role you do several things. As a group participant you add important ideas to the group discussions. You also are a vital part of helping the group meet its goals. Finally, as a group participant, you are necessary to the social functioning of a group. Remember, the most effective small groups are greater than the sum of their parts, meaning that although leadership is important, group members are equally important elements of the group.[4]

The success of a group depends on each of its members acting in ways that benefit the group. As such, group members take on specific roles that help the group succeed. For example, one person in the group might take notes at meetings, and another might tell jokes to lighten the mood. As you read the descriptions of the group member roles that follow, keep in mind that members may take on many roles and that at different times some roles will be more important than others.

There are three primary types of roles: group task roles, group building and maintenance roles, and egocentric roles.[5] The first two types help the group, whereas the third type causes problems for the group.

Help the Group Complete Tasks Successfully

Group task roles are positions that help the group achieve its task. These roles help the group manage cognitive constraints. Here is a description of some of these roles:

- The *initiator contributor* suggests new ideas related to the group's problem or goal or suggests a new solution that has not been considered.

- The *information seeker* asks for clarification of issues discussed, questions the accuracy of statements made, or seeks out facts related to the group's task.

- The *opinion seeker* asks for clarification of the values contained in the group's discussion and in the decisions made.

- The *information giver* offers facts relevant to the discussion or relates personal experiences to the group's goal.

- The *opinion giver* offers his or her opinion about what the values relevant to the group's discussion should be. This person does not discuss facts or information pertaining to the group's goal.

- The *coordinator* seeks to bring various groups or ideas together and looks for relationships among ideas discussed by other group members.

- The *energizer* stimulates the group to a higher level of activity when discussion slows or energy is at a low point.

- The *recorder* keeps a record of group actions, such as minutes for a meeting.

group task roles
Positions that help a group achieve its task.

Help Build and Maintain the Group

Groups also have members who take on **group building and maintenance roles.** These roles help strengthen, organize, and keep the group focused and moving forward. They help group members get along better and overcome affiliative constraints:

- The *encourager* praises the ideas of others and communicates warmth to the other group members so they will feel comfortable expressing their views.

- The *harmonizer* mediates differences between group members and seeks to relieve tension in the group.

- The *compromiser* adjusts his or her own status, previous statements, or positions to appease others and keep the group moving to its goal.

- The *gatekeeper/expediter* keeps communication channels open by watching the group's proceedings and making sure everyone has a turn to speak.

group building and maintenance roles
Positions that help strengthen, organize, and keep a group focused and moving forward.

Avoid Placing Individual Needs Above Group Needs

Egocentric roles place the group member above the group and are destructive to the group. Group participants who take on these egocentric roles want to have their own needs fulfilled before those of the group. Here is a description of some of these roles:

- The *aggressor* attacks other group members, deflates the status of others, or attacks the problem the group is discussing.

- The *blocker* resists movement by the group, disagrees with group discussion without reason, or attempts to bring back an idea that has already been dismissed.

egocentric roles
Positions that place the group member above the group and are destructive to the group.

- The *recognition seeker* calls attention to self through boasting and placing himself or herself in a superior position.
- The *self-confessor* discloses feelings, opinions, or ideologies not related to the group's task or mission.
- The *cynic* is pessimistic about the group and displays a lack of involvement in the group.
- The *dominator* asserts control over the group by manipulating the other group members.

Tips for Being an Effective Group Participant

It is probably easy to see how being a group leader requires a special set of skills. But being a group participant also has certain responsibilities and group members must also have special skills in order for the group to be effective. Here are some ideas to keep in mind as you interact in groups:

- *Always consider the goals of the group.* Act in ways that help the group achieve its goals. Seek to fulfill roles that other group members haven't already filled. Be flexible about which roles you are willing to play for the group. Do not be afraid to play a role that is outside your comfort area if you think it will help the group.

© CORBIS

- *Consider your nonverbal communication signals.* Although you might not intend to send negative messages to the group, crossed arms may signify you are closed to what is being discussed. Lack of eye contact might indicate you do not respect the other group members. Consistently being late for meetings might show you have more important priorities than the group. Keep in mind that nonverbal communication is somewhat subjective, and the meanings for nonverbal communication vary from culture to culture.

Being able to work effectively as part of a team is a valuable skill in today's workplace. There are many roles you can take on in a group that fit your particular personality, abilities, and contributions, such as an encourager. What role do you find yourself taking on in most small groups? What role would you most like to take on? What role would you least like to take on? Why?

- *Avoid interpersonal conflict.* When faced with group members who are enacting egocentric roles, consider the various ways you might confront them or their behavior, and guide the group back to a discussion of the issue at hand. Avoid adopting an egocentric role yourself to counter the disruptive group member. Such behavior may result in a downward spiral in which group task work suffers.

Speech Step 20.1 / Consider How Your Speaking Situation and Communication Affects a Group

Consider your next speech in a group. Is this a group you decided, have been asked, or are required to participate in? What effect does do you think this speaking situation will have on your participation in the group? What role will you likely take on in this group? Whatever that role is, how can you ensure your communication will help the group achieve its goals?

Group Problem Solving

With a better understanding of the structure of groups, we can now turn our attention to the task of groups: solving problems. One of the most widely used methods of solving problems is the reflective thinking method, developed by philosopher John Dewey.[6] The **reflective thinking method** is a five-step method for structuring a problem solving discussion. Reflective thinking involves taking a careful, systematic approach to a problem. The five steps of this model are:

- Identify the problem.
- Analyze the problem.
- Suggest possible solutions.
- Consider the implications of the solutions.
- Reach a decision about the best solution.

Many researchers have added a sixth step, implementing the solution, which we discuss later. To learn more about the philosophy of John Dewey, visit the Center for Dewey Studies Web site at http://www.siu.edu/~deweyctr/.

Let's explore how the reflective-thinking method works by taking a look at a real-world example. The Moorhead Public School District in Minnesota used a series of small groups to create a plan for its future. The task force was a group of fifteen people who met for three months in 2001 to help improve education and the cost of that education in Moorhead, Minnesota. The group was charged with making policy recommendations to the superintendent of schools and the local community. In essence, the group had to determine how the school district should manage deteriorating facilities and decreasing enrollments. To learn more about this initiative, visit the Moorhead Schools Web site at http://www.moorhead.k12.mn.us/www/district/superintendent/taskforces/index.htm.

reflective thinking method
Five-step method for structuring a problem solving discussion: identify the problem, analyze the problem, suggest possible solutions, consider the implications of the solutions, and reach a decision about the best solution.

Identify the Problem

The first step of the reflective-thinking model is problem identification. In this stage of the decision-making process, group participants identify the nature of the problem, the extent of the problem, who is affected by the problem, and the impact on those affected.

> The Moorhead Schools task force identified the problem as the cost to repair old schools, shifting demographics in the region which had resulted in decreasing enrollments, and problems with the current model for determining grade levels.

Once the group identified the problems that these issues presented to the school district and local community, it could move on to the next step of the model, problem analysis.

Analyze the Problem

It might be natural to jump to a discussion of solutions to the problems that have been identified. Instead, effective group communication starts by discussing why the problem exists. Much like a physician who must diagnose a patient's illness, the reflective thinker must understand the causes of the problem before moving on to discussing solutions. Besides helping the group arrive at a more reasoned solution, this step helps the group present its findings more successfully.

The task force isolated several reasons why the current school buildings and models for grade level were not working to provide a quality education. The school buildings were not designed for smaller classes, they did not allow the district to implement new programs, and they were not set up for new technology. The group's diagnosis was that the current school buildings could not solve the problems the district faced.

Suggest Possible Solutions

After group members have thought carefully about the reasons the problems exist, they can move on to suggesting solutions. A popular method used by groups at this stage of the problem analysis process is *brainstorming*. Recall from Chapter 4 that **brainstorming** is the process of generating ideas randomly and uncritically, without attention to logic, connections, or relevance. When groups brainstorm, they suggest as many ideas as they can think of without judging those ideas. After the group has listed as many ideas as possible, they can do two things. They can go through the list and eliminate those ideas that are not suitable until just a few options remain. Or the group may rank a longer list of options, then choose the solution that has the most support.

> The task force discussed several solutions to their problems. The task force considered building new schools, remodeling existing schools, and exploring a variety of grade-level configurations. It was tentatively decided that two new schools would be built, some existing schools would be converted to accommodate additional grades, and several schools would be demolished or sold.

A potential pitfall for groups as they generate solutions is a concept known as **groupthink**,[7] which occurs when the group conforms to a single frame of mind and chooses a solution without fully and objectively examining other potential solutions. Groups that fall victim to groupthink often are under a tight time line, are pressured by the leader, or are afraid to question each other's ideas. They also tend to get along well and favor consensus over conflict. Groupthink can be avoided by having a group member play the role of devil's advocate, questioning everything that is said; by removing the group's leader from discussions; or by taking time to fully evaluate each solution. To learn more about groupthink, complete Interactive Activity 20.1, "Avoiding Groupthink," found online at the *Invitation to Public Speaking* Web site under Student Resources for Chapter 20.

WEB SITE

> The task force avoided groupthink by having a reasonable time line for their discussions, not including the school superintendent in the discussion, and by weighing models from across the state of Minnesota. In the end, the group was fairly confident in its decision.

Consider the Implications of the Solution

After a group has arrived at a potential solution, it studies the implications of the solution. The group should avoid immediately enacting the solution and instead take time to examine its disadvantages or impact on others.

> For the task force, financing was an important consideration. The estimated cost for building new schools and renovating existing buildings was $64 million. Upon further investigation, the group discovered that the cost of renovating all the schools in the district, many of which were old, and maintaining them would be far greater than the cost of the new plan. Additionally, the task force learned the state would pay for half of the cost.

brainstorming
Process of generating ideas randomly and uncritically, without attention to logic, connections, or relevance.

groupthink
Act of a group conforming to a single frame of mind and choosing a solution without fully and objectively examining other potential solutions.

Reach a Decision About the Best Solution

Groups may use several methods to reach a decision about the best solution. For example, if the group has time and resources to implement a pilot study, it can study the effects of the decision over a period of time. Groups can also use reasoning to choose the solution that has the fewest detrimental effects.

> Upon further reflection, the task force reasoned that public support would be strongest for the most affordable plan and for one that provided maximum flexibility for future school district expansion or retraction. The tentative solution was sound, and the group chose to advocate this plan publicly.

Implement the Solution

Researchers often include a sixth step in Dewey's reflective-thinking model: implementing the solution. In this stage, the group determines how to carry out what it has decided. It is important for the group to consider who will be responsible for the different parts of the solution and when the solution should be implemented.

> The task force presented a final report to the school district, which voted to adopt the plan and call for a special bond election to determine if the local community would support the tax increase. The proposal passed, and work began on building new schools and renovating existing ones.

When you work in groups, you will be faced with a variety of problems to solve and issues to sort through. When you use six steps for solving problems, you can help your group arrive at a solution that will actually solve the problem and that should benefit all involved. Combined with your understanding of group dynamics, which includes the roles people in groups play as well as the constraints that prevent a group from working together well, you now are ready to begin planning your presentation. The speeches you will give in a group are as varied as the roles you may play, but each type involves using the skills for public speaking you have learned throughout this book.

Speech Step 20.2 / Practice Your Group Problem-Solving Skills

Identify the problem your group must solve. Follow the reflective-thinking process to solve this problem. What roles do you think you will take on to help your group solve its problem? How can you avoid cognitive, affective, and ego-centric constraints?

Conducting Meetings

One of the most common forms of public speaking in groups is conducting meetings. When you conduct a meeting, you assume the role of leader for a period of time. You prepare an agenda so people stay focused, and you manage the flow of conversation so people stay on track. To conduct a successful meeting, follow the guidelines outlined here.

Provide an Agenda in Advance

agenda
A list of topics that will be discussed in a meeting and for how long.

Several days before the meeting, provide meeting participants with an agenda. The **agenda** lists what topics will be discussed and for how long. If possible, gather topics for the meeting from group members before you pass out the agenda. Make sure the progression of items is logical (for example, follow a chronological pattern that moves from old business to new business, or another organizational pattern that helps the group stay focused). If you cannot distribute a copy of the agenda to the group before the meeting, pass it out at the start of the meeting so the group can follow your plan as the meeting unfolds.

Specify the Time and Location of the Meeting

Clearly state the start time, end time, and location for the meeting. Include this information on the agenda, or post it where group members will see it. Although it sometimes is difficult to specify an ending time, meetings that have one typically stay on topic, and groups are more likely to solve problems within the time frame they are allowed. In addition, group members need to know how long a meeting will last so they can schedule other meetings and events more accurately.

Be Prepared for the Meeting

The best meetings are meetings in which both the leader and the group members are prepared. When group members have not read meeting materials or have not thought about issues that will be discussed, an ineffective meeting is often the result. To avoid this, distribute important materials to group members beforehand so they have time to read them and think about them. Be sure you read the materials carefully ahead of time. Think carefully about the issues and how you will manage the discussion around them. Prepare any visual aids beforehand and check your equipment. Notify group members in advance if you want them to report on their activities to the group so they can prepare their presentations. Plan to follow the six steps for reflective thinking to help the group solve problems and stay focused.

Use an Effective Procedure for Conducting Meetings

Group members must know the rules governing who may speak, how decisions will be made, and how votes will be taken. Many groups use a form of *Robert's Rules of Order* to conduct their business. To learn more about *Robert's Rules of Order* and to modify this set of rules for a group, complete Interactive Activity 20.2, "Robert's Rules of Order Revised," online under Student Resources for Chapter 20 at the *Invitation to Public Speaking* Web site. Remember to appoint someone to take notes or to ask a volunteer to do so.

WEB SITE

Communicate Effectively as a Leader

Review the material discussed earlier in this appendix so you can communicate effectively as you conduct a meeting. Remember to ask questions, summarize the discussion at key points, involve everyone in the process, and keep the group focused.

Distribute the Minutes of the Meeting to Group Members

After the meeting, provide copies of the minutes to group members. The minutes, or notes, of a meeting should clearly identify what the group discussed and any action taken by the group. Be sure to identify group members who are responsible for certain tasks and assignments. Provide reports of these actions at future group meetings.

Making Group Presentations

As a member of a group, you may be called on to make formal group presentations. There are four common formats that you may be asked to follow: oral reports, panel discussions, symposiums, and team presentations. These four types of presentations are briefly described and summarized in Table 20.1.

Oral Reports

Oral reports are speeches given by an individual that present a group's findings, conclusions, or proposals to other members of the group or to a larger audience. When you present an oral report, use the skills you have learned in this book for giving a speech to present your report. Remember to write your general purpose, specific purpose, and thesis statement. Outline your main points and select your pattern of organization. Be sure to prepare an introduction that catches your audience's attention, reveals the topic of your report, establishes your credibility, and previews your main points. Include connectives during your report and write a conclusion that reinforces your thesis statement and brings your presentation to a close.

oral report
Speech given by an individual that presents a group's findings, conclusions, or proposals to other members of a group or to a larger audience.

For example, a consulting company might make an oral report to a university that is considering a move to Division I athletics. The consultant responsible for the study could hold a public presentation in which members of the university, local media, and public were invited. The consultant could present the rationale for the recommendation to switch to Division I and field questions from the audience.

Table 20.1

Types of Group Presentations

Oral report	• Speech given by one member of a group in order to present findings, conclusions, or proposals to an audience.
Panel discussion	• Informal discussion among group members in which they respond and react to each others' ideas.
	• Often includes comments and responses from the audience.
Symposium	• Formal presentations on the same topic by group members.
	• Group members do not necessarily have the same goal or purpose. They may disagree with one another.
Team presentation	• Well-coordinated, formal presentations on the same topic by group members.
	• Each presentation builds support for the goal of the presentation.

A panel discussion allows group members to interact with each other and an audience. Despite its somewhat informal format, group members should use appropriate verbal and nonverbal communication when they are communicating, but also when they are listening and responding to other panel members. What is the panelist on the left communicating through his nonverbal communication? Is he interested in the speaker's ideas? How can you tell?

© Reuters NewMedia Inc./CORBIS

Panel Discussions

A **panel discussion** is a structured discussion, facilitated by a moderator, among group members that takes place in front of an audience. When you are part of a panel discussion, you not only share your ideas with the other members of your group, you also share them with a larger audience. A panel discussion typically begins with brief opening statements by each of the panelists, followed by an informal discussion among them about their ideas. A moderator, who may be a member of the panel, facilitates the discussion. Usually the discussion becomes more focused as group members learn from each other and the audience. Occasionally the moderator or panel members may wrap up the discussion and summarize what has been said, but just as often, the discussion ends without resolution or summary. Because the goal of the panel discussion is to react to the ideas of another person, it is an ideal setting for invitational speeches. Group members can present their current thinking on a topic, learn from each other and the audience, and refine their ideas for future decision making.

When you are a part of a panel discussion, prepare your opening remarks beforehand, thinking of your speech as a short informative speech that previews what you hope to discuss during the session. Then view your participation in the discussion as a series of short speeches in which you develop a particular idea, invite others to understand your perspective or explore an issue with the other panel members, or encourage others to adopt your views. For example, the student government on your campus might hold a panel discussion to explore an issue such as parking or tuition increases. Representatives of various groups, including students, administrators, faculty, and staff, would briefly offer their reactions to the issue and then discuss the issue with the others and with the audience. The discussion would help the panelists and audience to better understand the implications of the issue.

Symposiums

A **symposium** is a public discussion in which several people each give speeches on different aspects of the same topic. Unlike panel discussions, which usually feature short opening statements by the participants, symposium speakers usually have fully prepared speeches that are formally presented. At a symposium, speakers either are experts in a particular subject area, or a topic may be divided into different areas so the audience can learn about many aspects of a single topic. If you are a part of a symposium, a moderator usually introduces each speaker, their topics, and facilitates audience questions and comments if appropriate. Symposiums typically feature three to five speakers with each person speaking for ten to fifteen minutes. Typically a symposium session lasts anywhere from one to two hours, with the time divided between the participant and audience questions.

For example, a group of scientists might hold a symposium in which they talk about a topic, such as the advantages and disadvantages of genetic cloning. Each scientist would offer his or her perspective on the topic, and the audience would then respond and react to the presentations. One scientist may focus on the medical benefits of cloning, and another could address the research procedures, including costs and risks. A third might focus on the ethical implications of cloning while a fourth could address the ways scientists from various nations have and could work together with respect to cloning research. Taken together, the audience would hear a wide range of perspectives on cloning and then ask questions of each presenter.

If you are a part of a symposium, follow the procedures for giving your speech outlined in this text. You probably will find that you use a manuscript for this presentation or that your speaking outline is quite detailed. Remember to stay within your time limits so other speakers can present their speeches and to ensure time for the question-and-answer session. Typically, a moderator will time the speeches and give signals to the speakers as their time reaches the end. Be sure to practice your presentations before you give the speech and to anticipate questions from the audience so you can formulate your answers.

Team Presentations

A **team presentation** is a presentation made by several members of the group, with each person presenting a different speech on a single topic. For instance, you might make a team presentation with other members of your group so you can present a solution to a problem you have solved. Each of the speeches is formal, with speakers addressing different parts of the solution and each speaker using similar delivery styles. There also is a continuous flow from one speaker to another. To make sure the presentation flows smoothly, team presentations usually have one group member acting as the moderator.

If you give a team presentation, it should be well organized, using one of the organizational patterns discussed in this book. Ask each group member to give a speech on a single main point, and ask one group member to present the introduction and conclusion. This person usually is the moderator, and she or he may introduce each speaker and their topics. If your group used the reflective-thinking model to solve a problem, the steps of the process make excellent main ideas in a speech.

For example, an advertising team could make a team presentation to a client proposing a specific ad campaign. One team member would introduce the group and briefly describe the presentation (similar to a speech preview). Another would identify and describe the target market for the advertising campaign. A third speaker would showcase the television ads that will be part of the campaign, and a fourth would show the print ads that would be used. Finally, a fifth team member (or perhaps the first speaker) would summarize the group's proposal and facilitate questions from the potential clients. All members of the group would participate in the discussion and question-and-answer session.

team presentation
Presentation made by several members of the group, with each person presenting a different speech on a single topic.

Tips for Effective Group Presentations

Whatever type of group presentation you make, keep in mind some general tips. These tips will help you organize your ideas and work together as a group so each group member can deliver an effective speech.

- *Consider the group's purpose when selecting a presentation format and audience.* If the group is in the preliminary stages of identifying a problem, the panel discussion may be the best format to use. Later, the group may wish to use the symposium format to air ideas for a more particular audience. When finished with the task, the group may choose to make a team presentation or an oral presentation to the audience that will enact the group's solution.

- *Use appropriate delivery style and skills.* Panel discussions usually consist of impromptu and extemporaneous speeches. Symposiums and team presentations are usually extemporaneous or they are delivered from a manuscript or even memorized. In addition, group members must remember that even when they are not speaking, they still are communicating with the audience. Facial expressions or gestures or body postures that contradict another speaker's message send confusing signals to the audience. Note that small group formats often foster invitational speaking, so make sure your nonverbal and verbal messages reflect this approach.

- *Organize your presentation.* For each type of small group presentation, one group member should introduce the speakers. Likewise, one group member should offer concluding remarks. Organize the rest of the presentation in a format consistent with the purpose of the presentation and the type of format used. Panel discussions will have a looser organization than a symposium. Team presentations and oral reports will be highly structured so the group can achieve its goal and present its information effectively.

- *Use effective visual aids as needed.* If visual aids are used, all members of the audience should be able to see them. For a team presentation, in particular, coordinate visual aids so they have similar backgrounds, colors, and fonts.

 Speech Step 20.3 / Design a Group Presentation Speech

Select the format you will use for your next speech in a group. Do you think the goals of the presentation best match an oral report, panel discussion, symposium, or team presentation? Once you have decided on the format, identify the speaking role each member of the group will take on (moderator, first main point, second main point, and so on). Using the skills you've learned throughout this course and in this appendix, design your group presentation speech.

Invitation to Public Speaking Online

After reading this chapter, use your CD-ROM and the *Invitation to Public Speaking* Web site to review the key concepts, access the online review questions, and complete the suggested Web Link questions, Interactive Activities, and InfoTrac College Edition Exercises. You can access the book's Web site via your CD-ROM or at http://www.wadsworth.com/product/griffin.

Key Concepts

small group speaking (465)
small group (466)
roles (468)
leadership behaviors (469)
cognitive constraints (469)
affiliative constraints (469)
egocentric constraints (469)
group task roles (471)
group building and maintenance roles (471)
egocentric roles (471)
reflective thinking method (473)
brainstorming (474)
groupthink (474)
agenda (476)
oral report (477)
panel discussion (478)
symposium (478)
team presentation (479)

Web Links

20.1: National Breast Cancer Coalition (467)
20.2: The Philosophy of John Dewey (473)
20.3: Moorehead, Minnesota, Schools Task Force (473)

InfoTrac College Edition Exercises

20.1: **Improving Leadership** (470)
Purpose: To learn strategies by which to become a more effective leader.

Interactive Activities

20.1: Avoiding Groupthink (474)
Purpose: To understand groupthink, its effects, and solutions..

20.2: Robert's Rules of Order Revised (476)
Purpose: To create a modified version of Robert's Rules of Order for use in a small group.

Glossary

abstract word Word that refers to ideas or concepts but not to specific objects.

abstract Summary of the text contained in an article or publication.

acceptance speech A speech that acknowledges gratitude, appreciation, and pleasure at receiving an honor or a gift.

ad hominen fallacy Argument in which a speaker attacks a person rather than that person's arguments.

affiliative constraints Problems that come about as a result of power dynamics in a group, particularly when the connections and affiliations within a group are causing problems for the members of the group.

affirmations Positive, motivating statements that replace negative self-talk.

agenda A list of topics that will be discussed in a meeting and for how long.

alliteration Repetition of a particular sound in a sentence or a phrase

analogical reasoning Process of reasoning suggesting that because two conditions or events resemble each other in ways that are certain, they will resemble each other in other ways that are less certain.

antithesis Placement of words and phrases in contrast or opposition to one another.

argument Set of statements that allows you to develop your evidence in order to establish the validity of your claim.

articulation Physical process of producing specific speech sounds in order to make language intelligible.

attitude General positive or negative feeling a person has about something.

audience Group of people who gather to listen.

audience centered Acknowledging your audience by considering and listening to the unique, diverse, and common perspectives of its members before, during, and after your speech.

audience centered Considerate of the positions, beliefs, values, and needs of an audience.

audience The complex and varied group of people the speaker addresses.

auditory listener Listener who needs to hear verbal explanations and descriptions to learn well.

balance Relationship of the items on a visual aid to one another.

bandwagon fallacy Argument that something is correct or good because everyone else agrees with it or is doing it.

bar graph A graph that compares quantities at a specific moment in time.

behavioral objectives The actions a speaker wants the audience to take at the end of a speech.

belief A person's idea of what is real or true or not.

bias Unreasoned distortion of judgment or prejudice about a topic.

bibliographic database A database that indexes publishing data for books, periodical articles, government reports, statistics, patents, research reports, conference proceedings, and dissertations.

bookmark A menu entry or icon that allows you to return directly to a site without typing in its URL or linking to it through other sites (also called a *favorite*).

Boolean operators Words you can use to create specific phrases that broaden or narrow your search on the Internet.

brainstorming Process of generating ideas randomly and uncritically, without attention to logic, connections, or relevance.

brainstorming Process of generating ideas randomly and uncritically, without attention to logic, connections, or relevance.

brief narrative Story that takes only a short time to tell and illustrates a specific point (sometimes called *vignette*).

browser Software program that allows you to search for, find, and display information on your computer screen.

call to action Request that an audience engage in some clearly stated behavior.

canon of arrangement Guidelines for ordering the ideas in a speech.

canon of delivery Guidelines for managing your voice, gestures, posture, facial expressions, and visual aids as you present your speech.

canon of invention Guidelines for generating effective content for a speech.

canon of memory Guidelines for the time taken to rehearse a speech and the ways you prompt yourself to remember the speech as you give it.

canon of style Guidelines for using language effectively and appropriately.

canon Authoritative list, an accepted principle or rule, or an accepted standard of judgment.

causal pattern Pattern of organization that describes a cause-and-effect relationship between ideas.

causal reasoning Process of reasoning that supports a claim by establishing a cause-and-effect relationship.

channel Means by which the message is conveyed.

character Audience's view of a speaker's sincerity, trustworthiness, and concern for the well-being of the audience.

character Audience's view of a speaker's sincerity, trustworthiness, and concern for the well-being of the audience.

chronological pattern Pattern of organization that traces a sequence of events or ideas.

civility Care and concern for others, the thoughtful use of words and language, and the flexibility to see the many sides of an issue.

claim Assertion that must be proved.

close-ended question Question that requires the respondent to choose an answer from two or more alternatives.

cognitive constraints Problems that affect how a group thinks about its tasks

cognitive restructuring A process that helps reduce anxiety by replacing negative thoughts with positive ones, called affirmations.

colloquialism Local or regional informal dialect or expression.

commemorative speech Speech that praises, honors, recognizes, or pays tribute to a person, an event, an idea, or an institution.

commemorative speech Speech that praises, honors, recognizes, or pays tribute to a person, an event, an idea, or an institution.

common ground Similarities, shared interests, and mutual perspectives a speaker has with an audience.

communication apprehension The level of fear or anxiety associated with either real or anticipated communication with another person or persons.

comparative advantages organization Organizational pattern that illustrates the advantages of one solution over others.

competence Audience's view of a speaker's intelligence, expertise, and knowledge of a subject.

competence Audience's view of a speaker's intelligence, expertise, and knowledge of a subject.

conclusion Logical outcome of an argument that results from the combination of the major and minor premises.

concrete word Word that refers to a tangible object—a person, place, or thing.

condition of equality Condition of an invitational speech that requires the speaker sees audience members as holding equally valid perspectives and positions that are worthy of exploration.

condition of self-determination Condition of an invitational speech that requires the speaker recognizes that people know what is best for them and have the right to make choices about their lives based on this knowledge.

condition of value Condition of an invitational speech that requires the speaker recognizes that the views of the members of the audience, although they may differ from the speaker's, have inherent value.

confirming Recognizing, acknowledging, and expressing value for another person.

connective A word or a phrase used to link ideas in a speech.

connotative definition The subjective meaning of a word or phrase based on personal experiences and beliefs.

considerate speech Speech that eases the audience's burden of processing information.

context Environment or situation in which a speech occurs.

conversational style Speaking style that is more formal than everyday conversation but remains spontaneous and relaxed.

coordination The process of arranging points into successive levels, with points on a specific level having the same weight or value.

counterarguments Arguments against the speaker's own position.

credibility Audience's perception of a speaker's competence and character.

credibility Audience's perception of a speaker's competence and character.

critical listener Listener who listens for the accuracy of a speech's content and the implications of a speaker's message.

culturally inclusive language Language that respectfully recognizes the differences among the many cultures in our society.

database Collections of information stored electronically so they are easy to find and retrieve.

decoding Translating words, sounds, and gestures into ideas and feelings in an attempt to understand the message.

deductive reasoning Process of reasoning that uses a familiar and commonly accepted claim to establish the truth of a very specific claim.

definition Statement of the exact meaning of a word or phrase.

delivery Action and manner of speaking to an audience.

demographic audience analysis Analysis that identifies the particular population traits of an audience.

demonstration Display of how something is done or how it works.

denotative definition The objective definition of a word or a phrase you would find in a dictionary.

derived credibility Credibility a speaker develops during a speech.

dialect Pattern of speech that is shared among ethnic groups or people from specific geographic locations.

dialogue An interaction, connection, and exchange of ideas and opinions with others.

direct quotation Exact word-for-word presentation of another's testimony.

drawing Diagram sketch of someone or something.

effective listener Overcomes listener interference in order to better understand a speaker's message.

egocentric constraints Problems that come about when a person puts herself or himself ahead of the group.

egocentric roles Positions that place the group member above the group and are destructive to the group.

either-or fallacy Argument in which a speaker claims our options are "either A or B," when actually more than two options exist. Sometimes called a *false dilemma*.

empathy Trying to see and understand the world as another person does.

encoding Translating ideas and feelings into words, sounds, and gestures.

ethical listener Listener who considers the moral impact of a speaker's message on one's self and one's community.

ethnocentrism Belief that our own cultural perspectives, norms, and ways of organizing society are superior to others.

ethos The word Aristotle used to refer to the speaker's credibility.

etymology The history of a word.

euphemism A word or phrase that substitutes an agreeable or inoffensive expression for one that may offend or suggest something unpleasant.

evidence The materials that speakers use to support their ideas.

example Specific instance used to illustrate a concept, experience, issue, or problem.

experiential listener Listener who needs to touch, explore, and participate in what is being described.

expert testimony Testimony of someone considered an authority in a particular field.

extemporaneous speech A speech that is carefully prepared and practiced from brief notes rather than from memory or a written manuscript.

extended narrative   Story that takes longer to tell and can be integrated into a speech more fully.

eye contact   Visual contact with another person's eyes.

fallacy   Argument that seems valid but is flawed because of unsound evidence or reasoning.

false cause   Error in reasoning in which a speaker assumes that one event caused another simply because the first event happened before the second.

fear appeal   Threat of something undesirable happening if change does not occur.

feedback   Verbal and nonverbal signals an audience gives a speaker.

flow chart   A chart that illustrates direction or motion.

font size   Size of the letters in a particular font, measured in *points*.

font   Type or style of print.

full-text database   A database that indexes the complete text of newspapers, periodicals, encyclopedias, research reports, court cases, books, and the like.

gain immediate action   Motivate an audience to engage in a specific behavior or take a specific action.

gain passive agreement   Ask an audience to adopt a new position without also asking them to act in support of that position.

gender-inclusive language   Language recognizing that both women and men are active participants in the world.

general purpose   A speech's broad goal: to inform, invite, persuade, introduce, commemorate, or accept.

gestures   Movements, usually of the hands but sometimes of the full body, that express meaning and emotion or offer clarity to a message.

global plagiarism   Stealing an entire speech from a single source and presenting it as your own.

graph   Visual comparison of amounts or quantities that show growth, size, proportions, or relationships.

group building and maintenance roles   Positions that help strengthen, organize, and keep a group focused and moving forward.

group communication   Communication among members of a team or a collective about topics such as goals, strategies, and conflict.

group task roles   Positions that help a group achieve its task.

groupthink   Act of a group conforming to a single frame of mind and choosing a solution without fully and objectively examining other potential solutions.

hasty generalization   Error in reasoning in which a speaker reaches a conclusion without enough evidence to support it.

hearing   Vibration of sound waves on our eardrums and the impulses then sent to the brain.

hypothetical example   Instance that did not take place but could have.

idiom   Fixed, distinctive expression whose meaning is not indicated by its individual words.

impromptu speech   Speech that is not planned or prepared in advance.

incremental plagiarism   Presenting select portions from a single speech as your own.

index   Alphabetical listing of the topics discussed in a specific publication, along with the corresponding year, volume, and page numbers.

inductive reasoning   Process of reasoning that uses specific instances, or examples, to make a claim about a general conclusion.

inferences   The mental leaps we make when we agree that a speaker's evidence supports his or her claims.

inflection   Manipulation of pitch to create certain meanings or moods.

information overload   When we take in more information than we can process but realize there still is more information we are expected to know.

informative speaking environment   Environment in which a speaker has expertise or knowledge that an audience needs but doesn't already have.

informative speech   A speech that communicates knowledge and understanding about a process, an event, a person or place, an object, or a concept.

informative speech   Speech that communicates knowledge and understanding about a process, an event, a person or place, an object, or a concept.

initial credibility   Credibility a speaker has before giving a speech.

interference   Anything that stops or hinders a listener from receiving a message.

internal preview   A statement in the body of a speech that details what the speaker plans to discuss next.

internal summary   A statement in the body of a speech that summarizes a point a speaker has already discussed.

Internet   An electronic communications network that links computer networks around the world via telephone lines, cables, and communication satellites.

interpersonal communication   Communication with other people that ranges from the highly personal to the highly impersonal.

intertextuality   Process in which stories reference other stories or rely on parts of other stories to be complete.

interview   Planned interaction with another person that is organized around inquiry and response, with one person asking questions while the other person answers them.

intrapersonal communication   Communication with ourselves via the dialogue that goes on in our heads.

introductory speech   Speech that gives the audience a sense of the unique perspective of the person introduced or that welcomes and familiarizes the audience with an event.

invitational environment   Environment in which understanding, respecting, and appreciating the range of positions possible on an issue, even if those positions are quite different from the speaker's own, is the highest priority.

invitational speaking   A type of public speaking in which a speaker enters into a dialogue with an audience in order to clarify positions, explore issues and ideas, or articulate beliefs and values.

invitational speech   A speech that allows the speaker to enter into a dialogue with an audience in order to clarify positions, explore issues and ideas, or share beliefs and values.

jargon   Technical language used by a special group or for a special activity.

language   System of verbal or gestural symbols a community uses to communicate with one another.

leadership behaviors   The ability to make sense of information and solve problems.

line graph   A graph that shows trends over time.

links   Icons or highlighted words and phrases that take you from site to site or from one part of a site to another.

list   Series of words or phrases that organize ideas one after the other.

listenable speech   Speech that is considerate and delivered in an oral style.

listening   The process of giving thoughtful attention to another person's words and understanding what you hear.

logos   The word Aristotle used to refer to the logical arrangement of evidence in a speech.

main points   The most important ideas you address in your speech.

major premise   Claim in an argument that states a familiar, commonly accepted belief. Also called the *general principle*.

manuscript speech   Speech that is read to an audience from a written text.

map   Visual representation of geographic features, urban areas, roads, stars and planets, and the like.

mass communication   Communication generated by media organizations that is designed to reach large audiences.

master statuses   Significant positions occupied by a person within society that affect that person's identity in almost all social situations.

mean   Average of a group of numbers.

median   Middle number in a series or set of numbers arranged in a ranked order.

memorized speech   Speech that has been written out, committed to memory, and given word for word.

message   Information conveyed by the speaker to the audience.

metaphor   A figure of speech that makes a comparison between two things by describing one thing as being something else.

minor premise   Claim in an argument that states a specific instance linked to the major premise.

mixed metaphor   Metaphor that makes illogical comparisons between two or more things.

mnemonic device   Rhyme, phrase, or other verbal device that makes information easier to remember.

mode   Number that occurs most often in a set of numbers.

model   Copy of an object, usually built to scale, that represents an object in detail.

monotone   A way of speaking in which a speaker does not alter her or his pitch

Monroe's motivated sequence   Sequential process used to persuade audiences by gaining attention, demonstrating a need, satisfying that need, visualizing beneficial results, and calling for action.

multiple perspectives pattern   Organizational pattern that allows the speaker to address the many sides and positions of an issue.

mythos   Interrelated set of beliefs, attitudes, values, and feelings held by members of a particular society or culture.

narrative   Story that re-creates or foretells real or hypothetical events.

noise   Anything that interferes with understanding the message being communicated.

object   Something that can be seen or touched.

objective   Having a fair and undistorted view on a question or issue.

open-ended question   Question that allows the respondent to answer in an unrestricted way.

oral report   Speech given by an individual that presents a group's findings, conclusions, or proposals to other members of a group or to a larger audience.

oral style   Speaking style that reflects the spoken rather than the written word.

organization   Systematic arrangement of ideas into a coherent whole.

organizational chart   A chart that illustrates the makeup of groups.

panel discussion   Structured discussion, facilitated by a moderator, among group members that takes place in front of an audience.

parallelism   Arrangement of related words so they are balanced or of related sentences so they have identical structures.

paraphrase   Summary of another's testimony in the speaker's own words.

patchwork plagiarism   Constructing a complete speech that you present as your own from portions of several different sources.

pathos   The word Aristotle used to refer to emotional appeals made by a speaker.

pauses   Hesitations and brief silences in speech or conversation.

peer testimony   Testimony of someone who has first-hand knowledge of a topic, sometimes called *lay testimony*.

personal appearance   Way speakers dress, groom, and present themselves physically.

personal testimony   Your own testimony that you use to convey your point.

personification   A figure of speech that attributes human characteristics to animals, objects, or concepts.

persuasive speech   A speech whose message attempts to change or reinforce an audience's thoughts, feelings, or actions.

persuasive speech   Speech whose message attempts to change or reinforce an audience's thoughts, feelings, or actions.

picture graph   A graph that presents information in pictures or images.

pie graph   A graph that shows the relative proportions of parts of a whole.

pitch   Highness or lowness of a speaker's voice on the musical scale.

plagiarism   Presenting another person's words and ideas as your own.

posture   Way speakers position and carry their bodies.

preliminary bibliography   List of all the potential sources you'll use as you prepare your speech.

preparation outline   Detailed outline a speaker builds when preparing a speech that includes the title, specific purpose, thesis statement, introduction, main points and subpoints, connectives, conclusion, and source citations of the speech.

preview   Brief overview in the introduction of a speech of each of the main points in the speech.

probe   Question that fills out or follows up an answer to a previous question.

problem-and-solution pattern   Pattern of organization that identifies a specific problem and offers a possible solution.

problem-cause-solution organization   Organizational pattern that focuses on identifying a specific problem, the causes of that problem, and a solution for the problem.

problem-solution organization   Organizational pattern that focuses on persuading an audience that a specific problem exists and can be solved or minimized by a specific solution.

pronunciation   Act of saying words correctly according to the accepted standards of a language.

proxemics   Use of space during communication.

public communication   Communication in which one person gives a speech to other people, most often in a public setting

public dialogue   The civil exchange of ideas and opinions among communities about topics that affect the public.

public speaking anxiety (PSA)   The anxiety we feel when we have to give a speech or take a public speaking course.

question of fact   Question that addresses whether something is true or not.

question of policy   Question that addresses the best course of action or the best solution to a problem.

question of value   Question that addresses the merit or morality of an object, action, or belief.

rate   Speed at which a speaker speaks.

real example   Instance that actually took place.

reasoning by sign   Process of reasoning that assumes something exists or will happen based on something else that exists or has happened.

red herring fallacy   Argument that introduces irrelevant information into an argument in order to distract an audience from the real issue.

referent   Object, concept, or event a symbol represents.

reflective thinking method   Five-step method for structuring a problem solving discussion: identify the problem, analyze the problem, suggest possible solutions, consider the implications of the solutions, and reach a decision about the best solution.

repetition   Repetition of keywords or phrases at the beginnings or endings of sentences or clauses to create rhythm.

research inventory   List of the types of information you have for your speech and the types you want to find.

rhetorical question   Question a speaker asks that an audience isn't supposed to answer out loud but rather in their own minds.

rhythm   Arrangement of words into patterns so the sounds of the words together enhance the meaning of a phrase.

roles   Positions members of a group must fill in order for the group to accomplish its goals.

search engines   Sites that index Web pages and, based on subjects you provide, search them to locate relevant sites.

sign   Something that represents something else.

signpost   A simple word or statement that lets an audience know where a speaker is in a speech or that indicates an important idea.

simile   Figure of speech that makes an explicit comparison of two things, using the words *like* or *as.*

slang   Informal nonstandard vocabulary, usually made up of arbitrarily changed words.

slippery slope fallacy   Argument in which a speaker claims that taking a first step in one direction will lead to inevitable and undesirable further steps.

small group speaking   Speaking to give a presentation to a small collection of individuals or speaking as part of a small group of people.

small group speaking   Speaking to give a presentation to a small collection of individuals or speaking as part of a small group of people.

small group   Three to fifteen people who must work together to achieve a common goal and who have the ability to influence one another through verbal and nonverbal communication.

spatial pattern   Pattern of organization in which ideas are arranged in terms of location or direction.

speaker   Person who stimulates public dialogue by delivering an oral message.

speaking outline   Condensed form of a preparation outline, used to help a speaker remember his or her ideas when speaking.

specific purpose   Focused statement that identifies exactly what a speaker wants to accomplish with a speech.

speech about a concept   Informative speech about an abstraction, such as an idea, a theory, a principle, a worldview, or a belief.

speech about a place or a person   Informative speech that describes a significant, interesting, or unusual place or person.

speech about a process   Informative speech that describes how something is done, how something comes to be, or how something works.

speech about an event   Informative speech that describes or explains a significant, interesting, or unusual occurrence.

speech about an object   Informative speech about anything that is tangible, that can be perceived by the senses.

speech of award   Speech given to present a specific award to someone and describe why that person is receiving the award.

speech of tribute   Speech given to honor someone. Speech that acknowledges gratitude, appreciation, and pleasure at receiving an honor or a gift.

speech to articulate a position   Invitational speech for which the speaker invites an audience to see the world as she or he does and to understand issues from her or his perspective.

speech to entertain   Lighthearted speech that addresses issues or ideas in a humorous way.

speech to explore an issue   Invitational speech for which the speaker attempts to engage an audience in a discussion about an idea, concern, topic, or plan of action.

speech topic   Subject of your speech.

spotlighting   Practice of highlighting a person's race or ethnicity (or sex, sexual orientation, physical disability, and the like) during a speech.

standpoint   Perspective from which a person views and evaluates society.

state, or **situational, anxiety**   Apprehension about communicating with others in a particular situation.

statistics   Numerical summaries of facts, figures, and research findings.

stereotype   Broad generalization about an entire group based on limited knowledge or exposure to only certain members of that group.

subordination   The process of ranking ideas in order from the most to the least important.

subpoints   A point in a speech that develops an aspect of a main point.

sub-subpoints   A point in a speech that develops an aspect of a subpoint.

summary   Concise restatement of the main points at the end of a speech.

symbol   Word or phrase spoken by a speaker.

symposium   Public discussion in which several people each give speeches on different aspects of the same topic.

systematic desensitization   A technique for reducing anxiety that involves teaching your body to feel calm and relaxed rather than fearful during your speeches.

team presentation   Presentation made by several members of the group, with each person presenting a different speech on a single topic.

terminal credibility   Credibility given to the speaker at the end of a speech.

testimony   Opinions or observations of others.

thesis statement   Statement that summarizes in a single declarative sentence the main proposition, assumption, or argument you want to express in your speech.

thought, or reference   Memory and past experiences that audience members have with an object, concept, or event.

timing   Way a speaker uses pauses and delivery for maximum effect.

topical pattern   Pattern of organization that allows the speaker to divide a topic into subtopics, each of which addresses a different aspect of the whole topic.

trait anxiety   Apprehension about communicating with others in any situation.

transition   Phrase that indicates a speaker is finished with one point and moving on to a new one.

two-sided message   Persuasive strategy that addresses both sides of an issue, refuting one side to prove the other is better.

URL (uniform resource locator)   Address of a specific Web site or page.

value   A person's idea of what is good, worthy, or important.

verbal clutter   Extra words that pad sentences and claims but don't add meaning.

visual listener   Listener who needs to see something to understand how it works.

visualization   Process in which you construct an image of yourself in your mind's eye giving a successful speech.

vocal variety   Changes in the volume, rate, and pitch of a speaker's voice that affect the meaning of the words delivered.

vocalized pauses   Pauses that speakers fill with words or sounds like "um," "er," or "uh."

volume   Loudness of a speaker's voice.

Web page   Individual screens that represent specific parts of a Web site.

Web site   Location on the World Wide Web.

World Wide Web   System that allows users to easily navigate the millions of sites on the Internet.

Notes

CHAPTER 1

1. Frederick Douglass, "I Have Come to Tell You Something About Slavery," Lynn, Massachusetts, October 1841. In John W. Blassingame, ed., *The Frederick Douglass Papers,* vols. 1–5 (New Haven: Yale UP, 1979).

2. Rudolph Giuliani, "Address to the United Nations," New York City, October 10, 2001. http://www.nytimes.com/2001/10/01/nyregion/01CND-GTEXT.html

3. Abraham Lincoln, *The Examiner* (September 13, 1862), p. 579.

4. Harold Barrett, *Rhetoric and Civility: Human Development, Narcissism, and the Good Audience* (New York: SUNY Press, 1991), p. 147.

5. Deborah Tannen, *The Argument Culture: Moving from Debate to Dialogue* (New York: Random House, 1998), pp. 1–4.

6. See, for example, Shawn Spano, *Public Dialogue and Participatory Democracy: The Cupertino Community Project* (Cresskill, NJ: Hampton, 2001); William Isaacs, *Dialogue and the Art of Thinking Together* (New York: Currency, 1999); Stephen L. Carter, *Civility: Manners, Morals, and the Etiquette of Democracy* (New York: Basic, 1998); Linda Ellinor and Glenna Gerard, *Dialogue: Rediscover the Transfrming Power of Conversation* (New York: John Wiley and Sons, 1998); Jeffrey C. Goldfarb, *Civility and Subversion: The Intellectual in the Democratic Society* (Cambridge: Cambridge University Press, 1998); Josina M. Makau and Ronald C. Arnett, *Communication Ethics in an Age of Diversity* (Chicago: University of Illinois Press, 1997); Ivana Markova, Carl F. Graumann, and Klaus Foppa, eds. *Mutualities in Dialogue* (Cambridge: Cambridge University Press, 1995); Douglas N. Walton and Erik C. W. Krabbee, *Commitment in Dialogue: Basic Concepts of Interpersonal Reasoning* (New York: State University of New York Press, 1995); Rob Anderson, Kenneth N. Cissna, and Ronald C. Arnett, *The Reach of Dialogue: Confirmation, Voice, and Community* (Cresskill, NJ: Hampton Press, 1994); and Harold Barrett, *Rhtoric and Civility: Human Development, Narcissism, and the Good Audience* (New York: State University of New York Press, 1991).

7. For an excellent discussion of the public dialogue, see Shawn Spano, *Public Dialogue and Participatory Democracy: The Cupertino Community Project* (Cresskill, NJ: Hampton, 2001).

8. Adapted from Kenneth Burke, *The Philosophy of Literary Form: Studies in Symbolic Action,* 3rd ed. (1941; reprint, Berkeley: University of California Press, 1973), pp. 110–111.

9. Melbourne S. Cummings, "Teaching the African American Rhetoric Course." In James W. Ward, ed., *African American Communications: An Anthology in Traditional and Contemporary Studies* (Dubuque, IA: Kendall/Hunt, 1993), p. 241.

10. Adapted from Janice Walker Anderson, "A Comparison of Arab and American Conceptions of 'Effective' Persuasion," *Howard Journal of Communications* 2 (Winter 1989–1990): 81–114. Reprint, Larry A. Samovar and Richard E. Porter, *Intercultural Communication: A Reader,* 7th ed. (Belmont, CA: Wadsworth, 1994), 104–114; and A. J. Almaney and A. J. Alwan, *Communicating with the Arabs: A Handbook for the Business Executive* (Prospect Heights, IL: Waveland, 1982), p. 79.

11. Bonnie Dow, "Ann Willis Richards: A Voice for Political Empowerment." In Karlyn Kohrs Campbell, ed., *Women Public Speakers in the United States, 1925–1993* (Westport, CT: Greenwood, 1994), p. 456.

12. Material for this section is from Ward, *African American Communications*; Mary Jane Collier, "A Comparison of Conversations Among and Between Domestic Culture Groups: How Intra- and Intercultural Competencies Vary," *Communication Quarterly* 36 (1988): 122–144; Larry A. Samovar and Richard E. Porter, *Communication Between Cultures* (Belmont, CA: Wadsworth, 1991); Anderson, "A Comparison"; Samovar and Porter, *Intercultural*

Communication; and Almaney and Alwan, *Communicating with the Arabs.*

13. Charmaine Shutiva, "Native American Culture and Communication Through Humor." In Alberto Gonzalez, Marsha Houston, and Victoria Chen, eds., *In Our Voices: Essays in Culture, Ethnicity, and Communication,* 3rd ed. (Los Angeles: Roxbury, 2000), pp. 113–117.

14. Bonnie J. Dow and Mari Boor Tonn, " 'Feminine Style' and Political Judgment in the Rhetoric of Ann Richards," *Quarterly Journal of Speech* 79 (1993): 286–302; Julia T. Wood, *Gendered Lives: Communi-cation, Gender, and Culture,* 4th ed. (Belmont, CA: Wadsworth, 2001); Marsha Houston, "When Black Women Talk with White Women: Why the Dialogues Are Difficult." In *In Our Voices,* pp. 98–104.

15. Lois Gibbs, *Love Canal: My Story* (Albany: SUNY Press, 1982).

16. Lois Gibbs, *Dying from Dioxin* (Boston: South End, 1995).

17. "On the Cover: The Quiet Victories of Ryan White," http://www.elibrary.com/s/edumark/; Ryan White and Ann Marie Cunningham, *Ryan White: My Own Story* (New York, Dial, 1991), p. 256.

18. http://web.lexis-nexis.com/univers.

19. Rebecca Vollelker, "Ryan White, 18, Dies After 5-Year Battle with AIDS," *American Medical News* (April 20, 1990): 11.

20. Thomas C. Reeves, *The Life and Times of Joe McCarthy: A Biography* (New York: Stein and Day, 1982), pp. 630–631.

CHAPTER 2

1. James C. McCroskey, "Oral Communication Apprehension: A Summary of Recent Theory and Research," *Human Communication Research* 4 (1977): 78. Italics added.

2. Ralph R. Behnke and Chris R. Sawyer, "Milestones of Anticipatory Public Speaking Anxiety," *Communicaiton Education* 48 (1999): 164–172; Amy M. Bippus and John A. Daly, "What Do People Think Causes Stage Fright? Naïve Attributions about the Reasons for Public Speaking Anxiety," *Communication Education* 48 (1999); 63–72; Thomas E. Robinson II, "Communicaiton Apprehension and the Basic Public Speaking Course: A National Survey of In-Class Treatment Techniques," *Communication Education* 46 (1997), 190–197.

3. Michael J. Beatty, "Situational and Predispositional Correlates of Public Speaking Anxiety," *Communication Education* 37 (January 1988): 29–30. Amy M. Bippus and John A. Daly, "What Do People Think Causes Stage Fright?: Naïve Attributions About the Reasons for Public Speaking Anxiety," *Communication Education* 48 (1999): 63–73.

4. Murray B. Stein, John R. Walker, and David R. Forde, "Public-Speaking Fears in a Community Sample: Prevalence, Impact on Functioning, and Diagnostic Classification," *Archives of General Psychiatry* 53 (1996): 169–174.

5. John A. Daly, Anita L. Vangelisti, and David J. Weber, "Speech Anxiety Affects How People Prepare Speeches: A Protocol Analysis of the Preparation Processes of Speakers," *Communication Monographs* 62 (December 1995): 383–397.

6. See Karen Kangas Dwyer, *Conquer Your Speechfright: Learn How to Overcome the Nervousness of Public Speaking* (Fort Worth, TX: Harcourt, 1998); Karen Kangas Dwyer, "The Multidimensional Model: Teaching Students to Self-manage High Communication Apprehension by Self-Selecting Treatments," *Communicaiton Education* 49 (2000): 72–81; and James C. McCroskey, "The Implementation of a Large Scale Program of Systematic Desensitization for Communicaiton Apprehension," *Speech Teacher* 21 (1972): 255–264.

7. Michael T. Motley, "Public Speaking Anxiety Qua Performance Anxiety: A Revised Model and an Alternative Therapy," *Journal of Social Behavior and Personality* 5 (1990): 85–104.

8. Joe Ayres and Theodore S. Hopf, "Visualization: A Means of Reducing Speech Anxiety," *Communication Education* 34 (1985): 318–323; Joe Ayres and Theodore S. Hopf, "Visualization: Is It More Than Extra-Attention?" *Communication Education* 38 (1989): 1–5; Joe Ayres and Theodore S. Hopf, "The Long-Term Effect of Visualization in the Classroom: A Brief Research Report," *Communication Education* 39 (1990): 75–78; Joe Ayres, Tim Hopf, and Debbie M. Ayres, "An Examination of Whether Imaging Ability Enhances the Effectiveness of an Intervention Designed to Reduce Speech Anxiety," *Communi-cation Education* 43 (1994): 252–258; Robert McGarvey, "Rehearsing for Success: Tap the Power of the Mind Through Visualization," *Executive Female* (January–February 1990): 34–37.

9. Adapted from Ayres and Hopf, "Visualization: Is it More Than Extra-Attention?" pp. 2–3.

10. Joe Ayres, "Coping with Speech Anxiety: The Power of Positive Thinking," *Communication Education* 37 (October 1988): 289–296.

11. William J. Fremouw and Michael D. Scott, "Cognitive Restructuring: An Alternative Method for the Treatment of Communication Appre-hension," *Communication Education* 28 (1979): 129–133.

CHAPTER 3

1. William Isaacs, *Dialogue and the Art of Thinking Together* (New York: Currency, 1999), pp. 17–18.
2. Lyman K. Steil, Larry L. Barker, and Kittie W. Watson, *Effective Listening: Key to Your Success* (Reading, MA: Addison-Wesley, 1983), p. 51.
3. Martin Buber. In Rob Anderson, Kenneth N. Cissna, and Ronald C. Arnett, eds., *The Reach of Dialogue: Confirmation, Voice, and Community* (Cresskill, NJ: Hampton Press, 1994), p. 23.
4. Michael P. Nichols, *The Lost Art of Listening* (New York: Guilford, 1995), p. 3.
5. Ronald R. Sims and Serbrenia J. Sims, *The Importance of Learning Styles: Understanding the Implications for Learning, Course Design, and Education* (Westport, CT: Greenwood, 1995). Auditory and visual learning styles also have been labeled "verbalizers" and "visualizers." Verbalizers will sometimes talk to themselves as they work through problems, whereas visualizers will attempt to create a mental image of the thing they are attempting to learn. See also David A. Kolb, *Experiential Learning: Experience as the Source of Learning and Development* (Englewood Cliffs, NJ: Prentice-Hall, 1984). For an alternative categorization of listening styles, which focuses on message content and listener focus, see Kittie W. Watson, Larry L. Barker, and James B. Weaver III, "The Listening Styles Profile (LSP-16): Development and Validation of an Instrument to Assess Four Listening Styles," *The International Journal of Listening* 9 (1995): 1–13.
6. This definition is adapted from Donald L. Rubin, "Listenability=Oral-based Discourse+Considerateness." In Andrew D. Wolvin and Carolyn Gwynn Coakley, eds., *Perspectives on Listening* (Norwood, NJ: Ablex, 1993), pp. 261–281.
7. Adapted from Amy Tan, *The Kitchen God's Wife* (New York: G.P. Putnam's Sons, 1991), pp. 71–72.
8. The debate over the role of language in constructing or reflecting reality is centuries old, beginning with Plato and Aristotle. For a summary of this debate and the implications of the many positions, see Ann Gill, *Rhetoric and Human Understanding* (Prospect Heights, IL: Waveland, 1994). James L. Golden, Goodwin F. Berquist, and William E. Coleman offer an anthology of some of the primary texts in this debate in their book *The Rhetoric of Western Thought*, 6th ed. (Dubuque, IA: Kendall/Hunt, 1997).
9. Adapted from Arthur K. Robertson, *Listen for Success: A Guide to Effective Listening* (New York: Irwin Professional Publishing, 1994), pp. 25–26.
10. Geneva Smitherman, *Black Talk: Words and Phrases from the Hood to the Amen Corner*, 2nd ed. (Boston: Houghton Mifflin, 2000), p. 118.
11. Julia Wood, *Gendered Lives: Communication, Gender, and Culture*, 4th ed. (Belmont, CA: Wadsworth, 2001), pp. 109, 110.
12. Diana K. Ivy and Phil Backlund, *Exploring GenderSpeak: Personal Effectiveness in Gender Communication*, 2nd ed. (Boston: McGraw-Hill, 2000), pp. 175–176.
13. Ibid., p. 174.
14. Adapted from Amy Einsohn, *The Copyeditor's Handbook* (Berkeley: University of California Press, 2000), pp. 404–416.
15. U.S. Census Bureau, Table 621: Full-Time Wage and Salary Workers—Number and Earnings: 1985–2000, *2001 Statistical Abstract of the United States*. Last revised 1 May 2002. Accessed 4 June 2002. http://www.census.gov/prod/2002pubs/01statab/labor.pdf.
16. Andrew D. Wolvin and Carolyn Gwynn Coakley, *Listening*, 2nd ed. (Dubuque, IA: William C. Brown, 1985), p. 177.

CHAPTER 4

1. Alfred Rosa and Paul Escholz, *The Writer's Brief Handbook*, 2nd ed. (Scarborough, Canada: Allyn & Bacon, 1996) p. 7.

CHAPTER 5

1. Adapted from Harold Barrett, *Rhetoric and Civility: Human Development, Narcissism, and the Good Audience* (New York: SUNY Press, 1991), p. 4.
2. Vincent Mosco and Lewis Kaye, "Questioning the Concept of the Audience." In Ingunn Hagen and Janet Wasko, eds., *Consuming Audiences? Production and Reception in Media Research* (Cresskill, NJ: Hampton, 2000), pp. 31–46.
3. For an excellent summary and discussion of the various theories that attempt to explain social development, see Julia Wood, *Gendered Lives: Communication, Gender, and Culture*, 5th ed (Belmont, CA: Wadsworth, 2002), pp. 37–59.
4. Gordon Marshall, ed., *The Concise Oxford Dictionary of Sociology* (New York: Oxford University Press, 1994), p. 315.
5. See, for example, Angela. Browne, "Violence Against Women by Male Partner: Prevalence, Outcomes and Policy Implications," *American Psychologist* 48 (1993): 1077–1087; Angela Browne and Kirk. R. Williams, "Gender, Intimacy, and Lethal Violence: Trends from 1976–1987," *Gender and Society* 7 (1993): 78–98; Bureau of Justice Statistics, "Violence Against Women: A National Crime Victimization Survey Report," 1994 [Online] Available: http://www.ojp. usdoj.gov; Eve. Buzawa, Thomas L. Austin, and Carl G. Buzawa,

"Responding to Crimes of Violence Against Women: Gender Differences Versus Organizational Imperatives," *Crime and Delinquency* 41 (1995): 443–466; Leandra Lackie and Anton F. de Man, "Correlates of Sexual Aggression Among Male University Students," *Sex Roles* 37 (1997): 451–457; Russell P. Dobash, R. Emerson Dobash, Kate Cavanagh, and Ruth Lewis, "Separate and Intersecting Realities: A Comparison of Men's and Women's Accounts of Violence Against Women," *Violence Against Women* 4 (1998): 382–414; Federal Bureau of Investigation, *Crime in the United States. Uniform Crime Reports* (Washington, DC: U.S. Department of Justice, 1989); Federal Bureau of Investigation, "Violence Against Women: Estimates from the Redesigned Survey," August 1995 [Online]. Available: http://www.ojp.usdoj.gov; U.S. Bureau of Labor Statistics, "The Employment Situation News Release," 1998 [Online]. Available: http://stats.bls.gov; "The Wage Gap," *Ms.* (1996, March–April), pp. 36–37.

6. Alice A. Egly and Shelly Chaiken, "Attitude Structure and Function." In *Handbook of Social Psychology* 1 (1998): 323–390; and James M. Olson and Mark P. Zanna, "Attitudes and Attitude Change," *Annual Review of Psychology* 44 (1993): 117–154.

7. Rushworth M. Kidder, *Shared Values for a Troubled World* (San Francisco: Jossey-Bass, 1994); Milton Rokeach, *Beliefs, Attitudes and Values: A Theory of Organization and Change* (San Francisco: Jossey-Bass, 1970); Milton Rokeach, *The Nature of Human Values* (New York: Free Press, 1973); Shalom H. Schwartz and Wolfgang Blisky, "Toward a Theory of the Universal Content and Structure of Values: Extensions and Cross-Cultural Replications," *Journal of Personality and Social Psychology* 58 (1990): 878–891.

8. Phyllis M. Japp, "Esther or Isaiah?: The Abolitionist-Feminist Rhetoric of Angelina Grimke," *Quarterly Journal of Speech* 71 (1985): 335–348; and Larry Ceplair, *The Public Years of Sarah and Angelina Grimke: Selected Writings: 1835–1839* (New York: Columbia University Press, 1989), pp. 318–323.

9. His Holiness The Dalai Lama and Howard C. Cutler, *The Art of Happiness: A Handbook for Living* (New York: Riverhead Books, 1998), pp. 1–2.

10. Kenneth Burke, *Counter-Statement* (Berkeley: University of California Press, 1968), p. 31.

11. Lyman K. Steil, Larry L. Barker, and Kittie W. Watson, *Effective Listening: Key to Your Success* (Reading, MA: Addison-Wesley, 1983), p. 91.

CHAPTER 6

1. Alvin Toffler, *Future Shock* (New York: Random House, 1970), p. 350.

2. Patricia Senn Breivik, *Student Learning in the Information Age* (Phoenix: Oryx Press, 1998), p. xi.

3. Randolph Hock, *The Extreme Searcher's Guide to Web Search Engines: A Handbook for the Serious Searcher* (Medford, NJ: CyberAge Books, 1999), p. 13.

4. Adapted from Myrtle S. Bolner and Gayle A. Poirier, *The Research Process: Books and Beyond* (Dubuque, IA: Kendall/Hunt, 1997), pp. 111–112, and Shirley Dughlin Kennedy, *Best Bet Internet: Reference and Research When You Don't Have Time to Mess Around*, Chicago: American Library Association, 1998, pp. 144–145

5. Breivik, *Student Learning*, p. 2.

6. Bolner and Poirier, *The Research Process*, p. 249.

7. Adapted from Bolner and Poirier, *The Research Process*, p. 125, and Christine A. Hult, *Researching and Writing Across the Curriculum* (Boston: Allyn & Bacon, 1996), pp. 28–29.

8. Adapted from Charles J. Stewart and William B. Cash Jr., *Interviewing: Principles and Practices*, 9th ed. (Boston: McGraw-Hill, 2000), p. 1.

9. Larry King, *The Best of Larry King Live: The Greatest Interviews* (Atlanta: Times, 1995). Review this book and notice the depth of knowledge King possesses over a wide range of subjects and topics. His preparation beforehand enables him to ask relevant, informed questions of each of his interviewees.

10. Adapted from George Killenberg and Rob Anderson, *Before the Story: Interviewing and Communication Skills for Journalists* (New York: St. Martin's, 1989).

CHAPTER 7

1. Adapted from James Crosswhite, *The Rhetoric of Reason: Writing and the Attractions of Argument* (Madison: University of Wisconsin Press, 1996), pp. 51, 55, 56.

2. Adapted from Edward S. Inch and Barbara Warnick, *Critical Thinking and Communication: The Use of Reason in Argument*, 3rd ed. (Boston: Allyn & Bacon, 1989) pp. 194–197.

3. Walter R. Fisher, *Human Communication as Narration: Toward a Philosophy of Reason, Value, and Action* (Columbia: University of South Carolina Press 1987), p. 58.

4. Kathleen Hall Jamieson, *Eloquence in the Electronic Age: The Transformation of Political Speechmaking* (New York: Oxford, 1988), p. 140.

5. Cynthia Crossen, *Tainted Truth: The Manipulation of Fact in America* (New York: Simon & Schuster, 1994), p. 42.

6. Reza Fadaei, ed., *Applied Algebra and Statistics* (Needham Heights, MA: Simon & Schuster, 2000), pp. 544, 545.

7. Phillip H. Taylor, Philip F. Rice, and Roy H. Williams, *Basic Statistics* (Cincinnati: Thompson Learning, 2000), Chapter 2, pp. 1–4. The author would like to thank the reference librarians at the Fort Collins Public Library for their help with this example.

8. Barbara Kantrowitz and Pat Wingert, "Teachers Wanted," *Newsweek*, October 2, 2000, p. 40.

9. Adapted from Inch and Warnick, *Critical Thinking and Communication*, p. 154.

10. Adapted from bell hooks, *Talking Back: Thinking Feminist, Thinking Black* (Boston: South End, 1989), pp. 3, 107, 109, 110.

11. The discussion over the type of language used by Truth, and whether or not she actually did repeat the phrase "ain't I a woman" is nicely summarized in Suzanne Pullon Fitch and Roseann M. Mandziuk, *Sojourner Truth as Orator: Wit, Story, and Song* (Westport, CT: Greenwood, 1997).

12. For more information about Katz's approach and his definition of feminism, log on to www.jacksonkatz.com; www.mediaed.org; or www.cavnet.org.

13. I. A. Richards, *The Philosophy of Rhetoric* (New York: Oxford University Press, 1965) (Original work published 1936); C. K. Ogden and I. A. Richards, *The Meaning of Meaning; A Study of the Influence of Language upon Thought and of the Science of Symbolism* (New York: Harcourt, Brace & World, 1923).

CHAPTER 8

1. Adapted from Stephen Toulmin, *The Place of Reason in Ethics* (Chicago: University of Chicago Press, 1950), p. 72.

2. For a discussion of the importance of maintaining Aristotle's distinction between *logos* and logic, see Joseph Little, "Confusion in the Classroom: Does *Logos* Mean Logic?" *Journal of Technical Writing and Communication* 29 (1999): 349–353. Aristotle suggested that *logos* refers to the process of reasoning as well as establishing credibility, or *ethos*, and using emotional appeals, or *pathos*. See also George Kennedy's translation of Aristotle: *On Rhetoric: A Theory of Civic Discourse*, George Kennedy, Trans. (Oxford: Oxford University Press, 1991), p. 37.

3. See Chaim Perelman and Luce Olbrechts Tyteca, *The New Rhetoric: A Treatise on Argumentation*, John Wilkinson and Purcell Weaver, Trans. (Notre Dame: University of Notre Dame Press, 1969), pp. 31–35, for a discussion of the universal audience, or that group of imagined listeners to which we submit claims and test their "logic."

4. Adapted from Stephen Toulmin, Richard Rieke, and Allan Janik, *An Introduction to Reasoning* (New York: Macmillan, 1979).

5. Perelman and Olbrechts-Tyteca identify approximately twenty-two different argument schemas in *The New Rhetoric*, and Douglas N. Walton, in *Argumentation Schemes for Presumptive Reasoning* (Mahwah, NJ: Lawrence Erlbaum, 1996), offers twenty-five different argumentation schemes. Although all of these schemes are important, students in a beginning public speaking course do well to rely on the five basic schemes or types discussed in this chapter and in most other public speaking texts.

6. The material in this section and the section on deductive reasoning is taken from Lester Faigley and Jack Selzer, *Good Reasons* (Needham Heights, MA: Allyn & Bacon, 2000); Howard Kahane and Nancy Cavender, *Logic and Contemporary Rhetoric: The Use of Reason in Everyday Life,* 8th ed. (Belmont, CA: Wadsworth, 1998); and Stephen Toulmin, *The Uses of Argument* (London: Cambridge University Press, 1969).

7. See, for example, David Vancil, *Rhetoric and Argumentation* (Boston: Allyn & Bacon, 1993), p. 134, who suggests that argument by example is "one of the archetypal forms of the inductive process," and David Zarefsky, *Public Speaking: Strategies for Success* (Needham Heights, MA: Allyn & Bacon, 2002), pp. 153–154.

8. Aristotle, *Rhetoric*, II, 20, 1394a, cited in Perelman and Olbrechts-Tyteca, p. 358. See also Aristotle, *The "Art" of Rhetoric*, John H. Freese, Trans. 1926 (Cambridge, MA: Harvard University Press, 1982), p. 265, for a slightly different translation of Aristotle's view on examples.

9. For an excellent compilation of women's speeches related to their right to vote, as well as other rights, including Anthony's speech, see Karlyn Kohrs Campbell, ed., *Man Cannot Speak for Her: Key Texts of the Early Feminists* (New York: Praeger, 1989).

10. See Faigley and Selzer, Kahane and Cavender, as well as Edward S. Inch and Barbara Warnick, *Critical Thinking and Communication: The Use of Reason in Argument*, 3rd ed. (Boston: Allyn & Bacon, 1998).

11. False causes are also know by their Latin name, *post hoc, ergo propter hoc*, which means "after this, therefore because of this." For a succinct discussion of false causes, see Inch and Warnick, pp. 208–209.

12. Cited in Paul Rogat Loeb, *Soul of a Citizen: Living with Conviction in a Cynical Time* (New York: St. Martin's Griffin, 1999), pp. 68–69.

13. Inch and Warnick call reasoning by sign "coexistential" reasoning, suggesting "an argument from coexistence reasons from something that can be observed (as sign) to a condition or feature that cannot be observed." See Inch and Warnick, p. 201.

14. Toulmin, *The Uses of Argument*; and Toulmin, Rieke, and Janik, *An Introduction to Reasoning*. See also

Mary M. Gleason, "The Role of Evidence in Argumentative Writing," *Reading & Writing Quarterly* 14 (1999): 81–106.

15. For a discussion of the characteristics of credibility, see James B. Stiff, *Persuasive Communication* (New York: Guilford, 1994), pp. 89–98.

CHAPTER 9

1. For a historical overview of the research on organizing speeches, see Ernest Thompson, "Some Effects of Message Structure on Listener's Comprehension," *Speech Monographs* 34 (1967): 51–57; James C. McCroskey and R. S. Mehrley, "The Effects of Disorganization and Non-Fluency on Attitude Change and Source Credibility," *Communication Monographs* 36 (1969): 13–21; Arlee Johnson, "A Preliminary Investigation of the Relationship Between Organization and Listener Comprehension," *Central States Speech Journal* 21 (1970): 104–107; and Christopher Spicer and Ronald E. Bassett, "The Effect of Organization on Learning from an Informative Message," *Southern Speech Communication Journal* 41 (1976): 290–299. For a more recent discussion of the importance of organization in speeches, see Patricia R. Palmerton, "Teaching Skills or Teaching Thinking," *Journal of Applied Communication Research* 20 (1992): 335–341; and Robert G. Powell, "Critical Thinking and Speech Communication: Our Teaching Strategies Are Warranted—Not!" *Journal of Applied Communication Research* 20 (1992): 342–347.

CHAPTER 10

1. Bas A. Andeweg, Jaap C. de Jong, and Hans Hoeken, "'May I Have Your Attention?': Exordial Techniques in Informative Oral Presentations," *Technical Communication Quarterly* 7 (1998): 281.
2. Mark L. Knapp, Roderick P. Hart, Gustav W. Friedrick, and G. M. Shulman, "The Rhetoric of Goodbye: Verbal and Nonverbal Correlates of Human Leave-Taking," *Speech Monographs* 40 (1973): 182–198.

CHAPTER 11

1. Adapted from Jonathan Price, *Outlining Goes Electronic* (Stamford, CT: Ablex, 1999), pp. 115–136.
2. See Price, Chapter 4, especially pp. 65, 68, and 74.

CHAPTER 12

1. Ann Gill, *Rhetoric and Human Understanding* (Prospect Heights, IL: Waveland, 1994), p. 11.
2. C. K. Ogden and I A. Richards, *The Meaning of Meaning: A Study of the Influence of Language upon Thought and of the Science of Symbolism* (New York:

Harcourt, Brace, 1930). (Original work published 1923).

3. For an excellent discussion of signifying, see Henry Louis Gates, *The Signifying Monkey: A Theory of Afro-American Literary Criticism* (New York: Oxford University Press, 1988), and Geneva Smitherman, *Talkin and Testifying: The Language of Black America* (Boston: Houghton Mifflin, 1977).
4. The material in this section is taken from Khosrow Jahandarie, *Spoken and Written Discourse: A Multi-Disciplinary Perspective* (Stamford, CT: Ablex, 1999), pp. 131–150; Eckart Scheerer, "Orality, Literacy, and Cognitive Modeling." In Boris M. Velichkovsky and Duane M. Rumbaugh, eds., *Communicating Meaning: The Evolution and Development of Language* (Mahwah, NJ: Lawrence Erlbaum, 1996), pp. 211–256; M. A. K. Halliday, "Spoken and Written Modes of Meaning." In Rosalind Horowitz and S. Jay Samuels, eds., *Comprehending Oral and Written Language* (New York: Harcourt Brace Jovanovich, 1987), pp. 55–82; Wallace Chafe and Jane Danielewicz, "Properties of Spoken and Written Language." In *Comprehending Oral and Written Language*, pp. 83–113.
5. Eric Partridge, *Usage and Abusage: A Guide to Good English* (New York: Norton, 1995), p. 182. (Original work published 1942)
6. Rigoberta Menchu, "Five Hundred Years of Sacrifice Before Alien Gods." Interview, 1992. http://indy4.fdl.cc.mn.us/~isk/maya/menchu.html
7. Richard Lederer, *The Bride of Anguished English: A Bonus of Bloopers, Blunders, Botches, and Boo-Boos* (New York: St. Martin's Press, pp. 33, 44.
8. Audley "Queen Mother" Moore. In Toyomi Igus, ed., *Book of Black Heroes: Vol. 2, Great Women in the Struggle: An Introduction for Young Readers* (Orange, NJ: Just Us Books, 1991), p. 12.
9. Partridge, p. 14.

CHAPTER 13

1. Patsy Rodenburg, *The Need for Words: Voice and the Text* (New York: Routledge, 1993), pp. 5–6.
2. Herbert W. Hildebrant and Walter W. Stevens suggest that no one method is better than another. Rather, "it is the ability of the individual speaker in using a particular method" that is influential. See Hildebrant and Stevens, "Manuscript and Extemporaneous Delivery in Communicating Information," *Speech Monographs* 30 (1963): 369–372.
3. Robert J. Branham and W. Barnett Pearce, "The Conversational Frame in Public Address," *Communication Quarterly* 44 (1996): 423.
4. Peter A. Andersen, Michael L. Hecht, and Gregory D. Hoebler, "The Cultural Dimension of Nonverbal Communication." In William B. Gudykunst and Bella

Moody, eds., *Handbook of International and Intercultural Communication* (Thousand Oaks, CA: Sage, 2002), pp. 89-106, and Larry A. Samoar and Richard E. Porter, *Communication Between Cultures* (Belmont, CA: Wadsworth, 1991), pp. 205–206.

5. Stephen E. Lucas, *The Art of Public Speaking*, 7th ed. (New York: McGraw-Hill, 2001), p. 290.

6. Paul L. Soper, *Basic Public Speaking*, 2nd ed. (New York: Oxford, 1956), p. 151. Soper also cites Ambrose Bierce as suggesting, with regard to too high a pitch, that *positive* is "being mistaken at the top of one's voice." See Soper, p. 150.

7. Adapted from Soper, p. 143.

8. Nicholas Christenfeld, "Does it Hurt to Say Um?" *Journal of Nonverbal Behavior* 19 (Fall 1995): 171–186. Christenfeld's study also found that audiences prefer no pauses to empty pauses.

9. See, for example, Stephanie Martin and Lyn Darnley, *The Teaching Voice* (San Diego: Singular Publishing Group, 1996), p. 60; Rodenburg, *The Need for Words*; Linda Gates, *Voice for Performance* (New York: Applause, 2000); and Richard Dowis, *The Lost Art of the Great Speech: How to Write One, How to Deliver It* (New York: American Management Association, 2000).

10. Many communication scholars define nonverbal communication as all aspects of communication other than words. In a public speaking course, the distinction between vocalized communication as verbal and nonvocalized communication as nonverbal seems pedagogically useful. A similar distinction is made in many other public speaking texts.

11. Ray Birdwhistell, *Kinesics and Context* (Philadelphia: University of Pennsylvania, 1970); Albert Mehrabian, *Silent Messages: Implicit Communication of Emotion and Attitudes*, 2nd ed. (Belmont, CA: Wadsworth, 1981).

12. See, for example, April R. Trees and Valerie Manusov, "Managing Face Concerns in Critics: Integrating Nonverbal Behaviors as a Dimension of Politeness in Female Friendship Dyads," *Human Communication Research* 24 (1998): 564–583; James C. McCroskey, Aino Sallinen, Joan M. Fayer, Virginia P. Richmond, and Robert A Barraclough, "Nonverbal Immediacy and Cognitive Learning: A Cross-Cultural Investigation," *Communication Education* 45 (1996): 200–211; and Mary Mino, "The Relative Effects of Content and Vocal Delivery During a Simulated Employment Interview," *Communication Research Reports* 13 (1996): 225–238. See also Julia T. Wood, *Interpersonal Communication: Everyday Encounters*, 2nd ed. (Belmont, CA: Wadsworth, 1999), p. 148.

13. For an excellent discussion of variations in nonverbal expectations across cultures, see William B. Gudykunst and Bella Moody, eds., *Handbook of International and Intercultural Communication*, 2nd ed. (Thousand Oaks, CA: Sage, 2002).

14. For example, see "Good-Looking Lawyers Make More Money, Says a Study by Economists," *Wall Street Journal* (January 4,1996), p. A1; Patricia Rozell, David Kennedy, and Edward Grabb, "Physical Attractiveness and Income Attainment Among Canadians," *Journal of Psychology* 123 (1989): 547–559; Tracy L. Morris, Joan Gorham, Stanley H. Cohen, and Drew Huffman, "Fashion in the Classroom: Effects of Attire on Student Perceptions of Instructors in College Classes," *Communication Education* 45 (1996): 135–148.

15. Arthur J. Hartz, "Psycho-Socionomics: Attractiveness Research from a Societal Perspective," *Journal of Social Behavior and Personality* 11 (1996): 683.

16. Paula Morrow writes that even though physical attractiveness is difficult to "quantify," "people within a given culture tend to agree with each other regarding whether a person's facial appearance is physically attractive or not and they tend to be consistent in their judgments over time." See Morrow, "Physical Attractiveness and Selection Decision Making," *Journal of Management* 16 (1990): 45–60, esp. p. 47. See also Ruth P. Rubinstein, *Dress Codes: Meanings and Messages in American Culture*, 2nd ed. (Boulder, CO: Westview, 2001); and, C. Peter Herman, Mark P. Zanna, and E. Tory Higgins, *Physical Appearance, Stigma, and Social Behavior: The Ontario Symposium*, Vol. 3 (Hillsdale, NJ: Lawrence Erlbaum, 1986).

17. Mark T. Palmer and Karl B. Simmons, "Communicating Intentions Through Nonverbal Behaviors," *Human Communication Research* 22 (1995): 128–160.

18. Steven A. Beebe, "Eye Contact: A Nonverbal Determinant of Speaker Credibility," *Speech Teacher* 23 (1974): 21–25; Steven A. Beebe, "Effects of Eye Contact, Posture and Vocal Inflection upon Credibility and Comprehension," *Australian Scan Journal of Nonverbal Communication* 7–8 (1979–80): 57–70; and Martin Cobin, "Response to Eye Contact," *Quarterly Journal of Speech* 48 (1963): 415–419.

19. See, for example, Peter E. Bull, *Posture and Gesture* (New York: Pergamon, 1987).

20. See, for example, Gilbert Austin, In Mary Margaret Robb and Lester Thonssen, eds., *Chironomia or A Treatise on Rhetorical Delivery* (Carbondale: Southern Illinois University Press, 1966) (Original work published 1806); and John Bulwer, In James W. Cleary, ed., *Chirologia: Or the Natural Language of the Hand, and Chiromomia: Or the Art of Manual Rhetoric* (Carbondale: Southern Illinois University Press, 1974) (Orginal work published 1644).

21. Adapted from Herbert W. Simons, *Persuasion: Understanding, Practice, and Analysis,* 2nd ed. (New York: Random House, 1986), p. 138.

CHAPTER 14

1. J. Anthony Blair, "The Possibility and Actuality of Visual Arguments," *Argumentation and Advocacy* 33 (1996): 23.
2. Will Linkugel and D. Berg, *A Time to Speak* (Belmont, CA: Wadsworth, 1970), pp. 68–96. See also Elena P. Zayas-Bazan, "Instructional Media in the Total Language Picture," *International Journal of Instructional Media* 5 (1977–1978): 145–150, and Emil Bohn and David Jabusch, "The Effect of Four Methods of Instruction on the Use of Visual Aids in Speeches," *Western Journal of Speech Communication* 46 (1982): 253–265.
3. Raymond S. Nickerson, "Short-Term Memory for Complex Meaningful Visual Configurations: A Demonstration of Capacity," *Canadian Journal of Psychology* 19 (1965): 155–160.
4. Bohn and Jabusch, p. 254.
5. William J. Seiler, "The Effects of Visual Materials on Attitudes, Credibility, and Retention," *Speech Monographs* 38 (1971): 334.
6. Seiler, pp. 331–334.
7. Joe Ayres, "Using Visual Aids to Reduce Speech Anxiety," *Communication Research Reports* 8 (1991): 73–79.
8. Myles Martel, *Before You Say a Word: The Executive Guide to Effective Communication* (Upper Saddle River, NJ: Prentice Hall, 1984).
9. Wilma Davidson and Susan J. Klien, "Ace your Presentation," *Journal of Accountancy* 187 (1999): 61–63.
10. For a nice discussion of using lists as visual aids, see Margaret Y. Rabb, *The Presentation Design Book: Tips, Techniques and Advice for Creating Effective, Attractive Slides, Overheads, Multimedia Presentations, Screen Shows and More* (Chapel Hill, NC: Ventana, 1993).
11. For example, see Lynn Kearny, *Graphics for Presenters: Getting Your Ideas Across* (Menlo Park, CA: Crisp, 1996); Claudyne Wilder, *The Presentations Kit: Ten Steps for Spelling Out Your Ideas* (New York: Wiley, 1994); and Rabb, *The Presentation Design Book.*
12. For example, see Rabb, Wilder, or Russell N. Baird, Duncan McDonald, Ronald H. Pittman, and Arthur T. Turnbull, *The Graphics of Communication: Methods, Media and Technology* (New York: Harcourt Brace Jovanovich, 1993).
13. Hans Biedermann, *Dictionary of Symbolism: Cultural Icons and the Meanings Behind Them,* trans. James Hulbert (New York: Facts on File, 1992).

CHAPTER 15

1. Conversation with Jennifer McMartin, student at Colorado State University, on June 6, 2001.
2. John R. Johnson and Nancy Szczupakiewicz, "The Public Speaking Course: Is It Preparing Students with Work Related Public Speaking Skills?" *Communication Education* 36 (1987): 131–137.
3. Andrew D. Wolvin, "The Basic Course and the Future of the Workplace," *Basic Communication Course Annual* 10 (1998): 1–6. See also Sherwyn P. Morreale, Michael M. Osborn, and Judy C. Pearson, "Why Communication Is Important: A Rationale for the Centrality of the Study of Communication," *Journal of the Association for Communication Administration* 29 (2000): 1–25.

CHAPTER 16

1. Deborah Tannen, *The Argument Culture: Stopping America's War of Words* (New York: Ballantine, 1999), p. 26.
2. The theory of invitational rhetoric was initially proposed by Sonja K. Foss and Cindy L. Griffin in "Beyond Persuasion: A Proposal for an Invitational Rhetoric," *Communication Monographs* 62 (1995): 1–18. That theory has been modified here so it is applicable to public speaking practices.
3. For more discussion on the conditions of equality, value, and self-determination, see the following sources: Harold Barrett, *Rhetoric and Civility: Human Development, Narcissism, and the Good Audience* (New York: SUNY Press, 1991); Seyla Benhabib, *Situating the Self: Gender, Community, and Postmodernism in Contemporary Ethics* (New York: Routledge, 1992); Linda Ellinor and Glenna Gerard, *Dialogue: Creating and Sustaining Collaborative Partnerships at Work* (New York: Wiley, 1998); William Isaacs, *Dialogue and the Art of Thinking Together* (New York: Currency, 1999); Paul Rogat Loeb, *Soul of a Citizen: Living with Conviction in a Cynical Time* (New York: St. Martin's Griffin, 1999); M. Scott Peck, *The Different Drum: Community-Making and Peace* (New York: Simon & Schuster, 1987); Carl R. Rogers, "The Interpersonal Relationship: The Core of Guidance," *Harvard Educational Review* 32 (1962): 416–429; and M. U. Walker, "Moral Understandings: Alternative 'Epistemology' for a Feminist Ethics," *Hypatia* 4 (1989): 15–28.
4. My thanks to Marko Mohlenhoff, former campaign associate at the Fort Collins Area United Way for sharing his approach to public speaking and working with me in this example.
5. bell hooks, *Outlaw Culture: Resisting Representations* (New York: Routledge, 1994), p. 241.

CHAPTER 17

1. Timothy C. Brock, Sharon Shavitt, and Laura A Brannon, "Getting a Handle on the Axe of Persuasion." In Sharon Shavitt and Timothy C. Brock, eds., *Persuasion: Psychological Insights and Perspectives* (Needham Heights, MA: Allyn & Bacon, 1994), p.1.

2. Adapted from Bruce E. Gronbeck, Raymie E. McKerrow, Douglas Ehninger, and Alan H. Monroe, *Principles and Types of Speech Communication*, 11th ed. (Glenview, IL: Scott, Foresman/Little, Brown Higher Education, 1990), pp. 180–205.

3. Numerous scholars, beginning with Aristotle, define persuasion as a process, as something that takes place over time. For example, see Gerald R. Miller and Michael E. Roloff, eds., *Persuasion: New Directions in Theory and Research* (Beverly Hills, CA: Sage, 1980); Kathleen Kennedy Reardon, *Persuasion in Practice* (Newbury Park: Sage, 1991); and James B. Stiff, *Persuasive Communication* (New York: Guilford, 1994), for three examples of this processual definition of persuasion.

4. See Stiff, *Persuasive Communication*, pp. 117–119.

5. Bryan B. Whaley and Lisa Smith Wagner, "Rebuttal Analogy in Persuasive Messages: Communicator Likability and Cognitive Responses," *Journal of Language and Social Psychology* 19 (2000): 66–84.

6. Connie Roser and Margaret Thompson, "Fear Appeals and the Formation of Active Publics," *Journal of Communication* 45 (1995): 103–121.

7. Patricia A. Rippetoe and Ronald W. Rogers, "Effects of Components of Protection-Motivation Theory on Adaptative and Maladaptive Coping with a Health Threat," *Journal of Personality and Social Psychology* 53 (1987): 596–604.

8. Hong Chyi Chen, Richard Reardon, Cornelia Rea, and David J. More, "Forewarning of Content and Involvement: Consequences for Persuasion and Resistance to Persuasion," *Journal of Experimental Social Psychology* 28 (1992): 523–541.

9. Vincent R. Waldron and James L. Applegate, "Person-Centered Tactics During Verbal Disagreements: Effects on Student Perceptions of Persuasiveness and Social Attraction," *Communication Education* 47 (1998): 55–56.

10. Jack W. Brehm, *A Theory of Psychological Reactance* (New York: Academic Press, 1996), and Patricia Kearney, Timithoy G. Plax, and Nancy F. Burroughs, "An Attributional Analysis of College Students' Resistance Decisions," *Communication Education* 40 (1991): 325–342.

CHAPTER 18

1. Adapted from Jay A. Conger, "The Necessary Art of Persuasion," *Harvard Business Review* (May–June 1998): 86, 87.

2. Deborah L. Shelton, "Twice a Victim: Battered Women and Insurance," *Human Rights: Journal of the Section of Individual Rights and Responsibilities* 23 (1998): 26–28.

3. For a nice discussion of the importance of maintaining Aristotle's distinction between logos and logic, see Joseph Little, "Confusion in the Classroom: Does Logos Mean Logic?" *Journal of Technical Writing and Communication* 29 (1999): 349–353. Aristotle suggested that logos refers to the process of reasoning as well as establishing credibility, or *ethos*, and using emotional appeals, or *pathos*. See also Aristotle, *On Rhetoric*, vol. 8, George Kennedy, Trans. (Oxford: Oxford University Press, 1991), p. 37.

4. Awareness, understanding, agreement, acceptance, and enactment are based on William J. McGuire's phases describing the process of persuasion. See William J. McGuire, "Attitudes and Attitude Change." In Gardner Lindzey and Elliot Aronson, eds., *Handbook of Social Psychology*, vol. 1 (New York: Random House, 1985), pp. 258–261.

5. See John C. Reinard, "The Empirical Study of the Persuasive Effects of Evidence: The Status After 50 Years of Research," *Human Communication Research* 15 (1988): 3–59.

6. Donald Dean Morely and Kim B. Walker, "The Role of Importance, Novelty, and Plausibility in Producing Belief Change," *Communication Monographs* 54 (1987): 436–442.

7. See Edward S. Inch and Barbara Warnick, *Critical Thinking and Communication: The Use of Reason in Argument*, 3rd ed. (Boston: Allyn & Bacon, 1998), p. 159.

8. See, for example, Peter A. Andersen and Laura K. Guerrero, eds., *Handbook of Communication and Emotion: Research, Theory, Applications, and Contexts* (San Diego, CA: Academic Press, 1998), especially Chapters 16 and 17; Kathleen Kelley Reardon, *Persuasion in Practice* (Newbury Park, CA: Sage, 1991), pp. 108–110; and James B. Stiff, *Persuasive Communication* (New York: Guilford Press, 1994), pp. 119–131.

9. Laura K. Guerrero, Peter A. Andersen, and Melanie R. Trost, "Communication and Emotion: Basic Concepts and Approaches." In Peter A. Andersen and Laura K. Guerrero, eds., *Handbook of Communication and Emotion: Research, Theory, Applications, and Contexts* (San Diego, CA: Academic Press, 1998), p. 6.

10. Richard E. Porter and Larry A. Samovar, "Cultural Influences on Emotional Expression: Implications for Intercultural Communication." In *Handbook of Communication and Emotion*, p. 452.

11. "Top 100 American Speeches of the 20th Century," News and Public Affairs, University of Wisconsin-

Madison, http://www.news.wisc.edu/misc/ speeches/.

12. See Richard M. Perloff, *The Dynamics of Persuasion* (Hillsdale, NJ: Lawrence Erlbaum, 1993), pp. 136–155; and Stiff, *Persuasive Communication*, pp. 89–106.

13. Stiff, pp. 102–104.

14. Perloff, *Dynamics of Persuasion*, pp. 170–179.

15. "Top 100 American Speeches of the 20th Century," *News and Public Affairs*, University of Wisconsin–Madison, http://www.news.wisc.edu/misc/ speeches/

16. Marian Friestad and Peter Wright, "Everyday Persuasion Knowledge," *Psychology & Marketing* 16 (1999): 185.

17. Friestad and Wright, p. 188.

18. For a nice discussion of the logic of mythos, see Glenn W. Most, "From Logos to Mythos." In Richard Buxton, ed., *From Myth to Reason? Studies in the Development of Greek Thought* (Oxford: Oxford University Press, 1999), pp. 25–47.

19. See Frans H. van Eemeren and Rob Gootendorst, *Argumentation, Communication, and Fallacies: A Pragma-Dialectical Perspective* (Hillsdale, NJ: Lawrence Erlbaum, 1992), and Howard Kahane and Nancy Cavender, *Logic and Contemporary Rhetoric: The Use of Reason in Everyday Life*, 8th ed. (Belmont, CA: Wadsworth, 1998).

CHAPTER 19

1. Sting, Commencement Address at Berklee, May 15, 1994. http://www.berklee.ed/html/lab_sting.html

2. Introduction from Dennis Choi, no date, http://apacure.com/cr/speeches.cfm?storyID=242

3. Nelson Mandela, "Now is the Time to Intensify the Struggle." In Steve Clark, ed., *Nelson Mandela Speaks: Forging a Democratic, Nonracial South Africa* (New York: Pathfinder, 1993), pp. 23–28.

4. Mandela, p. 25.

5. Congressman Bobby Rush, "Tribute to Mrs. Rosa Parks," April 20, 1999, http://www.house.gov/rush/ pr42099s.htm.

6. http://ourworld.compuserve.com/homepages/ rmt-paz/bioeng.htm

7. http://aol.eonline.com/News/Items/0,1,5285,00.html. "Rock Throws Stones at MTV Video Music Awards," Joal Ryan, September 9, 1999, 11:15 p.m. PT. E! Online. Accessed 17 June 2002.

8. Stephen E. Lucas, *The Art of Public Speaking*, 7th ed. (Boston: McGraw-Hill, 2001), p. 445.

9. Jerry Palmer, *Taking Humor Seriously* (London: Routledge, 1994), p. 161.

10. See, for example, Charles R. Gruner, "Advice to the Beginning Speaker on Using Humor—What the Research Tells Us," *Communication Education* 34 (1985): 142–147; Christie McGufee Smith and Larry

Power, "The Use of Disparaging Humor by Group Leaders," *Southern Speech Communication Journal* 53 (1988): 279–292; Elizabeth E. Grahm, Michael J. Papa, and Gordon P. Brooks, "Functions of Humor in Conversation: Conceptualization and Measurement," *Western Journal of Communication* 56 (1992): 161–183; Frank J. MacHovec, *Humor: Theory, History, Applications* (Springfield, IL: Charles Thomas, 1988); and Palmer, *Taking Humor Seriously.*

11. Jeffrey H. Goldstein, "Theoretical Notes on Humor," *Journal of Communication* 26 (1976): 104–112. See also Barry Alan Morris, "The Communal Constraints on Parody: The Symbolic Death of Joe Bob Briggs," *Quarterly Journal of Speech* 73 (1987): 460–473.

12. Even experienced comedians can go too far for their audiences. Consider the example of Joe Bob Briggs in Barry Alan Morris, "The Communal Constraints on Parody: The Symbolic Death of Joe Bob Briggs," *Quarterly Journal of Speech* 73 (1987): 460–473.

13. For an interesting discussion of gender differences in humor, see M. Alison Kibler, "Gender Conflict and Coercion on A & E's *An Evening at the Improv*," *Journal of Popular Culture* 32 (1999): 45–57.

14. See Joan B. Levine, "The Feminine Routine," *Journal of Communication* 26 (1976): 173–175; Lawrence La Fave and Roger Mannell, "Does Ethnic Humor Serve Prejudice? *Journal of Communication* 26 (1976): 116–123; and Dolf Zillmann and Holly Stocking, "Putdown Humor," *Journal of Communication* 26, 1976)129–133.

15. See Palmer, *Taking Humor Seriously*, and Joseph Alan Ullian, "Joking at Work," *Journal of Communication* 26 (1976): 129–133.

16. Victor Raskin, *Semantic Mechanism of Humor* (Dordrecht: D. Reidel, 1985).

17. Sylvia Simmons, *How to Be the Life of the Podium: Openers, Closers and Everything in Between to Keep Them Listening* (New York: AMACOM, 1991).

CHAPTER 20

1. Karen Stabiner, *To Dance with the Devil: The New War on Breast Cancer* (New York: Delacorte Press, 1997).

2. J. Kevin Barge, *Leadership: Communication Skills for Organizations and Groups* (New York: St. Martin's, 1994).

3. Ibid.

4. Kenneth D. Benne and Paul Sheats, "Functional Roles of Group Members," *Journal of Social Issues* 4 (1948): 41–49.

5. Adapted from Ibid., pp. 42–44.

6. John Dewey, *How We Think* (Boston: D.C. Heath, 1910).

7. Irving L. Janis, *Groupthink*, 2nd ed. (Boston: Houghton Mifflin, 1982).

Index

Consistency
    of Internet information, 133
    listening for, 63, 66
    of main points of a speech, 214,
        215
    in outlines, 257–258
Constraints, on small groups,
    469–470
Content, listening for consistency of,
    63, 66
Context
    defined, 14
    speaking goals and, 79–81
    for speeches, 37, 79–81
Contractions, in spoken language,
    283
Conversational style, of
    extemporaneous speech, 297
Conversations, public speaking
    versus, 10
Cool colors, 342
Coordination, in outlines, 253
Coordinator, as group task role, 471
Copying, in research, 146
Counterarguments, to persuasive
    speeches, 415
Counterexamples, importance of,
    159–160
Creativity in speeches, 238, 242
Credibility, 156, 429
    citing sources and, 220, 221
    of definitions, 174–175
    enhancing, 430–432
    in ethical reasoning, 195–197
    ethos and, 182
    through examples, 159–160
    expertise and, 236
    persuasion and, 428–432
    of sources, 427–428
    in speech introduction, 33, 229
    of testimony, 171
    types of, 429–430
    via visual aids, 324
    Web site on, 427
Crediting sources, 220–221
Critical listeners, 65–66
    guidelines for, 66
Crossen, Cynthia, 163–164
Crosswhite, James, 156
Cues for delivery, in speaking outline,
    266
Culturally inclusive language,
    improving listening via, 58–59

Cultural Rhythms of Time Web site,
    390
Cultures
    appropriate labels for, 279
    language and, 276, 278–279
    meanings of color in different, 341
    mythos and, 436–438
    speaking style and, 7–9
    visual, 322
Currency, of Internet information,
    131, 132
Cynic, as egocentric role, 472

D
Dalai Lama, 311
Daley, Eric, 297
Dangerous objects, as visual aids, 325
D'Arcy, Jan, 205
Databases, 135–137
    bibliographic, 136
    full-text, 136
DataTimes, 137
Decoding, defined, 13
Deductive reasoning (deduction),
    182–183, 185–188
    guidelines for, 187–188
Definitions
    avoiding circular, 175
    defined, 172
    emotions and, 173–174
    by negation, 174
    in support of speeches, 32, 156,
        172–175
    tips on, 174–175
    types of, 172–173
Definitive sentences, in public
    speaking, 92–93
Delivery, 296–316
    advantages and disadvantages of
        methods, 301
    as canon of public speaking, 28,
        36–37, 38
    defined, 296
    of entertaining speeches,
        462–463
    extemporaneous, 296–297, 301
    impromptu, 296, 297–299, 301
    listening for consistency of, 63
    manuscript, 296, 299–300, 301
    memorized, 296, 300–301
    methods, 296–302
    of narratives, 163
    nonverbal components of, 306–311

practicing, 40–41
    in presentations to small groups,
        480
    at speech conclusion, 239
    verbal components of, 302–306
Delivery cues, in speaking outline,
    266
Demographic audience analysis,
    105–107
Demonstrations, 325
    catching audience attention with,
        232–233
    as visual aids, 324, 325–326
Demonstration speeches, 365
Denotative definition, 172
Derived credibility, 429–430
Descriptions, on slides, 330
Design
    balanced, 343–344
    of drawings, 337
    of graphs, 335–336
    with poster boards, 328
    of visual aids, 332–339, 340–344,
        345–346
Dewey, John, 473
Dialect, in speeches, 306
Dialogue
    as battle, 6, 7
    defined, 102
    differences and, 62
    encouraging, 12
    in invitational speeches, 374–375
    public speaking as, 6–7, 37–38
    United Nations Year of, 24
Dictionaries
    as research sources, 138
    linguistic accuracy via, 280–282
Dictionary.com, 172
Dictionary definition, 172, 173
Differences
    as impediment to listening, 60–62
    inability to get beyond, 51–52
    in listening styles, 52–53
    testimony as illustrating, 169
Dillon, Matt, 307
Direct quotations, 169, 220–221
Disabilities, appropriate labels for
    people with, 279
Discussion
    in invitational speeches, 389–390
    leadership and leading, 470
    in Speech Evaluation Checklist, 69
Disgust, as primary emotion, 432

McMartin, Jennifer, 352
Mead, Margaret, 465
Mean, statistical, 164
Median, statistical, 164–165
Meetings, of small groups,
    475–477
Memorization, of speeches, 35–36
Memorized delivery, 296, 300–301
Memorized speech, 300
Memory
    as canon of public speaking, 28,
        35–36, 37
    in language, 277
Memory techniques, Web site on, 301
Menchú Tum, Rigoberta, 285,
    458–459
Merriam-Webster Online Web site,
    281
Messages, defined, 12–13
Metaphors, 285–286
    mixed, 286
Microsoft Internet Explorer, 129
Microsoft PowerPoint. *See*
    PowerPoint technology
Minor premise, in deductive
    reasoning, 186–187
Minutes, of meetings, 477
Mixed metaphors, 286
Mnemonic devices, 105, 288
Moakley, Joe, 287
Mobs, speaking before, 109
Mode, statistical, 164, 165–166
Models, 324
    as visual aids, 324–326
Monotone, speaking in, 303–304
Monroe, Alan, 412–413
Monroe's motivated sequence
    for question-of-policy speeches,
        412–413
    Web site for, 413
Morality, questions of value and, 403
Morella, Constance A., 426
Mother Teresa, 288
Multiple perspectives organizational
    pattern, 385–388
Mumbling, avoiding in speeches, 305
Mythos, 426, 436
    logic of, 437
    persuasion and, 436–438

N
Narratives. *See also* Storytelling
    audiences for, 161–162, 163
    brief and extended, 160

defined, 160
delivery of, 163
emotions and, 161–162
length of, 162
personalizing points via,
    160–161
in support of speeches, 31–32, 156,
    160–163
tips on, 162–163
Narrowing topics, 88–89
National Breast Cancer Coalition
    (NBCL) Web site, 467
Native Americans
    myths of, 437
    speaking styles of, 8, 9
Need, in Monroe's motivated
    sequence, 413
Negation, definition by, 174
Negative self-talk, 42–43
Nervousness
    overcoming, 38–45, 324
    visual aids as reducing, 324
Netscape Navigator, 129
NetZero Web site, 129
NewsBank, 137
NewsLink Web site, 129
Newton, John, 232–233
New York Times Index, 137
Nichols, Paul, 51
Noise, defined, 13
Noninclusive language, as
    impediment to listening,
    57–59
Nonthreatening objects, as visual
    aids, 325
Nonverbal communication, in small
    groups, 472
Nonverbal speech components,
    306–311
not Boolean operator, 130
Note cards, 269–270
Notes
    for speeches, 36, 37, 263. *See also*
        Outlines
    in research, 146
    taking during speeches, 63
Novel information, in speeches,
    427
Novelty, public speaking anxiety and,
    38, 39
Nujoma, Sam, 24
Numbers. *See* Statistics
Numerical evidence, statistics as,
    166–167

O
Objective testimony, 171–172
Objects, 324
    speeches about, 352, 357
    as visual aids, 324–326
Occupation, as impediment to
    listening, 61
Offensive language
    in speeches, 35, 37
    paraphrasing of, 170–171
Ogden, C. K., 175, 276, 277
Online catalogs, 135
Opelt, Jon, 241
Open-ended questions, 106, 143
Opening statements, catching
    audience attention with, 233–234
Opinion giver, as group task role,
    471
Opinion seeker, as group task role,
    471
Opposition, public speaking and, 5
Oral cultures, storytelling in, 283
Oral message, 12
Oral reports, to small groups, 477
Oral style, in public speaking, 282
or Boolean operator, 130
Organization
    of presentations to small group,
        480
    of speeches, 204–221, 358–363,
        382–388, 406–413
Organizational charts, as visual aids,
    334
Organizational patterns
    for informative speeches, 358–363
    for invitational speeches, 382–388
    for persuasive speeches, 406–413
Orientations, for libraries, 133–134
Outliers, statistical, 164
Outlines, 250
    body in, 256, 260–262, 267–269
    citing sources in, 255
    conclusions in, 254, 256, 262–263,
        269
    connectives in, 254–255, 256
    consistent labeling and notation for,
        257–258
    history of, 250
    introductions in, 251–252, 256,
        260, 267
    main points and subpoints in,
        252–253, 257–258
    note cards and, 269–270
    preparation of, 250–263

Reference works
  as research sources, 138–140
  Web sites for, 138–139
Referents, in language, 277
Reflective thinking method, 473
Rehearsing speeches, 36, 311–312.
  See also Practicing speeches;
  Preparation
Reinforcement, as goal of speaking,
  433
Reinforcing points
  via examples, 158
  via statistics, 167–168
  via testimony, 172
Relaxation, visualization and, 41–42
Relevance
  of examples, 159
  of Internet information, 133
Reliability
  of Internet information, 131, 132
  of signs, 191–192
Remembrance, as goal of speaking,
  433
Repetition, linguistic rhythm and,
  287–288
Repetitiveness, of spoken language,
  283–284
Reporters, 141
Research, 126–149
  acknowledging and thanking for,
    147–148
  filing system for, 146–147
  in libraries, 133–140
  on Internet, 129–133
  interviews in, 141–145
  inventorying for, 126–128, 145
  note-taking in, 146
  personal experience and knowledge
    in, 128
  plagiarism in, 146
  for public speaking, 39–40
  tips on, 145–149
Research inventory, 126–128, 145
  sample, 127
Research Inventory Worksheet, 126,
  128, 149
Response, to speeches, 68, 71
Reverence, as emotion, 432
Reviews, as research sources, 139
Rhetoric, 28, 37
Rhetorical questions, 230
  Web site on, 230
Rhyme, as mnemonic device, 288
Rhythm, 287

in language, 284, 287–290
in speeches, 35, 287–290
Richards, Ann, 8, 158, 283
Richards, I. A., 276, 277
Richards, J. A., 175
Richness of speech, clutter versus, 60
Ridiculously Enhanced Pi Page Web
  site, 262, 269
Robert's Rules of Order, 476
Roles, in small groups, 468,
  470–472
Roosevelt, Franklin Delano, 287
Rush, Bobby, 456–457
Rushing to judgment, 67
Rutgers University Web site, 403

S
Sadness, as primary emotion, 432
Salcido, Jose, 160–161
Sale, Jamie, 158
Sans serif fonts, 340
Satisfaction, in Monroe's motivated
  sequence, 413
Scale, in maps, 338
Scanning of images, 336
Scared Speechless Web site, 250
Schaaf, William, 263, 269
Scheduling interviews, 142
Scope of a speech, main points and,
  207–208
SearchBank, 137
Search engines, 84, 87–88
  table of Internet, 130
  using, 130–131
Secondary emotions, 432
Self, introducing, 452
Self-confessor, as egocentric role,
  472
Self-determination, in invitational
  speech environment, 376–377
Semantic triangle of meaning,
  276–277
Sentence structure, in public
  speaking, 92–93. *See also*
  Cluttered sentences; Complete
  sentences; Definitive sentences;
  Uncluttered sentences
Serif fonts, 340
Sexual orientation, appropriate labels
  for people of different, 279
Shame, as secondary emotion, 432
Shibata, Hidetoshi, 404
Sign, 191
  reasoning by, 182–183, 191–192

Signifying, 278
Signposts, in speeches, 218–219
Similes, 284–285
Sincerity, in commemorative
  speeches, 458
Situational anxiety, 38, 39
Size of audience, 110–111
Slang, as impediment to listening, 57
Slides. *See also* Transparencies
  photographs on, 337
  as visual aids, 329–330
Slippery slope fallacy, 441
Small groups
  conducting meetings of,
    475–477
  constraints on, 469–470
  defined, 466
  goals of, 472
  interpersonal conflict in, 472
  leadership of, 468–470
  nonverbal communication in, 472
  participating in, 470–472
  presentations to, 477–480
  problem solving by, 473–475
  public dialogue and, 466–468
  reasons for speaking to, 467–468
  roles in, 468, 470–472
  speaking in, 28, 30, 465–480
Small group speaking, 28, 30,
  465–480
  Web site for, 28
Society. *See also* Arab society;
  Communities; Cultures;
  Ethnicity; People
  attitudes, beliefs, standpoints, and
    values in, 104–105
  master status within, 103–104
  surveys of, 106, 107
"Some Notes on Gender-Neutral
  Language" (Jacobson), 58
Sound waves, 50–51
Sources. *See also* Internet; Libraries;
  Research
  citing, 220–221
  citing orally, 146, 221, 255
  credibility of, 427–428
  listening for, 63, 66
  speech outline and, 255
Spatial organizational pattern, 359,
  360–361, 384
  of main points of a speech,
    209–211
Speaker. *See also* Public speaking;
  Speaking; Speeches

in inductive reasoning, 185
as numerical evidence, 166–167
sparing use of, 167–168
in support of speeches, 32, 156,
163–168
tips on, 167–168
types of, 164–166
Statistics Homepage Web site, 166
Status, master, 103–104, 117–118,
119
Stereotypes, 106–107
Stewart, Martha, 437
Stillman, Courtney, 409
Sting, 451
Storage, of poster boards, 329
Storytelling. *See also* Narratives
catching audience attention by, 231
in oral cultures, 283
public speaking as, 7–9
Style, as canon of public speaking,
28, 34–35, 37
Subcultures, languages of, 278
Subordination, in outlines, 257–258
Subpoints
dividing main points into, 258
in outlines, 252–253, 257–258
Sub-subpoints, in outlines, 252–253,
257–258
Suggesting solutions to problems,
474–475
Summaries, 240. *See also* Internal
summaries
leadership and making, 470
at speech conclusion, 240–241
statistics as, 164, 166
Supporting evidence, listening for,
63, 66
Supporting materials. *See also*
Evidence
defined, 126
gathering, 31–32, 37, 126–149,
156–176
in speech conclusion, 242
Supportive climate, in invitational
speech environment, 376
Surprise, as primary emotion, 432
Surveys, 106, 107
Suspending judgment, 67–68
Symbolic interactionists, 276
Symbols, in language, 276–277
Symposiums, for small groups, 477,
478–479
Synopsis, speech outline as, 250
Systematic desensitization, 40

T

*Tainted Truth: The Manipulation of
Fact in America* (Crossen),
163–164
Tan, Amy, 53
Tannen, Deborah, 6, 374
Team presentations, for small groups,
477, 479
Technical language, as impediment to
listening, 55–57
Technology
brainstorming by, 87–88
problems with, 112–113
for public speaking, 112–113
Terminal credibility, 429, 430
Testimony
credibility of, 171
defined, 168
expert, 169
in inductive reasoning, 185
as supporting material, 32, 156,
168–172
tips on, 171–172
types of, 169
Thesaurus, 281
Thesis statement, 94
in causal organizational pattern,
361
in chronological organizational
pattern, 359, 382–383
in invitational speeches, 378, 380
main points of a speech and,
205–213, 215–216
in multiple perspectives
organizational pattern, 386–387
in question-of-fact speeches,
405
in question-of-policy speeches,
408–412
in question-of-value speeches,
406–407
in spatial organizational pattern,
360–361, 384
of a speech, 30, 37, 94–96,
204–205
at speech conclusion, 239–240
in speeches about concepts, 358
in speeches about events, 355
in speeches about objects, 357
in speeches about places and
people, 356
in speeches about processes,
353–354
speech outline and, 251

in topical organizational pattern,
362, 385
writing, 96
Thomas, Marlo, 289
Thought, in language, 277
Threatening themes, avoiding in
speeches, 434
Tilde (~), in URL, 131
Time. *See also* Timing
length of speeches in, 114–115
for meetings, 476
order of speeches in, 114
when speeches are given, 113–114
Time limits. *See also* Brevity
of acceptance speeches, 459
on classroom speeches, 81,
114–115
main points of a speech and, 207
on narratives, 162
Timing, in entertaining speeches,
460–461. *See also* Time
Title, of a speech, 251
Toastmaster Web site, 17
Toffler, Alvin, 128
Topical organizational pattern, 359,
362, 384–385
of main points of a speech,
212–213
Topics, 78–96
brainstorming, 85–88
bringing to life, 363–364
in causal organizational pattern,
361–362
in chronological organizational
pattern, 359–360, 382–383
of entertaining speeches, 462
introducing to audience, 228–238
in invitational speeches, 377–379,
379–382
for involuntary audience, 109–110
in multiple perspectives
organizational pattern, 385–388
narrowing, 88–89
for question-of-fact speeches,
405–406
for question-of-policy speeches,
408–412
for question-of-value speeches,
406–407
selecting, 14–15, 28–29, 37, 81–89
in spatial organizational pattern,
360–361, 384
for speeches about concepts, 358
for speeches about objects, 357